Colonial Ste. Genevieve

Colonial
Ste. Genevieve

An Adventure on
the Mississippi Frontier

Carl J. Ekberg

The Patrice Press
Gerald, Missouri

Library of Congress
Cataloging In Publication Data

Ekberg, Carl J.
    Colonial Ste. Genevieve: an adventure on the
    Mississippi frontier.
    Bibliography: p.
    Includes index.
    1. Sainte Genevieve (Mo.)—History. 2. Frontier
and pioneer life—Missouri—Sainte Genevieve.
3. Missouri—History. I. Title. II. Title: Colonial
Sainte Genevieve.
F474.S33E43 1985 977.8'692 85-29801
ISBN O-935284-41-9

Published by
The Patrice Press
Box 42 / Gerald MO 63037

Printed in the United States of America

For Abraham P. and Ida Nasatir

Contents

Part 1
The Illinois Country and Ste. Genevieve

Part 2
Fundamentals of Life

Part 3
Community Organization

Acknowledgments

I N DOING RESEARCH for this book in far-flung places, many persons facilitated my work by feeding and housing me: Daniel and Ruth-Christine Beveraggi in Paris; Joe and Christine Castle in New Orleans; Nat and Lottie Gilbert in Los Angeles; Rod and Anne Johnson in St. Louis; Abe and Ida Nasatir in San Diego; Bernie and Vion Schram in Ste. Genevieve; and Fred and Sandy Ward in Washington, D.C. Without the generous assistance of these persons, I could not have accomplished the research for this study.

Friends and colleagues at Illinois State University have rendered invaluable assistance in the preparation of this book: Ed Jelks, a historical-archaeologist, who first encouraged me to study the Illinois Country; Roger Champagne, Ira Cohen, Sandra Harmon, Mark Plummer, Joanne Rayfield, Susan Westbury, and Mark Wyman, all American historians, who helped me — a Europeanist — through many entanglements of early American history; and Larry Walker and John Brickle, without whose counsel I could not have handled the statistical data in this study.

Students in my French Illinois course at Illinois State University have offered suggestions on various aspects of this book that have proved illuminating and helpful. Suzette Pierson McInerney of the university honors program deserves special mention in this regard for her work on the Ste. Genevieve parish records.

Many librarians and archivists in various repositories have rendered great service by sharing their knowledge of source materials with me. I wish especially to thank Garold Cole of the Illinois State University Library and John Hoffman of the Illinois Historical Survey in Urbana. Holly Johnson generously took of her precious time in Seville, Spain, to track down several important documents in the Archivo General de Indias.

In Ste. Genevieve the entire Foundation for Historic Preservation has supported my research on its town. Some individual members of this organization have been particularly supportive and cooperative: Ron Armbruster, past president of the Foundation, who first invited me to speak in Ste. Genevieve; Jeanette Basler, overseer of the local records, who always extended herself to aid my work in the county courthouse; Lucille Basler, local historian, who has kept interest in historic Ste. Genevieve alive for more than half a century; Father Gregory Schmidt, a priest whose humanity is enhanced by a keen interest in the history of his parish; and finally, Bernie and Vion Schram, impresarios of historic Ste. Genevieve, whose sensibilities, social graces, and wine cellar have stimulated numerous scholars over the years.

Many of the ideas presented in this book developed during the course of informal conversations with various persons who are actively engaged in research on the Illinois Country. These include Natalia Belting, Margaret K. Brown, Raymnond Hammes, Terry Norris, Osmund Overby, Anton Pregaldin, and Melburn G. Thurman. Without the cross-fertilization of ideas that came of these conversations, this book would never have appeared in its present form.

The history of the Illinois Country was new to me when I began work on this project some five years ago. Thus, in order to sift out as many errors of fact and interpretationas possible, I asked a broad range of persons to read the manuscript version of the book. Ruth-Christine Beveraggi, Margaret K. Brown, William E. Foley, Raymond Hammes, Ernest Liljegren, Abraham P. Nasatir, and Bernard K. Schram have all painstakingly gone through the manuscript and made numerous corrections and recommendations that have improved the book. The errors that remain are solely my responsibility.

Melburn G. Thurman of Ste. Genevieve also read the entire manuscript and offered innumerable intelligent suggestions. Indeed, over the past five years I have discussed and argued virtually every major idea in this book with Mel Thurman. His unusually keen critical capacities and vast knowledge of the Illinois Country have saved me from many serious mistakes.

My first research on colonial Ste. Genevieve was done in working on an environmental impact study that was funded by the the St.

Louis District, U.S. Corps of Engineers. I am also indebted to the
research program of the Graduate School at Illinois State University for having funded part of the research that went into this
study. Most of the expenses for this research came from the family
budget, and for this sacrifice I extend warmest thanks to my wife
Gloria and my children, Andrew and Hannah.

While doing research in several repositories in California, I
needed a fast and inexpensive method of transportation. This was
supplied by Professor Marc Gilbert of Beverly Hills, who generously loaned me his superb BMW 500 motorcycle, which proved
to be the ideal machine for expediting travel and research in
southern California.

Typists in the Department of History at Illinois State University
laboriously produced several drafts of this book. I wish especially
to thank Dorothy Haeffle and her assistant, Mary Koch, who displayed great patience in typing and retyping my rough drafts.

Finally, I must thank my editor and publisher, Gregory M.
Franzwa, who has encouraged me at every stage of my work, and
who has shown enerring critical judgment in deciding what belongs and does not belong in a book of this sort.

— Carl Ekberg
Normal, Illinois
November 1, 1985

Foreword

FOR MORE THAN TWO CENTURIES the little river town of Ste. Genevieve has exerted a special charm on visitors. Such diverse guests as Henry Brackenridge, Thomas Ashe, Mark Twain and even modern representatives of the generally unsentimental Army Corps of Engineers have fallen under the spell of this historic community whose population figures have hardly changed in over one hundred years.

Dr. Carl Ekberg, therefore, is another in a long line of willing victims of this non-fatal attraction. Several years ago, he launched what might have proved to be merely a mild academic flirtation with this community. However, this blossomed swiftly into an ardent love affair between a sensitive historian and his subject — as is brilliantly reflected in this history of the French Colonial period of our community.

In common with most such affairs, the course of true love has not always run smoothly.

Dr. Ekberg early upset Ste. Genevieve traditionalists by challenging some long-cherished beliefs. This was especially true regarding the founding date of the town — held over the years to have been 1735. His painstaking scholarship indicated that the accepted foundation date was based on misinterpretation of an early document and declared it was some fifteen to twenty years later that the French permanently settled here. This direct assault on a hallowed article of local faith scarcely ingratiated the academic interloper to a community which celebrated its "bicentennial" in 1935 and its 250th birthday in 1985.

Which is not to argue with Dr. Ekberg's demonstrated scholarship. The fact that the celebration of the 250th anniversary continues proves simply that the modern heirs of Ste. Genevieve's founding fathers remain determined to preserve old customs and beliefs, in the tradition of their forebears. It also goes to show that "lovers" can be compatible, regardless of differences.

Carl Ekberg, despite his iconoclastic irreverence, has become an affectionately welcome honorary citizen of Ste. Genevieve. He has patronized with equal zeal our courthouse recorder's office and our restaurants, our historic seminars and our homes, and even occasionally dropped in on our local saloons in the interest of scientific research.

His studies have taken him far afield — from Ste. Genevieve to Paris, from Randolph County, Illinois, to California. He has collected maps and manuscripts, fact and fiction, lore and learning from American, French, Spanish and Canadian sources. He has plowed through our 28,000-document archives, our parish records, transcripts of Spanish documents, and thousands of other printed and manuscript pages. He has visited our many extant eighteenth-century buildings and followed the archaeological traces of our earliest Indian settlers. He has participated in scholarly conferences on French Colonialism all over the nation. Above all, he has applied intelligence, scholarship and insight to winnow through this enormous mass of material in search of the historic reality that was early Ste. Genevieve. How well he has succeeded is handsomely demonstrated in this book.

It may be that current or future historians will take issue with some of his findings, in which case I am sure that Dr. Ekberg will be the first to welcome any new light cast upon his subject. But I am equally sure that nobody with the slightest interest in French colonization of the Mississippi Valley can ignore this significant work by a man who brings such scholarship and enthusiasm to this field.

I have enjoyed a close personal association with Carl Ekberg throughout the period of his mining and refining the material for this book. It has been an educational experience for me as well as a delightful friendship. I am pleased to see that the wit and wisdom of the man has blended well with the dedicated scholarship incorporated in this book.

On the basis of our association I can attest to something the author himself has not mentioned — that is the personal sacrifice he and his family have made in the creation of this work. Unsupported by grants or other outside funding, Carl traveled at his own expense across both the American continent and the Atlantic Ocean in pursuit of information. He spent not only his hardearned professorial stipend but much time away from his home and family in this quest.

In the course of his work, Carl Ekberg has endeared himself to many and alienated a few. The diverse personalities who have assisted him include the venerable Abraham P. Nasatir of California and our own local historian, Mrs. Lucille Basler, who staunchly maintains that Ekberg is wrong about the town's founding date. And Carl has left an indelible impression upon hundreds of us — laymen and scholars alike — whom he encountered during the long course of his project.

Out of all this has come what I am confident will be an enduring opus that will provide pleasure and knowledge to all who know and love Ste. Genevieve, which if not the actual "Mother of the West," as some claim, certainly must be the "Foster Mother."

My fond hope is that this splendid book will stimulate further study of our community extending into the Anglo-American and German immigration periods — and that it will lure more visitors to Ste. Genevieve, where the past merges gracefully with the present, both in the physical environment and in the native hospitality bequeathed by our long and varied history.

— Bernard K. Schram
Ste. Genevieve, Missouri

Introduction

ALMOST SIXTY YEARS AGO, I began collecting historical
source materials pertaining to the colonial history of the
Mississippi Valley. In addition to using documentary depositories
and libraries in the United States, I traveled to Spain, Mexico,
France, and England in pursuit of relevant manuscripts. I realized
in later years that in the course of publishing books, articles,
monographic studies, and collections of documents I would not
be able to use the entire contents of my collection during my
lifetime. Hence, I invited selected scholars and students to use my
materials.

Some five years ago, I received a request from Professor Carl
J. Ekberg of Illinois State University for assistance with his ongoing
study of colonial Ste. Genevieve. He told me of his delving into
the rich documentary collection at the Missouri Historical Society
in St. Louis, an institution which I have always considered my
second home in the United States. I suggested to Professor Ekberg
that he come out and see what relevant materials I had here from
the Spanish archives. During the next several years, Carl came
repeatedly to San Diego to pursue his research in my collections
of documents.

Professor Ekberg is a convert to the colonial history of the Mississippi River Valley. He earned his doctorate in Early Modern
European history at Rutgers University under the direction of
Herbert H. Rowen, and only recently has become interested in
the Mississippi Valley. With a superior knowledge of eighteenth
century French history and European politics, he entered his new
field of study well equipped to write the definitive history of Ste.
Genevieve during the French and Spanish periods. At my sugges-

tion, he incorporated into his local study the history of international policies and events, and he discovered that the local sources integrated admirably with the archival materials that I had collected.

During the second half of the eighteenth century, St. Louis and Ste. Genevieve were the anchors of Upper Louisiana. While the story of the founding of St. Louis is well known, the genesis of Ste. Genevieve has been a matter of conjecture and confusion. Professor Ekberg has carefully researched the earliest migrations from the east side of the Mississippi River to the site that became Ste. Genevieve. By the 1750s, there had been created a stable community that was in many respects the real nucleus of French culture and Spanish dominion in the region during the late eighteenth century.

Many of Ste. Genevieve's inhabitants were bound together by family and economic interests, and they were strongly inclined to defend those interests if the occasion required. During the 1790s, when there were French and American schemes to invade Upper Louisiana, Ste. Genevieve was the only community in the territory with a will and determination to defend itself. The citizens, led by town commandant François Vallé II, built a fort and prepared for any possible incursion from across the Mississippi. Located as they were across the river from Kaskaskia, the metropole of Anglo-American Illinois, the inhabitants of Ste. Genevieve were often able to gauge the activities and movements of the Americans, and persistent contact with the American outpost served to assuage fears and tensions on the Mississippi frontier.

The correspondence of the Vallé family, preserved in the Missouri Historical Society in St. Louis, plus the local civil and religious records, which remain in Ste. Genevieve, afford the scholar a good picture of the early community. There is, however, much more. During the late eighteenth century, colonial Louisiana was governed under the paternalistic Spanish regime. The government had a hand in most activities, and the simplest matter might well be referred up through the chain of command to the king of Spain himself. One result of this system was a vast amount of letters, dispatches, reports, memoranda, and other written communication. Enormous quantities of this correspondence have been preserved in the voluminous archives of Spain, and Professor Ekberg has drawn heavily from this material in painting his detailed portrait of colonial Ste. Genevieve. Simple lawsuits, trade and conflict with the Indians, colonial financial accounts, military affairs, immigrants, local censuses, relations with the British and Americans, educational proposals, even church affairs — all of these and more were continually included in the correspondence of colonial officials.

Professor Ekberg has had access to much of the Spanish archival material for use in his study of colonial Ste. Genevieve. He has made good use of that material, integrating it with local sources that were previously available to him. The result of Carl's labors in these diverse sources is a study of colonial Ste. Genevieve that goes far beyond anything that has heretofore been possible.

During the time that Carl worked in San Diego, I had the opportunity to observe that he was a highly competent and well-balanced scholar. He seemed to be an ideal person to continue my work on the colonial history of the Upper Mississippi Valley. He has agreed to revise and cooperate with me in completing my last study of Spain in the Mississippi Valley. That will be the story of Anglo-American rivalry on the Upper Mississippi during the last decade of the eighteenth century. This study will complete my work in a field that I began with *Spanish War Vessels on the Mississippi*.

I consider it a privilege and a pleasure to provide this introduction to Professor Ekberg's study of colonial Ste. Genevieve. This book will be of great interest to scholars — historians, geographers, anthropologists, archaeologists, and genealogists — but it will also provide a valuable resource for those who have a genuine interest in the roots of their community.

— Abraham P. Nasatir
San Diego, California

Maps, Figures, and Illustrations

Chronology of Events in the Illinois Country

1673	Marquette and Jolliet descend Mississippi to Arkansas River
1682	LaSalle and Tonti descend Mississippi to Gulf of Mexico
1699	French mission established at Cahokia
1703	Village of Kaskaskia founded
1717	Illinois Country incorporated into French Louisiana
1718	New Orleans founded
1719	First Fort de Chartres begun
1720s	Philippe Renaut mining lead west of the Mississippi
1724	Etienne Bourgmont expedition up the Missouri River
1730	Destruction of the Fox Indian threat to Illinois settlements
1740s	First land grants conveyed in Ste. Genevieve area
1750	Village of Ste. Genevieve founded
1756-63	French & Indian War in North America
1762	Louisiana west of Mississippi conveyed by France to Spain
1763	Great Britain acquires sovereignty east of the Mississippi
1764	St. Louis founded by Laclède and Chouteau
1765	British forces arrive in the Illinois Country
1770	Spanish garrison established at Ste. Genevieve
1778	George Rogers Clark conquers English Illinois
1780	Anglo-Indian attack repelled at St. Louis
1783	Illinois east of the Mississippi conveyed to the United States
1785	Devastating flood strikes Ste. Genevieve
1785-95	Nouvelle Ste. Geneviève established
1794	Fort built at Ste. Genevieve
1800	France reacquires *de jure* sovereignty of Louisiana
1803	Napoleon sells Louisiana to United States
1804	Arrival of American officials in Upper Louisiana

Abbreviations of Archives, Libraries, and Documentary Collections Used in Footnotes

AAE	Archives du Ministère des Affaires Etrangères, Paris
AG	Archives du Ministère de Guerre, Vincennes
AGI	Archivo General de Indias, Seville
AN	Archives Nationales, Paris
ASP	*American State Papers*
BL	Bancroft Library, Berkeley, California
BN	Bibliothèque Nationale, Paris
HMLO	Huntington Library Manuscripts, Loudon Papers, San Marino, California
IHS	Illinois Historical Survey, Urbana, Illinois
JR	Reuben G. Thwaites (ed.), *The Jesuit Relations and Allied Documents*
KM	Kaskaskia Manuscripts, Randolph County Courthouse, Chester, Illinois
LSM	Louisiana State Museum Archives, New Orleans
MHS	Missouri Historical Society, St. Louis
PC	Papeles Procedentes de Cuba, in AGI
PRO	Public Record Office, London
SGA	Ste. Genevieve Archives, microfilm in MHS
SGPR	Ste. Genevieve Parish Records, microfilm in WHMC
SMV	Lawrence Kinnaird (ed.), *Spain in the Mississippi Valley, 1763-1794*
SRM	Louis Houck (ed.), *The Spanish Regime in Missouri*
UNDA	University of Notre Dame Archives, South Bend, Indiana
WHMC	Western Historical Manuscripts Collection, Columbia, Missouri

Part 1
The Illinois Country and Ste. Genevieve

Chapter I
A Town Is Born

T HE ILLINOIS COUNTRY, "le pays des Illinois": this phrase was coined in the late seventeenth century to describe the center of North America. French Canadian traders, trappers, and missionaries, including Louis Jolliet and Father Jacques Marquette, traveled on the Mississippi and Illinois rivers during the 1670s, and in 1682 Robert Cavelier de La Salle built the first European outpost of a permanent character in Illinois — Fort St. Louis, at present-day Starved Rock on the Illinois River. By 1688 even Italian cartographers labeled the region south of lakes Superior and Michigan "Paesi degl[i] Illinois."[1]

Although the expression Illinois Country was first used to designate the territory occupied by the Illinois Indians, it soon came to encompass much more than that. There were never specific boundaries as such for the Illinois Country, but by mid-eighteenth century it was generally understood to consist of all French-claimed territory from the mouth of the Ohio River north to the Great Lakes, including the valleys of the Mississippi, Missouri, and Ohio rivers. Thus during the French colonial regime in North America all of what is now the State of Missouri lay in the Illinois Country. Only on rare occasions did Frenchmen use the word "Missoury" as the place name for a territory, although that appellation was commonly used for the river. One of these rare occasions occurred in 1724 when the French engineer who was developing New Orleans, Adrien Pauger, wrote: "I regard Missoury as a lost country, too distant to maintain, more ruinous than useful."[2]

1. See reprint of "America Settentrionale," 1688, by the Venetian cartographer Marco Vincenzo Coronelli in Tucker (ed.), *Indian Villages, Atlas,* Plate IX.

2. Pauger to Directors of the Indies Company, May 29, 1724, AN, C[13]A, 8:57

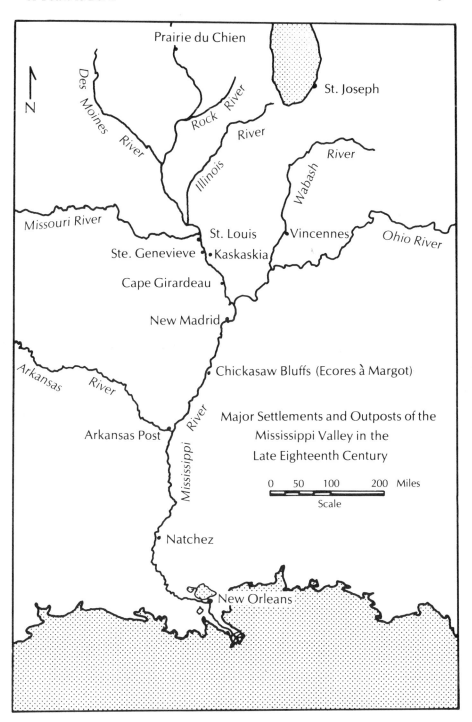

Prairie du Chien

St. Joseph

Des Moines River

Rock River

Illinois River

Wabash River

Missouri River

St. Louis

Vincennes

Ohio River

Ste. Genevieve

Kaskaskia

Cape Girardeau

New Madrid

Chickasaw Bluffs (Ecores à Margot)

Arkansas River

Mississippi River

Arkansas Post

Major Settlements and Outposts of the
Mississippi Valley in the
Late Eighteenth Century

0   50   100   200   Miles
Scale

Natchez

New Orleans

N

When the Spaniards acquired sovereignty over Louisiana in the 1760s, they continued to employ French geographic terms. Right on down to the time of the Louisiana Purchase, Spanish lieutenant governors in St. Louis governed a region that they called "Ylineuses." Thus for Ste. Genevieve's entire colonial history it is correct to refer to the town as Ste. Genevieve of the Illinois Country.[3]

In the seventeenth century, the major powers of northwestern Europe (Great Britain, France, and the Dutch Republic), began to compete seriously for New World empires with the first European colonizers, Spain and Portugal. The missionary impulse of the Catholic Reformation in France and the mercantile economic policies of the French absolute monarchy meant that France threw itself as heartily into the colonizing enterprise as any European state. This was especially true before Louis XIV's continental wars of the late seventeenth and early eighteenth centuries compelled the French to curtail their support for overseas colonies.

In any event, because the French had access to the heart of the North American continent via the St. Lawrence River and the chain of Great Lakes, they could cast their net of exploration and colonization more broadly than the Britsh. By the 1680s, the French, using their settlements on the lower St. Lawrence as a base, had dramatically outflanked the English (and their Iroquois allies) in North America by exploring the course of the Mississippi River from the Illinois Country to the Gulf of Mexico. In April 1682, La Salle planted the royal arms of Louis XIV at the mouth of the Mississippi and claimed all of Louisiana for France. By the end of the seventeenth century, French Jesuit missionaries and *coureurs de bois* had established outposts from the headwaters of the Mississippi at the Falls of St. Anthony (present-day Minneapolis), to the river mission of Cahokia in Illinois, and all the way to the Gulf of Mexico at Biloxi. The French empire in the center of the North American continent was sparsely populated; ultimately it proved to be fragile and vulnerable, but in 1700 it was breathtakingly vast and bold, given its narrow base of support in Quebec.[4]

---

3. Throughout this book Ste. Genevieve will be spelled without the *accent grave*, except when used in the context of a French phrase.

4. Recent surveys of French explorations in mid-America are found in Caruso, *Mississippi Valley Frontier;* Eccles, *Canadian Frontier;* Eccles, *France in America;* Folmer, *Franco-Spanish Rivalry.* Concerning the important issue of French explorations and Indian alliances, see Hunt, *Wars of the Iroquois,* 145 ff.; Jennings, *The Ambiguous Iroquois,* 172-213.

During the last two decades of the 17th century numbers of Frenchmen traveled through the Mississippi Valley and visited the region where Ste. Genevieve would later be founded. La Salle's loyal lieutenant, Henri de Tonti, traversed this area several times, but not having much of a literary impulse he left little record of what he saw. Another of La Salle's followers, Henri Joutel, continued northward after his leader had been murdered in what is now eastern Texas and eventually passed through the Illinois Country. Joutel later described the area that French Canadian colonists would one day turn into a thriving cluster of settlements:[5]

> We held on our way till the 25th [August 1687], when the Indians shew'd us a Spring of Salt Water, within a Musket Shot of us, and made us go ashore to view it. We observ'd the Ground about it was much beaten by Bullocks [bison] Feet, and it is likely they love that Salt Water. The Country about, was full of Hillocks, cover'd with Oaks and Walnut Trees....

Joutel's saline spring was perhaps the one located near the mouth of what later became known as the Saline Creek, which entered the Mississippi River just below the Old Town of Ste. Genevieve.

In 1698 three priests from the Seminary of Foreign Missions in Quebec, fathers Davion, Montigny, and St. Cosme, traveled west along the chain of the Great Lakes, crossed the portage from Lake Michigan to the Illinois River at "Checagou," and proceeded south into the Mississippi Valley. In a letter to the Bishop of Quebec, St. Cosme described their journey down the middle portion of the Mississippi. By December 1698 they had reached the area near present-day St. Louis, where they celebrated Mass. Continuing downriver, the missionaries erected a cross upon a high rock near the bank of the Mississippi. In his *History of Missouri* Louis Houck contended that this rock was the eminence now known as Grand Tower in Perry County, which may be correct; in any case it certainly was on the west bank of the Mississippi.[6]

In the autumn of 1700 a group of Kaskaskia Indians. French traders, and two Jesuit fathers, Jacques Gravier and Pierre Marest, left Fort St. Louis (at Peoria) on the Illinois River and headed south on what was becoming a well-traveled waterway. Entering

---

5. Stiles (ed.), *Joutel's Journal,* 186.
6. See St. Cosme's journal in Kellogg (ed.), *Early Narratives, 342-60;* also Alvord, *Illinois Country,* 116; Houck, *History of Missouri,* 1:241; Palm, *Jesuit Missions,* 31-2.

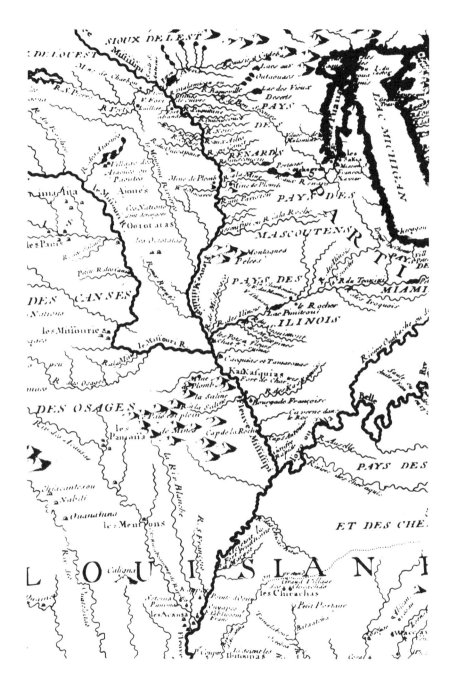

Detail of map of Louisiana by the royal cartographer Jacques-Nicolas Bellin, 1750. "La Saline" is shown but not Ste. Genevieve. Notice "Checagou" at the lower end of Lake Michigan. Original in Library of Congress, Division of Maps and Cartography.

out onto the Mississippi they proceeded downstream to the Tamaroa Indian village (Cahokia), where the missionary fathers Marc Bergier, Pierre Pinet and Joseph de Limoges were already at work. Father Marest and the Kaskaskia Indians soon moved across the Mississippi and settled down near the mouth of a small creek, creating a mission-trading community. This creek is now within the southern city limits of St. Louis and is named Des Peres in honor of the Jesuit fathers who served the tiny settlement.[7]

Within less than three years Father Marest led this French-Indian settlement sixty miles down the Mississippi and across to the east side, reestablishing it near the mouth of the Kaskaskia River. According to Father Bergier, the priest who served the mission center at Cahokia from 1700 to 1707, harassment by hostile Sioux Indians drove the Kaskaskia Indians and their French Canadian confreres from their location on Des Peres Creek and forced them to seek a more secure place for their settlement on the east bank of the Mississippi. Hostile Indians seem to have been a major reason why the center of the French Illinois Country developed on the east bank rather than the west bank of the Mississippi. In any case, by 1703 missionaries, *coureurs de bois*, and Indians had founded a new village in the North American empire claimed by King Louis XIV of France — Kaskaskia.[8]

Kaskaskia was a community of fur traders, farmers, priests, and Indians, and at first there was no French political or military presence in the area. Then, in 1717-18, the Bourbon monarchy revamped the administration of its mid-American possessions. The Illinois Country was removed from Canadian jurisdiction and became part of Upper Louisiana. A royal chartered enterprise, the French Company of the Indies, took charge of economic development in Louisiana, and in 1718 Jean-Baptiste Le Moyen, sieur de Bienville, founded New Orleans, which was destined to become the metropole of the colony. At the same time, officers, troops, and administrators were dispatched from the Gulf Coast to the Illinois Country to establish a civil government and a military presence. These men established Fort de Chartres — named in honor of Louis duc de Chartres, son of the regent of France, Philippe d'Orleans — some sixteen miles up the Mississippi from

7. Bannon, "Black-Robe Frontiersman," 359; Kenny, "Missouri's Earliest Settlement," 151-56; Palm 31-41; McDermott, *Old Cahokia*, 1-11.

8. Bannon, ibid., 360-61; Belting, *Kaskaskia*, 10; Garraghan, "Earliest Settlements," 351-62; Palm 42-45.

Kaskaskia. First built as a wooden palisaded structure during 1719-21, Fort de Chartres was repaired and rebuilt almost continuously until the 1750s, when the French government built a stone fort that it intended to be a keystone of the French empire in North America.[9]

The French settlements in the Illinois Country developed slowly during the first three decades of the eighteenth century. Fox Indians placed great pressure upon the French communities until 1730, when a combined expedition of French Canadians, soldiers from Fort de Chartres, and Indian allies of the French massacred a large number of Foxes in central Illinois. The next twenty-five-year period was a time of steady growth for French Illinois, with a vigorous birthrate and new settlers arriving. Most of the newcomers were French Canadians, although some Frenchmen who had come to Illinois via New Orleans also settled down to stay. In 1732 the total population of French Illinois, including slaves, approached 500 and by 1752 it was up toward 1400.[10]

During the first half of the eighteenth century, numerous exploratory thrusts were made from the French settlements on the east bank of the Mississippi into the vast unsettled territory west of the river. One of the best known of these was the Etienne de Bourgmont expedition up the Missouri River in 1723-24. On this occasion Bourgmont built Fort Orleans on the north bank of the river in what is now Carroll County, Missouri. For the purposes of this study, however, the shorter and less dramatic probes across the Mississippi in search of salt, lead, and agricultural land were more important, for they bore directly upon the early history of Ste. Genevieve.[11]

Joutel was the first Frenchman to describe the salt spring near the mouth of the Saline Creek, which he visited in 1687. André-Joseph Pénicaut, who traveled up the Mississippi about 1700-01, claimed that there was already an encampment of Frenchmen established on "La Petite Rivière de la Saline" at that time. These men probably were traders and trappers from the Cahokia area, who had come downriver a few leagues and camped long enough to boil out a year's supply of the essential mineral. "The Saline,"

---

9. Alvord, 152-53; Belting, 17-18; Giraud, *Histoire de la Louisiane française,* 3:3-60.

10. Alvord, 160-67; Peyser, "The 1730 Fox Fort," 201-13; Maduell (ed.), *Census Tables,* 150-53; "Recencement général du pays des Illinois en 1752," HMLO, 426.

11. On Bourgmont, see Nasatir (ed.), *Before Lewis and Clark,* 1:12-27.

as the salt springs, creek, and immediate environs were called in the eighteenth century, became an important adjunct to Ste. Genevieve once the village was founded, and it continued to be so throughout the entire colonial period.[12]

Lead was another mineral that attracted French explorers and entrepreneurs to the region where Ste. Genevieve would eventually rise. The French Jesuit, Father Jacques Gravier, noted in his journal for October 10, 1700, that "we discovered the River Miaramigoua [Meramec], where the very rich lead mine is situated, twelve or thirteen leagues from its mouth. The ore from this mine yields three-fourths metal." The present-day Big River was considered part of the Meramec in the eighteenth century, and Gravier seems clearly to have been describing the lead mines in the vicinity of what is now Old Mines in Washington County.[13]

Gravier no doubt heard about the Meramec mines from Indian sources, and Indians also probably told French explorers about the lead mines on the St. Francis River. In 1711, Governor Jean-Baptiste le Moyen de Bienville wrote: "Doubtless there are mines west of the Mississippi. All the tribes north of the Red River know about these mines." Antoine de La Mothe Cadillac became governor of Louisiana in 1713, and two years later he journeyed up the Mississippi to the Illinois Country in search of silver mines. Although disappointed in that search, La Mothe Cadillac did follow the Saline Creek westward from its mouth into what is now Madison County, where he conducted exploratory diggings for lead. Frenchmen in Louisiana were determined to find mineral wealth in their vast province, and if precious metals could not be found, lead would have to do. La Mothe Cadillac left his name to Mine La Motte in northern Madison County, Missouri.[14]

In 1719 Pierre Duqué, sieur de Boisbriant, builder of the first Fort de Chartres, visited the lead mining region near the St. Francis River. After this visit, Boisbriant descended the Saline Creek to the Mississippi, stood at the mouth of the creek, and remarked upon the desirability of having a permanent French outpost on the west side of the Mississippi: "My view would be to establish at

---

12. Stiles (ed.), *Joutel*, 186; McWilliams (ed.), *Fleur de Lys and Calumet*, 39-40.
13. *JR*, 65:101.
14. Bienville to minister, Oct. 27, 1711, BN, nouvelles acquisitions 9310:158; Cadillac to minister, Jan. 15 and May 18, 1715, AN, Archives des Colonies, C[13]A, 4:845-49, 855-58; La Harpe, *Journal historique*, 116; Hanley, "Lead Mining," 30-31; Rothensteiner, "Mine La Motte," 202.

this spot [the mouth of the Saline Creek] a settlement where we could have depositories in which to store the smelted metal. Transport from the mine [Mine La Motte] would be easy, for there is only one small mountain to cross." Boisbriant's comments tell us that Frenchmen first envisioned a settlement on the west bank of the Mississippi in the Illinois Country to serve as an entrepôt for the lead mines in the Missouri hinterland.[15]

This, however, was not to be. From the time that the well-known Philippe Renaut (sometimes Renault and Renaud) established his lead mining operation on the Mineral Fork of the Big River in 1723 until the end of the French regime in 1763, French colonists from the east bank of the Mississippi remained active in the two principal lead mining areas on the west bank — Mine La Motte and the Meramec Mine (Mineral Fork). The Kaskaskia Manuscripts contain the names and records of some of these early miners: In addition to Renaut, there was Antoine-Valentin de Gruy, Pierre Messager, Nicolas Drouen, Pierre de la Gautrais, and Joseph La Roche. But these men, with their seasonal mining activities, never extracted enough lead to require a permanent settlement west of the Mississippi — either at the mines or on the bank of the river. They crudely smelted the lead at the mines and transported it to Kaskaskia by pack animals and river boats. Contrary to widely accepted opinion, there is no evidence that lead miners founded Ste. Genevieve.[16]

French colonists from the east side of the Mississippi also crossed the river in search of something even more important to them than salt or lead — agricultural land. Around Fort de Chartres and Kaskaskia there was a growing number of colonists who required land for homesites and for farms, and that land was available on the alluvial flood plain across the river. Indeed, French colonial authorities at Fort de Chartres were conveying land grants on the *Grand Champ* (Big Field) in the 1740s, probably before any such village as Ste. Genevieve existed. The *habitants* who owned these arable lands eventually moved their residences from the east bank of the river to the west bank in order to be closer to their fields and their work. It was therefore agriculture, and not extrac-

---

15. AG, A¹2592:85.

16. See, for example, KM, 44:3:8:1 (8 March 1744, document 1); KM 44:2:10:1, Ekberg, "Antoine Valentin de Gruy," 136-50; Dorrance (*Survival of French*, 11) suggested that Ste. Genevieve was founded as a lead depot in the early 1720s. This suggestion was probably incorrect.

Commemorative plaque at Mine La Motte, Missouri. La Motte Cadillac visited the area in 1715. Photo by Holly Johnson.

tion of salt or lead, that prompted the founding of the first permanent European settlement west of the Mississippi in the Illinois Country. This was Ste. Genevieve, about whose founding there has been much confusion.

It is generally agreed that the "Old Town" of Ste. Genevieve, which was located on the Mississippi floodplain several miles below the present site of Ste. Genevieve, Missouri, was the first permanent European settlement west of the Mississippi River in the Illinois Country. At the time of its founding, Ste. Genevieve was clearly an offshoot of older French communities on the east bank of the Mississippi — Cahokia, Kaskaskia, Fort de Chartres, Prairie du Rocher, and St. Philippe. Kaskaskia was by far the most important of these parent communities, and the first official documents pertaining to citizens of Ste. Genevieve, whether for civil or religious affairs, were recorded in Kaskaskia. However, even before Ste. Genevieve had a capacity to maintain its own records it existed as a distinct village, if we define a village as a cluster of human dwellings continuously, rather than seasonally, inhabited over a period of years and that is large enough and independent enough to have a recognized name of its own.

There has been much controversy about when the French settlers from the east bank of the Mississippi planted their first permanent colony on the west bank, but the consensus has been that Ste. Genevieve was founded sometime in the 1730s. The historic monument in Ste. Genevieve states 1735. The founding date of Ste. Genevieve is an issue of some historical importance, for knowledge of when French settlers from the east bank of the Mississippi were obliged to cross the river and found a permanent village on the west bank will help us to understand the social and economic structures of French colonial society in the upper Mississippi Valley. Thus it is necessary to determine, as accurately as possible, the date when Ste. Genevieve was established.[17]

The great historian of early Missouri, Louis Houck, was the first scholar seriously to address the question of the date of Ste. Genevieve's founding. Houck adduced three pieces of evidence to make his case that the town was established as early as the 1730s. First, there was the case of the cut stone allegedly found in 1881 near the site of the Old Town. Houck never saw the stone but he was persuaded that the stone existed and that, as people said, the figures "1732" were cut distinctly on its top. It is slightly embarrassing to discover a historian of Houck's stature relying upon one of the cut-stone stories that have "proved" so many fabulous events over the years.[18]

Houck's other evidence for placing the founding date of Ste. Genevieve in the 1730s was documentary. He adduced a report made in 1798 by Zenon Trudeau, lieutenant governor of Upper Louisiana, which noted that Ste. Genevieve had been settled "for more than sixty years." Trudeau was a politician, not a historian, and his casual comment in 1798 about Ste. Genevieve's founding is hardly a firm basis upon which to argue that the village was established in the 1730s. One might just as well accept the remarks of the American Captain Amos Stoddard, who stated that Ste. Genevieve had been founded shortly after the peace treaties of 1763.[19]

---

17. Charles Peterson ("Early Ste. Genevieve and Its Architecture," 208-10) has been virtually alone in setting the town's founding date at about 1750.

18. Houck, *History of Missouri*, 1:338.

19. "Trudeau's Report Concerning the Settlements of the Spanish Illinois Country," January 15, 1798, in *SRM*, 2:247-58; Houck, 1:338; Stoddard, *Sketches*, 215.

Houck's final piece of evidence was a report written by the English Captain Philip Pittman, who was stationed across the Mississippi from Ste. Genevieve at Fort Cavendish (the former French Fort de Chartres) during the 1760s. Pittman's report on Ste. Genevieve was published in 1770 as part of his well-known, *The Present State of the European Settlements on the Mississippi,* but Pittman wrote it in 1766. Houck quoted Pittman's published work that "the first settlers of this village (Ste. Genevieve) removed about twenty-eight years ago from Cascasquias," and used this passage to support his contention that Ste. Genevieve was founded in the 1730s. Interestingly, however, Pittman's original manuscript report on Ste. Genevieve, which he sent to General Thomas Gage in February 1766 reads differently than his published description: "Ste. Genevieve . . . had its first establishment about 20 years ago." In any case, Pittman was unsure of the date ("about twenty-eight years ago" or "about 20 years ago") and probably had relied upon nothing but hearsay evidence. As a military engineer, Pittman was obviously more concerned with providing accurate descriptions of the Illinois settlements than he was in ascertaining their founding dates. However, if we wish to use Pittman as a source, we had best use the description that he sent to General Gage in February 1766, for it was written from the Illinois Country shortly after Pittman visited Ste. Genevieve and has the greater immediacy. This description: "Ste. Genevieve . . . had its first establishment about 20 years ago," would leave us with a founding date of about 1746 instead of 1738.[20]

Houck did not know of documents that were left by another British officer who visited the Illinois Country before Philip Pittman. Captain Thomas Stirling was dispatched from Fort Pitt with a detachment of men from the 42nd Regiment of Foot (the Black Watch) and arrived in October 1765 at Fort de Chartres, which he rechristened Fort Cavendish. In two letters written in 1765 to his superior, General Gage, Stirling mentioned Ste. Genevieve. The first of these letters stated that the village had been settled fourteen years earlier, placing the founding date in 1751, and the second stated that Ste. Genevieve had been settled thirty years earlier, placing the founding date in 1735. There is

---

20. Pittman, *European Settlements,* 50; Pittman to Gage, Feb. 24, 1766, papers of General Thomas Gage, William L. Clements Library, University of Michigan, Ann Arbor (photostat in IHS); Houck, 1:338. For more on Pittman, see Thurman, "Cartography of the Illinois Country."

no apparent way to resolve this inconsistency except to note that Stirling remained only briefly (two months) in the Illinois Country, and that there is no evidence that he even visited Ste. Genevieve; thus his comments concerning dates cannot be taken very seriously. The writings of neither Pittman nor Stirling constitute source documents on the subject of Ste. Genevieve's founding because neither officer was living in the Illinois Country at the time the village was established. For the historian their comments constitute mere casual hearsay.[21]

Ida M. Schaaf, a serious amateur historian, also took up the task of assigning a date for the founding of Ste. Genevieve. She accepted all of Houck's arguments, and then proceeded to buttress the case for an early founding date (1730s) by doing some dubious editing of the writings of Father Philibert Watrin. Watrin, a French Jesuit, served in the Illinois Country from 1747 to 1763, when the Society of Jesus was suppressed in France and in all French colonies. Watrin eventually returned to France and wrote an apology for the missionary work done by the Jesuits in Upper Louisiana. In this apology, written in 1764, Watrin remarked that Ste. Genevieve had been established "fifteen years ago," or 1749. Schaaf managed to misconstrue Watrin's comments and finally concluded that there had been **three** eighteenth century Ste. Genevieves: The original village dating from the 1730s; Watrin's Ste. Genevieve founded in 1749; and finally the new Ste. Genevieve established after the severe flooding of the 1780s.[22]

The third author to tackle the case of placing the founding of Ste. Genevieve in the 1730s was Father Francis J. Yealy. Yealy, unlike Houck and Schaaf before him, cast a cold eye on the issue; he refused to be swept away by what seems to be a virtually irresistible antiquarian impulse to push foundation dates of towns and production dates of artifacts back, and back, and back. Yealy acknowledged that a careful investigation of French archives had turned up no mention of Ste. Genevieve during the 1730s. He was also skeptical of the cut-stone evidence, recounting the story "for what it may be worth." But Yealy had other evidence for a founding date of 1732, evidence that neither Houck nor Schaaf had adduced.[23]

---

21. Stirling to Gage, Oct. 18, 1765, in Alvord and Carter (eds.), *The New Regime*, 108; Stirling to Gage, Dec. 15, 1765, ibid., 125.

22. Schaff, "Ste. Genevieve," 145-50; Watrin in JR, 70: 232-33.

23. Yealy, *Ste. Genevieve*, 25-27.

Yealy began his case with maps drawn by the French royal cartographer Jacques-Nicolas Bellin and printed in Paris in 1755. One of these maps labeled Ste. Genevieve as a "village francois establi depuis 3. ans" (French village founded 3 years ago). Yealy concluded that, although this would seem to set the founding date of the village in 1752 instead of 1732, "the period following the numeral may . . . indicate an abbreviation for 30 or 33. Or the engraver may by mistake have omitted another numeral either before or after the figure 3. If these maps were the only evidence available, the matter would call for more thorough investigation." Yealy did not, however, have available for examination a version of the 1755 Bellin map, which instead of labeling Ste. Genevieve as "village establi depuis 3. ans," labeled it as "village establi depuis trois ans," thus spelling out the figures and eradicating any doubt as to the intention of the cartographer, who clearly wished to indicate that Ste. Genevieve had been founded in 1752. A cartographer working in Paris had of course only outdated and fragmentary information, and we cannot take this Bellin map as proof positive that Ste. Genevieve was founded in 1752. It should be noted, however, that the Bellin maps of 1755 are the first known maps to identify a village of Ste. Genevieve in the Illinois Country.[24]

In any case, after a judicious survey of materials, Yealy adduced a "conclusive piece of evidence" for asserting that 1732 must be taken as the latest possible date for the founding of Ste. Genevieve. This was a letter written on May 25, 1732 by Father Mercier, who was a priest at the Seminary of Foreign Missions in Cahokia. Father Mercier wrote to a fellow priest stationed at Quebec: "Scarcely a month ago I had the honor to send you with a certain Louis Poulin from the parish of Saint Joachim all the papers and documents that will help you. . . ." Joseph Schlarman was the first authority

---

24. Ibid., 22. There are at least three Bellin maps dated 1755 and labeled "Partie du Cours de fleuve St. Louis ou Mississippi depuis la Rivière d'Ohio jusqu'à celle des Illinois avec les habitations françoises." Yealy referred to the version printed in Villiers du Terrage, *Les dernières années*, 121. An earlier version, with "trois ans" spelled out is in the Karpinski Collection (copy in IHS, folder 7, no. 26), but this version has Ste. Genevieve located incorrectly. An amended version, with Ste. Genevieve located correctly, is reprinted in Tucker (ed.), *Indian Villages, Atlas*, Plate XXIV. The Bellin maps entitled "Carte de la Louisiane et des pays voisins," dated 1750, depict the Illinois Country in detail, but show no Ste. Genevieve.

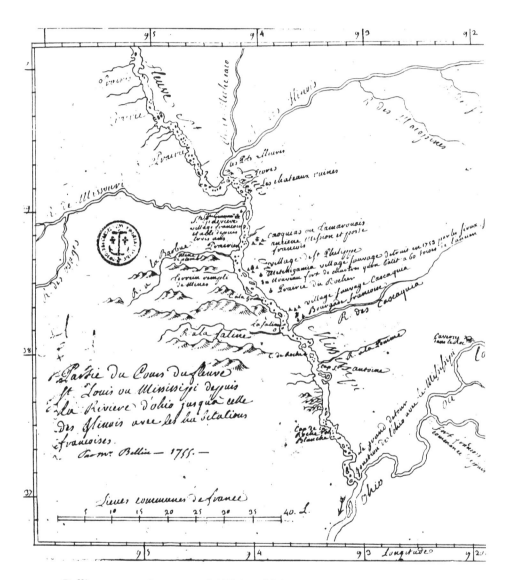

Bellin manuscript map of 1755, which states that Ste. Genevieve was
founded in 1752,"établi depuis trois ans." Notice that Ste. Genevieve is
located incorrectly, where St. Louis was founded in 1764. Original in the
Bibliothèque du Service Hydrographique, Paris.

Revised manuscript map by Bellen, 1755, showing Ste. Genevieve located correctly. Original in Bibliothèque du Service Hydrographique, Paris.

*Detail of Bellin map of Louisiana, 1755, showing Ste. Genevieve cor-
rectly located. Original in Library of Congress, Division of Maps and
Cartography.*

to identify the Saint Joachim of this 1732 letter with Ste. Genevieve. Yealy, following Schlarman's lead, pointed out that during the mid-eighteenth century the names St. Joachim and Ste. Genevieve were used interchangeably for the new French village on the west bank of the Mississippi River. Yealy used the original Ste. Genevieve parish records to demonstrate this interchangeability, and his work can be corroborated with the Kaskaskia Manuscripts now housed in the Randolph County Courthouse at Chester, Illinois. Indeed, between January 7, 1759 and August 9, 1763, Ste. Genevieve appeared as St. Joachim no fewer than ten times in the Kaskaskia civil records.[25]

But the precise dates when this usage began are important, for it is apparent that Father Mercier's mention of St. Joachim in 1732 was not a reference to the town of Ste. Genevieve in the Illinois Country, but rather a reference to the parish of St. Joachim in Quebec. Whether one uses the Ste. Genevieve parish records or the Kaskaskia Manuscripts, the first time that Ste. Genevieve appeared as St. Joachim was **1759.** The place name St. Joachim appeared in the Kaskaskia civil records before 1759, but in each of these instances St. Joachim was clearly the parish by that name in Quebec and not the French village on the west bank of the Mississippi in the Illinois Country. Cyprien Tanguay's *Dictionnaire généalogigue des familles canadiennes* tells us that the Louis Poulin of Father Mercier's letter was born in the parish of St. Joachim, Quebec, in 1710, and, after spending several years in the Illinois Country, returned there to die in 1733.[26]

Therefore we have a clear case of confused identity. Beginning with Schlarman, historians have not distinguished between the parish of St. Joachim in Quebec, from which numbers of Illinois settlers (including the well-known Louis Bolduc) came, and the French village on the west bank of the Mississippi, which between 1759 and 1767 was often called St. Joachim. This mistaken identity has had the unfortunate consequence of perpetuating the erroneous notion that Ste. Genevieve existed as a permanent settlement as early as the beginning of the 1730s; for the only substantial piece of evidence used to support the claim that Ste. Genevieve

25. Yealy, 24; Schlarman, *Quebec to New Orleans,* 287, n. 2; KM 59:1:7:1, for example.

26. KM 56:12:4:1, for example; Tanguay, *Dictionnaire,* 6:424-25. The parish of St. Joachim, Quebec was located just outside Quebec City, see Trudel, *Atlas,* 184.

existed at that time has been Father Mercier's letter of 1732 with its reference to St. Joachim.

The starting point for a fresh look at the origins of Ste. Genevieve is to clear up this issue of mistaken identity and move on to other sources and other perspectives. It is probably best to cease the quest for **the** document or **the** artifact that will provide a clear, crisp, and definitive date for the founding of Ste. Genevieve, and rather turn to an examination of the basic economic and demographic conditions in the Illinois Country during the mid-eighteenth century.

The Chevalier de Bertet (his given names are not known) was commandant at Fort de Chartres from 1742 until his death in January 1749. Sometime during his tenure in office, he, in conjunction with the civil judge of French Illinois, Joseph Buchet, granted one Antoine Heneaux (sometimes spelled Hunot) a strip of agricultural land on the alluvial bottom (later the Big Common Field of Ste. Genevieve) situated west of the Mississippi, just across from Kaskaskia. At that time Heneaux still resided in the Parish of Ste. Anne at Fort de Chartres, although he was later granted a piece of residential property in the village of Ste. Genevieve upon which he built a house. Heneaux's case is important because it demonstrates that agricultural land was being granted on the west bank of the Mississippi before 1750.[27]

By the mid-eighteenth century there was increasing demand for the rich alluvial agricultural lands located across the Mississippi from Kaskaskia. The year 1752 was one of severe drought in the upper Mississippi Valley, and that created special problems and demands. But it is also conceivable that declining agricultural productivity was becoming a chronic problem; the soil on the east side of the river was perhaps losing some of its renowned fertility after having been tilled for half a century. The primitive agricultural methods of the Indians and the French settlers, neither of whom knew how systematically to work nitrogen-fixing plants (such as clover) into a consistent pattern of crop rotation, were perhaps depleting the bottomlands around Kaskaskia and Prairie du Rocher. Major Jean-Jacques Macarty, who was commandant at Fort de Chartres from 1750 to 1760, wrote to Governor Vaudreuil in New Orleans on September 2, 1752, that the lands on the

27. Heneaux traded off his land in 1755, and the deed recounts the process by which he had acquired the property (see KM 55:2:3:1).

The foundations of the original parish church at St. Joachim, Quebec. This church, in which Louis Bolduc père *had been baptized, was burnt by British troops in 1759.*

east side of the Mississippi "were exhausted [*fatiguée*]" and that "most of the inhabitants are taking up lands on the side of Ste. Genevieve."[28]

More important than the condition of the soil on the east side of the Mississippi was the fact that there were more persons who craved land upon which to settle. The French colonial population in the Illinois Country was increasing, and colonists were moving to the west side of the Mississippi "near Ste. Genevieve," Macarty observed, "for there is no more land to sow or to allocate around here [i.e., on the east side of the river]." In April 1752, Jean-Baptiste Lasource, an *habitant* of Kaskaskia, petitioned Commandant Macarty on behalf of his two sons and one *beau-fils* (a son of Lasource's wife by her first husband). All three of these young men wished to settle in the Illinois Country close to their family, but, according to Lasource, "the large number of children here [i.e., near Kaskaskia] means that they cannot find enough land to

28. Macarty to Vaudreuil, Sep. 2, 1752, printed in Pease (ed.), *Illinois on the Eve of the Seven Years' War*, 693.

settle on in this area." Thus Lasource was asking Macarty for three homesites in the village of Ste. Genevieve and for three parcels of agricultural land outside of the village upon which the young men of his family could respectively live and farm. Lasource's petition represented a concern for the next generation of *habitants* in the Illinois Country and also his personal interest in maintaining the integrity of his extended family. Macarty granted the request.[29]

It would have been **convenient** for the French colonists in the Illinois Country to have had a permanent settlement on the west side of the Mississippi during the 1720s; such a settlement would have facilitated exploitation of the salt springs and the lead mines. However, it became **imperative** for them to have such a settlement by about 1750. The soil on the east side of the river was not as productive as it once had been, and, more importantly, there was a growing number of colonists who required land for homesites and for farms. That land was available on the alluvial plain west of the Mississippi River.

The oldest known document to use Ste. Genevieve as a place name is located in the Ste. Genevieve civil records and is dated April 27, 1751. This document, which must have been part of the Kaskaskia records originally, pertains to a survey that Antoine Heneaux requested for his land "located at Ste. Genevieve." Jean-Baptiste Bertlot *dit* Barrois, who was both a notary and a surveyor ("arpenteur") in Kaskaskia, responded to Heneaux's request and crossed the Mississippi in April 1751 to conduct the survey. This Heneaux was the same man who had received a grant of land on the Big Field from the commandant of Fort de Chartres, De Bertet, in the late 1740s, and he appears as a resident of Ste. Genevieve in the official census of 1752. Heneaux was clearly one of the first colonists to leave the parish of St. Anne at Fort de Chartres and move permanently to the west bank of the Mississippi. He sold his house near the fort in the spring of 1750, probably in preparation for moving across the river.[30]

In 1751, the surveyor Barrois described Heneaux as living at Ste. Genevieve. But the persons who owned land adjacent to Henaux's tract, Messieurs Desrousselles and Ossant, were not so

---

29. Ibid., see Lasource's petition, April 25, 1752, in MHS, Guibourd Collection.

30. SGA, Surveys, no. 75. See property transactions in Brown and Dean (eds.), *Village of Chartres*, 563-65. All citations of the SGA refer to the microfilm in the MHS. *Dit,* "called," introduced nicknames in colonial French parlance.

described. Their domiciles were not specified, and it is possible that though they owned land at Ste. Genevieve they continued to live on the east bank of the Mississippi. Indeed, neither Desrousselles nor Ossant were shown as residents of Ste. Genevieve in the 1752 census. Censuses were of course crude instruments in the eighteenth century, and Heneaux's neighbors may simply have been missed in the tally.[31]

Jean-Bernard Bossu was a French officer who ascended the Mississippi to Fort de Chartres with Major Macarty in 1751-52. In a letter written at the fort in 1753 Bossu commented that there were five French villages in the Illinois Country. When he first published his writings in 1768 he footnoted this letter with a remark that the five settlements were "Kaskaskia, Fort de Chartres, Saint Philippe, Cahokia, and Prairie du Rocher," and that "there is now a sixth one called Ste. Genevieve." In the early 1750s, when Bossu was in the Illinois Country, Ste. Genevieve was apparently small enough and new enough altogether to escape the Frenchman's notice.[32]

Finally, there is a letter of Louis St. Ange de Bellerive, who served as the last French governor of Fort de Chartres (1764-65) and who then went into the service of Spain at the newly founded post of St. Louis, west of the Mississippi. In 1769 St. Ange wrote to the Spanish governor of Louisiana, General Alexandro O'Reilly, that Ste. Genevieve had been established fifteen or twenty years before, that is, in 1754 or 1749. St. Ange had been French commandant at Vincennes in the Illinois Country for many years (1736-64) and he may have had firsthand knowledge of the date when colonists from the east bank of the Mississippi moved as permanent settlers to the west bank. Although St. Ange's letter to O'Reilly does not have the force of a source document in the strict sense of the phrase, we may consider it as corroborative evidence for our case that Ste. Genevieve was founded about mid-eighteenth century.[33]

Barrois's record of the survey he ran for Antoine Heneaux in 1751; Major Macarty's letter to Governor Vaudreuil of 1752; the Lasource land grants of 1752; the census for the Illinois Country

---

31. SGA, Surveys, no. 75; "Rencement . . . 1752," HMLO, 426.

32. Bossu, *Travels*, 76.

33. St. Ange to O'Reilly, Nov. 23, 1769, PC, legajo 187 (hereafter numbers following PC are understood to be legajo numbers).

Je Bertlos Barrois nommé arpenteur a la requisition
des habitans des Illinois, certifie a tous qu'il
appartiendra, que ce jourd'hui xviii avril 1751 me
suis transporté exprès a la requisition de Sr. antoine Jena
habitant demeurant a Ste. Geneviève sur une terre
y Située du coté du orient Sud ouest ou fleuve du mississipi
appartenant audit Sr. henaux tenant d'un coté a
celle du Sr. Desrousselles d'autre coté a celle de Sr. offant
aboutissant audit fleuve du mississipi d'autre bout
aux cotes Contenant Deux arpens de face chaque
arpens de dix huit perches de dix huit pieds mesure
de Paris et posé trois bornes accompagnée chacune
de Deux témoins de pierre sous deux ou sur l'alignement
de ladite terre et celle de Sr. Desrousselles, et une dans
celui d'icelle et celle de Sr. offant lesquels alignement
Courrent ouest Sud ouest, et est nord est, celui du
trait quarré Courre Nord nord ouest et Sud Sud est
le tous operé au desir dudit Sr. henaux Ce que je
Verifieray au besoin Sera fait et passé aux Gascabias
les jour et an susdit temoins mon Seing.

Barrois

Record of Barrois's survey for Antoine Heneaux, 1751. This is the earliest known document to mention Ste. Genevieve by name. Original in Ste. Genevieve County Courthouse, Ste. Genevieve, Missouri. Copy courtesy of Ste. Genevieve County Court.

of 1752; the Bellin maps printed in 1755; Father Watrin's apology for the Jesuits published in 1764; and St. Ange's letter to O'Reilly of 1769 — all are documents of widely disparate nature. Yet, they converge in remarkable agreement to suggest that the Old Town of Ste. Genevieve was founded about 1750 or perhaps a few years earlier. This seems to be as far as documents will take us in pursuit of Ste. Genevieve's roots. Perhaps archaeological evidence will one day throw new or different light upon the town's origins.[34]

Ste. Genevieve was established, almost inevitably, once the population of the French settlements on the east bank of the Mississippi had attained a certain level, once the land surrounding these communities had lost some of its productive power, and once pressure from hostile Indians had subsided somewhat. All of these conditions were met by mid-eighteenth century. Then it became possible, indeed necessary, for some of the settlers to move to the west bank of the Mississippi, there to establish the village of Ste. Genevieve, dedicated to the patron saint of the capital of the settlers' ancestral country.

---

34. Dr. Melburn D. Thurman of Ste. Genevieve has begun archeological investigations at the Old Town site.

Chapter II
The Old Town

WHO WERE THE FIRST COLONISTS to settle on the west bank of the Mississippi in the Illinois Country, and what was the appearance of their village perched precariously upon the alluvial bank of the river? Captain Philip Pittman, who was stationed across the river in English Illinois, claimed that "Ste. Genevieve or Misère had its first establishment . . . by an Inhabitant of Cascasquias, who through poverty was obliged to remove, thinking to better his circumstances by industry and being at a distance from any temptation of expence." One does not usually think of mid-eighteenth-century Kaskaskia as a fleshpot whose temptations could destroy a man's fortune and family, and it is likely that in this description Pittman was simply reaching to explain Ste. Genevieve's nickname, "Misère," meaning either misery or poverty.[1]

Pittman continued his account of Ste. Genevieve's founding with more cogency:

> The only thing I think that could have made him [i.e., the first settler] fix on this place for his residence is the convenience of the carrying place from Cascasquias, which without doubt has given the greatest facility to the establishment of the Village. This carrying place cuts off 6 leagues [approximately 20 miles] in distance by water as Sainte Genevieve is 4 leagues above the River Cascasquias. The goodness of the Soil and plentiful Harvest determined many others in some years after to cross the Mississippi and settle with him; thus by degrees this Village has rose to be of some consideration.

1. Pittman to Gage, Feb. 24, 1766, Clements Library (photostat IHS).

Pittman was correct on both points: There was an easy route — one league overland and a river crossing — between Kaskaskia and the Old Town of Ste. Genevieve, and the rich bottomlands were an incentive for colonists on the east bank of the Mississippi to move to the west bank in order to pursue their agriculture.

In 1825 Theodore Hunt was working for the U.S. government as recorder of land titles in eastern Missouri. One of the stops on his circuit was Ste. Genevieve, where he interviewed one Julien Labrière (or Labruyère). Labrière turned out to be a gold mine of information about the early history of Ste. Genevieve:[2]

> Julien Labriere being duly sworn, says He is fifty Six years of age, and that he was born in the old village of S'Genevieve, which place was built about where the lower ferry is at present, that when He first had any recollection, He remembers seeing A man then very old named Baptiste LaRose, who was the first settler in the Old Village. . . . About fifty years ago there was fifty or Sixty Cabens in the old village.

The Labrière family had settled in the Old Town during the 1750s. Julien was born there in January 1770 and married in the New Town in August 1794. His memory was good, and the information that he gave Hunt in 1825 was generally correct: the Old Town had been located just below the New Town, and in 1775 (i.e., fifty years before Hunt's interview with Labrière) the village had consisted of fifty or sixty residences, or perhaps a few more. The Baptiste La Rose of Hunt's "Minutes" was probably Jean-Baptiste Deguire *dit* La Rose, who had been an early settler in the Old Town. Or Labrière may have been confusing Jean-Baptiste with his kinsman, Andre Deguire *dit* La Rose, who had also lived in the Old Town during Labrière's boyhood.[3]

The French census of the Illinois Country in 1752 is an essential document for studying the first citizens of the Old Town. This census is especially valuable because in addition to listing the heads of household in early Ste. Genevieve it provides detailed information on the families and their worldly possessions. The first and wealthiest head-of-household listed on the census was La Rose. This was surely André Deguire *dit* La Rose and *not* Jean-Baptiste Deguire *dit* La Rose of Hunt's "Minutes." Jean-Baptiste, who ap-

2. "Hunt's Minutes," typescript MHS, archives.
3. SGPR, Baptisms, Book A:40; Marriages, Book B:27.

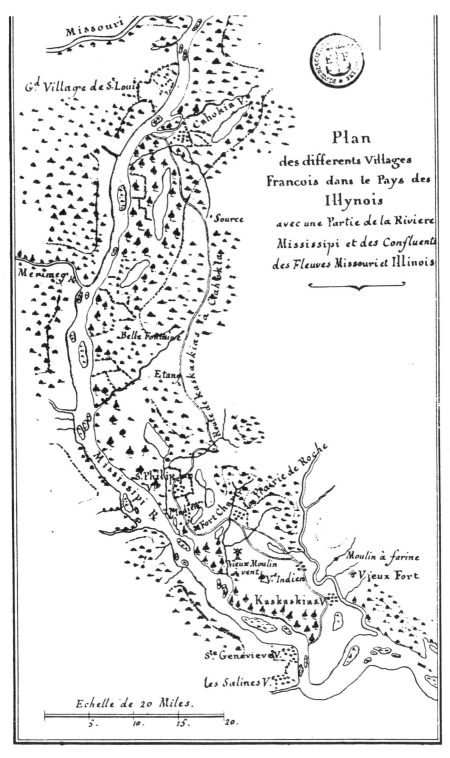

French map of the Illinois Country by an unknown cartographer. It would seem to date from the mid-1760s. Notice St. Louis at the top, and Ste. Genevieve at the bottom. Original in Bibliothèque du Service Hydrographique, Paris.

pears on the Kaskaskia census for 1752, was probably André's cousin, and he moved to Ste. Genevieve some years later. The Deguires were a French-Canadian family who had settled in Kaskaskia early in the eighteenth century. From later documents it appears that André Deguire *père*, who was the La Rose shown on the Ste. Genevieve census of 1752, was born in Canada about 1692, and was therefore an elderly man when he became a pioneer settler on the west bank of the Mississippi in the early 1750s.[4]

The Kaskaskia Manuscripts contain a bill of sale dated October 17, 1751, for a house located near Kaskaskia. The owner, André Deguire *dit* La Rose, was selling it to the surgeon in Kaskaskia, Louis Chancellier. Interestingly, the house was encumbered with a mortgage, and in order to clear the title for sale Deguire had to transfer the mortgage to "the house and other buildings that he has constructed at the village of Ste. Genevieve." Thus André Deguire, farmer from Kaskaskia, was selling out and taking himself and his family to the west bank of the Mississippi in search of greener pastures. André Deguire La Rose was clearly one of the pioneer settlers in Ste. Genevieve.[5]

The 1752 census indicates that André Deguire *père* had quite a household to manage as the first citizen of fledgling Ste. Genevieve: a wife, three sons old enough to bear arms (fifteen or older), two pre-pubescent daughters, one indentured servant, and one black slave. This household was established on seven arpents of land along the Mississippi, and tended an assortment of cattle, horses, and hogs. Deguire was certainly the most important man in the village, being the only one to own gunpowder and shot, although his fellow citizens did have muskets in which to use the ammunition. The Deguire-La Rose family was large and remained important in Ste. Genevieve throughout the colonial period.[6]

The second head-of-family in the census was one Antoine Obichon. Major Macarty, who drafted the census, was a whimsical speller, and this individual was probably Antoine Aubuchon. Au-

---

4. "Recencement . . . 1752," HMLO, 426. In 1777, André Deguire *père* gave a legal deposition and stated his age as eighty-five years (PC 1).

5. KM 51:10:17:1.

6. "Recencement . . . 1752," HMLO, 426. André Deguire may already have been captain of a small militia in Ste. Genevieve, which would explain his possession of powder and shot. The arpents of the 1752 census were apparently linear arpents facing the Mississippi, and it was understood that the property ran back to the hill line. Concerning units of measure, see below, Appendix G.

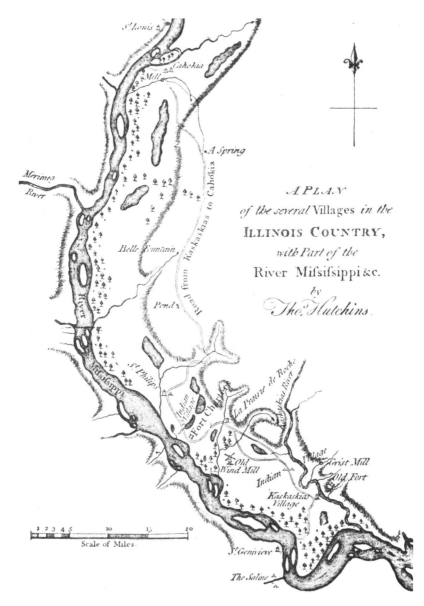

Thomas Hutchins' map of 1771. It is apparent that Hutchins used the preceding French map when drafting this one. Notice the road leading from Kaskaskia toward Ste. Genevieve. Photo from Hutchins, Topographical Descriptions, *1778.*

buchon's wife Elizabeth was the daughter of Deguire's wife Elizabeth by her first husband. Thus the Aubuchons fell within the extended family of André Deguire and probably considered Deguire their patron and protector. Aubuchon had only his wife, one pre-pubescent daughter, and an indentured servant to make up his household, and he held three arpents of land. Like the Deguires, the Aubuchons remained one of the foremost families of Ste. Genevieve throughout the colonial period.[7]

Rather oddly, the census next shows a household consisting of two adult male *habitants* (farmers), Duboy and Truto. These men were apparently partners and had pooled their resources; they controlled six arpents of agricultural land, instead of the customary concession of three arpents. Duboy and Truto (probably Dubois and Truteau) were horse breeders and they owned more horses than all other residents of Ste. Genevieve combined. French *habitants* in the Illinois Country routinely relied upon oxen rather than horses as draft animals. But they did use horses extensively for milling grain, and, like the French Canadians, they were expert horsemen and had a passion for spirited mounts. Dubois seems to have sold out in 1758 and left Ste. Genevieve. Truteau may have been Louis Truteau, who was originally from Kaskaskia and who eventually raised a family in Ste. Genevieve. Or Truteau may have been Pierre Truteau, a blacksmith who appears in later civil records.[8]

A single man, Ledoux, appears next in the census. Probably a French Canadian from Kaskaskia, he made up a single-member household on three arpents of bottom land. Perhaps this Ledoux was the Louis Ledoux who appeared as a "voyageur" on the Ste. Genevieve militia roster in 1779.[9]

Antoine Eneo (Antoine Heneaux), a pig farmer, followed Ledoux on the census. It is a bit of mystery why Heneaux, who had been a prosperous man at Fort de Chartres, crossed the river into Indian territory in order to settle down and raise his pigs and his family on three arpents of Mississippi mud. Perhaps he had fallen on hard times in the late 1740s, or perhaps he simply thirsted for adventure. In any case, Heneaux was one of the first settlers to own one of the small cluster of houses that constituted the

---

7. "Recencement . . . 1752"; Belting, Kaskaskia, 119.

8. "Recencement . . . 1752"; KM 58:7:15:1.

9. "Recencement . . . 1752"; "Relation de la compagnie de milice du post de Ste. Geneviève," Nov. 29, 1779, PC 213.

original village of Ste. Genevieve. He sold his land and his house near Fort de Chartres in the spring of 1750, and there is no record of his having built or purchased another residence on the east side of the Mississippi. Like Aubuchon, Heneaux was connected to the Deguire clan, for his first wife had been a sister to André Deguire's wife. After his first wife's death, Heneaux married Charlotte Chassin, with whom he moved to Ste. Genevieve.[10]

Antoine Heneaux was clearly well-established in Ste. Genevieve when the census of 1752 was taken. In January 1752 one Toussaint Heneaux petitioned Benoist St. Claire, commandant at Fort de Chartres before Macarty took over in March 1752, for land at Ste. Genevieve on the basis that he wished to settle close to his brother. Toussaint did not fulfill St. Claire's conditions for receiving the land (the grantee had to live on the land for a year and a day) and later in the year Macarty granted the parcel to someone else. Antoine Heneaux, however, continued to reside in Ste. Genevieve until his death in 1773, when he left a widow, four children, and an estate worth 5,000 livres.[11]

Jaque (Jacques) Chouquet (sometimes Duchouquet or Duchoquette) appears next on the census list. He was the son of a French-Canadian merchant and had immigrated to Kaskaskia before settling in Ste. Genevieve. Although Chouquet owned only three arpents of land, he had the second largest (after André Deguire) herd of domestic animals and owned one black slave. Joseph Chouquet, probably Jacques' brother, was also a resident of Ste. Genevieve by 1753. Joseph had married Marie Rose Deguire in 1747, and thus the Chouquets were also part of the Deguire family network.[12]

With the name of J. B. Beauvay (Jean-Baptiste Bauvais) we come upon one of the most important family names of colonial Ste. Genevieve. The French-Canadian Bauvais family moved to the Illinois Country in the early eighteenth century, and by mid-century Jean-Baptiste St. Gemme Bauvais *père* was probably the wealthiest merchant in Kaskaskia. When the Society of Jesus was

---

10. "Recencement . . . 1752"; Brown and Dean (eds.), 563-65; Belting, 91, 119-20.

11. Toussaint Heneaux's petition, Jan. 20, 1752, MHS, Guibourd Collection; SGA, Estates, no. 127. A royal decree of 1743 (AAE, Mémoires et Documents, Amérique 8:26) gave French colonial governors the right to repossess unused parcels of land.

12. "Recencement . . . 1752"; KM 53:9:16:1; Belting, *Kaskaskia*, 82, 120.

abolished and their property sold in 1763, Bauvais bought the property. By the 1760s, the Bauvaises owned so much real estate on both sides of the Mississippi that it is sometimes difficult to place them precisely as residents of Kaskaskia or of Ste. Genevieve. The Bauvais man shown on the 1752 Ste. Genevieve census was almost surely Jean-Baptiste *fils,* for Jean-Baptiste *père* appeared on the Kaskaskia census for that year. Perhaps the son had been sent temporarily to the west side of the Mississippi to serve as the family agent for the new land concessions opening there. After returning to Kaskaskia, Jean-Baptiste *fils,* along with his brother Vital St. Gemme Bauvais, finally moved to New Ste. Genevieve in the late 1780s; they both immediately became leading citizens of the town.[13]

The last individual listed on the 1752 census was Bon *dit* Simon, a soldier. He possessed the usual three arpents of land, but had no family, no hired hands, and no slaves residing in his household. Some soldiers from Fort de Chartres took leave of the French army to become permanent citizens of Ste. Genevieve. Simon apparently did not, and his appearance in the 1752 census is the one brief reference we have to him.[14]

There they were clustered together on the frontier west bank of the Mississippi in the Illinois Country — nine property owners with their families, their volontaires, and their black slaves. Twenty-three human souls — white and black, free and slave — who were the first official non-Indian residents of what became the State of Missouri. They surely did not think of themselves as persons whose activities were worthy of historical note. But their decision to move across the Mississippi in mid- eighteenth century made them pioneer settlers in a newly established village, a village that would grow, prosper, and play a vital role in the colonial history of the Mississippi River Valley.[15]

These nine families were official because they were the only

---

13. "Recencement . . . 1752"; Alvord and Carter (eds.), *The Critical Period,* 127-31; Alvord (ed.), *Kaskaskia Records,* passim. Members of this family in the Illinois Country always spelled their name Bauvais, not Beauvais. Their move to the New Town of Ste. Genevieve is dealt with below, chap. xiii.

14. "Recencement . . . 1752."

15. The three white *volontaires* on the 1752 census, who lived respectively with André Deguire, Antoine Aubuchon, and Jean-Baptiste Bauvais, did not own land at that time and were left nameless on the census. *Volontaires* were landless, white laborers.

families credited to Ste. Genevieve on the French census for Louisiana in 1752. There were, however, additional persons who owned land in or around Ste. Genevieve. And some of these property owners probably lived there but were somehow omitted from the census. Census-taking was a newfangled device of civil governments in the eighteenth century, and censuses from that era are notoriously inaccurate. Take, for example, the following case: Nicolas Albain *dit* La Feuillade, a soldier from Fort de Chartres, who according to Major Macarty's notes of September 1752 had already been granted land at Ste. Genevieve. It is apparent from other records that Albain did move to Ste. Genevieve at least as early as 1753, although the exact date is not known. Conceivably, Albain was, in 1752, still residing at Fort de Chartres and was only preparing to move to Ste. Genevieve. However, it seems more likely that Albain, for one reason or another, was simply omitted from the 1752 census, although already a citizen of the town.[16]

Or take the sons of Jean-Baptiste Lasource of Kaskaskia — Jean-Baptiste *fils,* Dominique, and Joseph Lamy — to whom Macarty granted both residential and agricultural land at Ste. Genevieve in April 1752 on the condition that they homestead ("maintain hearth and habitation") there for a year and a day. Perhaps the data for the 1752 census were gathered before they received their grants in April. This may also be true for François Rivard, a *volontaire* from the east side of the river, who was granted land at Ste. Genevieve in May 1752 on the same condition that he homestead it.[17]

Also of interest for the early history of the Old Town are two men, Janis and Chaponga, who were mentioned in Rivard's grant as adjoining property owners and must therefore have owned land in the Big Field before Rivard requested his grant. It seems certain that Janis was Nicolas Janis, who married a sister of the Lasource brothers, Marie-Louise, in April 1751, and who probably moved to Ste. Genevieve with his new bride. Logically, Janis and his wife should have appeared in the town's census for 1752. On the other hand, Chaponga was probably the Jean-Baptiste Chaponga who appears on the Kaskaskia census for 1752. In this case Chaponga's land grant was apparently not tied to a condition of occupying the property and he continued to live in Kaskaskia

16. Macarty's "Signalement," HMLO, 568; KM 53:11:28:1.

17. Lasource grant, Apr. 25, 1752, MHS, Guibourd Collection; Rivard grant, May 1, 1752, ibid.

while improving his land at Ste. Genevieve, and perhaps even pasturing domestic animals on it.[18]

Jean-Baptiste Lasource's wife, and the mother of the three young men represented in Jean-Baptiste's petition to Macarty, was Marie-Françoise Rivard. It seems likely that she was the sister of the earlier petitioner, François Rivard. Since all four petitioners were granted their requests for land, François and these three nephews became neighboring pioneers in the emerging village of Ste. Genevieve. One of the nephews, Dominique Lasource, later married Elizabeth Aubuchon, daughter of another pioneer settler, Antoine Aubuchon.[19]

It is apparent that most of the original residents of the Old Town of Ste. Genevieve were a closely-knit group of French Canadian *habitants,* or children of such *habitants,* who migrated from the east to the west bank of the Mississippi in pursuit of agricultural land. In these respects the migration that created the Old Town of Ste. Genevieve closely resembled the migrations that, as described by Jacques Mathieu, created new towns within the St. Lawrence River Valley.[20]

Ste. Genevieve of the early 1750s was far from a boom town. At this early stage of its development, the village had neither its own civil nor parish records. Its history must be pieced together from the records that were kept in the established communities on the east bank of the Mississippi, Fort de Chartres and Kaskaskia. Indeed, throughout the 1750s the new village on the west bank of the river was often called "Ste. Geneviève des Cascakias," which phrase reveals the village's status as a satellite of Kaskaskia. The latter was always referred to as "la ville," the city, while Ste. Genevieve was merely "le village."[21]

People from the east bank did, however, continue to spill over onto the west bank, and Ste. Genevieve, satellite though it was, grew steadily during the 1750s. Take, for example, two soldiers who had made up part of the garrison at Fort de Chartres. Nicolas

---

18. Rivard grant, ibid.; Belting, 83, 89; "Recencement . . . 1752," HMLO, 426. Nicolas Janis moved back to Kaskaskia and in 1760 sold his house and property in Ste. Genevieve (see KM 60:8:14:1). The Janis family moved to the New Town of Ste. Genevieve in the late 1780s (see below, chap. xiii).

19. Belting, *Kaskaskia,* 85, 89, 119.

20. Mathieu, "Familles et colonisation."

21. See, for example, KM 58:6:15:1; KM 58:7:15:1; KM 58:7:26:1; KM 60:8:14:1.

MARRIAGE ALLIANCES BETWEEN SOME OF STE. GENEVIEVE'S EARLIEST FAMILIES

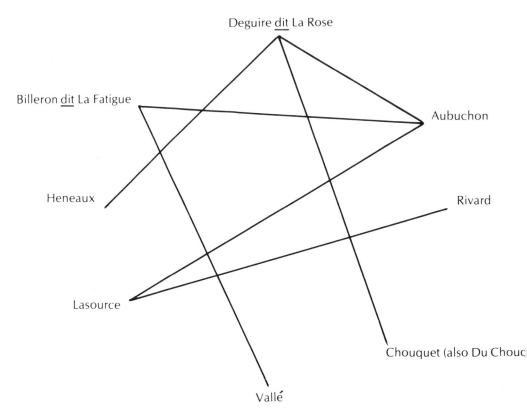

Albain, who was mentioned above, had been granted land at Ste. Genevieve in 1751 but was not included as a resident of the village in the 1752 census. Later civil records show that he had constructed some buildings on his property at Ste. Genevieve, and it seems likely that he lived in the village, at least for a time. Albain's comrade-in-arms, Jean-André Vignon *dit* Vicontant, was granted a plot of land next to Albain, and Vignon stayed on to become one of the solid citizens of early Ste. Genevieve.[22]

---

22. Macarty's "Signalement," HMLO, 568; KM 53:11:28:1. Vignon was sergeant in the Ste. Genevieve militia in 1766, see "Etat de la milice de Ste. Geneviève," PC 187.

These two soldiers are worth examining, for Major Macarty provided detailed biographical data on them. Insofar as Albain from Louisiana and not from French Canada, they were unique among their fellow settlers in the new village. Indeed, they were probably the only early settlers to have been born in France rather than North America, for French Canadians like André Deguire were generally already second or third generation North Americans. Because Albain and Vignon had been born and raised in France, their customs, mannerisms, and speech were perhaps rather odd among the French Canadians who were their neighbors in early Ste. Geneviève.[23]

In physical characteristics, Albain and Vignon were also probably somewhat different than their fellow townsmen of French Canadian extraction. Albain was five feet, three inches in height and had a long face with chestnut hair and eyebrows; Vignon was five feet, four inches tall, had black hair, eyebrows, and a beard. He also had a pug nose. Albain's height represents the average for the six soldiers whom Macarty described, and it is safe to assume that this was the average height for settlers in the Illinois Country who had been reared in France. On the other hand, the French Canadians and creoles in Illinois were probably larger in stature, for they had been raised on better diets than the Frenchmen, diets that were richer in proteins. Although they always made up a small minority of the town's population, metropolitan Frenchmen continued to immigrate to Ste. Geneviève throughout the colonial period.[24]

New settlers continued to trickle into Ste. Geneviève from Kaskaskia and Fort de Chartres during the 1750s. Despite the growing tensions between Great Britain and France and the war that finally erupted between them in 1756, the Illinois Country was relatively tranquil during the 1750s. Not even the Osage Indians seemed to trouble the settlers in the new village during its first decade of existence. Laurant Gaboury moved over from Fort de Chartres and began to build a new house, but died before it was completed. Jean-Baptiste Bauvais bought the house, and the Gaboury name disappears from the written records, only to acquire its own little piece of immortality in being affixed to a tiny tributary of the Mississippi, Gabouri Creek.[25]

---

23. Macarty's "Signalement," HMLO, 568.
24. Ibid.
25. KM 54:12:15:1.

François Vallé *père*, who was destined to become the leading citizen of Ste. Genevieve, had migrated to the Illinois Country from Canada in the 1740s and married at Kaskaskia in 1748. He owned property at Ste. Genevieve as early as 1753. Vallé sold his house in Kaskaskia in 1754, and it would seem that it was in the summer of that year that Ste. Genevieve acquired its future leader. At Ste. Genevieve's first recorded auction sale in March 1755 Vallé appeared in the column of purchasers as an *habitant* of the area. Vallé's wealth and prominence made him virtually a seigneur in the community, although the seigneurial class did not officially exist on the French-Illinois frontier.[26]

The record of the auction sale of 1755 is one of the more interesting and valuable documents on the early history of Ste. Genevieve. The occasion for the auction was the death of one François Laroque, who had been the village blacksmith. Items to be sold consisted of his possessions, mostly tools of the smithy's trade. The sale of Laroque's estate was conducted by a royal clerk dispatched from Fort de Chartres. This clerk, Joachim Gérard, was an agent of the civil judge of the French-Illinois Country, Joseph Buchet, who had served at Fort de Chartres since the early 1730s. Gérard carefully recorded his arrival on the morning of March 17, 1755, at "the house of Sieur Deguire La Rose [i.e., André Deguire], captain of the militia, with my two witnesses." But it is clear that in 1755 there was virtually no local government in Ste. Genevieve; government had to be brought in from across the river in order to conduct the auction.[27]

It is easy to imagine this auction as one of the major social events in the early history of Ste. Genevieve: friends and relatives came across the river from Kaskaskia; everyone took the day off to bid, gossip, and exchange news. Probably someone broke open a keg of tafia, that powerful and ubiquitous cheap rum of the Mississippi River Valley French, to chase away the chill of the March air. Women as well as men called out their bids, and Laroque's estate brought a total of 498 livres, 10 sous. An anvil, which had been Laroque's most precious possession, brought 140 livres. Its value stemmed from the travail of transporting such a heavy and necessary tool up the Mississippi from New Orleans. Pierre Trudeau, listed as a resident blacksmith of Ste. Genevieve, brought the anvil; perhaps he had been Laroque's partner before the latter's death.

---

26. KM 53:5:16:5; KM 54:6:3:1; KM 55:3:17:1; Belting, 86-87.
27. Ibid.
28. Ibid.

The Vallé (La Vallée) ancestral home in Beauport, Quebec. This late seventeenth century structure has stone walls covered with stucco (pierre crépie).

Gérard, with a mentality typical of a minor French bureaucrat, was clearly pleased to have been dispatched across the river to Ste. Genevieve in order to conduct the auction with "his" two witnesses, and he drafted up the proceedings with a flourish.[28]

The Deguire clan was expanded and the population of Ste. Genevieve enlarged when in 1756 André Deguire *fils* married Marguerite Gouvreau of Kaskaskia and became the second Deguire head-of-household in the village. The other leading family, Vallé, however, also had its extensions, for François Vallé's brother-in-law, Pierre Billeron *dit* Lafatique, moved to Ste. Genevieve with his wife Elizabeth Aubuchon. Thus we come full circle and complete the marriage relationships among the three most prominent families of early Ste. Genevieve — Deguire, Vallé, and Aubuchon. The Aubuchons were the connecting link, being related by intermarriage to both of the other two, and also to the large but less affluent Lasource clan.[29]

---

29. André Deguire *fils* married in Kaskaskia, see Belting, 84. In 1765, Louis Bolduc married Deguire's sister-in-law, Agathe Gouvreau, in Ste. Genevieve, SGPR, Marriages, Book A:131. SGPR, Book A, contains marriage and baptismal records to 1786. On Aubuchon marriages, see Belting: 83, 84, 86, 89, 94, 119.

Eighteenth-century people placed greater weight on extended family relationships than do their twentieth-century descendants, and the citizens of Ste. Genevieve were deeply concerned with who married whom in their families. The pattern of intermarriage among the prominent families of Ste. Genevieve, which continued throughout the colonial period, was a cement that helped to maintain social cohesiveness and stability in a frontier community. When in 1798 Lieutenant Governor Trudeau in St. Louis described the communities in Spanish Illinois, he remarked that the inhabitants of Ste. Genevieve "are united by the most narrow bonds. For nearly all of them being related, blood binds them to maintain the fast friendship and harmony which has always existed among them." Obviously Trudeau knew of what he wrote.[30]

In 1763 the Treaty of Paris ended the French and Indian War (Seven Years' War in Europe), and diplomats in Europe parceled out the territory in the heart of the North American continent to new owners: the Illinois Country east of the Mississippi River became English territory and the Illinois Country west of the river became Spanish. This juggling of the geopolitics of North America had profound consequences for the village of Ste. Genevieve. The most obvious one, that Ste. Genevieve was now under Spanish sovereignty instead of French, mattered little at first; the population remained French, and the Spanish monarchy did not assume command of its new province for years to come. More important was the fact that, as the French lost possession of the territory around Fort de Chartres and Kaskaskia, the new overlords, Englishmen, arrived in the Illinois Country. The Englishmen were immediately unpopular with the French colonists there. Unpopular because they were English; unpopular because they were Protestants; and unpopular because, not caring much about the remote Illinois Country, the English did not exercise effective government in their newly acquired territory on the Mississippi.[31]

On the other hand, the Spanish regime on the west side of the Mississippi was not at all inhospitable or alien to the French colonists in the Illinois Country. The Spanish monarchy had close blood ties to the French monarchy — they were both Bourbon family governments; the Spaniards were of course Roman Catholics like the French; and the Spanish colonial authorities wel-

---

30. *SRM*, 2:248.

31. See Alvord, *Illinois Country*, 246-328; Carter, *Great Britain and the Illinois Country*.

comed the French colonists from the east side of the river. In 1765 Captain Thomas Stirling, a royal officer in British Illinois, described the problem to his superior, General Thomas Gage:[32]

> The Settlement [i.e., British Illinois] has been declining Since the Commencement of the War [French and Indian War], and when it was Ceded to us many Familys went away for fear of the English, and want of Troops to protect them from the Indians; they have formed a Settlement Since the Peace [of Paris] Opposite to Caho [Cahokia] called St. Louis, where there is now [1765] about Fifty familys, and they have another opposite to Caskaskias [Ste. Genevieve], which has . . . about the same number of Familys, to these two Places they have retired.

This description of the state of affairs in the Illinois Country during the mid-1760s is accurate and enlightening. French colonists were fleeing the east side of the Mississippi for the west side, and one of the principal loci of their resettlement was Ste. Genevieve.

In November 1766 François Lalumandière *dit* Lafleur sent a petition from Ste. Genevieve to St. Ange de Bellerive, provisional commandant at St. Louis. Lalumandière, who had just crossed the Mississippi from Kaskaskia, wished to settle in Ste. Genevieve and he was applying for a piece of residential property. He explained to St. Ange that he had lived for many years in the village of Kaskaskia but that he wished to leave that community "to take refuge in his fatherland" because Kaskaskia had been "ceded to the enemies of the religion and the fatherland." Lalumandière probably was not sure which European state, France or Spain, possessed the west side of the Mississippi, but in any case Ste. Genevieve was preferable to British-held Kaskaskia. St. Ange, in the absence of any Spanish authority, granted Lalumandière a residential lot "next to Monsieur Lasource."[33]

It is difficult to trace the growth in population of Ste. Genevieve between 1752, when the French census of that year showed a grand total of twenty-three inhabitants, black and white; and 1772, when the first comprehensive Spanish census showed a total of

---

32. Stirling to Gage, Dec. 15, 1765, Alvord and Carter (eds.), *The New Regime*, 125.

33. See Lalumandière's petition, Nov. 27, 1766, and St. Ange's approval of the grant, Dec. 4, 1766, in SGA, Concessions, no. 57.

691, black and white. It is, however, apparent that Ste. Genevieve's population was growing very slowly during the first decade of that period, 1752-1762, and very rapidly during the second decade, 1762-1772. Indeed, the growth was so rapid during the later phase that one can fairly speak of a demographic explosion, which changed dramatically the size and makeup of the Old Town. The flood of new inhabitants that swept into Ste. Genevieve from the east side of the Mississippi during the 1760s created the mature Old Town, the Old Town that was not abandoned until after the severe flooding of the late 1780s.[34]

No census was taken in the Illinois Country during the last decade of the French regime because disruptions brought on by the French and Indian War precluded effective functioning of the civil government. When the British officers, Pittman and Stirling, arrived at Fort de Chartres in the mid-1760s, however, they observed the settlements on the Spanish side of the river and presented estimates of their sizes. Stirling wrote in December 1765 that there were fifty families in Ste. Genevieve, and Pittman, writing just two months later, estimated that there were seventy families. Ensign Thomas Hutchins, who was stationed in Illinois from September 1769 to September 1770, remarked that "Ste. Geneviève, or Misère, [contains] One Hundred and Fifty Houses, Four Hundred and Sixty Inhabitants, besides Three Hundred and Seventy Negro Slaves." Hutchins exaggerated the number of houses, but his population figures seem fairly accurate.[35]

A good guide to Ste. Genevieve's population during the mid-1760s is the muster roll of the town militia for 1766. The militia was composed of virtually every male citizen old enough to bear arms and the muster roll contains 115 names. Extrapolating from this figure, Hutchins' estimate of 460 total inhabitants, including slaves, for Ste. Genevieve seems about right. These figures are more or less consistent with the Spanish census of 1772, which gave a population of 691, slaves included, and reveal Ste.

34. Some immigrants (Louis Bolduc for example) came to Ste. Genevieve from Canada during the 1760s, and some (Jean-Baptiste Datchurut for example) even came from France. Most, however, were natives of the Illinois Country.

35. Stirling to Gage, Dec. 15, 1765, Alvord and Carter (eds.), The *New Regime*, 125; Pittman, *European Settlements*, 50; Hutchins, "Remarks Upon the Illinois Country," PRO, Colonial Office 5, vol. 89 (photostat in IHS); see also Hutchins, *Topographical Description*, 110, for a slightly different version of Hutchins' comments about Ste. Genevieve.

Genevieve's rapid growth during the mid-1760s.[36]

The growth of Ste. Genevieve during the 1760s was not only quantitative but in a sense qualitative, for many well-to-do and prominent colonists, merchants and traders as well as agriculturists, came to settle in the town (no longer a mere village) during that decade. The militia roll for 1766 reveals the names of many important men who had not lived in Ste. Genevieve in the early years: Bolduc (originally Boisleduc from the French town of that name), Datchurut, Hubardeau, Lalumandière, Pratte, and Viviat. François Vallé *père* had risen by 1766 to be captain of the militia, and the former soldier from the French garrison at Fort de Chartres, André Vignon, was sergeant. Most important of all the newcomers, at least for the immediate future, was the commandant who drafted the muster roll for the militia in 1766, aristocratic Philippe de Rocheblave. It was thus as a Spanish town, but with an overwhelmingly French population, that Ste. Genevieve began to amount to something, with a resident commandant, its own parish priest, Sebastian Meurin, and a depository for civil records.[37]

No detailed plan of the Old Town has been discovered, but land records permit the construction of a reasonably accurate picture of the settlement. Already by the 1760s, the Old Town was shaped basically in the configuration of a "string town." That is, it was strung out along a main road that in turn ran parallel to the Mississippi River. In 1766, Pittman described it as "about one mile in length and [containing] about seventy families." At the lower end of town, La Petite Rivière, which seems to have been a stream consisting of waters from the present-day Mill and South Gabouri creeks, entered the Mississippi. The docking area for riverboats (the Old Town was a river port) and for the Kaskaskia ferry was located at the mouth of La Petite Rivière.[38]

As early as the 1750s, there were secondary roads intersecting the Old Town's main street, although only the Grande Rue had a name. Residential lots were laid out on both the major axis and the minor axes. One of the most remarkable facts about the Old Town is that it was a planned community at a very early stage of its development. The land grants of 1752 were uniformly contingent upon the grantee accepting a designated building site *(emplacement)* from "Ms. Sausier"; François Saucier was the royal en-

---

36. "Etat de la milice de Ste. Geneviève," PC 187; census of 1772, *SRM*, 1:53-54.

37. "Etat de la milice," PC 187.

38. Pittman, 50.

gineer who in the 1750s was occupied with planning the new, stone Fort de Chartres. Thus did the Renaissance notion of urban planning penetrate the American wilderness under the sponsorship of the centralizing French monarch. The Bourbon government installed at the highly geometrized Versailles was not going to abide any helter-skelter development of its colonial settlements. Sloppiness in residential patterns might create unruly subjects or even breed seditious political ideas.[39]

Beyond the village proper was the Big Field Commons, which consisted of long, narrow strips of arable land running back to the hills. This vast and rich agricultural area was the true basis of the economy of early Ste. Genevieve. It was enclosed by a single, continuous fence set back from the Mississippi, which was maintained as a community enterprise. This common fence is the source of the expression "Big Field Commons," for the strips of arable land themselves were *not* held in common but were freehold possessions of individual *habitants*. Most adult male citizens owned, in addition to their respective residential lot (*un terrain* or *emplacement*) in the village, a strip of plowland (*une terre*) within the Big Field Commons. For the pasturing of domestic stock there was a true commons, land held in common, which was located between the Mississippi and the fence that enclosed the arable fields. Thus the pattern of agricultural settlement was more European than American, or even French Canadian. Many of the cultivators (*habitants*) lived clustered together in the village, from which they would go out to work their fields, rather than on isolated farmsteads in the midst of their arable lands. Like the early English settlers near Jamestown, the residents of early Ste. Genevieve had perhaps been forced by the threat of hostile Indians to live fairly close together. This pattern of community continued until the 1790s, when, after the founding of the New Town and New Bourbon, the settlement pattern in the Ste. Genevieve District became more diffuse and dispersed.[40]

---

39. Some idea of the Old Town's configuration during the 1750s can be obtained by perusing the property transactions in KM. However, the land records from that period are not complete enough to permit an accurate mapping of the town. The residential lots granted to François Rivard and the Lasource family in 1752 were laid out by François Saucier (MHS, Guibourd Collection). By the 1760s, Saucier's plan for the Old Town was probably forgotten, and the community was free to grow in more randy fashion.

40. The pattern of settlement in Ste. Genevieve was markedly different than in French Canada, where the *habitants* had "an aversion to villages" and lived

Although Ste. Genevieve was sometimes called "Fort Misère" or "Fort St. Joachim" during the 1750s and 1760s, it is apparent that the Old Town never possessed a fort or any other kind of fortifications. St. Ange de Bellerive was the last French commandant at Fort de Chartres. After he turned the fort over to British troops in October 1765, St. Ange crossed the Mississippi to St. Louis, where he became interim governor of Upper Louisiana, for no Spanish authorities had yet arrived in the territory. In November 1769, St. Ange, who was still quartered in St. Louis, wrote to the new governor of Spanish Louisiana, Alexandro O'Reilly:[41]

> In this district [i.e., Upper Louisiana] . . . there are only two villages: Ste. Geneviève or Misère and St. Louis or Paincourt. The former was established fifteen or twenty years ago and the latter five years ago. Each one has seventy or eighty houses without any means of defense — not even a prison to punish crime and maintain good order. The former has never had a garrison and the latter is guarded by only ten or twelve unfortunate soldiers. . . .

Within a year after St. Ange wrote this letter, Ste. Genevieve did receive a small garrison of Spanish soldiers. But no fort was ever built in the Old Town, and the Spanish garrison was quartered in a house rented from François Vallé for sixty pesos per year. A royal Spanish flag flew in front of this makeshift barracks.[42]

In the absence of a fort, the largest and most important building in the Old Town was the parish church. Father Philibert Watrin, the former Jesuit who retired to France when the Society of Jesus was suppressed in 1763, knew this first church intimately because he often crossed the Mississippi from Kaskaskia to celebrate Mass in it. In his later writings he did not describe the structure but he did explain the circumstances of its erection: "The pastor of Kaskaskia found himself obliged to go there [Ste. Genevieve] to administer the Sacraments at least to the sick; and, when the new

---

on dispersed farmsteads (Harris, *The Seigneurial System*, 176-86). Margaret K. Brown (personal communication) claims that the French colonial communities east of the Mississippi were originally dispersed settlements in the French-Canadian fashion. The Puritans in New England also established, for religious and social reasons, nucleated villages not unlike early Ste. Genevieve.

41. St. Ange to O'Reilly, Nov. 23, 1769, PC 187.

42. See PC 81 for correspondence concerning Vallé's rent.

inhabitants saw their houses multiplying, they asked to have a church built there." The first church in the Old Town was built either in 1752 or 1753, for in the summer of 1752 Major Macarty at Fort de Chartres was making land grants in Ste. Genevieve contingent upon the grantees furnishing logs for the new church. These logs were probably set upright in the ground, creating a vertical-log church that would have looked much like the residences surrounding it, although larger and without galleries. The parish church was the focal point of community life in the Old Town, and in front of the church door most public business, including auction sales, was conducted.[43]

By the early 1770s, the Old Town of Ste. Genevieve had reached maturity in extent and in population. Eighteenth-century censuses were always incomplete and inaccurate, but the data they contain are nevertheless important. The Spanish census for Ste. Genevieve of 1772 shows a total population, free and slave, of 691 persons, an enormous increase over the twenty-three souls who had comprised the embryonic settlement in 1752. The 1779 census shows an increase of only seven persons, bringing the total to 698. Thus after a dramatic spurt during the 1760s, the town's population remained steady during the 1770s. The rapid development of St. Louis, founded in 1764, helped to curb the growth of Ste. Genevieve.[44]

More informative than the 1779 census is the Ste. Genevieve militia roster for the same year. Of the 175 militiamen listed in 1779, the overwhelming majority were either natives of the Illinois Country (sixty-five) or had come from Canada (seventy-one). There were also seventeen Frenchmen, a surprising fifteen Englishmen (which means that Americans were still considered Englishmen), and a scattering from other locations, including the Canary Islands.[45]

The militia roster of 1779 reveals the interesting fact that more

---

43. Watrin in *JR*, 70:232-33; Rivard and Lasource grants, MHS, Guibourd Collection.

44. Printed copy of 1772 census, *SRM*, 1:553-54; 1779 census, PC 193 A.

45. "Relation de la compagnie de milice du poste de Ste. Geneviève," Nov. 29, 1779, PC 213.

than one-third of the militiamen (sixty-four) were "voyageurs," itinerant traders and boatmen. This suggests that a large part of Ste. Genevieve's early population was mobile, containing a sizeable group of men ready and willing to pull up stakes and move on at a moment's notice. Of the more sedentary townspeople, by far the largest number (fifty-two) were either agriculturists or agriculturists with an off-season sideline like blacksmithing or brewing beer (luckily, there was a German farmer who also brewed). These farmers together with the rest of the citizens — day laborers, hunters, merchants, blacksmiths, carpenters, cabinetmakers, and other artisans — reveal the essence of the Old Town of Ste. Genevieve: it was a frontier agricultural community that was largely self-sufficient, but which had substantial intercourse with the outside world via the Mississippi River.[46]

When Spanish soldiers ascended the Mississippi to take possession of Upper Louisiana in 1767, they pulled around a bend in the river to view this scene: a background of hills covered with clusters of hardwoods and cedars; a vast expanse of arable fields running in narrow strips from the hills down to the river; vertical log, whitewashed houses more or less regularly laid out along the bank of the river; picket fences surrounding each substantial resi-dence; domestic livestock grazing at will on the unenclosed areas of the bottomland. An agreeable landscape, a landscape that human toil had made both productive and pleasing to the eye. The Spaniards called Ste. Genevieve "Misery," but they were undoubtedly content to see the town materialize over the bows of their riverboats as they rounded the last bend, after having spent several back-breaking weeks on the Mississippi, and headed for the Old Town docks.

---

46. Ibid.

Chapter III
Ste. Genevieve and the
Competition for Empire

SPAIN AND PORTUGAL were the great explorers and colonizers of the sixteenth century. In the seventeenth century, northern European powers — England, France, and the Dutch Republic also plunged into the enterprise of overseas colonization. European colonization was driven by many factors — religious, economic, political, demographic — but certainly competition between the great powers of western Europe endowed the colonization effort with a particular fervor and urgency. Louisiana, including the Illinois Country, was a focal point for this competition during much of the eighteenth century.[1]

Competition for empire helped impel Frenchmen into the vast, uncharted territory of North America, where they vied with Spaniards and Englishmen for land, precious metals, pelts, and prestige. That the French empire in North America should eventually extend in a great arc from Quebec City in the northeast to New Orleans in the southwest was due in part to the waterways — the Great Lakes and the Mississippi River — that gave some cohesiveness to the arc and in part to the individual daring and genius of Robert Cavelier, sieur de La Salle. In 1682 La Salle completed his epic journey from the St. Lawrence Valley to the Gulf of Mexico, planted the royal arms of France at the mouth of the Mississippi, and claimed all of Louisiana (named after King Louis

---

1. A good survey of the competition between European states during this period is Zeller, *Les temps moderne;* on French colonization in North America see Eccles, *France in America;* for European rivalry over Louisiana see DeConde. *This Affair;* Folmer, *Franco-Spanish Rivalry.*

XIV) for France. Two years later, Louis XIV's minister of the marine, the marquis de Seignelay, expressed the French government's view of La Salle's feat: "The principal purpose of Sieur de La Salle in making this discovery [of the mouth of the Mississippi] was to find a port on the Gulf of Mexico on which could be formed a French settlement to serve as a base for conquests upon the Spaniards at the first outbreak of hostilities." Seigneley had obviously inherited some of the competitive spirit of his father, the renowned mercantilist Jean-Baptiste Colbert, and his comments reveal the combative nature of the European competition for empire in North America throughout the seventeenth and eighteenth centuries.[2]

During Ste. Genevieve's colonial existence, four nations (not including the Indian nations of the Illinois Country) — France, Spain, Great Britain, and the United States — fought over the ground upon which the town lay. A certain dramatic irony inheres in the fact that the ultimate victor in this violent competition did not exist at the time of the town's founding in the mid-eighteenth century. No resident of Ste. Genevieve in 1753 could have conceived that in the following fifty years sovereignty over the town would change three times, and that at the end of that half-century Ste. Genevieve would become part of a new republic established upon secular and anti- monarchical principles.

Ste. Genevieve was founded during a brief respite in the almost continual warfare of the eighteenth century. In 1748, the War of the Austrian Succession (King George's War in America) ended and Count Wenzel von Kaunitz was beginning his diplomatic strategems to reverse the alliance system in Europe. No one doubted, however, that bloody conflict would soon descend once again upon Europe. And because war in Europe meant war between England and France, European hostilities would inevitably arrive in America, where both nations possessed colonies. Whatever the structure of the European alliance system, pre- or post-Kaunitzian diplomatic revolution, Anglo-French rivalry was a constant factor in eighteenth-century war and diplomacy.[3]

The French and Indian War (Seven Years' War in Europe, 1756-63) was, however, more than simply a spilling over into

---

2. The latest survey on La Salle and his impact is Galloway (ed.), *La Salle and His Legacy;* see also Eccles, *France in America* and *The Canadian Frontier.*

3. An excellent account of European war and diplomacy during the mid-eighteenth century is Dorn, *Competition for Empire;* see also Zeller, chap. viii.

America of European rivalries, for the territory of North America was a central bone of contention between Great Britain and France. Since the beginning of the seventeenth century there had been friction along the frontier between New France and New England, and further south English trappers and traders competed with their French counterparts in the area between the Gulf Coast and the Carolinas. But the Anglo-French rivalry in North America heated to the flash point in the upper Ohio River Valley during the mid-1750s. English colonial land speculators supported by the colony of Virginia, and ultimately the English crown, were pushing over the Allegheny Mountains into the upper Ohio Valley, where they encountered French traders and soldiers who were determined to maintain control of the region.[4]

Horace Walpole claimed that the "world was set on fire" when young George Washington ambushed a party of encamped French soldiers in May 1754. The French and Indian War was decided, however, on the Plains of Abraham, just west of Quebec City in September 1759. Wolfe's British army decimated the French forces led by Montcalm, and French hopes for an ongoing empire in North America were shattered forever.[5]

There has been much scholarly argument as to what dashed French prospects in North America. The great French historian of Louisiana, Marcel Giraud, argued that the French inability to hold a North American empire was rooted in the very fabric of French government and society: chronic financial problems, short-sighted political leadership, and general moral slackness throughout French society. The Canadian historian, William Eccles, on the other hand suggests that a mere difference in outcome on the Plains of Abraham could have dramatically influenced Anglo-French rivalry, that had the French won the big battle their North American empire might have survived. Another distinguished Canadian scholar, Guy Frégault, probed deeper to analyze the outcome of the Anglo-French struggle "one had only to compare the forces that the rival empires had at their disposal in the New World when the War of the Conquest began. The superiority of the British was overwhelming." The ratio of Anglo to French

---

4. The standard work on the Seven Years' War is Waddington, *La Guerre de Sept Ans;* on the war in America the best account is Frégault, *Canada: The War of Conquest;* see also Eccles, *France in America,* chaps. vii, viii; Kopperman, *Braddock at the Monongahela;* DeConde, chap. ii.

5. Frégault, *Canada: The War of Conquest,* chaps. viii, ix; Stacey, *Quebec 1759.*

population in North America at mid-eighteenth century is reckoned to have been about twenty to one. Thus basic demography militated heavily in favor of eventual Anglo-American domination of eastern North America.[6]

Although the French built the mighty stone Fort de Chartres in preparation for the French and Indian War, the Illinois Country remained beyond the range of the fighting. Ste. Genevieve was during the 1750s a passive pawn in the Anglo-French rivalry upon the chessboard of North America. Yet it was this very rivalry that decided the town's fate.[7]

During the Seven Years' War British forces never invaded French Louisiana, including the Illinois Country. Nevertheless in 1760 the war in North America was all but over. England had crushed French power on the American continent and in the sea-lanes surrounding it. The war in Europe continued, however, and King Louis XV's foreign minister, Duke Etienne-François de Choiseul, chose to use Louisiana as a bargaining chip to ease France's embarrassment in foreign affairs. It was natural that Choiseul should turn to Spain with a proposition concerning Louisiana. Spain was ruled by the same Bourbon family that ruled France, and, furthermore, Louisiana was adjacent to Spanish-held territory in North America and thus of primary interest to Spain.[8]

In the summer of 1761, Choiseul lured Spain into negotiations by dangling Louisiana as bait, and in August of that year the two Bourbon states of Europe concluded an alliance that renewed their Family Compact. This agreement stipulated that Spain, in return for a loan to France or a declaration of war against England, would receive Louisiana. Although Choiseul has been much criticized for agreeing to sacrifice Louisiana, his decision was based upon the hard fact that France could no longer defend the colony.[9]

The war and diplomacy concerning North America was complex during the early 1760s, but Choiseul's position remained unswerving: France would dispossess herself of all her continental North American territories in order to achieve peace in Europe and maintain a grip on her lucrative Caribbean sugar islands. By the

---

6. Giraud, "France and Louisiana," 657-74; Eccles, 208; Frégault, 35; see also Wells, *Population of the British Colonies*, 64, 283; Henripin, *Population Canadienne*, 119.

7. Pease (ed.), *Illinois on the Eve of the Seven Years' War*, xlix, 881-82.

8. Lyon, *Louisiana in French Diplomacy*, chap. i; DeConde, 26.

9. Lyon, 20, 27, 33; DeConde, 27.

secret treaty of Fontainebleau (November 1762), Louis XV ceded all Louisiana west of the Mississippi, plus New Orleans, to his "brother and cousin," Carlos III of Spain. (They were in fact first cousins.) Once English power had penetrated the Caribbean (British forces captured Havana in August 1762), Great Britain's demand for Florida could not be denied, and Choiseul mollified Spain for the loss of Florida by ceding Louisiana to her. Although France did not divulge the nature of this gift to Spain until October 1763, it was the Treaty of Paris (February 1763) that effectively ended the French empire in North America. France lost Canada in battle; Louisiana she forsook at the bargaining table in order to achieve peace in Europe and maintain friendship with Spain.[10]

Spain's seaborne empire, which had commenced with the voyages of Columbus, extended by 1763 to the very heart of North America. Spanish Louisiana was a distinct province of the Spanish monarchy, adjacent to but not part of New Spain (Mexico). The northern and western boundaries of Louisiana, although not precisely defined, were commonly deemed to extend to the northern and western limits of the watershed of the Mississippi River.[11]

But imperial Spain was a hollow giant. She was not prepared to take possession of western Louisiana, and thus the colony remained temporarily in French hands. Indeed, the French governor of Louisiana, Jean-Jacques d'Abbadie, did not learn until the summer of 1764 that his capital city of New Orleans and all of western Louisiana had become *de jure* Spanish possessions. In January 1864 D'Abbadie, knowing that all former French territory *east* of the Mississippi (except New Orleans) had become British, wrote to Paris that "of all the Illinois establishments there remains to us today . . . only the village of Ste. Genevieve on the right bank of the river, where there are about 100 persons in all." When, one month after D'Abbadie wrote these words, Pierre Laclède Liguest founded St. Louis, he did not know that he was founding a settlement upon Spanish soil. Indeed, when in 1767 Father Sebastien Meurin wrote to Bishop Jean-Olivier Briand at Quebec, he explained: "In the French or Spanish territory beyond the river are situated the villages of Ste. Geneviève; . . . and at thirty leagues

---

10. Aiton, "Diplomacy of the Louisiana Cession," 701-20; Sheperd, "Cession of Louisiana to Spain," 439-58.

11. Nasatir (ed.), *Before Lewis and Clark*, 1:70-74; Nasatir, *Borderland in Retreat*, 2-5; Bjork, "The Establishment of Spanish rule in . . . Louisiana"; Caughey, "Louisiana Under Spain."

above is the new village called St. Louis." Thus during the mid-1760s no one in the Illinois Country seemed to know exactly who did possess sovereignty west of the Mississippi.[12]

For four decades, Ste. Genevieve was, together with New Orleans and St. Louis, a Spanish possession. Long ago Frederick Billon emphasized how western Illinois remained thoroughly French during the period of Spanish dominion. "The intercourse of the people with each other, and their governors, their commerce, trade, habits, customs, manners, amusements, marriages, funerals, services in church, parish registers, everything was French. . . . The country was only Spanish by possession, but practically French in all else." Billon's remarks are in large measure accurate, and as a matter of fact there was no one in Ste. Genevieve at the end of the colonial period who could write Spanish. Nevertheless, as will be shown, Ste. Genevieve could not develop for forty-odd years under Spanish rule without there taking place some hispanicization of law and administration, marginal though it may have been.[13]

Ste. Genevieve's citizens probably learned in the spring or summer of 1765 that they had become subjects of the king of Spain, although Spanish government had not yet arrived in Louisiana. How they reacted to this news is not known. In New Orleans influential Frenchmen held mass meetings to protest the transfer of Louisiana to Spain, and eventually they revolted against Spanish rule. Ste. Genevieve did not follow New Orleans' lead, for Ste. Genevieve was too rural, too illiterate, and too remote to become agitated over distant political changes. Few persons in Ste. Genevieve cared whether Louis XV at Versailles or his Bourbon cousin Carlos III in Madrid exercised *de jure* sovereignty over their town. There was virtually no sense of nationalism in the eighteenth century, and in Ste. Genevieve the pace of life and standard of living were not materially affected by the change of rulers.[14]

A story later circulated in Ste. Genevieve that some local men who sympathized with the anti-Spanish revolt had attempted to

---

12. D'Abbadie to Minister, Jan. 10, 1764, Alvord and Carter (eds.), *The Critical Period*, 210; McDermott (ed.), *French in the Mississippi Valley*, 10; Meurin to Briand, Mar. 23, 1767, Alvord and Carter (eds.), *The New Regime*, 523.

13. Billon (ed.), *Annals of St. Louis*, 1:76-77. Abraham P. Nasatir (*Borderland in Retreat*, 3-4) has popularized the useful name Spanish Illinois.

14. Moore, *Revolt in Louisiana*.

force François Vallé I to join their cause. Vallé, so the story went, armed his faithful black slaves and disbanded the group, thus remaining loyal to his legitimate Spanish masters. Whether or not the story is true, there is no doubt that Vallé served the Spanish newcomers with fidelity if not with genuine enthusiasm.[15]

When in the autumn of 1767 the Spaniards finally arrived in the Illinois Country, they were cordially received in Ste. Genevieve. Don Francisco Ríu commanded the first Spanish expedition to ascend the Mississippi from New Orleans. Ríu soon established Spanish headquarters for Spanish Illinois at St. Louis, which was strategically located near the mouth of the Missouri River. Before he could do this, however, Ríu tied up his small flotilla of riverboats at the Old Town of Ste. Genevieve. The Spaniards needed time to recuperated from the three-month river journey and to gather badly needed provisions.[16]

Ríu and company arrived in Ste. Genevieve on August 30, 1767, and remained there for several days. Although they called the town "Misera," — Misery — some of the Spanish soldiers liked the area well enough to desert their command; three months on the Mississippi had been too much for them. One of the deserters was later captured by townspeople and returned in chains to Ríu.

Ste. Genevieve's two leading citizens, military commandant Philippe Rastel de Rocheblave and civil Judge François Vallé, did their utmost to assist the Spaniards and to ingratiate themselves with Don Ríu. Vallé provided Ríu with foodstuffs on credit, and Rocheblave accompanied him as a guide upriver from Ste. Genevieve to St. Louis. Vallé continued to court Ríu by correspondence, and Ríu graciously responded: "I see with much pleasure by your letter of the seventh of this month [December 1767] the true zeal that you have for the service of the king [Carlos III]. Nothing could increase my sense that you have done everything possible to assist me with my problems . . . ."[17]

Papa François Vallé was off to a flying start in unabashedly currying favor with the new overlords of Upper Louisiana, and he and his sons would continue this policy throughout the period of Spanish rule. It was this Spanish connection that helped to keep the Vallé family at the head of politics and society in colonial Ste.

---

15. Delassus de Luzières to Carondelet, Feb. 1, 1794, PC 210.

16. Trenfel, "The Spanish Occupation of Western Louisiana," 70-75.

17. Francisco Ríu to Antonio de Ulloa, Nov. 12, 1767, PC 109; Ríu to François Vallé, Dec. 14, 1767, PC 187.

Genevieve. Rocheblave, who was not so prudent as Vallé, argued with Spanish authorities and in 1772 took a post as British commandant at Kaskaskia, just across the Mississippi from Ste. Genevieve.[18]

European states, and their respective colonies in North America, remained at peace with one another for more than a decade after the Seven Years' War. Although there was constant competition for the Indian trade and friction over commerce on the Mississippi, the Spanish subjects of Ste. Genevieve lived in peace with the British subjects and soldiers across the river. Indeed, during the 1760s and the early 1770s, merchants in Ste. Genevieve like Jean Datchurut maintained close business connections with British merchants in British Illinois, and the wealthy Bauvais family of Kaskaskia owned and exploited land on both sides of the Mississippi.[19]

Although at peace with the British, the citizens of Spanish Illinois faced ongoing hostility from various Indian tribes, and during the 1770s the formal military organization of Ste. Genevieve was accomplished. André Deguire and then François Vallé had served in turn as captains of the town militia during the French regime, but there is no evidence that this militia ever turned out as an organized body of fighting men during that time. Spanish authorities in Louisiana provided a formal structure for Ste. Genevieve's defensive forces, and these forces were eventually employed to defend Spanish Illinois.[20]

General Alexandro O'Reilly had in 1769 succeeded in imposing Spanish rule upon Lower Louisiana, and in February 1770 he dispatched instructions for the military organization of Spanish Illinois. Ste. Genevieve would, for the first time in its history, receive a garrison of regular soldiers: one lieutenant, one corporal, and seven enlisted men. In the summer of 1770, Lieutenant Governor Piernas reported from St. Louis that he had carried out O'Reilly's orders and sent the nine Spanish soldiers to their new post; thus was created the Ste. Genevieve detachment of the royal Spanish army. These soldiers were members of the 2nd company, 3rd battalion, of the fixed regiment of Louisiana. The first lieutenant to command this detachment was Louis Dubreuil Villars, one of the many French creoles who entered Spanish service in

---

18. On Rocheblave, see below, chap. xi.

19. Moore, "Anglo-Spanish Rivalry"; Carter, *Great Britain and the Illinois Country;* Alvord and Carter (eds.), *Trade and Politics.*

20. See "Etat de la milice de Ste. Geneviève," 1766, PC 187.

Louisiana during the 1760s. Villars married a local girl, Louise Vallé, daughter of François Vallé I.[21]

From 1770 until the end of the colonial regime in Louisiana, Ste. Genevieve was home for a small Spanish garrison. Even after a small fort was built near the New Town in 1794, this garrison had no formal barracks, and the soldiers were billeted in a house rented from the Vallés for sixty pesos per year. Occasional glimpses of the Spanish soldiery pop up in documents from colonial Ste. Genevieve. Some of the Spaniards were literate, and names like Juan Puñzada and Josef del Prado appear as witnesses in legal records. As usual, soldiers were one of the disorderly elements in society, and in 1775 one Esteban Denisas was sent to New Orleans for court martial after having killed Francisco Vial in a drunken knife fight.[22]

Probably the most enduring contributions these Spanish soldiers made to the community of Ste. Genevieve were the children they fathered by black slave women. Many illegitimate mulatto children were born in colonial Ste. Genevieve, and though their fathers are hard to trace, Spanish soldiers did a fair share of the siring. In a community where women of pure European stock were scarce and almost always married, slave women provided the soldiers with most of their female companionship. A specific case will be examined in a later chapter.[23]

In addition to the professional Spanish soldiers in town, Ste. Genevieve had its local militia company, which was comprised of all male citizens between the ages of fifteen and fifty; men of such age were deemed able to bear arms. General Alexandro O'Reilly's orders of February 1770 confirmed François Vallé I as captain of this local military body; Henri Carpentier was appointed lieutenant; and Francois Duchoquette *père* named second lieutenant. With the death of Duchoquette in 1772, François Vallé's son Charles, whom Piernas described as "robust, honorable, and able," became second lieutenant. When Henri Carpentier died in 1777, Charles Vallé was promoted to lieutenant and his younger brother François II appointed second lieutenant. The youngest of the three brothers, Jean-Baptiste, had been appointed cadet in 1774. Thus

---

21. "General Instructions of O'Reilly, . . . " Feb. 17, 1770, *SRM*, 1:79; Piernas to Unzaga, June 24, 1770, PC 81; Holmes, *Honor and Fidelity*, 18-19.

22. See correspondence concerning Vallé's contracts in PC 81 and PC 538 B; Piernas to Unzaga, Jan. 6, 1775, PC 81 concerning the knife fight.

23. Below, chap. vii.

at the time that international warfare was again flickering in North America the Vallé family occupied all of the commissioned ranks in the Ste. Genevieve militia. This time around, the war and bloodshed would not bypass the Illinois Country.[24]

For the purpose of examining the role that Ste. Genevieve and its citizens played in the American Revolution, it is best to view that revolution as part and parcel of European rivalry, war, and diplomacy. The constant factor of eighteenth-century hostilities — Anglo-French competition — was a central element in the American Revolution. Great Britain had humiliated France in the territorial settlements of 1763, and during the following decades France longed to wreak revenge and gain position upon Britain. The American Revolution provided her with an opportunity that was too enticing to pass up, and in 1778 France signed an alliance with the American rebels. This alliance brought a French royal army, commanded by the comte de Rochambeau, to North America, which meant that France became directly involved in the conflict. Surely the leading and literate citizens of Ste. Genevieve were not insensible of the fact that their mother country had taken up the American cause in a serious way.[25]

But Ste. Genevieve was under Spanish sovereignty, and Spain's position was more complicated than that of France. The Spaniards were trapped in the dilemma of being hostile to Great Britain but hostile to the Americans as well. Since Spain had acquired Louisiana in the 1760s, she had had constant trouble with Anglo-American traders encroaching upon her territory. American westerly migration was just as threatening to Spain as the British military outpost at Pensacola in west Florida. Thus, when Spain joined the war against Great Britain as France's ally in 1779, she did so only to recover Gibraltar, Minorca, and Florida, and to stop British contraband commerce in the Gulf of Mexico. Spain continued to refuse American requests for a military alliance and did not officially recognize the United States as a sovereign and independent

---

24. "Instructions of O'Reilly, . . . " *SRM*, 1:81; Piernas to Unzaga, June 11, 1770, PC 81; Piernas to Unzaga, July 13, 1772, PC 81; "Compañías de Milicias del Pueblo de Santa Genoveva," PC 131 A; Holmes, 225.

25. Billington, *Western Expansion,* 174-98; Darling, *Our Rising Empire,* 1-26; DeConde, 34-40; Nasatir, "The Anglo-Spanish Frontier," 291-358; Zeller, chap. x; Sosin, *Whitehall and the Wilderness,* passim.

26. DeConde, 36; Nasatir, "Tha Anglo-Spanish Frontier," 308-09; Whitaker, *The Spanish American Frontier,* 6-8; Zeller, 278-79.

state until after the signing of the Peace of Paris in 1783.[26]

The citizens of Ste. Genevieve were thus caught up in a complex situation during the American Revolution. As Spanish subjects they were the enemies of America's enemy, Great Britain, but they were not therefore officially friends of the infant United States. It was from this ambiguous position that Ste. Genevieve contributed to the cause of American independence.

Spanish colonial authorities in Louisiana were less reluctant than their superiors in Madrid to support the Americans in their war with Great Britain. Even before Spain declared war upon Great Britain in 1779, New Orleans had become an entrepôt for supplying American revolutionaries with war matériel. During the 1770s, Philippe de Rocheblave, former commandant at Ste. Genevieve, was serving as commandant of British Illinois. Rocheblave was an eighteenth-century soldier of fortune of the purest variety and he always placed his own honor and interest above any kind of national allegiance. Rocheblave wrote to Spanish Governor Unzaga from Illinois in September 1776 and complained of the fact that American riverboats from Fort Pitt (Pittsburgh) were procuring gunpowder in New Orleans to use against the British. An intelligent man, Rocheblave concluded his letter to Unzaga by making an astute geopolitical point: if the Americans achieved their independence from England no European power would long be able to maintain colonies on the North American continent. Rocheblave was probably sincere — and prophetically correct — in this argument, and the Spaniards surely knew this. Yet there was no easy solution to their difficult position in the cockpit of North American politics. In 1777 Bernardo de Galvez replaced Unzaga as governor of Louisiana, and Spanish aid to the American revolutionaries increased.[27]

The first British official to be adversely affected by this increased aid was Rocheblave himself. When the American General George Rogers Clark seized Kaskaskia in July 1778, Rocheblave was captured in his nightshirt. At that moment he probably wished that he had been discreet enough to maintain his position as commandant in Spanish Ste. Genevieve. Rocheblave was packed off to prison in Williamsburg, from where he eventually escaped to join the British forces in New York.[28]

---

27. See Caughey, *Bernardo de Gálvez;* James, *Oliver Pollock;* Rocheblave to Unzaga, Sep. 16, 1776, PC 189.

28. Alvord, *Illinois Country,* 322-28; James, *Life of Clark,* 118-19; Seineke, *The*

The sometime priest in Ste. Genevieve, Father Pierre Gibault, assisted General Clark during the Illinois campaign of 1778 by persuading the creole inhabitants that American rule would be preferable to British. Gibault, "the patriot priest," surely did play some role in these dramatic events of the American Revolution, but more important than Gibault was the logistical support that Clark received from Spanish Illinois. It is clear that much of this support was funneled through Ste. Genevieve. As riverboats laden with supplies came up the Mississippi to the Illinois Country, Ste. Genevieve was the first town and entrepôt at which they put in. Moreover, Ste. Genevieve was conveniently located just across the Mississippi from the metropole of eastern Illinois, Kaskaskia.[29]

After Clark seized control of British Illinois in the summer of 1778, his principle supplier was Gabriel Cerré, a merchant from Kaskaskia who conducted business affairs all up and down the Mississippi. Cerré had not at first been sympathetic to the American cause, but after the seizure of Kaskaskia he soon threw his lot in with the Virginians. In July 1779 Cerré informed Clark that he "had paid for with peltries all the supplies I took from Ste. Genevieve." Cerré ran these business affairs in close coordination with Ste. Genevieve merchants, although his principal base of operations was in St. Louis. Clark's bills of exchange, which were usually handled by an American agent in New Orleans, Oliver Pollock, reveal that half a dozen merchants in Ste. Genevieve were happy to turn a profit by supplying the Americans with war matériel. These men included Jean-Baptiste Pratte, René Rapicault, Charles Charleville, and André Fagot. The American Revolution in the western theater of action depended heavily upon Ste. Genevieve as a logistical base of support.[30]

When Clark captured Kaskaskia in July 1778, Fernando de Leyba had only recently arrived in St. Louis, having replaced Francisco Cruzat as lieutenant governor of Upper Louisiana. Although Spain was not yet officially at war with Great Britain, De Leyba wrote to Clark on 8 July to express his esteem for Clark

---

Clark Adventure, 92-3; De Leyba to Gálvez, July 11, 1778, in Kinnaird, "Clark-Leyba Papers," 95; Mason, "Rocheblave," 372-74; Surveyer, "Rocheblave," 237-38.

29. On Gibault see Donnelly, "Pierre Gibault," 81-92; Rothensteiner, *Archdiocese of St. Louis,* 1:132-39.

30. Alvord (ed.), *Kaskaskia Records,* 48, 102; Illinois State Archives, Draper Collection, series J, 48:37; Seineke, 94-96.

personally and his sympathy for the American cause in general. There was no question on whose side Spanish officials in Louisiana were; they clearly viewed the English as their profound enemies. Spain declared war upon Great Britain only in July 1779, however, and even then the news traveled slowly to the remote Illinois Country.[31]

Some of General Clark's American troops did not have as much affection for their commander as Lieutenant Governor De Leyba did, for the first taste that Ste. Genevieve got of the American Revolution came in the form of fifty deserters from Clark's army. These "turbulent and lawless fellows . . . were greatly troubling that town, eating without paying, and going out to assassinate any countryman or soldier from the other side whom they might find wandering around." Such a band of roughnecks and cutthroats perhaps prompted the citizens of Ste. Genevieve to wonder about the value of a revolution that Americans were conducting in the name of liberty and republican virtue. De Leyba ordered the American deserters to leave Spanish Illinois, and they obliged him by crossing back over the Mississippi to the eastern side.[32]

News that Spain and Great Britain were officially at war arrived in the Illinois Country early in 1780. François Vallé, who was captain of the Ste. Genevieve militia, was informed directly from New Orleans that his town could forthwith commence hostilities with the British. But Vallé must have been puzzled by just how and where he and his fellow citizens could pursue combat with Englishmen, for at that time the closest British outposts were at St. Joseph, Detroit and Michilimackinac, all hundreds of miles from Ste. Genevieve.[33]

Frontier guerilla soldiers with their Indian allies moved across the face of colonial North America with amazing speed and agility, however, and Spanish officials began to fear an Anglo-Indian attack upon Spanish Illinois almost as soon as Spain declared war on Great Britain in July 1779. It was this fear that persuaded Lieutenant Governor De Leyba to build the first road between St. Louis and Ste. Genevieve. De Leyba explained his reasons for this project to Governor Gálvez in a letter of July 1779: "A road has been constructed from this town [St. Louis] to Ste. Genevieve,

---

31. De Leyba to Clark, July 8, 1778, printed in Kinnaird, "Clark-Leyba Papers," 94; Nasatir, "Anglo-Spanish Frontier," 308.

32. De Leyba to Gálvez, July 13, 1779, PC 1.

33. Piernas to Vallé, Jan. 17, 1780, PC 147 A.

from which will result to the district under my command the following benefits: to be able to help that town with the new cavalry company if necessary; to have communication with it all the year around." Thus for strategic reasons, the linking together of the two principal towns in Spanish Illinois, St. Louis and Ste. Genevieve, De Leyba created the first government roadway in Spanish Illinois. By the end of the colonial era, this roadway (probably more a blazed trail) had been extended from Ste. Genevieve to the new settlements of Cape Girardeau and New Madrid.[34]

The main purpose of this military road, as De Leyba explained, was to enable St. Louis to provide assistance to Ste. Genevieve should the latter be attacked during the winter, when ice blocked the Mississippi and rendered useless the usual avenue of transportation and communication in the Illinois Country. Ironically, events turned out very differently, for it was St. Louis, not Ste. Genevieve, that required emergency assistance, and the emergency came in the spring, not the winter, of 1780.

In February 1780, the British command at Michilimackinac began actively to plan an attack upon St. Louis, the seat of Spanish government in Upper Louisiana. The British, with their various Indian allies, proposed to descend from the north via the Mississippi and its tributaries, in order to proceed with the "reduction of Pencour [i.e. St. Louis] by surprise." Although events did not transpire as the British had planned, an Anglo-Indian force did attack St. Louis on May 26, 1780. This attack was one of the most dramatic events in the colonial history of the Illinois Country and has been treated with great skill and precision by two eminent historians, Abraham P. Nasatir and John Francis McDermott. Both these scholars focused their attention, naturally enough, upon St. Louis and Lieutenant Governor De Leyba, and Ste. Genevieve's role in the events of May 26 thus received short shrift in their excellent general accounts.[35]

At midnight on May 8, 1780 a scout slipped into St. Louis and informed De Leyba that an Anglo-Indian force of 900 men was on the Mississippi at the mouth of the Rock River, near present-day Rock Island, Illinois. De Leyba, who already was too ill to write, awakened his secretary and by flickering candlelight dictated two letters that saved his command and his reputation. The letters

---

34. De Leyba to Gálvez, July 13, 1779, *SMV*, pt. 1:348.

35. Sinclair to Haldimand, Feb. 17, 1780, quoted in Nasatir, "The Illinois Country," 311; McDermott, "Captain De Leyba," 314-406.

were to Don Silvio de Cartabona, military commandant of Ste. Genevieve, and to François Vallé I, captain of the town's militia. These two leaders were ordered immediately to assemble the Ste. Genevieve garrison of regular Spanish troops (six men) together with sixty militiamen. This assembly of warriors was to embark on two riverboats with rations for twenty-four days and head immediately upriver for St. Louis. Cartabona and Vallé worked with amazing speed and efficiency, for the two-boat flotilla from Ste. Genevieve arrived in St. Louis on 13 May, which was only three days after De Leyba's emergency orders had arrived in Ste. Genevieve. Citizens of Ste. Genevieve were about to step onto the stage of world affairs by participating in events of the American Revolution.[36]

François Vallé I was too infirm to make this trip, but his two eldest surviving sons, Charles and François *fils*, went as officers in the militia and as representatives of Ste. Genevieve's first family. Cartabona commanded the combined Ste. Genevieve contingent, consisting of Spanish regulars and militiamen, and when he arrived in St. Louis on 13 May he became De Leyba's lieutenant for the entire garrison.[37]

It would be of interest to know precisely which sixty men from the Ste. Genevieve militia participated in this historic expedition, and how they were selected for this duty. A detailed comparison of Spanish muster rolls from St. Louis and the roster of the Ste. Genevieve militia of November 1779 suggests these facts: other than the two Vallé brothers, Charles and François II, the major families of Ste. Genevieve were not represented in the expedition; the men of the Ste. Genevieve contingent who can be identified were mostly *voyageurs*, i.e. men who were mobile, were good shots, and who probably had experience fighting Indians. Furthermore, it seems that whether they volunteered or were picked by Cartabona and Vallé the members of the Ste. Genevieve militia who went to St. Louis in May 1780 were those who were not tied down to any gainful employment at *that* moment. The *habitants*, merchants, and craftsmen from the established Ste. Genevieve families remained in town to pursue their labors. The Big Field was going

36. De Leyba to Vallé, May 9, 1780, printed in Nasatir, "St. Louis during the British Attack," 4-5 (pagination according to reprint); Nasatir, "Anglo-Spanish Frontier," 317.

37. "Relation de la compagnie de milice du poste de Ste. Geneviève," Nov. 29, 1779, PC 213; Nasatir, "Anglo-Spanish Frontier," 318-20.

to be plowed and planted whether or not there was a military emergency at St. Louis, for no armed enemy could threaten Ste. Genevieve as seriously as a year without crops. The following is a partial list of the men, with their occupations, from the Ste. Genevieve militia who served at St. Louis in May 1780:[38]

Officers
Charles Vallé [lieutenant] . . . . *habitant*
François Vallé II [sub-lieutenant] . . . . *habitant*
Enlisted Men
Charles Vallé [cousin of the above] . . . . *voyageur*
Etienne Parent . . . . *voyageur*
Raymond Govrau . . . . *voyageur*
François Lebeau . . . . *voyageur*
Louis Morissaux . . . . *voyageur*
Jean Baudoin . . . . *journalier* [day laborer]
Joseph Courtois . . . . *voyageur*
Joseph Morancy . . . . *voyageur*
Lafleur . . . . *voyageur*
Louis Ledoux . . . . *voyageur*
Jean Fortin . . . . *voyageur*
Jean-Baptiste Becquet . . . . *habitant*
Pierre Placet . . . . *journalier*
Pierre Duchêne . . . . *voyageur*
Nicholas Mercier . . . . *journalier*
Pierre Roy . . . . *habitant*
Louis Cavalier . . . . *chasseur* [hunter]
Charles Bellemard . . . . *voyageur*
Paul St. Jean . . . . *voyageur*

Once the men from Ste. Genevieve disembarked in St. Louis, they had two weeks during which to help prepare the defense of the town before the English and the Indians arrived. This time was largely spent working on jerry-built fortifications, for up to this time St. Louis had not been a fortified post. From the extant descriptions, it is difficult to visualize the fortifications as they were accomplished prior to the Anglo-Indian attack, but they seem to have consisted of a rough quadrilateral: the Mississippi served as the defensive barrier on the east; to the west was a hastily constructed stone tower in which were mounted five light cannons;

---

38. "Relation de . . . milice," PC 213; McDermott, "Captain De Leyba," 381-86.

on the north and the south earthen entrenchments projected inland from the Mississippi. Precisely how these entrenchments were tied into the stone tower to provide a closed, defensible perimeter remains unclear. Within the defensive compound the most substantial structure was the stone governor's mansion, which was the trading post built by Pierre Laclède in the mid-1760s and which the Spaniards rented for use as the lieutenant governor's residence.[39]

On May 23, De Leyba's scouts told him that the Anglo-Indian force had been spotted only twenty leagues (sixty to seventy-five miles) from St. Louis. It is clear that the British plan to take the Spanish post "by surprise" was ludicrous. De Leyba routinely had scouting parties out, and it was almost inconceivable that a large body of armed men could move about on the Mississippi frontier without being detected.[40]

The Anglo-Indian force — it could hardly be called an army — closed on St. Louis during the morning of May 26 and at about midday began its attack by assaulting the northern entrenchment. The attacking force was composed of a few British soldiers, a handful of French Canadians who were loyal to Great Britain, and a large component of Sauk, Sioux, Fox, and Menominee Indians. This disparate and polyglot group of temporary allies perhaps numbered 1,000 men in all. The fighting men who defended St. Louis, including the Ste. Genevieve contingent, consisted of twenty-nine Spanish regulars, plus 281 militiamen, *voyageurs*, hunters, trappers, and others.[41]

It is impossible to reconstruct clearly the battle for St. Louis that was fought during the afternoon of May 26, 1780. De Leyba's report to Governor Gálvez on June 8 is the most complete extant description of the battle, and it is a classic view of Indian warfare as seen through the eyes of a European. The enemies attacked "like madmen, with unbelievable boldness and fury, making terrible cries." When the savages failed to penetrate the defensive compound by storm they took to ravaging the environs, "massacring persons in the fields who had not had sufficient time to take

39. De Leyba to Gálvez, June 8, 1780, printed in Nasatir, "St. Louis During to British Attack," 5-11. Concerning St. Louis's fortifications, see Musick, *St. Louis as a Fortified Town,* 27-31.

40. De Leyba to Gálvez, June 8, 1780, in Nasatir, "St. Louis . . . Attack," 5-11.

41. Ibid.; Nasatir, "Anglo-Spanish Frontier," 318-19. McDermott, "Captain De Leyba," 373-80; "Relation de . . . milice," PC 213; "Report of Intendant Navarro," Aug. 18, 1780, printed in *SRM,* 1:167-79.

Stone tower (Fort San Carlos) begun at St. Louis in 1780. Notice De Leyba's mansion (originally Laclede's trading house) to the right. Courtesy of Missouri Historical Society.

refuge." To De Leyba, it was "a horrible spectacle" to see "these poor corpses cut to pieces; their entrails torn out; and their limbs, heads, arms, and legs scattered all over." De Leyba was forced to invent a new French verb, "savagaient" (were savaging) to describe the frightful actions of the attacking Indians.[42]

Little is known about the role of the Ste. Genevieve contingent in this successful defense of Spanish St. Louis. De Leyba assigned Silvio De Cartabona and twenty men to guard the women and children in the stone governor's mansion, but the remaining fifty odd men from Ste. Genevieve were presumably in the thick of it. The defending forces were outnumbered at least three to one, and the defense of the crude fortifications must have been a desperate struggle, in which there was no place for malingers. If as royal intendant Martín Navarro reported from New Orleans, De Leyba's total defending garrison was 310 men, the Ste. Genevieve contingent, composed of sixty militiamen and six Spanish regulars,

42. Nasatir, "St. Louis During . . . Attack," 5-11.

made up almost one quarter of the defensive force. Given the fact that the battle of May 26 was a close-run affair, it does not seem excessive to claim that the men from Ste. Genevieve added the weight that tipped the scale of battle in favor of the defenders.[43]

The Vallé family was singled out for praise by Spanish colonial officials: Papa François I for sending militiamen and provisions from Ste. Genevieve to St. Louis; his two sons, Charles and François II, for their active participation in the battle itself. Governor Gálvez (or Intendant Navarro) wrote personally to François I and assured him that King Carlos III of Spain would hear of Vallé's loyalty and service to the Spanish crown. The Spanish official kept his word, for by royal decree on April 1, 1782 Carlos conferred upon François I the rank of lieutenant in the regular Spanish army. François Valle, French Canadian *habitant*, thus became a Spanish don. Governor Gálvez remarked upon the "splendid actions" of the two Vallé sons and declared that they had "ignited in Illinois courage, zeal, industry, and love for service to Spain." It would be a good bet, however, that prudent self-interest rather more than burning loyalty to Spain motivated the Vallé men in their actions of May 1780.[44]

In August 1780, Intendant Navarro sent from New Orleans to Madrid the following casualty figures for the battle of May 26:

killed	wounded	captured
	Whites	
5	6	11
	Black Slaves	
7	1	13

There is no way to determine how many of these casualities came from the Ste. Genevieve contingent. One man surnamed St. Jean was killed, and another with the same name taken prisoner. Given the fact that the militia muster rolls for Illinois from November 1779 list one St. Jean at St. Louis and another at Ste. Genevieve, it may be presumed that Paul St. Jean, *voyageur* from Ste. Genevieve, was either killed or captured in defending St. Louis on May 26, 1780.[45]

---

43. "Navarro's Report," Aug. 18, 1780, *SRM*, 1:167-68.

44. Gálvez to Vallé, July 25, 1780, PC 113; Gálvez to Cartabona, July 25, 1780, PC 2; Cartabona to Piernas, Oct. 1, 1780, PC 113.

45. Gross casualty figures in "Navarro's Report," Aug. 18, 1780, *SRM*, 1:168;

On June 24, 1780 Silvio de Cartabona returned to his post at Ste. Genevieve with some of the militiamen. Part of the Ste. Genevieve contingent, including Lieutentant Charles Vallé, remained in St. Louis, for De Leyba was on his death bed and the Anglo-Indian presence in the Illinois Country was still ominous. On June 28 Cartabona received an express dispatch from St. Louis informing him of De Leyba's death at 4:00 a.m. that day; Cartabona forthwith departed for St. Louis to take charge as interim commandant of Spanish Illinois. By September 1780, the Anglo-Indian threat had diminished and Cartabona sent the entire Ste. Genevieve militia under Charles Vallé's command back home. Cartabona himself remained in St. Louis until Francisco Cruzat, who was reappointed lieutenant governor of Illinois, arrived from New Orleans in late September 1780.[46]

At the same time that the Franco-Spanish garrison repelled the Anglo-Indian attack on St. Louis, Colonel John Montgomery and General George Rogers Clark fended off a secondary British thrust at Cahokia across the Mississippi. These British setbacks in the western theater of action are a little-known part of the history of the American Revolution. Nonetheless, they prevented Great Britain from seizing control of the lucrative fur trade of the lower Missouri River, and even permitted a militia force from St. Louis and Cahokia to seize (and hold for twenty-four hours!) the English outpost at St. Joseph (Michigan) in January 1781. The Franco-American-Spanish successes in the Illinois Country did not destroy the British presence in the Mississippi Valley. They did, however, have a bearing upon the territorial settlement arrived at in Paris during the peace negotiations that concluded the American Revolution: Louisiana remained in Spanish hands, and the Northwest Territory became American.[47]

The violent competition for empire in North America during the 1770s and 1780s, which we call the American Revolution,

Nasatir first published the detailed casualty lists in "St. Louis During . . . Attack," 11-13; see also McDermott, "Captain De Leyba",: 386-88; "Relation de . . . milice," PC 213.

46. Cartabona to Gálvez, June 28, 1780, PC 113; Cartabona to Gálvez, July 10, 1780, PC 113; Cartabona to François Vallé, Sept. 7, 1780, PC 113.

47. See Nasatir, "Anglo-Spanish Frontier," 321-51; Kinnaird, "Spanish Expedition Against Fort St. Joseph," 173-81; Sosin, *Revolutionary Frontier,* chaps. viii, ix; Alvord, *Illinois Country,* 350-57; DeConde, 35-39. Spain claimed the valley of the Illinois River as a consequence of the raid on St. Joseph; see Spanish claim, Feb. 12, 1781, *SMV,* pt. 1:418.

resolved *some* of the political complexity in Louisiana: henceforth Great Britain would no longer continuously compete for sovereign control of the Mississippi Valley. In the peace treaties of 1783, Great Britain retained her rights to navigation — and therefore trade and commerce — on the entire course of the Mississippi. She also dominated the fur trade of the upper Mississippi Valley and even, contrary to the peace agreements, refused to give up her outposts there. Nonetheless, although Great Britain several times threatened to attack Spanish Louisiana, after 1783 she was no longer a persistent contender to become sovereign master of the colony.[48]

The period 1783-1803 would determine which of the other contenders — Spain, France, or the United States — could impose its rule upon the uncharted vastness of western Louisiana, which included the important river town of Ste. Genevieve. When Arthur P. Whitaker wrote that "north of New Orleans the only Spanish posts of any consideration in 1783 were Natchez, Arkansas and St. Louis, . . . " he neglected to mention Ste. Genevieve. But in 1783 Ste. Genevieve was as large as St. Louis and was a vital part of the trans-Mississippian West, a West that some Americans already coveted as a region for an American empire. As the American Revolution ended, however, the townspeople of Ste. Genevieve did not foresee the time when they would become citizens of the aggressive new republic that had just been established east of the Mississippi.[49]

The decade following the American Revolution was a period of relative political and military calm for Ste. Genevieve. The increasing numbers of energetic and land-hungry Americans pushing up to the Mississippi frontier from the east aroused uneasiness in Spanish colonial officials, including the commandant at Ste. Genevieve, but Americans did not become a clear and present danger to Spanish Louisiana until the 1790s. From 1783 to 1792, the citizens of Ste. Genevieve were preoccupied with the local, domestic issue of moving their community from the eroding mud flats of the Mississippi to higher ground near Gabouri Creek.

---

48. DeConde, 36-40; Nasatir, "Anglo-Spanish Rivalry," 355-58; Wright, *Britain and the American Frontier*, 1-10.

49. Whitaker, *Spanish-American Frontier*, 21.

Despite an occasional Indian scare and some friction with American Illinois, the townspeople were not much concerned with defense and politics during this era.[50]

During this quiet time, the small Spanish garrison remained quartered in Ste. Genevieve and the local militia continued to exist — at least on paper, for it seems never to have been mustered for duty. The Spanish commandants of Ste. Genevieve changed, Antonio de Oro replacing Cartabona in 1784, and Peyroux de la Coudrenière replacing De Oro in 1787, but their functions were more civil than military. Leadership of the town's militia evolved a little unpredictably. In 1783 François Vallé I, captain of militia died and was replaced by his oldest son Charles. Charles was destroying his marriage and his career with liquor and sexual license, however, and never exercised power as captain. He was an increasing embarrassment to his family and he finally moved to Lower Louisiana in the late 1780s. For a time the Vallés' position in Ste. Genevieve was seriously weakened. The family began to reassert itself in the early 1790s, when François Vallé II was appointed captain of the militia and his younger brother, Jean-Baptiste, lieutenant.[51]

The last decade of Ste. Genevieve colonial history, in marked contrast with the decade that preceded it, was a period of virtually constant turmoil, as the town experienced repeated threats and alerts. During the 1780s the town had been battered by the unchained natural force of the rampaging Mississippi; during the 1790s Ste. Genevieve was threatened by a series of man-made upheavals — Indian incursions, American immigration, and fantastic French Revolutionary schemes. The interaction of these apparently disparate elements was complicated, but at some level they were all related: American westward expansion placed pressure on the Indian tribes, whose upheaval in turn threatened Ste. Genevieve. Meanwhile, French Revolutionaries indulged themselves with the wishful thought that they could use rambunctious American republicans to help them seize Spanish Louisiana on

---

50. Peyroux de la Coudrenière nervously reported (Peyroux to Miró, Aug. 4, 1787, PC 199) an American settlement at Ecores à Margot [Memphis] and the appointment of Arthur St. Clair as governor of the Northwest Territory (Peyroux to Miró, Mar. 8, 1788, PC 201); see also DeConde, chap. iii; Whitaker, *Spanish-American Frontier*, chaps. i-viii.

51. Officers of Ste. Genevieve militia listed in Miró to Cruzat, Mar. 26, 1784, PC 117 B; on town commandants see below, chap xi; on Charles Vallé's personal life, see below, chap. vi.

EL REY.

Por quanto *atendiendo al merito, y servicios de Dn. Juan Bautista Vallee, y al q.e contraxo en la Conquista de los Fuertes, y Establecim.tos Yngleses del Rio Misisipi, he venido en confirmarle el Empleo de Subtent.e de la Compañia de Milicias de S.ta Genoveva de Ylinoa en la Luysiana con la antiguedad desde 1.o de Sep.re de 1780. q.e le sirve con Despacho del Govierno de la misma Provincia* ~ ~

Por tanto mando al *Capitan Qual interino de ella* ~ ~ ~ ~ ~ ~ ~ ~ dé la orden conveniente para que se le ponga en posesion del mencionado Empléo, guardandole, y haciendole guardar las preeminencias y exenciones, que le tocan, y deben ser guardadas, que así es mi voluntad; y que el *Yntendente de la propia Provincia* ~ ~ dé asimismo la orden necesaria para que en los Oficios principales de mi Real Hacienda se tóme razon de este Despacho, y se le forme asiento; con prevencion, de que siempre que mánde juntar *dho Cuerpo* ~ ~ ~ para acudir á los parages, que convenga á mi Real Servicio, se le asistirá con el sueldo que á los demás *Subtent.es de Ynfanteria* de las Tropas regladas, en consequencia de lo que tengo resuelto. Dado en *S.t Yldefonso* á *diez y siete* de *Septiembre* de mil setecientos *ochenta y siete.*

Yo El Rey

Nombramiento de *Subtent.e de la Compañia de Milicias de S.ta Genoveva de Ylinoa en la Luysiana p.a D.n Juan Bautista Vallee.*

Jean-Baptiste Vallé's appointment as second-lieutenant of the Ste. Genevieve militia, September 17, 1787, by King Carlos III of Spain. Courtesy of Missouri Historical Society, St. Louis.

behalf of the newly created French republic. Ste. Genevieve's citizens surely did not understand the large forces — demographic, political, nationalistic, and military — that were shaping their destiny during the 1790s, but they did know that their town was in danger.[52]

By 1793, continual depredations throughout Spanish Illinois by Big Osage Indians provoked Governor Carondelet into formally declaring war upon the tribe. This was largely an empty and vainglorious gesture, for the Indians were not about to be drawn into a pitched battle that they knew would destroy them. Yet Carondelet's action does reveal the extent of his exasperation with the Big Osages, and this subject will be dealt with more fully in a later chapter.[53]

The Osage threat had not fully passed when news of a more complex and potentially dangerous threat struck Spanish Illinois. The French Revolution had awakened strong imperialistic impulses in the French nation, and these in turn rekindled ideas of a French Louisiana in the minds of some Hispanophobes in Lower Louisiana; if French kings had not been able to keep Louisiana French perhaps French republicans could. In early 1793, 150 citizens of New Orleans petitioned the French Revolutionary government, asking it to take Louisiana under its protective custody. For Spanish subjects in the colony this was of course an act of treason; but the Bourbon Family Compact had disintegrated with the coming of the French Revolution, and the Revolutionaries were not uninterested in regaining Louisiana. The Revolutionary government sent an agent, François de Chasseboeuf, comte de Volney, to Louisiana for the purpose of testing the political waters there, and in the spring of 1793 a new French minister to the United States, Citizen Edmond C. Genêt, arrived in North America with more ambitious plans.[54]

Genêt was a representative of the expansionist Girondin party in France, and he hoped to sponsor a joint Franco-American assault upon Spanish Louisiana. As part of this plan he made contact with the American general, George Rogers Clark. That old and alcoholic campaigner was hankering to lead an army again. Genêt's famous plot soon collapsed: The fiery Frenchman alienated U.S.

---

52. A brilliant introduction to all of these issues is in Nasatir (ed.), *War Vessels*, 1-21; see also Turner, "Origins of Genêt's Projected Attack," 650-71.

53. See below, chap. iv.

54. DeConde, 79.

President George Washington and his Federalist government; Genêt's Girondin party lost power in France to the Jacobins; and there was in fact no American army on foot during the early 1790s with which to mount an invasion of Spanish-held territory. Nevertheless, before the plot collapsed, rumors of an imminent invasion of Louisiana ran up and down the Mississippi Valley.[55]

News traveled slowly in the eighteenth century, and at the very time that Genêt's hare-brained scheme collapsed toward the end of 1793, word spread in the Illinois Country that an invasion force was on its way. Rumor had it that Clark might lead his frontiersmen across the Mississippi even without French support or approval from the U.S. Government. In December 1793, Pierre Menard returned to Kaskaskia from Philadelphia and reported that the Kentuckians were ready to march. Peyroux, commandant at Ste. Genevieve, said that this news had frightened his townspeople, who feared to lose "their slaves and other property." French creoles viewed American frontiersmen as ruffians — "Whiskey Boys" one observer called them — who were hotheaded and lawless. New Madrid was considered the most vulnerable post in Spanish Illinois, and the Ste. Genevieve militia was ordered to prepare itself to march southward to help defend its sister settlement.[56]

Early 1794 was therefore a time of hurried military preparation in Ste. Genevieve. The Vallé family had no sympathy for either French or American republicans, for the Vallé men entertained no radical political ideas, and, moreover, they had thrived and prospered by currying favor with the Spanish monarchy. If the townspeople possessed loyalty to any entity larger than the town itself it was to the Bourbon family, which during the 1790s ruled Spain but not France. In 1794 Ste. Genevieve, under Vallé leadership, prepared to defend itself as a loyal crown colony of Spain.

The only fort ever built at Ste. Genevieve was erected in response

---

55. DeConde, 57-58, 78-79; James, *Life of Clark*, chap. xviii; Lyon, *Louisiana in French Diplomacy*, 68-79; Whitaker, *Spanish-American Frontier*, chap. xiii; Turner, "Policy of France toward the Mississippi Valley," 249-79.

56. Peyroux to Carondelet, Dec. 26, 1793, PC 207 A; Carondelet to Trudeau, Dec. 22, 1793, PC 20; Bonnevie de Pogniat, "Mémoire sur la Louisiane, . . ." Archives Nationales, section Outre-Mer, DFC Louisiane 26:30.

The site of New Madrid had originally been a trading post known as l'Anse à la Graisse, greasy cove. In 1789 George Morgan founded a settlement there and named it New Madrid. Thomas Portell was Spanish commandant there during the early 1790s.

to rumors of a Franco-American invasion of Upper Louisiana. Lieutenant Governor Trudeau explained the circumstances of its construction in a letter to Carondelet: "The inhabitants of the towns of Ste. Genevieve and New Bourbon, having informed me of the danger to which they are exposed without a fort to defend themselves and protect their families, offered to construct one of solid wood. . . ."[57]

The fort was built under the direction of the young engineer-surveyor, Antoine Soulard, who arrived at Ste. Genevieve in February 1794. It was a wooden palisaded structure, one arpent (approximately 192 feet) square, with four corner bastions and a parapet. François Vallé shouldered the cost of construction and later submitted his itemized bill of expenses to Spanish officials in New Orleans. The total bill, including labor and materials, amounted to 1,442 pesos, 5 reales. At that time the peso had a value equivalent to the American dollar. Of this amount, 712 pesos, 1 real went for the supply of 630 oaken posts, the single most expensive item on the bill. Excavation and movement of earth "for leveling the banquette and the bulwarks," amounted to 166 pesos, 7 reales. The cost of labor to erect the fort, once the site had been prepared and the materials cut and assembled, was only 214 pesos, of which ninety went to the master carpenter and 124 to common laborers. Labor made up a remarkably small part of the total cost of the fort, although no doubt much of the cost of the oaken posts was the labor of cutting, trimming, and transporting the posts to the constuction site. Christian Schultz, who visited Ste. Genevieve in 1807, recounted the local story that François Vallé padded his bill for the fort and thus embezzled funds from the Spanish government. There is no evidence in the source documents to substantiate this story.[58]

The four small cannons (probably two-pounders) known to have been in Ste. Genevieve were perhaps mounted in the corner bastions, where they could be manned by the troop of Spanish regulars. These Spanish soldiers continued living in quarters rented from Jean-Baptiste Vallé, for there is no record that any kind of a barracks was ever built within the fort.[59]

---

57. Trudeau to Carondelet, Jan. 28, 1794, PC 1447.

58. Soulard to Gayoso de Lemos, Dec. 15, 1797, PC 123; Vallé to Trudeau, Jan. 27, 1794, PC 209; Carondelet to Francisco Rendón, July 7, 1795, PC 618; Schultz, *Travels*, 68-69.

59. Charles Delassus to Jean-Baptiste Vallé, Aug. 10, 1804, MHS, Vallé Collection, Box 3. Ste. Genevieve first received several small cannons when the French

The fort built at Ste. Genevieve in 1794 was one of the largest and most curious structures erected in colonial Ste. Genevieve. We know that by the end of the colonial era it was decrepit and falling down (oaken posts will not last more than ten years sunk in the ground), and there are few eyewitness descriptions of it. From the comments of Christian Schultz concerning "the eminence" upon which it was located, and from the location of a fort shown on maps done by General Victor Collot and Nicolas de Finiels (see map) it seems apparent that the fort was situated on the hill immediately south of South Gabouri Creek. Precise determination of the fort's location would enhance our understanding of Ste. Genevieve's history in the late eighteenth century. Perhaps historical-archeology will one day reveal the fort's exact site and provide valuable information on the human activity that transpired in and around the structure during colonial times.[60]

The threat of a Franco-American invasion served as a catalyst for other actions at Ste. Genevieve. Fear that a fifth column of ethnic Frenchmen would rise up and assist the invaders in overthrowing the Spanish regime lead to a minor witch-hunt in Louisiana during 1794-95. One of the victims of this persecution was none other than the commandant of Ste. Genevieve, Peyroux de la Coudrenière, whose row with the Vallé family had already undermined his position in town. Lieutenant Governor Trudeau used the occasion of threat of invasion to smear Peyroux, remove him as commandant at Ste. Genevieve, and dispatch him to New Orleans. Once this was accomplished, Trudeau replaced Peyroux with François Vallé II, Trudeau's friend and ally. Peyroux, who had surely not conspired against Spain even though he was a maladroit commandant in Ste. Genevieve, was fully exonerated and later became commandant in New Madrid.[61]

January 1794 was as tense a time in Ste. Genevieve as the citizens had experienced since the Anglo-Indian attack on St. Louis in 1780. A French sponsored invasion of Upper Louisiana by Americans was expected at any time, and Ste. Genevieve and St. Louis were both vulnerable. Trudeau wrote to Carondelet that the situation in Spanish Illinois was perilous, for on the east side of the

---

abandoned Fort Massac on the Ohio River in 1763 and sent the ordnance to Ste. Genevieve (Villiers to D'Abbadie, Dec. 1, 1763, Alvord and Carter [eds.], *The Critical Period*, 53).

60. Schultz, 68; Collot map in Tucker (ed.), *Indian Villages, Atlas*, Plate XXVIII.

61. Liljegren, "Jacobinism," 47-97; on Peyroux's dismissal see below, chap. xi.

Mississippi was a population "composed in greater part of vagabonds, without manners and without laws, who own only a rifle and sometimes a horse and whose only ambition is to pillage, vandalize, and murder." Trudeau stood on the west bank of the Mississippi, as Romans once stood on the west bank of the Rhine, gazing across at the barbarians massing on the other side of the river. There is an unmistakable sense in Trudeau's prose that the prospect of an American invasion had aroused visceral fear in the lieutenant governor.[62]

In order to provide a more flexible defensive force, Trudeau decided in January 1794 to restructure the militia in the Ste. Genevieve District. Henceforth, instead of one there would be two militia companies in the district, which would be designated either "1" and "2" or "Ste. Genevieve" and "Nouvelle Bourbon." The officers of the first were François Vallé II, captain; Joseph Pratte, lieutenant; and François Vallé III, second lieutenant. And of the second company, Jean-Baptiste Vallé, captain; André Deguire II, lieutenant; and Jean-Baptiste Janis, second lieutenant. If Machiavelli's dictum that whoever controls the soldiery controls the community is valid, the Vallé family was clearly in control of Ste. Genevieve. Although Peyroux was still officially town commandant when Trudeau reorganized the militia, his days were numbered. André Deguire II was probably the only one of the six officers in the two militia companies to reside at New Bourbon in 1794, for De Luzières' settlement adjacent to Ste. Genevieve was just getting started.[63]

François Vallé, who was more a frontiersman than Trudeau, displayed calm mastery in his command at Ste. Genevieve. He proceeded with plans for the town's fort and also traveled downriver to Cape Girardeau to monitor events in the Ohio Valley. Louis Lorimier, who was commandant at Cape Girardeau, kept a journal during this period, and this document reveals the frenetic atmosphere in Spanish Illinois as preparations were made to fend off the expected invasion from the East: exhausted couriers rushing dispatches up and down the Mississippi between the outposts; hurried efforts to secure foodstuffs and munitions; obsessive analysis of news and rumors coming from the United States via

---

62. Trudeau to Carondelet, Jan. 28, 1794, PC 209; see also Carondelet to Las Casas (Feb. 9, 1794, PC 1447): "The commandant of Ste. Genevieve tells me that all of the citizens are highly alarmed, fearing pillage of their property . . . ."

63. Trudeau to Carondelet, Jan. 15, 1794, PC 122 A; "Milicias Sueltas Santa Genoveva," PC 131 A; on New Bourbon see below, chap. xiii.

the Ohio River; frustrating diplomatic work trying to keep the various Indian tribes in line. War seemed inevitable and imminent.[64]

The genuine, although largely unfounded, fear of invasion-cum-revolution that gripped Spanish Louisiana early in the year 1794 is perhaps best seen in Carondelet's "Warning Against Revolution," a circular that the governor addressed to all of the colony's citizens on February 12. Carondelet raised the specter of "torrents of blood" such as had inundated Revolutionary France, and "looting and loss of property" such as had occurred during the slave rebellion on the French island of St. Domingue.[65]

Yet by the time that Carondelet's circular arrived in the Illinois Country the crisis had begun to pass. While François Vallé was on watch at Cape Girardeau (February 6-13), Delassus de Luzières' daughter and son-in-law arrived there after having descended the Ohio River from Pittsburgh. The son-in-law, Pierre Derbigny, reported that in visiting American settlements along the Ohio he had seen no preparations whatsoever for an invasion of Louisiana, although there was still much talk of it. In late February, a spy whom Vallé had sent to Vincennes returned to Ste. Genevieve and reported that no army had gathered in the Indiana Territory. By May 1794 fear of invasion was dissipating, and one of the militia companies in the Ste. Genevieve District was taken off active duty. Trudeau reported with palpable relief on June 8 that "it has been a long time since the [Illinois] country has enjoyed such great tranquility." The panic of 1793-94 was over.[66]

Although the threat of imminent invasion had passed, there remained among Spanish officials in Louisiana a persistent anxiety that political radicals — French and/or Americans — were trying to subvert the Spanish regime in the colony. This anxiety meant that the witch-hunt penetrated into the Ste. Genevieve District.

Louis Coyteux was a craftsman of precious metals who had moved from British Montreal to Spanish Illinois sometime during the late 1780s. First he practiced his trade in St. Louis, but by 1792 he was living at Cape Girardeau, where he was involved in the Indian trade with the well-known Louis Lorimier. Coyteux

---

64. See "Journal of Lorimier," in *SRM*, 2:59-99; on Lorimier and the founding of Cape Girardeau, see Nasatir (ed.), *Spanish War Vessels*, 71-72, 297-98.

65. Printed in *SMV*, pt. 3:255-57.

66. Vallé to Trudeau, Feb. 14, 1794, PC 209; Vallé to Trudeau, Apr. 15, 1794, PC 209; Trudeau to Carondelet, June 8, 1794, PC 209; see also Nasatir, *War Vessels*, 1-21.

must have fought with Lorimier, for he left Cape Girardeau un-
expectedly in the spring of 1794 and moved to the Ste. Genevieve
District. There he built a log cabin in which to live and practice
his craft. Coyteux was a literate and able person despite his modest
circumstances, and Ste. Genevieve was fortunate to have such a
settler.[67]

On February 22, 1795, Lieutenant Governor Trudeau sent
François Vallé orders to arrest Coyteux and ransack his residence.
This was duly accomplished, and Coyteux was clapped in irons and
transported to New Orleans to face charges of subversive activities.
It is not clear what the basis of the charges was. Trudeau himself
did not know, but he surmised that the devious Lorimier was
behind them. François Vallé was sure that Coyteux was innocent
and he wrote directly to Governor Carondelet in defense of his
fellow townsman.[68]

Coyteux was in fact completely exonerated in New Orleans,
where Vallé's letter no doubt helped him. He was soon back in
Ste. Genevieve, and a year later he had a skirmish with the parish
priest for cohabitating with a woman out of wedlock. Under pressure, Coyteux married the woman, settled down, and within a
short while became one of the most solid citizens of Upper
Louisiana, even serving as a deputy law enforcement officer in
1800. Such was the fluidity of society on the Mississippi frontier —
a man doubly tainted one year could become a pillar of the community the next. In any case, Coyteux's ordeal demonstrates the
extent of Spanish fear about political subversion in Louisiana during the 1790s, and also reveals with what remarkable efficiency
the arm of the Spanish government could reach out and seize an
individual to face political charges. This betrays none of the slug-
gishness that supposedly plagued the Spanish colonial administration at that time.[69]

Although from the perspective of hindsight it seems slightly
absurd, there was genuine fear of revolution in Upper Louisiana
during the mid-1790s. Carondelet heard that a club of *sans-culotte*

---

67. Lorimier to Vallé, May 14, 1794, MHS, Vallé Collection Box 1; SGA,
Estates, no. 73; Tanguay, *Dictionnaire*, 3:108.

68. Vallé conducted the search on Feb. 24, 1795, SGA, Estates no. 73; Trudeau
to Vallé, Mar. 4, 1795, MHS, Vallé Collection, Box 2; Trudeau to Carondelet,
Mar. 12, 1795, PC 217; Liljegren "Jacobinism," 90; Vallé to Carondelet, Mar.
23, 1795, PC 2371.

69. On Coyteux's marriage, see below, chap. xi. In 1800 Coyteux was a deputy
in a rape case, see SGA, Litigations, no. 114

revolutionaries was active in St. Louis, and Jacobin agitators were reputed to be on the loose in the Illinois Country. Trudeau admitted that a rare "incendiary pamphlet" appeared in St. Louis, but it is doubtful if political radicalism was ever popular enough in Spanish Illinois to have occasioned the formation of a revolutionary party. There was, however, a small coterie of adventurers in the upper Mississippi Valley, and they, had the occasion arisen, might have served as radical operatives in Spanish Illinois. This group included André Michaux, Jean Pisgignoux, and Bonnevie de Pogniat.[70].

The Spaniards' fear of an insurrection in Upper Louisiana prompted them to dispatch war vessels up the Mississippi as far north as Ste. Genevieve and St. Louis. In October 1795, the governor of Natchez, Manuel Gayoso de Lemos, tied up his galiot *La Vigilante* on the riverbank at Ste. Genevieve and marched into town to visit Commandant François Vallé. This was a momentous occasion for the townspeople, and the local militia formed up to salute Gayoso with a volley of musket fire. Gayoso remained for several days as Vallé's houseguest and reconnoitered of Ste. Genevieve and its environs. He was favorably impressed, remarking that the townspeople were "blindly ready for whatever is required of them by the royal service. . . . Captain Don Francisco Vallé is a subject of very appreciable qualities, a lover of peace and of good order; all his actions are testimonies and proofs of the fervor with which he loves the king [Carlos IV]." Vallé's passion for a monarch upon whom he had never laid eyes may be doubted, but Gayoso's report made it clear that Ste. Genevieve was not seething with revolutionary ferment. Yet the political climate in Spanish Illinois during the mid-1790s was so baffling that even Delassus de Luziéres of New Bourbon, who was *plus royaliste que le roi*, momentarily came under suspicion because of a fleeting contact with the adventurer Bonnevie de Pogniat.[71]

By the end of 1795, the Jacobin revolution in France was over; the threat of a Franco-American invasion led by George Rogers

---

70. The extent of Spanish fear about the "red scare" of 1794-95 is revealed in the reams of correspondence it occasioned, which are preserved in the PC; the best accounts of this episode are in Liljegren, "Jacobinism," 47-97 and Nasatir, *War Vessels*; the latter contains both analysis and documents.

71. See Gayoso's diary for Oct. 24-28, 1795, in Nasatir, *War Vessels*, 300-04; Gayoso's report of Nov. 24, 1795, ibid., 332; Bonnevie to De Luzières, Aug. 27, 1795, PC 211; De Luzières to Carondelet, Oct. 2, 1795, PC 212 A; Holmes, *Gayoso*, chap. vi; Holmes (ed.), *Documentos*, 272, n. 24; 283, n. 45.

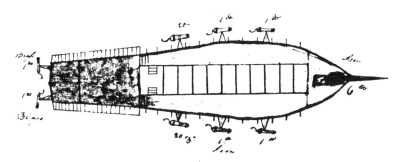

A Spanish galiot of the type that visited Ste. Genevieve in 1795. Notice the six-pound cannon in the prow and the eight little swivel guns. Courtesy of the Missouri Historical Society, St. Louis.

Clark had passed; and the United States and Spain had come to terms in the Treaty of San Lorenzo el Real (Pinckney's Treaty), which opened the Mississippi and New Orleans to American commerce. All this meant that tensions were momentarily reduced in Louisiana. Yet new circumstances soon had Governor Carondelet worrying about his province's security, and he was compelled to take vigorous action that involved the Illinois Country.[72]

In the summer of 1795, France and Spain made peace with the Treaty of Basel. This peace did not signify, however, that France had forsaken its desire to reacquire Louisiana; satisfaction was merely postponed. On the other hand, Spain broke her alliance with Great Britain in order to make peace with France and thereby rekindled Anglo-Spanish rivalry in Upper Louisiana. Spain's anxieties about Loiuisiana took particular and concrete form in the spring of 1796, when the French minister to the United States, Pierre-Auguste Adet, sent General Georges Victor Collot to the Mississippi Valley on a reconnaissance mission. Collot, a master at deception and intrigue, was able simultaneously to generate two worries in the minds of Spanish officials in Louisiana: His mere presence suggested that France still had designs upon Louisiana. But, to make matters worse, Collot spread rumors that a British army was preparing to attack Spanish Louisiana from Canada. Given the increasing tensions between Great Britain and Spain (war did break out between them in October 1796), Collot's rumors were not implausible.[73]

Governor Carondelet, besieged in New Orleans with rumors and difficulties, decided upon a bold stroke that was designed to protect Spanish Illinois against any English incursions from Canada; he created a new administrative position — military commandant of Upper Louisiana. Don Carlos Howard, an Irishman with many years in Spanish service, was appointed to this position, and in November 1796 Carondelet issued his secret orders to proceed to the Illinois Country. In Howard's orders, François Vallé was characterized as "a man of fine qualities although without military talent," and Delassus de Luzières as "a French émigré . . . living retired in Santa Genoveva."[74]

---

72. On the important diplomatic activity of the mid-1790s see Bemis, *Jay's Treaty* and *Pinckney's Treaty*; DeConde, chaps. iii-v; Lyon, chaps. iii, iv; Whitaker, *Spanish Frontier*, chap. xiv and *Mississippi Question*, pts. 1, 2.

When, in April 1796, François Vallé II heard about Pinckney's Treaty, he reported to Carondelet about the reduced tensions across the Mississippi frontier (Vallé to Carondelet, Apr. 5, 1796, PC 2371).

73. Lyon, 85-88; Whitaker, *Mississippi Question*, 119-120; DeConde, 60, 61, 80-82; Kyte, "Spy on the Western Waters," 427-42.

74. Liljegren, "Lieutenant-Colonel Don Carlos Howard"; Nasatir, *War Vessels*, 136-40; Houck, *History of Missouri*, 1:322-24.

Howard ascended the Mississippi during the winter of 1797. At New Madrid he left the river in order to proceed more rapidly by horse, and after a brief layover at Ste. Genevieve he arrived in St. Louis at the end of April. His small fleet soon joined him there. The Spanish war vessels (including three galleys) caused quite a stir in Spanish Illinois, where 1797 became in local legend *"l'année des galères,"* the year of the galleys. Howard set to work beefing up the fortifications of St. Louis in order to fend off a possible English attack from Canada. Such an attack was not in fact likely, for, as Howard himself pointed out, the closest British presence to St. Louis was 300 leagues away at Michilimackinac. But Spanish officials remembered the Anglo-Indian attack of 1780, and were worrying themselves into a frenzy: if not the French it was the Americans, and if not the Americans it was the English who were threatening Spanish Louisiana. Trudeau announced Spain's declaration of war against Great Britain in St. Louis on May 3, 1797 and sent a copy of the declaration to Ste. Genevieve, where the militia was put on alert. The Spaniards were trying desperately to keep the doors of invasion to their colony closed and guarded.[75]

Carlos Howard remained in Spanish Illinois until August 1797, when he departed downriver for New Orleans. By that time it had become clear that the British were not going to launch an attack upon Louisiana from Canada. Moreover, rumors were abroad that Spanish Louisiana was facing a new threat — this time in the form of a plot involving a United States senator. Senator William Blount of Tennessee had hatched a scheme to ally western Americans with British forces for the purpose of seizing Louisiana and the Floridas. This scheme, for which Blount was expelled from the United States Senate, collapsed, but it reveals the complexity of the threats that kept Spanish colonial officials in a perpetual state of perturbation.[76]

The last decade of Spanish rule in Louisiana was a time of constant tension as one crisis after another buffeted the government. Finally, however, European politics and American immigra-

---

75. By far the best study of the Howard expedition is Liljegren's thesis, "Lieutenant-Colonel Don Carlos Howard"; see also Nasatir, *War Vessels*, 137-39; Howard to Carondelet, May 13, 1797, printed in Nasatir, *Before Lewis and Clark*, 2:514-15; Houck, *History of Missouri*, 1:322-27; documents in *SRM*, 2:225-39; copy of Spain's declaration of war against England, SGA, Documents no. 17½.

76. Mueller, "The Blount Conspiracy"; Wright, *Britain and the American Frontier*, 108-17; Whitaker, *Mississippi Question*, 104-15; DeConde, 63.

tion rather than military invasion doomed the Spanish regime in Louisiana. Spain's weakness vis à vis Napoleonic France cost her Louisiana in the Treaty of San Ildefonso (1800). But Napoleon's ambitions were more European than colonial. His obsession with defeating Great Britain, his failure to control the high seas, his chagrin at French losses on St. Domingue, and his desire to remain on good terms with the Americans persuaded Napoleon to sell Louisiana to the United States in 1803 — despite the fact that he had promised Spain he would not do so.[77]

Since the end of the American Revolution, European statesmen had harbored uneasy premonitions about the energetic new republic in North America. In 1783, Count Pedro Aranda, who was Spanish ambassador to France, commented that "this federal republic is born a pigmy. . . . The day will come when she will be a giant, a colossus formidable even to those countries [France and Spain], . . . and will think only of her own aggrandizement." Twenty years after Aranda made these remarks, the *New York Evening Post* opined that "it belongs of right to the United States to regulate the future destiny of North America." American regulation of the territory west of the Mississippi began with the Louisiana Purchase, and this territory included the town of Ste. Genevieve.[78]

The Louisiana Purchase was a deal in global politics arranged by European and American diplomats over a three-year period. In essence, France bullied Spain into retroceding Louisiana in 1800, and Napoleon, breaking his word, sold the colony to the United States in 1803. These agreements concluded in far-off world capitals were, however, only the tip of the iceberg; for, at the very time the negotiations were taking place, a solid base of American settlers already occupied the land in question. Napoleon's awareness of this fact surely bore upon his decision to sell Louisiana to the United States in 1803.[79]

When the militia from Ste. Genevieve marched to New Madrid in December 1802 to participate in chastising the Mascouten Indians who had killed a white man, the militiamen marched under

77. Lyon, chaps. iv-x; DeConde, chaps. vi-ix; Turner, "Policy of France toward the Mississippi Valley," 249-79.

78. Aranda quoted in Houck, *History of Missouri* 1:303; *New York Evening Post* quoted in DeConde, 127.

79. Lyon, 115-16; DeConde, 158-59. On the arrival of American settlers in Upper Louisiana, see Kinnaird, "American Penetration"; Alvord, *Illinois Country*, 398-427; and below, chap. xiii.

the Spanish royal flag. This was so because Spain's retrocession of Louisiana to France in 1800 was done secretly and remained unknown in Upper Louisiana until May 1803. On 5 June of that year, François Vallé posted copies of the retrocession orders in front of his house and on the door of the parish church in Ste. Genevieve. The townspeople must have gazed in wonderment at this document as it dawned upon them that they had become Frenchmen once again. This time of course they were citizens of Napoleon's empire instead of subjects of a Bourbon king. The townspeople did not rejoice at this fact, for their political loyalties were old-fashioned and dynastic, rather than modern and nationalistic.[80]

Francois Vallé II wrote a marvelously diplomatic letter to Governor Manuel de Salcedo on the occasion of Louisiana's retrocession to France. Obviously, Vallé pointed out, the citizens of Ste. Genevieve were unanimously in favor of continuing to live under Spanish dominion, but, unfortunately, they were all agriculturists and thus would be obliged to remain with the land they tilled. As for Vallé himself, as civil and military commandant of Ste. Genevieve he very much wished to move to some region still under Spanish sovereignty, but his large family and impecunious circumstances precluded such a move. The fact of the matter was, of course, the François Vallé did not care a fig for His Most Catholic Majesty of Spain and was perfectly content to pursue his own interests in Ste. Genevieve under any flag, be it Spanish, French, or American.[81]

The people of Ste. Genevieve did not have long to gather their wits over their regained French nationality, for within a few months they were struck with more dramatic news — they had all become Americans. Although some families like the Vallés had prepared for it, most of the townspeople must have been thunderstruck. The twentieth century may be considered a time of continuous upheaval and political turmoil, but the colonial inhabitants of the Mississippi Valley experienced an equally bewildering series of changes. There were persons in Ste. Genevieve who had lived, in turn, under French Bourbon kings, Spanish Bourbon kings, a French emperor, and finally an American president.[82]

---

80. De Luzières to Charles Delassus, May 23, 1803, PC 218; François Vallé to Delassus, June 5, 1803, PC 217. Concerning the Mascouten affair, see below, chap. iv.

81. Vallé to Manuel de Salcedo, Oct. 8, 1803, PC 138.

82. The American acquisition of Louisiana was not formally proclaimed in

Jean-Baptiste Vallé was one of these persons. With the death of his older brother, François, on March 6, 1804, Jean-Baptiste had taken charge in Ste. Genevieve, and two weeks later he remarked: "We are now all Americans, and as such I will devote myself to my country's service and to the welfare of my fellow citizens as I have done under all other governments." A pragmatic and prudent man, Jean-Baptiste Vallé made the transition from Spanish officer to American commandant of Ste. Genevieve without so much as batting an eye. Sometime between March 10 and 19 (probably the 16th), 1804, Vallé ordered the flag of the Spanish Bourbon monarchy lowered and the stars and stripes of the American republic run up over his post. The only vestige left of Spanish rule in Ste. Genevieve was, in Vallé's words, "some remains of a decrepit fort."[83]

Everyone in the Ste. Genevieve area did not, however, take the arrival of American republican sovereignty with Vallé's equanimity. Delassus de Luzières in New Bourbon had fled republican government in France, and, in 1796, stated: "I continue to aver that I will live and die more attached than ever to the authority of kings and to nations governed by them." Exactly what De Luzières was thinking on this subject in the spring of 1804 is not known, but presumably he was not overjoyed with the prospect of having an American republican revolutionary, Thomas Jefferson, as his new leader.[84]

The American president was largely ignorant of the vast territory that he acquired for the United States in 1803. In July of that year, Jefferson sent a letter from Washington, D.C. to Peyroux de la Coudrenière, who was then commandant at New Madrid. Remarkably, Jefferson addressed the letter to "Mr. Peyroux Commandant of Upper Louisiana." Jefferson had met Peyroux in Philadelphia in 1793, and Peyroux must have been one of the few persons in Upper Louisiana whose name Jefferson knew. The American president had obviously not heard of the Vallés of Ste. Genevieve, and it must have tickled Peyroux to discover this fact

---

Ste. Genevieve until February 1804 (see De Luzières to Charles Delassus, Feb. 27, 1804), but it was known for months before that time. I am indebted to William E. Foley for the information that the Louisiana Purchase was known in St. Louis as early as August 1803.

83. Vallé to Delassus, Mar. 19, 1804, PC 197; "Inventaire des titres, actes, procédures, papiers du poste de Ste. Geneviève," Mar. 16-17, 1804, PC 142 A.

84. De Luzières to Carondelet, Aug. 1, 1796, PC 212 A. More on Delassus de Luzières and New Bourbon, below, chap.xiii.

when he broke open Jefferson's letter.[85]

President Jefferson learned quickly, however, and in 1805 he made up for his earlier blunder by appointing Louis Vallé, son of Jean-Baptiste, to the new American military academy at West Point. What better way to gain the loyalty of the important families of the newly acquired territory than to turn their sons into American officers. Louis Vallé did not long pursue a military career. After receiving his commission and doing a short tour of duty in the U.S. Army, he returned to his home town and became a merchant. But young Vallé had become Americanized at West Point, and by returning to Ste. Genevieve he helped to fulfill Jefferson's plan of turning the residents of Upper Louisiana into Americans.[86]

While dramatic political changes between 1763 and 1803 swept Ste. Genevieve from French to Spanish to French to American sovereignty, it is difficult to discover to what loyalties, if any, the townspeople have clung during these changes. The Vallé family adroitly served one sovereign after another, all the while remaining loyal to themselves and their town. If, anytime between 1750 and 1810, the townspeople had been polled on their political loyalties it seems likely that the poll would have revealed no trace of national sentiment or patriotism among them. Loyalties in Ste. Genevieve were intensely local; the people were loyal to their families, to their friends, to their church, and perhaps to their town. There may have been some lingering loyalty to the Bourbon family, if not to France as such. When, in the autumn of 1793, news arrived in the Illinois Country that King Louis XVI had been executed in Paris by French Revolutionaries, Trudeau wrote to Carondelet that "the sad end of Louis XVI . . . affected all the old Frenchmen here." This is one of the very rare known comments on political sentiment from colonial Illinois, and one suspects that it was a short-lived sentiment; with wood to cut for the coming winter there was little time to "sit upon the ground and tell sad stories of the death of kings."[87]

---

85. Jefferson to Peyroux, July 3, 1803, in Nasatir (ed.) *Before Lewis and Clark*, 2:721.

86. Houck, *History of Missouri*, 2:381; Dalton, "Genealogy of the Vallé Family," 65.

87. Trudeau to Carondelet, Oct. 2, 1793, PC 211.

O F THE THREE principal ethnic groups that inhabited Upper
Louisiana during the eighteenth century — white Europeans, black Africans, and red Indians — the last was the largest.
A history of colonial Ste. Genevieve must deal with the red men:
they had a direct and continuous bearing upon the community,
and no single topic occupies so large a place in the correspondence
of the Illinois Country as do Indian affairs. Here the Indians of
the Illinois Country will be treated strictly within the context of
their association with and their impact upon Ste. Genevieve, since
the town and its citizens, not the Indians, are the focus of our
attention.

Henry Brackenridge observed that sizeable Indian settlements
had once existed near the site of Ste. Genevieve: "This appears . . .
to have been one of those spots pitched upon by former and
numerous nations of Indians as a place of residence. In the bottom
[i.e., the Big Field] there are a number of large mounds. Barrows,
and places of interment, are every where to be seen." Brackenridge
was clearly referring to the Indian remains dating from the prehistoric era that dot the floodplain of the Mississippi River. Rem-
nants of a Mississippian mound complex can be seen in the agricultural land near U.S. Highway 61 south of Ste. Genevieve. The
Indians who had lived on the Big Field in late prehistoric times
were probably associated with the mound builders of Cahokia,
and they had long since disappeared when Frenchmen arrived in
the Mississippi Valley.[1]

---

1. Brackenridge, *Views of Louisiana*, 125; a team of archeologists from the
University of Missouri, Columbia, is now engaged in further study of prehistoric
Indian sites near Ste. Genevieve.

When Frenchmen first arrived in the Illinois Country, they established outposts in association with client Indian tribes. Starved Rock, Pimiteoui (Peoria), Cahokia, Kaskaskia, and Fort de Chartres were all settlements at which various tribes of Illinois Indians (Kaskaskia, Tamaroa, Peoria, and Michigamea) lived in close proximity with Frenchmen. At the time Ste. Genevieve was founded, however, no Indian tribe occupied the immediate vicinity. The maps of Upper Louisiana drawn in the 1740s and 1750s by Jacques-Nicolas Bellin, designated general areas inhabited by various Indian tribes and even located certain Indian villages. Bellin, who worked in Paris, had no firsthand information upon which to base his maps, and portions of them are wildly inaccurate; nonetheless, in mid-eighteenth century he was the most knowledgeable European cartographer on the subject of the Mississippi Valley. Bellin showed the Kaskaskia Indians on the east side of the Mississippi, but west of the river his maps depicted no Indian village within 100 miles of Ste. Genevieve.[2]

The absence of Indian villages in the vicinity of Ste. Genevieve did not mean that Indians from various tribes did not frequent the region, for Indian hunting and war parties were remarkably mobile. A French explorer, Antoine-Valentin de Gruy, wrote in 1743 that Foxes and Sioux had driven Philippe Renaut from his lead mines in the valley of the Big River. If that in fact occurred, those particular Indians had descended to the watershed of the Meramec River from much further north in the Mississippi Valley; perhaps they had even come down temporarily to exploit the lead deposits that Renaut was working. The Big Osage tribe, whose established villages were far west of Ste. Genevieve, eventually had great impact upon the town, although in the 1750s and 1760s they seem to have kept their distance from the French settlements.[3]

Historians' knowledge of Indian affairs derives largely from documents written by white men about Indians or from information gleaned from anthropologists and archaeologists. For the first twenty years of Ste. Genevieve's history, ca. 1750-1770, documents dealing with Indian affairs are scarce. The local civil and religious records for that period are incomplete, and administrative corre-

---

2. See, for example, the Bellin map of Louisiana, 1755, a part of which is shown above, chap. ii. See also Sturtevant (ed.), *Handbook of . . . Indians*, 15:594-601.

3. De Gruy's memoir, AN, G¹, 465:9, Din and Nasatir, *Imperial Osages*, chaps. ii, iii; Chapman, "Indomitable Osage," 287-90.

spondence dealing with the town and its environs is scanty: the French and Indian War disrupted communications during the last decade of the French regime in the Illinois Country, and Spanish administrators did not establish themselves in Spanish Illinois until the end of the 1760s. Substantial documentation on Indian affairs that pertain to the history of Ste. Genevieve thus begins with the early 1770s.

There were numerous, deep, and sustained amicable relations — sexual, marital, and commercial — between Indians and white men in the Illinois Country. The extent of the fur trade and the many racially mixed marriages and mixed-blood offspring testify to this. Yet the documentation on Indian-white relations in and around colonial Ste. Genevieve is largely a record of fear, distrust, tension, and hostilities.

The bloodiest massacre of white men by Indians during the Spanish regime in Upper Louisiana occurred at Mine La Motte in April 1774. Seven men, including Joseph Vallé, son of François Vallé I, were killed in this episode and some of them were buried in the Old Town of Ste. Genevieve. The circumstances of the massacre are not clear, for records pertaining to it are scarce. Louis Houck claimed, without citing a source, that Osages had massacred the French lead miners, but it seems more likely that it was Chickasaws; in June 1774 Lieutenant Governor Piernas reported to New Orleans from St. Louis that Chickasaws had perpetrated the massacre, and Piernas, who was close to the scene, probably had accurate information.[4]

Moreover, there is an interesting case in the Ste. Genevieve civil records which shows that Chickasaws, who were traditionally allies of the English and enemies of the French and Spaniards, were active near Mine La Motte during the early 1770s. This case, from 1771, tells how several black slaves belonging to the lead miners Pierre Gadobert and Jean-Baptiste Labastide were kidnapped by "Chiks" (Chickasaws) on the road between Ste. Genevieve and Mine La Motte. It is hard to say what the Chickasaws intended to do with the black slaves; perhaps they planned to sell them to English traders operating in Chickasaw territory east of the Mississippi and south of the Ohio River. In any case, two bounty hunters from Ste. Genevieve, Jean Lacroix and Jean Bertau, took

---

4. Houck, *History of Missouri*, 1:378, Unzaga to Piernas, Aug. 22, 1774, PC 81: "I was informed by your letter of June 5 of the death at the hands of the Chickasaws at the lead mine . . . of the seven persons who were working it, including the son of Don Francisco Vallé. . . ." SGPR, Burials, Book 1:20.

three "Arks" (Arkansas Indians) and an interpreter, pursued the Chickasaw raiding party, and successfully retrieved the slaves for their masters. Probably the English were encouraging the Chickasaws to conduct raids into Spanish Illinois during the 1700's. One year after his slaves had been abducted, Labastide himself was killed by the Chickasaws at Mine La Motte.[5]

Although it *may* have been true that French and Spanish colonists were less racist, and therefore more humane, than Anglo-Americans in their treatment of Indians, there is no doubt that Spanish officials in Upper Louisiana viewed Indians as adversaries to be dealt with in any way possible. In 1772 Lieutenant Governor Piernas in St. Louis attempted to sort out some of the complexity of intertribal relations in Spanish Illinois, and he described the process by which the Little Osages had in the past split off from the Big Osages and associated themselves with the Missouri tribe, "their ally and neighbor." Following this description, Piernas suggested that the Little Osages and the Missouris were "the least numerous of all and the easiest to reduce by means of extermination." Twenty years later, the Spaniards did attempt a war of extermination against the Big Osage tribe. Although this policy was perhaps not racially motivated and also proved an abysmal failure, Piernas's words have a chilling effect upon a reader familiar with genocidal policies of twentieth-century governments.[6]

The 1770s were years of continual Indian incursions into the environs of Ste. Genevieve, and occasionally into the town itself. These raids were overwhelmingly for the purpose of stealing horses and seem to have been largely bloodless. Indeed, there was remarkable forbearance on both sides. The Indians came to steal, not to kill, and if caught they gave up their booty and fled, without blood being drawn on either side.[7]

The Little Osage and the Missouri were the most persistently troublesome tribes for the people of Ste. Genevieve during this period. Why those particular tribes, and not for example the ferocious Big Osage, is difficult to explain, but perhaps this had to do with issues internal to the respective tribes — choice of hunting grounds or village sites, for example. In the spring of 1779, a

5. SGA, Litigations 129½; ibid., Estates no. 131. On Chickasaw activities during the early 1780s, see Din, "Loyalist Resistance," 159-70.

6. Piernas to Unzaga, July 4, 1772, *SMV*, pt. 1:204-05.

7. See for example, Piernas to Unzaga, July 30, 1772, ibid., 206-07; Cartabona to Unzaga, Apr. 1, 1776, PC 81.

large number of citizens in Ste. Genevieve petitioned Lieutenant Governor de Leyba to do something to stop pilfering by Little Osages and Missouris. The petitioners stated that "for the last seven or eight years these tribes have come each year to the out-lying areas of the post and have stolen the horses of the inhabitants. . . . But the said undersigned persons now find themselves totally without horses because of repeated thefts by the said nations. . . . They fear with reason that they will be unable, through lack of horses, to grind their wheat and accomplish their other labors." De Leyba did not give the petitioners from Ste. Genevieve much satisfaction, except to authorize them to defend their possessions against Indian incursions by force of arms.[8]

When an British-sponsored force attacked St. Louis in the spring of 1780, it consisted largely of Indians from northern tribes — Sioux, Foxes, Sauks, and Menominees. Local tribes, like the Osage and Missouri, hated Englishmen even more than they hated French-men and Spaniards and did not participate in the hostilities near St. Louis. In July 1780, Louis Bolduc found five men killed by Indians southwest of Ste. Genevieve, and it seems likely that this was the work of Chickasaws, who were allies of the English. And in December 1780 François Vallé reported from Ste. Genevieve that his town was "more threatened than ever by the savage tribes, who are provoked both by their misery and by the English." There is no evidence, however, that Ste. Genevieve itself was attacked during the violent years of the American Revolution.[9]

Great Britian recognized the independence of the United States in the Treaty of Paris (1783). The decade following this treaty witnessed streams of Americans moving into the territory north and west of the Ohio River. Pressure from the land-hungry new settlers drove the Indian tribes in that territory westward toward the Mississippi, and even across the river into Upper Louisiana. During the early 1780s, Shawnees and Delawares began to arrive on the west side of the Mississippi. They were unwelcome in Amer-ican territory because they had supported Great Britain during the American War of Independence. Spanish officials welcomed these new tribes, whom they hoped to use to check the power of the Osages and as a bulwark against encroaching Americans and

8. People of Ste. Genevieve to De Leyba, Mar. 28, 1779, *SMV*, pt. 1:335-36; De Leyba to Gálvez, July 13, 1779, *SRM*, 1:163-64.

9. Cruzat to Gálvez, Nov. 14, 1780, *SMV*, pt. 1:398-99; Vallé to Piernas, Dec. 27, 1780, PC 193 B; see SGA, Miscellaneous 2, no. 4.

Englishmen.[10]

Shawnees and Delawares first appeared in Spanish Illinois in the spring of 1782, when Shawnee, Loup, Chickasaw, and Cherokee chiefs arrived at St. Louis to offer Lieutenant Governor Cruzat peace necklaces. The migration of Shawnee and Delaware groups to the west side of the Mississippi continued during the mid-1780s, and by 1787 substantial numbers of these Indians began to establish villages south of Ste. Genevieve. These villages were located along the creeks that flowed eastward into the Mississippi — the Saline, Apple, Cinque Hommes, and Flora — with the western frontier of the settlements being the White River.[11]

During the late colonial period the Shawnees and Delawares lived in close proximity to each other and on all important issues coordinated their activities. The arrival of these two tribes meant that there were more Indians closer to Ste. Genevieve than there had ever been before. During the 1790s groups of Shawnees and Delawares often visited Ste. Genevieve; they conducted peaceful trade in town, and they played a major role in the complicated Indian diplomacy of Upper Louisiana during the last ten years of the colonial regime. The New Bourbon census of 1797 listed seventy Shawnee and 120 Delaware (Loup) families living on the north bank of Apple Creek, and their respective tribal villages were located several miles apart.[12]

The name Louis Lorimier is intimately linked to the settlement of Shawnees and Delawares in Upper Louisiana and to white relations with these tribes once they settled in the region south of Ste. Genevieve. Lorimier was a French Canadian by birth who had reconciled himself to British rule in his homeland. Loyal in his fashion to Great Britain, he had led Indian war parties against American settlements in the Ohio Valley during the American Revolution. Houck observed that Lorimier served as an agent of Lieutenant Governor Pérez during the late 1780s and worked to induce certain bands of the Shawnee and Delaware tribes to settle in Spanish Illinois. This was probably true, for Lorimier felt no

10. Sosin, *Revolutionary Frontier*, 17, 38, 57. On Shawnee and Delaware migrations, see Sturtevant (ed.), *Handbook of Indians*, 15:600-01, 623-35.

11. Cruzat to Miró, Mar. 18, 1782, *SRM*, 1:209. Captain Amos Stoddard, the first American commandant of Upper Louisiana, wrote (*Sketches*, 210): "A considerable number of Delawares, Shawanese [*sic*], and Cherokees, have built some villages on the waters of the St. Francis and White Rivers. Their removal into these quarters was authorized by the Spanish government. . . ."

12. New Bourbon census of 1797, PC 2365.

more at home in American territory than did the Indians. He was fluent in several Indian languages, despite his inability to write French or Spanish (he could barely scrawl his name), was adept at Indian relations, and lived with a full-blooded Shawnee woman. His first established residence in Spanish Illinois was in the Ste. Genevieve District on the Saline Creek. Lorimier picked this site, on the northern edge of the concentration of Shawnee and Delaware settlements, in order to facilitate his dealings with those particular tribes. Five years later, in 1792, Lorimier moved to the southern edge of this concentration and established a trading post at what soon became the settlement of Cape Girardeau.[13]

Spanish officials were intent upon maintaining good relations with the Shawnees and Delawares, and Lorimier's position as liaison between these Indians and the Spanish government was vital. Late in 1792, he petitioned Lieutenant Governor Trudeau for a license to conduct commerce with the Delaware and Shawnee tribes. Trudeau forwarded Lorimier's petition to Governor Carondelet with the recommendation that it be approved, for Lorimier was "a man of good conduct, who has been very useful." Carondelet reacted with alacrity and forthwith granted Lorimier exclusive trading privileges with the Shawnees and Delawares in the entire region between the Arkansas and Missouri rivers. This was a prudent decision, for when the Spaniards feared a British attack against St. Louis in 1797 Carondelet claimed that Lorimier could command 200 Shawnee and Delaware braves to help defend Spanish Illinois.[14]

The advancing Americans because of their numbers, and perhaps also because of their attitudes, made little attempt to live in harmony with the Indians. This is not the place to dwell upon the pathos of the American Indians as they were buffeted by white civilization, but the description of the Delawares given in the early 1820s by Paul Wilhelm, Duke of Württemberg, has a pathetic quality about it: "Crowded out by political conditions, the Delaware tribe . . . have settled in the westerly region of the Mississippi near the Meramec River. Here a pitiable remnant of this once powerful nation, the most dreaded enemy of the immigrated Europeans, barely ekes out a wretched existence near their oppressors, and

13. Houck, *Memorial Sketches*, 1-18; Lorimier's journal, Oct. 26, 1792, PC 208 B; Nasatir (ed.) *War Vessels*, 71, n. 27.

14. Trudeau to Carondelet, Nov. 12, 1792, PC 25; Douglas, *History of Southeast Missouri*, 1:69-71.

they will soon be given over to certain ruin."[15]

Available records strongly suggest that during the 1780s the Chickasaws, who ranged all the way from St. Louis to Mobile, became less of a problem for the white settlements in Spanish Illinois. This tribe, which for half a century had played havoc with the convoys that plied the Mississippi between New Orleans and the Illinois Country, repeatedly carried peace collars (wampum belts) to the Spanish lieutenant governor in St. Louis and seem to have stopped their depredations in the middle Mississippi Valley. What accounted for this change in behavior of a tribe that had been the terror of riverboatmen and that had perpetrated the massacre at Mine La Motte in 1774 is not known. Perhaps the English were no longer provoking the Chickasaws to attack creole settlements; perhaps the Chickasaws had reconciled themselves to living in peace with the creoles because they detested the advancing Americans more than they did the creoles; or perhaps it had something to do with the internal politics of the Chickasaw tribe.[16]

There is no doubt about the intense enmity that existed between most Indian tribes and the advancing Anglo-Americans. When in August 1784 representatives of the Iroquois, Cherokee, Shawnee, Chickasaw, Choctaw, and Loup tribes visited St. Louis in order to present Lieutenant Governor Cruzat with peace collars of porcelain beads, they addressed Cruzat with the following words: "The Americans, a great deal more ambitious and numerous than the English, put us out of our lands, forming therein great settlements, extending themselves like a plague of locusts in the territories of the Ohio River. . . . They treat us as their cruelest enemies are treated, so that today hunger and the impetuous torrent of war . . . have brought our villages to a struggle with death." Four years later, Peyroux de la Coudrèniere, who was then commandant at Ste. Genevieve, sent a medallion to Governor Miró and explained that it was "an authentic souvenir of the Indians' hate for Americans of the United States; it came from the Cherokees, who have mutilated an American with a kind of fury." Indian detestation of Americans meant that the creoles in Spanish Illinois had more Indians with whom to cope, for the deracinated redmen fled the United States and came flocking to the west side of the Mississippi.[17]

15. Württembourg, *Travels*, 175.

16. Cruzat to Miró, Aug. 8, 1782, *SMV*, pt. 2:49-54.

17. Cruzat to Miró, Aug. 23, 1784, ibid., 117-18; Peyroux to Miró, Dec. 5, 1788, PC 201.

Shawnee Indian as depicted by General Georges-Victor Collot in the 1790s. The Shawnees began to arrive in Upper Louisiana during the 1780s. Illustration from Collot's Journey in North America.

The variety of Indians with whom the townspeople of Ste. Genevieve dealt during the 1780s was greater than ever before. In addition to Shawnees and Delawares, other newcomers to the Ste. Genevieve District were the Peorias, who had acquired some notoriety when a member of their tribe killed the great Ottawa chief Pontiac near Cahokia in 1769. The Peorias began their migration to the west side of the Mississippi as early as the late 1760s. Precisely when they settled down near Ste. Genevieve is not known, but it seems to have been in the mid-1780s. At that time, a substantial number of Peorias were baptized in town. The Peorias were the red men with whom the townspeople had the closest relations during the last two decades of the colonial period, but little is known about the quality of these relations other than that they seem to have been entirely peaceful. Perhaps the vigor and aggressiveness of the Peorias had already been sapped by liquor, disease, and cultural disintegration.[18]

The Osages, both Big and Little, were still vigorous and active in the late colonial period, however, and Ste. Genevieve fell within their range of visitation. In May 1784, town commandant Silvio de Cartabona reported that a band of Big Osages had fallen upon two residents of Ste. Genevieve who were hunting in the "mountains" west of town, had stripped them of all possessions, including their clothes, and left them to make their way home naked and on foot. Two Robinson-Crusoe-like apparitions limped into Ste. Genevieve several days later. During the same spring of 1784, Big Osages were also roaming close enough to Ste. Genevieve to steal horses from *habitants* working their fields near town.[19]

But the most notorious Osage outrage of the 1780s was the killing of a creole hunter near Ste. Genevieve in March 1788. One Jean-François la Bûche was hunting near the "Fourche à Courtois" (Courtois Creek enters the Meramec River in present-day Crawford County) with two of his sons. The boys' mother was a black woman living in Ste. Genevieve. On the afternoon of March 8, La Bûche and his older son were out in the forest hunting, having left the younger boy back at camp. After seeing Indian signs in the woods, La Bûche became alarmed for his younger son's safety

---

18. Alvord, *Illinois Country*, 273; St. Ange de Bellerive reported a band of over one hundred Peorias near St. Louis in 1766 (Aug. 4, 1766, PC 187); SGPR, Baptisms, Book A. On the Peorias during the eighteenth century, see Temple, *Indian Villages* 11-55.

19. Cruzat reported this incident to Miró, June 23, 1784, PC 10. On the Osages, see the comprehensive new study, *Imperial Osages*, by Din and Nasatir.

and returned to camp, leaving the older boy at their hunting site. Hearing gunshots in the direction of the camp, the older boy ran back to camp to find the scalped body of his father near the fire and horse tracks leading off toward Osage territory.[20]

The younger boy had saved himself by scrambling into the bush, and both youths made it back to Ste. Genevieve and reported the incident to town commandant Peyroux. One month later, a fur trader informed Lieutenant Governor Pérez in St. Louis that a Little Osage brave had confessed to having been one of a party of nine of his tribe who had killed La Bûche, but the Indian had justified the killing on the grounds that La Bûche had fired on them first. Pérez explained all this in a letter to Governor General Miró. Miró, who ridiculed the notion that La Bûche would begin firing when the odds were so stacked against him, demanded that the killers be brought to justice, and Pérez duly confronted the Little Osages when they visited St. Louis. The Indians admitted that one of their tribe had killed La Bûche but insisted that the guilty individual was himself dying from a bullet wound. Then two weeks later two Little Osage chiefs came to Pérez to inform him that the wounded brave had died. Spanish officials, stumped with that turn of events, decided to drop the matter.[21]

The La Bûche killing is of interest because it reveals how the Indians could manipulate the Spanish officials and also because it confirms Houck's contention that remarkably few white settlers were killed by Indians in Upper Louisiana during the Spanish regime: when the killing of one itinerant hunter could provoke a flurry of correspondence from Ste. Genevieve to St. Louis to New Orleans and back, it is apparent that such killings were not an everyday — or even every-year — occurrence. La Bûche's black concubine was left to raise the dead man's sons by herself.[22]

The commandant at Ste. Genevieve not only had to contend with sporadic hostility from a variety of Indian tribes; he had also to monitor relations among the Indians themselves within the Ste. Genevieve District. In April 1788, for example, Peyroux reported that a war party of Sauks and Foxes secretly brought their canoes onto the bank of the Mississippi near Ste. Genevieve to attack the

20. Peyroux to Miró, Mar. 12, 1788, PC 201; Din and Nasatir, 184-85.

21. Pérez to Miró, Apr. 18, 1788, *SMV*, pt. 2:253; Miró to Pérez, May 7, 1788, PC 5; Pérez to Miró, Sept. 1, 1788, PC 2361; Miró to Pérez, Nov. 6, 1788, PC 119.

22. Houck, *History of Missouri*, 2:213; on La Bûche's wife and children, see SGPR, Baptisms, Book A:129 C.

A Kaskaskia Indian as depicted by General George-Victor Collot in the 1790s. The Kaskaskias were originally part of the large Iliniwek (Illinois) tribe. Illustration from Collot's Journey in North America.

Peorias who were living there. When one of the Peoria women was killed and scalped, the Peoria tribe asked Peyroux for a letter of recommendation so that they might retire in safety to the Arkansas District. And two years later Peyroux wrote to the governor of Louisiana that the Peorias, Loups (Abenakis) and Shawnees were all complaining to him about depredations by the Osages. The Shawnees went so far as to suggest that if the Spanish colonial government did not take action to pacify the Osages that the Shawnees would move back to the east side of the Mississippi, for they preferred to reconcile themselves with the Americans rather than be destroyed by the Osages. This was probably an empty threat, but in fact it was other Indian tribes who first suggested to the Spaniards that they conduct a war *à l'outrance* against the Osages.[23]

The decade of the 1790s was a period of almost continual tension and hostility between the townspeople of Ste. Genevieve and the Big Osage tribe. According to an anthropologist of the Osage, Carl H. Chapman, the Big Osages moved their villages increasingly south and west during the 1790s, therefore further away from Ste. Genevieve. Yet it seems apparent from historical documents that at the very time their villages were becoming more distant from town Osage raiding parties were visiting the area more frequently. It is difficult to ascertain clearly the internal dynamics of the Big Osage tribe, but perhaps the relocation of the villages and the movements of the raiding parties can be seen as interrelated reactions — one defensive and the other offensive — to the increasing numbers of white settlers on the west side of the Mississippi; the Big Osages moved their women and children further west for protection and simultaneously sent their warriors east against the white settlements.[24]

Although the Big Osages continued to make incursions into the Ste. Genevieve District throughout the colonial era — witness their raid at Mine La Motte in 1802 — their threats during the period 1790-94 created an atmosphere of veritable crisis within the community. In April 1790 a petition signed by thirty-four residents of Ste. Genevieve was sent to Governor Miró. It contained a litany of misdeeds committed by the Big Osages: they were stealing horses, killing cattle, waylaying hunters, and disrupting agricul-

---

23. Peyroux to Miró, Apr. 28, 1788, PC 119; Peyroux to Miró, Apr. 7, 1790, PC 203.

24. Chapman, "Indomitable Osage," 292; Din and Nasatir, chap. vii.

Cheveux Blancs (White Hairs), a principal chief of the Big Osage tribe during the late colonial period. He visited President Thomas Jefferson in Washington D.C. in 1804. Photo courtesy of the New York Historical Society.

ture. The immediate occasion for the petition was the arrival in Ste. Genevieve of Loups (Delawares), who pitiably came to town carrying their saddles because the Osages had stolen their horses; the Loups told the townspeople that Osages were still prowling in the area. The petitioners asked Miró to prohibit all trade up the Missouri River, for, according to the petitioners, this was the only sure means of driving the Osages into submission.[25]

This petition of 1790 had no immediate effect, and the Big Osage raids continued unabated. Correspondence of the period is replete with commentary on Osage activities: in April 1791 Lieutenant Governor Pérez in St. Louis addressed an open letter to the inhabitants of Ste. Genevieve, telling them that "it pains me, sirs, to see the injuries that the Osage Tribe causes for you, and I now see more clearly than ever that it is time to put a stop to them." In December 1791 Commandant Peyroux reported to Governor Miró that the Osages were stealing horses daily in the Ste. Genevieve District. In March 1792 François Vallé II, who was serving as commandant ad interim at Ste. Genevieve while Peyroux was out of town, complained to Pérez that the people of his district were being "tormented" by Osages, who were bold enough to enter villages at night in order to pilfer. In the hinterland the Osages roamed so freely that in 1793 Lieutenant Governor Trudeau called the Meramec (i.e., Big) River Valley, "la galerie des Osages," Osage Alley.[26]

Spanish officials in Upper Louisiana had always planned to use friendly tribes, such as the Loup and Shawnee, as allies against the Osages. But Indian allies did not necessarily take well to being manipulated by the whites and often proved difficult to manage. In September 1792, for example, a band of Loups came to Ste. Genevieve to look for food and to blow off a little steam. Vallé described their visit: "They drank for three or four days. At the Saline they killed a yearling calf . . . and several pigs. They were not yet sober, and I was unable to speak to them." Allies like these understandably made the townspeople a little nervous.[27]

In 1792 Spanish administrators changed in both St. Louis and New Orleans; Trudeau replaced Pérez at the former, and Caron-

25. Citizens of Ste. Genevieve to Miró, Apr. 9, 1790, PC 7.

26. Pérez to citizens of Ste. Genevieve, Apr. 26, 1791, MHS, Vallé Collection, Box 1; Peyroux to Miró, Dec. 2, 1791, PC 204; Vallé to Pérez, Mar. 15, 1792, PC 211; Trudeau to Carondelet, Sep. 28, 1793, PC 208 A; Din and Nasatir, chaps. vii, viii.

27. Vallé to Trudeau, Sept. 25, 1792, PC 207 B.

delet replaced Miró at New Orleans. The new men hoped to succeed where their predecessors had failed in pacifying the Big Osage tribe. In December 1792 Carondelet sent letters to both Trudeau and François Vallé ordering a war of annihilation against the Osages. The letter to Trudeau included the following remarks: "I have determined that you shall prohibit all . . . trade with the Great and Little Osages. . . . At the same time you will proclaim that any subject of His Majesty [Carlos IV], or individual of the other nations, white or red, may overrun the Great and Little Osages, kill them and destroy their families, as they are disturbers of the prosperity of all the nations." Carondelet was a greenhorn governor when he wrote this letter and he would soon learn that the Osage tribes were not to be destroyed so easily.[28]

Although Carondelet's orders to wage open war against the Osages arrived in the Illinois Country about April 1, 1793, Lieutenant Governor Trudeau did not declare war immediately, for to have done so would have jeopardized the traders who were in Osage territory at the time. Finally in June Trudeau reluctantly ordered war declared, and François Vallé II posted the declaration in Ste. Genevieve on Sunday morning, June 23, 1793. The townspeople had been clamoring for a war against the Osages, and, according to the parish priest, Father St. Pierre, Carondelet's decision to declare war was greeted in Ste. Genevieve with "great acclamations of joy and satisfactions."[29]

Lieutenant Governor Trudeau, however, felt differently. He had been reluctant to declare war against the Osages because he felt that it was positively dangerous to declare a war that could not be fought. As he explained in a letter to Valle: "It seems to me that to declare war and not prosecute it for lack of means is like declaring war upon ourselves." Less bluntly but in more detail, Trudeau explained the situation to Governor Carondelet: "With a population of 1250 men, young men, and warriors, they [the Big Osages] live all together in the same village in the midst of an immense prairie, an advantage which makes them formidable, and which will not permit in our time the accomplishment of what is desired for the good of the province." Trudeau's prophecy was abundantly borne out.[30]

28. Carondelet to Trudeau, Dec. 22, 1792, *SMV*, pt. 3:107.

29. Trudeau to Carondelet, Apr. 10, 1793, *SMV*, pt. 3:148-49; Trudeau to Carondelet, Apr. 16, 1793, PC 104; "Répertoire des archives du poste de Ste. Geneviève," PC 206; St. Pierre to Carondelet, May 29, 1793, PC 208 A.

30. Trudeau to Vallé, 1793, MHS, Vallé Collection, Box 1; Trudeau to Carondelet, Apr. 10, 1793, *SMV*, pt. 3:148; Din and Nasatir, chap. viii.

Carondelet was not deterred by Trudeau's reservations and he ordered Trudeau to organize a coordinated attack against the Osages — employing men from St. Louis, Ste. Genevieve, New Madrid, plus warriors from the friendly Indian tribes. This expedition was never mounted. Trudeau explained that the Indian allies were not reliable and that there were simply not enough white militiamen in Spanish Illinois to pursue such an enterprise with any hope of success. As for the people of Ste. Genevieve, they had no capacity to march against the Osages. Indeed, rather than going on the offensive, François Vallé reacted defensively by recalling to town the small Spanish garrison, which had temporarily been posted at Mine à Breton. In September 1793 Trudeau reported to Governor Carondelet that "the inhabitants of Ste. Genevieve, who cried out the loudest to punish this tribe [the Big Osage], are today ready to sacrifice even the remainder of their horses in order to have peace with them; formerly they feared only thieves, now they fear assassins."[31]

In 1797 Trudeau drafted a historical perspective on events in Upper Louisiana during 1793-94 and recalled that in January 1794 a hundred Big Osage braves had come into Ste. Genevieve and killed a man. The anthropologist Carl Chapman has interpreted this event as an example of the Osage mourning-war ceremony. But there is no documentation from January 1794 to corroborate Trudeau's story, which seems to be unfounded; such a dramatic event would surely have entered contemporary records had it in fact occurred. Smaller groups of Osages were active in the Ste. Genevieve District during February and March 1794, however. When one of three miners, who was returning to town from the lead mines, left his companions and went into the woods to hunt squirrels a party of Osages ambushed him, killed him, and cut off his head. His two companions fled back to Ste. Genevieve without taking the time to bury the headless corpse; a party of militia later rode out to perform a proper burial. The Osages also continued to steal horses in the town's environs, and at 2 a.m. on March 31 one Monsieur Pagé discovered Osage thieves in his barn, which was located on top of the hill just south of the Petite Rivière (now South Gabouri Creek) and virtually in view of Commandant Vallé's house across the creek. Pagé frightened them off with rifle shots, but not before the Osages had stolen several

31. Carondelet to Trudeau, May 6, 1793, *SMV*, pt. 3:155; Trudeau to Carondelet, Sept. 28, 1793, ibid., 206; Vallé to Trudeau, Apr. 9, 1793, PC 207 B; Trudeau to Carondelet, Sept. 28, 1793 [second letter of that date], PC 208 A.

horses. No doubt the fort that was begun at Ste. Genevieve in February 1794 was intended to protect the townspeople from Indians as well as from the feared Franco-American invasion.[32]

In any event, during the spring of 1794 all talk about a war of extermination against the Osages ceased. Carondelet was perhaps beginning to see the fatuousness of such a proposal, and, moreover, the threat of a Franco-American invasion of Spanish Louisiana began to loom as a greater danger than the Osages. When in early 1794 Trudeau and the Chouteau brothers in St. Louis conceived of a plan to pacify the Osages without a war, Carondelet jumped at the chance to get out of the embarrassing situation of having declared a war that could not be waged. Auguste Chouteau traveled to New Orleans in the spring of 1794 and in May signed a contract with Carondelet that permitted the Chouteau brothers to construct a combination fort and trading post, Fort Carondelet, on the Osage River in the midst of Big Osage territory.[33]

Although the Chouteaus' exclusive privilege for trading with the Big Osage tribe caused some discontent among other traders in St. Louis, Fort Carondelet was built, and the Chouteau policy of dealing with the Osages through quiet diplomacy instead of war worked reasonably well. The Big Osages continued to steal horses around Ste. Genevieve; they raided the lead mines in 1797, 1801, and 1802; and they occasionally engaged in highway robbery. In 1797, for example, on a road near Ste. Genevieve a party of Osages relieved one Henry Pagget of a substantial amount of goods — including horses, saddles, men's and women's clothing, shoes, and velvet cloth. Pagget, who was apparently an Anglo-American trader, argued unsuccessfully that Auguste Chouteau was responsible for his loss because Chouteau was charged with handling Osage affairs. But those who fell victim to the Osages in the late 1790s seem to have been mostly Anglo-Americans rather than French creoles — probably because the new settlers lived in the more outlying areas. And the Osages were remarkably restrained in their thieving enterprises, hardly ever killing the victims. In any case, the townspeople of Ste. Genevieve were never

---

32. Trudeau to Gayoso, Dec. 20, 1797, Nasatir (ed.) *Before Lewis and Clark*, 2:526-29; Chapman, "Indomitable Osage," 298; Vallé to Trudeau, Mar. 31, 1794, PC 209; concerning the fort built at Ste. Genevieve in 1794, see above, chap. iii.

33. See Din and Nasatir, chap. ix; Foley and Rice, *The First Chouteaus*, chap. iv; see also documents in *SRM*, 2:100-110.

again threatened as sorely by the Osages as they had been during the early 1790s.[34]

The "indomitable Osages" were not fully subjugated in the Ste. Genevieve District until after the Louisiana Purchase and the end of the colonial era. As Auguste Chouteau wrote to Governor Gayoso de Lemos in 1798, "one cannot hope to civilize such a nation [the Osage] except through the passage of time. My brother [Pierre, commandant at Fort Carondelet] is doing his best to keep them in line. . . ." Indeed, it took time and floods of American settlers to push the proud Osages out of their native territory, break their spirit and destroy their heritage, which may or may not be what the Chouteau brothers meant by the verb "civilize."[35]

The first full-blooded Indians to live in the town of Ste. Genevieve were slaves of the white *habitants*. Indian slavery had been practiced in New France during the seventeenth century and had become officially legal in 1709. French Canadian settlers in the Illinois Country had used Indian slaves since the earliest days of their communities, and French colonial authorities discussed Indian slavery at length. Those opposed to it argued with sound logic that the tribes from whom the slaves were taken (usually by other tribes) resented the practice and learned to despise the French, who purchased slaves from their Indian captors. Other officials argued just as plausibly that if the French refused to buy slaves they would alienate the stronger, more aggressive tribes, which was worse than gaining the enmity of the weaker tribes, like the Pawnee, from whom the slaves often came. Whatever the merits of the different viewpoints, Indian slavery persisted as a legal practice in Louisiana right down to the end of the French regime.[36]

---

34. Henry Pagget to Don Carlos Howard, Apr. 6, 1797, PC 35; Auguste Chouteau to Carlos Howard, May 4, 1797, ibid.

35. Auguste Chouteau to Gayoso, Nov. 29, 1798, PC 215 A. On the Chouteau brothers and their relations with the Indians, see Foley and Rice, passim.

36. On the white man's use of Indian slaves in North America, the following are the most valuable studies: Lauber, *Indian Slavery in Colonial Times*; Trudel, *L'Esclavage au Canada*; Jaenen, *Friend and Foe*. For an interesting French criticism of Indian slavery, see "Mémoire concernant les Illinois," 1732, AN, Colonies, F³24:236. See also Magnaghi, "Indian Slavery in St. Louis," 264-72.

No Indian slaves appeared on the Ste. Genevieve census of 1752, but both civil and parish records reveal that by the 1760s there were Indian slaves in town. These probably were used principally as domestic servants, and they were bought and sold as any other chattels. In 1768, for example, Simon Hubardeau sold a female Indian slave named Fanchon to François Poitou for 1,500 livres, which was about the same price that black slaves were bringing at that time.[37]

The French-creole practice of trading in Indian slaves ran into difficulties when Spain took possession of Louisiana, for the Spanish crown had frowned upon Indian slavery since the sixteenth century. In December 1769 General Alexandro O'Reilly issued an important decree concerning Indian slavery in Louisiana. Henceforth, no Indians could be enslaved on any grounds whatsoever, nor could any existing Indian slaves be bought or sold by any Spanish subject of Louisiana. The only manner by which owners of Indian slaves could dispossess themselves of their human property was by manumission. O'Reilly did not abolish Indian slavery as such at the time of this decree, for that would have constituted *ex post facto* legislation and would have infuriated the *habitants*. But the total prohibition on acquiring Indian slaves or trading in such slaves meant that Indian slavery should gradually disappear, and O'Reilly ordered a census of all Indian slaves in every post in Spanish Louisiana in order that the Spanish colonial government could monitor the situation.[38]

In May 1770, François Vallé I carried out O'Reilly's order and conducted what was the only census of Indian slaves ever taken in Ste. Genevieve.[39]

Indian slaves at Ste. Genevieve in 1770

Owners	Men	Women	Minors Below Age 15
Nicolas Boyer	1		2
Henry Carpentier		1	2
Louis Robinet			1

---

37. SGA, Slaves, no. 87.

38. Copy of O'Reilly's decree in *SMV*, pt. 1:125-26; also in SRM, 1:249-50. Stephen Webre's excellent article "The Problem of Indian Slavery in Spanish Louisiana," just appeared in *Louisiana History* 25:117-35.

39. Printed in *SMV*, pt. 1:167-70.

François Vallé	1	
Antoine Aubuchon	1	2
Antoine Diel	1	1
Widow Billeron	1	1
Laurent Truto	1	3
Pierre Gadobert		1
Michel Placet	1	3
J.-B. Larose [Deguire]	1	
François Poitou	1	
Widow Hubardeau	1	2

Note: Adult slaves living in the same house-hold as minors were not necessarily the parents of those minors.

The census of 1770 showed a total of twenty-nine Indian slaves owned by thirteen different owners. Of the twenty-nine, twenty-six were women and children, indicating that it was very difficult to keep adult male Indians in bondage, for they could so easily take to the woods and regain their freedom. Except for one nine-year-old Comanche boy, all those assigned tribal names were of the Pawnee or Panis Piqué (Wichita) tribes. The designation of Indian slaves as Pawnees can be misleading, however, for so many Indian slaves in the Illinois Country were Pawnees, that the term "Pawnee" often came to mean "Indian slave." The adult Indian slaves in Ste. Genevieve were valued at between 1,000 and 1,500 livres each, thus they had about the same value as black slaves in 1770. One of the Indian slave women had a black child, establishing that sexual liaisons between Indians and blacks, which were common in Lower Louisiana, occurred at least occasionally in the Illinois Country.

In conformity to the will of the Spanish monarchy, colonial officials in Spanish Illinois did take some positive steps to limit and discourage Indian slavery. In 1772, for example, a trader who was ignorant of O'Reilly's decree brought three Paducah children to St. Louis to sell. Because of his ignorance the trader was not charged with a criminal offense, but Lieutenant Governor Piernas confiscated the children. He then took two into his own household and gave one to Lieutenant Antonio de Oro (later commandant at Ste. Genevieve), in order to "undertake their education as freemen." A rather different case arose in 1777, when a band of Sauk Indians captured and enslaved a woman of the Illinois tribe and brought her to market in St. Louis. Lieutenant

Governor Cruzat purchased her (presumably with government funds) and commissioned François Vallé to repatriate her with the Illinois tribe. This action was legal, humane, and, of course, wise Indian diplomacy on Cruzat's part.[40]

Nevertheless, there is a good deal of evidence that O'Reilly's decree prohibiting the Indian slave trade in Louisiana remained largely a dead letter. The very fact that Cruzat had to republish the decree at St. Louis in 1787 suggests that O'Reilly's order was being ignored. Local civil records from Ste. Genevieve reveal that illegal trading in Indian slaves persisted on into the 1790s. In 1790, for example, town commandant Henri Peyroux purchased, illegally under O'Reilly's decree, an Indian woman and her nine-year-old son. Probably because this was an illegal transaction the contract-for-sale was done verbally and never put in writing, although Lieutenant Governor Pérez himself witnessed the sale. Before the transaction could be made final, however, the seller suddenly died, and Peyroux was unable to conclude the agreement satisfactorily with the heirs. Peyroux thereupon asked Pérez to intervene and settle the case. Pérez, perhaps already worried because he had witnessed an illegal transaction, washed his hands of it and told Peyroux that he would have to appeal the case to Governor Miró in New Orleans, which Peyroux did. Miró's response drafted in New Orleans in February 1791 was terse and definitive. He addressed Peyroux: "You should already know that Indians [in Louisiana] are as free as whites themselves, . . . and therefore I cannot deal with your case." Interestingly enough, Miró did not order Peyroux to free the two Indians. If Peyroux kept them, which he probably did, it was illegally and without either a certificate of title or a bill of sale.[41]

The case of Peyroux's Indian woman may have been resolved finally by Lieutenant Governor Trudeau in 1794. An Indian woman named Marguerite was living in Peyroux's household at that time but wished to leave in order to be gainfully employed elsewhere. Trudeau ordered François Vallé II, who had replaced Peyroux as commandant in Ste. Genevieve, to liberate Marguerite, and in May 1794 Vallé reported to Trudeau that he had "given

---

40. Unzaga to Piernas, Mar. 14, 1772, PC 81; Cruzat to Vallé, Aug. 26, 1777, PC 215 A. Webre's recent article deals with several interesting cases of Indian slaves obtaining their freedom.

41. Gayarré (3:334-35) claimed that O'Reilly's decree was never enforced in Lower Louisiana; Peyroux to Miró, Dec. 14, 1790, PC 204; Miró to Peyroux, Feb. ?, 1791, ibid.

her entire liberty to work for her own profit." Peyroux seems to have been a major user of Indian slaves in Ste. Genevieve, for in 1795 Vallé was ordered to free another Indian woman whom Peyroux had purchased illegally.[42]

Indeed, it is difficult to study the Indian slave trade in colonial Ste. Genevieve, interesting and important though the topic may be, because it was an illegal practice and thus had a shadowy existence. Indian slaves were not listed in official census reports, and, as the Peyroux case indicates, transactions in Indian slaves usually were concluded as verbal agreements. It is therefore only rarely and by chance that Indian slaves appear in official documents after 1770, although their use probably continued in Ste. Genevieve right down to the end of the colonial period. In 1796 Bernard Pratte and Jean-Baptiste Bauvais both had Indian slaves baptized by the parish priest. Indian slavery was increasingly less prevalent and important as time went on, however, and perhaps the twenty-nine Indian slaves living in Ste. Genevieve in 1770 were as many as the town ever had.[43]

Because of their uncertain legal status it is difficult to determine how Indian slaves were treated by their white masters in Ste. Genevieve. Perhaps Indian slaves were more abused than their black counterparts. The latter were at least sometimes protected by the Black Code, while Indian slaves, whose legal position was ambiguous, probably had none of those advantages. The 1770 census of Indian slaves in Ste. Genevieve, for example, suggests that the integrity of the conjugal family was not respected, that wives were separated from husbands and children from parents; this violence to Indian slave families was of course often perpetrated by other Indians at the time slaves were captured. Black slaves were at least sometimes protected from such abuses by the Black Code.[44]

A curious judicial inquest, recorded at Ste. Genevieve in 1773-74, reveals something about the condition of Indian slave women and children in town. This is one of the most touching series of

42. Vallé to Trudeau, May 26, 1797, PC 209; Trudeau to Vallé, Nov. 2, 1795, MHS, Vallé Collection, Box 2.

43. SGPR, Baptisms, Book B:65, 68; on the handling of Indian slavery in the Missouri Territory, see Catterall and Hayden (eds.) *Judicial Cases*, 5:104-110.

44. To what extent Indian slaves in Upper Louisiana fell under the jurisdiction of the Black Code remains unknown. In Lower Louisiana they did so fall at least on certain occasions (see Webre, "Indian Slavery," 3-4). Concerning black slave families in colonial Ste. Genevieve, see below, chap. vii.

documents contained in the civil records of colonial Ste. Genevieve. The inquest was prompted when Captain Hugh Lord, commandant of English Kaskaskia, complained to Lieutenant Louis Villars, military commandant of Ste. Genevieve, that a man named Céledon, who lived in Ste. Genevieve, had stolen a female Indian slave from Kaskaskia. Céledon, a mestizo huntsman who roomed off and on in the home of Jean-Baptiste Deguire Larose, had just left town on a hunting expedition when Captain Lord submitted his complaint.[45]

Upon Villars' request François Vallé, *lieutenant particulier* in Ste. Genevieve, sent Wassas, an Indian scout, to track Céledon. Hardly had Wassas left town on the morning of March 18, 1773, however, when he returned horrified to report that he had found a corpse about a league from town near the Rivière aux Vases. Thereupon François Vallé led a mounted posse of eight men out to retrieve the body, which turned out to be an Indian woman in men's clothing. By 5 P.M. that day, Jean-Baptiste Laffont, surgeon of Kaskaskia, had examined the body and proclaimed that the woman had been killed by a single musket ball to the right breast. Céledon was then wanted in Ste. Genevieve for theft of the slave woman *and* on suspicion of her murder.

Although neither Louis Villars nor François Vallé had the authority to hold court for a capital offense, Vallé was responsible for gathering all facts pertaining to the case; he forthwith began to take depositions from persons who knew or had spoken with Céledon. Céledon appears in the first depositions as a quite ordinary type for the Illinois Country. He roomed in Ste. Genevieve when not out hunting, and was known as a decent fellow. In his rented room he had left a large wooden chest containing his few worldly possessions.

Then, a month later, in April 1773 Céledon struck again, not to regain his belongings that remained *chez* Larose but instead to get the woman that he wanted and needed as a companion and partner in the outback. On April 24 François Vallé and two witnesses went to the residence of Widow Aubuchon (Lasource) to collect information from the widow and a nine-year-old Indian slave boy. Widow Aubuchon recounted that on the night of April 20-21 her Indian slave, Marianne, was tethered with a chain in a locked and barred room of the Aubuchon residence where she was supposed

---

45. SGA, Slaves, no. 196; see also on this case, Piernas to Unzaga, Dec. 26, 1773, PC 81.

to be sleeping with her nine-year-old son. On the morning of April 21 the widow discovered that the bars on the window of Marianne's room had been cut and that Marianne was gone, although her son was still there.[46]

Vallé next turned to the Indian boy, Baptiste, for information. Baptiste recalled that during the night of April 20-21, while he was sleeping with his mother, Céledon (the boy apparently knew the man) came to the window and called to his mother, begging her to come with him for he had good horses. Marianne had asked Baptiste to accompany them, but, according to Baptiste, he refused to go without his younger brother, six-year-old Louis. His mother replied that Louis could not come because he would encumber them and slow their flight from Ste. Genevieve. She, however, was going to flee to "her country" but promised to return with Indian braves the following winter to take her boys. She then cast off her chains (Céledon must have provided her with tools), slipped out of the window, and with Céledon raced for her freedom on the back of an Indian pony. A detachment of ten militiamen later pursued them in vain. As rustic as the townsmen might have been, they were no match in the bush for a mestizo woodsman and his Indian woman. In October 1773 Céledon's effects, taken from his wooden trunk, were auctioned off in front of the Ste. Genevieve church door for a total of 514 livres 10 sols. Presumably, this small sum went to Widow Aubuchon to help cover her loss of Marianne, who with her two boys was valued at 2,000 livres on the 1770 census of Indian slaves.[47]

The affair Céledon was not, however, finished, for François Vallé persisted in gathering information from other hunters and trappers who encountered Céledon and Marianne in winter camps or on traplines. Vallé had no difficulty gathering such information, for a steady stream of *coureurs de bois* moved between Ste. Genevieve and the hunting and trapping grounds in the hinterlands of Spanish Illinois. During the winter and spring of 1773-74 Vallé took deposition after deposition from men just returned from the backwoods, and these depositions reveal a great deal

---

46. Elizabeth Aubuchon Lasource's husband, Dominique Lasource, died in January 1773 (SGPR, Burials, Book 1:11), and it seems that the widow's brother, Antoine Aubuchon, then gave (or sold) her three Indian slaves — Marianne and her two sons, Baptiste and Louis. Those three Indians were listed on the Indian slave census of 1770 (*SMV*, pt. 1:168) as the property of Antoine Aubuchon.

47. *SMV*, pt. 1:168.

about Céledon, Marianne, and their life together on the trans-Mississippi frontier of colonial Missouri.

Céledon repeatedly insisted that the Indian woman found dead near the Rivière aux Vases in March 1773 had killed herself accidentally in seizing by the muzzle a flintlock that had a "tender" action. Although the precise truth of the matter will never be known, Céledon's account is plausible enough. The Indian woman was probably unaccustomed to handling firearms, and, moreover, Céledon had no motive for killing her after he had gone to the trouble of stealing her out of Kaskaskia. Other woodsmen from Ste. Genevieve clearly did not consider Céledon a murderer and did not hesitate to make camp with him on the Rivière de L'Eau Noire (Black River), which was his stamping ground. J.-B. Bequet *fils* from Ste. Genevieve frequently associated with Céledon (they wintered together in 1773-74) and provided the fugitive with provisions from town. Céledon also claimed that if he were not a fugitive from the law he would gladly work to pay for Marianne, for he understood that she belonged to Widow Aubuchon; the stealer of slaves had no quibble with the practice of slavery. Although he was unaware of it, Céledon's notion that he might purchase Marianne was illegal, for Governor O'Reilly's decree of 1769 had absolutely forbidden commerce in Indian slaves.

Commandant Vallé was also interested in Marianne in her own right and he routinely queried his deponents about their contacts with her. They informed him that Marianne was living with Céledon on the Black River and that both of them carried fusils, light muskets. Charles Boyer of Ste. Genevieve conversed with Marianne at a hunting camp and reported that she weepingly asked him about her two sons. Boyer told her that one remained with Widow Aubuchon and that the other had been placed *chez* Antoine Aubuchon, the widow's brother. There is no evidence that Marianne tried to retrieve her two boys, who were still slaves in Ste. Genevieve in 1778. Such a rescue mission would have been virtually assured of failure.[48]

Jean-Baptiste Bequet reported from the Black River that Marianne prayed for her children to be raised with the fear of God in their hearts, which suggests that although Marianne must have hated white civilization she accepted the white man's religion. In any event, Marianne told Mathieu Lafitte that she had made her choice and would not, even for her children, return to Ste.

---

48. Widow Aubuchon sold both of the Indian slave boys (Antoine Aubuchon Estate, January 1778, SGA, Estates, no. 4), back to her brother Antoine.

Genevieve. The creole practice of Indian slavery had contrived to present Marianne with a heart-rending dilemma, and it is difficult to fault her for the choice she made, knowing that it was made in moral anguish.[49]

In March 1774 François Vallé closed the Céledon case. He was almost certainly persuaded that Céledon had not murdered the Indian woman found at the Rivière aux Vases, that her death had in fact been accidental. Thus the fugitive was guilty merely of having stolen an Indian slave, of whose bondage the Spanish colonial government disapproved in any case. Moreover, given Céledon's honorable status in the confraternity of *coureurs de bois* there was small chance that he would ever be apprehended. Vallé prudently dropped the issue, and Céledon and Marianne, a gallant couple caught between two cultures, disappear from the historical record.

On balance it must be acknowledged that Indian slaves were not a significant part of the economy in colonial Ste. Genevieve. Nonetheless, their continued presence in town throughout the colonial period is worth remembering, for it reveals important aspects about society and government in the community.

The Peoria tribe, like the Kaskaskia tribe east of the Mississippi, probably originated as a band of the large Iliniwek group, which prior to the eighteenth century had split up into distinct tribes. As noted earlier, the Peorias seem to have settled near Ste. Genevieve during the mid-1780s. Henry Brackenridge, who knew Ste. Genevieve and its environs from the 1790s, observed in 1810 that Peorias had formerly occupied a village south of town, "but they abandoned it some time ago." In 1796 Abbé de St. Pierre drafted a census of his entire parish, which included outlying settlements like New Bourbon and the Saline as well as Ste. Genevieve proper. He listed 119 Indians as his parishioners, most of whom were surely Peorias, for the Ste. Genevieve parish registers indicate that the vast majority of Indians baptized in town were Peorias. Perrin du Lac visited Ste. Genevieve in 1802 and portrayed the Peorias as "entirely destroyed by war, smallpox, and, especially, by strong liquor, . . ." and "living in the center of

---

49. All of this material derives from depositions in SGA, Slaves no. 196.

the village."[50]

It is clear that deracination, alcohol, and the increasing crush of white culture were rapidly eroding the moral force and the tribal integrity of the Peorias. Spanish officials in St. Louis repeatedly tried to prohibit the purveyance of liquor to all Indians, including the Peorias, but the very proliferation of decrees forbidding such purveyance indicates the futility of government efforts. Tradesmen of Ste. Genevieve knew that liberal doses of alcohol made the Indians more docile and easier to manipulate.[51]

Little is known about the relationship of the Peorias to the town of Ste. Genevieve. For years the townspeople seem to have lived in relative harmony with the neighboring Indians. But by the end of the colonial period the situation had changed. In 1802, thirty-three *habitants* of Ste. Genevieve addressed a petition to François Vallé II. The *habitants* complained that the Peorias were ravaging their crops by cutting maize, pasturing horses on arable lands, and leaving open the gates in the fence around the Big Field. The petition continued: "The indolence of these Indians, who are not spread out like the tribes further away, creates in them a disposition to pillage." The petitioners also offered the commandant a solution to the Peoria problem: "If they [the Indians] were settled in places more distant and better suited to their manners and customs, they would not be in a position to pillage and inconvenience us either by their thievery or their drunkenness, which are their principal occupations."[52]

Therefore, in 1802 the Peoria Indians, who in the 1780s had been pushed to the west side of the Mississippi by advancing Americans, were about to be pushed away from Ste. Genevieve by creole farmers, whose agricultural practices did not mix with the Indian habit of foraging. When in 1810 Brackenridge returned to Ste. Genevieve after an absence of more than a decade, he noted that the Peorias had left the area, which was largely true. In November 1813 the *Missouri Gazette* in St. Louis reported on their pitiful remains: "The Peorians, . . . are now reduced to 10 or 15 heads

---

50. On the Iliniwek group of Indians, see Temple, *Indian Villages of the Illinois Country*, chap. i; Brackenridge, *Views of Louisiana*, 125; St. Pierre's parish census attached to St. Pierre to Bishop Peñalver, Sept. 30, 1796, UNDA, Diocese of Louisiana, IV-5-1, folios 508-09.

51. Lieutenant Goveror Cruzat traveled in person to Ste. Genevieve during September 1776 in order to proclaim an ordinance against selling liquor to the Indians (Ordinance of Sept. 8, 1776, PC 2358).

52. Petition of Aug. 30, 1802, PC 219.

of families and reside near Ste. Genevieve." Most of the Peorias had moved west and they soon lost their tribal identity as they became mixed with other uprooted tribes of American Indians in what was to become Oklahoma.[53]

In eighteenth-century Louisiana the relative shortage of white women meant that miscegenation between white men and Indian women was extremely common. Sometimes *voyageurs* and *coureurs de bois* preferred Indian women even when white women were available. In the early days of Louisiana, a boatload of nubile French women arrived in the colony, but a colonial official complained that they were so ugly ("laides") that the *voyageurs* in town preferred to seek out Indian women for mates. An observer at Kaskaskia in 1721 remarked that "the French *habitants*, even the substantial ones, marry Indian women, and they live very well together." Government officials discouraged mixed marriages on the basis that such alliances would dilute the strength of French civilization in North America. French missionary priests on the other hand sometimes advocated such marriages in order to reduce the vast amount of sinful concubinage. In any case, during the first half of the eighteenth century mixed marriages were common throughout Louisiana, including the Illinois Country.[54]

By the time Ste. Genevieve was founded, about mid-eighteenth century, the number of marriages between white men and Indian women (at least full-blooded) was waning, for there were more white and mestizo women available for matrimony. Nevertheless, a few white men in colonial Ste. Genevieve did marry pure-blooded Indian women. In December 1770, for example, Charles Aimé married an Osage woman, Marie-Anne Anouacou, who was bap-

53. Brackenridge, *Views of Louisiana*, 125; *Missouri Gazette*, Nov. 13, 1813.

54. Commissaire ordonnateur Duclos to Minister Pontchartrain, July 15, 1713, BN, nouvelles acquisitions 9310:166; M. Lallement to the directors of the Company of the Indies, Apr. 5, 1721, AN, Archives du Service Hydrographique de la Marine, 115x, no. 29. On the subject of mixed marriages in early Louisiana, see Gayarré, 1:392-93; Belting, *Kaskaskia*, 75. Cornelius Jaenen has pointed out (*Friend and Foe*, 164) that Jesuits in seventeenth century Canada were opposed to mixed marriages, but Jesuits in the Illinois Country sometimes advocated them. For an example of such advocacy, see comments made in 1738 by Father René Tartarin (An, C[13]A 23:24). On the general issue of miscegenation in early North America, see Nash, *Red, White, and Black*, chaps. v, ix.

tized three days before the marriage. They had ten children to-gether, became early residents in Petites Côtes (New Ste. Genevieve), owned a house near Gabouri Creek, and then moved to New Bourbon. Charles and Marie-Anne Aimé apparently lived quite normal and ordinary lives within the community.[55]

Although there were progressively fewer marriages between white creole men and full-blooded Indian women, much Indian blood flowed in the veins of Ste. Genevieve's citizens. How much would be impossible to ascertain; indeed the very issue is often meaningless. Mestizo children raised exclusively in French Cana-dian or French creole families carried no Indian culture with them; for all intents and purposes they were white children. It is likely, for example, that François Vallé I's illegitimate daughter, Marguerite, was born of an Indian woman whom Vallé had en-countered while on a trading expedition. Yet Marguerite's mestizo presence in Ste. Genevieve had very little cultural significance: she was raised in the Vallé household and married a respectable French creole, Louis Caron. In effect Marguerite became a white person, or at least as white as the rest of the creole townspeople.[56]

Sometimes, however, the issue was more complicated and in-teresting. Take the case of Marie-Josephe (sometimes Josette) De-guire Larose. She was the illegitimate daughter of Jean-Baptiste Deguire Larose, a former master tailor of Kaskaskia who died at Ste. Genevieve in 1781. Almost certainly Marie's mother was an Indian slave belonging to Joseph Buchet, a longtime notary at Fort de Chartres. In the autumn of 1747 Deguire paid Buchet one-hundred livres "to redeem" two children that he had had by one of Buchet's slaves. Apparently Deguire took it upon himself to raise the children from that time on, and the wishes of the Indian slave mother were simply ignored.[57]

In 1759 Marie-Josephe Deguire Larose married one Louis Tirart *dit* St. Jean in Kaskaskia and shortly thereafter moved to Ste. Genevieve. By 1774 Louis Tirart was dead, but Marie-Josephe,

55. SGPR, Marriages, Book A:147; SGPR, Baptisms, Book A:50; SGA, Deeds, no. 6; New Bourbon census of 1797, PC 2365.

56. No baptismal record survives for Marguerite Vallé, but her marriage con-tract (SGA, Marriage Contracts, no. 32) and her marriage record (SGPR, Mar-riages, Book A:165) contain much information about her. Jacques Boyer, whose mother, Dorothée Olivier Boyer, was half Indian (Belting, *Kaskaskia,* 87) was one of the many citizens of colonial Ste. Genevieve who had Indian blood coursing through her veins.

57. SGPR, Burials, Book 1:39; SGA, Estates, no. 80; KM 47:10:9:1.

widow Tirart, vouched for her daughter, Marie-Josephe also, when the latter married Joseph Joubert. Three years later, Joubert had a chance to return the favor when he witnessed the marriage of Marie-Josephe, widow Tirart, to Pierre Verrau of Ste. Genevieve. A week after this marriage, Alexis Griffard, a saltmaker in Ste. Genevieve, married Marie-Josephe Deguire's second daughter, Marie-Magdeleine Tirart. Obviously, Marie-Josephe and her daughters were marriageable women.[58]

When Jean-Baptiste Deguire Larose died in 1781 his illegitimate mestizo daughter, Marie-Josephe Verrau, claimed and received his entire estate as sole heiress. Then in 1786 Pierre Verrau died and left his wife Marie-Josephe as sole heiress. Thus Marie-Josephe outlived her natural father and two successive husbands and inherited their estates. She then went on to a third marriage, with François Bernier, before she died in 1788. The illegitimate mestizo girl had done very well for herself in the society of colonial Ste. Genevieve.[59]

In a speculative vein, and it can be little more than that, it is worthwhile to consider the possible effects of Indian culture upon society in colonial Ste. Genevieve. Brackenridge's description of the townspeople, for instance, tells us that Indian moccasins were standard footwear in the community. And estate inventories reveal that Indian as well as European-style saddles were used on riding horses. There is also some sketchy evidence that the interest of French creoles in Indian workmanship went beyond purely practical things like footwear and saddles, and that they became interested in Indian arts and crafts. In 1794, for example, one of François Vallé II's teenage daughters sent as a gift to the daughter of Governor Carondelet "a sample of work done by an Abenaki [Delaware] woman." There is no further information on this gift that had been produced by an Indian artisan, but probably it was fancy beadwork. Perhaps in cosmopolitan New Orleans, if not in Ste. Genevieve, there were by the end of the eighteenth century connoisseurs and collectors of Indian arts and crafts.[60]

At a deeper social level, there is some wonder about the influence

---

58. Marriage contract, Jan. 29, 1759, copy in SGA, Marriage Contracts, no. 134 a; marriage contract, Sept. 7, 1774, ibid., no. 75; marriage record, June 30, 1777, SGPR, Marriages, Book A:161; marriage record, July 7, 1777, ibid., 162.

59. SGA, Estates, no. 81; ibid., no. 231; marriage record, SGPR, Marriages, Book B:4.

60. De Luzières to Carondelet, July 17, 1794, PC 209.

of wives of Indian blood on domestic life within certain households. How did Marie-Anne Anouacou's Osage origins affect cooking, housekeeping, sexual relations, and child rearing in the household of Charles Aimé? Perhaps at the very least Aimé's diet was a bit more variegated and interesting than those of his neighbors who were married to white women. And there must have been some unusual customs in the households in which the mestizo Marie-Josephe Deguire served as housewife, for the illegitimate daughter of an Indian slave was raised by her mother before Jean-Baptiste Deguire acquired custody of her. Or, in another fashion, what effect did the Peoria Indian children have on the white creole children whom Perrin du Lac witnessed playing together "pell-mell" in the dusty streets of Ste. Genevieve? Du Lac, a Frenchman, did not like what he saw, for he believed that the white children acquired Indian "tastes, habits, but especially their indolence." Henry Brackenridge, always tolerant, commented that the Indian boys around Ste. Genevieve "often intermingled with those of the white village, and practiced shooting with the bow and arrow; an accomplishment which I acquired with the rest, together with a little smattering of the Indian language. . . ." No doubt the children of Ste. Genevieve picked up a fair amount of Indian lore, games, words, stories, and so on from their red-skinned playmates.[61]

On balance, it is clear that the conquering culture of the white men had a much larger influence, ultimately a devastating influence, upon the Indians than that of the Indians upon the white man. The cohesiveness and technological superiority of European civilization, plus European diseases and European-style alcoholic beverages, swamped the American aborigines. But the process of acculturation always works to some extent in both directions, and the culture of French Canadians and French creoles was clearly marked by the presence of American Indian society. Surely one of the important things that distinguished the residents of the Illinois Country from, say, prosperous peasants of eighteenth-century France was the degree to which the former had assimilated cultural traits from the Indians: dress, diet, modes of transportation, medicines, style of warfare, and so forth. This subject would be an entire study unto itself.

Certain persons in the Ste. Genevieve community developed special relationships to the Indians, learning to live like them, talk

---

61. Perrin du Lac, *Voyage,* 173; Brackenridge, *Recollections,* 26.

like them, and even think like them. Such a person was Hypolite Bolon, who lived with a Delaware woman and was a master of Indian languages. As early as 1784 Bolon was serving as an interpreter for the Spanish government in the Illinois Country. A lawsuit from 1796 reveals that Bolon, who moved easily between white and red society, could use the Indians for his own purposes. Bolon had become involved in a bitter dispute with Israel Dodge over some business affair, and, according to Dodge, Bolon threatened to have the Indians burn Dodge's brewery or even kill him ("terminer mes jours"). The outcome of Dodge's suit is not known, but it is a matter of record that Bolon prospered with his special skills right down to the end of the colonial era. In 1804 the Spanish government was paying him 200 piastres, plus firewood, annually for his services as an interpreter of Indian languages.[62]

Knowing from the perspective of the late twentieth century of the ravages inflicted upon Indian culture by the advancing white man, it might be supposed that the Indians of Spanish Illinois felt nothing but unrelieved hatred for all white men, including the citizens of Ste. Genevieve. That supposition would be incorrect. A complex and symbiotic relationship had developed between the French creoles and the Indians, and the latter came to depend upon many of the things that they received from white society, including foodstuffs and all of the usual trade goods. At the end of the colonial era, Lieutenant Governor Delassus estimated that the Spanish government conveyed 12,000 to 13,000 piastres worth of gifts to various Indian tribes in Upper Louisiana each year. By the end of the eighteenth century no Indian brave in the Illinois Country could have endured going without gunpowder, steel knives, and glass mirrors — not to mention frequent gifts of grain.[63]

To penetrate the red man's deepest thoughts and feelings about the white man is of course quite impossible. A Frenchman, Bonnevie de Pogniat, who traveled in the Illinois Country during the mid-1790s, claimed that the Indians were "fond of the French; they say that the English deceived them and that the Americans steal their land. The French alone are their true friends. . . ."

62. Cruzat to De Oro, Aug. 11, 1784, PC 117A; SGA, Litigations, no. 94.

63. Delassus to Stoddard, Mar. 6, 1804, Billon (ed.), *Annals*, 1:371.

Although Bonnevie had political motives in making such remarks, there was perhaps at least a grain of truth to them. During most of the eighteenth century the creole population in the Illinois Country was not growing fast enough to present a serious threat to the established Indian tribes, at least west of the Mississippi. Settlers from the Ste. Genevieve District did not make substantial inroads into Indian territory until the population boom and land speculation fever of the late 1790s.[64]

A commonplace event in the story of white-red relations in eighteenth-century North America is raised in the words of Bonnevie quoted above: that the Indians got along better with the French than with the English or the Americans. The statement is probably true. When chiefs from various tribes came to address Lieutenant Governor Cruzat at St. Louis in 1780, one of them proclaimed: "It is my father the Frenchman who hung the [peace] collar upon their necks [of his father and grandfather]. I am holding it firmly without letting it go. The Englishman has never been my father." These Indian chiefs had good reason to curry favor with Cruzat, for they had come to ask for foodstuffs. Yet their expressions of regard for the French and hatred of the English have a certain ring of truth to them.[65]

What the various Indian tribes in Spanish Illinois thought about the presence of the Ste. Genevieve community cannot be ascertained. Some of the tribes — Shawnee, Delaware, and Peoria — were more or less satellites of the community and were dependent upon it. The indomitable Osages kept their distance from the white settlements, yet they did engage in commerce with creole fur traders and came to depend upon certain trade goods provided by white civilization. The Osages liked to steal horses from Ste. Genevieve, and if they had had their choice they may well have preferred to see the community continue to exist within rather strict limits. It is worth observing that during the first two decades of Ste. Genevieve's existence, while it was still a very small settlement, the Osages almost never bothered it. And even during the continual depredations of the 1790s there is no evidence that the Osages wished literally to destroy the community. If such destruction had occurred the Osages would no longer have had a convenient reservoir from which to steal horses![66]

---

64. Bonnevie, "Mémoire su la Louisiane et les Illniois," 1.

65. Indian chiefs to Cruzat, *SMV*, pt. 1:401-03.

66. Ste. Genevieve's fort was never used to defend against an Indian attack.

Although the townspeople had daily contact with Indians, it is not easy to ascertain just what they thought about the red man. Interestingly, the citizens of Spanish Illinois did have some fleeting awareness that their own presence had contributed to making the Indians what they were. In a petition sent to Governor Carondelet in 1793 "the citizens and *habitants* of western Illinois" stated that "the Indians tribes are slowly destroying themselves. . . . They contract a large number of diseases for which nature, climate, and their life style did not prepare them. . . . Alcoholic beverages are a source of destruction that every day extends its empire further over the Indian tribes." The awareness revealed in this document was rare however. Despite the voluminous correspondence concerning Indians that came from the pens of leaders in Ste. Genevieve over the decades, virtually no appraisals of the red man and his plight are found. Official documents dealing with Indian trade and diplomacy tend to be terse and factual, and occasional opinions, as when De Luzières remarked in 1797 that the Shawnees and Delawares were "rather civilized and cause little trouble," are not very helpful.[67]

In his important study, *Friend and Foe,* Cornelius Jaenen has argued that Frenchmen in North America persistently thought of the American Indians as their inferiors. Yet the Frenchmen's notion of the red man's inferiority was based little upon racial grounds, and largely upon cultural and religious grounds. That is, the French did not think of Indians as inherently inferior beings but rather felt that they were inferior because they lacked the Christian religion and French civilization. The Indian therefore possessed the potential of becoming the Frenchman's equal, if only he would adopt the Frenchman's ways. There is a fair amount of evidence that Jaenen's general analysis works well for the community of Ste. Genevieve specifically.[68]

Because of the history of the American South during the nineteenth century, modern Americans almost inevitably associate racism with slavery. Yet that association was virtually absent from French colonial slave practices, involving both blacks and Indians, in the eighteenth century. The townspeople of Ste. Genevieve did not practice Indian slavery because they considered Indians inferior creatures. Had that been true it would be difficult to explain

---

67. Petition, 1739:, PC 2362; De Luzières' in New Bourbon census of 1797, PC 2365.

68. Jaenen, esp. 190-97

François Vallé I's year-long inquest into the death of the female Indian slave who has found shot near the Rivière aux Vases. Destruction of mere chattels would not have demanded so extensive an investigation; the death of a human being must have motivated Vallé. And in 1801, his son, François Vallé II, sent a special commissioner to Mine La Motte to investigate the report that a creole miner had used a knife to attack an Indian. The result of this investigation is not known, but Vallé's action reveals that Indian lives were not taken casually in colonial Ste. Genevieve.[69]

As pointed out earlier, Henri Peyroux de la Coudrenière, commandant at Ste. Genevieve from 1787 to 1794, was a persistent and even illegal user of Indian slaves. It might be supposed that he was a callous racist, who regarded Indians as inferior creatures. But this was not so. In a revealing letter to Governor Carondelet in November 1793 Peyroux urged the Spanish colonial regime in Louisiana to "encourage marriages between whites and Indians with gifts, which would be the best and the most humane way to civilize and subdue the Indians." Peyroux was not a tender-minded person, nor did he have any interest in or respect for Indian culture. But if Indian women were baptized, married white men, and became Europeanized they were quite the same as any other women to Peyroux. And in the words, "most humane," there is even the faintest suggestion that Peyroux had some sympathy for the plight of Indians whose culture was being shattered by the impact of the white man. Thus, contrary to our expectations about the man, Peyroux turned out to be an assimilationist, who wished literally to integrate the white and red races as quickly as possible.[70]

On the subject of Indian women and their marriages to white men, most persons in colonial Ste. Genevieve probably felt as Peyroux did: permit, or even encourage, white men to take Indian women as wives. Surely it was easier for the townspeople to condone that pattern of miscegenation than couplings between white women and red men. The latter circumstance seems never to have arisen (or at least was never recorded) in colonial Ste. Genevieve. But as for Indian and mestizo wives, the evidence suggests that they were the legal and social equals of their white counterparts.

Macsouten Indians, who have proved elusive for historians, mi-

---

69. Vallé to Monsieur de Provenchère (Vallé's deputy), June 29, 1801, PC 217.
70. Peyroux to Carondelet, Nov. 14, 1793, PC 207 B.

grated into Spanish Illinois sometime around the turn of the nineteenth century. The presence of the Mascoutens provided an occasion for a final *opera bouffe* performance by the Ste. Genevieve colonial militia. In January 1802 a group of Mascoutens killed a white man, David Trotter, near New Madrid and burned his house. Trotter was a well-known supplier of liquor to the Indians. Some Mascoutens became drunk on bad whiskey sold to them by Trotter and then killed him; an act that under the circumstances would hardly seem to have warranted a full-scale military retribution. But Charles Dehault Delassus, Spanish commandant of Upper Louisiana from 1799 until 1804, insisted that this tribe had been perpetrating "barbarities" for years, the length and breadth of Spanish Illinois, and that they had to be stopped. The result of Delassus's sentiments was the largest infantry maneuver in Upper Louisiana since the coordinated defense of St. Louis in 1780.[71]

Charles Delassus himself descended by riverboat from St. Louis to New Madrid in December 1803. Meanwhile, militia companies from Ste. Genevieve, Plattin Creek, and New Bourbon proceeded overland to the same outpost, picking up the militia from Cape Girardeau on the way. François Vallé II commanded the Ste. Genevieve company and was in charge of the combined overland march. François Vallé III, back from school in New York, commanded the company from Plattin Creek, and Camille Dehault Delassus, brother of Charles and son of Pierre Delassus de Luzières, commanded the New Bourbon company. What with their vanguards, rear guards, detachments, standard-bearers, aides- de-camp, and adjutants, Delassus's marching orders evoke images of a veritable Napoleonic campaign — but it must have been a pretty motley crowd that stumbled through snow, sleet, and rain from Ste. Genevieve to New Madrid in late December 1802. Perhaps Delassus was wishing that he had swallowed his monarchical principles and remained in France, for he then would have had the opportunity to command a genuine army.[72]

The Ste. Genevieve militia contingent left home December 13, 1802, and returned January 11, 1803. On January 3 the Mascouten

<hr />

71. There is a mass of correspondence concerning the Trotter killing and its consequences. Most of it is in the following: PC 219, PC 2372; MHS, Chouteau Collection, Box 4; MHS, Delassus Collection, Box 3; Billon (ed.), *Annals*, 1:316-32, contains some of this material.

72. Delassus to Peyroux, Dec. 10, 1802, PC 219; Vallé to Delassus, Dec. 12, 1802, PC 217, MHS, Delassus Collection, Box 3; Billon (ed.), *Annals*, 1:318-32.

killer, Tewanayé, was shot by firing squad in front of the assembled militiamen and witnesses from various Indian tribes. Tewanayé's body was then placed in a coffin and ceremoniously interred. Revenge and justice were thus accomplished in accordance with the instructions that Governor Manuel Salcedo had dispatched from New Orleans. This treatment of the Indians was moderate and civilized compared to the butcheries that Americans would soon inflict upon the red men of the western frontier.[73]

The men from Ste. Genevieve must have been bitter about being ordered to leave home and hearth during the height of the holiday season and march for two weeks (one each way) through wilderness in the nastiest weather of the year merely to witness the execution of a single Indian. The officers had at least one event to cheer them during the holidays however: Peyroux de la Coudrenière, commandant at New Madrid and ex-commandant at Ste. Genevieve, threw a dinner party on Christmas Day. While the rain beat down outside, the officers of the militia companies sat down to a feast that lasted well into December 26. One wonders what Peyroux and François Vallé II, old enemies and competitors for power in Ste. Genevieve, talked about as they broke bread and drank wine together that night. If Peyroux's Bordeaux vintages were smooth enough they perhaps washed away their animosities and toasted the coming of the new year, a year that would bring sweeping changes to Louisiana.[74]

During the last decade of Spanish control in Louisiana, everything, including the position of the red man, was being transformed by the massive immigration of Anglo-Americans. In February 1804, during the very last days of the colonial regime in Spanish Illinois (technically French once again), an event occurred in the Ste. Genevieve District that revealed the changing position of the Indians and provided a taste of what was in store for them in their American future. François Vallé II lay on his deathbed, and his brother Jean-Baptiste was conducting official correspondence for him. Jean-Baptiste wrote to Lieutenant Governor Delassus in St. Louis that ten Mascouten Indians had recently arrived in Ste. Genevieve and spent the night at the residence of Jean-Baptiste Pratte. The Mascoutens were seeking sanctuary because five

---

73. Billon (ed.), 327-8; Salcedo to Delassus, Aug. 31, 1802, MHS, Chouteau Collection, Box 4.

74. See Delassus's journal of the New Madrid expedition in MHS, Delassus Collection, Box 3.

of their tribe had just been killed on the "Marameck" (i.e., the Big River) by a group of Americans. "A Peoria woman who was with them verified the report and added that the Americans had opened fire on them." Americans arriving on the west side of the Mississippi did not attempt, as had Frenchmen and Spaniards, to live amicably with the red man and react only defensively to Indian aggression. The Americans had come to seize the land and, for all intents and purposes, eradicate the red man. As Gregory Franzwa has pointed out, the newcomers "regarded shooting Indians as somewhat akin to squirrel hunting."[75]

In his thoughtful study of race relations in colonial North America, *Red, White, and Black,* Gary B. Nash has argued persuasively that circumstances of colonization rather than differences of national character accounted for the different Indian policies of the Anglo-Americans on the one hand, and Frenchmen and Spaniards on the other. All European peoples were selfishly pursuing their own ends in North America. Given their numbers and their interests, the Anglo- Americans found it expedient to try to eliminate the red man, whereas Frenchmen and Spaniards found it more profitable to tolerate him. This argument may well be valid. But in any case, beginning in 1804 a new and desperate struggle was commencing for the Indians of Louisiana, a struggle they were destined to lose.[76]

75. Jean-Baptiste for François Vallé to Delassus, Feb. 14, 1804, PC 220; Franzwa, *Ste. Genevieve,* 60.

76. Nash, 67.

Part 2
Fundamentals of Life

Chapter V
Earning a Living:
Grain, Lead, and Commerce

I N 1746, SHORTLY BEFORE THE FOUNDING of Ste. Genevieve, someone in King Louis XV's ministry of foreign affairs drafted a twenty-page "Memoir Concerning the Colony of Louisiana in 1746." Commenting upon the Illinois Country [Upper Louisiana], the anonymous author remarked that "they sow much wheat for flour; they have much livestock; they have a salt spring that supplies the colony and even parts of neighboring Canada; abundant lead mines are being worked, and it is even in leaden kettles that the salt is produced." If the author had mentioned peltries, his summary of the Illinois Country's economy would have been complete. It is noteworthy that wheat was the first component of the economy that he listed.[1]

Long before the founding of Ste. Genevieve, the Illinois Country was viewed as the breadbasket of French Louisiana. The rich soil, the temperate climate, and the broad expanses of alluvial bottomland made the region the best place in all of French North America for the production of cereal grains. French colonial authorities in New Orleans nervously monitored production of grain and flour in the Illinois Country and eagerly awaited the arrival of the convoys of riverboats that carried these products to the metropole. Without the agricultural products of the Illinois Country the population in New Orleans would have faced starvation.[2]

---

1. "Mémoire sur la colonie de la Louisiane en 1746," in AAE, Mémoires et Documents, Amérique 2:208.

2. Governor Jean-Baptiste le Moyen de Bienville to Minister, Apr. 26, 1738, AN, C^{13}A, 23:48; see also Surrey, *Commerce of Louisiana*, chap. xvii.

An early historian of Louisiana, Le Page du Pratz, never visited the Illinois Country but he lived for years in the lower colony and gleaned information concerning the entire Mississippi River Valley. He was aware of how Louisiana depended upon the agriculture of the Illinois Country and described the region in this way:[3]

> The French Post of the Illinois is, of all the colony, that in which with the greatest ease they grow wheat, rye, and other like grain, for the sowing of which you need only to turn the earth in the slightest manner; that slight culture is sufficient to make the earth produce as much as we can reasonably desire. I have been assured, that in the last war [War of Austrian Succession], when the flour from France was scarce, the Illinois sent down to New Orleans upwards of eight hundred thousand weight thereof in one winter.

Eight-hundred thousand was probably an exaggeration, but in both 1738 and 1739 the Illinois Country did send 300,000 pounds of flour down to New Orleans.[4]

At the very time that Ste. Genevieve was emerging as a distinct settlement, Governor Vaudreuil wrote from New Orleans to the commandant at Fort de Chartres, Jean-Jacques Macarty, and urged him to increase the supply of wheat to the lower colony. Perhaps Vaudreuil's letter had a bearing upon Major Macarty's eagerness to convey land grants on Ste. Genevieve's Grand Champ during the spring of 1752, which he did to persons like François Rivard and Jean-Baptiste Lasource.[5]

When Spanish soldiers finally arrived in the Illinois Country in the autumn of 1767, they chose to establish their headquarters for Upper Louisiana in St. Louis — but they remained almost entirely dependent upon Ste. Genevieve for foodstuffs. On the way upriver to St. Louis, Spanish commander Francisco Ríu stopped at "Misera" to gather provisions "to survive in the new establishment." And once he was settled in St. Louis, Ríu sent repeated expeditions to Ste. Genevieve in order to secure food for the Spanish garrison. There was a certain irony, which the Spaniards did not seem to perceive, in their being dependent upon a place they called "Misery" in order to obtain the necessities of life to survive in St. Louis. The latter town was then known as

---

3. Le Page du Pratz, *History of Louisiana,* 182.

4. Surrey, 291-92.

5. Vaudreuil to Macarty, Aug. 8, 1751, HMLO 325.

"Paincourt" — short-of-bread.[6]

Colonial Ste. Genevieve was first, last, and foremost an agricultural community. The town was founded by agriculturalists, and at the end of the colonial period grain production from the Big Field remained the single largest component in the town's economy. Most adult males in eighteenth-century Ste. Genevieve were directly involved in agriculture, working the land themselves or overseeing their hired and slave labor. Those who were not directly engaged in cultivation, like the merchant Jean Datchurut for example, were involved insofar as their commercial activities controlled the shipment of agricultural products from the town.

Visitors to colonial Ste. Genevieve were struck by the primacy of agriculture in the life of the community. Perrin du Lac remarked that "the inhabitants of Ste. Genevieve are exclusively occupied with cultivation. . . . They possess a portion of the earth whose fertility transcends the imagination; in a few days they can sow and harvest their subsistence for the entire year." Du Lac, a Frenchman accustomed to the tiny plots of exhausted land in France, was awestruck by the productive capacity of the Big Field.[7]

Henry Brackenridge, who knew the area well, remarked that the fence around the arable lands of the Big Field enclosed 7,000 acres, and that "the principal employment of the inhabitants is agriculture." Brackenridge's description of agriculture in colonial Ste. Genevieve is the best eyewitness account that we have.[8]

> As the agriculture of St. Genevieve, is carried on more extensively, than in any of the other villages, I shall take this opportunity of giving a description of it. One fence encloses the whole village field, and this is kept up at the common expense. The river side is left open, the steepness of the bank rendering any enclosure unnecessary. This field is divided into a number of small lots, of an equal size; a certain number of arpents in front, and a certain number in depth. The more wealthy possess and cultivate several of these lots, while some of the poorer class do not own one entire. But nearly all the inhabitants have a share in them; they were ceded by the Spanish government, as an appendage to the possession of every residenter in the village. This mode has been practiced from the earliest settlements on both sides of Mississippi, and

6. Ríu to Ulloa, Nov. 12, 1767, PC 109; Ríu to Ulloa, May 12, 1768, ibid.

7. Perrin du Lac, *Voyage dans les deux Louisiane,* 172.

8. Brackenridge, *Views of Louisiana,* 127.

perhaps had its origin from necessary precaution against the Indians. Their agricultural labors commence in the month of April, when the inhabitants, with their slaves, are seen going and returning, each morning and evening, for eight or ten days, with their ploughs, carts, horses, &c. The ground is broken up with a kind of wheel plough, which enters deep into the soil. Corn, pumpkins, and spring wheat, compose the usual crop. It is now left entirely to nature, and no further attention is paid to it until harvest, when each villager, but without that mirth and jollity, which usually takes place on such occasions, in other countries, quietly hauls in his own crop.

In April 1751 Antoine Heneaux requested the notary from Kaskaskia, Bertlot Barrois, to survey a tract of agricultural land (*une terre*) in the Big Field of Ste. Genevieve. This was the first such survey known. Barrois duly measured off a narrow strip of land two arpents (one linear arpent equals about 192 English feet) wide that ran with a southwest-northeast orientation from the Mississippi to the hills (about sixty arpents). He then set stone monuments to mark the boundaries of the property. Heneaux's *terre* became a model for arable plots in the Big Field that persisted throughout the colonial period, and whose vestiges are still discernible in agriculture practices of that area. The strips of arable land, privately owned, were usually one, two, or three arpents wide. Their lengths, roughly from the Mississippi back to the hills, varied because the bottom land was not of uniform width along the river. The parcels of plowland had no fences between them and no habitations on them, and thus constituted a system of open field agriculture, which was traditional in much of Europe.[9]

These peculiar (to modern American eyes) strips of plowland had their origins in a number of factors — historical, geographical, and technical. That was the manner in which Frenchmen and French Canadians had customarily laid out their farm lands in the Illinois Country, in Canada, and in parts of northern France. The configuration of geographic features near Ste. Genevieve — the Mississippi River, alluvial bottom, distinct line of hills — meant that running the strips across the bottom from the river to the valley wall provided property owners with two convenient and

---

9. SGA, Surveys, no. 75; on the history of open field agriculture, see Bloch, *French Rural History*, 36-40; Hoffman, "Medieval Origins," 23-71; Slicher van Bath, *Agrarian History*, 54-58.

permanent boundaries. A plowman's most difficult task when working with draft animals is turning the beasts and plow at the end of each furrow; long narrow strips of land reduce the number of onerous turns required per unit of plowed land. The long narrow strips of privately owned arable land were the principal characteristic of man-made geography in Ste. Genevieve throughout the colonial period and on into the nineteenth century.[10]

The fence surrounding the arable lands in the Big Field was the single most important structure in the community, for without it the sown fields would have been ravaged by grazing livestock. This fence, which was probably made of wooden stakes driven into the ground and bound together with horizontal stringers, was maintained jointly by all persons who owned land within the enclosure. Thus it was the fence, and not the land enclosed, that was communal property. Brackenridge described the fence as having three sides, with the Mississippi River serving as the fourth boundary of the vast enclosure. This configuration was adopted, however, only in the early 1790s with the abandonment of the Old Town. Originally the fence ran on all four sides of the arable lands; when the Old Town was nearly deserted the lateral fence lines were simply extended down to the riverbank.[11]

It is impossible to say precisely when the big fence was first erected. Probably it began as an ad hoc and piecemeal affair in the 1750s, as the number of freely grazing cattle increased to the point that they were a clear and present danger to the crops. By 1776 the fence and its various gates had become thoroughly institutionalized features, with a complex of regulations governing their maintenance and use. The *habitants* (farmer-proprietors) of Ste. Genevieve elected syndics and arbiters to draft complex reg-

---

10. Strips of land running perpendicular to a river were characteristic of real estate patterns in the St. Lawrence Valley as well as in the Mississippi Valley. The Canadian pattern was significantly different than that in Ste. Genevieve, however, because French Canadians had their habitations dispersed on the land rather than clustered in villages. According to Harris (*The Seigneurial System,* 120-21), the Canadian pattern developed in part because each *habitant* wanted access to the river for transportation and fishing. This was not an issue in Ste. Genevieve, where the villagers had convenient access to the river at established communal sites.

11. Brackenridge, *Views of Louisiana,* 127; on the issue of changing the fence see the following documents in PC 208 B: Petition of citizens to François Vallé, Feb. 26, 1793; Trudeau to citizens, Mar. 7, 1793; Trudeau to Vallé, Mar. 16, 1793; regulations of citizens, Mar. 27, 1793.

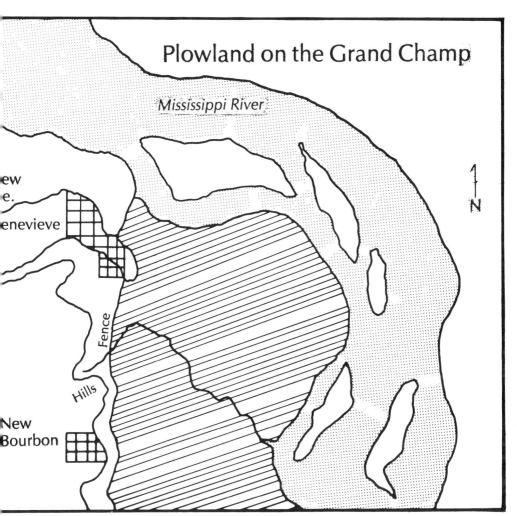

Strips of plowland on the Grand Champ at the end of the eighteenth century were individually owned but enclosed by a common fence. This illustration is based on the 1797 map of Nicolas de Finiels and a sketch drawn at Ste. Genevieve in 1793.

ulations and oversee their enforcement. Each owner of arable land was responsible for maintaining the sections of fence at both ends of his strip of land and for contributing to the maintenance of the in-common lateral fences. The entire fence had to be ready by April 15 of each year to hold out domestic stock, especially hogs. If grazing stock gained access to the arable lands through defective fencing and damaged the sown fields, the individual responsible for that section of fence was financially liable for damages. After the fence had been "received" by one syndic and six arbiters on the first Sunday after April 15, the arable lands became a sort of sacrosanct area that was off-limits to everyone. Anyone damaging the fences or entering the fields was liable to a series of fines and even to imprisonment. A paid gatekeeper was responsible for keeping the public gate to the fields guarded "day and night" during the entire sowing-growing-harvesting season and was liable for any damages caused by animals that strayed through the gate.[12]

The working of the soil — plowing, harrowing, planting, and harvesting — was done by the *habitant,* day laborers (*journaliers*), and black slaves. It is difficult to determine what proportion of the agricultural labor was carried out by these respective groups. Certainly many of the *habitants* toiled in their own fields, yet it is difficult to imagine civil judge François Vallé I, who was categorized as an *habitant,* working the land shoulder to shoulder with his black slaves. Probably the closest Papa Vallé ever got to field work was the occasional overseeing of his hired or slave labor. It is noteworthy that in the detailed Ste. Genevieve censuses of 1787 and 1791 nearly one-half of the crop-producing *habitants* owned at least one black or mulatto slave. Moreover, there was a close correlation between the number of slaves owned and the amount of grain produced; that is, the large slave holders — the Vallé brothers, the Bauvais brothers, Louis Bolduc, Jean-Baptiste Pratte, and François Moreau — were also the big grain producers. Clearly, much of the agricultural labor was slave labor, and probably at least some female slaves worked in the fields with the men.[13]

Agriculture as practiced on Ste. Genevieve's Big Field was primitive. None of the new methods of crop rotation, with intermixing of legumes, that Dutch and English farmers were using had penetrated to the remote Illinois Country. The alluvial soil of the Big Field was of course extremely fertile and was from time to time rejuvenated by the floodwaters of the Mississippi, just as the land in Egypt had been kept productive for millenia by the annual spring flooding of the Nile. It does not appear that the *habitants* of Ste. Genevieve even bothered systematically to fertilize their fields with waste from their domestic livestock. Cattle, horses, and hogs were allowed to graze freely upon the stubble of the arable

---

12. Ordinance of Cruzat, Sep. 7, 1776, PC 2358; regulations of citizens, May 9, 1778, SGA, Documents, no. 27; regulations of Cruzat, Apr. 27, 1784, ibid., no. 28; contract for gatekeeper, May 9, 1784; regulations of citizens, Mar. 27, 1793, PC 208 B; ordinance of Trudeau, Sep. 7, 1793, SGA, Documents, no. 30.

13. Copy of 1787 census in MHS archives (concerning this census, see below, chap. viii, n. 3); census of 1791 in *SRM,* 2:365-68.

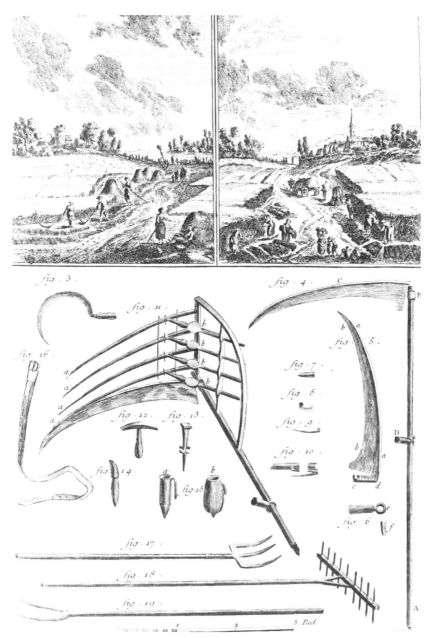

Diderot's Encyclopédie *depicted harvest scenes from eighteenth-century* France. Habitants *in colonial Ste. Genevieve used the same type of* implements.

fields from the end of the harvest until April of the next spring. These beasts probably kept the randy vegetation well-enough under control so that the plowing, harrowing, and sowing could commence as soon as the great fence was closed in April of each year. The increase in the amount of grain produced in the Ste. Genevieve District toward the end of the colonial period does not reflect improved agricultural techniques but merely an increase in the population and the amount of acreage sown in wheat and maize.

Plowing was done almost exclusively with oxen, teamed together with wooden yokes, and hitched to heavy-wheeled plows. Horses were rarely, if ever, used for this purpose. A good team of draught oxen was a precious possession for any *habitant*. In 1786 Pierre Verrau died and left an estate worth a total of 1,435 livres, 10 sols. His lot with a small *poteaux-en-terre* house and outbuildings was valued at 300 livres, his team of oxen at 250 livres. A good team of oxen probably comprised a larger percentage of an eighteenth-century farmer's capital investment than a good tractor does for the American farmer today.[14]

Once the fields had been planted it was up to God and the Mississippi to determine how the crop would fare each year. If there was enough rain and the river stayed within its banks, the harvest of wheat, maize, and tobacco — the three principal crops — was bountiful. During a bout of enthusiasm in 1750 the parish priest of Kaskaskia, Father Vivier, wrote that wheat returned five to eightfold per bushel planted and maize "yields a thousandfold." Vivier's estimate was probably a bit low for the wheat seed:yield ratio and about right for that of maize. Crows were a nuisance in the Illinois Country, and sometimes a bounty was placed on them.[15]

In 1769 Lieutenant Governor Piernas in St. Louis reported about Ste. Genevieve that "it has extensive fields and meadows suitable for all kinds of crops. The chief crop is wheat, which is yielded abundantly. It could be obtained in greater quantity if there were more farmers and its *habitants* applied themselves

---

14. Inventory of Pierre Verrau estate, March 6, 1786, SGA, Estates, no. 231.

15. *JR*, 69:219; on bounties for crows, see Peyroux to Casa-Calvo, Aug. 10, 1801, PC 220. Natalia Belting (personal communication) is studying the issue of crop yields in the Illinois Country and believes that on some occasions the seed/yield ratio of wheat was as high as one to twenty or twenty-five. The wheat raised in the Illinois Country, including Ste. Genevieve, was summer wheat.

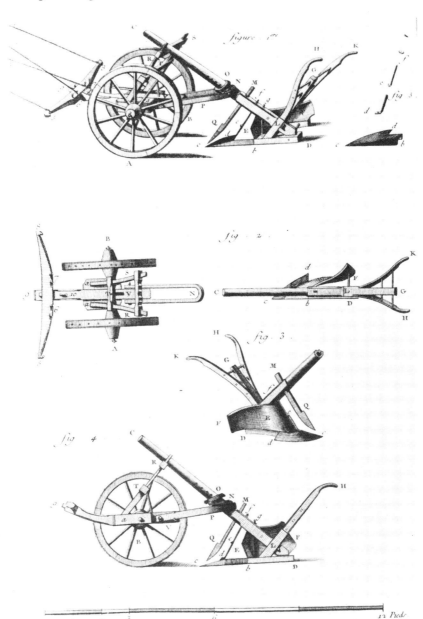

These illustrations of eighteenth-century French plows are taken from Denis Diderot's Encyclopédie. *Henry Marie Brackenridge remarked that the* habitants *of colonial Ste. Genevieve used "old fashioned wheel ploughs" when they cultivated their fields.*

[always the moralizer, Piernas]." Piernas was probably correct in designating wheat as the principal crop in Ste. Genevieve in 1769, although the harvest records from that year do not give detailed figures. By 1787, however, the maize harvest was one-third larger than the wheat harvest, 17,888 minots versus 11,402. The higher value of wheat probably meant that the cash value of the two harvests was about the same, 18,000 piastres (dollars). The proportion of maize continued to increase to the end of the colonial period — in 1791 and 1800 maize production was double that of wheat production in minots, and in 1796 triple. Perhaps the French in the Mississippi Valley, who had traditionally eaten wheat bread, had become accustomed to maize and were increasingly willing to consume it instead of wheat for their carbohydrate; or perhaps the surplus maize was shipped downriver for cattle and slaves, who had always been fed the coarser grain.[16]

Maize in the Illinois Country was not only plentiful; it was reputed to be an especially excellent variety. In 1795, Lieutenant Governor Gayoso de Lemos wrote to François Vallé and asked him to send "three minots of seed corn to Natchez so that we might have Illinois corn there."[17]

Ste. Genevieve's third crop in order of importance was tobacco, which was consumed by persons of all classes and colors up and down the Mississippi Valley. It is difficult precisely to compare the tobacco crops with the grain crops, for grains were measured in minots while tobacco was weighed in livres (French pounds). An approximate calculation for the 1787 harvest reveals the Ste. Genevieve wheat crop to have had a cash value of about 18,000 piastres and the tobacco crop a value of only about 700 piastres. Cotton, flax, and hemp were also raised but were even less important than tobacco. Rough though they are, the figures make it apparent that Ste. Genevieve's Big Field was used overwhelmingly to produce cereal grains. Maize and wheat were the mainstays of Ste. Genevieve's economy throughout the colonial period, although during the last two decades of this period lead played an

---

16. Piernas to O'Reilly, Oct. 31, 1769, *SRM,* 1:70; 1787 census, MHS archives; 1791 census, *SRM,* 2:365-68; 1796 census, ibid., 143; 1800 census, ibid., 1:facing 414. This is reckoning wheat at eight livres per minot, and corn at five livres per minot. For a summary of currencies, prices, weights, and measures, see Appendices G and H.

17. Gayoso to Vallé, Dec. 2, 1795, MHS, François Vallé Collection, Box 2.

These eighteenth-century style farm implements are displayed at the Bolduc House in Ste. Genevieve.

increasingly important role.[18]

In all areas of agricultural productivity Ste. Genevieve ordinarily outstripped St. Louis, often by whopping amounts. As soon as the Spanish garrison arrived in St. Louis in 1767 it became dependent upon Ste. Genevieve for foodstuffs and so it remained during the entire colonial period. Lieutenant Governor de Leyba reported to Governor Gálvez in New Orleans that the inhabitants of St. Louis neglected their farming because everyone in that settlement wished to be a merchant. It is clear that the economy of St. Louis was relatively more commercial and that of Ste. Genevieve relatively more agricultural: in 1791 Ste. Genevieve's production of

18. Census of 1787, MHS archives; wheat reckoned at eight livres per minot and tobacco reckoned at forty livres per hundredweight (quintal).

wheat and maize was two times that of St. Louis, in 1796, four times, and in 1800, three times.[19]

Agricultural productivity, of course, varied from year to year. Crops are always vulnerable to the whims of the weather, but they were especially so in the Illinois Country because the arable fields were located principally on the flood plain of the Mississippi. In 1778 De Leyba reported that constant rain during the harvest in Spanish Illinois had ruined one-half of the wheat crop. And the flooding Mississippi was more devastating than heavy rains. In 1785, 1794, and 1797 the rampaging river destroyed virtually all the crops sown on the Big Field. Lieutenant Governor Trudeau reported that the *habitants* of the Ste. Genevieve-New Bourbon area claimed that they customarily lost two out of five crops to the untamed Mississippi. The tendency of farmers to exaggerate their plight is universal and eternal; nevertheless the evidence is incontrovertible that floods often played havoc with the crops and the lives of Ste. Genevieve's *habitants*.[20]

For the last thirty-five years of the colonial period there is a good deal of evidence, both statistical and impressionistic, about the size of the grain harvest from Ste. Genevieve's Big Field. Roughly, the evidence leads to this breakdown: Good years — 1769, 1772, 1774, 1775, 1787, 1790, 1791, 1795, 1796, 1799, and 1800. Bad years — 1773, 1778, 1780, 1784, 1785, 1788, 1789, 1792, 1794, and 1797. These sort of data are, however, misleading, for the average to good years during which no statistics were gathered are missing. Marginally bad harvests were loudly proclaimed in correspondence from the Illinois Country, whereas only a real bumper crop would receive the same attention. Thus, employing the adage that no news is good news, it is probably safe to infer that most of the years missing from the above listings were at least decent years. If that was true, the average was about one bad year in three or four. Although slightly less dismal than the two bad years in five reported to Lieutenant Governor Trudeau by his informants in 1798, this was surely bad enough. And when the bad years came in clumps, as they did during the 1780s, the townspeople of Ste. Genevieve experienced tough

---

19. De Leyba to Gálvez, Nov. 16, 1778, *SMV*, 1:312; 1791 census *SRM*, 2:365-68; 1796 census, ibid., 143; 1800 census, ibid., 1:facing 414.

20. De Leyba to Gálvez, Nov. 16, 1778, *SMV*, 1:310; Trudeau to Gayoso, Jan. 15, 1798, *SRM*, 2:248.

This illustration of agriculture in eighteenth-century France is from Denis Diderot's Encyclopédie. *Horses were seldom, if ever, used as draught animals in colonial Ste. Genevieve.*

times.[21]

The tabulation of harvest years into good and bad is also artificial because of wide variations within those respective categories, and because a good year for maize was not necessarily a good year for wheat and vice versa. For example, in September 1792 Lieutenant Governor Trudeau reported to Governor Carondelet that a poor wheat harvest in the Illinois Country that year had pushed the price of flour to eight pesos per hundredweight, but that the good harvest of maize at Ste. Genevieve had compensated somewhat for the scarcity of wheat.[22]

In June 1795 De Luzières wrote to Carondelet from New Bourbon and predicted a better harvest of wheat and maize than had been "seen in thirty years." The prediction proved correct, for the recorded harvest of 1795 for Ste. Genevieve and New Bourbon totaled nearly 52,000 minots of wheat and maize. The harvest of 1796 went even higher, jumping to nearly 60,000 minots of grain, and that of 1800 rose to 64,000 minots. All three of these years were remarkable in view of the fact that in 1787, which was also a decent year, approximately only 29,000 minots were brought in by Ste. Genevieve's habitants. The abundant harvests of 1795, 1796, and 1800 were probably due largely to good weather, although new acreage being sown on the uplands by recent immigrants may have had some impact. In his report of 1798, Trudeau observed that the new American settlers "sow on the heights, . . . where they gain an abundant harvest of grain of a superior quality, and do not fear to lose it by the rising of the river."[23]

But despite the newly developed plowland on higher ground, Ste. Genevieve's Big Field remained the breadbasket of Spanish Illinois throughout the colonial period. This was apparent in 1797, when the Mississippi wiped out the grain crops on the alluvial bottomlands and the harvest from the upland fields could not prevent a genuine disaster from descending upon the Ste. Genevieve and New Bourbon districts. The horror began on June 4, 1797, when the Mississippi stormed over its banks and swept across the Big Field. The pitiable efforts of the *habitants* to stop

---

21. This information derives from a large variety of sources, such as census reports, memoranda, and official correspondence.

22. Trudeau to Carondelet, Sep. 24, 1792, PC 25.

23. De Luzières to Carondelet, June 9, 1795, PC 211; 1795 census, BL (wheat harvest of 1795 incorrect in *SRM*, 1:326, short 10,000 minots); 1796 census, ibid., 2:143; 1800 census, ibid., 1:facing 414; 1787 census, MHS archives; Trudeau to Gayoso, Jan. 15, 1798, *SRM*, 2:248.

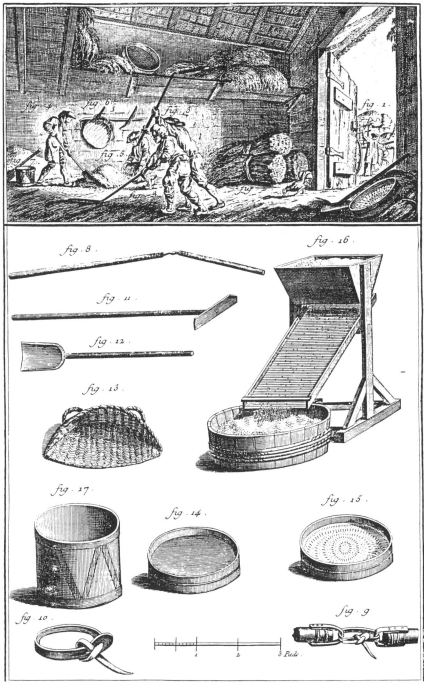

Diderot's **Encyclopédie** *illustrated threshing in eighteenth- century France, depicting the same tools and techniques which were used in colonial Ste. Genevieve.*

the river's destructive progress were futile, and soon the young wheat and maize plants were entirely submerged. Delassus de Luzières reported from New Bourbon on June 12 that the surface of the "*plaine basse* was one vast sea" and that the wheat and maize crops were "totally" destroyed. The same day François Vallé described the inhabitants of Ste. Genevieve scurrying to the outlying regions of the district in search of grain, for they knew that they were going to face famine during the coming winter.[24]

Indeed, during the winter of 1797-98 numerous habitants of Ste. Genevieve and New Bourbon were reduced to slaughtering their livestock and taking grain given in charity by those few fortunate enough to have reserves. François Vallé described "the cruel distress caused by a lack of food," and Delassus de Luzières called the situation "truly disastrous." The Spanish government at first sold foodstuffs at reduced prices, and then simply gave flour to the neediest families. These government actions tided the communities over until the 1798 harvest, which was apparently a good one. Then in 1799 and 1800 there were bumper crops, and the crisis of 1797-98 was long forgotten. When the Big Field was generous it could be extravagantly so, but if the Mississippi swept over it at the wrong time of year Ste. Genevieve's economy was temporarily devastated and the townspeople pushed to the brink of starvation.[25]

Although the economy of Ste. Genevieve the production of wheat and maize, the problem of getting the cereal grains milled into flour was never adequately resolved during the colonial period. The typical gristmill of the French Illinois Country was the horse mill. This was a primitive device that dated back to ancient times, before wind and water power had been effectively harnessed. In 1777 François Vallé I bought at auction from Madame Rocheblave a horse mill "all ready to grind flour." And in 1779 the townspeople were afraid they would not be able to mill their flour because Osage Indians had stolen twenty horses.[26]

24. De Luzières to Carondelet, June 12, 1797, PC 212 A; Vallé to Trudeau, June 12, 1797, PC 214.

25. Vallé to Gayoso, Dec. 2, 1797, PC 214; De Luzières to Gayoso, Jan. 7, 1798, PC 215 A; petition of citizens of Ste. Genevieve, Feb. 9, 1798, SGA, Documents, no. 24; Trudeau to Vallé, Nov. 30, 1797, MHS, François Vallé Collection, Box 2; Peyroux wrote from New Madrid (Peyroux to Charles Delassus?, Aug. 29, 1798, PC 261 A) that the harvest looked good for both wheat and maize.

26. Auction sale, Dec. 28, 1777, SGA, Public Sales, no. 108; citizens of Ste.

During the 1760s there was at least one water mill in Ste. Genevieve. Captain Philip Pittman described the town in 1766 as having "a very fine watermill, for corn [i.e., grain] and planks, belonging to Mons. Valet." The technology of water mills was difficult to maintain, however. Ste. Genevieve land records reveal that there were numerous attempts to establish water mills for grinding flour. Jean-Baptiste Bauvais *père*, who lived in Kaskaskia but owned much land on the west bank of the Mississippi, had a water mill built of stone on the Petite Riviere near the Old Town in the early 1770s. In 1783 Angélique Perodot purchased from Joseph Tellier one-half interest in a water mill located in Ste. Genevieve. And beginning in 1787 there was a flurry of development at a creek (probably Dodge Creek) flowing out of the hills. Both François Vallé and John Dodge were involved in this development, which included grist and saw mills as well as a brewery and a still.[27]

Despite all of these efforts, there apparently was not a single good water mill to grind flour at Ste. Genevieve during the 1790s. When Delassus de Luzières was at New Orleans in the spring of 1793 he became a partner with Barthélemy Tardiveau and Pierre Audrain in an ambitious scheme to build large flour mills at both New Madrid and Ste. Genevieve. This partnership had halting success at New Madrid, but when Spanish government financing fell through the whole project collapsed, and Ste. Genevieve did not get a new mill after all.[28]

The old-fashioned horse mills could not produce enough flour, which meant that Ste. Genevieve's producers had to resort to the wasteful method of shipping whole grain. Horse mills also turned out a less refined grade of flour. Governor Miró wrote to town commandant Peyroux in 1788 and told him that flour from Illinois tasted good, but that because it was not white it sold cheaply in New Orleans. In Miró's opinion, "someone there [Illinois] should speculate on a good mill," which remark may have prompted

Genevieve to De Leyba, Mar. 28, 1779, *SMV*, 1:335-36. The Jesuits in Kaskaskia had, at least for a time, a windmill at their establishment.

27. Pittman, *European Settlements*, 50; Bauvais's mill was listed in the inventory of his estate, Apr. 21, 1776, SGA, Estates, no. 20; Angélique Pérodot's purchase, Mar. 27, 1783, SGA, Deeds, no. 359; SGA, Concessions no. 28; Ste. Genevieve County Courthouse, Deed Book B: 118-119.

28. Concerning this enterprise, see documents printed in *SRM*, 1:373-409; Peyroux wrote (Peyroux to Miró, Mar. 8, 1788, PC 201) that "there are no good mills in Illinois."

Peyroux's purchase of a flour mill from Jean Datchurut in December 1789.[29]

In the New Bourbon census for 1797, Delassus de Luzières commented that water mills to produce flour and lumber were being built at Ste. Genevieve, New Bourbon, and New Madrid. De Luzières expected that these mills would produce "fine market flour, which up to this time the horse mills have not been able to accomplish." In all likelihood De Luzières' expectations never came to fruition during the colonial period. The large stone mill on the Saline Creek, whose spectacular remains are still to be seen, was erected early in the nineteenth century.[30]

The mining region in Upper Louisiana captured French imaginations during the early eighteenth century, and helped to promote several ambitious financial schemes. The mineral sources turned out to contain principally lead rather than the hoped-for gold and silver, but this was not known at first. Moreover, lead and silver sources are often associated, and if the first were plentiful the second might be discovered at any time — or so it was thought.

This wishful thinking was encouraged by an important gap in geographical knowledge. All literate persons in Europe knew of the fabled wealth of the silver mines in Spanish Mexico, but there was a general misapprehension that French Louisiana was not far removed from Spanish Mexico and that the mining areas in the respective colonies shared the same rich lodes. The Henrick de Leth map of 1710, for example, showed Santa Fe in New Spain only 300 miles distant from the mouth of the Missouri River. If the Illinois Country were indeed that close to Mexico, it was not delusional for the French to dream of great mineral wealth in Upper Louisiana.[31]

Even before Kaskaskia was founded in 1703, French explorers knew about the mines on the west side of the Mississippi. As early as 1700, the Jesuit missionary, Father Jacques Gravier,

---

29. Miró to Peyroux, Apr. 30, 1788, PC 201; Datchurut sold Peyroux two slaves and a horse mill, Dec. 24, 1788, SGA, Slaves, no. 40.

30. New Bourbon census of 1797, PC 2365.

31. Tucker and Temple (eds.), *Indian Villages, Atlas,* supplement, Plate LXV.

noted in his journal that rich lead deposits were to be found near the Meramec River. Indians had probably been extracting lead from the Meramec mines for centuries, but it was silver that French explorers sought. In 1715 the French governor of Louisiana, Antoine de La Mothe Cadillac, journeyed up the Mississippi to the Illinois Country in search of silver mines. In this search he was disappointed, but he did follow the Saline Creek westward into present-day Madison County and conduct exploratory diggings for lead.[32]

By 1716 dispatches were flowing from Louisiana to Paris that described the vast mineral wealth of the Illinois Country. Coincidentally, news of the Missouri mines arrived in the French capital at the same time that the Scottish financial wizard, John Law, was taking charge of royal economic policy. During 1717-18 a series of royal edicts restructured the administration of French North America. Illinois officially became part of Louisiana, which had a new capital at New Orleans (1718), and the entire economy of Louisiana was turned over to the direction of the newly-created Company of the West (later to become the Company of the Indies), commonly referred to as the Mississippi Company. The success or failure of John Law's financial schemes hinged largely upon tapping the supposed mineral wealth of Upper Louisiana, for a "big find" was necessary to maintain public confidence in the paper certificates circulating in France. This did not occur. Law's Mississippi Bubble burst in 1720, although the Company of the Indies struggled on in control of Louisiana for another decade.[33]

Fort de Chartres was built in 1719 in part because of the mines located across the Mississippi. At the time the fort was going up, there arrived in the Illinois Country one Philippe Renaut, a man from northern France with experience in mining. Lead mining in what became Missouri was associated almost exclusively with Renaut during the 1720s and 1730s. According to Pierre-François de Charlevoix, Renaut found a thick vein of lead on the Meramec (actually, the Big River) in the summer of 1720, and in 1723 he was awarded land grants on both sides of

---

32. See above, chap. i.

33. La Mothe Cadillac to minister, Jan. 2, 1716, AN, C[13]A, 4:509-12; Giraud, *Histoire de la Louisiane*, 3; Carré in Lavisse (ed.), *Histoire de France*, vol. 8, pt. 2:24-27; Eccles, *France in America*, 164. According to the Bowen and Gibson map of 1763 (Tucker and Temple (eds.), Plate LXXII), "the mines of the Marameg . . . gave rise to the famous Mississippi scheme in the year 1719."

the Mississippi to carry on his mining efforts. His grant north of Fort de Chartres became the village of St. Philippe (after Philippe Renaut), and his Meramec grant seems to have been located near where the Mineral Fork joins the Big River in Washington County.[34]

It has been frequently suggested that Renaut's lead mining operation gave rise to the establishment of Ste. Genevieve — that is, that Ste. Genevieve was founded in the 1730s as an entrepôt for the lead mines on the west side of the Mississippi. There is no evidence to support this thesis. Renaut's operations were primitive and sporadic, and the amount of smelted lead he produced was never enough to warrant creation of a river port to handle its shipment. Renaut went bust and returned to France in the early 1730s, but his old lead mine on the Mineral Fork continued to be worked, at least sporadically, during the 1740s.[35]

Antoine-Valentine de Gruy, an officer at Fort de Chartres, visited Renaut's old mine in 1743 and described its operation: the individual miners (eighteen or twenty of them) probed for veins of lead ore and extracted it with picks and shovels; they then crudely smelted the ore with a log fire set in a shallow earthen excavation; finally, the masses of lead were remelted and cast into small bars for transport to Kaskaskia. These bars weighed, according to De Gruy, sixty to eighty livres (sixty-five to eighty-six pounds) each and were carried out of the mining district on pack horses, for no wagon road existed at that time. De Gruy's account of his journey to the lead mines corrects the erroneous notions that lead was cast into leaden horse collars for transport and that Ste. Genevieve was founded as a lead-mining entrepôt in the 1730s. The lead horse collars should be put back into the barn for good, and Ste. Genevieve should be seen for what it was — as agricultural community founded at mid-century.[36]

Lead miners from Fort de Chartres and Kaskaskia carried out seasonal mining operations at Mine La Motte as well as at the Meramec (Mineral Fork) mines. There were high hopes for

---

34. See Ekberg, et al., "Pine Ford Lake Project," 10-15; Giraud, 3:179-80; Charlevoix, *Journal historique*, 6:139; Renault grants, KM 23:6:14:1.

35. Schaaf, "The Founding of Ste. Genevieve," 145-50; Swartzlow, "The Early History of Lead Mining," 295; Dorrance, *Survival of French*, 11.

36. Ekberg, "Antoine Valentin de Gruy," 136-50.

these mines, even after it became apparent that they produced only lead and not precious metals. Le Page du Pratz, the early historian of Louisiana, wrote that the lead mines in the Illinois Country were "so rich . . . as to vegetate, or shoot a foot and a half at least out of the earth." De Gruy claimed that more than 2,000 bars of lead were taken out of Mine La Motte alone in each of both years, 1741 and 1742. Lead from the Illinois Country was shipped both south to New Orleans and north to Canada. De Gruy began to mine lead himself, and in 1752 Major Macarty at Fort de Chartres reported that De Gruy had supplied Canada with 100,000 livres of lead.[37]

The hopes for heavy and continuous lead production in the Illinois Country were never realized during the first decades of effort, however. De Gruy wrote in 1743 that Philippe Renaut's operation collapsed because of constant harassment by Fox and Sioux Indians in the mining area. Macarty remarked in 1752 that De Gruy had twenty-five men working at his lead mines but that without slaves, labor costs were consuming all of his profits. The mines were too remote and difficult of access; labor costs were too high; Indians — Osage and Chickasaw as well as Fox and Sioux — were too eager to parry the thrust of Europeans into territory that the red man deemed to be his by prescriptive right.[38]

It is clear that from the early 1740s until the late 1770s Mine La Motte was the principal lead mine of the Illinois Country, but information on early mining at Mine La Motte is sparse. Daniel Blouin, an entrepreneur from Kaskaskia, was the most important lead miner of the late 1750s and early 1760s. In January 1767 he sold his property and possessions at Mine La Motte to Jean Datchurut of Ste. Genevieve. The possessions included tools as well as five black slaves and three slave cabins. Even before Datchurut got involved in lead mining, however, some lead miners lived at Ste. Genevieve when they were not working at Mine La Motte. In 1757, for example, Joseph Tassint, lead miner, sold his house in Ste. Genevieve to Antoine Thopart, lead miner, by verbal agreement. The contract of sale was put

37. Le Page du Pratz, *History of Louisiana*, 182; Ekberg, "De Gruy," 148; Macarty to Governor Vaudreuil, Mar. 27, 1752, Pease (ed.), *Illinois on the Eve of the Seven Years' War*, 563.

38. De Gruy's memoir, AN, G^1, 465:9; Macarty to Vaudreuil, Mar. 27, 1752, Pease (ed.), "Illinois on the Eve," 563.

into writing at Kaskaskia in 1759, and both parties were identified as living at Mine La Motte.[39]

By the late 1760s, several prominent citizens of Ste. Genevieve
were involved in lead mining at Mine La Motte — François
Vallé, Jean-Baptiste Datchurut, Henri Carpentier, Daniel
Fagot — as well as some less prominent men — Pierre Dagobert,
Nicolas Noël *dit* La Rose (no relative of the Deguire La Roses),
Pierre Messager, and Louis Chamard. Numerous documents testify to the legal entanglements that beset these miners, who
became embroiled in squabbles over land, partnerships, mining
rights, labor agreements, and investments. Mine La Motte was
worked sporadically throughout the colonial period, but the
Indian attack of 1774 (see above, chapter iv) and the discovery
of rich lead deposits near the headwaters of the Big River in
the same year did much to diminish its importance.[40]

A minor revolution in lead mining in the Ste. Genevieve District began in the mid-1770s with the discovery of rich lead
deposits near present-day Potosi in Washington County. These
were apparently discovered by François Azau *dit* Breton (because he was from Brittany) while he was hunting in 1774. This
became the most productive lead mining site of the late colonial
period in Upper Louisiana, and by the early 1790s a village,
Mine à Breton, had sprung up there. Mine à Breton was the
first permanent European settlement in the hinterlands of
Spanish Illinois, removed some thirty-five miles from the Mississippi River.[41]

Until the establishment of Mine à Breton, lead mining in the
Ste. Genevieve District was overwhelmingly seasonal, although
there were perhaps some men who lived more or less continuously at the mines. The seasonal period of work at the mines
was sometimes called "la campagne," the campaign, as the expression is used in military parlance. This expression conveys
much about the nature of the lead mining enterprise in the Ste.
Genevieve District before Moses Austin revolutionized the min-

---

39. Rothensteiner, "Earliest History of Mine La Motte"; Hanley, "Lead Mining," 30-35; see copy of the inventory of Blouin's property, Dec. 17, 1766, MHS,
St. Louis Archives no. 12; Blouin purchased this property at Mine La Motte in
1763 from Nicolas Noël *dit* La Rose (KM 63:12:28:1); Tassint to Thopart, KM
59:4:23:2.

40. La Rose to Rocheblave, Jan. 15, 1770, MHS, Vallé Collection, Box 1; La
Rose's deposition, Aug. 19, 1773, SGA, Mines, no. 27; Hanley, 75-80.

41. Hanley, 86-88; Houck, *History of Missouri,* 1:284.

ing industry in the late 1790s: a group of men leaving town and families to penetrate into the countryside, where they fought Indians and the natural elements in order to extract lead. The mining season evidently began about April 1 and ran for several months. This calendar permitted the miners to return to Ste. Genevieve in time to help with the harvest from the Big Field. According to Austin there was a second mining season, which ran from August to December, that is, from the end of the harvest to cold weather.[42]

Curiously, none of the official documents that list men by occupation contains a single individual designated lead miner. More than anything else, this probably reveals the seasonal nature of the lead-mining enterprise. Certainly some of the men listed as "journaliers," or day laborers, on the censuses worked seasonally at the lead mines as *engagés*. *Engagés* were persons who signed contracts (*engagements*) to work for a fixed period of time for fixed wages (*gages*). French settlers in the Illinois Country employed *engagés* for all kinds of purposes — agriculture, oarsmen on riverboats, construction, lead mining, and so on. The hallmarks of a typical *engagement* were the time period of the contract and the wages; the type of work to be accomplished was sometimes but not always mentioned, for that was not a fundamental issue.

In 1744, Nicolas Drouen of Fort de Chartres engaged himself to Pierre Messager, "miner at the Meramec Mine," for two months, with wages set at eighty livres per month. At Ste. Genevieve in 1770, Jean Duval engaged himself to Noël *dit* La Rose, lead miner at Mine La Motte. The contract of *engagement* was to run for one calendar year from the day it was signed, November 2, and Duval pledged himself "to do everything he was ordered that was honest and legal" for that period of time. Duval's year of labor was to begin with a boat trip to New Orleans, but because such an expedition would take at most six months Duval would remain engaged upon his return to the Illinois Country. Noël *dit* La Rose was a "miner resident of Mine La Motte," and it may be assumed that Duval spent at least part of his *engagement* working at La Rose's lead diggings. Duval was

---

42. François Vallé wrote to Lieutenant Governor Trudeau (Mar. 22, 1794, PC 209) in late March that the mining season was about to begin. Austin, on the other hand, wrote that "the time for working the mines, is from August to December (*Summary of the Lead Mines*, 10)."

paid 700 livres, of which 150 were paid before his departure for New Orleans. Three decades later, when Amable Partenay engaged Baptiste La Chapelle for a two-year term, the wages, 750 livres per year, were almost the same as they had been in 1770. Labor must have been more scarce, however, for in addition to wages Partenay had to furnish La Chapelle with board, room, clothes, and laundry.[43]

Engagés were used for various and sundry tasks, and they were often employed as lead miners. Mining records provide most of our information on the *engagés* of the Ste. Genevieve District. Because lead mining was largely a seasonal occupation the *engagements* for laborers at the lead mines were shorter term than the usual *engagements,* running for a month at a time instead of a year. The monthly wages varied between sixty and seventy livres, which, if projected to an annual rate, made them consistent with those of the longer *engagements.*

Payment of wages to *engagés,* as payment for virtually everything in colonial Ste. Genevieve, was often in kind rather than in coin, for the latter was in short supply. In the early 1770s, an interesting case arose when Indians attacked Mine La Motte and forced the temporary abandonment of the mine. These untoward circumstances caused the price of lead to double in a brief time. Some *engagés* under contract to Vallé and associates had been engaged to be paid in lead, which was worth five cents a pound at the time of *engagement* but ten cents a pound at the time of payment. Most of the *engagés* were amenable to Vallé's compromise, which was to pay the *engagés* in cash after calculating their wages in lead at the rate of eight cents per pound. One of the *engagés,* however, Pierre Massé, found the compromise unacceptable and wanted his payment in the highly valued lead. Vallé exploded, flung Massé against a tree, and compelled him to take the compromise wages. Massé filed suit against Vallé (who was after all the civil judge in Ste. Genevieve) in St. Louis, but Lieutenant Governor Cruzat ruled in Vallé's favor. So much for eighteenth-century labor relations.[44]

From an investment standpoint, wages for *engagés* could consume a big chunk of profits from lead mining. In 1773, for

---

43. Drouen *engagement,* KM 44:2:10:1; Duval *engagement,* SGA, Contracts and Agreements, no. 43; La Chapelle *engagement,* June 17, 1799, ibid., no. 28.

44. This account is taken from documents printed in Billon (ed.), *Annals,* 1:136-38; see also Hanley, 78-80.

example, Madame Pierre Gadobert was operating her absent husband's share of the Castor Vein at Mine La Motte. Her balance sheet for the four-month mining season was as follows:[45]

```
Value of lead delivered to Ste. Geneviève .  780.94  piastres
Wages for engagés, smelting, tools,
  and foodstuffs . . . . . . . . . . . . . . . . . . . 639.74
Payment for blacksmith for campaign  . . . . . . . . 18.00
Transport of lead  . . . . . . . . . . . . . . . . . . 69.85
    Total Expenses  . . . . . . . . . . . . . . . . . 727.59
Net Profit  . . . . . . . . . . . . . . . . . 53.35  piastres
```

If the investor had been a slave owner, he could have substantially increased his profit margin by using slaves instead of *engagés* and functioning as overseer himself.

Black slave labor played an important role in the lead mines of the Ste. Genevieve District throughout the entire second half of the eighteenth century. It is impossible to determine what percentage of the pick-and-shovel labor at the mines was made up of slaves, for slaves were often rented out by their owners and thus appear on lead mining accounts as *engagés*, whose wages of course went to the owners. Some of the wages for *engagés* shown on Madame Gadobert's account probably went to slave owners for the rent of their slaves. In 1757, François Vallé lent two black slaves to Messieurs Tassin and Thopart, lead miners of Ste. Genevieve, on condition that Vallé would receive one-half ownership of any lead veins they discovered. In this way Vallé obtained an interest in the well-known Castor Vein at Mine La Motte. And in 1772 Vallé, Pierre Gadobert, and Noël *dit* La Rosa formed a triparite partnership to mine at Mine La Motte. François Vallé's share of the investment was to provide two black slaves (one male and one female), ten horses with harness, hand tools, and himself as overseer. Surely the only women to work at the lead mines were slaves. When Moses Austin began mining at Mine à Breton in the late 1790s he used large numbers of black slaves, who lived the year around in quarters located near the mines. Black slaves made up a large percentage of the population in early Mine à Breton.[46]

---

45. Gadobert account for 1773, MHS, Vallé Collection, Box 1. Lead was cheap in 1773, bringing only a bit more than five cents (sous) per pound.

46. La Rose's deposition, Aug. 19, 1773, SGA, Mines, no. 27; Contract, Dec.

Lead ore was smelted on the spot at the mines. In 1743 De Gruy described a primitive bonfire method of smelting, which has been called the log-heap process. By the 1770s the miners had begun to use some crude stone furnaces, which Moses Austin likened to lime kilns. After smelting, the lead was remelted and cast into bars for transport. At the end of the eighteenth century, Austin introduced the more sophisticated and efficient log-hearth and reverberatory-ash furnaces.[47]

In the 1740s, there were no cart roads in what later became the Ste. Genevieve District, and lead bars were carried from the mining regions to the west bank of the Mississippi on pack animals. Ida M. Schaaf was correct to describe the road from Mine La Motte to Ste. Genevieve as the first road west of the Mississippi in the Illinois Country, if by *road* is meant a thoroughfare that will accommodate wheeled vehicles instead of merely pack animals, which can move on *trails*. Mrs. Schaaf did not hazard a guess as to when this first road was cleared, but probably it was accomplished during the 1760s. It was certainly done by the 1770s, for already at that time mining records employed the words "charroy" and "charroyer" to describe lead shipments. This means that lead was being transported from Mine La Motte to Ste. Genevieve in *charettes,* two-wheeled carts that resembled the well-known Red River carts of the early nineteenth century.[48]

In 1791 the commandant in Ste. Genevieve, Peyroux de la Coudrenière, reported that the miners had just built a "cart road of twenty-five leagues to go to the lead mine, which aids them in carting their lead with oxen."Although colonial cart roads were tortuous routes, Peyroux perhaps exaggerated the length of the road built in 1791, for he must have been describing the road from Ste. Genevieve to Mine à Breton. This road was improved during the 1790s, and in 1797 Moses Austin described it as "a good waggon road," about thirty miles in length. Austin himself was responsible for building a wagon road between Old Mines and Mine à Breton, which was later extended from Mine

---

7, 1772, SGA, Contracts and Agreements, no. 80; Moses Austin to John Brickey, Feb. 22, 1815, Barker (ed.) "Austin Papers," vol. 2, pt. 1:247-48; also see below, chap. vii.

47. Ekberg, "De Gruy," 147-48; Austin, *Summary*, 9; Schoolcraft, *View of Lead Mines*, 93-112; Hanley, 129-30.

48. Schaaf, "The First Roads," 92-99; see, for example, Gadobert account for 1773, MHS, Vallé Collection, Box 1, and Vallé-La Rose contract, Dec. 7, 1772, SGA, Mines, no. 29.

Two-wheeled cart much like the charettes *used in colonial Ste. Genevieve. Replica in National Park Service Museum, St. Louis.*

à Breton to Herculaneum. The latter town, which Austin began to develop on the west bank of the Mississippi between St. Louis and Ste. Genevieve in 1806, soon competed with Ste. Genevieve for the distinction of being the most important entrepôt of the Missouri lead mining district.[49]

Moses Austin's arrival at Mine à Breton in the late 1790s brought important changes in virtually every aspect of lead mining in Spanish Illinois: he extracted the mineral ore differently, sinking deep vertical shafts with extended horizontal drifts, instead of digging surface pits; he used improved smelting furnaces in order to extract a greater percentage of the ore's lead; he vastly increased the scale of mining operations, using both hired and slave laborers who remained at the mines the year around; he expedited the transport of lead from the mines to the Mississippi by building a road between Mine à Breton and

49. Peyroux to Miró, Dec. 2, 1791, PC 204; Garrison (ed.), "Memorandum of Austin," 540; Kedro, "The Three Notch Road Frontier," 189-204; Gardner, 94-95.

Herculaneum; he instituted a practice of freehold ownership of real estate in the mining regions, thereby raising havoc with the customary system of prescriptive mining rights.[50]

Between the time that Philippe Renaut received large concessions of land at both Mine La Motte and the Mineral Fork in 1723 and the time that Moses Austin arrived in the Illinois Country in 1797, no one had laid claim to large tracts of land in the lead mining districts. Small plots were claimed at Mine La Motte, but bases for the titles were often tenuous. In 1800, François Vallé explained to Lieutenant Governor Delassus that he did not know *what* title three residents of New Bourbon — Paul Deguire, François Lachance, and Jerome Matisse — had to land near Mine La Motte upon which they had built a cabin, "but I can tell you that their ancestors were old settlers at this post." Tradition, family name, and customary rights counted heavily in the Illinois Country.[51]

A revolution in land-holding practices at the lead mines began in 1797. From Ste. Genevieve, Moses Austin wrote to Governor Carondelet and asked for a concession of one square league (over 6,000 acres) near Mine à Breton. Austin's request was supported by Charles de Luzières and François Vallé, and Carondelet granted Austin the land. Boundaries for this vast tract were not immediately established, and Austin complained bitterly about trespassers violating his property; it was of course virtually impossible to maintain 6,000 sacrosanct acres in the wilderness. Finally, Antoine Soulard, the official surveyor for Upper Louisiana, went to Mine à Breton accompanied by François Vallé and surveyed Austin's tract.[52]

American officials eventually rejected Austin's claim to the square league of land near Mine à Breton. But before that occurred in 1816, much discontent and violence flared up in the mining district. The bitterness that traditional creole miners harbored toward Moses Austin and his mining enterprise was appar-

---

50. On Austin see, Houck, *History of Missouri,* 1:365-71; Hanley, 116-35; Gardner, *Lead King,* 84-97.

51. Vallé to Delassus, Nov. 25, 1800, PC 217; on early land claims at Mine La Motte, see Vallé to Trudeau, May 26, 1794, PC 209; Hanley, 50-55, 143-47; *ASP, Public Lands,* 3:667, 4:540.

52. Austin's petition, Jan. 26, 1797, BL; De Luzières to Carondelet, Jan. 28, 1797, PC 214; Austin to Delassus, Aug. 13, 1799, PC 216 A; François Vallé to Delassus, Aug. 19, 1799, ibid.; Vallé to Delassus, Aug. 25, 1799, ibid.; Vallé to Delassus, May 30, 1800; Nasatir, "Pedro Vial in Upper Louisiana," 101-04; Hanley, 123-28.

ent at Mine à Breton in 1802, when they refused to help defend Austin's settlement against an Osage raiding party. Austin's men luckily had a three-pound cannon with which to repel the Osage braves. Indians resented the white man for trying to possess the lead mines, and creole miners resented Austin for his apparent greed. Austin himself naturally felt that his substantial capital investment in labor and machinery justified a large freehold concession.[53]

French-creole entrepreneurs, prompted by Austin's vision and ambition, soon began to seek large concessions in the mining districts. These included many citizens of Ste. Genevieve — Jean-Baptiste Vallé, Jacques Guibourd, Amable Partenay, and Pascal Detchmendy. At the time of the Louisiana Purchase, disputes over real estate in the area around Mine à Breton were complicated and acrimonious. Small investors, both creole and American, confronted the big speculators, who were also both creole and American, and the big speculators fought with each other.[54]

Pascal Detchmendy came to Ste. Genevieve from southern France and married a Bauvais woman in 1798. Not long thereafter he received a large land grant at Belleview, south of Mine à Breton. In February 1804, just before the official transfer of Louisiana to the United States, Detchmendy tried to have his land surveyed by Thomas Maddin, who was assistant (to Antoine Soulard) surveyor for Upper Louisiana. An armed mob of Americans rose up and threatened Detchmendy and Maddin, driving them off the land in the name of the United States. Maddin was convinced that Austin was the man behind the mob, although that was never demonstrated. Jean-Baptiste Vallé called the mob action an "insurrection," and Charles Delassus called it a "revolt." Vallé ordered the police commissioner at Mine à Breton, Joseph Decelle Duclos, to investigate the situation, but the survey was not completed at that time. United States land commissioners finally confirmed Detchmendy's concession in 1835.[55]

In 1804 Mine à Breton consisted of twenty to thirty households, about half creole and half American. It was more a mining camp

---

53. *ASP, Public Lands*, 3:671; Garrison (ed.), "Memorandum of Austin," 519; Barker (ed.), "Austin Papers," vol. 2, pt. 1:2; Gardner, 74.

54. Hanley, 138-48; Gardner, 62-76.

55. Jean-Baptiste Vallé to Delassus, Feb. 14, 1804, PC 220; Vallé to Delassus, Feb. 25, 1804, PC 197; Delassus to Stoddard, Mar. 30, 1804, PC 220; *ASP, Public Lands* 8:73.

than a town, however, and it continued to be troubled with violence well on into the American period. Moses Austin was a focal point, if not precisely a cause, for much of the violence. He was the enemy of the small land holders on the one hand, while on the other he feuded with the notorious John Smith T. (T. for Tennessee). Smith was feared as a sharp-shooting duelist and unscrupulous land speculator, and both he and Austin had supporting gangs of thugs. In 1807, the inhabitants of Ste. Genevieve petitioned the new governor of the Louisiana Territory, Meriwether Lewis, to send regular troops to Mine à Breton in order to "prevent an effusion of blood." Lead mining in the Ste. Genevieve district had changed dramatically since the days when a few townspeople, with a handful of black slaves and *engagés*, conducted seasonal diggings at the mines.[56]

Evidence on the amount of lead produced in the Ste. Genevieve District during the colonial period is sketchy, but there is enough data available to make some generalizations. Antoine de Gruy claimed that in 1743 Mine La Motte produced 2,300 bars of lead. Reckoning the weight of each bar at seventy-five pounds gives a total of 172,500 pounds of lead for one year's production. In the early 1750s, at about the time that Ste. Genevieve was emerging as a distinct community, De Gruy reportedly contracted to supply Canada with 100,000 pounds of lead from his operations at the Meramec mines. These figures from the 1740s and 1750s seem high and may well have been inflated by persons (De Gruy and Macarty) who wished to cast the economic potential of the Illinois Country in a favorable light.[57]

The detailed Spanish census of Ste. Genevieve for 1772 shows 60,025 pounds of lead shipped to New Orleans during the year, while the following year the poundage dropped to 17,800 pounds. This precipitous drop probably reveals the extent of Indian troubles at the mines. The Osage and Chickasaw tribes seem virtually to have shut down the lead mines for several years during the early 1770s. François Vallé's son Joseph was killed by Chickasaws at Mine La Motte in 1774.[58]

---

56. Austin, *Summary*, 8; Hanley, 148; petition of citizens, MHS, Mines Envelope; Gardner, 110-21; in 1807 Timothy Phelps wrote to Moses Austin (Aug. 6, 1807, Barker [ed.], "Austin Papers," vol. 2, pt. 1:131) from Ste. Genevieve and described his revulsion over "the reign of Terror at the Mines."

57. Macarty to Vaudreuil, Mar. 27, 1752, Pease (ed.), *Illinois on the Eve of the Seven Years' War*, 563; Ekberg, "De Gruy," 148.

58. Census of 1772, *SRM*, 1:55; census of 1773, ibid., 87; on the Chickasaws, see below, chap. iv.

Receipt sent to François Vallé by his factor in New Orleans, Berte Grima, for a shipment of lead. Notice Vallé's commercial logo on the left. Copy courtesy of the Missouri Historical Society, St. Louis.

No data are available on lead production during the 1780s, but with the discovery of the rich veins of ore at Mine à Breton in the mid-1770s we may presume that production increased. By 1791, Ste. Genevieve was exporting 216,000 pounds of lead; by 1795, 327,300 pounds; by 1800, together with New Bourbon, 438,080 pounds. The sharp increases of the early 1790s represented steady exploitation of the rich deposits near Mine à Breton, and those of the late 1790s the advent of Moses Austin and his improved technology. In 1804, Austin estimated the annual potential of all the lead mines in the hinterlands of the Ste. Genevieve District at about 730,000 pounds. This again may have been an exaggerated figure, for Austin, like De Gruy and Macarty before him, had an interest in casting his mining operations in a favorable light. Yet, within the context of the earlier production figures, Austin's estimate does not seem wildly inflated.[59]

In brief, it appears that the decade from about 1798 to 1808 was the golden age of early lead production for Ste. Genevieve. Entrepreneurs like Austin and Amable Partenay directed flourishing operations, and there was a good wagon road from the lead mines to Ste. Genevieve, where the lead bars were loaded on riverboats for shipment to New Orleans. By 1800 there was a permanent settlement at Old Mines, as well as at Mine à Breton, and it is a bit disturbing to discover that already in 1804 there were complaints by the citizens of Old Mines about industrial pollution of their drinking water. Water pollution was of course a sure sign of industrial progress and increased lead production. Although data are very approximate, by the end of the colonial era, the lead produced in the Ste. Genevieve District probably had an annual market value somewhat less than the cereal grains produced in the region. But because a larger percentage of the lead was exported it generated more cash (or rather credit) for the community.[60]

Ste. Genevieve's early lead boom was, however, short-lived and was already subsiding by 1808. Austin's new town of Herculaneum was located closer to Mine à Breton than Ste. Genevieve and had a tower for producing lead shot. It may have superseded Ste. Genevieve as the principal entrepot for the lead industry in Upper Louisiana. Then the entire industry was hit by a recession in late 1812, when the War of 1812 disrupted commerce and severly deflated the price of lead. Lead was an important component in the economy of colonial Ste. Genevieve, but the town would have been founded and would have developed more or less as it did even if there had been no lead mines in the hinterlands of the district.[61]

The other local mineral that was central to the economy of colonial Ste. Genevieve was salt. Indeed, the salt springs of the

---

59. Census of 1791, *SRM,* 2:365-68; census of 1795, ibid., 1:326; census of 1800, ibid., facing 414; Austin, *Summary,* 20.

60. Petition of citizens at Old Mines, April 1804, SGA, Mines, no. 40; the pollution was allowed to continue, see Partenay vs. citizens of Old Mines, SGA, Litigations, no. 227.
Austin estimated (*Summary,* 20) the annual value of the lead produced at approximately $40,000. Reckoning the value of wheat at eight livres per minot and that of maize at five livres per minot, the harvest of Ste. Genevieve and New Bourbon for 1800 had a market value of about $74,291.00.

61. Gardner, 98-102.

Saline Creek were known and exploited before the deposits of lead ore, which were located farther from the Mississippi. Long before Ste. Genevieve was founded French Canadian settlers from the east side of the Mississippi had established temporary camps at the salt springs in order to extract from the saline waters a mineral essential to their existence.[62]

No good description of these salt works (such as they were) in colonial times has survived, but scattered documents permit the following picture to be drawn. Saline water was pumped out of the springs into kettles, which were made of an assortment of metals including lead, for a boiling away process of extracting the salt. The kettles were heated on stoves ("furnaces") that were fired with wood, which meant that the area around the salt springs was deforested. When in 1797 François Vallé II asked for a concession at another salt spring, located further up the Saline Creek, he requested an entire square league of land so that he might have "the wood necessary to exploit the saline." Once the water was boiled off, the remaining salt and other trace minerals were scooped out of the kettles and packed in containers (sacks or kegs?) that contained either seventy pounds (one minot) or one hundred pounds (one quintal). Salt was frequently used as a medium of exchange in the Illinois Country, and in 1779 one hundredweight of salt was worth forty livres, which was the same value as flour at that time.[63]

Alexis Griffard was the only resident of Ste. Genevieve on the militia roster of 1779 listed as a saltmaker ("sellier") by profession. Griffard was Canadian and had arrived in Ste. Genevieve sometime during the mid-1770s. In 1777 he married Marie-Magdaleine Tirard, daughter of the illegimate mestizo woman, Marie-Josephe Deguire Tirard, and took up salt making. It seems likely that the Griffards left Ste. Genevieve proper to settle near the Saline, for the name does not appear on the Ste. Genevieve censuses of 1787 and 1791. In 1797, however, the Griffard family of ten persons was included in the census of New Bourbon, and Alexis was still designated a saltmaker by profession. Griffard remains an important name in the region around the Saline Creek in the 1980s.[64]

---

62. For a good introduction to the Saline in colonial times, see Denman, "History of 'La Saline'," 307-20.

63. Vallé to Carondelet, June 23, 1797, PC 214; see SGA, Personalty, no. 10; on weight of salt, see Surrey, *Commerce of Louisiana*, 291.

64. "Relation de la compagnie de milice du poste de Ste. Geneviève," Nov.

In the early 1790s, most of the salt that came out of the Ste. Genevieve area was produced by a handful of important families — Vallé, Bolduc, Bauvais, Peyroux, and Pratte. These wealthy men were entrepreneurs, and they used either black slaves or hired *engagés* to work the salt springs on their behalf. Louis Bolduc *père* was the single largest producer in 1791, turning out 300 minots of salt. In the autumn of 1795, Gayoso de Lemos, lieutenant governor of the Natchez District, visited Ste. Genevieve and noted that production at "La Salina" was fifteen minots per day. That figure for daily production corresponds reasonably well with the annual total presented in the 1795 census, 5,400 minots, which was a large amount compared to the total from 1791, 1300 minots. By 1800 the number of minots of salt had jumped to over 11,000 and most of the producers were evidently Anglo-Americans. In 1797 the Saline fell under the jurisdiction of New Bourbon, and the New Bourbon census of that year lists nine saltmakers. Eight of these were Anglo-Americans, the ninth being the aging but still productive Alexis Griffard.[65]

Salt production at colonial Ste. Genevieve was never central to the town's economy. But salt was an essential mineral, and its availability at the nearby Saline was one of the reasons that the community of Ste. Genevieve developed where it did. Salt was not only a vital component of daily life for the townspeople, it was also used to cure meat and animal hides for local use and export to New Orleans. To cure a ham or a buffalo hide required literally pounds of salt.

As was the case with the lead mining districts, it is difficult to determine the land holding patterns at the salt springs. In 1766, Jean Datchurut of Ste. Genevieve purchased from Jean-Baptiste Lagrange of Kaskaskia "une Saline," a salt works, but no real estate was mentioned. Ten years later, Henri Carpentier purchased from the Jean-Baptiste Bauvais estate a log house (*pièce-sur-pièce*), a stable, and a salt furnace at the Saline. But once again it is not clear if Carpentier was acquiring title to the land itself or merely the structures and the equipment. In the 1790s, Henri Peyroux laid claim to a vast tract of land on the lower Saline Creek that

29, 1779, PC 213; SGPR, Marriages, Book A :162; New Bourbon census of 1797, PC 2365.

65. Census of 1791, *SRM,* 2:365-68; census of 1797, ibid., 1:326; census of 1800, ibid., facing 414; New Bourbon census of 1797, PC 2365; Gayoso's report from Nasatir (ed.), *Spanish War Vessels,* 33.

included the salt springs. Yet numerous other persons were operating furnaces and extracting salt on Peyroux's concession. As with the lead mines, there seems to have developed over time a customary system of prescriptive rights: the salt springs were controlled de facto by those individuals who were established there producing salt.[66]

In 1752, at the time that the first census was taken in Ste. Genevieve, all the heads of household in town were agriculturalists. As the community grew and the economy became more diverse, the spectrum of occupations broadened. By 1779 the muster roll of the Ste. Genevieve militia showed no less than eighteen different occupations in town — including brewing (the brewer, François Colmand, was perhaps an Alsatian), blacksmithing, cabinetmaking, and hatmaking. Much of the occupational diversity in Ste. Genevieve by 1779 can be attributed to the influx of skilled workers from Kaskaskia after that village became British in the 1760s. In any event, Ste. Genevieve had clearly become a largely self-sufficient community by the time of the American Revolution.[67]

Between 1779 and 1787, when a detailed census was compiled, the number and variety of occupations in Ste. Genevieve increased substantially. A schoolteacher (Louis Tonnellier) entered the ranks of the honorably employed in town, and so did two potters. There were also several other specialists in 1787 that had not been available in town in 1779. By the later date, one could have one's musket or shoes repaired right in the Old Town, for there were two cobblers and two gunsmiths. During the 1770s, Jean-Baptiste Laviolette was "master butcher" in Ste. Genevieve, but there were probably no bakers or candlestickmakers in town. Throughout the colonial period, households in Ste. Genevieve were overwhelmingly self-sufficient, and baking and candlestickmaking were domestic rather than entrepreneurial activities. Henry Brackenridge commented that "in none of the villages or towns [of Upper Louisiana] is there a market house; the reason I have already mentioned, the inhabitants raised their own provisions, and were

---

66. Account of Lagrange succession, Apr. 27, 1797, Louisiana State Museum, 1768092803; SGA, Public Sales, no. 81; on Peyroux's concession at the Saline, see the numerous documents in PC 214 A, including a copy of Peyroux's concession dated 1787.

67. Census of 1752, HMLO 426; militia roster 1779, PC 213.

all cultivators of the soil."[68]

A curious thing about the occupational listings of 1779 and 1787 is that in the former "voyageur," or riverboatman, looms large, while in the latter no *voyageurs* appear. In 1787, however, masses of day laborers (*journaliers*) are shown. The solution to this little riddle is probably that *voyageurs* and *journaliers* constituted the floating, mobile labor force in Ste. Genevieve, and that a young man who worked as a day laborer at the lead mines one month might well serve as a boatman on a trip to New Orleans the next.

One of the most valuable documents for examining the range of occupations in the Ste. Genevieve region during the colonial period is the detailed census of New Bourbon drawn up by Delassus de Luzières at the end of 1797. The Ste. Genevieve census for 1797 is not extant, but New Bourbon was close enough to Ste. Genevieve in location and character for its census to provide valuable information about the latter community. The majority of New Bourbons citizens were of course "cultivateurs," but there was also a substantial group of craftsmen: four coopers, three blacksmiths, two carpenters, one cartwright, and one gunsmith. These were essential craftsmen, without which no self-respecting community could function. Ste. Genevieve, which was somewhat larger and more sophisticated (if one may use such a word!) than New Bourbon had more of these basic craftsmen and, in addition, had specialists, like tailors and cobblers, for producing articles of a civilized society.[69]

There is only sketchy evidence concerning the wages of craftsmen and laborers in colonial Ste. Genevieve. As mentioned above, *engagés* received 700-800 livres per year on contract, but it would be virtually impossible to translate that amount into hourly or daily wages. François Vallé II's bill of expenses for the fort built in 1794 provides an indication of wages for certain types of workmen: common laborers received one peso (five livres or one dollar) per day on that project, and the master carpenter received twenty reales (12½ livres or $2.50) per day. Unless François Vallé was padding his bill, these figures are reliable for the 1790s. At that time, Paul Alliot reported that a day's wages in New Orleans was four escalins, which would mean that wages in Ste. Genevieve were twice as much. There must have been more laborers available

---

68. Census of 1787, MHS archives; inventory of Laviolette's estate, SGA, Estates, no. 164; Brackenridge, *Views of Louisiana*, 120.

69. New Bourbon census of 1797, PC 2365.

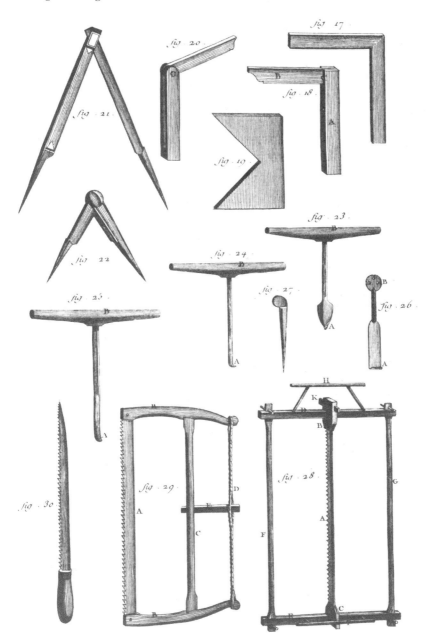

Woodworking tools of the type used by craftsmen in colonial Ste. Genevieve. Illustration from Denis Diderot's Encyclopédie.

in New Orleans, or perhaps there were more slaves to do ordinary labor, thus deflating wages.[70]

Two geographic features were essential to the existence of colonial Ste. Genevieve, the Big Field for agriculture and the Mississippi River for communication and transportation. Ste. Genevieve would have existed without the lead mines of the hinterland, and perhaps even without the nearby Saline Creek, but the Big Field and the river were the *sine qua non* of the town. The Mississippi was the commercial lifeline of Ste. Genevieve, linking the community with the outside world to the north, east, and south. Riverboats went north on the Mississippi to St. Louis and Prairie du Chien; they ascended the Ohio River to Louisville (the falls of the Ohio) and to Pittsburgh (the forks of the Ohio); and, most importantly, boats went down to New Orleans, where commercial contacts could be made with Europe, the Caribbean, and the East Coast of North America.

A multitudinous variety of boats plied the waterways of the Mississippi watershed in the eighteenth century: log rafts, bark canoes, dugout pirogues, barges, and, most important of all for commerce, the renowned *bateaux*. *Bateaux* came in different sizes, but the workhorse of the Illinois Country-New Orleans axis was a shallow-drafted vessel about ten feet by forty feet, which carried a commercial payload of up to fifteen or sixteen tons. Riverboats were always in short supply and sometimes they were built in Ste. Genevieve. *Voiture* was a generic word in Mississippi-Valley French meaning vessel, and in February 1796 François Vallé remarked that he had recently had two "voitures" constructed for carrying freight on the river.[71]

Guiding these bulky craft downriver required great skill. This was the task of a special group of men called "patrons," skippers, who were employees of the boat owners. A good skipper could jockey a *bateaux* from Ste. Genevieve to New Orleans in two or three weeks, but coming up the river was a different matter. *Engagés* and slaves were employed as oarsmen, and the trip required three or four months on the river. Sometimes, especially in time

---

70. Vallé's bill included in Carondelet to Rendón, July 7, 1795, PC 618; Alliot, "Reflections," 91; both the escalin and the reale were worth one-eighth of a piastre or dollar in the late colonial period (see Appendix H).

71. The best introduction to eighteenth-century river craft is in Surrey, *Commerce of Louisiana*, 55-76; Vallé to Thomas Portell, Feb. 14, 1796, PC 48.

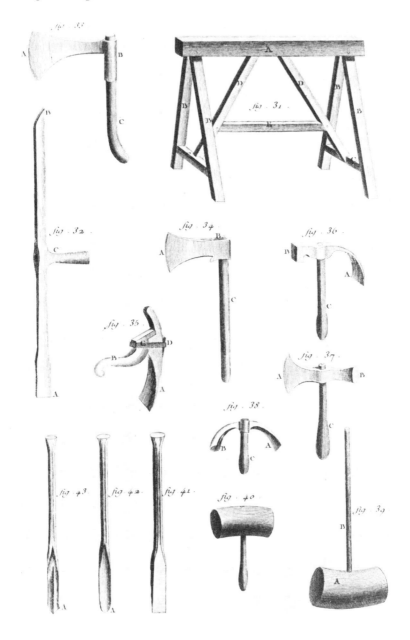

Woodworking tools of the type used by craftsmen in colonial Ste. Genevieve. Illustration from Denis Diderot's Encyclopédie.

of war or Indian troubles, the *bateaux* traveled in small convoys. Increasingly toward the end of the colonial period single boats could make the run to New Orleans without fear of being bushwhacked along the way.[72]

According to the Ste. Genevieve militia roll of 1779, *voyageur*, riverboatman, was the single largest occupational category in town, making up more than thirty percent of the adult male work force. Riverboatmen led arduous lives. Perrin du Lac who traveled on the Mississippi at the end of the colonial era, provided a vivid description of daily life for eighteenth-century boatmen:[73]

> No trips are more tiring than those on the Mississippi. The men who row up it are exposed to the weather, sleep on the ground, and eat nothing but maize and bacon. On long voyages ... they suffer indescribably. They wear no clothes except those necessary to provide decency, and their skins, burned by the sun, peel off several times. Nothing can refresh them, not even plunging into the river twenty times a day. It is not unusual for them to succumb to fatigue and die oar in hand. The incredible number of mosquitoes that infest the river banks increases their torment and prevents them from obtaining the rest at night that is required to restore their strength .... Their bed is a bear or buffalo hide in which they wrap themselves in the winter or place under themselves in the summer. They all have mosquito nets of rough canvas that they hang on four stakes to save themselves from the bites of the insects.

Huck Finn enjoyed his raft trip down the Mississippi in the mid-nineteenth century, but pulling and cursing a *bateaux* upstream from New Orleans to Ste. Genevieve in colonial times was no pleasure trip. A *voyageur* song described it this way:[74]

> Oh, it's like a marriage
> If to voyage you pledge yourself.
> I pity him who binds himself
> Without having been compelled.
> Rise early, turn in late,
> He must endure his fate,
> Expose himself to death.

---

72. In 1767 it took Francisco Ríu three months to get from New Orleans to the Illinois Country (Ríu to Ulloa, Nov. 12, 1767, PC 109); in the autumn of 1780 it took Francisco Cruzat only two months (Vallé to Piernas, Oct. 5, 1780, PC 193 B); see also Surrey, 75.

73. Militia roster 1779, PC 213; Perrin du Lac, *Voyage dans les deux Louisianes*, 166.

74. Barbeau, "Voyageur Songs," 349.

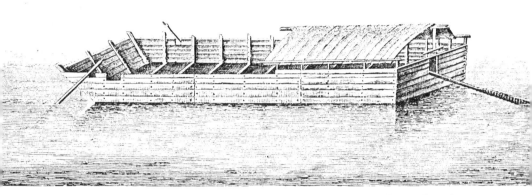

Flatboat of the type used by Americans to carry produce down the Ohio and Mississippi rivers. Creole bateaux *were quite different in appearance, being tapered on both ends. Illustration by Charles Warin from Georges-Victor Collot's* Journey in North America.

Ste. Genevieve exported raw materials and foodstuffs, which was perfectly consistent with the town's position as a rustic colonial outpost. Numerous bills of lading for riverboats loaded in Ste. Genevieve reveal the kind of products that were shipped to New Orleans: maize, wheat, flour, tobacco, salted meat, lead, hides, pelts, and occasionally butter and cheese. In February 1772, for example, Daniel Fagot, merchant of the Illinois Country and sometime resident of Ste. Genevieve, loaded his *chaland* (a smaller variety of *bateau*) at the Old Town docks for a trip to New Orleans. Fagot's cargo was typical for that time: fifty sheets of lead, thirty-one barrels of flour, nine bundles of beaver skins, four bundles of buckskins with the hair on, eleven bundles of buckskins with the hair removed, fifteen doeskins, and eighty-five buffalo robes. Foodstuffs shipped down river were consumed in New Orleans. Hides and pelts were largely sent on to Europe, where there was an insatiable demand for them. Commandant Louis Villars of Ste. Genevieve gave Fagot his shipping license, and the *chaland's* cargo was verified by the commandants at Pointe Coupée and Manchac before it arrived at New Orleans.[75]

---

75. Fagot bill of lading, PC 111. Daniel Usner ("Frontier Exchange in the Lower Mississippi Valley," 129-30) has pointed out that large quantities of deerskins were shipped from New Orleans to Europe during the eighteenth century.

In 1788, John Dodge, who was then living in Ste. Genevieve, asked Lieutenant Governor Pérez for a license to ship diverse agricultural products to New Orleans. In his request Dodge explained that when he sold out his possessions on the east side of the Mississippi he had been obliged to take payment in kind rather than in coin because there was a shortage of hard currency in the Illinois Country. Dodge wished to ship 110 barrels of tobacco, 50,000 pounds of flour, 10,000 pounds of bacon and hams, and 5,000 pounds of butter and cheese. This was a small fortune in agricultural products and would have required a veritable convoy of riverboats for transport to New Orleans. Pérez forwarded Dodge's request to Governor Miró with the advice that it would be prudent to accommodate a man as useful and influential as John Dodge.[76]

Flour shipments to New Orleans made up an important part of Ste. Genevieve's exports during the entire colonial period. A pattern developed whereby the Illinois Country withheld most shipments of grain and/or flour from one year's harvest until the next year's harvest was in and accounted for. In this way, food shortages were prevented in Upper Louisiana. During the early and mid-1770s, for example, harvests were generally good, and every autumn the Illinois Country shipped flour down river to New Orleans. In 1780, however, both weather and warfare militated against a good harvest. Thus in the autumn of 1780 Lieutenant Governor Cruzat forbade any export of flour from Spanish Illinois, and he did so again in the spring of 1786 as a consequence of the great flood of 1785.[77]

Ste. Genevieve produced more cereal grains than any other settlement in Spanish Louisiana. Flour, wheat, and maize were not only shipped to New Orleans but also to such nearby posts as St. Louis, Cape Girardeau, and New Madrid. During the winter of 1796-97, the commandant at New Madrid, Charles Delassus, reported that the citizens of his settlement were reduced to eating maize because the boats sent to Ste. Genevieve for flour were trapped by ice on the Mississippi. St. Louis did not have to import foodstuffs every year, but riverboats regularly carried flour, grain, and salted meat from Ste. Genevieve to its sister city in Spanish

---

76. Dodge to Pérez, Sep. 23, 1788, PC 14; Pérez to Miró, Oct. 12, 1788, ibid.

77. See statistics on flour shipments, *SRM*, 1:89, 95, 103; these statistics are not terribly reliable, indeed the figures for 1775 are way off base, but they are close enough to establish a general pattern for the period; Vallé to Piernas, Dec. 7, 1780, PC 193 B; Cruzat to De Oro, May 8, 1786, PC 117 B.

Illinois.[78]

Voluminous records document the shipment of various foodstuffs from Ste. Genevieve to St. Louis during the early 1780s. François Vallé, Louis Bolduc, Jean Datchurut, Simon Hubardeau, Louis Lalumandière, and René Rapicault were the merchants, *habitants,* and *voyageurs* most heavily engaged in this trade. And the products they most often handled were flour, maize, and salted pork bellies. Between December 1, 1780, and May 31, 1781, for example, Louis Bolduc shipped to St. Louis flour and pork worth a tidy 3,565 livres. There was of course no such amount of cash available in St. Louis, and thus Bolduc was paid in paper certificates backed by the Spanish treasury in New Orleans. Bolduc could then use these bills of exchange to pay for manufactured goods from Europe, which his riverboats would eventually pick up from the wharfs in New Orleans. Hard cash may have been scarce in Spanish Illinois, but commerce went on apace with the use of sophisticated paper transactions, bills of exchange and credit-book accounts.[79]

The *bateaux* that carried agricultural products from Ste. Genevieve to New Orleans did not reascend the Mississippi with empty hulls but rather were loaded to the gunwales with trade goods of all sorts. These goods were destined both for *habitants* in the Illinois Country and for barter with the Indians. During the last days of July 1768, a small convoy of riverboats was preparing to depart New Orleans for Ste. Genevieve, and their owners applied to Governor Ulloa for permission to load the vessels and head upriver. The owners were Carpentier (probably Henri), Chamard (probably Louis), and one Beaulieu, and all three had apparently made the trip to New Orleans in person. It is hard to say how often the important merchants of Ste. Genevieve made the journey to "la ville," as New Orleans was called, but certainly these trips were not unusual. Interestingly, each boat carried two passengers. One of those in Carpentier's craft was "Monsieur Bois-le-Duc," who was probably the wealthy merchant of Ste. Genevieve, Louis Bolduc.[80]

78. Charles Delassus to Carondelet, Mar.6, 1797, PC 35; see also Cruzat to François Vallé I, Nov. 26, 1782, PC 195; François Vallé II to Louis Lorimier (commandant at Cape Girardeau), Mar. 22, 1794, PC 209; Vallé to Portell (commandant at New Madrid), June 8, 1795, PC 192.

79. See Cruzat's account (Nov. 30, 1782, PC 702), which was sent to New Orleans.

80. The bills of lading for this convoy are all in PC 188 A.

The bateaux of this convoy were all flat-bottomed, broad of beam, driven by long sweeps, and featured primitive cabins in the afterquarters. Those belonging to Chamard and Carpentier were large craft and had crews of twenty-one men each — the skipper and twenty oarsmen. Chamard's oarsmen were all white *engagés*, while Carpentier had eighteen *engagés* and two black slaves. Beaulieu's smaller boat had a skipper and a crew of twelve *engagés* and one slave. Who the white man and two black slaves. Beaulieu's smaller boat had a skipper and a crew of twelve engages and one slave. Who the white men were that engaged themselves for these river trips between Ste. Genevieve and New Orleans is difficult to say, for there are very few extant contracts for such *engagements*. Given Perrin du Lac's description of the arduous lifestyle of boatmen, it would seem that only those men who had no other means of gaining a livelihood would take such a job. Or perhaps young men with a hankering to see New Orleans would sign on for one trip and then be grateful to return to farming. Little is known either about the skippers, but they were highly skilled men and their lives every bit as eventful as those of steamboat pilots in Samuel Clemens' time. Tropez Ricard, who had abandoned balmy St. Tropez on the French Mediterranean to become a resident of Ste. Genevieve, was listed on the 1787 census as a skipper. Unfortunately he did not retire from life on the river to write enthralling books about his experiences.[81]

When the three boat-owners requested permission to leave New Orleans in July 1768, they were required to submit bills of lading to the Spanish government. Thus there is a good record of the products that were routinely carried from "la ville" to Ste. Genevieve. The cargoes of the three boats were remarkably similar, and the large variety of products they carried can be grouped roughly in five categories:[82]

Household Goods

cloth [many varieties]	soap
woolen blankets	mirrors
cooking kettles	thread
iron	faïence
copper	earthenware
brass	cotton for candle wicks
ceramic	

81. Ibid.; Census of 1787, MHS archives; see Tropez Ricard's marriage record, SGPR, Marriages, Book A:123.

82. Bills of lading, PC 188 A.

A few French silver coins such as this one circulated in colonial Ste. Genevieve. The late Irven Peithmann discovered this Louis XV coin near the site of old Kaskaskia. Photo courtesy of the Illinois Department of Conservation.

Comestibles
  wine [many varieties]
  brandy
  tafia
  coffee
  sugar
  anisette liquor

Miscellaneous
  nails
  sickles
  ironware
  canvas
  gunpowder
  lead shot

Indian Trade Goods
  glass beads
  vermillion
  knives
  guns
  gunpowder
  lead
  shot
  cloth

Clothing
  shoes
  woolen stockings
  caps
  handkerchiefs

This categorization is somewhat arbitrary, for virtually any one of the items listed might have served as an item in the Indian trade.[83]

It is apparent that most of the products that came upriver to Ste. Genevieve in the summer of 1768 did not originate in the New Orleans area but had been shipped into "la ville" before

83. On the Indian trade, see Phillips, *The Fur Trade;* Surrey, *Commerce of Louisiana;* Nasatir, "Trade and Diplomacy in Spanish Illinois."

being transported up the Mississippi. The British had made large commercial inroads into Louisiana by the 1760s, and some of the manufactured goods, especially cotton cloth, probably originated in England. There are telltale indications, however, that many products shipped from New Orleans to Ste. Genevieve originated in France. Obviously the alcoholic beverages did, and so did the thread from Rennes, the handkerchiefs from Rouen, and the cloth from Beaufort. France maintained close commercial connections with its former colony of Louisiana, and Spain's manufactories were too weak to produce many exports. The large quantities of cloth in the convoy indicates that little or no weaving was being done in Upper Louisiana. This was largely a consequence of mercantile economic policy that obliged colonists to purchase cloth from Europe. Curiously, all three boats carried lead, which suggests two things: 1) The lead mines of the Ste. Genevieve District were so unproductive at that time that they could not even supply local needs. 2) Lead, principally for shot, was an indispensable item for the inhabitants of the Illinois Country.[84]

This small convoy of riverboats left New Orleans to ascend the Mississippi at a fortuitous time, about the beginning of August. This meant that the convoy was on the river during autumn, when the current was least forceful, but before the frosts came. There is no record of the convoy's arrival in Ste. Genevieve, but if the trip upriver went reasonably well it should have pulled up at the Old Town docks about the end of October. The convoy's arrival was a festive occasion for the townspeople, for the boats carried news of the outside world, and products — especially wine, liquor, coffee, and sugar — to take some of the sharp edge off winter in the Illinois Country.

During the 1790s, the New Orleans businessman Berte Grima became the factor *en ville* for several of Ste. Genevieve's wealthiest citizens. Grima, for example, purchased and loaded in New Orleans large quantities of products and materials that were sent to the Vallé brothers, François II and Jean-Baptiste, in Ste. Genevieve. François II and Grima kept up a continuous and cordial correspondence for ten years, 1794-1804, and they maintained their friendship by exchanging gifts — Vallé sent Grima the good apples of the Illinois Country, and Grima reciprocated

84. On English and French commerce with Spanish Louisiana, see Clark, *New Orleans, 1718-1812: An Economic History,* passim; Whitaker, *Mississippi Question,* chap. v.

by sending to his Ste. Genevieve friend anchovies imported from Europe.[85]

It is of some interest to compare the goods sent from New Orleans to Ste. Genevieve in the 1760s with those sent thirty years later. There is no doubt that at the end of the colonial period, as in the 1760s, New Orleans was principally an entrepôt and not a producer of the goods that were shipped to the Illinois Country. The riverboat cargoes of both eras contained large quantities of alcoholic beverages and cloth of different varieties. In the 1790s, Vallé's beverages — tafia, table wines, and dessert wines (Malaga) — came from France, Spain, and the Caribbean sugar islands, while the cloth — cottons, linens, and canvas — came from England and France.[86]

An obvious difference between the cargoes shipped from New Orleans to Ste. Genevieve in the 1760s and those shipped in the 1790s is that in the later period there was a much higher percentage of luxury household goods: fancy soaps, Havana cigars, hankerchiefs, parasols, fans, and crystal goblets. This difference may be simply because the bills of lading extant from the 1760s were for cargoes intended principally for the Indian trade, whereas the bills from the 1790s list products intended for the domestic use of Ste. Genevieve's wealthier citizens. Or the difference may be explained by the fact that New Orleans, which had grown steadily in size and importance, was increasingly able to furnish fine products to the various outposts of Louisiana. Finally, life in Ste. Genevieve, at least for some persons, had become more refined as time went on. It is hard to imagine those stylish parasols that were shipped to Ste. Genevieve in the 1790s having much of a place in the Old Town of the 1760s.[87]

A curiosity of Berte Grima's shipments to Ste. Genevieve was the large number of empty bottles and corks. Occasionally, a case of bottled wine (presumably fine vintages) was shipped from New Orleans, but overwhelmingly alcoholic beverages came in barrels and were decanted into smaller vessels after they had arrived in the Illinois Country. In 1803, for example, Berte Grima sent François Vallé II a shipment that included a barrel of wine and 525 empty bottles with corks. Vallé was to share this shipment with

---

85. See the Grima-Vallé correspondence in MHS, Vallé Collection, Box 2.

86. Ibid., bills of lading for shipments to Vallé in Ste. Genevieve.

87. See bill of lading, July 14, 1795, for a *berge* leaving New Orleans for Ste. Genevieve, ibid.

the then parish priest, Father James Maxwell. The wine was worth thirty piastres, and the bottles to contain it 23½ piastres. Given the travail of carrying goods up the Mississippi, one might suppose that the tipplers in Ste. Genevieve could have saved and reused their empties — or perhaps even have sponsored a local glass blowing industry.[88]

Merchants in Ste. Genevieve carried on some trade in furs and hides throughout the colonial period. Deer hides, for example, were a standard medium of exchange in a community that was chronically short of hard cash. When Henri Peyroux was appointed town commandant in 1787, Governor Miró specifically allotted him one share in the fur trading privilege of Upper Louisiana as part of his official remuneration.[89]

Yet the famous fur trade of Upper Louisiana was largely an enterprise of St. Louis as agriculture was of Ste. Genevieve. When in 1790 Lieutenant Governor Pérez in St. Louis allocated the Indian trade of the Missouri River to merchants of Spanish Illinois only two men from Ste. Genevieve, Jean-Baptiste Pratte and Henri Peyroux (as town commandant) were included in the allocation. During the mid-1790s, the whole fur trade of Spanish Illinois was reorganized by Lieutenant Governor Trudeau and the entrepreneur Jacques Clamorgan, and a total of twenty-eight merchants were included in the distribution; only three of these, Louis Bolduc, Simon Hubardeau, and Jean-Baptiste Pratte were from Ste. Genevieve. And in 1795 Trudeau reported to Governor Carondelet that one of these three, whom he did not name, had not traded for four years.[90]

No doubt geography — St. Louis's proximity to the mouth of the Missouri River — determined that Ste. Genevieve would play a secondary role in the fur trade. If a French or creole merchant wished to trade in furs he established himself in St. Louis rather than in Ste. Genevieve; that, after all, was the specific purpose for which Pierre Laclède Liguest and the young Auguste Chouteau

---

88. Grima to Vallé, May 30, 1803, ibid.

89. Miró to Cruzat, Apr. 20, 1787, PC 4.

90. Allocation of Pérez, attached to Pérez to Miró, Aug. 23, 1790, PC 16; Clamorgan to Trudeau, May 3, 1794; BL; Trudeau to Carondelet, Oct. 26, 1795, PC 211; Nasatir, "Jacques Clamorgan"; Foley and Rice, *The First Chouteaus,* 76-78; numerous documents pertaining to the Missouri River Valley and the fur trade of Spanish Illinois during the 1790s are printed in Nasatir (ed.), *Before Lewis and Clark,* 2: passim.

had founded St. Louis in 1764.[91]

The last decade of the colonial era was a time of stress and turmoil for Ste. Genevieve's economy, as indeed it was for almost every facet of the town's existence. Probably in 1794 (the document is undated) a group of important citizens of St. Louis and Ste. Genevieve petitioned Governor Carondelet, complaining of the economic plight in Upper Louisiana. The declining fur trade and falling flour prices were the two principal issues raised in the petition. Problems with the fur trade were real, but these were largely the concern of entrepreneurs in St. Louis. Falling flour prices, however, adversely affected virtually every person in Ste. Genevieve.[92]

Increasing quantities of American flour from the Ohio Valley drove down flour prices in New Orleans. Spain had outlawed this commerce in 1784. Although Americans had been adept smugglers and sold contraband flour in New Orleans, the American flour trade increased in 1788 when it became legal upon payment of import duties in New Orleans. Thus American flour competed in the metropole of Louisiana with flour from Spanish Illinois and helped to drive the price down. In 1782 flour had been worth forty livres per hundredweight, whereas the petitioners of 1794 asked Governor Carondelet to provide price supports for flour at 22½ livres per hundredweight. There is no evidence that Carondelet did this. Probably he did not have to because the increasing population of New Orleans and environs soon increased the demand for flour and drove the price up. After the Treaty of San Lorenzo in 1795, Americans had free access to the markets of Lower Louisiana for their agricultural products. Nevertheless, in 1796 there was a serious food shortage in New Orleans, and grain and flour from Ste. Genevieve fetched high prices despite competition from American produce. In 1798, good plowland at Ste. Genevieve was bringing nearly 600 livres per facing arpent, which suggests that the town's farmers were not in dire financial straits during the late 1790s.[93]

91. On the reasons for the founding of St. Louis, see McDermott, "Myths and Realities," 8-10; see also the excellent recent study of the Chouteaus by Foley and Rice.

92. Citizens and *habitants* of western Illinois to Governor Carondelet, 1794?, PC 2362.

93. On the complicated issues of the grain trade, flour prices, and navigation of the Mississippi see: Clark, *New Orleans*, 208-18, 258; Clark, "The New Orleans

With a growing population, large cereal grain production, and the lead mines booming, the Ste. Genevieve District was prosperous during the last years of the colonial era. The quantity and quality of goods that François Vallé was buying in New Orleans at the turn of the nineteenth century indicate that the Vallé family was living better than ever before. Whether this was true for a majority of the townspeople in Ste. Genevieve is difficult to judge. The Vallés were prospering, but was their affluence created at the expense of other citizens? Were the rich getting richer and the poor poorer in Ste. Genevieve, or was there enough opportunity within the socio-economic structures of the colonial town for the average *habitant* to participate in the prosperity.

When Peyroux de la Coudrenière was about to lose to François Vallé II his position as commandant in Ste. Genevieve, he complained that François Vallé I had exercised power to benefit a few at the expense of the many:[94]

> The father of the Valles [Francois I] introduced the practice of having a large part of the arable field fencing built by the people who had only a little land, or no land at all. . . . Likewise, work on the church, the cemetery, the rectory, and other things was the responsibility of all household of free persons, a poor widow paying as much as a rich habitant who had more slaves. In this fashion, the rich have crushed the poor.

François Vallé I had certainly used his position as civil lieutenant to promote his family's interests. He sometimes did this up to the edge of legality, and he was twice accused of conducting auction sales in such a way as to favor members of his family. François I kept his office, however, and the Vallés remained the most prominent political family in Ste. Genevieve to the end of the colonial era. Did Vallé leadership, despite its apparent popularity, in fact serve to weaken the economic fabric of colonial Ste. Genevieve by serving the interests of a small wealthy elite? Probably data are not available to answer this question with certainty.

Throughout the colonial period a relatively small group of entrepreneurs exercised a preponderant share of economic power in Ste. Genevieve. These individuals — the Vallés, the Bauvaises,

---

Cabildo," 208; DeConde, *This Affair of Louisiana*, chap. iii; Whitaker, *The Spanish American Frontier*, 93-96, 220-22. One and one-half facing arpents of land in the Big Field brought 850 livres, Nov. 8, 1798, SGA, Deeds, no. 329.

94. Peyroux to Carondelet, Nov. 14, 1793, PC 207 B.

Jean-Baptiste Datchurut, Jean-Bapiste Pratte, Louis Bolduc, Henri Carpentier, François Moreaux — in order to maximize their profits and minimize their risks invested in a variety of enterprises: agriculture, lead mining, salt making, and commerce. This diversification, however, should not obscure the fact that Ste. Genevieve's economy was based more upon agriculture than anything else. Everyone who counted in the community (except perhaps Datchurut) invested in arable land, and tabulations of the harvests from the Big Field between the early 1770s and early 1790s suggest that there was not a significant tendency toward increased economic concentration. The wealth coming from wheat and maize production was no more unevenly distributed in the 1790s than it had been in the 1770s.[95]

Peyroux was probably wrong to claim that in colonial Ste. Genevieve the rich were crushing the poor. If the community had been milked and exploited by a selfish few, Frederick Bates, secretary of the Louisiana Territory, could not have written in 1807 that Ste. Genevieve was "the most wealthy village in Louisiana."[96]

---

95. Indeed, the tendency may have been toward *less* concentration of economic power. During the early 1770s, the four top grain producers regularly produced one-third of the total crop. In 1791, one-third of the crop was produced by eight farmers. See census reports cited above in *SRM*.

96. Frederick Bates to William Hull, June 17, 1807, Marshall (ed.), *Bates Papers*, 1:144.

Chapter VI
Society on the French Frontier

T HE STRUCTURE OF SOCIETY in colonial Ste. Genevieve was unique — it was not quite like that of any other European or colonial society in the eighteenth century. Metropolitan France had, until 1789, a society of well-defined orders or estates based upon clear legal distinctions between clergymen, nobles, and commoners. Furthermore, commoners were divided rigidly into bourgeoisie and peasantry. In Ste. Genevieve these socio-legal distinctions, were never systematically maintained or observed.[1]

The people of colonial Ste. Genevieve were largely of French Canadian stock, although frequently second or third generation Illinoisans. In Canada the Bourbon monarchy of France had attempted to introduce a seigneurial system consisting of lords and settlers. Such a legal, economic, and social system could not be transplanted from the compost heap of Europe to the virgin wilderness of New France, but at least in theory French Canadians were saddled with a social structure vaguely resembling that of France. The imposition of this bastard seigneurial system was not even attempted in the Illinois Country, and the citizens of Ste. Genevieve were never divided into seigneurs and commoners.[2]

Lower Louisiana, and to a lesser extent military outposts such as Fort de Chartres, contained a scattering of persons from aris-

---

1. On the medieval origins of the three-order society, see Duby, *The Three Orders*.

2. Eccles, *France in America*, 34-35, 79-80; Adair, "The French Canadian Seigneury"; Diamond, "An Experiment in 'Feudalism'"; Harris, *The Seigneurial System*, 20-25; Moogk, "Rank in New France."

tocratic French families. Sometimes these persons passed through Ste. Genevieve, and one of them, Louis Dubreuil de Villars, married a Vallé woman. For the most part, however, Ste. Genevieve was a frontier community where the class distinctions of highly-structured European society were virtually obliterated.[3]

This is not to say that society in the colonial village was perfectly leveled and egalitarian, for the first census of the community, in 1752, revealed important economic and social differences within a group of fewer than thirty persons. André Deguire was the preeminent citizen of the fledgling village, owning land worth four times more than that owned by anyone else in town and having both a black slave and an indentured servant in his household. There were then gradations of wealth, and presumably social status, down to the three *volontaires*, landless men who often became settlers and acquired land of their own. The human beings at the bottom of the social hierarchy were of course the two black slaves, one owned by André Deguire and the other by Jacques Chouquet; these slaves, too, could conceivably gain their freedom, either by gratuitous manumission or through self-purchase, but there was little likelihood of that happening. Ste. Genevieve's social structure soon became more diverse, rich, and complex with the addition of merchants, lead miners, skilled artisans, freed blacks, and Indians of one kind or another, but already in 1752 there was a wide spectrum of economic power and social status in the hamlet.[4]

In 1778, Lieutenant Governor de Leyba remarked that in Upper Louisiana "the classes of people are so mixed up that one cannot tell who is a farmer and who is a merchant." Speaking as a European aristocrat, De Leyba was a bit distraught to see social distinctions blurred on the Mississippi Valley frontier. Henry Brackenridge, on the other hand, noted with approbation that "there was scarce any distinction of classes in the society [of the Illinois Country]. . . . They all associated, dressed alike, and frequented the same ball room." Thus it is somewhat artificial to describe or analyze colonial Ste. Genevieve in terms of social classes. Yet, for the sake of convenience, we shall examine the town's society by dividing its citizens into four rough categories: upper crust, yeomen farmers and craftsmen, landless laborers, and slaves. There were in fact representatives of all of these groups (none

---

3. See Arthur and Kerwin, *Old Families of Louisiana*.

4. For an analysis of the Old Town's early settlers, see above, chap. ii.

identified as craftsmen) included in the Ste. Genevieve census of 1752, although a total population of less than thirty souls does not lend itself to accurate analysis by social class.[5]

Throughout much of the colonial period Ste. Genevieve society was dominated by a handful of established and wealthy families, most of which had come to the Illinois Country via French Canada and had been settled for some time on the east bank of the Mississippi before moving to Ste. Genevieve. Vallé, Deguire, Aubuchon, Carpentier, Pratte, Bauvais, Janis, Bolduc, Datchurut, and Lachance were the families that supplied the personnel for the power elite in colonial Ste. Genevieve. These families were not aristocratic; indeed, their origins in France were largely peasant. But in Ste. Genevieve members of these families had money, status, and power, and they dominated the cadre of the local militia. Wealth was important but it was not the only factor that conveyed prestige in the community. Neither the Deguires nor the Aubuchons, for example, had great wealth like the Vallés, but they were old, respectable, and well-to-do families.

Surviving marriage contracts reveal how important families were bound together by blood, friendship, and self-interest. In 1777, François Vallé II, son of militia captain and civil judge François Vallé, married Marie Carpentier, daughter of Henri Carpentier, who was wealthy and a lieutenant in the militia. As witnesses on his behalf, young Vallé had his father, several brothers, and Jean Datchurut. And among Marie's witnesses were three Aubuchon men and André Deguire *père,* all four her uncles. In 1797, Louis Bolduc *fils,* son of the builder of the restored Bolduc House, married Marie-Louise St. Gemme Bauvais. Louis's witnesses included his brother Etienne and his uncle André Deguire *fils.* Marie Louise's witnesses were her uncle Vital Bauvais, her brother Vital St. Gemme Bauvais, Jean-Baptiste Pratte, and Jean-Baptiste Vallé. The principals, families, and witnesses of these two marriage constitute a veritable social register of colonial Ste. Genevieve.[6]

Although French-Canadian families dominated the society of Ste. Genevieve, well-to-do males from outside these families were permitted to marry into the group. These outsiders were often French and were always literate and Roman Catholic. In 1771

---

5. De Leyba to Gálvez, Nov. 16, 1778, *SMV,* pt. 1:313; Brackenridge, *Views of Louisiana,* 135; census of 1752, HMLO, 426.

6. Vallé contract, Jan. 18, 1777, MHS, Vallé Collection, Box 1; Bolduc contract, Aug. 29, 1797, SGA, Marriage Contracts, no. 17.

Signatures of principals and witnesses on the parish record of the marriage of Louis Bolduc fils *and Marie-Louise St. Gemme Bauvais, 1797. With a heroic effort Louis Bolduc* père *signed his son's marriage record rather than leaving his usual mark. Copy courtesy of Father Gregory Schmidt.*

Louis de Villars of New Orleans married Marie-Louise Vallé; in 1776 François Leclerc from Rouen married Marie-Louise Vallé (cousin of the above); in 1795 Guillaume Giroüard from Normandy married Marie Hubardeua; in 1798 Pascal Detchemendy from Bayonne married Thérèse St. Gemme Bauvais; and in 1801 Walter Fenwick, an Anglo-American, married Julie Vallé. In the relatively fluid society of colonial Ste. Genevieve, these outsiders immediately became members of the town's upper crust.[7]

In addition to the influential families that were imbedded in the social and economic fabric of the town, there were transient persons, who, while they resided in Ste. Genevieve or its immediate environs, must be viewed as having been part of the upper crust of society. These were the offical commandants of Ste. Genevieve: Philippe François de Rocheblave (1760-70), Silvio de Cartabona (1776-84), Antonio de Oro (1784-87), Henri Peyroux de la Coudrenière (1787-94), and the commandant of New Bourbon, Pierre-Charles Delassus de Luzières (1793-1804). All of these men were genuine European aristocrats and during their sojourn in the Ste. Genevieve area enjoyed a status even more elevated than that of the bourgeois power elite. The citizens of colonial Ste. Genevieve (like their Anglo-American counterparts) were not terribly impressed with European noblemen, however. Moreover, the relatively brief periods that the aristocratic commandants resided in town and their usual lack of ties to the economic and social infrastructure of the powerful local families meant that they did not exercise great influence on society in Ste. Genevieve.[8]

Beneath the upper crust of society the economic and social gradations were so fine that there was an essentially unbroken continuum down to the disenfranchised slaves. The detailed Spanish census of 1791, which includes information on slave ownership and economic productivity, provides a convenient overview of the range of economic positions and social levels occupied by the citizens of Ste. Genevieve. Agriculture was the single most important economic activity in the community, employing the the largest number of people and producing the most revenue, and the three principal crops were wheat, corn, and tobacco. Most of the most prestigious families were engaged in agriculture, as well as other things like trade, lead mining and salt production, and used slaves to work their crops. François Vallé II had the largest number of black and mulatto male slaves, twenty-four. Beneath the upper crust of society existed a large group of farmers (*habitants* or *cultivateurs*). These men owned few or no slaves and yet they produced sizeable quantities of wheat, corn, and tobacco. This

7. SGPR, Marriages, Book A : 148, 158; Book B : 31, 49, 77-78.

8. On the aristocratic commandants at Ste. Genevieve, see below, chap. xi.

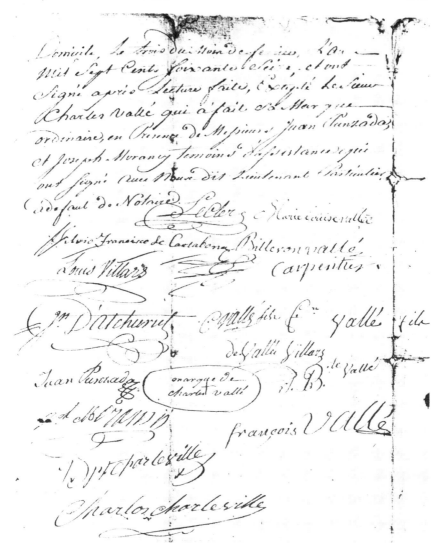

Signatures of principals and witnesses on the marriage contract of François Leclerc and Marie-Louise Vallé, 1776. Of the eight Vallés who signed this document, only one, Charles Vallé, nephew of François Vallé I, could not write his own name. Copy courtesy of Ste. Genevieve County Court.

group of sturdy yeomen farmers constituted the single largest economic and social category in colonial Ste. Genevieve and must be considered to have been the backbone of the community. They were not members of the upper crust but they freely associated with persons from the power elite and would have been scorned by no man in Upper Louisiana. Many of the Aubuchons, Deguires, and Lalumandières fell into this grouping.[9]

At the time of its first census, 1752, Ste. Genevieve had no craftsmen or artisans; all of the town's citizens were agriculturalists. By the end of the colonial era, however, there was a whole gamut of specialized craftsmen in town: blacksmiths, coopers, carpenters, masons, cartwrights, cabinetmakers, and even two goldsmiths. It is difficult to say exactly where these craftsmen and artisans fitted into the social rankings of Ste. Genevieve. Probably they were about on a par with the yeomen farmers. Because the craftsmen had no guilds and because the farmers lived in town rather than on isolated farmsteads there was no clear distinction between the two groups of citizens, and no town-country animosities split the community.[10]

All members of the social groups described above owned real estate of one kind or another — farm land, lot and workshop, personal residence, or a combination of these. Beneath these established landowners was a social group of less substantial persons: contract laborers (*engagés*) and day laborers (*journaliers*), and itinerant hunters, trappers, miners and boatmen. Sometimes these were young men from good families who had not yet settled down in the family enterprise; sometimes they were doubtless drifters and ne'er-do-wells. The large number of *voyageurs* and *journaliers* listed on the Ste. Genevieve militia roll in 1779 indicates that transient, landless men made up a large part of the town's population at that time. Although there were certainly exceptions, these men fell largely at the bottom of free, white society in colonial Ste. Genevieve.[11]

Black slaves as a group fell into a social category beneath all free, white society, although in rare cases a slave might possess more wealth than some white day laborers; slaves did occasionally purchase their own freedom. Their low legal and social status meant that female slaves were vulnerable to sexual exploitation

---

9. Census of 1791, *SRM,* 2:365-68.

10. Compare the census of 1752 (HMLO, 426) with that of New Bourbon in 1797 (PC 2365) for a glimpse of how the labor force in the Ste. Genevieve region changed during the second half of the eighteenth century.

11. Ste. Genevieve militia roster for 1779, PC 213.

and that male slaves could not participate in the town meetings that sometimes determined community policy.[12]

Within the ranks of the black slaves there were surely social gradations, although these are difficult to ascertain. Slaves belonging to powerful families, favorite domestic servants and concubines, perhaps mulattoes in general, had higher status than the average black field hand. The firearms that François Vallé II's slaves frequently carried must have served as emblems of their superior status in the pecking order of colonial Ste. Genevieve's black society.[13]

During the colonial era there were always large numbers of nomadic unmarried hunters, trappers, miners, and *voyageurs* living in Ste. Genevieve. Nonetheless, the established conjugal household was the basic building block of society in the colonial town. Married couples, whose marriages were prescribed in a civil contract and performed by a Roman Catholic priest, and legitimate children, baptized by a priest and raised in the household, were fundamental to Ste. Genevieve. This was true even though the family was not the neat and tidy affair familiar to our middleclass society. Families in colonial Ste. Genevieve were messier groupings parents, stepparents, grandparents, legitimate children, natural children, aunts, uncles, cousins, nephews, nieces, and often unrelated boarders likely to be mixed together in some combination or other within the same household. The corrected 1787 census for Ste. Genevieve (excluding slaves) shows the two most common household types to have been those consisting of a married couple and children (twenty-three percent) and those consisting of a married couple and children plus boarders (thirty-three percent).[14]

The traditional Christian marriage was central to family life and society in Ste. Genevieve. Marriage ceremonies were conducted in accordance with the canon law of the Roman Catholic Church as decreed by the Council of Trent in the sixteenth century, which meant that marriages were valid only if performed by a legitimate priest in the presence of witnesses.[15]

---

12. Concerning black slave society in colonial Ste. Genevieve, see below, chap. vii.

13. The controversy over slaves carrying firearms is dealt with in chap. xi, below.

14. MHS, archives. Concerning the 1787 census, see below, chap. viii, n. 3.

15. Baade, "Marriage Contracts," 13.

The fundamental civil law that governed wealth and power within families in colonial Ste. Genevieve was the *coutume de Paris*. This was the traditional matrimonial property law of north-central France, which was under the jurisdiction of the *Parlement de Paris* (a law court). This "law" did not exist as a single codified text but was rather a complex congeries of customary laws dating back to medieval times. A legal historian, Hans W. Baade, has referred to the *coutume de Paris* as a pattern of "French legal folkways." The French monarchy officially introduced the practices of the *coutume de Paris* to all Louisiana in 1712. Although the Spanish regime altered some aspects of matrimonial property law in Louisiana in order to make it conform to the laws of Castile, the *coutume de Paris* remained a vigorous model that governed civil marriage contracts in Ste. Genevieve throughout the colonial period.[16]

In all areas where the *coutume de Paris* was practiced, the marriage contract was vitally important because it was the chief instrument for transmitting family wealth. This was in contrast to regions, such as parts of southern France and Castile, where matrimonial property law was based upon the written Roman Law; in those areas the will rather than the marriage contract served as the principal device governing family wealth.[17]

In the absence of an official notary, marriage contracts in colonial Ste. Genevieve were almost always drafted by the civil commandant or *lieutenant particulier* in the presence of witnesses. The contracts generally contained the following provisions: 1) The married couple (*la compagnie conjugale*) pooled their wealth to form an economic community (*la communaté*). It was understood that upon the death of one spouse this community of family wealth would be divided, with one-half going to the surviving spouse and the other half to the legitimate adult children of the marriage, including the females. Upon the death of the second parent, the children received the remainder of the estate. Because legitimate female children inherited a share of their parents' wealth, dowries (*dots*) do not ordinarily appear in the marriage contracts.[18]

---

16. Olivier-Martin, *Histoire de la Coutume de la Prévoté et Vicomté de Paris;* Baade, 27, 68-69, 77.

17. Baade, 44-48; Olivier-Martin, 2:369. Billon (*Annals,* 1:88) was wrong in stating that the marriage laws of Paris and Castile were the same.

18. Most of the marriage contracts for colonial Ste. Genevieve are located in the SGA. François Vallé II's, however, is in the Vallé Collection (Box 1) at the MHS.

2) Although *dots* were not usual in marriage contracts governed by the *coutume de Paris, douaires préfixs* were always included. The *douaire préfix* was the amount of wealth dowered by the bridegroom to the bride, separate from the *communauté,* to provide for her support should her husband precede her in death. *Douaires préfixs* as stipulated in Ste. Genevieve marriage contracts varied depending upon the wealth of the respective families. In 1794, François Duquette provided the handsome sum of 3000 livres when he married Marie-Louise St. Gemme Bauvais.[19]

3) The *préciput* was another parcel of family wealth that marriage contracts decreed to be independent of the *communauté.* This sum, usually 500-1500 livres, was reserved for the benefit of either spouse upon the death of the other and was not included in the children's share of the estate's *partage.* Thus a wife whose husband preceded her in death would in law automatically receive, in addition to her share of the *communauté,* the *douaire préfix* and the *préciput* to provide for her future sustenance.[20]

According to the *coutume de Paris* as practiced in Louisiana, wives retained the right to renounce the marriage contract and withdraw their share of the *communauté* of goods and property. Sometimes this right of renunciation was specified in the marriage contract and sometimes not, but in any case the contract could not deny the wife's right of renunciation. This right protected the interests of the wife's family.[21]

Not all couples who were married in colonial Ste. Genevieve went to the trouble of drafting a civil contract of marriage. Among poorer folks, for whom disposition of family wealth was not of great importance, the civil contract was often dispensed with. The evidence strongly suggests, however, that the "French legal folkways" incorporated in the customary law of Paris were in fact the guiding rules that governed inheritance, even in marriages for which no formal civil contract was drafted.

In practice, the transmission of family property under the customary law of Paris was often a complicated affair, as it is under any legal system. After Madame François Billeron Vallé died in 1781, a complete inventory of the Vallé estate was compiled in order that the estate might be divided between her four adult

---

19. SGA, Marriage Contracts no. 59. *Douaires préfixs* usually ran between 1,000 and 3,000 livres.

20. Baade, 15-17. *Préciputs* usually ran between 500 and 1,500 livres.

21. Ibid., 17, 25.

children and her surviving husband. Her daughter, Marie-Louise Vallé Villars, had moved to New Orleans with her husband, however, and therefore the partage of the Vallé estate was postponed. François Vallé I then died in 1783 and his half of the total estate had to be included in the partage among the four legitimate children. François Vallé I also had a surviving natural daughter, Marguerite. She, as illegitimate, was not included in the *partage* of the family estate, but she had been taken care of earlier, at the time of her marriage to Louis Caron in 1778. Their marriage contract was unusual in that it contained a handsome dowry (*dot*) brought into the marriage community as a gift from her father. In this way, the illegitimate daughter, who could not technically inherit, received her share of the Vallé estate.[22]

The prohibition on inheritance by illegitimate children was occasionally lifted, however. Marie-Josette Deguire was the illegitimate daughter of Jean-Baptiste Deguire by an Indian slave woman. In 1781 Jean-Baptiste died in Ste. Genevieve, and Marie-Josette was living in town with her husband Pierre Verrau. Deguire had no legitimate children, and Marie-Josette petitioned the government, asking for his entire estate as his natural daughter. Lieutenant Governor Cruzat recognized her claim and granted her request, but there is some question as to what would have happened in this case if Deguire had had legitimate children. Probably Marie-Josette as an illegitimate mestizo would have been entirely excluded from the *partage* of the estate.[23]

Children in colonial Ste. Genevieve were legally minors until they reached the age of twenty-five years, and if one or both of their parents died while they were minors their financial interests were looked after by a legal guardian of some sort. When one parent died, the guardian of the minor children was generally the surviving parent; when both parents died, a gathering of "friends and relatives" selected guardians for the orphaned minors, and these guardians were usually either relatives or other reputable citizens.

A striking example of how estates were divided and the interests of minor children protected arose in 1774, when both Jacques Lacourse and his wife Charlotte died. They left five surviving

22. Vallé estate papers and the letter to Cruzat requesting postponement of the *partage* are in MHS, Vallé Collection, Box 1; Caron-Vallé marriage contract, SGA, Marriage Contracts, no. 32.

23. SGA, Estates, no. 80.

children and an estate worth 17,832 livres, 10 sous. Under the supervision of *lieutenant particulier* François Vallé I, the real and personal property of the estate was divided into five lots, and five slips of paper were numbered respectively 1 through 5. The slips were then given to a young boy, Henry Deguire, who scrambled them in his hat and handed one to each of the five heirs. How Henry, who was then only four years old, must have relished his participation in the world of adult affairs! The number that each heir received represented that individual's particular share of the estate. Two of the Lacourse children, Jacques *fils,* who was the oldest, and Marie, already married to Louis Lasource, received their shares outright. Elizabeth, who was twenty years old, also received her share but was assigned a *curateur,* Henri Carpentier, to assist her with its management. The youngest children, Antoine and Louise, were assigned Louis Lasource, their brother-in-law by virtue of his marriage to their older sister Marie, as *tuteur.* When Antoine reached the age of twenty-one he received his share of the estate along with a *curateur* to help him manage it. Louise got her share after she married Jean-Baptiste Bequet in 1778. It was a complicated system — but it seemed to work and it testifies to the concern that the townspeople had for the care of minor children and the equitable distribution of family wealth.[24]

As viewed through marriage contracts, marriages in colonial Ste. Genevieve were purely and simply financial agreements; they smacked nothing of the love and romance now associated with marriage. Of course, even if persons did occasionally marry out of blind passion, this passion would not have appeared in the marriage contract. Very largely, however, eighteenth-century sensibilities did not foster romantic marriages. Marriage without doubt presumed some measure of mutual attraction and affections, but for the most part marriages were intended to produce legitimate offspring and to further the economic interests of the respective families.

The Ste. Genevieve local records contain one case that might be called an affair of the heart, which, at the end of a fittingly romantic struggle, led to marriage. The orphaned teenager Louise Lacourse, who was being raised in the household of her *tuteur,* Louis Lasource, fell in love with Jean-Baptiste Bequet *fils.* Jean-Baptiste was a sound fellow with a good heart, although he was

---

24. Ibid., no. 136. Orphaned children under twenty-one years usually required *tuteurs,* while those twenty-one and over received *curateurs.*

something of a roughneck. He courted Louise, but Louis Lasource would not permit the couple to marry, for Louise was only twenty years old in 1778 and needed her *tuteur's* permission to marry. The young couple decided upon a dramatic course of action.[25]

On Sunday, November 1, 1778, All Saint's Day, the residents of Ste. Genevieve were basking in the sun of an Indian summer. Neither whites nor blacks worked on Sundays, for the Black Code designated the Sabbath as a day of rest for slaves. No one in Ste. Genevieve paid any particular attention to Baptiste, a black slave belonging to Louis Lasource, when he strolled across town and chatted briefly on the street with Jean-Baptiste Bequet *fils*. Baptiste was in fact carrying a message from Louise to her paramour Jean-Baptiste: meet me at the Big-Field rendezvous tonight and bring horses.

Sunday night Louise slipped out of the Lasource house unnoticed and met Jean-Baptiste, who was assisted by his cousin Jacques Boyer *fils,* as agreed upon. The couple mounted horses and took to the woods near the Old Town. Many persons in town were sympathetic to the plight of the youngsters, for a half-dozen persons assisted them with food and clothing during their ten days in the wilderness. Bequet *fils* also obviously had received his father's agreement for the "elopement," for no sooner had the couple disappeared into the woods than Bequet *père* appeared at the house of Louis Lasource to request, on his son's behalf, permission to marry Louise Lacourse. Lasource, however, remained obstinate and refused to grant the permission — at least at first.

The young couple were finally apprehended in the woods by civil lieutenant François Vallé I and questioned about their flight from town. Jean-Baptiste and Louise replied that they had intended harm to no one and that their only desire was to marry as soon as possible. At that point Louis Lasource was persuaded to relent and agree to the marriage, for on November 24, 1778 Jean-Baptiste Bequet and Louise Lacourse were married in the parish church of Ste. Genevieve. Three months later Louise became of age and received her share of her parent's estate, 3566 livres 14 sous, and by October 1779 the couple had their first child, Jean-Baptiste III. Jean-Baptiste and Louise lived happily thereafter. But thereafter was often a short period of time in colonial Ste. Genevieve, and by January 1786 Louise was dead of

---

25. This entire case is revealed in SGA, Marriage Contract, no. 144, which is not in fact a marriage contract at all.

one of the numerous maladies that afflicted eighteenth-century people. Jean-Baptiste Bequet II was destined to marry twice more in Ste. Genevieve, but he did not have much luck in marriage, losing three wives to early death within a five-year period.[26]

In the case of Jean-Baptiste Bequet and Louise Lacourse we have a marriage that was based upon mutual affection and mutual choice. How often this was true in colonial Ste. Genevieve is impossible to determine. Surely there were fewer arranged marriages in the Illinois Country than in France, but the important families in town probably exercised substantial influence when their young people selected mates. Peter Kalm observed that in French Canada "persons who wish to be married must have the consent of their parents. However, the judge may give them leave to marry if the parents oppose their union without any valid reason." Marriages in traditional societies usually represent alliances between families, and no doubt this was often the case in colonial Ste. Genevieve.[27]

Females in colonial Ste. Genevieve ususally married for the first time in their late teens, which was younger than in eighteenth-century Canada or France. This pattern of relatively early marriage for women in Ste. Genevieve was probably a consequence of the persistent shortage of white females in the community. Males married older than females, usually marrying for the first time in their mid-twenties, and virtually never before age twenty. Teenage males were required at home for family chores, and, moreover, there were not enough nubile white girls to go around. The corrected 1787 census, which lists sixty-three married couples, shows the average age of husbands to have been forty-one and of wives thirty-four. Of the sixty-three couples, in only eight cases were wives older than husbands.[28]

Favorite months for marriage in Ste. Genevieve were January, February, and November. The distinct seasonality of marriages was based upon two fundamental aspects of life in the town: it was an agricultural community and a Roman Catholic community. Couples married during the slack season for agricultural labors

26. SGPR, Marriages, Book A : 165; ibid., Baptisms, Book A : 94; inventory of Bequet estate, Jan. 18, 1786, SGA, Estates, no. 26.

27. Kalm, *The America of 1750*, 2:536. On marriage strategies in Old Regime France, see Bourdieu, "Marriage Strategies as Strategies of Social Reproduction," 117-44.

28. SGPR, Marriages; Charbonneau, 166-68; Henripin, *Population Canadienne*, 18; Goubert, "Historical Demography," 42; census of 1797, MHS, archives; Several wives listed in the 1787 census were Indian women.

but not often during Lent and Advent. Thus January was the favorite month for marriage, while December was the least popular month. Double marriages were common in colonial Ste. Genevieve as they were in French Canada. On February 13, 1798, for example, two children of Jean-Baptiste St. Gemme Bauvais married — Vital to Marie-Thérèse Pratte, and Thérèse to Pascal Detchemendy. And on November 13, 1798 two sons of André Deguire II married — Louis to Mary Dodge, and Jean-Baptiste to Eulalie Bernier. Such double marriages served to buttress the extended family social structure in the community.[29]

Marriages, even of young folks, ended with death rather than divorce in colonial Ste. Genevieve because divorce as such was not possible for the Roman Catholic citizens of the town. In extreme circumstances and rarely, however, the civil authorities would grant legal "separation of goods and persons." In 1770, Genevieve Heneaux, daughter of one of Ste. Genevieve's founding fathers, Antoine Heneaux, asked Lieutenant Governor Piernas in St. Louis for an official separation from her husband Louis Courtois. François Vallé I investigated the case on Pierna's behalf, and on the basis of this investigation Piernas found no reason to grant Geneviève Heneaux's request. Rather, Piernas directed Geneviève to rejoin her husband and ordered Geneviève's mother Charlotte Chassin Heneaux to cease disturbing the tranquility of her daughter's household. End of case, with Lieutenant Governor Piernas functioning as judge, jury, and marriage counselor.[30]

A much more serious case arose, however, in 1783. Pélagie Carpentier Vallé, wife of Charles Vallé and daughter-in-law of *lieutenant particulier* François Vallé I, asked Lieutenant Governor Cruzat for a separation on the following grounds: her husband was continually drunk; he beat her; he gambled; he kept a mulatto mistress in Kaskaskia; he had fornicated several times with his mistress in his wife's presence and threatened to kill his wife should she divulge his activities; he was alienating property belonging to the *communauté* of their marriage. In short, Charles Vallé, member of Ste. Genevieve's best family and defender of St. Louis in 1780, was guilty of a "débauche continuelle."[31]

---

29. SGPR, Marriages, Book B : 47-48, 53-54. The seasonality of marriages in French Canada (Charbonneau, *Vie et Mort,* 181) was similar to that in colonial Ste. Genevieve.

30. SGA, Marriage Contracts, no. 41 a.

31. This case is found in SGA, Marriage Contracts, 138 a and b.

Charles Vallé did not contest his wife's charges or fight her request for a legal separation, even though their marriage contract did not contain the formal renunciation clause. The *communaute* of Charles Vallé and Pélagie Carpentier was divided, and, in addition to her share, Pélagie was granted resources to support their two children, who were nine and three. Charles soon left Ste. Genevieve and moved to Lower Louisiana. He died at Opelousas in 1796, a man who was perhaps broken by the demands of being scion-apparent to an important family.[32]

By the mid-1790s, with the arrival in the Ste. Genevieve District of many Americans, there was a sharp increase in the number of disintegrating marriages. In 1795 Lieutenant Governor Trudeau sent commandant François Vallé II instructions from "Monsieur le curé" [?], which were supposed to "prevent the scandal of divorces *volontaires*. The pressures of frontier life may have been driving men and women apart in Ste. Genevieve toward the end of the colonial period, but it is clear that divorce was never a major social problem in the French Canadian and creole community.[33]

The customary law of Paris and the marriage and separation proceedings from local civil records provide some basis upon which to speculate about the position of women in colonial Ste. Genevieve. Marriage contracts make it clear that wives, with rights to *douaire prefix, preciput* and at least one-half of the *partage* of the family estate, had much financial security and were in general the economic equals of their husbands. When important family business was conducted — the sale or purchase of real estate or a slave — husband and wife were considered co-owners and both signed the contract of exchange.

François Vallé I's wife, Marianne Billeron Vallé, had a large hand in family financial dealings. She traveled to St. Louis to transact family business, and at public auctions in Ste. Genevieve she appeared in person to bid along with other citizens of the town. In December 1777, for example, Madame Vallé bought at auction the estate of Philippe de Rocheblave, the former town commandant. The minutes of that auction, which describe Mme. Vallé out there in front of the parish church matching wits and trading bids with her male competitors, certainly convey the im-

---

32. Ibid.; for more on Charles Vallé, see above, chap. iii.
33. Trudeau to Vallé, Apr. 20, 1795, MHS, Vallé Collection, Box 2.

pression that women were very much the equal of men in colonial Ste. Genevieve, and that economic status was much more important than sex in determining a person's position in the community.[34]

The wives' financial equality, insofar as it existed, was rooted in the fact that in marriage contracts wives represented another family (the Billerons in Mme. Vallé's case), which wished to protect its interests when one of its members married. It would be wrong to think that society in colonial Ste. Genevieve was precociously modern in its view of sexual equality. Probably when Mme. Vallé conducted family business and participated in auction sales she did so only with her husband's explicit permission. That would have been in accordance with the traditional *coutume de Paris*, and, from another family in Ste. Genevieve, there is an example of such permission being granted. When in 1774 the lead miner Pierre Gadobert left Ste. Genevieve on business, he expressly stated in an affidavit that he had turned his affairs over to the charge of his wife, Anne Normand Gadobert. Thus, the business activities of wives in Ste. Genevieve seem to have been contingent on their husbands' permission, but once that permission was granted the wives did excercise real financial power.[35]

The *communauté*, the common ownership of family property by husband and wife, was *the* central concern of marriage contracts in colonial Ste. Genevieve. In practice, however, the *coutume de Paris* gave husbands more control than wives over the *communauté* When, for example, Charles Vallé was squandering his family's fortune on wine, women, and cards, his wife Pélagie was obliged to sue for a legal separation in order to stop the hemorrhage and preserve the integrity of the family estate. There is no evidence that François Vallé I needed his wife's agreement to provide his bastard daughter with a substantial dowry (three black slaves and an arpent of land), which certainly was conveyed at the expense of the family *communauté*. Given the fact that the daughter was raised within the Vallé household, Mme. Vallé probably would have agreed in any case, but such agreement may not have been necessary within the context of French legal folkways.[36]

The case of François Vallé I's bastard daughter, Marguerite,

---

34. Rocheblave auction, December 1777, MHS, Vallé Collection, Box 1. On the legal status of married women in French Louisiana, see Baker et al., "Le Mari est Seigneur."

35. See SGA, Mines, no. 24, no. 25.

36. For Marguerite Vallé's dowry, see SGA, Marriage Contracts, no. 32.

raises a collateral issue about rights, privileges, and power within the family. While Marguerite, as François's daughter, was raised within the Vallé household as a legitimate daughter would have been, it is difficult to conceive of the situation reversed, with a bastard child of the wife being accepted in the household by the husband. And while men in Ste. Genevieve did take black concubines it is unimaginable that their wives took black lovers. Black women, not white women, bore the mulatto children. Thus women of the community were indeed the victims of a double standard; what husbands could often do, wives could not.[37]

After Cruzat had granted Pélagie Carpentier Vallé a separation from Charles Vallé, an interesting case of child custody arose that reveals much about the position of women in colonial Ste. Genevieve. Pélagie had plans to gather up her two children and return to Canada, from whence she had come to the Illinois Country. Hearing of this plan, Charles Vallé's two brothers, François and Jean-Baptiste, petitioned Cruzat to forbid Pélagie to remove their nephew and niece from Ste. Genevieve. François and Jean-Baptiste argued that Pélagie should not subject the children to the hardships of a journey to Canada, and that if Pélagie were determined to make the trip the children should be left in Ste. Genevieve to be raised "in the bosom of our family." Cruzat, who had granted Pélagie's request for a separation, immediately authorized the Vallé brothers to seize her children should she attempt to take them out of Upper Louisiana. The larger rights of the extended family prevailed over the personal feelings and interests of the mother. Pélagie's two children did live on and marry in Ste. Genevieve. Pélagie herself disappeared from the historical record in 1783 and perhaps did flee back to Canada, leaving her two children to be raised by her brothers-in-law.[38]

The French legal historian, François Olivier-Martin, remarked that in the regions governed by the *coutume de Paris* "very ancient traditions gave the husband power over his wife that approached harshness." This observation does *not* accurately portray the domestic situation in colonial Ste. Genevieve. It seems apparent that on the trans-Mississippi frontier, where white women were scarce, wives were better off than they were in north-central France. Brackenridge noted that "the women make faithful and

37. Concerning black concubines, see below, chap. vii.

38. See Vallé brothers' petition and Cruzat's decree in SGA, Marriage Contracts, no. 138 a.

affectionate wives, but will not be considered secondary personages in the matrimonial association."[39]

Women in colonial Ste. Genevieve acquired most power and authority as widows. Although they were usually called widow so-and-so, and thus lost the identity of their own family and Christian names, widows had full rights to conduct business, make contracts, and serve as legal witnesses. When François Leclerc died in 1789, his widow, Marie-Louise Vallé Leclerc, who was henceforth called Widow Leclerc, inherited an estate worth over 50,000 livres with which to raise her two children. This large estate meant that Widow Leclerc was one of the powerful figures in the community. Widows such as Marie-Louise Vallé Leclerc may even have had the legal right to participate in civic political deliberations where community issues were discussed and often voted upon, although they do not seem to have done so in colonial Ste. Genevieve. Madame Leclerc thrived on widowhood and outlived her husband by thirty-seven years, dying in 1826 at age eighty-seven, matriarch of the town.[40]

---

39. Olivier-Martin, 2:182; Brackenridge, *Views of Louisiana,* 135.

40. Inventory of Leclerc estate, Sep. 3, 1792, SGA, Estates no. 166. Widows did not always go by their late husbands' surnames, however. Elizabeth Aubuchon Lasource, for example, was called Widow Aubuchon after her husband Dominique Lasource died in 1773. SGPR, Burials, Book 2:135. In southern France, where the customs of Paris were not employed, the husband's will governed family wealth, and widows had less power and autonomy (see Davis, *Martin Guerre,* 30-31).

Chapter VII
Black Slavery French Style

WHEN FRENCHMEN WERE ESTABLISHING COLONIES in the
New World, chattel slavery had disappeared from Western
Europe. The reknowned French jurist, Antoine Loisel, declared
in 1608 that all Frenchmen were free. Yet at the same time most
Europeans accepted the enslavement of non-European pagans as
a perfectly normal aspect of civilized Christian society. There were
few critics of slavery in the seventeenth century, and slaves were
routinely used in European colonies, in the Americas and elsewhere, when such usage was deemed profitable.[1]

French colonies in the New World were chronically short of
labor. Indian slaves were used in Canada as early as the 1670s,
and there were even spasmodic attempts to bring black slaves to the
St. Lawrence Valley. But it was in the Antilles of the Caribbean,
the famed and lucrative Sugar Islands, where French slavery
flourished most luxuriantly during the course of the seventeenth
and eighteenth centuries. Sugar cane was brought into Martinique,
Guadeloupe, and Saint- Domingue from Brazil about 1640, and
at the same time black slaves were introduced to the islands. The
indigenous Indian population in the Caribbean had not proved
satisfactory as a slave labor force: there were too few Indians,
especially after such devastating European diseases as smallpox
began to take their toll, and the Indians were temperamentally
unsuited for slavery because they had not been pre-conditioned

---

1. The best introduction to slavery in the western world is Davis, *The Problem
of Slavery in Western Culture*. For a broader, more speculative approach, see
Patterson, *Slavery and Social Death*.

for it by their own cultures. Black Africans, on the other hand, better withstood European diseases and had become accustomed to the institution of slavery within Africa. During the course of the seventeenth century, black slave labor became as much a part of the human landscape of the Caribbean Islands as sugar cane was of the physical landscape.[2]

French colonists in Louisiana sought a supply of black slave labor from the earliest days of the colony. The heat and insects of the Gulf Coast were punishing for men accustomed to the temperate climate of France, and orphans, convicts and vagabonds sent as laborers to Louisiana died in droves. The experience of the plantation owners on the Sugar Islands taught colonists in Louisiana to look to black Africans to fill their need for labor. Years before New Orleans was founded in 1718, Jean-Baptiste Le Moyen de Bienville, first royal governor of Louisiana, conceived an interesting scheme to supply black slaves for his colony. He looked about himself and saw an abundance of North American Indian flesh that might be harnessed for some useful purpose, and he proposed to the royal government in France that an exchange might be arranged whereby Indians could be traded for blacks. The Indians in Louisiana did not serve well as slaves there because they had a habit of fleeing back to their native tribes, but Bienville reckoned that the Indians could be put to good use elsewhere. Louis XIV's ministers, however, were having none of Bienville's salesmanship and in 1710 they bluntly informed him that if the French colonists in Louisiana wanted black slaves they would have to pay for them in sound merchandise or hard cash. In any event, a scattering of black slaves had arrived in Louisiana, probably via the Caribbean Islands, as early as 1712.[3]

When the first French-Canadian missionaries and fur traders settled near the mouth of the Kaskaskia River in 1703, they did not bring slaves with them from Canada. Thus the first black slaves to arrive in the Illinois Country came from Lower Louisiana via the Mississippi. By 1719, shortly after New Orleans was founded, several shiploads of blacks arrived in Louisiana under the auspices of the Company of the West, which was the royal chartered company that had assumed control of the colony in

2. Martin, *Histoire de l'esclavage dans les colonies françaises,* 11-32; Trudel, *L'Esclavage au Canada français,* 19-36.

3. Minister to Bienville, May 10, 1710, abstract of letter in BN, nouvelles acquisitions 9310:141; Usner, "From African Captivity to American Slavery," 26; Hardy, "Transportation of Convicts to Colonial Louisiana," 207-20.

1717. It seems likely that Jesuit missionaries were the first owners of black slaves in the Illinois Country. Slaves were in short supply, and there was a heavy demand for them. The Jesuits with their substantial financial resources and powerful political connections were in the best position to purchase slaves and have them shipped up the Mississippi. In the French archives there is a description of Illinois dating from 1720 that mentions the Jesuits to be the owners of sixteen to eighteen slaves, "negros and savages." It is impossible to determine from this description the number of black slaves in this grouping, but the Society of Jesus in Kaskaskia was surely the single largest owner of slaves in the Illinois Country at that early time.[4]

The Jesuits used their slaves principally as agricultural laborers and domestic servants, but there were plans to use slave labor on other projects. The most important of these was mining. For years the French had known about the lead mines in what are now St. Francois and Washington counties in Missouri and they fervently hoped to find silver there as well. All Frenchmen who were interested in these mining operations agreed that black slaves were required to work the mines, for the work was both backbreaking and dangerous. It was once thought that an early French lead miner, Philippe Renaut, brought literally *hundreds* of black slaves up the Mississippi to work his mines in Missouri. Given the meager supply of blacks in Louisiana during the 1720s, Renaut would have had to have commandeered virtually every slave in the entire colony in order to have employed the 500 slaves he has been credited with having. Nonetheless, Renaut was certainly one of the early and important slave holders in the upper Mississippi River Valley, and the 1726 census of the Illinois Country listed twenty blacks in his possession.[5]

In October 1720, sieur de Boisbriant, royal commandant at Fort de Chartres, wrote from Kaskaskia that "100 negros would be marvelous for this settlement [i.e. the Illinois Country]." Boisbriant went on to explain that black slaves could be used in clearing land

---

4. Usner, "African Captivity," 25-28; "Etat de la Louisiana au mois de Juin, 1720," AG A¹ 2592:93.

John Mason Peck, an abolitionist, was the first person to present a history of slavery in Illinois. He did so in a series of newspaper articles written in 1847, and his first several articles dealt with slavery in the Illinois Country during the French regime. See Bridges (ed.), "John Mason Peck on Illinois Slavery," 179-217.

5. Alvord, *The Illinois Country*, 154, 202, n. 34; Maduell (ed.) *Census Tables*, 57.

for agricultural purposes and that Illinois would then be able to furnish foodstuffs for most of Louisiana. Boisbriant never received the requested 100 blacks, but it is clear that a number of black slaves was brought into the Illinois Country during the 1720s.[6]

In April 1721, Governor Bienville reported the arrival in Biloxi of three slaving ships from the coast of Angola. These slavers contained a cargo of 925 black slaves, and though many were ill Bienville was confident that a diet of maize (which Frenchmen did not normally eat) would soon restore the blacks to good health. We know that some of these blacks wound up in Illinois, for one month after the arrival of the slave ships in Louisiana Bienville commented on the allocation of the newly arrived blacks: "The distribution has been made with great fairness. The colonists from Illinois who were in the lower colony have participated and are willing to testify to it. . . . Forty of these negroes are reserved to row in the boats that will ascend [the Mississippi] to the Illinois Country." From Bienville's report it is impossible to determine if all forty of the black oarsmen had been allotted permanently to settlers from Illinois. However, given the fact that these settlers had traveled to Biloxi for the distribution of slaves, it seems likely that many of the blacks were destined to remain in Illinois.[7]

A detailed, though not entirely accurate, census of the Illinois Country was conducted in 1732. The total human population of the entire region, from Cahokia in the north to Kaskaskia in the south, was 471. This number included men, women, and children; white, red, and black; free and slave. The black slaves, adults and children, numbered 168, which means that they constituted somewhat more than one-third of the total population of the Illinois Country. The Society of Jesus in Kaskaskia and Philippe Renaut at his mine in Missouri were the largest slave holders, each commanding twenty-two blacks. Renaut's black slaves were the first black inhabitants of what is today the state of Missouri. They were not, however, permanent residents on the west side of the Mississippi, for the lead mining operations there were only seasonal in nature and Renaut's enterprise soon collapsed. When Antoine Valentin de Gruy visited the Missouri lead mines in 1743, Renaut was long gone and no black laborers remained at the diggings.[8]

---

6. Boisbriant to Company of the Indies?, Oct. 3, 1720, AG, A¹2592:97-98.

7. Bienville to Company of the Indies?, Apr. 25, 1721, A¹2592:106-08.

8. Maduell (ed.), *Census Tables,* 151-53; Ekberg, "Antoine Valentin de Gruy," 146.

The 1737 census of the Illinois Country listed a total of 314 blacks, indicating that the black population of the region had almost doubled in five years. This marked increase was due largely to continuing imports of blacks from Lower Louisiana rather than an exploding birth rate within the existing black population of Illinois, for the ratio of children to adults was about the same in 1732 and 1737. Yet life for slaves was certainly less harsh in the Illinois Country than on the Caribbean Islands; if blacks were not reproducing rapidly in Illinois during the 1730s they at least were not dying like flies as they did on the notorious sugar plantations in the West Indies.

In 1747, Governor Vaudrueil of Louisiana issued an order forbidding all shipments of blacks and mulattoes from "New Orleans and other places on the lower river to Illinois." Vaudrueil explained that slaves shipped north up the Mississippi could not readily be replaced in the lower colony (war with England was disrupting commerce on the high seas) and that the slaves working in the area around New Orleans were being used more efficiently than they could be used in Illinois; presumably Vaudreuil meant that the larger the agricultural enterprise the more efficient slave labor was, and plantations on the lower river thus got first priority in the allocation of black slaves. It is not known how effective Vaudreuil's order was. But the persistent warfare between England and France for the duration of the French regime in Louisiana meant that there was a general shortage of slaves in the colony and that few were shipped north to the Illinois Country. Increases in the black slave population of Illinois after 1747 were therefore generated largely by reproduction within the existing population.[10]

Major Macarty's census of 1752 listed 768 Europeans, 445 black slaves, and 147 Indian slaves for the entire Illinois Country. It is therefore clear that by the time that the village of Ste. Genevieve emerged as a distinct community on the west bank of the Mississippi (ca. 1750) there was a large population of black slaves in the Illinois Country.[11]

The census of 1752 showed two adult slaves in Ste. Genevieve. Over the following two decades this number grew dramatically, as did the European population of the new town. Captain Philip

9. Census of 1737, AN, C[13]C, 4:197.

10. Vaudreuil's order, May 1, 1737, AN, F[3],243:13.

11. HMLO 426.

Pittman reported that in 1766 François Vallé *père,* Ste. Genevieve's leading citizen, had "one hundred negroes, besides hired white people, constantly employed." Pittman grossly exaggerated the number of Vallé's blacks, but in any case it is clear that Vallé had a large enough mass of black slaves to make a big impression upon the English officer. Data on Ste. Genevieve's black population are less complete, and probably more imprecise, than those on the white population, yet there is substantial documentation available concerning the blacks. The following figures derive from extant Spanish censuses of Ste. Genevieve:[12]

1773

Total human population 676
Total number of black and mulatto slaves . 276   (41% of total)

1787

Total human population 670
(including 10 free blacks and mulattos)
Total number of black and mulatto slaves . 256   (38% of total)

1800 (Ste. Genevieve District)

Total human population 1,163
(including 5 free blacks and mulattos)
Total number of black and mulatto slaves . 350   (30% of total)

The lower proportion of blacks in the 1800 census probably does not reveal a declining proportion of black slaves within the town of Ste. Genevieve per se, but rather the fact that recent American immigrants to the outlying regions of the district were not great slave holders. Census figures suggest that throughout the colonial period about forty percent of the town's population consisted of black slaves, and in every eighteenth century census of Spanish Illinois Ste. Genevieve had a higher proportion of black slaves than did its sister settlement of St. Louis.[13]

The heretofore neglected black people of colonial Ste. Genevieve deserve study, not only because they made up a significant segment of the town's population but because their history sheds new light on the history of the entire town and its people. What C. Vann Woodward wrote about Southerners and blacks

---

12. Pittman, *European Settlements,* 50; census of 1773, *SRM,* 1:61; census of 1787, MHS archives; census of 1800, *SRM,* 1:facing 414.

13. This was because Ste. Genevieve was preponderantly agricultural.

applies just as well to the two principal races of colonial Ste. Genevieve: "They . . . shaped each other's destiny, determined each other's isolation, shared and molded a common culture. It is, in fact, impossible to imagine the one without the other and quite futile to try."[14]

Historical records do not reveal much movement of black slaves into or out of colonial Ste. Genevieve, although there was some trading with external markets and sources. When the Bauvais brothers, Jean-Baptiste and Vital, moved to Ste. Genevieve from Kaskaskia in the late 1780s they brought with them a substantial number of black and mulatto slaves, twenty and thirteen respectively. For the most part, however, the 350 slaves that lived and worked in Ste. Genevieve in 1800 were descendants of the 276 slaves that appeared on the 1773 census. It is virtually impossible to trace the lives of individual slaves because they had no surnames, but civil and parish records do permit us to make some general observations about the black population in the community.[15]

Although both French and Spanish law encouraged masters to have their slaves marry, only fourteen black slave marriages were recorded in the colonial parish records of Ste. Genevieve. Significantly, the last one took place in 1783, which suggests that masters increasingly discouraged marriages among their slaves. The reason for this was probably that under both French and Spanish law it was illegal to break up a conjugal slave family by selling individual members, and thus it was in the masters' commercial interests to discourage slave marriages. Being obliged to buy and sell slaves in family units was an impediment to sharp business practice.[16]

Documents are not available from which to derive a clear picture of the black slave family, such as it existed, in colonial Ste. Genevieve. The fact that few slave marriages were formalized by church ceremony does not necessarily mean that there were not sustained conjugal relationships between black men and women, although such relationships are difficult to trace. Of the somewhat less than 500 black and mulatto children baptized in Ste. Genevieve during the colonial period, only about eleven percent of them had both parents listed in their baptismal record. This may mean that sexual relations were so casual among black slaves that the fathers

---

14. Woodward, quoted in Genovese, *Roll, Jordan, Roll,* xv.

15. *SMV.* 2:290.

16. SGPR, Marriages.

of the children were not known. More likely, however, it reveals that the parish priests simply did not list fathers unless the parents of the child had been formally married in the church. In any case, the constitution of the black slave family in colonial Ste. Genevieve remains an elusive aspect of the town's social history.[17]

According to the civil censuses and the parish records the black population of colonial Ste. Genevieve was healthy and vigorous enough to perpetuate itself, and even to sustain some modest growth. Although the figures are only approximate, the parish records show a birth-to-death ratio for black slaves of 1.36 from 1780 through 1804, compared to a ratio of 1.66 for the white population during the same period. Because blacks were generally less well fed, clothed, and housed than whites they were more vulnerable to diseases such as pneumonia and influenza. On the other hand, blacks withstood malaria better than whites. Many were immune to the *vivax* species, and they also tolerated *falciparum* better than did whites. At birth, life expectancy for black slaves in Ste. Genevieve was less than twenty-five years, compared to about twenty-seven for whites. But in regard to health, diet, standard of living, and longevity the black slaves of colonial Ste. Genevieve were perhaps as well off, relative to their white masters, as any slaves on earth during the eighteenth century. Edmund Flagg, with a touch of the newspaperman's hyperbole, remarked in the mid-1830s that the slaves he had seen in the French communities of the Mississippi Valley were "a sleeker, fleshier, happier-looking set of mortals" than any he had seen elsewhere in the West.[18]

The black slavery practiced in Ste. Genevieve throughout the colonial period was a Franco-Spanish brand of slavery. To understand this system of human bondage, it is necessary to begin by commenting upon the famous *Code Noir*, the Black Code. This law code was first promulgated by the French crown for the West Indian Islands in 1685. It was reissued, *mutatis mutandis*, for French Louisiana in 1724, and was reaffirmed by the Spanish Governor Alexandro O'Reilly in 1769.[19]

17. SGPR, Baptisms.

18. SGPR, Baptisms and Burials; on the resistance of blacks to malaria, see Rutman, "Agues and Fevers," 35; Flagg, "The Far West," 56.

19. "Edit concernant les Nègres à la Louisiane," 75-90; in a stimulating article ("The Law of Slavery in Spanish Luisiana," 54), Hans Baade has raised the

The Black Code was a product of the centralizing Bourbon monarchy in France. Although not promulgated until two years after Jean-Baptiste Colbert's death in 1683, the code was established by the legal reforms instituted in France by that ramrod of Louis XIV's bureaucracy. Historians have argued about whether the intention of the Black Code was humanitarian or whether the code was simply a hardheaded legal-economic document. The word humanitarian did not exist in the seventeenth century, and, moreover, Colbert was not the sort of person to sit around fretting about the plight of unfortunate slaves. Surely the eminent French historian of slavery, Gaston-Martin, was correct to argue that the intention of the code was purely economic and not at all humanitarian. However, it must also be acknowledged that enlightened economic interest (which the code represented) and more humane treatment of slaves were not necessarily incompatible.[20]

The Black Code defined the legal status of French black slaves: they were chattels that could be bought and sold like other personal property. Yet the code also clearly recognized slaves as human beings. Colbert and Louis XIV were not racial supremacists who attempted to justify slavery on racial grounds. Indeed, there was no need for them to adopt that position for the simple reason that there was no need to justify or explain slavery. The compulsion to justify slavery on one ground or another was more characteristic of the Anglo-Saxon sensibility and the eighteenth-century frame-of-mind. To seventeenth-century Frenchmen like Colbert, the institution of human bondage was part and parcel of human society; it was normal and usual and therefore did not have to be justified. Like all documents drafted under Colbert's auspices, the Black Code is a dispassionate and tightly reasoned document — reasoned to serve not the slaves, nor even their masters, but rather the interests of the absolute French state.[21]

The Code is a lengthy document containing fifty-five articles, which make the following salient points: slaves had to be properly housed, clothed, and fed; slave children could not be sold away

---

question of the exact significance of O'Reilly's reaffirmation of the Black Code, especially for Lower Louisiana.

20. Eccles, *France in America*, 152; Martin, *Histoire de l'esclavage*, 25-30. On the Black Code in Lower Louisiana, see McGowan, "Creation of a Slave Society," chaps. i, ii.

21. Concerning the acceptance of slavery during the sixteenth and seventeenth centuries, see Davis, *The Problem of Slavery*, 106-07, 118-21, 191-92.

from their parents until they had arrived at puberty; masters could whip and bind their slaves, but the slaves could not be imprisoned, mutilated, or put to death without due process of the law; slaves could not be worked before sunrise or after sunset; old and infirm slaves had to be cared for; slave women were not to be sexually exploited; slaves were to be baptized and instructed in the Christian (i.e. Roman Catholic) faith; slaves could not carry firearms, or even "large sticks"; slaves were to be encouraged to marry with their masters' consent but could not be compelled to marry against their will; interracial marriage and cohabitation were forbidden; masters could not manumit slaves without government permission. Finally, the code provided slaves with the right to take their masters to court at no cost if they felt that their masters were abusing them in violation of other articles. If not the entire code, this last provision was surely an example of Colbert's over-confidence in the ability of government to control the actions of refractory men. It is difficult to imagine a black slave in French Louisiana bringing suit against his master for breach of the Black Code.[22]

Whether the Black Code was genuinely effective in regulating relations between French colonists and their black slaves is a grave question. Some colonial administrators in Louisiana took the code seriously, however, and attempted to enforce it. In 1751 Governor Vaudreuil issued on behalf of King Louis XV of France a "Règlement sur la police pour la province de la Louisiane." In eighteenth-century France the word "police" did not have the narrow meaning that we assign to it; rather it meant everything concerned with the upkeep, cleanliness, and security of the public domain. Vaudreuil's "Règlement" of 1751 dealt mostly with slavery. The thirty-first article referred "all other matters pertaining to negros to the Black Code, which has provided for all cases." Once again we encounter the French bureaucrat's confidence that if the laws are on the books everything is provided for.[23]

In any case, the "Règlement" of 1751 reflected Vaudreuil's ruminations about how to strike a proper balance between severity and humanity in dealing with black slaves. Few French colonials in the

---

22. Article II, "Edit concernant les Nègres," 81; on the administration of the Black Code in French Louisiana, see two recent studies: Brasseaux, "The Administration of Slave Regulations in French Louisiana," 139-58; Allain, "Slave Policies in French Louisiana," 127-37.

23. "Règlement," AN, C^{13}A, 35:40-51; Allain, 127. Concerning Vaudreuil's "Règlement" and its enforcement in Lower Louisiana, see McGowan, "Creation of a Slave Society," 145-55.

Mississippi Valley meditated upon this issue the way Vaudreuil did, but the governor was experiencing some of the confusion of modern parents, who seem to be losing control of their children and do not know whether to react by becoming more severe or more permissive. Vaudreuil clearly felt that Louisiana colonists were losing their grip on their slaves, and his "Règlement" represented an effort to clamp down on such nefarious activities as consumption of alcohol, nocturnal roaming, frequenting of disreputable establishments (operated by freed negroes), and reckless horse racing. One can well imagine modern American parents drawing up a similar list about their children. Indeed, the "Règlement" of 1751 was expressly paternal in its wording, Article 19 admonishing slave owners to discipline their negroes "en bon père de famille," as a good father of the family. Yet Article 28 brings us back to the realities of eighteenth-century slave-holding society, for that article prescribes "fifty lashes and branding of the *fleur-de-lys* on the buttocks for any negro or other slave who is insolent, forgets he is a slave, and does not show appropriate submissiveness." After all, a good father must not spare the rod or, in this case, the branding iron.[24]

The patently paternal attitude of the French colonists toward their black slaves was best expressed in the writings of Le Page du Pratz. Du Pratz was one of the many Netherlanders who took France as his adopted country during the Old Regime. In 1718, the year New Orleans was founded, Du Pratz sailed for French Louisiana to make his fortune. He failed in this attempt and returned to France in 1734, disenchanted with colonial adventures. Du Pratz did not, however, lose interest in Louisiana and during the 1750s he began to write about the colony in which he had once lived. The most important of his writings on Louisiana was published in Paris in 1758 under the title, *Histoire de la Louisiane*. This title was a bit of a misnomer, for large sections of this "history" contain practical advice for persons considering immigration to Louisiana. One of these sections tells the French colonist how to handle black slaves, and this portion of Du Pratz's *Histoire* gives us a fair indication of what eighteenth-century Frenchmen thought about their slaves.[25]

Du Pratz's advice on handling slaves echoed much of the *Code*

---

24. "Règlement," 35: 46, 49-50.

25. Louisiana State University Press has recently published a facsimile of the 1774 English edition, *History of Louisiana*, edited by Joseph G. Tregle.

Noir on such matters as careful attendance to the slaves' physical and spiritual needs. Du Pratz's views were, however, less coldly bureaucratic and more personal and specific. For example, he was persuaded that blacks smelled differently and stronger than Europeans and recommended that slave owners prudently locate their slave quarters in accordance with the prevailing winds so that the owners "be as little incommoded as possible with their natural smell. . . ." But, although Du Pratz took some time to delineate physiological differences between blacks and whites, he never continued on this tack to the point of claiming that blacks were racially inferior. As with most eighteenth-century Frenchmen, Du Pratz did not justify slavery on racial grounds but deemed it part of the natural order of the universe. Indeed, when paternally discussing the housing for "my people" after he had settled upon his concession at Natchez, Du Pratz seemed to lump French *engagés,* Indian slaves, and black slaves altogether as indistinguishable members of his "family" of laborers. Du Pratz concluded his *Histoire de la Louisiane* with the remark that "one may, by attention and humanity, easily manage negroes; and, as an inducement, one has the satisfaction to draw great advantage from their labors." This remark is probably an accurate summation of the enlightened French colonists' view of their black slaves: practical, reasonable, non-racist, and unsentimental.[26]

Under the Spanish regime in Louisiana, black slaves in Ste. Genevieve continued to be sold "in conformity to the Black Code." But simple reference to the Black Code did not solve all problems relating to black slavery in Upper Louisana — far from it. First, on some critical issues the Black Code conflicted with Spanish laws and practices. The French code proscribed miscegenation, which had never much bothered the Spaniards, and also discouraged slaves from purchasing their own freedom, which Spanish laws specifically condoned. Second, the Black Code did not prove to be an instrument that could, in Governor Vaudrueil's hopeful words, "provide for all cases" pertaining to black slaves in Louisiana. Vaudrueil's own "Règlement" of 1751, plus a continuing flow of local, regional, and provincial decrees dealing with blacks and black-white relations, attest to three facts: the Black Code was often not enforced; it was largely unenforceable; and slavery constituted the most difficult legal and social problem in

---

26. Le Page du Pratz, *History of Louisiana,* 382.

colonial Louisiana.[27]

Between 1776 and 1781, during Cruzat's two terms as lieutenant governor of Spanish Illinois, he issued four ordinances dealing with blacks in Upper Louisiana. These forbade whites from fraternizing with blacks or supplying them with alcoholic beverages; forbade blacks from crossing the Mississippi without first obtaining permission from their masters and the commandant; forbade blacks from leaving their cabins after the sounding of retreat in the evening or from holding nocturnal assemblies; forbade blacks from dresssing "in barbarous fashion, adorning themselves with vermillion and many feathers." Cruzat's ordinances suggest that the black population in Spanish Illinois was giving the lieutenant governor the jitters, that he expected the blacks at any minute to become rebellious and threaten the stability of his regime. Cruzat's apprehensions were unfounded, however, for there was never a slave revolt in Upper Louisiana.[28]

Local regulations for black slaves in the Ste. Genevieve District were promulgated under the Spanish regime in 1794. François Vallé II had just become town commandant when he issued these regulations, which have been preserved in the town archives. None of them contravene the Black Code, and most of them are reaffirmations of ordinances that Lieutenant Governor Cruzat had earlier issued: blacks were required to have passports in order to cross the Mississippi; they were forbidden to congregate in their cabins or on the streets; they could not leave their cabins after the sounding of retreat; and no white person could use another person's slave without first obtaining permission. Not surprisingly, blacks who broke the regulations were to be whipped, while white violators could only be fined.[29]

Vallé's regulations curtailing the activities of black slaves in the Ste. Genevieve area were posted at the same time that the townspeople decided to build a fort, and the two issues were related. In 1794 Spanish Illinois was on alert to ward off a potential Franco-

---

27. Despite references to the Black Code in contracts for sales of slaves in Ste. Genevieve (SGA, Slaves, Bills of Sale, no. 105) there is some question about how well the code was known in the outposts of Louisiana. On conflicts between Spanish slave law and the Black Code, particularly in Lower Louisiana, see Baade, "The Law of Slavery in Spanish Luisiana."

28. Two of Cruzat's ordinances concerning black slaves are published, *SRM*, 1:244-45; two are found in PC 2358.

29. Vallé's ordinance, Jan. 14, 1794, SGA, Slaves, no. 199½.

American invasion from the east side of the Mississippi. And together with rumors of invasion were rumors to the effect that the republican invaders intended to free the creole slaves and use them to further their designs on Spanish territory. In the minds of the townspeople of Ste. Genevieve, American imperialism and American notions about liberty were joint threats to the security and prosperity of their community.[30]

What with provincial, regional, and local laws and ordinances, there was a surfeit of regulations for controlling black slaves in colonial Ste. Genevieve. But the regulations were not so easy to enforce, as the two following cases demonstrate.

In 1786, town commandant Antonio de Oro was distraught because the Vallé brothers, François II and Jean-Baptiste, were allowing their black slaves to carry firearms. This practice was a clear violation of Article XII of the Louisiana Black Code, and De Oro complained about it to both the lieutenant governor in St. Louis and the governor general in New Orleans. The Vallé brothers in turn remonstrated that their slaves were obliged to carry firearms in order to defend themselves against hostile Indians and wild beasts, including "tigres" (apparently cougars). The Vallés pleaded their case cunningly, arguing that it was ultimately the owners of the slaves who lost if their laborers could not defend themselves on the job. De Oro lost the argument, and henceforth the Vallé slaves carried firearms in open violation of the Black Code. The Vallé brothers had political clout, and they also apparently had great faith in the loyalty of their black slaves.[31]

An interesting legal case from 1796 reveals how the changing makeup of the population in the Ste. Genevieve District made enforcement of slave regulations more difficult. Delassus de Luzières, commandant at New Bourbon, had sent François Vallé II a report concerning a slave named Sem, who belonged to De Luzières. This Sem, according to his owner, was being "debauched" by Englishmen living at the nearby Saline. The white men were harboring the black man, providing him with whiskey, and employing him to play the violin for their amusement. Sem, fully occupied with these high jinks, was unable to get on with the urgent work of sowing crops. Vallé was thereupon moved to post a formal notice that the activities of the Englishmen were a contra-

---

30. Peyroux to Carondelet, Dec. 26, 1793, PC 207 A; Carondelet to Luis de Las Casas, Feb. 9, 1794, PC 1447.

31. Correspondence concerning this affair is in PC 12, 199, 200.

vention of Article 7 of his ordinance of January 14, 1794, and that anyone found guilty of such illegal activities would be liable to a 100-livre fine, one-half of which would be paid to the informer. Vallé's last provision, the paying of informers, reveals the difficulty of cracking down on the seemingly harmless, though surely aggravating, "debauching" of black slaves in the Ste. Genevieve District. There is no evidence that Vallé and De Luzières were able ever to bring the guilty Englishmen to justice.[32]

Toward the end of the colonial era, Delassus de Luzières summed up his view of black slavery in the Ste. Genevieve region:[33]

> Most thieveries are committed by slaves, and it is only too evident that this sort of person is naturally inclined to thievery, brigandage, and disorders. But that which contributes to their excesses in this area is the extreme liberty that they enjoy and which they abuse. There are no rules or police concerning them. The slaves are almost all armed, and they circulate almost every night . . . committing disorders.

If Colbert, in his grave, could have seen De Luzieres' remarks, he would have rolled over and drafted another set of unenforcable regulations.

During the 1780s and '90s roughly forty percent of all households in Ste. Genevieve owned at least one black or mulatto slave, and these slaves were used for a wide variety of tasks: field work, clearing land, cutting wood, mining lead, rowing *bateaux,* salt making, domestic help, and some skilled labor. But as the economy of Ste. Genevieve was predominantly agricultural, so black slaves functioned principally as agricultural laborers — field hands. The censuses of 1787 and 1791 reveal that the town's six top agricultural producers owned roughly one-half of all the black and mulatto slaves.[34]

Henry Brackenridge had an omnivorous curiosity and a compelling need to describe everything that his hungry eyes took in. In commenting upon the agriculture of Ste. Genevieve he noted that "their agricultural labors commence in the month of April, when

32. Vallé's proclamation, Apr. 2, 1796, SGA, Documents, no. 199.

33. De Luzières, "Observations, . . ." attached to the 1797 New Bourbon census, PC 2365. 34. Census of 1787, MHS, archives; census of 1791, *SRM*, 2:365-68.

34. Census of 1787, MHS archives; census of 1791, SRM, 2:365-68.

the inhabitants, with their slaves, are seen going and returning, each morning and evening, . . . with their ploughs, carts, horses, etc." There is a curious democratic aura about Brackenridge's scene; one can imagine the closeness and camradarie among those common tillers of the soil — French colonial *habitants* and their black slaves. Perhaps farm lore — how deep to plant the seeds, what was the most effective way to hoe the fresh sprouts — from France and Africa was exchanged between blacks and whites there on the Big Field of Ste. Genevieve. Certainly Brackenridge's description (and Brackenridge knew the area and the people) does not bring to mind the Anglo-American plantations of the Eastern Seaboard.[35]

After agriculture, lead mining was the most important heavy labor for which black slaves were used by the citizens of Ste. Genevieve. As mentioned above, Philippe Renaut had introduced black slave labor to his lead mines on the Big River as early as the 1720s. Renaut's enterprise was sporadic and short-lived, however, and his base of operations was St. Philippe, near Fort de Chartres, and not Ste. Genevieve. We know that persons from Ste. Genevieve were engaged in lead mining, probably both on the Big and St. Francis rivers, in the late 1750s. These were small operations, however, and there is no evidence that slave labor was used at that early time. The entrepreneurs worked the lead diggings themselves, or perhaps with the assistance of an *engagé* or two. By the mid-1760s, however, there were several small slave quarters at Mine La Motte.[36]

About 1770, lead mining near the St. Francis River entered a small boom period, and persons from Ste. Genevieve went out to work diggings at Mine La Motte and Castor Mine. At least as early as 1772, François Vallé I was involved in the lead mining business. Given the fact that he was the largest slave holder in Ste. Genevieve at that time, it was natural that he should have used slave labor at the mines. When François Vallé agreed to enter into a joint mining operation with two other men, his committment to the joint enterprise consisted of himself as overseer, two black slaves (one male and one female), ten horses with harness, and tools. The three men were clearly going to engage in a seasonal mining

---

35. Brackenridge, *Views of Louisiana*, 127.

36. See MHS, St. Louis Archives, no. 12, for a property transaction at Mine La Motte that included slave quarters.

operation, employing themselves as supervisers and their slaves as laborers. Perhaps the female slave served as camp cook and laundress, or perhaps she even worked the veins of lead ore along with the men.[27]

By the 1780s, Mine à Breton (near present-day Potosi) had become the most intensely worked lead mine for miners from Ste. Genevieve, and some of these miners used black slave labor. In 1789 Charles Charleville, inhabitant of Ste. Genevieve, filed a complaint with acting town commandant François Vallé II against one Lafforêt, whom Charleville accused of claim-jumping at Mine à Breton. Given the absence of freehold property in the mining area at the time, Charleville's complaint is not remarkable. More interesting is that Charleville accused Lafforêt of having "chased his [Charleville's] negros from their work site" during Charleville's absence from the mining district. Charleville must have had re-markably docile and obedient slaves in order to have left them unsupervised at their work while he returned to Ste. Genevieve.[38]

At the end of the eighteenth century Moses Austin introduced modern, large scale mining techniques to Mine à Breton, and along with those techniques came large numbers of black slaves. In 1803 Austin agreed to rent a black youth from William Reed, a local slave owner, and Reed wrote in awkward English to confirm the agreement: "I have sent the negar boy agreeabell to promise and you May Keep him unto I send for him that is if he will suite you at 15 Dollars per Month he is like the moust of negars you will have to mind him." Although at that early stage of his enter-prises at Mine à Breton Austin was reduced to hiring black-slave labor, by 1814 he was in a position to invest $24,000 in a lump sum for fifty-two blacks — men, women, and children. Austin's operations are beyond the scope of this study on colonial Ste. Genevieve, but it is worth remembering that the French colonists had been using black slaves in the lead mines for more than fifty years when Austin arrived on the scene, and that he merely ex-panded a system that was already in place.[39]

Black slaves sometimes served as domestic servants in colonial Ste. Genevieve. The parish priests, for example, used their slaves exclusively in this manner, for the priests were not actively engaged

37. SGA, Contracts, no. 80, Dec. 7, 1772.

38. SGA, Mines-Miscl., no. 5, Aug. 8, 1789.

39. William Reed to Moses Austin, Sep. 25, 1803, Barker (ed.), *Austin Papers*, 1:88; Moses Austin to James Bryan, Nov. 25, 1814, ibid., 243.

in agriculture, lead mining, and so forth. There is a veritable sociology of slavery in the Big House from the Anglo-American South, but remarkably little is known about domestic black slaves in the households of the Illinois Country. How did they live, work, and relate to their masters and to other slaves in the community? Precious few records exist with which to answer these important questions. One thing, however, stands out: black slaves, including domestic servants, usually were quartered in freestanding slave quarters independent of the master's residence. The residences of which there are descriptions simply were not commodious enough to house live-in servants, free or slave. There is no record of a residence in which space was allocated for servants' quarters. The townspeople did not live in manor houses bustling with man- and maidservants, for Ste. Genevieve was a rustic frontier town even if some households possessed great wealth in slaves.[40]

After agriculture, lead mining, and domestic chores, which were the three most common slave occupations, slaves were employed in various and sundry other tasks. In 1776, for example, the merchant Jean Datchurut rented two slaves to serve as oarsmen on a riverboat that he was sending to New Orleans on a commercial trip. Datchurut, who was the wealthiest merchant in Ste. Genevieve at the time of his death in 1789, may have used many slaves in this fashion, but the ordinary black slave in Ste. Genevieve probably never made the journey back and forth to New Orleans during the course of his lifetime. Datchurut, and certainly others as well, also used black slaves for working the salt furnaces at the Saline, but little is known about that activity.[41]

Available records do not reveal how often black slaves were trained for skilled tasks such as cabinetmaking, cooperage, carpentry, boatmaking, blacksmithing, candlemaking, and other trades. In contracts drawn up for the construction of houses in Ste. Genevieve, blacks sometimes appear as part of the labor component for the project, but it seems likely that they were used for common rather than skilled labor. On the Anglo-American plantations of the Eastern Seaboard, black slaves often became skilled craftsmen. A scholar once remarked that "it is hard to see how the eighteenth-century plantation could have survived if the negro

---

40. In 1775, Father Hilaire, parish priest in Ste. Genevieve, reported to Governor Unzaga (June 20, 1775, PC 192) that it would cost him six to eight pesos per month to rent a black slave for use as a domestic servant.

41. SGA, Slaves, no. 57.

slave had not made his important contributions as an artisan. . . ." But the situation was quite different in the Illinois Country. Rather than being composed of many outlying and isolated plantations, each requiring its own laborers, skilled and unskilled, colonial Ste. Genevieve was a concentrated community with an adequate supply of white artisans for hire. There was little need to train black slave craftsmen in Ste. Genevieve. Occasionally, however, black slaves did become skilled artisans whose services were sought.[42]

In the summer of 1773, a resident of Ste. Genevieve, Jean-Baptiste Labastide, was killed by Chickasaw Indians at Mine La Motte. When Labastide's estate was settled his creditors submitted their claims against the estate. Interestingly, one of the claimants was one "Colas nègre," who was presumably a black slave. At the time of his death, Labastide had owed Colas 40 livres for a small bed, a fine table, and a partition wall that the black man had made for him. This case is revealing, for it shows that black slaves had legal rights in financial matters, that they were sometimes skilled craftsmen, and they had a right to earn money on their own account. Colas, not his master, made the claim against Labastide's estate. Dumont de Montigny had earlier remarked about French slavery in Louisiana that "the negros have Saturdays and Sundays for themselves, during which time their masters are not obliged to feed them. They [the slaves] then work for other Frenchmen who do not have slaves and who pay them." Article V of the Black Code in fact forbade owners to work their slaves on Sundays and holidays, and on their free time slaves were at liberty to engage in gainful employment. Article XXII, which prohibited slaves from working for themselves in order to acquire property, was apparently simply ignored. The living system of slavery was, in this instance, more humane than the law.[43]

Because slaves were, as Aristotle called them, "animate articles of property," they could be used for non-labor purposes. In November 1771, for example, the lead miner Louis Chamard borrowed money from both François Vallé and Jean-Baptiste Lacroix (a total of over 1300 livres) and put up his negress Jeanette

---

42. Marcus W. Jernegan quoted in Genovese, 389.

43. SGA, Estates, no. 131. Colas seems to have been a slave, for no free blacks were listed in the 1773 census (*SRM*, 1:61). Perhaps this was the same Colas that François Vallé I gave in dowry to his illegitimate daughter Marguerite in 1778 (SGA, Marriage Contracts, no. 32). Dumont de Montigny, *Mémoires*, 2:242-43.

as security on the loans. Chamard must have had a good year at the mines, for the mortgage on Jeanette was released in July 1772.[44]

The selling price of a black slave depended upon age, health, and sex, and the circumstances of supply and demand at any given time. Although there were doubtless short-term fluctuations, prices seem to have remained fairly constant over extended periods of time. French colonists in the Mississippi Valley called a prime, mature black slave of either sex a *pièce d'Inde*, and in Ste. Genevieve during the 1760s and '70s *pièces d' Inde* were fetching 1500-2000 livres if they were "sound and free of all illnesses." In 1768, one Antoine Renaud gambled and purchased a twenty-two-year-old black male named Michel for "400 pounds of good tobacco." The contract specified that Renaud had to assume the "risk and the danger of the illness that now attacks him [the slave]." If Michel recovered Renaud clearly had struck a good bargain; if not he would have to work his tobacco field with extra diligence the next year.[45]

In 1783, several Vallé slaves were valued at 2,000 livres each, and in 1788 a healthy thirty-five-year-old male sold in Ste. Genevieve for 2,500 livres. Slave prices (in French livres) rose a bit in the Illinois Country during the 1780s. This may have been due to increased demand or to economic dislocation wrought by the American Revolution. With the coming of the Spanish regime in Louisiana, the piastre was used as well as the livre in Ste. Genevieve, and there was remarkable consistency in the price of slaves in piastres throughout the 1790s; *pièces d'Inde* usually fetching about 500 piastres (2500 livres). By 1803, prime males and females sold for 3000 livres in Ste. Genevieve.[46]

Slaves seem to have been slightly more expensive in Upper Louisiana than on the lower Mississippi, probably because they were more scarce. This scarcity in the Illinois Country perhaps explains why female slaves, who sold cheaper than males in Lower Louisiana, brought the same price in Ste. Genevieve: the value of the childbearers was substantially higher in the region where

44. SGA, Contracts, no. 55.

45. SGA, Slave Sales, no. 138. Four hundred pounds of tobacco was worth 160 livres. Technically a *pièce d'Inde* (from Spanish *pieza de India*) was a unit of labor, and to qualify as a *pièce* a slave had to be young and robust (see Curtin, *Slave Trade*, 22).

46. Inventory of Vallé estate, MHS, Vallé Collection, Box 1; SGA, Slave Sales, no. 18; Simon Hubardeau estate, SGA, Estates, no. 125.

Bill of sale for a black female slave, Pelagie, age about twenty-five years. Father Pierre Gibault sold her to town commandant Antonio de Oro in 1784 for 525 piastres. Copy courtesy of Ste. Genevieve County Court.

black slaves were most scarce.[47]

On the subject of slave treatment in colonial Ste. Genevieve, there is the perennial problem of theory versus practice, of how slaves were supposed to be treated as opposed to how they were treated in fact. This is a particularly vexatious issue because there is more information on theory than on practice. The theory was laid out in governmental ordinances and regulations, and in homilies written by well-meaning moralists, whereas the practice must be teased out of an assortment of source documents that deal with disparate topics.

It is perhaps well to begin the subject of slave treatment by adducing the truism that simple self-interest encouraged masters to treat their slaves well, for the slaves were valuable articles of property. This generalization does not require much elaboration except to say that it was probably more valid in the slave-owning society of Ste. Genevieve than it was on the large plantations of the lower Mississippi or the Eastern Seaboard; more valid because in Ste. Genevieve's relatively small scale enterprises slave owners usually worked closely with their slaves and were not distanced from them by the use of intermediate overseers. Thus the owners, the persons who had most to lose from physical abuse of their slaves, usually functioned themselves as overseers. No doubt there were some sadistic slave owners, who by reason of their emotional maladies were capriciously brutal in dealing with their own slaves. But such owners existed in all slave societies, and on balance sadistic behavior was probably less common among the owner-overseers of Ste. Genevieve than among the hired overseers on large plantations.

Perhaps the most important provision of the Black Code was Article XLIII, which prohibited the breaking up of the nuclear slave family if all family members were owned by the same master. Contract after contract for the sale of slaves in colonial Ste. Genevieve demonstrates that this article was often adhered to: April 1766 — sale of a negro family consisting of father Baptiste, mother Angelique, and daughter (ten or twelve years old) Elizabeth; March 1774 — sale of negro family consisting of father Jean Baxe, mother Madeleine, and a "little mulatto at the breast named Joseph", April 1800 — sale (by Father James Maxwell,

---

47. Holmes (*Gayoso*, 118) states that in Lower Louisiana during the 1790s female slaves brought about $300 and males about $400; see also Fiehrer, "African Presence," 12.

parish priest of Ste. Genevieve) of a black woman named Deltée with her three children, a female mulatto of four years, a male mulatto of about two years, and a negro girl of one month. In all of these instances the slave family, or at least the mother and her prepubescent children, was maintained as an integral unit in the sale.[48]

In colonial Louisiana slave children were considered to have achieved puberty at age fourteen. Eighteen-year-olds were adults. as can be seen in the sale of two slave women by Auguste Aubuchon in 1797 and 1802. On the first date Aubuchon sold an eighteen-year-old named Esther for 500 piastres and on the second date a forty-five-year-old named Nanette, who was Esther's mother, for 350 piastres in lead and furs, the younger woman being substantially more valuable. Charles Dehault Delassus, who was Spanish commandant at New Madrid, bought Esther, and François Vallé II, commandant at Ste. Genevieve, bought Nanette. No government regulation prohibited the separation of mother and daughter at that stage in their lives, although the forced separation was likely painful for the two black women.[49]

To complicate matters, however, there were also numerous cases in the Ste. Genevieve District of the separate sale of slave children who were patently prepubescent: April 1798 — sale of a four-year-old female mulatto at New Bourbon; March 1799 — sale of a two-year-old negro boy to Louis Bolduc; September 1801 — sale of a negro girl of "three or four years." The human merchandise of these transactions were perhaps illegitimate slave children, and the sales thus did not technically violate Article XLIII of the Black Code, which only prohibited the breaking up of an integral conjugal family: "the husband, the wife, and the prepubescent children." If, as was suggested above, slave owners in Ste. Genevieve increasingly discouraged such conjugal families from developing within the slave population, they were free to sell off the young children. In this way they probably increased the market value of their slaves.[50]

There is little evidence of physical brutality to slaves in colonial Ste. Genevieve. Masters did not have legal power of life and death over their slaves, and Article XXXVIII of the Black Code forbade

---

48. "Edit concernant les Nègres," 86-87; SGA, Slave Sales no. 126; to Louis Lasource, Mar. 5, 1774, MHS, Guibourd Collection; SGA, Slave Sales, no. 112.

49. Ibid., no. 4, no. 5.

50. Ibid., no. 109, no. 19, no. 133.

masters to torture or mutilate their slaves under penalty of confiscation of their human property. Disciplining of slaves by individual masters was legally limited to chastisement with "rod or rope."[51]

In 1783 an interesting case arose when the overseer of Jean Datchurut, one of the few masters who owned enough slaves to require an overseer, became embroiled in an argument with a black slave at the Saline. The overseer, Jean-Baptiste Lacroix, arrived at the salt furnaces one morning and was not satisfied with the work of one Tacouä, a slave who had been at work during the night pumping saline water into the boiling-off kettles. In the course of their argument Lacroix struck Tacouä on the head with a pickaxe *(pioche)*, and the slave died fourteen hours later. That Tacouä's death was not taken lightly is revealed by the record of the inquest concerning it. Town commandant, Silvio de Cartabona, ordered the town surgeon, Jean-Baptiste Laffont, to examine the corpse, and Cartabona also interrogated another slave who had witnessed the fatal blow. The inquest clearly demonstrated that Lacroix had killed Tacouä in violation of the laws of colonial Louisiana, but there is no evidence that Lacroix was brought to justice for the killing. In fact, he remained on as Datchurut's overseer. The inquest was apparently prompted by Datchurut's loss of a valuable piece of property, Tacouä, but Tacouä's life was not important enough in Ste. Genevieve for justice to be pursued, out of a sense of equity, revenge, or deterrence.[52]

Slaves' deaths at the hands of masters or overseers were rare events in colonial Ste. Genevieve. Whippings on the other hand were certainly routine. In 1776, François Vallé I took it upon himself to supply Lieutenant Governor Cruzat with a slave for the modest price of 250 piastres. Vallé was doing Cruzat a favor in supplying a good slave at that price, and the two men agreed that if Cruzat should decide to sell the slave that Vallé could buy him back at the original price. In August 1777 Cruzat decided that he had to sell the slave because he was departing for New Orleans and he was sure that his slave did not wish to leave his father and mother and go down river. Moreover, Cruzat wanted to acquire a more docile slave, one which he would not have to "order about and whip all the time, which I absolutely detest." Cruzat had heard that Vallé knew of a mulatto slave "who is docile and industrious and knows how to perform his duties without

---

51. "Edit concernant les Nègres," 85.

52. SGA, Slaves, no. 197.

having to be told every day what he is supposed to do." Cruzat was hoping that he might be able to trade in his intractable black on the more submissive mulatto slave.[53]

The outcome of Cruzat's proposal to Vallé is not known, but Cruzat's letter is nonetheless revealing. Cruzat did not object to slavery as such, but he was apparently a tender-minded person who blanched at slavery's concomitant but disagreeable details, the whippings and continual bullying. In short, Cruzat had not learned the lesson that Charles Pettigrew, a planter from North Carolina, lectured on in 1806: "It is a pity that agreeably to the nature of things, Slavery & tyranny must go together — that there is no such thing as having an obedient & useful slave without painful exercise of undue & tyrannical authority." One can well imagine tough-minded François Vallé I quietly sneering at Cruzat, for Ste. Genevieve had not been built by men with Cruzat's delicate sensibilities. Vallé had probably killed Indians and flogged black slaves and he had succeeded in carving out a piece of the Mississippi frontier for himself and his family; newcomers like Cruzat could be damned for all that Vallé cared. In any case, Cruzat was unusual in evincing humanitarian compassion for his black slave at a time and in a place that did not often show that compassion. This is true even though Cruzat seemed to be moved more by his own visceral discomfort in whipping his slave than by the welts raised on the black man's back.[54]

Henry Brackenridge lived with the Vital St. Gemme Bauvais family in Ste. Genevieve for several years during the mid-1790s. Brackenridge came from a non-slave state, Pennsylvania, and was repelled by slavery, but he loved the Bauvaises, who owned numerous slaves. In his descriptions of life with the Bauvais family therefore, Brackenridge adopted the euphemistic device of calling slaves "domestics." He portayed his hostess in this fashion: "Madame Bauvais was a large fat lady, with an open cheerful countenance, and an expression of kindness and affection to her numerous offspring, and to all others excepting her coloured domestics, towards whom she was rigid and severe." Thus we see the two sides of Madame Bauvais, the warm, affectionate, and hospitable hostess, and the scowling, sharp-tongued, switch-wielding mistress of her "domestics."[55]

53. Cruzat to Vallé, Nov. 11, 1776, PC 112; Cruzat to Vallé, Aug. 1, 1777, PC 207 B.

54. Pettigrew quoted in Genovese, 87.

55. Brackenridge, *Recollections of the West,* 23.

Although it seems to have happened but rarely, slaves in Ste. Genevieve were sometimes punished publicly by the civil authorities. In October 1767, eight slaves, four blacks and four Indians, went on a drunken spree and decided to take a pirogue for a ride on the Mississippi. Fleuri, an Indian slave belonging to Charles Bauvais, stood up in the pirogue, lost his balance, fell into the river and drowned. The boating party came to an abrupt end. But when the party goers had sobered up they discovered that Charles Bauvais was angered over the loss of his slave and had gone to town commandant Rocheblave with a complaint. After a thorough investigation, Rocheblave handed down this judgment: the surviving slaves were given 100 lashes each in the town square; and two white men, Joseph Segond and André Vignon, who had supplied the slaves with liquor, had each to pay Charles Bauvais 400 livres as compensation for the dead Fleuri plus a fine of 300 livres each. The 600 livres of fine were donated to the parish church. The seven slaves who were publicly flogged belonged to Pierre Aubuchon, Widow La Fatigue (Billeron), and Jean-Baptiste Datchurut, and one supposes that these owners saw to it that the lash was not too heavily laid on. After all, the flesh that was being shredded in the town square was their valuable property.[56]

Article XXI of the Black Code required that old and/or ill slaves be cared for in an adequate and humane fashion. In practice, this surely meant that old and sick slaves simply continued to live in the quarters and were ministered to by friends and relatives. A curious, perhaps unique, case arose at Ste. Genevieve in 1790, however. Jean-Baptiste Datchurut, who had been a bachelor and one of the town's wealthiest citizens, died in December 1789 and left in his estate an "old negro, blind and infirm," named Nago. How would this man be cared for during his remaining days? The town commandant at the time, Peyroux de la Coudrenière, decided to hold an "adjudication aux rabais" in front of the parish church after mass on Sunday. "Adjudication aux rabais" is an untranslatable phrase, which seems virtually to have been invented for this event in Ste. Genevieve, but means something like "auction sale to the lowest bidder." In this fashion, money from Datchurut's estate would be used to pay someone on a monthly basis for the task of providing the dead man's slave with food, clothing, and heat. The person who was willing to do this for the lowest price was the "winner" of the auction. Jean-Baptiste Vallé started the

---

56. SGA, Slaves, no. 189.

bidding out at eight piastres a month; Charles Aimé countered with an offer of six; Vallé went to five; Aimé came down to four, and at noon he was adjudged the winner. Thus is seen a fascinating case of social welfare functioning through the free enterprise system in old Ste. Genevieve. Let us hope that in the last dark days of his life old blind Nago was well-served by Charles Aimé, who was himself in his mid-60s in 1790. Henceforth Aimé's household consisted of Aimé, his Osage Indian wife, six mestizo children, and the old black man — not a typical American household in any era or region.[57]

Article II of the Black Code required that black slaves be baptized and instructed in the Roman Catholic religion, which was the only legal religion in Franco-Spanish Louisiana. This article demonstrates that the French did consider blacks to be human and possessed of souls that were worthy of salvation. The parish records of colonial Ste. Genevieve reveal that most, perhaps virtually all, blacks were in fact baptized. Thirty-five percent of all baptisms performed in town during the period 1760-1804 were of blacks, and blacks constituted 35-40 percent of the town's population. Slave owners in Ste. Genevieve surely did not attempt to prevent baptisms of their slaves on the grounds that they were somehow less than human.[58]

As for the blacks' instruction in the Roman Catholic faith and their practice of it once they had been baptized almost nothing is known. There is an entire literature on slave religion in the American southeast, but our ignorance of this subject for Upper Louisiana is nearly complete. How often, if ever, the slaves attended mass; where they sat, or stood, in the parish church; how seriously they took the religion of their masters are all questions that remain to be answered. Given the fact that black and mulatto slaves represented an important percentage of colonial Ste. Genevieve's total population, our ignorance of their religious lives is a serious gap in our knowledge of the community's history.[59]

How the black slaves were housed, clothed, and fed is also largely a matter of conjecture. As mentioned above, slaves seldom if ever seem to have lived in the masters' houses, even domestic slaves.

---

57. SGA, Slaves, no. 42.

58. "Edit concernant les Nègres," 76; SGPR, Baptisms.

59. Raboteau (*Slave Religion*, 75-80) and Fieher ("African Presence," 25-30) have remarked that slave religion in Lower Louisiana was influence by African religious practices. This has not been established for Upper Louisiana.

The freestanding slaves' quarters located near major residences were often substantial structures. When former commandant Rocheblave's house was sold in 1777 the "cabanne à nègre" was included in the property settlement. This building measured 23.39 feet (twenty-two French feet) by 19.14 feet (eighteen French feet) and had two stone fireplaces within. This was a sturdy and commodious building, but it is impossible to ascertain how many slaves were required to live in it. Archaeological excavation of some of these slaves' quarters could be a great boon to the knowledge of the quality and texture of slave existence in old Ste. Genevieve.[60]

There is no detailed information about slave diet in the Illinois Country. The Ste. Genevieve District was one of the important granaries of Louisiana, producing large quantities of maize and wheat for export and for local consumption. Black slaves routinely ate maize (perhaps in the form of some sort of cornbread), which the French creoles themselves did not find acceptable except in time of wheat shortages. With the usual steady supply of cereal grains available — plus some domestically raised meats (chicken and pork at least), fish from the Mississippi, and wild game from the neighboring forests — it may be conjectured that the slaves in Ste. Genevieve often had an abundant and rather well-balanced diet. In 1815 Moses Austin allotted three-quarters pound of meat per day and a peck of Indian (corn) meal per week for each black slave at his lead mine at Mine à Breton; sometimes hominy, potatoes, and beans took the place of Indian meal. Austin's slaves were eating better than many European peasants. It is difficult to say if the quantity and variety of foods that Austin furnished his slaves were in the tradition of the Ste. Genevieve District, within which Mine à Breton fell, or whether Austin had brought his notions of slave diet with him from Virginia, where he had previously mined·lead. However, the foods he selected for his blacks, basically pork and maize, were produced in great quantities in the Ste. Genevieve District, and it does not seem far-fetched to suppose that the slaves in the region had been subsisting on those products since the 1750s.[61]

---

60. Rocheblave auction, MHS, Vallé Collection, Box 1.

61. As early as 1721 maize was deemed the nutrient of preference for black slaves. Governor Bienville wrote (Apr. 25, 1721, AG, A¹2592:107) that the black Africans recently arrived in Louisiana needed maize to restore their health. Moses Austin to John Brickey, Feb. 22, 1815, Barker (ed.), *Austin papers*, vol. 2, pt. 1:247-48.

During the American Civil War, an aristocratic lady from South Carolina, Mary Boykin Chesnut, described the pattern of slave society that she knew from the American South. She remarked with disapproval that "our men live all in one house with their wives and their concubines, and the mulattoes one sees in every family exactly resemble the white children — and every lady tells you who is the father of all the mulatto children in everybody's household, but those in her own she seems to think drop from the clouds. . . ."[62]

Interracial sex and cohabitation were forbidden by Article VI of the Black Code of Louisiana. This article had been framed not in pursuit of racial purity but rather on grounds that miscegenation disrupted society and threatened the stability of the family, which was deemed fundamental to the colony's prosperity. Up and down the Mississippi, from the Gulf Coast to the Illinois Country, this article of the Black Code was consistently violated. It was violated because there was a shortage of white women and because such laws are always ignored by wayward humankind. Further inducement to its violation came in the late 1760s, when Spanish authorities arrived in Louisiana. For although the Spaniards reaffirmed the Black Code, which forbade interracial marriages, the Spanish colonial Law of the Indies did not. Thus the very government of Louisiana was ambivalent about miscegenation, which became more acceptable and widespread in the colony after 1770.[63]

A *very* rough measure of miscegenation in the Illinois Country is available in the colonial census records. The detailed French census of 1752 included no independent category for mulattos. Insofar as they existed, which they surely already did, they were simply included with the blacks. The general Spanish census for Louisiana in 1771 included a category for mulattos, but none was listed for either St. Louis or Ste. Genevieve. By 1787, however, Ste. Genevieve's census showed thirty-nine mulattos, nine free and thirty slave, constituting fifteen percent of the non-white population. And by 1800 this number has risen to eighty-eight, three free and eighty-five slave, or twenty-five percent of the non-white population in town. The approximate nature of these figures need

---

62. Woodward (ed.), *Mary Chesnut's Civil War*, 29.

63. "Edit concernant les Nègres," 77; Moore, *Revolt in Louisiana*, 141. Regarding miscegenation and the Black Code in Lower Louisiana, see Allain, "Slave Policies," 134.

not be dwelt upon, but they nevertheless indicate that there was a fair amount of white-black miscegenation in colonial Ste. Genevieve.[64]

The persistent shortage of white women, the general absence of racism, and the institution of black slavery, which permitted slave women to be exploited, all conspired to make interracial sexual relations an ordinary phenomenon in Spanish Illinois. There were some notorious keepers of black concubines like Jacques Clamorgan, a St. Louis businessman, who purchased a twenty-five-year-old negress at Ste. Genevieve in 1791. Although no citizen of Ste. Genevieve acquired Clamorgan's reputation as a connoisseur and consumer of black women, miscegenation was no stranger to the town. We have already seen how Charles Vallé's notorious relationship with a black concubine destroyed his marriage and a promising career.[65]

During the 1770s, Jean-François la Bûche, a hunter and trapper, took up residence in the Old Town with a black woman named Elizabeth. It is not clear whether she was La Bûche's slave or a free concubine, but in any case she was his woman. In 1778 four of their illegitimate children, two boys and two girls, were baptized in Ste. Genevieve. La Bûche and his two mulatto sons were hunting west of Ste. Genevieve in 1788 when a party of Osages descended upon them and killed the father. The two boys managed to make their way safely back to Ste. Genevieve, where they rejoined their mother and told their story of the Osage terror.[66]

In the early 1780s, Antoine Aubuchon, a member of one of Ste. Genevieve's oldest (if not best) families began a liaison with a free black woman named Elizabeth. The records do not tell us, but it seems likely that Aubuchon purchased Elizabeth as a concubine and then emancipated her. Probably Elizabeth, "free negress," who appears on the 1787 census with her two sons was the mistress of Antoine Aubuchon. Before Antoine died in 1798 at age forty-eight, he and Elizabeth had had ten children, and in March of that year Elizabeth sued Antoine's estate on behalf of those mulatto children. In the settlement she collected thirty-five minots of wheat, ten minots of maize, a carbine, and a rifle. This was not a munificent inheritance upon which to raise ten children,

---

64. Census of 1787, MHS, archives; census of 1800, *SRM,* 1:facing 414.

65. On Clamorgan, see Nasatir, "Jacques Clamorgan," 101-112; concerning the Vallé case, see above, chap. vi.

66. SGPR, Baptisms, Book A:129c; on the La Bûche killing, see below, chap. iv.

but in any event Elizabeth had been able to demonstrate to the judge (Delassus de Luzières in this case) that her children had been sired by Antoine Aubuchon and that they deserved a share of his estate.[67]

In the 1790s, a case of white-black miscegenation occurred in Ste. Genevieve that sent shock waves from New Orleans all the way to St. Charles on the Missouri River. The case is fascinating and reveals so much about society in Upper Louisiana that we must quote extensively from a document that summarizes the case. This is a letter from Governor Carondelet to Lieutenant Governor Trudeau in St. Louis dated January 16, 1796:[68]

> Antoine Janis, son of Nicolas and brother-in-law to Vital Bauvais, all inhabitants of Ste. Genevieve, has with no discretion and in front of all the people of that parish maintained a scandalous relationship with Marie-Louise, a mulatto slave of Vital Bauvais. Despite all the painstaking efforts of the Janis family, the parish priest, and the most respectable persons of that district to end this relationship, it continued and two children were born of it. This has compelled the mulatto woman's owner to rent her to his son-in-law . . . at St. Charles, thirty leagues from Ste. Genevieve, in order to separate them.
>
> Antoine Janis has since fled to the American side [of the Mississippi], from where he has supplied friends with a considerable amount of money to purchase the mulatto so that he can live with her freely and without restrictions. The respectable Janis family is very sensitive about the situation because they fear the shame that will stain their reputation. Therefore they have had the priest [Abbé St. Pierre] ask me to intercede in order to stop this shameful and criminal affair. This he has correctly done out of concern for the future corruption of his parishioners.
>
> It is undeniable that the government should use all of its authority to prevent such illegal affairs, that are harmful to society, destructive of the fortunes of its members, contrary to good order, and even more if we consider the just complaints of families who wish to preserve their good names intact.
>
> The Royal Decree that speaks of emancipation for slaves says they may acquire it if they have money obtained by honest means. Since this entire affair is not exactly an honest one, she living with him as a concubine, her owner is not obliged to sell her into liberty so that she may continue concubinage

---

67. Census of 1787, MHS, archives; SGA, Litigations, no. 80.
68. Carondelet to Trudeau, Jan. 16, 1796, PC 23.

with her [new] master. . . .

This has all been explained to the commandant of Ste. Genevieve, François Vallé, and in conjunction with him you will strive to stop the emancipation of this slave.

Marie-Louise must have been quite a woman to have provoked her lover into such outrageous actions. However, Carondelet's letter makes it clear that the outrage was not interracial sex per se but rather the scandal caused by the flagrantness of the affair. Indeed, the remark about the "families who wish to preserve their good names intact" intimates that many prominent families had members involved in similar affairs. And the parish priest's concern about the "future corruption of his parishioners" suggests that those who were not already engaged in interracial sexual affairs had the desire to become so engaged and were merely waiting for an open precedent to clamber aboard the bandwagon of carnal delight.

Local records from colonial Ste. Genevieve and St. Charles shed some light on this curious case. A mulatto woman named Marie-Louise, who belonged to Vital St. Gemme Bauvais, bore illegitimate children at Ste. Genevieve in 1792 and 1795. Presumably these were the children of Antoine Janis to whom Carondelet referred in his letter. On October 5, 1794 Marie-Louise St. Gemme Bauvais, Antoine Janis's niece, married François Duquette in Ste. Genevieve, and Antoine served as one of the bride's witnesses. The very next day François Duquette contracted with Vital St. Gemme Bauvais to rent the mulatto Marie-Louise for a term of 15 years. The Duquettes were then moving to St. Charles, where François soon became a pillar of the community. His statue still graces the picturesque town on the Missouri River.[69]

In April 1796, Governor Carondelet wrote a second letter to Lieutenant Governor Trudeau on the subject of Antoine Janis and Marie-Louise. It was apparently an issue that engaged the governor. In the second letter Carondelet explicated a Spanish royal decree of 1778 that granted all slaves the right to purchase their freedom if they had the necessary funds acquired by legitimate means. Marie-Louise, Antoine Janis's mulatto concubine, had petitioned for her freedom, but Carondelet was not sure if she had acquired her purchase price by legitimate means. After ruminating upon this matter for several pages, Carondelet con-

---

69. SGPR, Baptisms, Book B:37; ibid., 56; SGA, Marriage Contracts no. 59; SGA, Slaves, no. 168.

cluded his letter by ordering Trudeau to make the final decision on the issue in St. Louis.[70]

Documents do not exist to inform us of the exact outcome of this case, but the records strongly suggest that love triumphed over all obstacles. Antoine Janis bought land in St. Charles, whither Marie-Louise had gone with the Duquette family, and settled down there as a merchant. In 1802 a free colored woman named Marie-Louise bore a child in St. Charles, and though there is no proof it seems likely that Antoine Janis and Marie-Louise picked up in St. Charles what they had earlier left off in Ste. Genevieve. Much later, in 1817, Antoine Janis finally married a creole woman in St. Charles. Probably Marie-Louise had died by then, and the wayward Antoine was ready to become respectable. Ste. Genevieve's intolerance had cost the town a solid citizen who had indulged himself in one randy passion. Whatever became of Antoine Janis's children by Marie-Louise remains unknown.[71]

Charles Vallé, Jean-François la Bûche, and Antoine Janis were all residents of colonial Ste. Genevieve who entered into extended intimate relations with black or mulatto women outside the bonds of marriage. Sometimes miscegenous affairs went as far as matrimony, however. In 1796, John Burk, a German Lutheran, settled in Ste. Genevieve as a blacksmith. In November 1796, Burk purchased Rachel, a "mulatto healthy and sound," from Joseph Coulton for the reasonable sum of 475 piastres. By August 1797 Burk and Rachel had had their first child, and a second followed in December 1799. In August 1801, Father James Maxwell, parish priest in Ste. Genevieve, married John Burk and Rachel Prior, "daughter of Thomas Prior" and "native of Virginia in the United States of America." Although a Roman Catholic priest married them, John Burk and Rachel Prior were married as non- Catholics, for he was a Lutheran and she a Presbyterian. The parish record of the marriage does not reveal that Rachel was a former slave nor that she was a mulatto, for once she had been freed, these facts about her were of little or no consequence to Father Maxwell.[72]

70. Carondelet to Trudeau, Apr. 30, 1796, PC 23; the Spanish royal decree to which Carondelet referred was at odds with the Black Code, which contained no provision for slaves to purchase their own freedom. On this issue, see Baade, "The Law of Slavery," 67-70; McGowan, "Creation of a Slave Society," chap. iv.

71. MHS, St. Charles Parish Records, Baptisms; St. Charles Historical Society, St. Charles Deed Book A:53.

72. SGA, Slaves, no. 35; SGPR, Baptisms, Book B: 79, 120, 153, 201; SGPR, Marriages, Non-Catholic (hereafter cited as Book D):41-43.

An even more unusual mixed marriage took place at Mine La Motte in May 1801. This marriage was doubly mixed, for it involved two religions and two races. Pierre Viriat (sometimes Vériat), a lead miner from Lorraine and a Roman Catholic, married Roddé Christi, who was a daughter of Israel Christi, a native of Virginia , and a Protestant. Viriat had purchased Roddé, a mulatto slave, in July 1800 at Ste. Genevieve and emancipated her on May 7, 1801, just two days before their marriage. Viriat was an old and respected citizen of the Ste. Genevieve District and he owned sizeable amounts of real estate in the district, including a one-fifth share in Mine La Motte. The list of witnesses for his marriage constitutes a veritable who's who of Ste. Genevieve's power elite: François Vallé, Jean-Baptiste Vallé, Jean-Baptiste St. Gemme Bauvais, and Jean-Baptiste Pratte. It is obvious that none of these men, who apparently traveled from Ste. Genevieve to Mine La Motte for the marriage, cared whether their old friend Pierre Viriat was marrying a mulatto and a former slave. Again we see that once the woman was freed these facts did not matter; she was not stigmatized by her race or by her late position as a slave.[73]

Although the relatively few extant records on miscegenous relationships make generalizations risky, there is some evidence for these observations: mulatto women were deemed more desirable than black women by white men in the Illinois Country, and mulatto women from Virginia were the most desirable of all. The only two recorded cases of racially mixed marriages in colonial Ste. Genevieve involved such women. John Burk and Pierre Viriat bought, manumitted, and married such women. Mulattos from Virginia were perhaps viewed as slave aristocrats, who possessed lighter skins and more polished manners than the other slaves.

The shortage of white women and the availability of slave women created some odd situations in colonial Ste. Genevieve. In February 1784, Jean-Baptiste Vallé, who was one of the town's largest slave holders, made an unusual agreement with one Pierre Taurique, who was a soldier stationed in the Spanish garrison at St. Louis. The contract concerned the future of a mulatto infant, Jean-Baptiste, who had been born of Vallé's negress slave, Marguerite Catin, in January, 1784. The contract was initiated at the request of Pierre Taurique, who agreed to pay Vallé 200 piastres in May 1784, in return for which sum Vallé agreed to bear the costs of supporting the mulatto boy, Jean-Baptiste, until he reached the

---

73. SGA, Slaves, no. 78, no. 180; SGPR, Marriages, Book D:46.

age of seven. At that time, Pierre Taurique would have the right and the obligation to take the boy, if he were still living, as his own and raise him as a free person. If Marguerite Catin, the mulatto boy's mother, were sold, the boy would nevertheless remain with the Vallé family as a free person, for as soon as Taurique paid the 200 piastres the infant Jean-Baptiste would be considered emancipated. Taurique, an enlisted man, was not able to raise the 200 piastres by May as he had contracted to do, but he did pay Vallé the full amount in cash in February 1785, thereby purchasing the freedom of the then one-year-old Jean-Baptiste. That is the last we hear of the boy, but Billon's *Annals of St. Louis* reveals that one Pedro Torrico (surely Pierre Taurique) purchased a house in St. Louis in 1785. Thus it seems that Taurique took his son and settled down at St. Louis in the mid-1780s to raise the boy.[74]

Pierre Taurique surfaced once again at Ste. Genevieve in the spring of 1804. In May of that year he married a mestizo woman, Marguerite-Joseph, embarked upon a domestic life, and had several children. But it is Taurique's contract with Jean-Baptiste Vallé that is of most interest to the historian. Some obvious conclusions can be drawn from the contract: Taurique, who often served as a courier between St. Louis and Ste. Genevieve, had sexual relations in Ste. Genevieve with Vallé's black slave, Marguerite Catin. The mulatto boy, Jean-Baptiste, was Taurique's son by Marguerite. As a slave, Marguerite had no maternal rights to keep or raise Jean-Baptiste once Taurique had paid for his emancipation.[75]

Such were the bare facts of the Taurique-Vallé agreement of 1784. But this particular case raises far-reaching questions about slavery and white-black relations in colonial Ste. Genevieve that cannot be clearly answered at this point. How often were such contracts made? Was it customary for white soldiers to take black slave women as concubines? Did slave owners like Jean-Baptiste Vallé acquiesce in such practices, or even encourage them, for the sake of breeding their female slaves and thus increasing their holdings of human property? Had Marguerite Catin been a willing sexual partner of Taurique's or had Vallé ordered her to sleep with him? "Catin" in French means a woman of ill repute. Did Jean-Baptiste Vallé make a profit when he agreed to raise the mulatto boy at his own expense for seven years? As important as they may be, these questions must remain largely unanswered,

---

74. SGA, Slaves, no. 179; Billon (ed.), *Annals*, 1:71.

75. SGPR, Marriages, Book B:99; SGPR, Baptisms, Book B:196, 225.

although it would seem likely that Vallé did in fact stand to turn a nice profit on his contract with Taurique. After all, the purpose of slaves, infants as well as mothers, was to be *profitable* articles of animate property.

It is obvious that there was a considerable amount of miscegenation in colonial Ste. Genevieve. But it is also apparent that most such cases remained, at least on the part of the white males, affairs of the glands and not of the heart. Antoine Janis emerges from obscurity, into scandal in the eighteenth century and onto the printed page in the twentieth century, because he did not take seriously enough the unwritten code of his society: black women are available but never get your anatomy mixed up; your loins and your heart are distant parts of your body. Most of Antoine's compatriots stuck to the code; just how much emotional wreckage they left behind — in their black concubines, in their bastard mulatto children, and in themselves — can only be surmised.

From time to time masters in colonial Ste. Genevieve manumitted black slaves, although there is no indication that French colonial society considered such acts virtuous. In 1779, Jacques Billeron and his wife Louise-Marguerite drew up a legal instrument providing for the freedom of their thirteen-year-old female mulatto slave, Marie-Reine, when she attained the age of twenty-five years. If both husband and wife died before that time, Marie-Reine would automatically become free, and none of the Billeron heirs could lay claim to her as family property. The document of manumission does not reveal what motivated the Billerons in drafting it, but they may have been rewarding loyal service and/or attempting to assure themselves of loyal service for 12 years to come.[76]

Spanish law, unlike French law, specifically provided slaves with the opportunity to purchase their own freedom. Although laws on this issue were never promulgated in colonial Ste. Genevieve, there was obviously some awareness of them in the community. In 1787, Marianne, a negress belonging to Louis Deloriers, a merchant of Ste. Genevieve, purchased her future freedom for 400

---

76. SGA, Slaves, no. 170½. Article L of the Black Code sanctioned manumission but required approval of the colonial Superior Council for all manumissions. By 1779 the Superior Council no longer existed, and Spanish policy seemed to permit voluntary manumissions without governmental approval (see Baade, "The Law of Slavery," 60).

piastres. Because Deloriers had paid 600 piastres for Marianne, however, she was obliged to serve him until his death before achieving her freedom. Four hundred piastres was a substantial sum, and it is apparent that slaves in colonial Ste. Genevieve had enough discretionary time and liberty of movement to earn, if they were ambitious, considerable wages by doing odd jobs in town. In 1788, Charles Vallé, oldest son of François Vallé I, owned two slaves, François Jasmin and his wife Catherine, who had accumulated enough cash to pay 800 piastres for their freedom in order that they could "enjoy in the future all the privileges and duties that are entailed in the free condition."[77]

An unusual emancipation of two mulatto children occurred at Ste. Genevieve in 1806. We have seen that Pierre Viriat purchased the mulatto woman Roddé Christi in 1800, emancipated her in 1801, and shortly thereafter married her. Roddé Christi's past can be traced back further than 1800 however. Her marriage record stated that she was originally from Virginia, and the Ste. Genevieve civil records indicate that she and her two children, a boy of fifteen months and a girl of six weeks, were sold to Guillaume Girouärd at Ste. Genevieve in September 1797. When Pierre Viriat bought Roddé Christi from Girouärd in 1800, the two children remained in Girouärd's possession. This was a specific case when a slave mother and her children were separated by the market place in Ste. Genevieve. Technically this was not a violation of Article XLIII of the Black Code because Roddé Christi's family had no husband and father, but it was surely a violation of the code's spirit. In any case, before Pierre Viriat died in early 1806, he and his wife, Roddé Christi Viriat, began negotiations to acquire Roddé's two children, who were still living as slaves in American Ste. Genevieve. Shortly after Viriat's death, Roddé succeeded in purchasing her two children, Orange, age ten and Marie, age nine, from John Calloway for $600 cash. Thus, after nine years of imposed separation, Roddé Christi's family was reunited in Ste. Genevieve as a free mulatto household. Roddé Christi, Orange, and Marie had come a long way since they had been sold down the Tennessee River back in 1797.[78]

---

77. SGA, Slaves, no. 172, no. 178. These documents of manumission were similar to, but not precisely the same as, *the cartas de libertad* that were employed in Lower Louisiana during the Spanish period (Baade, "The Law of Slavery," 67-68). Article XXIII of the Black Code ("Edit concernant les Nègres," 82) permitted slaves to earn money on their own time.

78. SGPR, Marriages, Book D:46; SGA, Slaves, no. 145, no. 146, no. 181; Ste.

Free blacks and mulattoes never made up a substantial portion of the population in colonial Ste. Genevieve. The census of 1791 listed twenty-six free blacks and mulattoes in the entire Ste. Genevieve District, but for some reason, the census of 1800 listed only ten in Ste. Genevieve and New Bourbon. This marked decline in the number of free blacks and mulattoes in and around Ste. Genevieve may indicate that many of the freed persons had moved to St. Louis, where they perhaps found the more cosmopolitan atmosphere better to their liking. Or the sudden decrease may simply indicate careless record keeping.[79]

According to Article XLV of the Black Code, freed slaves in French and Spanish Louisiana possessed all the "rights, privileges, and immunities" that white, freeborn persons did, although Article LIII stipulated that freed slaves should show "singular respect" for their former masters. There is evidence that Article XLV was in fact adhered to in Spanish Illinois. In 1782, a freed negress named Yaneta went to Lieutenant Governor Cruzat in St. Louis with a promissory note signed by one Maluen (?), who was a resident of Ste. Genevieve at that time. According to Yaneta, Maluen was refusing to pay her the sum prescribed on the note. Cruzat sent the woman back to Ste. Genevieve and dispatched François Vallé orders to see to it that justice was done in the case. Thus we see that not only did the freed negress have money to lend out but she also had available a system of justice that permitted her as a creditor to collect outstanding debts.[80]

Historians have often remarked that a three-caste pattern of society — consisting of whites, black and mulatto slaves, and black and mulatto freed persons — developed in Louisiana during the French and Spanish periods. Authorities in New Orleans were persistently plagued by the association of black slaves with "free persons of color." The latter often operated clandestine taverns, gaming houses, and even fencing operations for stolen goods that catered to the slaves. Although the free black population in Ste. Genevieve was not large, François Vallé's town ordinance of 1794

Genevieve County Courthouse, Deedbook A:60-65. The Franco-Spanish brand of slavery practiced in Upper Louisiana probably accounts for the fact that it was easier to manumit a slave in nineteenth-century Missouri than in the states of the southeastern United States (see Foley, "Slave Freedom Suits," 1-23; Oberholzer, "Legal Aspects of Slavery." 544-45).

79. Census of 1797, *SRM*, 2:365-68; census of 1800, *SRM*, 1:facing 414.

80. "Edit concernant les Nègres," 87, 89; Cruzat to Vallé, Oct. 1, 1782, PC 195.

indicates that some of New Orleans' problems may have existed in Ste. Genevieve: Article 3 forbade any inhabitant to invite slaves into his residence at night for the purpose of assembling or dancing. And Article 5 forbade any inhabitant from buying anything from a slave without written permission from the slave's owner. Perhaps by the end of the colonial period there was a small ghetto of free blacks in Ste. Genevieve, and in this area slaves could congregate to escape the oppression of their workaday situation and engage in illicit dancing, drinking, and gambling.[81]

Black slaves in Louisiana who fled captivity and tried to survive in the backwoods were called *marrons. Marronage* was widespread in the lower colony, where the climate made life in the wildnerness easy to support; occasionally, *marrons* appeared in the Illinois Country as well. Indeed, the first free black person known to have lived in what is now the state of Missouri was a black man named Lusignan who seized his own freedom. Lusignan had been a slave of the Bauvais family in Kaskaskia before he fled across the Mississippi in the early 1750s and became a *marron.* To flee was not, however, necessarily an easy decision for slaves to make; being unaccustomed to the American wilderness, they sometimes could not cope with freedom in the forest and died, free but desitute. Lusignan was no ordinary fellow however. He not only survived in *marronage* but became the leader of a band of Indians that brazenly harassed French lead miners on the Big River. It is not known what became of Lusignan after 1752, when he was reported to be on the loose with his band of Indians in the lead mining district of Upper Louisiana.[82]

Blacks and Indians did not, however, usually get along as friends and/or allies in the Ste. Genevieve District. There was, for example, a notorious case of *marronage* in 1785. In early May of that year, as the citizens of the Old Town fled in the face of the rising flood waters, five black slaves took advantage of the chaos and ran for the woods. But before they ran, they plundered the commandant's house of assorted commodities, including a keg of brandy, a case of soap, and twelve pounds of sugar. These *marrons* remained on the loose for several months, but on August 19, town commandant Antonio de Oro reported that they had been captured by Cherokee

---

81. SGA, Slaves, no. 199½.

82. Concerning marronage in general, see Price (ed.), *Maroon Societies;* regarding Lusignan, see Macarty to Vaudreuil, Dec. 7, 1752, Pease (ed.), *Illinois on the Eve of the Seven Years' War,* 756- 57, 776.

Indians. Lieutenant Governor Cruzat ordered the blacks sent to St. Louis to face justice, although there is no record of their punishment. Article XXXII of the Black Code called for clipping of ears, cutting of hamstring tendons, and branding with the *fleur-de-lis* for the crime of extended *marronage*. Surely, however, the slave owners in Ste. Genevieve did not wish to see their valuable property mutilated and disabled.[83]

A similar case occurred in 1800. In August of that year, five *marrons*, two men and three women, appeared in the New Bourbon District. Delassus de Luzières, commandant at New Bourbon, reported that the five runaways had been circulating in the area of Mine La Motte, when the "little chief of the Peorias" caught one of the women. She belonged to a man living at the Little Saline, and the chief was asking him for three blankets and a shirt as a reward. The miners at Mine La Motte were also asking compensation from the owners of the black *marrons* for the "one hundred pounds of gunpowder" that the runaways had stolen from the mining camp. *Marrons* frequented the lead-mining areas as easy places from which to steal commodities for survival in the Missouri wilderness; the mining camps were remote and vulnerable.[84]

Lusignan's case notwithstanding, there is no evidence that the Indians of the area harbored any notions of brotherhood with the black slaves on any grounds, either color of skin or shared sense of exploitation by the white man. Most of the *marrons* in the Ste. Genevieve area were apprehended sooner or later, and when they were it was often with the assistance of Indians who were seeking rewards. The Indians were interested in bounties, not in helping their "brothers." Two blacks from Ste. Genevieve who were abducted by Chickasaws on the road to Mine La Motte in 1771 no doubt understood this well enough.[85]

If in Spanish Illinois there were isolated slaves, or small groups of slaves, who fled for their freedom, there was never a general slave uprising in Upper Louisiana. In December 1793, when there was fear of a Franco-American invasion of Spanish Illinois, town commandant Peyroux de la Coudrenière wrote that the citizens

---

83. Cruzat to De Oro, May 19, 1785, PC 117 B; De Oro to Miró, Aug. 6, 1785, PC 11; Cruzat to De Oro, Aug. 23, 1785, PC 117 B.

84. De Luzières to Charles Dehault Delassus, Aug. 24, 1800, PC 217.

85. SGA, Litigations, no. 129½. Sexual relations between blacks and Indians, which were common in Lower Louisiana (Usner, "Frontier Exchange," 253), were rare in Upper Louisiana.

of Ste. Genevieve were threatened with "pillage and a freeing of our slaves." The invasion never occurred, however, and the slaves showed no interest in rising to overthrow their masters. In 1795 there was a serious though abortive slave rebellion in Lower Louisiana, but the rebels had no ties with slaves in the upper colony. All slave owners in Ste. Genevieve were assessed a tax of six escalins per slave to reimburse the owners of the twenty-three slaves hanged for sedition in the aftermath of the rebellion *manquée*.[86]

The total absence of any threat of slave rebellion in colonial Ste. Genevieve is remarkable and warrants some comment. There was a large proportion of black slaves in the population, and, according to Delassus de Luzières, many of them habitually carried firearms. Why the slaves did not revolt is something of a mystery. Perhaps they were so isolated and lacking in leadership that organized rebellion was simply inconceivable. Or perhaps, given the *relatively* benign Franco-Hispanic system of slavery and the general absence of racism within the colonial creole population, the slaves were treated well enough so that they had no desire to revolt. Delassus de Luzières wrote of the "extreme liberty" that slaves in the Ste. Genevieve region enjoyed. If this was in fact true, the slaves had little reason to risk death in rebellion in order to pursue something they already largely enjoyed. Many slaves, however, probably did not agree with De Luzieres' assessment of their condition.[87]

Given the almost total lack of extant personal literary records — letters, diaries, and memoirs — and the absence of a continuous oral tradition among the blacks of the area, it is extremely difficult

---

86. Peyroux to Carondelet, Dec. 26, 1793, 207 A; Carondelet to Trudeau, June 4, 1795. Concerning this slave uprising, see Holmes, "Abortive Slave Revolt," 341-62; McGowan, "Creation of a Slave Society," 347-93.

87. De Luzières' remarks quoted here concerning slaves were made in his "Observations, . . ." attached to the New Bourbon census of 1797, PC 2365. Not only did De Luzières remark that slaves in Ste. Genevieve frequently carried firearms, there was in 1786 a fierce dispute (see below, chap. xi) between town commandant Antonio de Oro and the Vallé brothers about slaves carrying firearms.

This study of the town of Ste. Genevieve is not the appropriate place to take up the lively debate concerning the relative merits and demerits of the respective varieties of slavery practiced in the New World. At this point I am inclined to think that the brand of human bondage practiced in colonial Ste. Genevieve was less repressive and more humane than that practiced in the Anglo-American colonies. For an introduction to this important subject, see: Tannenbaum, *Slave and Citizen;* Elkins, *Slavery,* esp. chap. ii; Davis, *The Problem of Slavery,* esp. chap. viii; Nash, *Red, White, and Black,* 172-82.

to determine just how the different races viewed each other in
colonial Ste. Genevieve. Beyond mere sexual liaisons, it is clear
that whites often trusted and respected blacks. Several of the manumissions cited above were the results of such feelings. But there
are other subtle indications that strong emotional ties developed
between whites and blacks. Five years before his death for example,
François Vallé I provided a dowry for his illegitimate daughter,
Marguerite, who was marrying Louis Caron. Part of the dowry
consisted of a black slave family, but François Vallé specifically
reserved one of the family's sons, Colas. Colas was to remain with
Vallé until Vallé's death, at which time he would be reunited with
his family. What motivated Vallé in framing this unusual clause
in his daughter's dowry will never be known, but it seems likely
that he had become attached to the black boy Colas and did not
wish to part with him. Vallé's arrangement was of course entirely
selfish, for it apparently did not take into account the feelings of
Colas or his parents.[88]

If strong affective bonds sometimes developed between whites
and blacks, an occasional white expressed his distrust, fear, and
loathing of blacks. Delassus de Luzières thought that blacks were
"naturally inclined to thievery, brigandage, and disorder," and
was appalled by the extent of liberty that slaves enjoyed in Ste.
Genevieve. De Luzières was a newcomer to the region, however,
did not understand slave society, and was ignorant of the subtleties
of local black-white rélations. Obviously the Vallés, who permitted
many of their black slaves to carry firearms, did not think that
blacks were stained with inherently criminal characters.[89]

Of the vast array of documents pertaining to colonial Ste.
Genevieve, few of them divulge anything about the feelings and
thoughts of the black slaves in the community. One which does,
however, is the record adduced earlier of the official inquest
conducted after Jean Datchurut's overseer killed a black slave at
the Saline. At 11:00 a.m. on November 6, 1785, town commandant
Don Silvio de Cartabona interrogated a slave who had witnessed
the fatal scene. The witness's name was Jacob; he was fifty years
old; he was a Roman Catholic. Jacob testified in detail about the
altercation that had taken place between his friend, Tacouä, and
Datchurut's overseer, Jean-Baptiste Lacroix. Lacroix hit Tacouä
with a pickaxe, Tacouä was stunned but not unconscious. At that

88. SGA, Marriage Contracts, no. 32.

89. De Luzières, "Observations, . . ." New Bourbon census of 1797, PC 2365.

stage of the story, Jacob made his critical point: Tacouä fell, "where he lay, refusing to be intimidated [*où il a laissé sans paraître intimidé*]." Tacouä died within hours, and there was nothing that Jacob could do to bring his friend back to life; it was clear that the white man had power over the black man's physical being. But Jacob wanted the record kept straight; the white overseer had never broken the black man's spirit. To his credit, Cartabona kept the record straight, and it is because of that record that we now have some faint glimmering of how black slaves felt in colonial Ste. Genevieve. They wished to demonstrate that though enslaved they had refused to be intimidated; they had refused to let the white man destroy their pride and honor.[90]

---

90. SGA, Slaves, no. 197. Regarding the legal aspects of this case, see below, chap. xi.

Chapter VIII
Life, Death, and Doctoring

W HEN SPANISH SOLDIERS ARRIVED to take command of Upper Louisiana in the late 1760s, the Old Town of Ste. Genevieve was a mature community. It had been in existence for nearly two decades, and the population had grown — slowly at first and then with a spurt as French-speaking residents of English Illinois flocked to the west bank of the Mississippi during the mid-1760s. In October 1769 the lieutenant governor of Spanish Illinois, Pedro Piernas, estimated the total population of Ste. Genevieve to be 600 persons. A few years later Spanish colonial officials began to compile censuses of their settlements throughout Louisiana, and many of these records have survived.[1]

Census taking was a new instrument of government for European states in the eighteenth century, and it was a very crude and imprecise exercise indeed. Nonetheless, the censuses that the royal Spanish government compiled for colonial Ste. Genevieve are rich historical records. These censuses usually divided the town's population into categories by sex, by race, by status (free or slave), and by age group. Three age groups were presented: up to fourteen years, fourteen to fifty, and over fifty. Such divisions by age possessed a certain rationale for both males and females: the middle grouping, which was of course always the largest, contained the fertile females and the males able effectively to bear arms. The totals for the following five years, years for which there are extant censuses, contain figures for the free white population only:[2]

---

1. Piernas's report, Oct. 31, 1769, *SRM,* 1:70.

2. Census of 1773, *SRM,* 1:61; census of 1779, PC 193 A; census of 1787, MHS, archives; census of 1795, *SRM,* 1:324-25; census of 1800, ibid., facing 414. On the move from the Old Town to the New Town and the development of New Bourbon, see below, chap. xiii.

1773
Males	251
Females	149
Total	400

1779
Males	254
Females	154
Total	408

1787 (corrected census, including Petites Côtes)
Males	263
Females	141
Total	404

1795 (New Town, excluding New Bourbon)
Males	312
Females	225
Total	537

1800 (New Town, excluding New Bourbon)
Males	461
Females	345
Total	806

These figures are only approximate, for the one detailed census, that of 1787, contains numerous errors and omissions and reveals the imprecision of colonial censuses. Eighteenth-century people simply did not have our passion for precise record keeping. Nonetheless, the census figures, with all their imprecision, do provide some essential facts: 1) For almost two entire decades, the 1770s and '80s, Ste. Genevieve's white population remained more or less unchanged. 2) There was a significant and persistent imbalance in numbers between the sexes throughout the colonial period, although it became less marked at the end of the period. These facts are important for understanding the flow and tenor of everyday life in colonial Ste. Genevieve, and they must be examined within the general demographic history of the town.

Some salient aspects of the structure of Ste. Genevieve's population can be seen at a glance by using an age pyramid, and the following pyramid is based upon the households listed in the 1787 census. This census contains numerous errors, many of which were corrected for the pyramid by using other available records

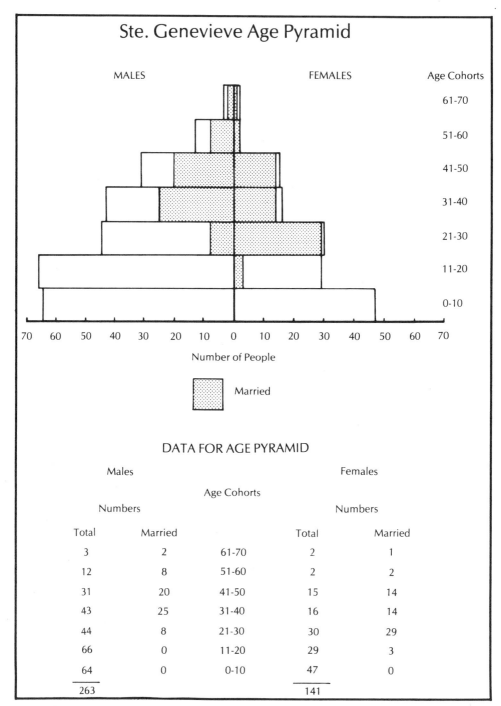

Ste. Genevieve Age Pyramid

MALES   FEMALES   Age Cohorts

61-70

51-60

41-50

31-40

21-30

11-20

0-10

70 60 50 40 30 20 10   0   10 20 30 40 50 60 70

Number of People

Married

DATA FOR AGE PYRAMID

Males		Age Cohorts	Females	
		Numbers		
Total	Married		Total	Married
3	2	61-70	2	1
12	8	51-60	2	2
31	20	41-50	15	14
43	25	31-40	16	14
44	8	21-30	30	29
66	0	11-20	29	3
64	0	0-10	47	0
263			141	

Spanish census of St. Louis and Ste. Genevieve compiled by Lieutenant Governor Fernando de Leyba in December 1779. Notice the breakdown of the population by age, sex, and status (free or slave). Photo courtesy of the Archivo General de Indias, Seville, Spain.

—parish registers, legal depositions, estate papers, and so forth — to obtain correct names and birth dates. The pyramid still has only approximate accuracy and is skewed because of the arrival of immigrants to Ste. Genevieve. Nevertheless, the general configuration of the pyramid is accurate enough to make it useful for casting some demographic facts into relief. The town had many more men than women, and therefore a much higher percentage of the women were married. More significantly, while parish records show 199 births between 1777 and 1787, the age pyramid for 1787 shows only 111 children through age ten. Some of the differential between the two figures is due to careless tabulation of the census, but most of it testifies to alarmingly high rates of infant and child mortality. Notice that few persons lived past the age of fifty, especially women. In 1777, François Rivard, one of the earliest settlers in the Old Town, was described as a "decrepit sexagenarian." Virtually all persons over sixty years of age were decrepit in colonial Ste. Genevieve, although André Deguire *père* lived to the age of ninety.[3]

The male side of the pyramid is abnormal from age eleven upward in part because Ste. Genevieve was a frontier town and single males tended to congregate there. In this way, the town's indigenous population pool was "contaminated." Many of the males shown in the pyramid for the cohort ages eleven through twenty were not native sons but rather were immigrants of one kind or another that fill out the pyramid in that section and make male youngsters appear inordinately healthy. Of the ninety-two males listed in the parish records as having been born from 1767 through 1776 (i.e., cohort ages eleven through twenty on the pyramid) many of them had died by the time the census was taken at the end of 1787, but immigrants replaced them in the town's aggregate population.

A perplexing issue that arises in studying the population of colonial Ste. Genevieve was the persistent imbalance between males and females. Part of this imbalance can be explained by Ste. Genevieve's role as a frontier town, where an excess of adventuresome males inevitably gathered. This aspect of Ste. Genevieve is apparent in the town's first census, that of 1752, in which only eight females were listed in a total population of twenty-three, and also in the militia roster of 1779, in which more than one-third of the militiamen were designated as *voyageurs*. But a greater proportion of males existed in all age categories, even in the zero to ten-year-old group, as the age pyramid for 1787 reveals. Indeed, there were consistently more males than females baptized by the various parish priests in the colonial town.[4]

Parish records indicate that between 1765 and 1804 approximately twenty-two percent more males than females were born in Ste. Genevieve and its environs. And for the Old Town during the period for which there are reasonably complete records, 1765-1787, the ratio of male to female births is yet more abnormal, forty-seven percent more male births having been recorded. Some of the abnormality in these ratios may be explained by the fact that is is usual in the ordinary course of human affairs that 105

---

3. The 1787 census of Ste. Genevieve in the MHS archives is a copy *of* a copy *of* the original and contains many errors. I am greatly indebted to Anton J. Pregaldin, master genealogist of French Illinois, for having helped me in correcting many of these errors. Concerning Rivard's age, see Gálvez to Villars, June 25, 1777, PC 190.

4. Census of 1752, HMLO 426; militia roster of 1779, PC 213; SGPR, Baptisms. Concerning the SGPR, see below, chap. xii, n. 43.

males for every 100 females are born, but the odds are extremely remote that such ratios could have developed by chance. It is barely conceivable that the extant data are so wildly inaccurate, that the parish records were so badly kept, that the anomalous ratios of male-female births did not exist in fact. This seems unlikely, however, for the markedly abnormal sex ratios that appear in the records for white births do not appear in the records of black slave births. Would the parish priests have been more careless in recording white than black female births?[5]

It seems likely that in the society of colonial Ste. Genevieve male children were more highly valued than female children. Males were more useful in the annual routine of extracting sustenance from the soil. Moreover, many more sons than daughters continued to live at home into early adulthood, for suitable brides were hard to find. Females married earlier than males and in marriage were more likely to move away from home. The young men were helpful to their parents in working the land, and, even in marriage, generally settled down near home and took up the family farming enterprise. Sons thus provided security for their parents that daughters could not provide.[6]

Given this situation, did some families in colonial Ste. Genevieve somehow arrange to have more male than female children? One conceivable option, female infanticide, cannot absolutely be ruled out, although it is hard to believe that the townspeople resorted to it. The parish priests would *never* have acquiesced in such a practice, and, moreover, the usual abundant supply of food in colonial Ste. Genevieve should have forestalled parents from going to the extreme of infanticide. Through abstinence from sexual intercourse, or conceivably *coitus interruptus,* couples could have practiced some sort of family planning that would have given their households more male than female children. For example, once a couple had had a number of male children they might have begun a regime of marital discipline that reduced the number of conceptions. The problem of the anomalous sex ratios in both parish and civil records is important and difficult to solve. We

---

5. Priests recorded baptisms, not births, but the baptismal records (SGPR) usually include a date of birth. In French Canada, slightly more males than females were born (Henripin, 54).

6. The corrected census of 1787 shows thirty-five unmarried sons age fifteen and over living at home and eighteen such daughters (MHS, archives). On the issue of the age at which males and females married in colonial Ste. Genevieve, · see above, chap. vi.

must be content at this time to raise the issue without resolving it. Perhaps a more detailed and penetrating demographic analysis will one day cast light on this cloudy problem.[7]

In his study, *The Structures of Everyday Life*, Fernand Braudel described the biological *ancien régime* of Europe in these words: "A number of deaths roughly equivalent to the number of births; very high infant mortality; chronic undernourishment and formidable epidemics." Braudel's description was of Europe and not the Mississippi River Valley, but colonial Ste. Genevieve, especially the Old Town, had its own grim biological *ancien régime* that was not much different from that of Europe: short life expectancy, high infant mortality, and a birth rate not much higher than the death rate.[8]

In all societies, whatever the life expectancy, infants and small children run a high risk of death. In colonial Ste. Genevieve, with its short life expectancy, the toll of death among infants and small children was awesome. Probably one-third of the children born died before their first birthdays (the rate in the United States is now 1.25 percent). Although children's risk of death diminished each year until they reached their mid-teens, there was heavy mortality throughout early childhood. Marie Carpentier Vallé, wife of Commandant François Vallé II, bore fourteen children between 1778 and 1801, and only seven of them lived to age five. The Vallés were especially unlucky in this regard, but less than half of the children born in colonial Ste. Genevieve lived to reach maturity. There was so much burying of children that it may have become a routine act that evoked little or no mourning.[9]

The annual number of births per 1000 residents in the parish of Ste. Genevieve averaged between forty and forty-five and the number of deaths between twenty-five and thirty, with significant yearly fluctuations for both births and deaths. Life expectancy at birth was less than thirty years for the white townspeople. Male children who survived through their fifth year could expect to live to about age forty-seven, female children only to about age

---

7. Historians have understandably been reluctant to deal extensively with the tricky problem of infanticide. For a recent survey of the topic, see Langer, "Infanticide: A Historical Survey."

8. Braudel, *The Structures of Everyday Life*, 91.

9. SGPR, Baptisms and Burials. Life expectancy in all societies is greatest for persons in their early teens (Wrigley, 8-9).

forty. The shorter life expectancy for women was rooted in the rigors of childbirth, plus the fact that women in their childbearing years are especially vulnerable to malaria, which was endemic in the Ste. Genevieve region.[10]

The demographic profile of colonial Ste. Genevieve was not unlike that of the colonial Chesapeake Bay region, of northern France during the seventeenth century, and of equatorial African states in mid-twentieth century. Demographic similarities do not, however, mean that human existence was harsh and brief in these disparate populations for precisely the same reasons. Famine, warfare, and roving bands of soldiers and freebooters contributed to the high mortality rates in many European peasant populations. Ste. Genevieve was largely spared those particular scourges. France is reckoned to have undergone sixteen *general* famines during the eighteenth century, and in some localities severe food shortages occurred more often. The usual bountiful supplies of food in the Illinois Country protected the townspeople from downright famine, although the winter of 1797-98 was difficult. And Ste. Genevieve was far removed from European style warfare, with its marauding and disease-carrying soldiery. All of these factors meant that the town suffered fewer savage epidemics than Europe. Only three times during the colonial era — in 1781, 1788, and 1797 — did Ste. Genevieve experience dramatically increased mortality. On these occasions the number of annual deaths in the parish shot up to more than double the usual number.[11]

Medical history is at best a slippery business, and it is often wildly misleading to try to diagnose illnesses that afflicted peoples in centuries past. This is especially true for the diseases that struck

---

10. SGPR, Baptisms and Burials. Birth rates were higher, and death rates lower, in French Canada, which was largely free of the river-valley fevers that plagued the Illinois Country (Charbonneau, *Vie et mort*, 34; Henripin, 14-15, 39-40; Henripin and Peron, "Demographic Transition," 218-19). The birth-death ratio in colonial Ste. Genevieve would have been more favorable had there not been a persistent shortage of women.

11. Walsh and Menard, "Death in the Chesapeake," 211-17; Goubert, *L'Ancien Régime* 1:35-47; *Demographic Yearbook*, 1970; Braudel, *Structures*, 74; on the relationship between famine and mortality in Early Modern France, see Meuvret, "Crisis in France," 513-19. Ordinarily, there were about fifteen deaths per year in Ste. Genevieve's white population during the 1780s and 1790s. In 1781, 1788, and 1797, however, the number of deaths rose to over thirty each year (SGPR, Burials, Books 1 and 2).

down large numbers of citizens in Ste. Genevieve in 1781, 1788, and 1797, for we have very few descriptions of the symptoms that appeared. In February 1782 an observer at Vincennes in the Illinois Country reported that "there has been a contagious disease at Ste. Genevieve and at Kaskaskia; fifty-four persons have died, among them the elder Madame Valé [sic]." What contagious disease carried off the wife of François Vallé I in October 1781 at age fifty-two is not known, but the Ste. Genevieve parish records reveal that some killer disease sent twenty townspeople to their graves in the Old Town during September and October 1781.[12]

A vicious epidemic of "fevers" swept through Spanish Illinois in the autumn of 1788. Lieutenant Governor Pérez in St. Louis reported that everyone was ill, even the soldiers in the garrison, and that there was no one left strong enough to harvest the crops. Ste. Genevieve was especially hard hit, and Pérez said he feared that fully one-half of the town would be buried. The parish burial records are incomplete for 1788 and it is impossible to determine just how many townspeople did die or what the month of highest mortality was. Town commandant Henri Peyroux reported that 1788 was the worst year that Ste. Genevieve had ever experienced, but surely mortality did not leap to the level suggested by Pérez; colonial administrators always exaggerated their problems.[13]

In 1797 a similar situation occurred in the New Town of Ste. Genevieve. Lieutenant Governor Trudeau, who visited Ste. Genevieve, reported to Governor Carondelet that "the village . . . is today changed into a hospital; everyone has the fever, doubtless occasioned by the stagnant waters that the floods have created." Delassus de Luzières' New Bourbon census of 1797 reported the scarcity of foodstuffs caused by the floods of that year. De Luzières further lamented that "the plague of scarcity has been followed by one even more disastrous of illnesses caused by the putrid and unhealthy exhalations of the stagnant waters. . . . Almost all the inhabitants of these villages [New Bourbon and Ste. Genevieve] have been afflicted with epidemic diseases."[14]

---

12. See McNeill, *Plagues and People,* for a brilliant overview of the history of diseases and their impact on human society. Legras to Clark, Feb. 15, 1782, James (ed.), *George Rogers Clark Papers,* 2:38.

I wish to thank Glenn R. Conrad, director of the Louisiana Studies Center, Lafayette, Louisiana, for his helpful criticism of this section.

13. Pérez to Miró, Oct. 12, 1788, PC 14; Miró to Peyroux, Jan. 22, 1789, PC 202.

14. Trudeau to Carondelet, Aug. 31, 1797, PC 121; New Bourbon census 1797, PC 2365.

Burial record of Marie-Anne Billeron Vallé, wife of François Vallé I, who died during the great mortality of 1781. Father Pierre Gibault performed the burial in the Old Town cemetery, 22 October 1781. Photo courtesy of Father Gregory Schmidt of Ste. Genevieve.

In both 1781 and 1797, the months of highest mortality in Ste. Genevieve were September and October. Burial records for 1788, the third year of extraordinary mortality in town, are not complete, but Lieutenant Governor Pérez bemoaned the high death rate at Ste. Genevieve in October of that year. The marked seasonality of deaths during the three years of great mortality, plus the fact that both Trudeau and De Luzières associated illness with stagnant waters, suggest that colonial Ste. Genevieve was suffering from mosquito transmitted diseases — malaria and/or yellow fever. Malaria is more often a debilitating than a mortal disease, but it is possible that some other disease — influenza, pneumonia, typhus, typhoid fever, diptheria, or especially dysentery — in association with endemic malaria accounted for the periods of high mortality. Dysentery, which in temperate climates also hits hardest in late summer and early autumn, may have been the killer culprit at Ste. Genevieve during 1781 and/or 1788. Yellow fever was rampant in North America during the 1790s, and an epidemic of this disease began at New Orleans late in 1796. It seems likely that the deadliest disease at Ste. Genevieve in 1797 was yellow fever.[15]

Persons in colonial Ste. Genevieve died by drowning in the Mississippi, in falling off their horses, in firearms accidents, in being crushed by falling trees, at the hands of hostile Indians, and, on at least one occasion, by apparent suicide. But accidental and/or violent deaths did not account for the generally high level of mortality in the town. The fragility and brevity of life were due to the usual diseases of eighteenth-century Europeans — plus, in Ste. Genevieve, endemic malaria. Rarely can the historian speak with so much confidence about the presence of a particular disease in a particular community at a particular time in the past, but the case for malaria in colonial Ste. Genevieve is overwhelming. Endemic malarial fevers, more than famines or epidemic diseases, were the health bane of the town's citizens.[16]

Malaria is characterized by intermittent fever, headaches, and general malaise. It is caused by the entry into the bloodstream of parasites of the genus *Plasmodium* through the bite of female *Anopheles* mosquitos. For the existence and spread of malaria, there must be both infected human hosts and *Anopheles* mosquitos to transmit the parasites to other humans. It is likely that malaria did not exist in the Americas before European contact. Probably

---

15. SGPR, Burials, Books 1 and 2; Pérez to Miró, Oct. 12, 1788, PC 14; Gayarré, 3:375. On yellow fever during the eighteenth century, see Ackerknecht, *History of Diseases*, 50-59; Duffy, *Epidemics in Colonial America*, chap. iv; McNeill, 280-82. Hans Zinsser (*Rats, Lice and History*, 238) has called the eighteenth century "the Century of Typhus par excellence," and it is possible that typhus struck Ste. Genevieve in one of the years of great mortality. On the other hand, typhus was known as a disease especially associated with soldiers and famines, neither of which afflicted colonial Ste. Genevieve.

16. Nicolas Paquin left home on the morning of Feb. 5, 1792 "in an excess of frenzy" and was later found with his head blown off and his *fusil* lying beside him (SGA, Inquests, no. 97). Paquin's burial record (SGPR, Burials, 2:19) stated that he had always led a "good, Christian life."

both of the common species of *Plasmodium, vivax,* and *falciparum,* had arrived in the Illinois Country by the late eighteenth century. *Vivax,* for which the mortality rate is less than five percent when untreated, was widespread in Europe during the entire period of New World colonization and arrived in North America early. *Falciparum* is more virulent, with an untreated mortality rate of up to twenty-five percent; this species probably originated in Africa and arrived in North America somewhat later than *vivax.*[17]

The first detailed description of malaria in the Upper Mississippi Valley was written by the businessman-adventurer, George Morgan, at Kaskaskia in October 1768:[18]

> Since Colonel Wilkins Arived He, every officer & almost every private Man, have been most Violently attacked with a Feaver. . . . They continued helthy until about the 20th of September, When they Were Attack'd by twentys in a day & so severely that in the Course of about a Week there was but Nineteen Men capable of Duty at Fort Chartris. . . . At present there are about fifty Men capable of Duty & the Violence of the Disorder is greatly abated.

In his study, *Malaria in the Upper Mississippi Valley, 1760-1900,* Erwin Ackerknecht claimed that the Illinois Country was almost entirely free of malaria until the 1760s. He argued that there was an "epidemiological latency period" between the time that whites began to settle in the Mississippi Valley and the time that malaria became epidemic. That may be so, or it may be simply that good descriptions of malaria were not written in the Illinois Country until the 1760s. In 1722, Marc-Antoine de La Loëre des Ursins, an official of the French Company of the Indies, reported from the Illinois Country that "recurring illnesses this year have prevented M. Renaut from going to the mines." It was perhaps no coincident that La Loëre wrote this in early October, which was toward the end of the malaria season in the Illinois Country. In any case, malaria was certainly active in Ste. Genevieve from the earliest days of the community.[19]

Evidence for malaria in colonial Ste. Genevieve is manifold:

17. On the history of malaria, see Ackerknecht, *Malaria in the Upper Mississippi Valley;* Duffy, 204-14; McNeill, 211-15, 179-83; and, most especially, the excellent and stimulating article by Darrett B. and Anita H. Rutman, "Of Agues and Fevers: Malaria in the Early Chesapeake," 33-43.

18. Morgan to Bayton, Wharton and Morgan, Oct. 30, 1768, Alvord and Carter (eds.), *Trade and Politics,* 439-40.

19. Ackerknecht, *Malaria,* 21, 58; La Loëre des Ursins to Minister, Oct. 3, 1722, AN, C[13]A, 6:405.

existence of good breeding grounds for *Anopheles* mosquitos in stagnant ponds along the banks of the Mississippi; optimal weather conditions for *Anopheles* activity, with frequent evenings of temperature and humidity in the mid-to low-eighties; seasonal mortality rates with peaks that correspond to the malaria season in temperate climates; numerous literary references to symptoms typical of malaria cases; similar conditions and descriptions in the colonial Chesapeake Bay region, where malaria was endemic; and the established fact that malaria was widespread throughout much of the Mississippi Valley during the nineteenth century. Black people, for several reasons mentioned in the previous chapter, were less vulnerable to malaria than whites.[20]

The first attack of malaria triggers a reaction in the human body, which gradually acquires immunity. Relapses occur in hosts of the *vivax* species and strengthen the immunity until overt signs of the disease disappear, although the parasite remains in the liver. Malaria is therefore most pronounced and painful in those persons acquiring it for the first time, and it was the newcomers to the Mississippi Valley who suffered most acutely. These afflicted newcomers provided most of the literary references to malaria in Spanish Illinois.[21]

In 1769 Father Sebastien Meurin wrote to Bishop Jean-Olivier Briand of Quebec about his colleague Father Pierre Gibault, who was serving Ste. Genevieve at that time: "M. Gibault since his arrival in this country has nearly always been ill, with fevers at first high and dangerous, and then slight and slow, against which his courage has always upheld him. . . ." This is the first description of *Plasmodium vivax's* activity in Ste. Genevieve, although Gibault was surely not the first person in town to contract the disease. It is noteworthy that Meurin was writing about Gibault's recurring fevers at the very time of year, June, when *vivax* relapses are most frequent in temperate climates.[22]

---

20. Significantly, blacks in Ste. Genevieve, who were more resistant to malaria than whites, died in the largest numbers during the winter, not in the autumn. In northern France during the 1770s and 1780s there was no distinct seasonal pattern for deaths (Goubert, *Malades et médecins*, graph facing 456). Chad McDaniel of the University of Missouri-Columbia first noticed that seasonal death rates in colonial Ste. Genevieve strongly suggested a community afflicted with endemic malaria. He presented his findings at a meeting of the Foundation for Historic Preservation in Ste. Genevieve.

21. Rutman, 33-34.

22. Meurin to Briand, June 14, 1769, Alvord and Carter (eds.), *Trade and Politics*, 549.

WHITE BURIALS IN STE. GENEVIEVE, 1780-1804

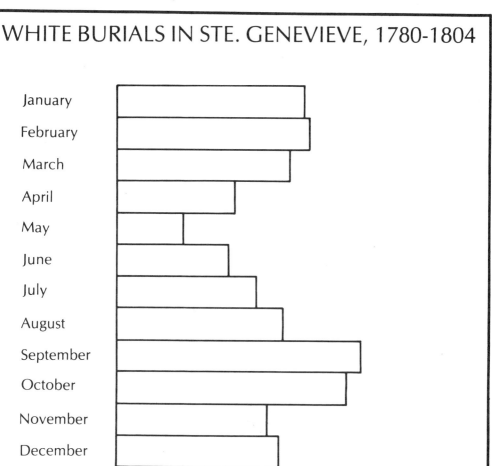

During the early 1790s, a number of distinguished settlers arrived in the Ste. Genevieve area, and for that era the source documents are replete with descriptions of malaria symptoms. Delassus de Luzières was stricken almost immediately upon his arrival in 1793, and in September of that year Lieutenant Governor Trudeau filed this report from St. Louis: "Having been in Ste. Genevieve several days ago, . . . I had the satisfaction of seeing M. Delassus, who had just arrived and whom was reported to have died. It is true that I found him in a deplorable condition. His confidence in my ability to cure him induced me to play the role of charlatan, and I succeeded in cutting and stopping his fever."[23]

The bark of the South American cinchona tree, from which quinine is derived, had long been used as a drug for fevers, and some forms of quinine were apparently available in the Illinois Country. It seems unlikely, however, that Trudeau was carrying drugs with which to treat De Luzières. More likely, from the tone of Trudeau's account of the incident, that De Luzières' malarial fever simply went into periodic remission, which is entirely characteristic of the disease, and De Luzières was deceived by the coincidence of Trudeau's visit and his own relief. Politicians in Spanish Illinois had to be multifaceted men, with talents for witchdoctory as well as for statesmanship.[24]

When the malaria season of 1794 hit the Illinois Country, De Luzières' family had already arrived in New Bourbon via Pittsburgh and the Ohio River. The entire household was in desperate straits, as De Luzières reported to Governor Carondelet in September:[25]

> I cannot describe to you the frightful position in which we have found ourselves during the past three months. Of the twelve members who compose my household, 11 have been attacked by the most violent and stubborn fever. It has overtaken me on two different occasions and did not leave me for several days. . . . I say that one must have strength and courage in order not to succumb to it.

Malaria-bearing mosquitos were probably unknown in De Luzières' Flemish homeland, and he was thus utterly mystified by the fevers that struck down his family. De Luzières' descriptions of the fevers — and the fall season in which he wrote of them — however, make it clear that it was malaria, probably of the *vivax* species, that had smitten his household.

About the same time that Delassus de Luzières arrived in Ste. Genevieve from France, Henry Brackenridge arrived in town to take up his study of the French language. Much later, in his *Recollections of the West,* Brackenridge described his health problems in

---

23. Trudeau to Carondelet, Sep. 28, 1793, PC 208A.

24. For a sketch of the history of quinine treatment for malaria, see Ackerknecht, *Malaria,* 98-110. In 1797, Father Pierre Didier listed "sel de Kinquina" as one of the drugs lacking at the hospital in St. Louis (May 13, 1797, PC 35).

25. Trudeau to Carondelet, Sep. 1, 1794, PC 210.

Ste. Genevieve:[26]

> During the second summer of my residence at this place, I
> was overtaken by a bilious fever, which had well nigh put an
> end to all my wanderings. . . . The disease was permitted to
> run its course, until there was scarcely sufficient vitality left
> for it to feed upon. . . . It was some time after the fever left
> me before I could walk, but afterwards my recovery was rapid.
> This was a seasoning, which I have no doubt was of service
> to me afterwards; subsequent attacks of fever, at different
> periods of my life, appearing in mitigated form, and yielding
> more readily to medicine.

This is a clinically accurate description of *Plasmodium vivax*
malaria, and Brackenridge carried the parasite in his liver until
the day he died. The "seasoning" of which Brackenridge wrote
was the period of first exposure to malaria that newcomers to the
Mississippi Valley almost inevitably experienced. In another context, Brackenridge wrote about the Illinois Country that "there is
no doubt, but that . . . autumnal fevers will prevail. . . . From the
first of August to the last of September, is considered the most
unhealthy." No one could swat the female *Anopheles* mosquitos
fast enough, as they swarmed off the stagnant waters near Ste.
Genevieve on warm evenings during the late summer and early
autumn months, to avoid being bitten. Moreover, the residents of
Ste. Genevieve had no idea that the bites of those little buzzing
insects were the source of those big throbbing headaches and
paroxysms of fever that plagued them during the autumn.[27]

One of the earliest descriptions of mosquitos in Louisiana was
provided by a French officer, Dumont de Montigny, who arrived
in the colony in 1719. When he wrote his memoirs, Dumont remarked: "In Louisiana there are numerous flying insects that are
a real nuisance. Among these are mosquitos, which are an almost
invisible little fly. Their bite is like a spark of fire on the skin."
Frenchmen and Spaniards in Louisiana were irritatingly aware of
mosquitos, but they never associated these insects with the various
diseases transmitted by them.[28]

When in October 1788 Lieutenant Governor Pérez reported

---

26. Brackenridge, *Recollections*, 30-31.

27. Brackenridge, *Views of Louisiana*, 111.

28. Dumont de Montigny, *Mémoires historiques*, 1:112.

what was probably a surge of malaria in Spanish Illinois, he associated the disease with the flooding of the Mississippi that spring, remarking that "the stagnant waters had become corrupt and infested the air." Malaria means "bad air" in Italian, and eighteenth-century people were persuaded that seasonal fevers were caused by noxious mists rising off the water. Indeed, a common English name for malaria in the eighteenth century was "marsh miasma." In Spanish Illinois everyone was convinced that stagnant pools of water along the floodplain, created by the rising and receding Mississippi, turned the air bad. During flood years, De Luzières repeatedly spoke of water "standing in stagnation and putrefaction" in the Big Field, and he was certain that it was the "true cause of the maladies." Much of the correspondence from the Illinois Country that complains of "the fevers" was written in the autumn of the flood years; by that time the flooding river had subsided, the stagnant pools formed, and the clouds of malaria-bearing mosquitos hatched. No one at that time, however, associated the chronic fevers with mosquitos. Rather, "corrupted air" was universally blamed for causing the illnesses. Old ideas die hard, and it was not until the end of the nineteenth century that *Anopheles* mosquitos were identified as the carriers of malarial fevers.[29]

There are many unanswered, perhaps unanswerable, questions about malaria in colonial Ste. Genevieve. These questions are important, for the annual cycle of malarial fevers was central to the rhythms of human existence in the community. Numerous species and varieties of *Anopheles* mosquitos with different characteristics of range and biting are indigenous to North America. Which one, or ones, inhabited the Ste. Genevieve region? We know that mosquito nets were used in the colonial Mississippi Valley. Did the townspeople of Ste. Genevieve use them over their windows or beds during the summer months? How much quinine or other anti-febral drugs were used to provide some symptomatic relief from malaria? Was the incidence of malaria reduced, at least marginally, when the New Town of Ste. Genevieve was established further than the Old Town from the *Anopheles* breeding grounds along the Mississippi? Finally, what effects did endemic malaria have upon the general tenor of life in colonial America?

With regard to the last question, Darrett and Anita Rutman

---

29. Pérez to Miró, Oct. 12, 1788, PC 14; De Luzières to Carondelet, Sep. 1, 1794, PC 210; De Luzières in New Bourbon census of 1797, PC 2365.

have proffered some fascinating speculations for the Chesapeake Bay region, suggesting that Virginians' attitudes toward both life and death may have been colored by the presence of an endemic disease that both shortened their lives and clouded their thought processes. While the Rutmans' suggestions are highly speculative, even playful in nature, they must be taken seriously, for they may help us to penetrate areas of colonial mentalities that have remained heretofore unplumbed. In the case of Ste. Genevieve, take for example Brackenridge's remarks about harvest time on the Big Field: "No further attention is paid to it [i.e. the crop] until harvest, when each villager, *but without that mirth and jollity* which usually takes place on such occasions in other countries, quietly hauls in his own crop." (Italics mine.) After Henri Peyroux had left Ste. Genevieve to become commandant at New Madrid, he wrote in August 1802 that "we are now in the season of fevers and harvest. . . ." Is it not likely that the somber rather than mirthful mood that Brackenridge perceived in the harvesters on the Big Field was rooted in the fact of life that Peyroux noticed — that harvest time was also the time when the endemic fevers of the Mississippi Valley gripped the population of Ste. Genevieve? Victims of malaria were simply in no mood to be so mirthful as Brackenridge would have had them.[30]

With the exception of malaria, for which there is extensive documentation, the written records provide only sketchy information about disease and illness in colonial Ste. Genevieve. Town commandant Antonio de Oro was suffering from an inflamed colon in 1785 and died in the Old Town two years later; perhaps he was prone to dysentery or perhaps he had cancer of the colon. There is no way to diagnose Oro's maladies, but doubtless Ste. Genevieve had its share of both cancer and dysentery.[31]

In 1795, Lieutenant Governor Trudeau reported from St. Louis that the only dangerous contagious disease that afflicted Spanish Illinois was "fluxiones al pecho," fluxions of the chest. This general definition probably meant any severe upper respiratory infection, which might have included pneumonia, tuberculosis, diptheria, influenza, or perhaps some combination of the four. The high death rates in Ste. Genevieve during January and February, which were second only to the malaria months of September and Oc-

30. Rutman, 58-60; Brackenridge, *Views*, 127; Peyroux to Manuel de Salcedo, Aug. 7, 1802, PC 219.

31. Cruzat to De Oro, May 4, 1785, PC 117 A.

tober, suggest that the cold winter season, which mercifully halted the activity of the *Anopheles* mosquitos, brought on a rash of lung infections. These would have been most troublesome for, and caused most mortality among, the older citizens in town.[32]

The most frightening disease throughout the Western World in the eighteenth century was smallpox. Smallpox was a mortal disease in both Europe and America, and even those who survived it were often left, as was George Washington, disfigured with facial pockmarks. Colonial Ste. Genevieve was fortunate to have escaped this curse. Smallpox symptoms are distinct and were well known in the eighteenth century; if the disease had visited Ste. Genevieve, it would have appear somewhere in the extant records.[33]

In 1777-78, a smallpox epidemic hit New Orleans and swept away, along with scores of others, three children of Don Pedro Piernas, the former lieutenant governor from St. Louis. There is no evidence, however, that this epidemic reached up the Mississippi to the Illinois Country. During the summer of 1793, Ste. Genevieve experienced a smallpox scare when it was reported that a band of Miami Indians with smallpox symptoms had been seen at Kaskaskia. François Vallé II wrote to Louis Lorimier, commandant at Cape Girardeau and a specialist in Indian affairs, and asked him to prevent the Indians on the *west* bank of the Mississippi from having any commerce with those who might have the small pox. Perhaps this was a false alarm, for in the eighteenth century the fear of smallpox was such as to give rise to alarms; or perhaps the quarantine of the Miami Indians was effective. In any case, the disease, *la picotte* in creole French, did not arrive in Ste. Genevieve that summer.[34]

According to Louis Houck, smallpox first appeared at St. Louis in 1799, and therefore that year acquired the epithet, *Année de la picotte*. This may well be true, for there certainly was an outbreak of the disease at St. Louis in the spring of 1801. In late April and early May 1801, Commandant François Vallé II decided to try to seal off Ste. Genevieve by halting all movement of persons both into and out of town. He posted guards on the roads and at the docking areas along the Mississippi, and asked Lieutenant Gover-

---

32. Trudeau to Carondelet, Nov. 28, 1795, PC 110.

33. Concerning smallpox in the eighteenth century, see Ackerknecht, *History of Diseases*, 61-66; Duffy, *Epidemics*, chap. ii; McNeill, *Plagues and People*, 249-56.

34. Gayarré, 3:120-21; Dan Murray to Thomas Bentley, May 25, 1777, Alvord (ed.), *Kaskaskia Records*, 8; Vallé to Lorimier, July 20, 1793, *SRM*, 2:53.

nor Charles Delassus to deny passports for travel to Ste. Genevieve. The guards whom Vallé posted at Little Rock Landing just north of Ste. Genevieve became overzealous and refused to admit not only travelers but also official correspondence arriving from St. Louis. When Delassus got wind of this, he exploded and sent a furious letter to François Vallé, informing him that official correspondence could *never* be interrupted, not even in time of plague, much less of smallpox. Delassus suggested that Vallé order his guards at Little Rock Landing to dip official letters in vinegar to disinfect them without damaging them. Whether the quarantine and the vinegar trick worked or whether Ste. Genevieve was just lucky will never be known, but the town escaped smallpox in the spring of 1801 even though the citizens decided to reject inoculation.[35]

Inoculation with smallpox virus to ward off the dread disease had been advocated by Lady Mary Wortley Montagu in England during the 1720s. In New Orleans inoculation was practiced as early as the late 1780s, but it is not known if anyone in Spanish Illinois submitted himself to the procedure at that time. There was, however, wide use of inoculation at St. Louis in the spring of 1801, for in May François Vallé wrote to Delassus that he was "glad to hear that the smallpox has worked to everyone's satisfaction in St. Louis." On May 5, 1801 Commandant Vallé called a meeting of *habitants* at his residence in Ste. Genevieve, but the townspeople decided to postpone inoculation. They claimed that the malaise brought on by inoculation might interfere with the sowing of the Big Field, and thus bring on a second scourge — that of famine. Probably this justification for postponing inoculation was a rationalization for the townspeople's fear of a new and exotic medical procedure. In any case, their gamble paid off, and they were spared smallpox in the year 1801.[36]

Whether *inoculation* was ever widely used in Ste. Genevieve is not known. But by 1802 Edward Jenner's improved technique of

35. Houck, *History of Missouri*, 2:62-63; Vallé to Delassus, Apr. 29, 1801, PC 217; Vallé to Delassus, May 6, 1801, ibid.; Vallé to Delassus, May 18, 1801, PC 218; Vallé to Delassus, May 28, 1801, PC 217; Delassus to Vallé, June 8, 1801, MHS, Vallé Collection, Box 2.

36. The famous Lady Mary learned about inoculation when she was living in Turkey as the wife of the English ambassador, Edward Wortley Montagu (McNeill, 253). On inoculation in New Orleans, see Gayarré, 3:190; Vallé to Delassus, May 18, 1801, PC 218; Vallé to Delassus, May 6, 1801, PC 218.

smallpox prevention, *vaccination* with virus from a cow, had arrived in Ste. Genevieve. In a public notice posted on May 1, 1802 François Vallé and Delassus de Luzières advised the citizens of Ste. Genevieve and New Bourbon "to address themselves confidentially to Doctor Walter Fenwick, who has received from Kentucky all the details of the operation." The "confidentially" was presumably intended to prevent anyone who dared to undergo the newfangled procedure from being disgraced in the public's eye. It is a good bet that vaccination did not become widespread in Ste. Genevieve until after the end of the colonial regime, for the traditionally-minded townspeople were suspicious of new things.[37]

The germ-theory of disease was not conceived until Joseph Lister's famous work in the mid-nineteenth century, and the residents of colonial Ste. Genevieve had no clear idea of what caused the diseases that beset them and often killed them. For most of its existence the colonial town struggled along in a medical dark age. Yet this ignorance did not prevent the town commandants from attempting to do *something* to prevent the diseases that plagued the community. In 1785 Antonio de Oro posted a town ordinance that ordered all dead animals found in the town or its environs to be thrown into the Mississippi. This ordinance reflects some vague notion about the sources of infection and disease, for it noted that dead animals could cause "epidemic diseases." Obviously Oro did not know precisely what the relationship was between carrion and disease, but he acted upon the scant knowledge he possessed.[38]

In 1797, Commandant François Vallé II attempted a much more ambitious undertaking, the first of its kind in Ste. Genevieve. In July of that year he ordered all households of the community to provide a proportion of their men to engage in a project for draining the stagnant pools and water-filled ditches near Ste. Genevieve and New Bourbon. Vallé justified this commandeering of labor by explaining that "experience has convinced us that the flooding of the Pointe Basse, as has occurred this year during the hottest season, has always been followed by cruel illnesses and epidemics caused by the noxious and infectious exhalations coming from the waters that have collected in the ditches and pools

---

37. SGA, Documents, no. 80. Jenner, an English country doctor, made public his vaccination procedure in 1798.

38. SGA, Documents, no. 7.

of the Pointe Basse." Although in focusing upon "noxious exhalations" instead of mosquitos Vallé revealed his ignorance of the true danger presented by the stagnant waters near Ste. Genevieve, his attempt to harness the resources of the community to drain the pools and ditches was an enlightened effort. How far this project proceeded is not known, but the community obviously lacked technical resources to make much headway on the drainage project.[39]

In his ordinance for draining pools and ditches, Vallé noted that he was initiating the project on the advice of "educated doctors," who had reported to him that "these injurious diseases are caused by nothing else than these putrid exhalations. . . ." One of these doctors must have been the newly-arrived Dr. Walter Fenwick, who probably settled at Ste. Genevieve sometime during the first half of 1797. Who Vallé's other physician may have been remains a mystery, for when Walter Fenwick arrived in 1797 Ste. Genevieve had been without a medical doctor for years.[40]

Indeed, for long periods of its colonial history Ste. Genevieve had no physician. Claude Dupré, "master surgeon," appears in the Ste. Genevieve parish records for 1774, but Dupré seems to have practiced his profession in town only briefly, if at all. When François Vallé I was investigating a possible homicide in 1773, he brought Kaskaskia's surgeon, Jean-Baptiste Laffont, to Ste. Genevieve to serve as coroner in the case. Sometime during the mid-1770s, Bernard Gibkins, a German physician, came to Ste. Genevieve and apparently practiced medicine there until his death in 1783. During the mid-1780s, Ste. Genevieve had no medical doctor. But in the spring of 1788, Laffont, who had moved from Kaskaskia to Vincennes, arrived in Ste. Genevieve "with his family and a slave" and settled down to practice medicine. Laffont lived less than two years, however, dying in the winter of 1790 at age forty. Once again Ste. Genevieve was without a resident doctor, and apparently remained so deprived until 1797, when Dr. Walter

---

39. Ordinance of François Vallé, July 20, 1797, SGA, Documents, no. 10.

40. In the Illinois Country, including Ste. Genevieve, some distinction was made between medical doctors (*docteurs, docteurs en médecine, médecins*) and surgeons (*chirurgiens*). But it is clear that the sharp distinction drawn in eighteenth-century France between doctors and surgeons (see Goubert, *Malades et médecins*, 129) was not made in the Mississippi Valley. On physicians and surgeons in Spanish Louisiana, see Holmes, "Medical Practice," 335.

Fenwick arrived from the United States.[41]

De Luzières was worried about the lack of a doctor in Ste. Genevieve. In May 1793, he wrote to Governor Carondolet about hiring Sieur Le Moine, a surgeon living in the French community of Gallipolis on the upper Ohio River, to move to Ste. Genevieve and practice medicine at a salary of fifteen piastres per month. But Le Moine never came. De Luzières later explained that Sieur Le Moine "married in America, operates an inn at Gallipolis, and appears to have no intention of coming to settle in New Bourbon." Perhaps the citizens of New Bourbon and Ste. Genevieve were just as well off without the tender ministrations of Sieur Le Moine, whose preferred *métier* was that of barkeep, not physician.[42]

De Luzières continued to worry about the lack of medical care in the Ste. Genevieve-New Bourbon region. In 1797, he complained: "I have lived for five years in the Illinois Country where there are many illnesses from which persons often perish for lack of assistance from the art [of medicine]. I am more than ever convinced of the importance of having a good doctor-surgeon to care for the sick and wounded at Ste. Genevieve and New Bourbon, which are today heavily populated." The plight of the two communities and De Luzières' preoccupation with the public good, as he put it, finally impelled him to look across the Mississippi to the United States. "There," he remarked, "are a large number of persons very learned in medicine and surgery." De Luzières' long and frustrating search finally came to a happy conclusion in 1797.[43]

Living in Kentucky was an American Roman Catholic named Joseph Fenwick, who wanted to settle at New Bourbon with his slaves and establish a plantation. Somehow De Luzières had heard about Fenwick and struck up a correspondence with him, for De Luzières knew that Fenwick had a son who was a physician. In a letter to Governor Carondelet, De Luzières described his efforts to bring a doctor to Ste. Genevieve, a community that had been without one for seven years:[44]

41. SGPR, Marriages, Book A : 154; SGA, Slaves, no. 196; SGPR, Marriages, Book A: 156; ibid., Burials, Book 1: 33; Miró to Peyroux, Sep. 6, 1788, PC 201; SGPR, Burials, Book 2:12. On the earlier career of Laffont, see Alvord (ed.), *Kaskaskia Records*, xxx. Gibkins also lived for several years in St. Louis, Billon (ed.), *Annals*, 1:392.

42. De Luzières to Carondelet, May 1, 1793, PC 214; De Luzières to Carondelet, Aug. 17, 1797, PC 204.

43. Ibid.

44. Ibid.

> Having learned sometime ago that the honest M. Fenwick
> had an eldest son in Philadelphia, where he practiced the two
> professions [i.e. medicine and surgery] with success and dis-
> tinction, I wrote to him [Fenwick] before he left Kentucky, . . .
> asking him to engage his son the doctor to join him in Illinois,
> where he could advantageously practice the double profession
> of surgery and medicine. . . . Pursuant to my urgent requests,
> M. Fenwick succeeded in persuading his son to leave Philadel-
> phia and come and settle in Illinois in order to exercise here
> his talents in the art of surgery and medicine.

The son of M. Fenwick would have been better off had he never
come to the Illinois Country, for this son was the famous and ill-
fated Dr. Walter Fenwick, who was tragically killed in a notorious
duel on Moreau's Island in 1811. He was a healer of bodies, whose
own body was shattered by the harsh frontier code of honor.[45]
The fatal duel was a long way off in 1797, however, and De
Luzières was overjoyed with his success in bringing Walter Fenwick
to Ste. Genevieve. The year 1797 was one of much illness in the
community, probably because it was a flood year and disease-bear-
ing mosquitos bred prolifically on the flood plain of the Mississippi.
But De Luzières was convinced that the "mortality would have
been much more considerable without the assiduous cares of the
honest and able Dr. Fenwick."[46]
If Walter Fenwick did well by the citizens of Ste. Genevieve, the
town also did well by him, for he thrived and prospered. In 1800
Commandant François Vallé II granted him a free concession of
real estate in Ste. Genevieve, and a year later Fenwick married
Vallé's fifteen-year-old daughter, Julie. Fenwick was the first of a
new kind of person to enter the upper crust of Ste. Genevieve
society, a member of a wealthy and elite professional class, for
when he arrived in 1797 there were no trained doctors, lawyers,
or teachers in town.[47]
Fenwick's professional seriousness and his intellectual curiosity
are attested to by the fact that he performed dissections in order
to study human anatomy; in 1810, for example, he won permission
to dissect the body of the convicted murderer Peter Johnston,
who had been hung. Fenwick may have been about as competent

---

45. Houck, *History of Missouri*, 3:76.
46. De Luzières to Carondelet, Aug. 17, 1797, PC 204.
47. SGA, Concessions, no. 31; SGPR, Marriages, Book B:78.

as any physician working in America at the turn of the nineteenth century, and there is no doubt that the citizens of Ste. Genevieve mourned his death in 1811. A serious question, however, is what in fact a doctor, any doctor, could do for most illnesses in the late eighteenth century. As William McNeill has observed about pre-modern medical practice: "It is very doubtful whether the physiological benefits of even the most expert medical attention outweighed the harm done by some of the common forms of treatment. The practical basis of the medical profession rested on psychology. Everyone felt better when self-confident. . . ."[48]

Guillaume Clouet took ill at Ste. Genevieve in October 1774 and began a regimen of treatments with the then-town physician, Bernard Gibkins. One cannot even guess at the nature of Clouet's illness, and Gibkins' treatments were not described with great clarity or precision. Gibkins treated Clouet a total of fourteen times during an eleven-month period and administered, among other things: eight doses of febrifuge, eight enemas, eight doses of anodyne, and seven doses of astringent. Given the fact that blood-letting (phlebotomy) was the sovereign cure for virtually all illnesses at the time, it is curious that Gibkins did not bleed Clouet, for whatever ailed him. Gibkins may have been an eccentric physician in that he did not practice bleeding. In any case, Clouet died after eleven months of treatment, more likely because of than despite the medical attention he had received. Gibkins filed a claim against Clouet's estate for 244 livres, a not insubstantial sum of money for the time. Treatments change over the centuries, but some aspects of doctoring remain the same.[49]

As another case makes clear, Gibkins did in fact have a mercenary streak in him. Patients in Spanish Illinois had the right, however, to contest his bills. In 1775, Pierre Massé was locked up in the Ste. Genevieve jail as a consequence of an altercation he had had with civil lieutenant François Vallé. Massé took ill while in jail, and town commandant Louis Villars directed Gibkins to treat him. According to Massé's suit, which he filed with Lieutenant Governor Cruzat at St. Louis in 1777, Gibkins overtreated him. Massé claimed that he had taken two doses of medicine and felt better, but that Gibkins had pushed additional medications upon him on the basis that Commandant Villars was going to foot the bill in any case; if two doses of medicine had made Massé feel

48. Houck, *History of Missouri*, 3:81, n. 59; McNeill, *Plagues and People*, 237.
49. SGA, Estates, no. 67.

better, a dozen would make him feel wonderful. Villars in fact paid none of Massé's medical expenses, and Gibkins presented Massé with an itemized bill for 230 livres. The good doctor had administered numerous doses of "anodynes," "febrifuges," and "electuaries" over a period of several weeks. Upon receiving Massé's suit, Cruzat had Gibkins' bill audited by a physician in St. Louis, who judged that Massé owed Gibkins only 120 livres. The effect of Gibkins' medications was problematical, and his bill was inflated, but in any event Pierre Massé found some justice in Spanish Illinois.[50]

Walter Fenwick was probably a better doctor than Bernard Gibkins. Fenwick surely knew his anatomy and could set bones, lance boils, extract teeth, sew up lacerations, and so forth. On the other hand, major surgery, an amputation for example, had slim chance of success without sterile instruments, and many patients would have died of hemorrhage, shock, or infection.

As for medicine as opposed to surgery, one wonders what Fenwick could have done for the malaria and yellow fever victims of 1797 that so pleased De Luzières. De Luzières himself complained about the lack of drugs in Ste. Genevieve and New Bourbon because "the country is still not sufficiently populated to have druggists and apothecaries." In 1797, Father Pierre Didier, parish priest in St. Louis, drew up a list of medicines required in the hospital at St. Louis. This list included such sure-fire remedies as "prepared red coral, distillation of stag horn, powdered rhubarb, syrup of peach blossoms, and prepared crayfish eyes." This outlandish pharmacopoeia may persuade one that Ste. Genevieve and New Bourbon were indeed fortunate to be short on medicines. However, Didier's inventory also included "sel de Kinquina," which was a form of quinine. Quinine was already known as an anti-fever drug, but it was almost certainly not available for Fenwick to prescribe to combat malarial fever; there was no quinine even in St. Louis, and De Luzières noted in 1797 that "medicines are rare and often non-existent at this edge of the universe."[51]

The French traveler, Jean-Bernard Bossu, commented in the

---

50. SGA, Litigations, no. 142. On Massé's dispute with Vallé, see above, chap. vi, and Billon (ed.) *Annals*, 1:136-37.

51. De Luzières, "Observations, . . ." attached to the New Bourbon census of 1797, PC 2365; Didier, "Etat des drogues qui manquent à l'hôpital de St. Louis des Illinois," May 13, 1797, PC 35. For more on medications in Spanish Louisiana, see Holmes, "Medical Practice," 334.

mid- eighteenth century that "the French who have settled among the Illinois Country have learned to prepare [maple] syrup as a cure for colds and tuberculosis." Maple syrup cured neither colds nor tuberculosis, but when mixed with suitably large quantities of tafia the syrup certainly provided much comfort for those citizens of Ste. Genevieve who were afflicted with coughs, colds, sore throats, or anything else, physical or spiritual, that ailed them. French creoles had doubtless learned the use of maple syrup from Indians, and perhaps the townspeople used an assortment of other native American potions to ease the pain of their many illnesses.[52]

Midwives were probably more important for sustaining human life in colonial Ste. Genevieve than medical doctors. Midwives were not bound to the usual treatments of bleeding, purging, and doses of bizarre medications. Rather, they practiced simple, manipulative procedures based upon an intimate and practical knowledge of female physiology, which meant that they certainly saved lives of both mothers and infants. The importance of midwives to the well-being of the community had long been recognized in the Illinois Country, and during the French regime the royal government provided a stipend for the midwife in Kaskaskia, who was therefore an official of the crown.[53]

In 1793, Delassus de Luzières, who was determined to improve the quality of life in the Ste. Genevieve-New Bourbon region, reported to Governor Carondelet that there was but a single midwife in Ste. Genevieve and that she was old and incompetent. Moreover, she refused to move from the Old Town to the New Town, where most of the citizens lived by 1793. De Luzières explained that he was especially concerned about the situation because his daughter had recently married, and he suggested that one Madame Lacaisse, a midwife residing in Gallipolis, might be induced to come to Ste. Genevieve for the "modest salary of six to seven piastres a month." It is of interest to note that on De Luzières' scale of values a midwife was worth about one-half what a physician was, for in the same letter he suggested fifteen piastres a month for a doctor's salary in Ste. Genevieve.[54]

De Luzières had some luck with this project. Madame Lacaisse did in fact move to Spanish Illinois, although she established her

---

52. Bossu, *Travels*, 108.

53. Belting, *Kaskaskia*, 72-73.

54. De Luzières to Carondelet, May 1, 1793, PC 214.

practice in St. Louis rather than in Ste. Genevieve. De Luzieres reported to Carondelet's successor, Gayoso de Lemos, in December 1797 that Carondelet had promised to provide Madame Lacaisse, who had taken it upon herself to train other midwives to work throughout Spanish Illinois, with a salary of *thirty* piastres per month. War had prevented the government in New Orleans from carrying out Carondelet's promise, but De Luzières implored Gayoso "in the name of humanity" to accord Madame Lacaisse a salary retroactive to January 1797. Whether this was done or whether one of Madame Lacaisse's students eventually wound up delivering babies in Ste. Genevieve is not known.[55]

For nonprofessional but experienced medical advice, the townspeople relied upon Madame François Vallé II during the 1790s. Perrin du Lac provided an unforgettable description of "la Commandante," Mistress Commandant, as he called her: She, "to whom long experience has given some knowledge of childhood diseases, never refuses her aid when an aggrieved mother comes to her. Day and night she serves the sick, from whom she does not even ask for thanks." What a treasure trove of folk culture we would have if Madame Vallé had written down her cures for children and her counsel for their parents; it would be a veritable eighteenth-century version of Dr. Benjamin Spock's *Baby and Child Care.* Madame Vallé did not, however, have a literary impulse. And had she had, with her own large brood plus the children of her relatives and friends to care for, she would have had neither the time nor the energy to indulge it.[56]

At the beginning of this chapter Fernand Braudel was quoted on the subject of the biological *ancien régime,* a regime that was characterized by such high risks of death that society could barely perpetuate itself. Although this grim picture is a generally accurate portrait of Ste. Genevieve during most of its colonial existence, there is *some* evidence that as the colonial era was ending, the grimness of the biological *ancien régime* was moderating. During the 1780s the annual birth-death ratio as revealed in the Ste. Genevieve parish records averaged only about 1.39, while during the last decade of the colonial era it averaged 1.83. In short, the people seemed to be somewhat healthier, although in both 1797

---

55. De Luzières, "Observations, . . ." New Bourbon census, PC 2365.

56. Perrin du Lac, *Voyage,* 169-70.

and 1804 there were more deaths than births in the parish.[57]

Part of the explanation for the improving birth-death ratio may be that by the end of the colonial era the parish of Ste. Genevieve included numerous persons living in the outlying areas of the district. In general those areas were healthier than the banks of the Mississippi. New Ste. Genevieve on the Petites Côtes was in a more salubrious location than the Old Town had been. The drinking water was better and the town was less accessible to malaria-bearing mosquitos, whose range of flight is only one or two miles from their breeding grounds. Or perhaps the program begun in 1797 by François Vallé II and Dr. Walter Fenwick to drain the stagnant water from the ditches and ponds on the Mississippi flood plain was partly realized, and had the unwitting success of curtailing the breeding of *Anopheles* mosquitos. Fenwick, who came to Ste. Genevieve from Philadelphia, brought certain knowledge and skills to the Mississippi Valley that improved the health of the citizens of Ste. Genevieve. We saw that he promoted smallpox vaccination in town, and although there had never been a smallpox epidemic in Ste. Genevieve some persons must have occasionally fallen victim to the disease. Because the data are meager these remarks are speculative, but it certainly appears that the population of Ste. Genevieve was healthier at the time of the Louisiana Purchase than it had ever been before.

57. SGPR, Baptisms and Burials.

Chapter IX
Parent and Child

I N 1744 AN OFFICIAL in King Louis XV's foreign ministry drafted a memoir on French Louisiana and remarked that "the earth is very fertile, the climate salubrious, and the women fecund." The climate in the Mississippi Valley was not in fact all that healthy because it favored malaria and yellow fever. The soil was rich, however, and women in colonial Ste. Genevieve were fecund enough to bear one child every four years per married woman. This fertility rate was substantially lower than in French Canada, but it was high enough to give the community a favorable birth-death ratio. In other words, the population could sustain itself and show some modest growth.[1]

Children began to arrive soon after marriage, the first child usually coming nine to twelve months after wedlock. Traditional morality, relatively young brides, and the fact that virtually all white women in town married meant that there were few illegitimate white children in colonial Ste. Genevieve. The numerous illegitimate children in town were usually mulattos or mestizos born of Indian, black, or mulatto women. The occasional white illegitimate birth did not, however, seem to reflect ill on either the mother or the child. Marie-Louise Caron was from a perfectly

---

1. AAE, Mémoires et Documents, Amérique 2:220; Charbonneau, 193-210; Henripin, 57-89. In 1787, for example, sixty-three married women bore sixteen live children, giving a crude fertility rate of .254. The lower fertility rate in Ste. Genevieve was somewhat compensated for by the fact that virtually all women of marriageable age were married (see Age Pyramid, above, chap. viii), thus raising the birth rate.

respectable French Illinois family and bore an illegitimate son at Ste. Genevieve in 1784. She went on to marry Antoine Thaumur in 1786 and, after Thaumur's death, Antoine Dufour in 1789. The records do not reveal if the illegitimate boy had been sired by Thaumur.[2]

The parish records suggest that there was not even much premarital sex, for few children were born before the eighth month after marriage, and birth control of any kind was practiced rarely if at all. In the eighteenth century, the sheep-gut condom was used only by sophisticates like Jacques Casanova, who took the canons of the Roman Catholic Church rather lightly, and not by ordinary folks who attended Mass and confessed regularly. For the latter, even *coitus interruptus*, the biblical sin of Onan, was out of bounds and probably not often practiced in Ste. Genevieve. For fertile couples the alternatives were to continue having children or to refrain from sexual intercourse.

The baptismal records of colonial Ste. Genevieve, which provide much though not complete data on births, reveal that most conceptions occurred during the winter and spring months, and that there was a sharp slump in conceptions from July through October. These four months of summer and autumn represented the harvest and malaria seasons, during which time the townspeople had little energy or inclination to engage in sexual relations. This pattern of sexual activity was quite different from that in French Canada, where most conceptions occurred during the spring and summer months.[3]

The interval between births was often a little less than twenty-four months. André Deguire *fils* and his wife Marguerite had twelve children between 1763 and 1784, which was very tight spacing. The Vallé family had several sturdy and prolific women. Marie Carpentier Vallé, wife of François II, was said by Perrin du Lac in 1802 to have had eighteen children. But Du Lac exaggerated, for the Ste. Genevieve parish records show that Marie mothered *only* fourteen children between 1778 and 1801. Theoretically, births could have been spaced even closer than they were, and the birth intervals suggest that it was customary in colonial

---

2. SGPR, Baptisms, Book A:204; SGPR, Marriages, Book A:126; SGA, Marriage Contracts, no. 57. Concerning the issue of low rates of illegitimacy in premodern western society, see Shorter, *The Making of the Modern Family*, 80-98.

3. SGPR, Baptisms:passim; Henripin, 42. It is possible that malaria affected fertility as well as sexual desire.

Ste. Genevieve for couples to abstain from sexual intercourse at least during the first phase of the nursing period. Menopause ordinarily set in at about age forty-five and halted the child bearing process.[4]

The extremely high rates of infant and child mortality meant than many of the children born in Ste. Genevieve never even reached puberty. Despite all of the children being conceived and born, the families in town were not all that large. The 1787 census shows that for the fifty-nine free white households with children and at least one parent living at home, the average number of children per household averaged only 3.2, with a range of one to nine. These figures do not include orphans or other boarders.[5]

Untoward mortality did not affect only children. It was not uncommon in colonial Ste. Genevieve for both parents to die and leave children to be cared for. An interesting case of the care of orphans is revealed in the 1787 census. Etienne Gouvreau, a village blacksmith, died in 1781 at age forty-five, and his wife, Marie-Jeanne La Vallée Gouvreau, died a short time later at age forty. Seven children survived, all boys. There was no family in town in a position to take in seven boys as boarders, so the children were farmed out to four different households. Three of them — Louis, Jean-Baptiste and Pierre — went to live with the family of an older married cousin, Elizabeth Bolduc Parent. Two, Etiennne *fils* and Michel, moved in with a widowed aunt, Marie-Louise Gouvreau Lacroix, to help her out around the house. Henri, age nine, was taken in by Louis Bolduc, an uncle-in-law, to be raised up with his two Bolduc cousins. And Antoine, age fifteen, went to live with another cousin, Jean-Baptiste Deguire Larose, who had just married Marie Roy and who had no children of his own yet. In this distributive fashion were the Gouvreau orphans cared for without being an excessive burden to any single household. The many Gouvreaus and Govros living in and around present-day Ste. Genevieve are likely descendents of these eighteenth-century orphan boys.[6]

During the mid-eighteenth century, Jean-Bernard Bossu visited Louisiana three times as a French naval officer. Bossu's curiosity about social customs and mores was omnivorous, and when he

---

4. Perrin du Lac, 169; SGPR, Baptisms; concerning fertility in nursing mothers, see Henripin, 86.

5. Corrected census of 1787, MHS, archives.

6. SGPR, Burials, Book 1:30, 40; census of 1787, MHS, archives.

wrote his travel accounts of Louisiana he remarked upon a broad range of human behavior, for both white men and red men. On the issue of feeding infants, Bossu commented that "Indian women would consider themselves disgraced if they abandoned their children to the care of a far-off nurse.... The pleasure of perpetuating the race and of seeing themselves live once again, day by day, in this little creature to which they have given life more than makes up for any hardship they may have to bear. The white women, who are called Creoles, follow European custom in America and do not nurse their children. As soon as a child is born, they give it to a black, colored, or Indian slave. . . ."[7]

Bossu was living at the beginning of the back-to-nature movement that was being promoted in France by Jean-Jacques Rousseau and his followers, and Bossu's proto-Romantic sentiment is apparent in his remarks about nursing in Louisiana. In any event, the creole women whom Bossu saw turning their infants over to the care of wetnurses were probably a small minority of the white mothers in Louisiana, for most of the women did not have slaves available to serve as nurses. Certainly the vast majority of white mothers in colonial Ste. Genevieve, as in French Canada, nursed their own children. When Perrin du Lac visited Commandant François Vallé II's household in 1802, he met Madame Vallé with an infant "à la mamelle." Perhaps, however, some women from families with many slaves (Bolduc, Vallé, Pratte, Bauvais) occasionally made use of black wetnurses.[8]

The fact of the matter is that on the subject of infant feeding, as with virtually everything else pertaining to child rearing in colonial Ste. Genevieve, we are woefully ignorant. Philippe Ariès, the French historian of childhood, has argued that a revolution in the concept of childhood was occurring during the Early Modern Period, that by the eighteenth century there was a much richer sense of the particular nature of childhood than there had been in centuries past. Children became central to family life; they were coddled and taken by adults to be objects of delight and amusement. The extent to which this revolution had come to pass in the French- creole society of the Mississippi Valley is simply not known, and may never be known.[9]

---

7. Bossu, *Travels*, 101.

8. Perrin du Lac, 169; concerning breast feeding in French Canada, see Henripin, 86.

9. Ariès, *Centuries of Childhood*, esp. 128-33.

One of the few sure things about children in colonial Ste. Genevieve is that, as in all premodern societies, many of them did not live to reach maturity. Perhaps the high rate of infant and child mortality meant that parents largely neglected their children during the first five or ten years of life. After all, why invest much time and energy in creatures who were likely to disappear at any moment? Our ignorance of childhood is doubly unfortunate, for it means that our knowledge of both children and adults is impoverished: we do not know how parents interrelated with their children or how methods of child rearing created the emotional matrix of the adult world. To know something about toilet training, early education, and patterns of work and play would enormously enrich our knowledge of society in colonial Ste. Genevieve. It seems likely, however, that no sources exist to reveal this kind of information.[10]

When Perrin du Lac visited Ste. Genevieve at the end of the colonial period he remarked that the children in town were "raised pell-mell with the little savages." One could interpret this to mean that children in Ste. Genevieve received a healthy and robust upbringing in the fresh air of a frontier settlement. Du Lac did not intend his remarks to be taken that way, however, for he also described the young people of Ste. Genevieve as "without schooling and with no desire to acquire it." The Frenchman was in fact appalled by the lack of formal education in Ste. Genevieve.[11]

Du Lac was not entirely correct when in 1802 he described the youth of Ste. Genevieve as being "without schooling," for by that time many youngsters in town had received some formal education. Had he visited Ste. Genevieve twenty-five years earlier, however, his remarks would have been closer to the mark. The Old Town of Ste. Genevieve was overwhelming a community of illiterates. It is not possible to state precisely what percentage of the residents of the Old Town were illiterate at any given time. But reckoning from the number of persons who could not sign legal documents — marriage contracts, petitions, bills of sale, and so forth — and rather had to affix their marks it is safe to say that fully three-quarters of the Old Town's population could neither read nor write. This percentage was roughly the same as in rural eighteenth-century France, whereas in colonial New England,

10. On infant and child mortality, see above, chap. viii.

11. Perrin du Lac, 172-73.

where the Puritans advocated individual Bible reading, the literacy
rate ran as high as sixty percent.[12]

Residents of the Old Town who could not sign their names
included influential person, such as Louis Bolduc *père* and the
André Deguires, *père* and *fils*. Beginning with François I, however,
the Vallé men were literate and signed their names with flourishes
as elaborate as those of educated Parisians. In general, women
were less likely than men to be literate in colonial Ste. Genevieve.
But the wives of François Vallé I and II, Marianne Billeron and
Marie Carpentier, could sign their names, although not with the
ornamentation that characterized their husbands' signatures. The
literacy of the Vallés, both males and females, surely contributed
to the power and influence that that family exercised in Ste.
Genevieve.[13]

Few residents of the Old Town owned books. Rather surprisingly, the detailed inventory of the estate of François Vallé I, who
was after all civil judge and captain of the militia in Ste. Genevieve,
does not include a single volume. This disdain for books continued
in Ste. Genevieve's first family to the end of the colonial period.
Bills of lading for goods shipped to the Vallé family from New
Orleans during the 1790s contain numerous luxury items but
never any books. With all of the effervescence — intellectual, political, and economic — that characterized European civilization at
that time, one would think that the Vallés might have shown some
interest in events that were transpiring in Paris or London. Evidently they had little or no intellectual curiosity. Books, even more
than literacy, were a function of a family's origin in colonial Ste.
Genevieve. The only persons in town who possessed small libraries
were those who had come from France via New Orleans or
Philadelphia. French Canadians, like the Vallés, had generally not
lugged books with them on the long trip from the St. Lawrence
Valley to the Illinois Country.[14]

The wealthy merchant of French origin, Jean Datchurut, had

---

12. Goubert, *L'Ancien Régime*, 2:244 ff.; Lockridge, *Literacy in Colonial New
England*.

13. François Vallé I learned to write as an adult after he had moved to Ste.
Genevieve, for when he lived in Kaskaskia during the early 1750s he still employed his mark on legal documents. It is interesting that Louis Bolduc *père*
could not sign his name, even though he came from a parish in Quebec, St.
Joachim, where a well-known school existed (Kalm, 2:452).

14. Inventory of Vallé estate, MHS, Vallé Collection, Box 1; see bills of lading
in ibid., Box 2.

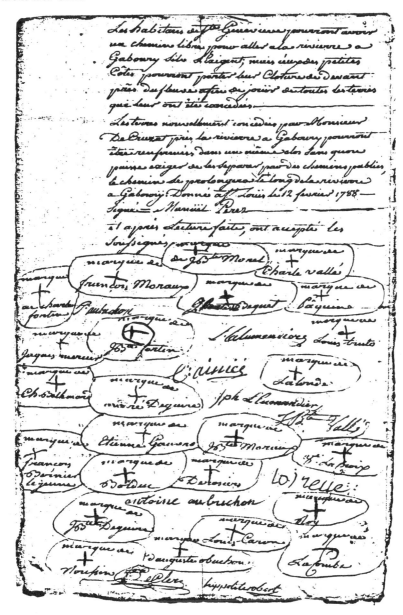

Signatures of townspeople on regulations for community fences,1788. Few of the habitants *could sign their names. Original in Ste. Genevieve County Courthouse. Copy courtesy of Ste. Genevieve County Court.*

a collection of some forty volumes that included a French grammar, six volumes of *Spectacle de la Nature*, four volumes of *Philosophe Chrétien*, and fourteen volumes of *Histoire Universelle*. Jean Datchurut's library consisted of standard, old-fashioned reference works, and in striking contrast to some libraries in St. Louis contained no modern authors of the French Enlightenment such as Voltaire, Montesquieu, or Buffon. Surely the Abbé de St. Pierre, who was an educated and cosmopolitan man, had a small library when he was parish priest in Ste. Genevieve, but the titles are not known. Charles Delassus de Luzières and his son, Charles Dehault Delassus, brought libraries with them when they settled at New Bourbon in 1793-94. These were the largest and most varied libraries in the area at that time. In 1793, the brother of Henri Peyroux, Pierre-Charles Peyroux, bequeathed "one chest of classics" and "two chests of books on agriculture and the arts" to Lieutenant Governor Trudeau with the expressed intention that the books should be used to aid education in the parish of Ste. Genevieve, but the fate of these books is unknown.[15]

Ste. Genevieve of the 1760s contained very few books, but by the late 1790s there were perhaps 500 to 1000 volumes in the Ste. Genevieve-New Bourbon area. John Francis McDermott studied the libraries of colonial St. Louis and discovered that the private libraries in the capital of Upper Louisiana contained several thousand books on a wide range of subjects — chemistry, botany, medicine, poetry, history, political economy and so on. The large number and variety of books in colonial St. Louis as opposed to Ste. Genevieve was likely due to two factors: there were more educated persons of French origin in the former than in the latter, and St. Louis was a commercial town that had more continuous contact with the cosmopolitan world of New Orleans than did Ste. Genevieve, which was more an agricultural community.[16]

The high rate of illiteracy and relative scarcity of books in colonial Ste. Genevieve did not, however, mean that the town was totally benighted and without regard for education. As early as 1787 there was a schoolmaster in Ste. Genevieve. This man, Louis Tonnellier, had immigrated to Spanish Louisiana from his native parish of St. Germain de l'Auxerrois, near the Halles quarter of

---

15. Datchurut estate, SGA, Estates, no. 77; McDermott, "Diary of Charles Delassus," 362; McDermott, *Private Libraries in Creole St. Louis,* 113-28; Liljegren, "Frontier Education," 365; Peyroux' will, SGA, Wills, no. 38.

16. McDermott, *Private Libraries.*

Paris. He married at Ste. Genevieve in 1786, probably not long after he had arrived in town. It is impossible to say who induced this educated young Parisian to take up school teaching. Probably it was either the town priest, St. Pierre, or the town commandant, Peyroux de la Coudrenière, both of whom were interested in education.[17]

In 1793, Judge H. H. Brackenridge of western Pennsylvania sent his seven-year-old son, Henry Marie, to Ste. Genevieve in order to learn French, an action that seems at once both callous and enlightened. It is not known whether Judge Brackenridge had heard about the existence of a school in Ste. Genevieve or whether he simply intended that his son should learn French by living with a creole family and conversing with the town's citizens. In any case, when young Henry took up his lodging *chez* Vital St. Gemme Bauvais in the New Town of Ste. Genevieve he knew, according to his own account, exactly two words of French — *oui* and *non*.[18]

Curiously, the schoolmaster who taught Henry Brackenridge in Ste. Genevieve remains unknown. Francis J. Yealy suggested that it was François Moreaux, but Moreaux seems an unlikely candidate since he could not even sign his own marriage contract. It is possible that Louis Tonnellier was still teaching at Ste. Genevieve during the mid-1790s. Tonnellier appeared as a small-time lead miner on the census of 1791, and in 1797 he was living as a farmer at New Bourbon. In February 1794, Catherine Millet Barsaloux, widow of Gérard Barsaloux, died in Ste. Genevieve, and the inventory of her estate included "an account book for her school." Catherine Barsaloux was a French Canadian woman who had moved to Ste. Genevieve during the winter of 1787-88. Her husband died in November 1788, and it is possible that Widow Barsaloux supported herself thereafter by operating some sort of an elementary school in Ste. Genevieve. But it is apparent that Catherine Barsaloux was not Henry Brackenridge's schoolteacher, who was assuredly a man. Although Brackenridge did not in his writings mention his teacher's name, he did recount that the teacher sometimes whipped him "for the edification of *his* other

---

17. Tonnellier was shown on the 1787 census (MHS, archives) as a schoolmaster; he signed his marriage contract (SGA, Marriage Contracts, no. 136) in 1786 with a handsome flourish. Yealy (p. 79) thought that St. Pierre was in charge of the school at Ste. Genevieve.

18. Brackenridge, *Recollections,* 22.

scholars." (Italics mine.)[19]

The whippings must have motivated Brackenridge, for the young American was soon judged the best reader in the school and awarded a set of teacups and saucers. This reward prompted Henry to remark that "from the nature of the prize, the presumption is, it was intended for the other sex." In another context, Brackenridge wrote about his "school-fellows, . . . who must now be the men and women of Ste. Genevieve." Thus it is apparent that the village school in Ste. Genevieve during the mid-1790s was a progressive, co-ed institution. Attendance was certainly voluntary, and it may be assumed that only a handful of the town's citizens sent their children to school. Book learning was for a small minority on the Mississippi Valley frontier.[20]

A fleeting opportunity for further educational opportunities at Ste. Genevieve arose with the arrival in the district of refugees from the French Revolution. When Delassus de Luzières' family joined him at Ste. Genevieve in early 1794, Madame de Luzières was accompanied by three Clarisse nuns, who had journeyed with her from Pittsburgh by riverboat. In February 1794, François Vallé wrote that the three nuns were going to devote themselves to "the education of young girls and care of the sick." Vallé also thought that the nuns "seemed very decent and enlightened" and that their settlement in Ste. Genevieve would be "precious for the colony." But the unstable political climate in Upper Louisiana prompted Governor Carondelet to recall the nuns to New Orleans. He described the circumstances in Ste. Genevieve as "little favorable" for the nuns' settlement there and felt that the well-known Ursuline Convent in New Orleans would be a more suitable place for them to live. By September 1794 the three nuns were on their way down to New Orleans, and De Luzières warned Carondelet about one of them, Mme. Le Blond: "It would be difficult to find a person more loquacious, more indiscreet, more tyrannical, and more stubborn." Her personality made De Luzières fear that she would not be "happy in the peaceful and honorable refuge to which you have destined them [the nuns]." Perhaps the children of Ste. Genevieve were fortunate that Mme. Le Blond did not stay on to become schoolmistress in town.[21]

19. Yealy, 124; census of 1791, *SRM*, 2:366; New Bourbon census of 1797, PC 2365; Barsaloux estate, SGA, Estates, no. 15; SGPR, Burials, Book 2:9; Brackenridge, *Recollections*, 204.

20. Brackenridge, *Recollections*, 28, 240.

21. Vallé to Trudeau, Feb. 24, 1794, PC 209; Carondelet to Trudeau, May 16, 1794, PC 21; De Luzières to Carondelet, Nov. 1, 1794, PC 210.

The mystery about the identity of Henry Brackenridge's schoolmaster in Ste. Genevieve is deepened by the "Observations on the Characteristics, Qualities, and Occupations of the White Settlers" that Delassus de Luzières appended to the New Bourbon census of 1797. In these observations, De Luzières remarked that when he had arrived at Ste. Genevieve (1793) there had been "a lack of public education for the youth" in the town. De Luzières then went on to say that he had engaged "Monsieur Frémon de Laurière, a young Breton gentleman who was very well-behaved and well-educated" to take up the profession of teaching school, and that this young man had been "successfully teaching for about two years to the satisfaction of the citizens in Ste. Genevieve and New Bourbon." De Luzières made these remarks in December 1797, which means that Augustin-Charles Frémon de Laurière probably began teaching in Ste. Genevieve sometime in 1795. If this is true, then Henry Brackenridge, who resided in Ste. Genevieve from 1793 to 1796, may have had several schoolmasters during his sojourn in town. This would explain why Brackenridge, who made repeated remarks about his schooling at Ste. Genevieve, never once mentioned a particular schoolmaster. Sources are lacking to clear up this confusion about the teaching profession in Ste. Genevieve during the mid-1790s. All that is known for certain is that by 1795 Frémon de Laurière, an aristocratic refugee from the French Revolution, was in fact the town schoolmaster.[22]

When in December 1797 De Luzières described Frémon de Laurière's position as schoolmaster in Ste. Genevieve, he mentioned that Frémon had been teaching his pupils "according to a rational plan of education." In the hope of persuading Governor Carondelet to provide a small stipend for Frémon, De Luzières sent the governor a copy of Frémon's rational plan. This educational prospectus, a rare document for having come from the Mississippi Valley frontier in the eighteenth century, has been translated and elucidated by Ernest Liljegren.[23]

Frémon began his plan by insisting that a good education must be something more than mere occupational training, that it must inculcate "the principles of virtue and the true philosophy." Next came an outline of eight fundamental points: 1) Classes to meet twice each week, On Wednesday evenings and Friday mornings. 2) Emphasis to be placed upon written composition with correct

---

22. De Luzières, "Observations, ..." PC 2365.

23. Ibid.; "Plan d'éducation propre à la jeunesse des Illinois, proposé par M. de Frémon," Apr. 1, 1796, PC 212 A; Liljegren, "Frontier Education," 358-70.

spelling. 3) Grades to be assigned each month on the basis of examinations and written compositions. 4) Prizes to be awarded every three months for best performance on public examinations. 5) Pupils to be divided into three classes according to level of achievement. 6) Instruction in the principles of the Roman Catholic faith not to be forgotten. 7) Physical education to include dancing, wrestling, running, foot races, etc. 8) Pupils to be helped to instruct themselves in the principles of drawing, painting, music, and classes to be held on the best principles of agriculture as practiced in France and England. In conclusion, Frémon recommended that instruction should soon be expanded to include instruction in both English and Spanish.[24]

Frémon's plan for educating the youth of colonial Ste. Genevieve was idealistic and ambitious, and surely was better suited for implementation in Europe than on the trans-Mississippian frontier. Nevertheless, it was a progressive and enlightened proposal for its time, and included the eminently practical goals of teaching young people to write and to learn something about the new agricultural techniques that were being used in western Europe. For modern eyes, surely the most conspicuous lacunae in Frémon's educational plan is its failure to mention any training in mathematics or science. Nowadays, first-graders learn about the heliocentric universe and memorize the names and locations of the various planets. Probably the youngsters of colonial Ste. Genevieve continued to believe in the Ptolemaic, geocentric universe, which is what the Catholic Church wanted them to believe.

Frémon's plan does not reveal whether or not girls were included in the educational system that he was implementing in Ste. Genevieve. Brackenridge's description of elementary education in town reveals that schooling was coeducational even before Frémon arrived in Ste. Genevieve, however, and it seems likely that that pattern would have persisted.

Ernest Liljegren has remarked that "of the Creole towns outside of New Orleans, Ste. Genevieve had the fullest measure of cultural advantages and made the greatest effort to foster education and learning. In truth, Ste. Genevieve was the cultural center of upper Louisiana." This contention might be disputed by pointing out that St. Louis possessed many more books dealing with a wider range of subjects, but it does seem clear that there was more concern for schooling in Ste. Genevieve than in any other town in Upper Louisiana.[25]

24. Ibid.
25. Liljegren, "Frontier Education," 372.

Schoolteaching in colonial Ste. Genevieve was not, any more than today, a lucrative occupation. Young, literate men newly arrived from France engaged in it only long enough to find work that promised better returns. Louis Tonnellier remained a schoolmaster only until he could get a start in lead mining and farming. And Frémon de Laurière taught in Ste. Genevieve for no more than four years, 1795-99. According to De Luzières, Governor Carondelet had promised to provide a government stipend for Frémon "in order to encourage him to continue an establishment so precious for the education of the youth," but Carondelet was succeeded by Gayoso de Lemos in 1797 and the stipend never materialized. It is not known who paid Frémon's salary during the time he taught in Ste. Genevieve; perhaps the parents of the pupils made contributions to sustain the school.[26]

It would be of interest to know just where in Ste. Genevieve Tonnellier and Frèmon conducted their classes. In 1791 Marguerite-Susanne Peyroux, mother of town commandant Henri Peyroux, drafted a will in which she bequeathed her residence in the Old Town and most of her possessions for the purpose of establishing a school ("maison d'education") for poor orphans. But Widow Peyroux changed her will three years later, and nothing seems to have come of her intended project. In 1793 Widow Peyroux's son, Pierre-Charles Peyroux, brother to Henri, bequeathed several tracts of land, as well as the three chests of books mentioned above, to help create a boys' school ("college de garcons") for the parish of Ste. Genevieve. Pierre Peyroux had a clear idea of what kind of an establishment this school was going to be, for his will proscribed tobacco smoking, "which is entirely prejudicial to learning." Peyroux's project fared no better than his mother's, and Ste. Genevieve was without an official school building until the famous Louisiana Academy was built in 1810. Perhaps the parish church, or a room in one of the larger houses, served as a school house during the 1790s.[27]

In June 1797, Governor Carondelet granted Frémon de Laurière permission to serve as unofficial town clerk in Ste. Genevieve, unofficial because Frémon had not been trained as a notary. From 1797 until 1802, Frémon functioned as *greffier* and drafted many of the legal documents in Ste. Genevieve, contracts, bills of sale, and so on. He also signed documents as an official witness (*témoin d'assistance*), although François Vallé as town commandant remained ultimately responsible for the validity of the

---

26. De Luzières, "Observations, . . ." PC 2365.
27. Peyroux wills, SGA, Wills, no. 36, no. 37, no. 38.

Petition by residents of the Ste. Genevieve District requesting that the General Court for Upper Louisiana be moved from St. Louis to Ste. Genevieve. Drafted shortly after the Louisiana Purchase, this petition shows a majority of Anglo-American names. Louis Bolduc père *was one of the few signers who could not write his own name. Courtesy of Missouri Historical Society, St. Louis.*

documents. Whether Frémon's income from his paralegal work permitted him to abandon schoolteaching altogether is not known. In any case, he did not remain long in the teaching profession and was soon involved in land development and salt-making. Formal education was simply not valued highly enough in colonial Ste. Genevieve to permit the retention of a permanent schoolmaster. For the last six years of the colonial period the youth of Ste. Genevieve were free, in the words of Perin du Lac, "to occupy themselves exclusively with hunting, horseback riding, and dancing."[28]

It would seem that sporadic but persistent elementary education of some sort was being offered in Ste. Genevieve from the time of Louis Tonnellier's arrival in town (1785?) until the time that Frémon de Laurière gave up teaching (1799?). The subject matter was obviously very limited, for when François Vallé II wanted his son François III to learn English the boy had to be sent to New York City in 1796. Yet the continued efforts to provide at least some skills did apparently pay off. The literacy rate within the creole population of Ste. Genevieve was higher in the 1790s than it had been in the 1770s. This can be seen in petitions signed by the citizens of Ste. Genevieve at different times. Toward the end of the colonial era significantly more of the petitioners signed their names than had twenty years earlier. Some of this change can be attributed to the immigration to Ste. Genevieve of literate persons, both Anglo-Americans and creoles, from the east side of the Mississippi. But some of the change was brought about by increasing literacy within the indigenous population of Ste. Genevieve. Louis Bolduc *père* and the André Deguires I and II could not sign their names, but Louis Bolduc *fils* and André Deguire III could.

One can only guess at the other salutary effects Ste. Genevieve's colonial schools may have had upon life in the community. Perhaps the conversation and demeanor of young persons in town were superior to those of the youth at other posts in Spanish Louisiana; perhaps a civilized quality of life existed in Ste. Genevieve during the late colonial period that was unique to the Mississippi frontier at that time; perhaps Ernest Liljegren was even correct to claim that for several years Ste. Genevieve was "the cultural center of upper Louisiana."[29]

28. Carondelet to De Luzières, June 3, 1797, PC 214; Perrin du Lac, 172.
29. Liljegren, "Frontier Education," 372.

Chapter X

Daily Life in the Colonial Community

COLONIAL STE. GENEVIEVE, whether Old Town or New Town, had a strongly rural flavor. Fernand Braudel has remarked about Early Modern European villages that "the towns urbanized the countryside, but the countryside 'ruralized' the towns too . . . . In fact town and countryside never separate like oil and water." This observation is *a fortiori* true for Ste. Genevieve because the residential lots *(terrains)* were larger than they were in European villages. Although by the end of the colonial period some of the larger lots were already being subdivided, the standard residential lot in both Old Town and New Town was a square arpent (approximately .85 acre). In addition to the main house, these lots often contained a cow barn, a stable, a henhouse, a corncrib, an orchard, a vegetable garden, a bake oven, a well, sometimes a slave's quarters, and occasionally a detached free-standing kitchen.[1]

Henry Brackenridge remarked upon the aspect of Ste. Genevieve with which he was familiar:[2]

> Although there is something like regularity of streets, and the houses are built in front of them, they do not adjoin, while the gardens, orchards, and stables, occupy a considerable extent of ground. Each house with its appurtences, has the appearance of one of our farm-yards. All kinds of cattle, cows, hogs, sheep, mingle with the passengers, in the streets.

1. Braudel, *The Structures of Everyday Life*, 486.
2. Brackenridge, *Views of Louisiana*, 119.

With their outbuildings, animals and their usual enclosure of picket fencing, the major residences of colonial Ste. Genevieve were like small rural estates. Clearly the sounds, sights, and smells of the town were those of the barnyard: cocks crowing, calves bawling, pigs squealing, urine sizzling, and manure steaming. Some of this rural flavor is still discernible at the restored Jean-Baptiste Vallé residence, although the number of animals there has been reduced to one friendly dog and one spoiled cat.

Around most residential lots in Ste. Genevieve ran a picket fence, for the French Canadian settlers in the Mississippi Valley did not fence their grazing animals in, instead they fenced them out. That is, instead of fencing in pasture lands, the system of husbandry was to permit the animals to graze freely in and around the village and on the village commons; stock was only fenced out of the arable lands (the Big Field) and individual residential lots.

But the enclosed residential compounds involved another issue, which was a matter of taste and not merely of practicality. The French creoles apparently had a passion for picket fencing around their residences. This was perceived by the Anglo-American merchant, George Morgan, who was living in English Illinois in 1770. At Fort de Chartres (Cavendish), Morgan recorded a conversation with Colonel Wilkins about the pros and cons of picketing in one's property: "I told him that I would Picket in my Lott . . . . He answered it was not worth while as no one would buy my Lott after the Troops went home from here. I answered that the Pickets would always be an inducement for Some of the French to Purchase my House and Lott, *even if it was only for the sake of the Pickets.*" (Italics mine) Thus the picket fences that the French colonists in the Illinois Country insisted upon building around their residential lots served for something more than control of foraging animals: in pursuit of privacy, or because they wished literally to stake out what belonged to them, these settlers demanded picket fencing.[3]

When François Vallé ordered posts for a *poteaux-en-terre* house in 1781, he also ordered 1,243 pickets eight feet (seven and one-half French feet) long. Reckoning each picket at between seven and eight inches in diameter (Brackenridge said they were eight to ten inches at the Vital St. Gemme Bauvais residence),

---

3. Morgan memorandum, Sep. 30, 1770, Morgan Papers, IHS.

and assuming that they were set picket-to-picket two feet into the ground, these 1,243 pickets would have enclosed a plot almost precisely one arpent square (192 feet per side) with a fence six feet high. The picket fences surrounding the houses in Ste. Genevieve were a distinctive feature of the town's landscape, and the demand for such fencing drove up the price of cedar, which by the 1790s cost three times as much as oak.[4]

Colonial Ste. Genevieve consisted of a broad array of human habitations. It would be an error to conceive of the town as having been made up uniformly of substantial dwellings of the sort that still exist. People lived in picket lean-tos, barken shanties, rough log cabins, and thatched-roof sheds as well as in the more solid and permanent houses that are familiar to us. The humbler dwellings have of course long-since disappeared.

The better houses in colonial Ste. Genevieve, whether Old Town or New Town, were remarkably similar in shape and style, although not in size. Brackenridge noted that the "houses are built in a very singular form, and it is said, copied after the fashion of the West Indies. They do not exceed one story in height, and those of the more wealthy are surrounded with spacious galleries; some only on one or two sides, while the poorer class are obliged to put up with naked walls, and a poor habitation." Charles Peterson traced the origins of various elements of the French Illinois house to eastern Canada, northern France, Lower Louisiana, and the West Indies. More recently, Melburn Thurman has emphasized the way in which these borrowed elements were combined to create a style of architecture unique to the Illinois Country.[5]

Houses in colonial Ste. Genevieve were usually rectangular, vertical-log structures. The interstices between the logs were filled with saplings and nogging made of straw and clay *(bouzillage)* or stones and mortar *(pierrotage)*, and whitewash was smeared over the exterior to seal the walls. In the early nineteenth century, the American preacher Timothy Flint remarked about Ste. Genevieve that "the greater proportion of the houses have mud walls, whitened with lime, which have much the most pleasant appearance at a distance." Flint was seemingly unaware of the sophisti-

---

4. Vallé's order, Oct. 2, 1781, MHS, Vallé Collection, Box 1.

5. Brackenridge, *Views of Louisiana,* 119; Peterson, "Early Ste. Genevieve," 207-32; Peterson, "The Houses of French St. Louis," 17-40; Thurman, *Building a House,* 25.

cated framing that underlay the whitewash. This framing was erected in one of two ways.[6]

The simplest procedure required a rectangular trench of the desired dimensions. Dressed logs were then inserted upright in the trench, after which they were backfilled. French colonists in the Mississippi River Valley called this type of construction, *poteaux-en-terre* — posts in the earth. In 1781 François Vallé I bought eighty-four "seddre" posts 11.70 feet (eleven French feet) long in order to build a house. Cedar was the most rot-resistent and the most desirable wood to use for the palisade-style house walls, but it was also the most expensive, and often other woods like white oak or mulberry were substituted. The still-standing Bequette-Ribault House has walls of the long-lasting cedar posts. *Poteaux-en-terre* was the most popular method of house construction in Ste. Genevieve throughout the colonial period.[7]

The more sophisticated method of construction, in which squared vertical logs were joined to wooden sills that in turn rested on a stone foundation (*poteaux-sur-solle* or *maison à colombage*), was also used in Ste. Genevieve, although somewhat less commonly. *Poteaux-sur-solle* construction was much like *poteaux-en-terre*, both utilizing vertical logs, but was more complicated, more expensive, and had two distinct advantages: structures built in this fashion were more resistant to rot and insects because their wooden members were not planted in the earth; secondly, they could be more readily dissembled and their components reused elsewhere. Because in this style construction the timbers did not come into contact with the soil, there was no need to use a thoroughly rot-resistant wood like cedar, and oak was most often used for the vertical posts. Placement on sills, however, meant that there was less lateral stability than in *poteaux-en-terre* construction. To solve this problem some of the vertical members were placed at angles, thus triangulating the wall structure to provide greater strength.[8]

One of the largest and most unusual houses in the Old Town was that of the wealthy merchant Jean Datchurut. Datchurut was an unusual figure in many ways: he came to the Illinois Country straight from France (instead of via Canada); he was purely and simply a merchant, not engaging in agriculture; he had no family;

6. Flint, *Recollections*, 100.

7. Vallé's purchase order, Oct. 2, 1781, MHS, Vallé Collection, Box 1.

8. Peterson, "Early Ste. Genevieve," 217; Peterson, "Houses of French St. Louis," 26-27; Moogk, *Building a House in New France*, chap. ii.

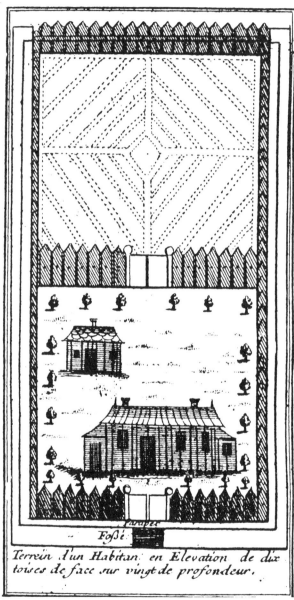

Terrein d'un Habitan en Elevation de dix
toises de face sur vingt de profondeur.

A French colonial residence in New Orleans as depicted by Dumont de Montigny. Notice the formal garden, the picket fence surrounding the property, the appentis *on the ends of the house, and what is perhaps a slave quarters behind the house. Residences in colonial Ste. Genevieve were similar to this but had larger lots and more outbuildings.*

and he had an unusual house. This structure, which was probably built when Datchurut arrived in the Old Town about 1766, was long and narrow (47.85 x 21.27 English feet) and was apparently a kind of transitional house, for on one side of it the vertical posts were set in the ground and on the other upon sills. How these two different forms of construction were tied together at the corners is not known, but in any case, Datchurut's *maison mixte* was probably unique in the Old Town.[9]

At least two galleries projected from the better houses in colonial Ste. Genevieve, front and back, and often there were galleries on all four sides. These galleries were usually five or six feet wide and served two purposes: they provided additional living space in fair weather, and their roofs protected the main body of the house from both sun and rain. In lieu of galleries, usually on the ends of the house, were often *appantis* (or *appentis*), which were shed-like projections that provided additional space within the houses. None of these have survived, and it is not known just how they looked or how they were integrated with the galleries.

Houses with walls of mortared limestone (*maison en pierre*), which were common in French Canada and also appeared in Kaskaskia, were rare in Ste. Genevieve during the colonial period. The Indian Trading Post and the so-called Hubardeau House date from the early nineteenth century. Just south of town, the Vital Bauvais House with its beautifully trussed roof is probably the oldest stone house in the area, and it may have been built late in the colonial era. A French Canadian version of horizontal log construction, with finely dressed logs slotted into upright posts at regular intervals (*pièce-sur-pièce*), appeared occasionally in colonial Ste. Genevieve. The well-known St. Louis merchant, Jacques Clamorgan, had such a building constructed on Rue à l'Eglise (now Market) adjacent to Jean-Baptiste Vallé's property in the late 1790s. Buildings covered with clapboards or constructed of brick were probably not seen in Ste. Genevieve until the early American period. The Guibourd House, which was built in 1805 or 1806, originally had a hipped instead of a gable roof, and the clapboards were probably added later. It is questionable whether there was any sawmill in Ste. Genevieve capable of cutting clapboards during the colonial period. Perhaps John Price built the Old Brick House facing the Place de l'Eglise (Courthouse Square) shortly before the Louisiana Purchase, as is claimed locally, but it seems more

9. Description of Datchurut's house in SGA, Estates, no. 78.

likely that he built the house after 1804, when he bought land on what is now Third Street from Nicolas Roussin. Brackenridge remarked that early in the nineteenth century "some alteration is perceptible in the general appearance of the villages, from the introduction of a new mode of building by the Americans, of frame, stone, or brick."[10]

Whether of *poteaux-en-terre* or *poteaux-sur-solle* construction, the walls of most of the early houses were surmounted by roof framing of wooden trusses, heavy members pegged together. Over the main portion of the house, these trusses were designed to create a steeply pitched roof because the roofing material, either straw or wood, required such a pitch to shed rain without leaking. Over the galleries or porches, where weather-tightness was less important, the pitch of the roofs was much less steep and was uniform on ends and sides if the galleries extended around the entire house, such as on the restored Bolduc house.

Although the houses were occasionally thatched above the trusses, thatching had two disadvantages: it was vulnerable to fire and provided an excellent habitat for vermin. If thatching continued to be used for outbuildings and slave *cabanes*, the primary dwellings of both the Old and New Towns were roofed with *bardeaux*, wooden shingles. The assumption would be that they were split rather than sawn, but the contract for the Bolduc house of 1770 obliges Bolduc "to have sawn [*scier*] and delivered the shingles required for the house." Perhaps the sawing referred to here was merely the sectioning of a tree trunk from which sections the shingles were later split.[11]

Over forty years ago, Charles Peterson noted that "toward the end of the colonial period, there is ever increasing mention of the *maison en boulins*" in the Ste. Genevieve civil records. This is true, and furthermore these "maisons en boulins" were often roofed with "mairins" instead of the usual "bardeaux." In 1796, for example, Jean-Baptiste Bequet sold a house built "en boulins" and roofed with "mairins" for 150 livres. The fact that even a modest

10. A University of Missouri research group is working to ascertain the construction date of the Vital Bauvais stone house, but has not yet published its results. The *pièce-sur-pièce* building on Clamorgan's property also had an *appanti* on one end (SGA, Deeds, no. 90); on *pièce-sur-pièce* construction in French Canada, see Moogk, *Building a House*, 28-35. Roussin to Price, Mar. 28, 1804, SGA, Deeds, no. 333.

11. SGA, Contracts, no. 5. On the roofing of French creole houses, see Peterson, "Houses of French St. Louis," 19-23; Peterson, "Early Ste. Genevieve," 216-17.

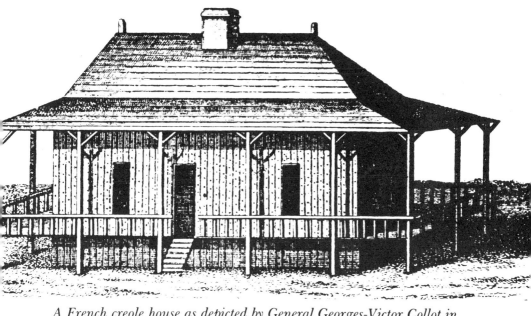

A French creole house as depicted by General Georges-Victor Collot in the mid-1790s. In this illustration the vertical posts are placed too close together.

Model of a French creole house built by the National Park Service. This is of the poteaux-en-terre *type, which was the most common in colonial Ste. Genevieve. Notice the shutters on both windows and doors.*

house of vertical logs and shingles was bringing 500-600 livres at that time demonstrates that the houses "en boulins" and roofed with "mairins" were lesser structures. None of these have survived and no one seems to know just what "boulins" and "mairins" were. Peterson thought that "boulins" were simply undressed logs laid horizontally in American fashion, and Peter Moogk, an expert on French Canadian houses, agrees. No conclusive evidence has been adduced for this contention, but there is sound logic behind it given the increased American influence in Ste. Genevieve toward the end of the colonial period. "Mairins" seem to have been boards or slats of some sort, and they were probably laid down vertically, creating a board-and-batten style roof. These unsolved problems are merely indicative of the large lacunae in our knowledge of creole material culture for the Upper Mississippi Valley.[12]

In layout the houses of both the Old Town and the New Town were overwhelming rectangular, single-story structures. The smallest were as small as 10 x 15 French feet, more cabins than houses. The largest house on record was one in the Old Town belonging to Jean-Baptiste Bauvais that measured 30 x 50, plus galleries. But there were a number of large residences in the Old Town. In addition to the Bauvais house, Henri Carpentier's measured 25 x 30, Commandant Rocheblave's was 20 x 50, Jean Datchurut's 20 x 45, Jean-Baptiste Morel's 23 x 40, and Simon Hubardeau's 25 x 30. And to those dimensions must be added the galleries, which provided additional living space during much of the year.[13]

Residential floor plans in colonial Ste. Genevieve were starkly simple. Most dwellings were one or two room affairs, and all household activities — cooking, eating, sleeping, and socializing — took place in close proximity to each other. Even the wealthy Louis Bolduc had a residence in the New Town that was basically a two-room structure, and this served as Bolduc's office as well as his residence. The smaller Bequette-Ribault house on St. Mary's Road is an excellent example of the two-room variety with a fireplace in each room. The galleries, which the Bequette-Ribault house had on all four sides, provided substantial additional living

---

12. Peterson, "Early Ste. Genevieve," 218; SGA, Deeds, no. 39. Peter Moogk, personal communication.

13. One French foot equals 12.76 English inches (see below, Appendix G). SGA, Estates, no. 19; ibid., no. 51; MHS, Vallé Collection, Box 1; SGA, Estates, no. 78; SGA, Deeds, no. 431; ibid., Contracts, no. 20.

The Bequette-Ribault House in process of restoration. This poteaux-en-terre *house on St. Mary's Road is now owned by Royce and Margaret Wilhauk. When Jesse Francis, Jack Luer, and Melburn Thurman complete the restoration, this structure will have a hipped roof and galleries on all four sides.*

space in fair weather.[14]

The large houses of colonial Ste. Genevieve tended to be long and narrow in configuration, with rooms set end to end and side to side. A new architectural notion, the hallway, was just coming into use in Europe during the eighteenth century and appeared only rarely in the Mississippi Valley. The residence of former town commandant, Philippe de Rocheblave, in the Old Town, which was sold at public auction in 1777, was described as having "two interior walls across and then two more intersecting walls, with a double stone chimney." Vital St. Gemme Bauvais's house

14. The Bolduc House and the Bequette-Ribault House were catalogued and described by the Historic American Buildings Survey in the 1930s (HABS survey numbers MO-1105, MO-1114). Dr. Melburn Thurman has determined that the Bequette-Ribault House had originally only one room and one fireplace (*Building a House*, 14-19).

in the New Town had a floor plan similar to Rocheblave's in the Old Town, although it was somewhat smaller and had only two instead of four *cabinets* or small bedrooms. Brackenridge described the Bauvais house in this way: "The house . . . was a long, low building, with a porch or shed in front, and another in the rear; the chimney occupied the centre, dividing the house into two parts, each with a fireplace. One of these served for dining room, parlour and principal bed chamber; the other was the kitchen; and each had a small room taken off at the end for private chambers or cabinets." The general-purpose living room in the Bauvais house, as in most residences in colonial Ste. Genevieve, was called the *salle.*[15]

The house that Louis Bolduc *père* had built at the Old Town in 1770-71 had two doors, presumably front and rear, and five windows, probably one for each of five rooms arranged as in Rocheblave's house. The 1769 contract for Simon Hubardeau's house called specifically for glazed windows, "fenêtres vitrées," and doubtless Bolduc's house had the same. Lesser houses likely had windows covered with oiled skin or cloth instead of expensive imported glass. Bolduc's windows were probably of the casement type and may have been built by Pierre La Chapelle or François Chauvin *père,* who were cabinet makers in Ste. Genevieve at that time. Windows in the substantial residences had exterior shutters (*volets* or *contrevents*) in the French and French Canadian manner, and shutters required expensive, imported hardware. The expense of glass and hardware, in addition to the difficulties of heating in winter months, meant that windows were kept to a minimum in the houses of colonial Ste. Genevieve. Most of the better houses were "planchée haut et bas," that is they had planked floors (instead of earthen or puncheon) and also had floor boards in the *grenier* (attic) to provide storage space and separate that area from the main living quarters below. Interior walls were daubed with clay, which when dry was coated with whitewash.[16]

Paradoxically, life in the houses of frontier Ste. Genevieve was in many respects like life in the royal chateau at Versailles: crowded and cold in the winter and crowded and hot in the summer. Widow François Vallé II, who died in 1811, had a Franklin stove

15. MHS, Vallé Collection, Box 1; Brackenridge, *Recollections of the West,* 24.

16. SGA, Contracts, no. 5 and no. 20. La Chapelle and Chauvin were listed on the 1779 militia muster roll (PC 213) as "menuisiers." See also Green, "Material Culture of a Pre-enclosure Village."

Hand-hewn oak truss in the roof of the Bequette-Ribault House. Notice the pegged mortise-and-tenon joints. Photo courtesy of Holly Johnson.

("cheminée à la franclin") to comfort her in her last years, but there were no stoves in colonial Ste. Genevieve. Fireplaces, even several of them per house, do not keep a dwelling very comfortable, for they tend to provide more smoke than warmth. And during the summer months, in addition to oppressive heat unknown in France or Canada, there was the plague of flying insects. Fly screens had not yet been invented, but mosquito netting was known and surely it was used over the beds during the summer. Winter, even with cold, smoky, and crowded houses, must have been a welcome respite after months of swatting mosquitos and flies.[17]

The large families living in relatively small houses (even those of the wealthy) meant that things were usually crowded at home. The average household in Ste. Genevieve consisted of five white persons, and the average house contained only about 600 square feet. Compare that to modern American conditions, in which a family of five is likely to have 1,500-2,000 square feet of living space. The wealthy Jean Morel had a family of nine persons living in a residence of less than 1,100 square feet in the Old Town, and in the New Town Hypolite Robert had his family of ten living in less than 700 square feet.[18]

Premodern people, including the well-to-do, cared very little about domestic privacy as we know it today, and that insouciance helped the townspeople of colonial Ste. Genevieve endure living circumstances that we would consider intolerable. As the French historian of the Early Modern family, Phillipe Ariès, has remarked: "In the same rooms where they ate, people slept, worked, danced, and received visitors." A few married couples had their own tiny *cabinet* to themselves, but conjugal intimacy was more often confined to under-the-covers, or sometimes, to the privacy of a four-poster bed equipped with draw curtains. Big feather beds play a prominent role in the inventories of family estates, and each big bed inevitably included its "traversin," the long, sausage-like pillow that often perplexes American tourists on their first trip to Europe. Sleeping conditions within the households were much like those described by Laura Ingalls Wilder in *Little House in the Big Woods*: "Alice and Ella and Mary and Laura all [slept] in one big bed on

---

17. SGA, Estates, no. 227.

18. Family sizes based upon SGPR and the census of 1787 (MHS archives); SGA, Deeds no.431; ibid., no. 327.

The Louis Bolduc house as restored by Ernest Allen Connally with funds provided by the Matthews family. The house is now owned and operated as a historic site by the Colonial Dames of America.

the floor. Peter had the trundle bed. Aunt Eliza and Uncle Peter were going to sleep in the big bed, and another bed was made on the attic floor for Pa and Ma." Well-to-do folks in Ste. Genevieve used linen bedsheets on their featherbeds.[19]

Domestic furniture other than beds tended to be sparse and crude. Concerning the wealthy Vital Bauvais household, Brackenridge recalled that "the furniture, excepting the beds and the looking glass, was of the most common kind, consisting of an armoire, a rough table or two, and some course chairs." Estate inventories confirm Brackenridge's recollections and suggest that stuffed chairs were rare and chests with pull drawers virtually unknown in colonial Ste. Genevieve. Local craftsmen certainly did, however, turn out beautiful armoires of native black walnut and wild cherry. When former commandant Henri Peyroux moved to New Madrid in 1799, he found the ceilings in the house he had rented too low to accommodate his massive armoires, and

19. Ariès, *Centuries of Childhood*, 394; Wilder, *Little House in the Big Woods*, 67.

his only option was to seek another dwelling place.[20]

Neither interior walls nor woodwork of the residences was painted. The principal ornamental as well as practical furnishing in many Ste. Genevieve households was a mirror. These were expensive, and a large one with a good frame was worth 100-200 livres. Many households also contained some small religious artifacts. Henri Carpentier, a wealthy individual, had for example little paintings of Christ and St. Anne in gilded frames. The impression remains, however, that the interiors of the houses were simple though not Spartan. Interior lighting was accomplished largely with candles, and both candelabra and candle molds played a prominent role among household possessions. Wealthier households had window curtains for decoration and to provide a bit of privacy.[21]

Food was most often prepared in the general purpose room of the houses, and the cooking was done in the central fireplace located there. Some residences had detached, freestanding kitchens, although they were never as lavish as the one to be seen at the Pierre Menard house on the east side of the Mississippi. The restoration of the kitchen behind the Bolduc house was largely conjectural, but Henri Carpentier had a detached kitchen sixteen feet square behind his residence in the Old Town. Most residences had a bread oven made of baked clay located outside the main house. An occasional wealthy household (Rocheblave, Datchurut, Carpentier) had a bake oven of bricks, which were probably fired in a clamp on the site.[22]

The cooks, white housewives or black slaves, commanded quantities of implements and utensils with which to prepare, cook, and serve food. An inventory of a modest household in 1770 included a large wooden trough for kneading bread dough (*une huche*), a hutch for dishes (*un vaisselier*), six plates, three platters and a bowl of pewter, six pewter spoons, six steel forks (pewter does not work well for forks), three iron kettles, and a large frying pan. A wealth-

---

20. Brackenridge, *Recollections of the West*, 24; Peyroux to Delassus ?, Nov. 12, 1799, PC 216 A. Concerning creole furniture of the Illinois Country, see the excellent article by Charles Van Ravenswaay, "The Creole Arts and Crafts of Upper Louisiana," 213-48; see also Lessard and Marquis, *Encyclopédie des antiquités du Québec.*

21. SGA, Estates, no. 50.

22. SGA, Estates, no. 50, no. 78; auction of Rocheblave residence in MHS, Vallé Collection, Box 1. An interesting study of French Canadian bake ovens is Boily and Blanchette, *Les fours à pain au Québec.*

The rebuilt free-standing kitchen behind the Louis Bolduc house. Although some of the wealthier residents of colonial Ste. Genevieve did have such kitchens, this reconstruction is largely conjectural.

ier household like the Carpentier's had in addition numerous bowls and platters of faience, several copper kettles, and two deep-dish pans (*tourtières*) with covers.[23]

The townspeople were not of the sort to write down recipes, and no recipe from colonial Ste. Genevieve had survived. Yet there is a fair amount of scattered information about the food they ate. Brackenridge remarked that "with the poorest French peasant, cookery is an art well understood. They make great use of vegetables, and prepared in a manner to be wholesome and palatable. Instead of roast and fried, they had soups and fricasses, and gumbos, (a dish supposed to be derived from the Africans) and a variety of other dishes." Gumbo — from an African word for okra, *quingombo* — may indeed have originated in Africa. Perhaps the Bauvais's black cook had something to do with turning out gumbos for the family, for her ancestry was from Africa, or perhaps Lower Louisiana, whereas the Bauvais family was French Canadian in origin. Only by virtue of domestic black slaves did African-creole cooking from the Gulf Coast arrive in the upper Mississippi Valley.[24]

Regarding French colonial concern for good food, Meriwether Lewis recorded a revealing case that arose during the Lewis and Clark Expedition. The expedition's cook, Charbono (Charbonneau), was preparing a sausage of bison flesh, and he began by taking "about six feet of the lower extremity of the large gut of the Buffaloe . . . [that] the cook makes love to." When Charbono had finished the sausage, "it is taken and fryed with bears oil until it becomes brown, when it is ready to esswage the pangs of a keen appetite or such as travelers in the wilderness are seldom at a loss for." It is difficult to imagine an Anglo-American frontiersman making love to a bison colon in order to produce a toothsome sausage for supper.[25]

No doubt the townspeople of Ste. Genevieve ate bison on occasion, as well as other game: deer, squirrels, bears, ducks, and geese. What percentage of their meat intake consisted of game cannot be said, but probably they ate more beef, pork, and domes-

23. SGA, Contracts, no. 17; SGA, Estates, no. 50; for French Canadian household items, see Genêt, et. al., *Les objets familiers de nos ancêtres.*

24. Brackenridge, *Recollections of the West,* 25. On African influence in French Louisiana, see Fiehrer, "African Presence," 3-31.

25. This story is recounted in McDermott, *Glossary of Mississippi River Valley French,* 32-33. Charbonneau was married to the famous Sacajawea.

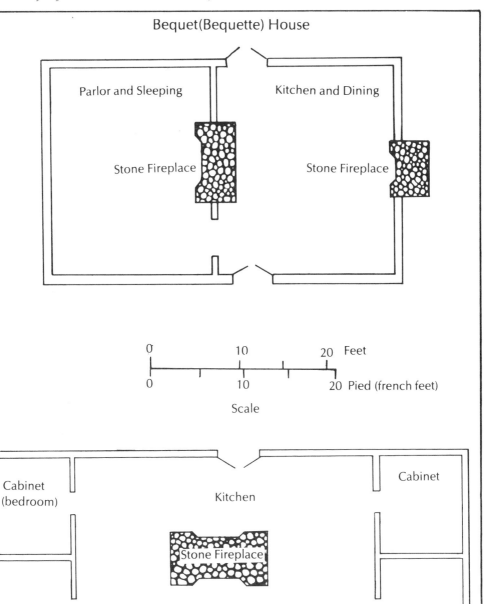

Bequet(Bequette) House

Parlor and Sleeping

Kitchen and Dining

Stone Fireplace

Stone Fireplace

0   10   20   Feet

0   10   20   Pied (french feet)

Scale

Cabinet
(bedroom)

Kitchen

Cabinet

Stone Fireplace

Cabinet

Salle (Parlor and Dining)

Cabinet

Rocheblave House

tic fowl than game. Pork may have been the favorite meat of Frenchmen in the Illinois Country. Smoked hams were a specialty of the region, and many were shipped downriver to New Orleans. In the autumn of 1795, the founding father of Cape Girardeau, Louis Lorimier, invited François Vallé II to come down for a visit in order to feast on suckling pig, for Lorimier had "many fine, fat ones ready to slaughter." In 1799 Pascal Detchemendy, a relative newcomer to Ste. Genevieve from France, was granted a concession of land for raising beef cattle in order that he might open a butcher shop to supply the town with fresh meat the year around. It is not known if Detchemendy's enterprise succeeded, but if so it was surely the first such business in Ste. Genevieve.[26]

Bear oil was a delicacy throughout the Mississippi Valley, and according to Paul Alliot was produced in large quantities by the townspeople of Ste. Genevieve. "In their forests they find bears prodigiously fat and large, the oil from which is much sought after by the inhabitants, even by those of New Orleans. Although it is very bitter to the taste, it is preferred to the poor oil of Provence." Bear oil was used for shortening, for seasoning, and even for salad dressings.[27]

Fish for human consumption were taken from numerous rivers and streams, and the North American fish that most impressed Frenchmen was the catfish. They adopted the Indian name for this fish, *barbüe* or *barbel,* and found its flesh "very good and delicate." Evidence that catfish were plentiful in the Ste. Genevieve region is seen in an early name for the Meramec River, "Rivière à la Barbüe," Catfish River.[28]

Residents of the Illinois Country during the eighteenth century did not enjoy three of the summer specialties that people in that area enjoy today — sliced tomatoes, corn on the cob, and potato salad. Indian corn (maize), of which great quantities were grown in the Big Field of Ste. Genevieve, seems to have been used largely for feeding domestic stock and black slaves and for producing corn liquor. Only as a last resort was corn rather than wheat used to make bread. In 1797 the commandant at New Madrid, Charles

---

26. Lorimier to Vallé, Aug. 16, 1795, MHS, Vallé Collection, Box 2; Detchemedy to Delassus, Sep. 27, 1799, MHS, Delassus Collection, Box 3.

27. Alliot, "Historical and Political Reflections on Louisiana," 133.

28. Dumont de Montigny, *Mémoires historiques,* 1:95; Le Page du Pratz, *History of Louisiana,* 286-88; Bellin map of 1755, Tucker (ed.), *Indian Villages, Atlas,* Plate XXIV.

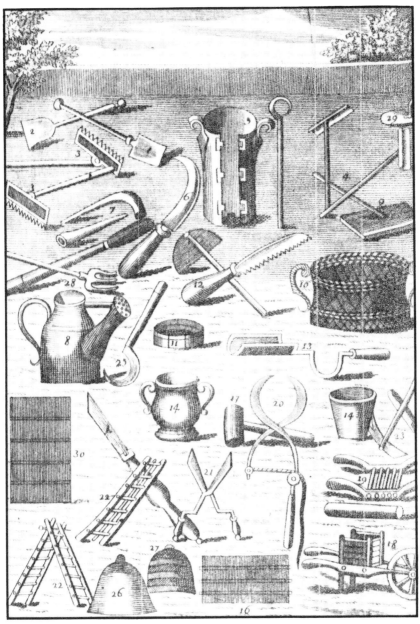

Household tools and implements as shown in **La Nouvelle Maison Rustique,** *a popular book in eighteenth-century France. Many of the objects shown here appear in estate inventories from colonial Ste. Genevieve. Notice the sprinkling can on the left.*

A typical huche *of French North America. They were used for kneading bread dough. This one is made of pine and is in the collection of the Missouri Historical Society in St. Louis.*

A freestanding oven from Quebec. In colonial Ste. Genevieve bread was baked in ovens like this, some made of clay and some of brick. Notice the long-handled pelle, *which was used to insert and extract the loaves from the oven. Photo courtesy of the National Museums of Canada.*

Delassus, reported to Governor Carondelet that ice floes on the Mississippi had prevented boats from going to Ste. Genevieve for foodstuffs and that the residents of New Madrid had for six weeks been "reduced" to eating corn bread. Potatoes were apparently not grown in the Illinois Country during most of the colonial period, for in 1770 the English trader George Morgan ordered seed potatoes shipped to Kaskaskia from Pennsylvania. By 1797, however, Delassus de Luzières, described experiments in raising "patates anglaises," English potatoes, in the New Bourbon District. Tomatoes remained virtually untouched by human lips in the eighteenth century, for they were usually deemed to be poisonous.[29]

Despite the absence of maize, potatoes, and tomatoes in their diets, the townspeople of Ste. Genevieve were not lacking for fruit and vegetables. When Jean-Baptiste Bauvais's residence in the Old Town was sold in April 1776 it included a "kitchen garden [*jardin potager*], already planted." And Henry Brackenridge described the yard of Vital Bauvais's home in the New Town like this: "It was, indeed, a garden — in which the greatest variety, and the finest vegetables were cultivated, intermingled with flowers and shrubs: on one side of it, there was a small orchard containing a variety of the choicest fruits."[30]

Although Frenchmen in the Mississippi Valley were reluctant to consume some New World products, others they learned almost immediately to savor. One of the latter was watermelon. Early in the eighteenth century, Dumont de Montigny described with relish the "melons d'eau" of which he partook in Louisiana: "They are called this because in eating them it seems as if you have a sponge soaked in Alicante wine dissolving in your mouth, for the juice is crimson and exquisitely flavored . . . . You pick these melons in the morning before sunrise and place them in the shade. In this fashion they maintain perfectly their freshness, which they then transmit to those who eat them." One can well imagine a housewife in colonial Ste. Genevieve sending a domestic slave to the melon patch early on an August morning to select a plump watermelon that could be hung in the well to cool during the day. Then in the evening the family would gather on the front porch to munch succulent slices of melon and contentedly spit the black seeds over

29. Delassus to Carondelet, Mar. 6, 1797, PC 35; Morgan to Wilkins, Sep. 16, 1770, Morgan Papers, IHS.

30. SGA, Estates, no. 19; Brackenridge, *Recollections of the West*, 24. Curiously, Brackenridge did not mention herbs, such as sage, which were surely present in the Bauvais garden.

Walnut armoire made in colonial St. Louis and now in the Missouri Historical Society at the Jefferson Memorial. Few families in Ste. Genevieve would have had armoires this large and elaborate.

the railing of the *galerie*.[31]

Apples were a specialty of the Illinois Country, and their qualities had been praised in New Orleans since the 1720s. If someone in Ste. Genevieve wished to send a gift to a person in "la ville," a usual choice was apples. In July 1786, for example, town commandant Antonio de Oro dispatched "a little crate of summer apples" to the financial intendant of Louisiana, Don Martín Navarro. It would be interesting to know just what varieties of apples were raised in the orchards of colonial Ste. Genevieve. Likely the French Canadians had taken apple seeds with them from Canada, where they had been brought from France. Apples were peeled and eaten *crude*, fermented and turned into cider, and no doubt sliced, cooked, and used to make *tartes aux pommes*. All of the basic ingredients — flour, butter, and apples — for these wonderful pastries the townspeople of Ste. Genevieve possessed in abundance, and one may be sure that the ingredients were not wasted in a region where delicacies were in short supply.[32]

The single most important item of diet in colonial Ste. Genevieve was bread. In writing about the history of Europe, Braudel has remarked that "the trinity of grain, flour, bread is to be found everywhere . . . . It was the major preoccupation of towns, states, merchants, and ordinary people for whom life meant 'eating one's daily bread.'" These remarks are wholly applicable to the Illinois Country. It was a universally accepted fact in colonial Louisiana that the best wheat in North America came from the Illinois Country, and by the 1770s much of that wheat was produced on the Big Field of Ste. Genevieve. Because the townspeople potatoes or maize and because most of their wheat was turned into bread, rather than pasta for example, bread was overwhelmingly the most important source of carbohydrates in their diets. Indeed, bread probably constituted the single largest component of their total caloric intake. The flour mills in Ste. Genevieve did not turn out highly refined flour, so the large round loaves *(miches)* that were pulled out of each *habitant's* bake oven were course, dark, and wholesome. It was the staff of life for the townspeople and was probably eaten at virtually every meal.[33]

Let us imagine a Sunday dinner menu for a well-to-do family

31. Dumont de Montigny, *Mémoires historiques*, 1:19-20.
32. De Oro to Navarro, July 24, 1786, PC 602 A.
33. Braudel, *Structures of Everyday Life*, 143.

A French creole chair, with carved legs and a rawhide seat, owned by the Missouri Historical Society of St. Louis. Stuffed chairs were unknown in colonial Ste. Genevieve.

A French creole chair, with turned legs and a split-hickory seat, owned by the Missouri Historical Society of St. Louis. By the 1770s, lathe-turned chair legs were being made in Ste. Genevieve by the local tourneur.

in colonial Ste. Genevieve:[34]

Vegetable soup, depending heavily upon peas, cabbage, and
  onions
Catfish fried in refined bear oil
Boudin (probably the traditional French blood sausage)
Roast suckling pig
Dessert of fresh fruits, fruit *tartes*, custards and cheeses (dairy
  products were abundant in Ste. Genevieve)

All of this was accompanied by wheat bread, washed down with
French or Spanish wine, local beer, cider and wild cherry liqueur,
and followed by coffee. An acceptable repast.

After dinner the men of the household would stuff their clay
pipes with locally grown tobacco and light up, for smoking was a
favorite pastime for males of all classes in colonial Ste. Genevieve.
Brackenridge recounted that Vital Bauvais had his pipe "continually in his mouth, except while in bed, or at mass, or during meals."
And when Delassus de Luzières drafted "Observations on the
Character, Qualities, and Professions of the White Inhabitants of
the New Bourbon District" he complained bitterly about the fires
ignited in surrounding fields, woods, and meadows by the "negli-
gence of the numerous smokers of this country, whites, Indians,
and slaves, . . . who always put down their pipes without taking
care to extinguish them . . . ." Who would have thought that
America's first Smokey Bear was a French aristocrat living in

---

34. We know that households in Ste. Genevieve made *boudin,* for the implement
used in filling the sausage casings, *une boudinière,* appears in inventories of household possessions. A French-Canadian recipe for *boudin* is given in Gagné, *Recettes
typiques de la Côte-du-Sud,* 71.

*A pewter soup spoon of the type used in colonial Ste. Genevieve. Photo
courtesy of Dominique Tinel.*

Eighteenth-century French clay pipe showing an Indian woman on a chamber pot. The late Irven Peithmann found this artifact near the site of old Kaskaskia. The pipe's motif reveals the earthy tastes of the French creoles. Photo courtesy of the Illinois Department of Conservation.

Spanish Illinois?[35]

The townspeople regularly drank wine, beer, and cider with their meals, the latter two lending themselves readily to local production because grain and apples were available in large quantities. Wine in barrels was imported from France and Spain via New Orleans and bottled locally. French colonists in the Illinois Country had early tried to produce wine from local grapes but the product seldom proved satisfactory.[36]

---

35. Brackenridge, *Recollections of the West*, 23; "Observations . . ." attached to the 1797 New Bourbon census, PC 2365.

36. On wine shipments to Ste. Genevieve, see bills of lading (MHS, Vallé Collection, Box 2) for cargoes arriving from New Orleans during the late 1790s.

Distilled beverages as well as wine were shipped up the Mississippi, brandy coming from France and rum (tafia) from the French sugar islands in the Caribbean. The townspeople also distilled some of their own spirits. It is hard to say when the first still was set up in Ste. Genevieve, but it was probably done rather early. François Vallé II bought two stills from John Dodge and his wife in 1789, and in 1798 Delassus de Luzières boasted to Gayoso, the governor of Spanish Louisiana, that in a few years the citizens of New Bourbon would be producing their own "strong liquors like good whiskey, and peach and wild cherry brandy." The "good whiskey" was doubtless to be produced from the corn grown on the Big Field, and thus we have our first distinct reference to Bourbon (corn whiskey) in the Ste. Genevieve area.[37]

Coffee, and to a lesser extent tea, were also popular beverages in colonial Ste. Genevieve, but apparently not always readily available. Brackenridge's account from the mid 1790s that "tea was not used at meals, and coffee for breakfast, was the privilege of M. Bauvais only" suggests that the ingredients for those beverages were not deemed essential enough for human happiness in Ste. Genevieve to bear the financial burden of shipping them up the Mississippi from New Orleans. Yet, by 1808, when the English traveler Thomas Ashe visited Ste. Genevieve, coffee was a popular drink, and Ashe partook of a cup that was as good "as ever I drank . . . at the Palais Royale, or at the foot of Pont Neuf." Coffee mills appear routinely in estate inventories, and in 1797 François Vallé had an entire barrel of coffee sent from New Orleans to Ste. Genevieve.[38]

Virtually all families in colonial Ste. Genevieve possessed some pewter and ceramic tableware. Wealthy families had crystal and sterling silver to boot. The inventory of goods that went to François Vallé I after his wife died in 1781 included: twenty-four table settings of silver, six large silver stew spoons, a silver coffee pot, a silver eating bowl, six silver goblets, a large silver platter, six silver candelabra, and two silver salad bowls. And in 1797 François Vallé II received a shipment of commodities from New Orleans that included four dozen crystal goblets, doubtless imported from Europe. When dignitaries like Lieutenant Governor Manuel Gayoso de Lemos visited the Vallé household, they ate and drank

---

37. SGA, Concessions, no. 28; De Luzières to Gayoso, Mar. 6, 1798, PC 2371.

38. Brackenridge, *Recollections,* 25; Ashe, *Travels in America,* 288; see Berte Grima's bill to Vallé, June 3, 1797, MHS, Vallé Collection, Box 2.

as if they were in Paris — or at least New Orleans. By the mid-1790s, Ste. Genevieve boasted two gold/silversmiths, Louis Coyteux and Louis Robitaille, and their handiwork must soon have begun to grace a few tables in town.[39]

How family members comported themselves at the dinner table is difficult to say. It is apparent from the inventories cited above, which include numerous dinner plates, that table manners for the comfortably well-off families in colonial Ste. Genevieve had progressed past the stage of eating out of a common pot placed in the center of the table; there was a place setting for each individual. Probably, however, that was a rather new and fancy custom, and the more humble families still took their meals by digging into a central pot. Forks and spoons appear routinely in inventories, but table knives do not. This suggests that individuals used their own hunting knives at the table, that people gnawed off bits to eat instead of cutting them off, or that everything, including meats, was cut up and cooked down to the consistency of bite-sized morsels. The numerous bowls, tureens, and large spoons that appear in listings of household possessions indicate that many meals consisted of stews or thick soups of some sort. Pepper mills were used to grind the spice directly onto the food; salt was usually spooned (not shaken) out of a small vessel (*salière*) placed in the center of the table. Wealthy folks had plentiful supplies of napkins and tablecloths, which were usually of fine linen imported from Beaufort, France. Humble folks had to make do with calico cotton or a shirtsleeve to remain seemly at the dinner table.[40]

The man of the household occupied the central position during mealtime. An eighteenth-century Frenchman from the provinces, Rétif de la Bretonne, described his family this way:[41]

> When he [the father] arrived home he was a king, a god before whom all took flight. He was greeted with the utmost solicitude — in a cool place during the summer, at the hearth during the winter. A comfortable chair, warm slippers, a fur cap, and mulled wine were brought to him before he was embraced . . . . This father, this husband, so beloved was left quietly to warm himself while supper was prepared. The table was pushed up close to him, and when he turned to it supper began. Madame served her master; she tenderly assisted him

39. MHS, Vallé Collection, Box 1; ibid., Box 2.
40. SGA, Estate inventories, passim.
41. Rétif de la Bretonne, *La vie de mon père*, 188-190.

prepare to eat, and then she sat down next to him, in the second place. She served him what he desired and experienced the inexpressible pleasure of seeing him content . . . . When he, as well as the rest of the family, had eaten, the table was cleared . . . . The entire family, children and domestics, formed a circle around the gigantic ancient fireplace. It was while the entire family experienced this pleasure, so great in winter, . . . that the father of the family played his most beautiful role: he talked, recounted stories, and gave orders. Everyone listened with rap attention, the wife providing an example.

Rétif's description of mealtime and social life within the household for a French rural family may be as close as we will ever come to seeing family ways in colonial Ste. Genevieve. The two salient points of his description are the preeminent role of the father in the family and the unforced affection shown for him by the rest of the family. If the father of the family was a kind of despot, he was a benign and beloved despot.

On the subject of clothing and styles of dress, we must rely upon inventories of personal property and rare eye-witness accounts, Peter Kalm for the French Canadians in mid-eighteenth century and Brackenridge for Ste. Genevieve during the 1790s. As for male attire, Brackenridge described his host, Vital St. Gemme Bauvais, as garbed with "a blue cotton handkerchief on his head, one corner thereof descending behind and partly covering the eel skin which bound his hair; a check shirt; course pantaloons on his hips; and the Indian sandal, or moccasin, the only covering to the feet worn here by both sexes." Bauvais's clothing strikes one as imminently comfortable and practical dress: medium length hair bound into a single pigtail with an eel skin and covered with a handkerchief; a calico cotton shirt open at the neck; full-length, rough-woven cotton trousers ("course pantaloons" were surely not the *culotte* knee britches of the eighteenth century) not unlike our dungarees; and soft leather moccasins on his feet. In wet weather, Bauvais exchanged his moccasins for wooden sabots to keep his feet dry.[42]

This was, however, Bauvais's ordinary casual dress, for on Sundays and other important occasions a man of his status would shed his *sans-culotte* garb for knee britches, frock coat, silk stockings and cravat, silver-buckled shoes, and a ruffled linen shirt. All wealthy men in Ste. Genevieve possessed these articles of clothing.

42. Brackenridge, *Recollections,* 23.

Brackenridge's description is also clearly of summer attire, and in winter months Bauvais probably donned the traditional *capot* of the Illinois Country, which was not unlike a monk's habit — a knee-length, belted and hooded outer garment of coarse wool. In bitter cold weather the men of Ste. Genevieve also put on leather mittens, "mitaines de cuir." For Bauvais's forays into the outback, when he went hunting or visited the lead mines, he wore the *voyageur's* tassled stocking cap and buckskin leggings. The latter prevented Bauvais's stockings and trousers from being shredded in the underbrush. Different garb served for different seasons and on different occasions for the men of Ste. Genevieve, and except for their Sunday-go-to-meeting outfits — which were much the same as those worn in Philadelphia, London, or Paris — their clothing styles were dictated entirely by the practical demands of the Illinois Country.[43]

There is not a single detailed firsthand account of female clothing fashions for the Illinois Country. Estate inventories reveal that the ladies of colonial Ste. Genevieve had skirts made of plain cotton, calico, gingham, and mohair; cotton and silk dresses; cotton and linen blouses; sleeveless cloaks of calico, cotton, and silk; and cotton corsets and stockings. The large amounts of cloth, as opposed to finished goods, that were shipped from New Orleans to Ste. Genevieve, indicate that the ladies in town did their own sewing, and they must have hungered for news of the latest fashions appearing in European capitals.[44]

Peter Kalm observed women's fashions in mid-eighteenth century French Canada, and he emphasized the wearing of hats, claiming that "all women in the country without exception, wear caps of some kind or another." Kalm then described the women's skirts, "which scarcely reach down to the middle of their legs." Kalm exhibited a healthy interest in women's legs, and he returned time and again to describe the shortness of skirts in Canada: "Every day but Sunday they wear a neat little jacket and a short skirt which hardly reaches halfway down their leg, and sometimes not that far." On Sundays and feast days the ladies of colonial Ste. Genevieve donned their dresses, which were probably ankle-length. The best dresses were made of silk taffeta, and were often trimmed with fur. Over the dress was worn some sort of shawl, cape, or cloak, of which French ladies were very fond. It is not clear what kind of dress shoes the women wore. Kalm noted that

43. For a listing of male clothing, see SGA, Estates, no. 67.
44. For a listing of female attire, see ibid., no. 44.

Canadian habitant in winter dress by Francis Ann Hopkins. All of the items of clothing shown in this painting appear in inventories of personal possessions in the Ste. Genevieve Archives. Photograph courtesy of the Canadian National Archives, Ottawa, Canada.

French Canadian women wore dress shoes with very high heels, "and it is surprising how they can walk in them." If the ladies of colonial Ste. Genevieve wore such shoes on Sundays, they were certainly happy to return to their moccasins or *sabots* on Monday.[45]

In his *Pioneer History of Illinois,* John Reynolds claimed that the French Canadians of the Illinois Country had "a strong predilection for the blue color." This observation is born out in records from Ste. Genevieve, where clothes, both male and female, are often described as blue or red.[46]

When Perrin du Lac paid a social call at the home of Commandant François Vallé in the 1790s, he was flabbergasted by the appearance of Madame Vallé, which struck him as so odd ("grotesque") and so far removed from the usual apprehension of reality that he declined to describe it. "It would have been impossible," Du Lac claimed, "to have clothed her in a fashion so at odds with the adopted customs of the civilized world." Perhaps Madame Vallé's attire was aberrant even in Ste. Genevieve, but more likely the women of the frontier town had adopted enough Indian clothing styles, moccasins and buckskin jerkins for example, so that they appeared bizarre to a metropolitan Frenchman like Du Lac. Du Lac was too sophisticated, however, to judge Madame Vallé merely on the basis of her appearance and he went on to point out that she was a "humane, generous, and compassionate" person.[47]

How the residents of colonial Ste. Genevieve took care of their bodies and practiced personal hygiene within their households is largely a matter of conjecture. There was lots of soap available, for soap kettles, "marmites à savons," are a standard item in estate inventories. Moreover, fancy soap was imported from Europe and cases of it appeared often on the bills of lading for riverboats leaving New Orleans for Ste. Genevieve. Water was stored in faïence jugs and pitchers within the houses, but it seems that washing and shaving (the men were clean shaven for the most part) were usually done in copper, tin, or pewter rather than ceramic basins. For Saturday night baths, if such an institution existed in town, the large wooden wash tubs, *cuves,* were probably the facility of choice.[48]

45. Kalm, *Travels in North America,* 2:402-03, 417, 525-26.

46. Reynolds, *Pioneer History of Illinois,* 51.

47. Perrin du Lac, *Voyages dans les deux Louisianes,* 169.

48. In July 1795, the Vallés were sent two cases of soap from New Orleans (MHS, Vallé Collection, Box 2).

Chamber pots were inevitably of faïence, for metals could not withstand the corrosive effects of excrement. There is, however, a mystery about excrement in the French Illinois Country, which is not lending itself readily to solution. Were there privies out in the yards beyond the wells and the bake ovens? If so, it seems strange that they never appear in the detailed descriptions or inventories of property that include wells, dilapidated henhouses, and small sheds. The failure of privies to appear on listings has nothing to do with shyness about such matters, for the townspeople were not inhibited by any sense of false modesty. Perhaps the contents of chamber pots were simply flung into the muddy streets, which was the usual practice even in most European cities. Perhaps historical-archaeologists will one day solve this mystery and thus provide us with important information about daily life in colonial Ste. Genevieve.[49]

Households in colonial Ste. Genevieve had few books for recreational reading and few musical instruments to break the daily routine with tunes. Some singing, dancing, story telling, and card playing no doubt went on in homes, but most recreation and socializing took place outside of the households. The public places in town where people most frequently congregated were: the parish church, especially in front of the main entrance; the commandant's house, which served as town hall and county court house; billiard parlors, which began to appear at least as early as the 1790s; the docking areas along the Mississippi, especially the two from which ferries did a brisk business with the east side of the river; and of course the streets of the town itself, where there was often animated, and sometimes angry, social intercourse.[50]

The parish church in Ste. Genevieve was the focal point of community life for both religious and secular affairs. It was at the church door, for example, where virtually all public auctions were cried and where all public notices were posted. A parish church for the New Town had been planned as early as 1793, but in August 1794 Lieutenant Governor Trudeau had to travel from St. Louis to Ste. Genevieve in order to help the town's citizens resolve the myriad disputes that surrounded the building of the first church in the new community. Trudeau's description of this

---

49. A plan of the mission at Cahokia from 1735 (McDermott, *Old Cahokia,* facing 16) shows a "latrine."

50. On books and education in Ste. Genevieve, see above, chap. ix.

visit contains valuable information about the new church building:[51]

> The purpose of my trip was to examine the old church
> [built in 1787] to see if it could not be moved to the new
> village, for . . . all of the wood in it was good and excellent,
> and to see if it might be lengthened 12 feet. That would make
> it 84 feet by 28 feet, which is its present width. I had calculated
> that . . . it would burden the citizens at least 80 piastres apiece,
> without counting their time, to build an edifice such as was
> at first projected. . . . The church will have nine more pews
> than it has at present, where there are still some that rent for
> 30 sols. . . . It is apparent that it will be large enough without
> the enlargement that had been planned . . . . The present
> curate [St. Pierre] complains and wants a much larger edifice.
> I too would prefer that, but I see the impossibility of ac-
> complishing it.

The materials that the townspeople supplied for the new
church's construction — logs, stone, lath, shingles, beams, and
planks — reveal that the new parish church in Ste. Genevieve was
a *poteaux-sur-solle* structure with a wooden shingled roof. Although
we have no contemporary description of it, it probably looked
much like the restored chapel at Cahokia. Its remains are today
buried beneath the present Victorian-Gothic edifice, for the last
three parish churches of Ste. Genevieve — the log structure of
1794, the stone structure of 1837, and the present building —
seem to have been built on the same site.[52]

In modern American society religious holidays are less important than they once were; the World Series and Superbowl Sunday
have become as important as Christmas and Easter in serving to
break up the dull grind of the calendar year. Colonial Ste.
Genevieve was still of the Old World, still French and still Roman
Catholic, and the townspeople celebrated numerous religious holidays during the course of the year. The better known were
Epiphany, Ash Wednesday, Easter, Ascension, Pentecost, Corpus
Christi, Assumption, All Saint's, Advent, and Christmas. The religious quality of holidays was reinforced by virtue of the fact that
individuals celebrated their saint's day rather than their birthday.
On July 5, 1771, Lieutenant Governor Pedro (Peter) Piernas wrote

---

51. Trudeau to Carondelet, Sep. 1, 1794, PC 197. Concerning the transfer of
the parish from the Old Town to the New Town, see below, chap. xiii.

52. The building materials are described in SGA, Litigations, no. 25.

to François Vallé I and thanked him for the greetings that Vallé had sent on the occasion "du jour de ma fete." St. Peter's day falls on June 29. With all the Françoises and Jean-Baptistes in Ste. Genevieve, half the town must have gotten drunk each January 24 and June 24.[53]

The Christmas-Epiphany season was the festive highlight of the year in Ste. Genevieve. Christmas Day began with High Mass at midnight on Christmas Eve. Schoolboy Henry Brackenridge trudged up the Rue à l'Eglise from Vital Bauvais's residence to attend this service at the parish church in the New Town. Young Henry, just recently arrived from Protestant Pennsylvania, was transfixed by the trappings of a Roman Catholic High Christmas Mass:[54]

> At Christmas eve, it was the custom to keep the church open all night, and at midnight to say mass. On this occasion, I found myself alone for nearly an hour before that time, seated on a high chair, or stool, with a cross in my hand, in front of the altar, which was splendidly decorated, and lighted with the largest wax candles the village could afford. My imagination was at first filled with an indescribable awe, at the situation in which I was placed, and I gazed upon the sacred images about the altar as if they were in reality what they represented.

Christmas Mass was followed by *Le Reveillon*, the "wake-up" breakfast that lasted the remainder of the night and on into the following day. New Year's did not have the religious focus that Christmas did, centering rather upon the revelry that attended the singing of *La Guignolée* on New Year's Eve. New Year's was devoted principally to the youth. The town's young men visited the girls during the rounds of *La Guignolée,* and St. Nicholas showered the children with gifts on New Year's Eve rather than at Christmas.[55]

The French Canadian tradition of *La Guignolée* probably descended from an ancient Gallic custom of distributing mistletoe *(gui)* at the time of the winter solstice. In Ste. Genevieve it took the form of young men donning costumes and going from door

---

53. Piernas to Vallé, July 5, 1771, PC 190.

54. Brackenridge, *Recollections*, 30.

55. Belting (*Kaskaskia*, 68-70) contains a good description of the religious holidays in the French Illinois country.

to door in quest of donations for the Twelfth Night celebrations. The young men sang *La Guignolée* as they made their rounds.[56]

La Guignolée

Bonsoir le maître et la maîtresse
   Et tout le monde du logis!
Pour le premier jour de l'année
La Guignolée nous vous devez.
   Si vous n'avez rien à nous donner
Dites-nous le!
   Nous vous, demandons pas grand 'chose
Une échinée
   Une échinée n'est pas grand 'chose
De quatre-vingt dix pieds le long;
   Encore nous demandons pas grand 'chose,
La fille ainée de la maison
   Nous lui ferons faire bonne chère
   Nous lui ferons chauffer les pieds
Nous salvons la compagnie
   Et la prions nous excuser.
Si l'on à fait quelque folie
   C'étoit pour nous des ennuyer
Une autre fois nous prendons garde
   Quand sera temps d'y revenir
Dansons la Guenille, dansons la Guenille, dansons
   la Guenille!

Chorus

Bonsoir le maître et la maîtresse
   Et tout le monde du logis!

Good evening master and mistress,
   and to everyone else who lives with you.
For the first day of the year,
   You owe us *La Guignolée*
If you have nothing at all to give,
   Tell us of it right away.

---

56. This version of *La Guignolée* was taken from a transcript in the IHS (Forbes). The rough translation is mine.

We're not asking for very much,
  A chine of meat or so will do.
A chine of meat is not a big thing,
  only ninety feet long.
Again, we're not asking for very much,
  only the oldest daughter of the house.
We will give her lots of good cheer,
  and we will surely warm her feet.
Now, we greet your company,
  and beg you to forgive us please.
If we have acted a little crazy,
  we only meant it in good fun.
Another time we'll surely be careful
  to know when we must come back here again.
Let us dance la Guenille, la Guenille, la Guenille!

Chorus

Good evening master and mistress
  and to everyone else who lives with you!

Sunday was the only day of the week when High Mass was normally celebrated in the parish church of Ste. Genevieve, and thus it was a day infused with special religious significance. Nonetheless, Sunday was not a day during which all non-religious activities were proscribed as they were in Puritan New England. Indeed, Sundays were a time for business and socializing in Ste. Genevieve, much like Saturdays were in nineteenth-century American towns. For example, Sunday was *the* day for auction sales in town, and auctions commenced immediately following the morning's mass.

Real estate auctions were the most important kind of sales, and they were announced on several successive Sundays before the sale took place. On December 7, 1777 civil lieutenant François Vallé I, accompanied by two witnesses, appeared after mass "at the principal door of the parish church." As the crowd poured forth into the sunlight, Vallé "read, posted, publicized, and cried out in a loud and intelligible voice in order to let the assembled public know" that there was going to be an auction of land, house, and outbuildings belonging to Madame Rocheblave, wife of the former town commandant. Vallé repeated this procedure on successive Sundays until December 28, when the public announcement was made for the last time and the real estate went on the block. After a brisk exchange of bids on that frosty December morning, the Rocheblave property was knocked off at noon to Madame Vallé (probably François's wife) for the sum of 600 livres, payable in deerskins or beaver pelts. Scarcity of hard currency meant that residents of colonial Ste. Genevieve depended heavily upon a barter economy. Virtually any commodity might serve as a medium of exchange on a given occasion, but the most popular were deer skins, lead, salt, and flour.[57]

On Sunday, October 8, 1775, François Vallé appeared "at the issue of the Grand Mass" in front of the church door in the Old Town to announce the sale of the personal property of Guillaume Clouet, who had recently died and left no heirs in the community. The auction was to take place forthwith at Vallé's residence just up the "Grande Rue" from the parish church, where Clouet's belongings had been assembled and where "everyone will be received in order to bid." Louis Lasource bought a brown *capot* of Spanish wool for twenty livres; François Leclerc two linen shirts for fifteen livres; Antoine Aubuchon three clay pipes and an Indian calumet for four livres; François Vallé himself a pair of deerskin *culottes* for forty livres. The auction at Vallé's house went on "until sunset" on that October afternoon, by which time "there was nothing left to put up for sale." Purchasers of goods were to make payment in "good wheat" at the exchange rate of fifteen livres per hundredweight of wheat. Clouet's property was sold for a total of 1,131 livres, much of which was used to cover the debts he had outstanding at the time of his death.[58]

In November 1779, one Jean-Louis de Noyon, an itinerant peddler from Vincennes, arrived in Ste. Genevieve to sell "diverse clothing of decorated deerskin and silk." François Vallé declared the sale in front of the parish church on Sunday, November 21, and once again the event was held at Vallé's residence. The entire day was probably a festive occasion — with much eating, drinking, and a dance in the evening. The holiday atmosphere of Sundays was a persistent aspect of town life, for on those occasions when no auction took place a wedding usually did. Marriages were customarily celebrated on Sundays after the last ban had been proclaimed at mass in the morning, and the wedding festivities went

---

57. MHS, Vallé Collection, Box 1. For a summary of currencies, prices, weights, and measures, see Appendices G and H.

58. SGA, Estates, no. 67.

on until well into the night.[59]

After the parish church, the most important social, economic, and political focal point in Ste. Genevieve was the commandant's residence, which was sometimes called "la chambre du gouvernement." This residence, as well as the house where the small Spanish garrison was billeted, was distinctive by virtue of the royal Spanish flag that fluttered in front of it. These flags were small splashes of color in a community that had no billboards or street signs, and where there were no shops with brightly painted placards hung in front. On special occasions, to decide upon the building of a new church for example, town meetings were held at the commandant's house. Moreover, there was a daily parade of people to Commandant François Vallé II's residence on the north side of South Gabouri Creek. They came with requests for land grants, with lawsuits and petitions, to have contracts drafted in official form, and no doubt sometimes simply to socialize and gossip. On the morning of Monday, November 11, 1794 six residents of New Bourbon appeared at Vallé's house with a petition for the commandant to appoint someone to mark off property lines in their new village. After talking to the commandant, the petitioners probably sat around the rest of the morning on the front gallery of his house and chewed the fat with their friends and relatives from Ste. Genevieve. The Vallés were renowned for their hospitality and did not seem to resent the fact that their residence was a quasi-public building.[60]

The New Town of Ste. Genevieve had several public establishments for recreation and entertainment, features that distinguished it from the Old Town. St. Louis had had a billiard parlor as early as 1770, but that was because a sizeable Spanish garrison was quartered in the capital of Spanish Illinois. There is no evidence that the Old Town ever had a billiard parlor, a card room, or a tavern, although the house where the Spanish soldiers were billeted certainly was the scene of much debauchery.[61]

By the early 1790s, however, the New Town had several "billards," or billiard parlors. Nicolas Caillot *dit* Lachance *fils,* who had come with his father to Ste. Genevieve in the late 1780s, may have been the first entrepreneur to open a billiard parlor in town. Late in 1792 Lachance sold a house in Ste. Genevieve to François

59. SGA, Personalty, no. 10.
60. MHS, Documents, no. 23.
61. Billon (ed.), *Annals,* 1:72-73.

Lalumandière that was fitted out with a parlor. At about the same time, a Spanish merchant and civil servant from St. Louis, Joseph Alvarez Hortiz, who was married to a Bequet woman, also opened a billiard parlor in Ste. Genevieve. Hortiz must have become fed up with being an absentee landlord, however, for in 1794 he sold his establishment, which was equipped with "six new balls and three old ones," to the first vice king of Ste. Genevieve, François Lalumandière.[62]

During the mid-1790s, Lalumandière was apparently running two billiard parlors close to the center of Ste. Genevieve. The parlor he bought from Hortiz in 1794 was located near Church Street (now Market), and it is possible that there was in fact a small entertainment area in that part of town. Such immoral go-ings-on were not to be ignored by the parish priest, Abbé de St. Pierre, and the reverend father complained of the situation to Governor Carondelet in 1792. St. Pierre pointed out that there were already two billiard parlors in Ste. Genevieve and then launched into a diatribe about the pernicious effects on the community of such dens of iniquity. Billiards was "causing discord among neighbors, disputes within marriages, poverty to some families, and will perhaps be the ruination of the town . . . ." St. Pierre's puritanical attitude may have stemmed from his German background, for his attitude appears to be distinctly un-French. The priest acknowledged that vices such as billiards were necessary in large cities to cater to tourists and to entertain a sedentary population, but in a small town of farmers and merchants like Ste. Genevieve billiards were an evil. In St. Pierre's words "the cries of poor housewives and the tears of half-naked children" called out for a prohibition of billiard parlors.[63]

The dens of Father St. Pierre's letter were probably drinking and gaming establishments as well as billiard parlors. Delassus de Luzières reported in 1794 that all the inhabitants of the Illinois Country "prefer any kind of strong liquor to beer," and Ste. Genevieve was no stranger to problem drinkers, who included Charles Vallé and Father Gibault. The early nineteenth-century traveler, Christian Schultz, remarked upon the passion for gam-bling in Ste. Genevieve: "*Vingt-un* [the card game Twenty-one] is the word; and never did I see people embark with so much spirit and perseverance to win each other's money, as in this little village.

---

62. SGA, Deeds, no. 227; ibid., no. 335, no. 188.
63. St. Pierre to Carondelet, Oct. 1, 1792, PC 206.

I have frequently known them to sit thirty hours at the same table without any other refreshment than a dish of miserable coffee, or a glass of sour claret; and I even recollect one instance of an infatuated young man, who could ill afford it, having lost eleven hundred dollars at one sitting." Back in 1766, the English officer, Philip Pittman, remarked that the first settlers in Ste. Genevieve had been sent there from Kaskaskia in order to remove those persons weak in the flesh from temptations presented in a large town. By the end of the colonial period, Ste. Genevieve had itself become one of the sin centers of the Illinois Country.[64]

Not everyone in Ste. Genevieve viewed billiard parlors in the same light as Father St. Pierre. In 1800 Guillaume Girouärd, a native of Normandy who had moved to Ste. Genevieve in the early 1790s and married Marie Hubardeau, approached Commandant François Vallé with a request to establish a billiard parlor. Vallé forwarded the request to his superior, Lieutenant Governor Charles Delassus, in St. Louis, and included a cover letter on behalf of Girouärd: "I believe that you should have no objections to his [Girouärd's] request, since I am very content with the inn or tavern that he has run here for several months. Quantities of strangers pass through here daily and stay with him instead of bothering the citizens as they used to. I have nothing but praise for the peace and good order that he maintains at his establishment." Perhaps, Girouärd, who was a shrewd businessman, had sweetened his petition to Vallé with a small gratuity, but in any case it seems likely that Delassus permitted "Girouärd to open a new billiard parlor in Ste. Genevieve.[65]

Vallé's letter to Delassus on Girouärd's behalf reveals the interesting fact that sometime during the year 1800 Girouärd had opened the first public inn at Ste. Genevieve. There is no information as to where precisely this inn and tavern were located or how long they remained in business. When Thomas Ashe visited Ste. Genevieve in the autumn of 1806, he stayed at an "inn which had strong indications of comfort," and which was operated by "a lively Frenchman." This could not have been Girouärd's establishment, however, for Girouärd had died in 1805. But it may have been the Green Tree Tavern, which François Janis supposedly opened on the south edge of town sometime shortly after the turn of the

---

64. De Luzières to Carondelet, Oct. 17, 1794, PC 209; Schultz, *Travels on an Inland Voyage,* 61; Pittman to Gage, Feb. 24, 1766, Clements Library (photostat in IHS).

65. Vallé to Delassus, Sep. 20, 1800, MHS, Chouteau Collection.

nineteenth century.[66]

In 1798 Governor General Gayoso de Lemos promulgated a set of regulations for controlling recreation centers in Spanish Louisiana. Among other things, these regulations prohibited "card or dice games in houses, especially those called *Lansquenet, Monte, Albures, Primera, Rolina,* and *Crabs,* for only too often do they harm the youth." Gayoso also decreed that taverns and billiard parlors had to close, during all seasons, at the hour of retreat, and that no tavern could open without government permission.[67]

Spanish colonial officials in Louisiana had long been concerned with taverns and with controlling the sale and consumption of alcoholic beverages. Their motives seem to have been partly paternal, in that they wished to exercise some control on public morality; partly economic, for they wished to levy taxes on the sale of wine and liquor; and partly political, as they wished to prevent Indians from becoming drunk and destructive. When the trader David Trotter was killed by an Indian near New Madrid in 1802, after having sold liquor to the Mascouten tribe, the lieutenant governor of Spanish Illinois, Charles Delassus, issued extensive regulations for the sale of alcoholic beverages. Each community would have a strictly limited number of taverns that would pay a license fee of thirty piastres per year. Who received the license or licenses for Ste. Genevieve is not known, but perhaps both Guillaume Girouärd and François Janis became responsible for controlling the flow of booze in town. Indians and black slaves were forbidden to buy alcoholic beverages, but it is apparent that by the end of the colonial period taverns were an established feature of white social life in Ste. Genevieve.[68]

The parish church, the commandant's house, and the taverns notwithstanding, most public life in colonial Ste. Genevieve transpired on the streets and byways of the town. The French historian Lucien Febvre has reminded us that "we must remember that we are all, like it or not, hothouse products; the man of the sixteenth century grew in the open air." This was just as true for men of the eighteenth century, especially in a frontier community like Ste. Genevieve. On the streets the townspeople met, argued, and transacted business, and on the streets processions took place on

66. Ashe, *Travels in America,* 288; Yealy (105) claimed that Ashe did in fact put up at the Green Tree Tavern but cited no source.

67. Gayoso's regulations, Jan. 1798, MHS, Chouteau Collection, Box 3.

68. Delassus, "Ordre général concernant les aubergists cantiniers de tous les postes de cette haute Louisiane," Jan. 5, 1803, PC 220.

special occasions.[69]

Corpus Christi, the moveable feast of late May or early June, had acquired a special significance in the French New World, where local militias accompanied the procession of the Blessed Sacrament through the streets of the villages. An interesting example of how the Illinois Country changed with the coming of the English to the east bank of the Mississippi arose in the summer of 1768 when Father Meurin, who served both banks of the river, wished to parade the Sacrament in Kaskaskia. Meurin wrote to the bishop of Quebec that early on the morning of Corpus Christi Day he had officiated at the procession of the Sacrament in Ste. Genevieve but that English officers in Kaskaskia had forbade such a procession on the east bank of the river. The French settlers in the Illinois Country placed great stock in the salutory effects of parading the Blessed Sacrament, but in Kaskaskia Father Meurin had to be content with a celebration within the church walls. No wonder English rule in Kaskaskia drove many settlers across the Mississippi to St. Louis and Ste. Genevieve.[70]

Simon Hubardeau was a wealthy man, but he was also one of the town eccentrics in colonial Ste. Genevieve. On Corpus Christi Day in June 1786, Hubardeau thought it would be cute to make some obscene and blasphemous gestures during the passing of the Host. This stunt so infuriated town commandant Antonio de Oro, who was a sober Spanish Catholic, that he had Hubardeau thrown in the town jail and reported the matter to Lieutenant Governor Cruzat in St. Louis. Cruzat decided that a couple of days in jail was enough to teach Hubardeau a lesson, and he ordered De Oro to release him. Blasphemous, adolescent acts, even by adults, were less heinous offenses in Ste. Genevieve than in France, where in 1766 a young man had been tortured and executed for an infraction that brought Hubardeau only several days in the calaboose.[71]

Hubardeau not only liked to cut up in public, he was also a thin-skinned and litigious fellow. In 1789 he and Jean-Baptiste Bequet became embroiled in a violent argument on the "Grand Chemin" of Ste. Genevieve, and Bequet called Hubardeau a "damned, fucking faggot [*sacre, fouta Berdache*]." Jean-Baptiste

---

69. Febvre, *Life in Renaissance France,* 23.

70. Meurin to Briand, June 11, 1768, Alvord and Carter (eds.), *Trade and Politics,* 308.

71. Cruzat to De Oro, June 27, 1786, PC 117 B; on the La Barre case, see Gay, *Voltaire's Politics,* 278-82.

Pratte testified that he had heard Bequet roar his epithets from over 300 feet away. Hubardeau sued Bequet, but apparently got no satisfaction from town commandant Peyroux. The case is revealing in several ways, however. It indicates that maledictory street language in Ste. Genevieve had a sexual orientation; Bequet impuned Hubardeau's masculinity rather than cursing his ancestors or the like. This suggests that society in Ste. Genevieve had a machismo orientation. Secondly, it is worth noting that despite the undoubted violence of the argument between Bequet and Hubardeau the two men never came to blows. French officers in New Orleans and at Fort de Chartres fought duels to the death over personal slights, real or imagined, but French Canadian habitants showed little inclination to inflict bodily harm on one another. Ste. Genevieve became more violent when the Americans arrived, for they, like French aristocrats, did not shrink from killing and maiming one another on the streets.[72]

In the autumn of 1792 there occurred a public holiday unique in the annals of colonial Ste. Genevieve. François Vallé II, commandant of the town, received news and an order from Governor Carondelet in New Orleans: the news was that the queen of Spain had given birth to a son, Prince Philipe Marie François, and the order was that the parish priest of Ste. Genevieve was to have sung a solemn Te Deum Mass in celebration of the princely birth. Vallé pitched in by having the town's artillery mounted on "small plow wheels" in order to boom out the civic joy over the glad tidings. The citizens of Ste. Genevieve must have been monumentally bored with the whole affair, for they were not passionately attached to the Spanish royal family. Nonetheless, they probably took advantage of the occasion to get gloriously drunk in toasting the infant Prince Philipe — a bizarre scene on North American soil.[73]

When Thomas Ash visited Ste. Genevieve in September 1806, he was impressed with the variety and vivacity of casual street entertainment in the town:[74]

> I . . . heard the guitar resound after sun-set, with the complaints and amorous fables of the village swains, and heard

---

72. SGA, Litigations, no. 26. Concerning the use of the word *berdache* for homosexual, see McDermott, *Glossary of Mississippi Valley French*, 22-23. On insulting language in French Canada, see Moogk, "Thieving Buggers."

73. Vallé to Trudeau, May 10, 1793, PC 207 B. This Spanish Bourbon prince was the son of King Charles IV and Queen Marie Louise of Parma.

74. Ashe, *Travels*, 289.

the same hand, which toiled all day in the wilderness and in
the waste, strike the tender notes of love in the evening. The
custom seemed to pervade all ranks. Nearly every house had
its group, and every group its guitar, fiddler, story-teller, or
singer. As the evening advanced and the heat diminished,
walking commenced, and towards midnight the music of the
village united, the little world crowded to the spot and danced
with infinite gaiety and mirth till past one in the morning.

This is our first description of Ste. Genevieve by a full-blown
romantic sensibility; the nineteenth-century had indeed arrived.
In any case, the passion of the townspeople for dancing, in winter
as well as in summer, is indisputable. Christian Schultz observed
that "one ball follows another so close in succession, that I have
often wondered how the ladies were enabled to support themselves
under this violent exercise, which is here [Ste. Genevieve] carried
to extremes. The balls are generally opened at candlelight, and
continue till ten or twelve o'clock the next day." Schultz's mildly
censorious tone makes one suspect that he was either a bad dancer
or a sourpuss. Brackenridge, more complaisant than Schultz, was
favorably disposed to the dancing in Ste. Genevieve: "The dances,
were cotillions, reels, and sometimes the minuet. During the car-
nival, the balls followed in rapid succession. They have a variety
of pleasing customs, connected with this amusement. Children
have also their balls, and are taught a decorum and propriety of
behavior, which is preserved through life."[75]
    Much of the recreation for the townsmen took place in the out-
of-doors. The abundance of good horse flesh, the fine forests and
prairies, and the variety of wild game meant that most men in
Ste. Genevieve were inveterate sportsmen. Virtually all outsiders
who visited Upper Louisiana during colonial times commented
upon the passion of its inhabitants for riding and hunting. When
the British officer Thomas Stirling arrived in the Illinois Country
in 1765, he remarked that it was difficult to ascertain the exact
size of the population because so many of the men were out in
the woods hunting, "which they go to as regularly as the Savages."
And thirty years later, toward the end of the colonial era, a French
visitor to Ste. Genevieve, Perrin du Lac, remarked that "the youth
are occupied exclusively with riding, hunting, and dancing."[76]

---

75. Schultz, *Travels*, 60; Brackenridge, Recollections, 29.
76. Stirling to Gage, Dec. 15, 1765, Alvord and Carter (eds.), *The New Regime*,
125; Perrin du Lac, *Voyage*, 172.

The overwhelmingly popular image of the French-creole settlers in the Mississippi Valley is that they were happy-go-lucky, frivolous free spirits. Natalia Belting summed this view up when she wrote that "the Illinois habitant was a gay soul; he seemed shockingly carefree to later, self-righteous puritans from the American colonies." This notion seems to be rooted in a variety of facts and Anglo-American fancies, of which one of the latter is that all Frenchmen are slightly giddy personalities. French tourists in this country joke about having to do their frivolous routine in order to meet the expectations of their American hosts. It is a fact, however, that the French Canadian settlers in the Illinois Country used many nicknames that convey the impression of a happy-go-lucky people: La Chance, the lucky one; Sans Chagrin, the carefree one; Beau Soleil, the sunny one; La Framboise, the raspberry; Sanspeur, the fearless one; Joyeux, the joyful one. One can well imagine the greetings that rang out over the water as canoes passed on the Mississippi: "Hey, La Chance how did you make out in town last night?" And Belting's remark distinguishing colonists of the eastern seaboard from those in the Mississippi Valley is surely correct: the French settlers in the Illinois Country were not Anglo-American Puritans; they did dance and conduct business on Sundays, and drink and play cards in the evenings.[77]

Peter Kalm made the same point in the mid-eighteenth century, remarking that "the manners and customs of the French in . . . Canada, and those of the English in the American colonies, is as great as that between the manners of those two nations in Europe." Kalm was particularly interested in observing the ladies of French Canada, whom he found "well bred and virtuous, with an innocent and becoming freedom." The young women liked to gossip, laugh, and joke and, their good breeding notwithstanding, "invent 'double-entendres.'" Kalm was fond of French Canadian ladies, who could flirt tantalizingly within the bounds of propriety. And the men he found "extremely civil," with the custom of doffing their hats to everyone they met on the roads and byways. The frontiersmen of the Ste. Genevieve region were perhaps not so refined in their public demeanor, but Timothy Flint remarked about the town that "in this place [Ste. Genevieve], we were introduced to amiable and polished people, and saw a town evidencing the possession of a considerable degree of refinement."[78]

---

77. Belting, *Kaskaskia*, 68.
78. Kalm, *Travels*, 2:402-03, 525-26; Flint, *Recollections*, 99.

Characterization of personality or temperament by group is at best a dubious and slippery enterprise. Nonetheless, it seems fair to describe the townspeople of colonial Ste. Genevieve as a civil and relatively (relative, say, to the New England colonists) cheerful and light-hearted group of people. There were of course always notable exceptions. In reading François Vallé II's letters one never finds a crack of good humor or bonhomie; he never let down his guard. And we have Brackenridge's description of Vital St. Gemme Bauvais: "He was a man of a grave and serious aspect, entirely unlike the gay Frenchmen we are accustomed to see...." Whether grave or gay, however, the citizens of colonial Ste. Genevieve possessed a certain openness of personality that often struck visitors from the outside. Again we rely upon the remarks of that sharp observer of human kind, Perrin du Lac, who was so favorably impressed with François Vallé's reception of him: "He received me with that open courtesy and that unaffected honesty which long ago were replaced in France by devious politeness and dull ceremony." Ste. Genevieve was a far cry from Versailles, and at least in some respects Du Lac preferred the former.[79]

The phrase "colonial Ste. Genevieve" inevitably evokes in the minds of many persons images of better known colonial settlements — Jamestown, Williamsburg or Plymouth Colony. Such associations are of course misleading, for Ste. Genevieve was radically different than its Anglo-American cousin communities on the eastern seaboard of North America; different in ethnic composition, language, religion, architecture, social customs, and patterns of everyday existence. Indeed, the texture of daily life in Ste. Genevieve during the 1790s was so exotic that some leap of the imagination is required to think of the town either as part of colonial America or part of the American Midwest: a Spanish fort overlooking the community from the south; a babble of French, English, and Spanish languages, plus several Indian dialects, mixing in street conversations; parish priests who owned and traded in black slaves; Te Deum services being sung to honor the birth of European princes; Indians living in and around town; numerous households composed of racially different or racially mixed persons; white, black, and Indian children playing together pell-mell in the dusty streets; aristocratic *émigrés* from the French Revolution rubbing shoulders with illiterate trappers and riverboatmen; black slaves carrying muskets and rifles; bundles of deerskins, lead in-

---

79. Brackenridge, *Recollections*, 23; Perrin du Lac, *Voyage*, 168.

gots, and bags of salt serving as mediums of exchange. Social customs and daily life in colonial Ste. Genevieve were unique and were as exotic as any that ever existed in a European community in North America.

Part 3
Community Organization

Chapter XI
Town Government

IN THE 1750s, during Ste. Genevieve's first decade of existence, there was virtually no local civil government, for the fledgling town on the west bank of the Mississippi continued to be administered as an adjunct to the French colonial communities on the east bank of the river. We have seen, for example, that when an auction sale was held at Ste. Genevieve in 1755 an agent of the civil judge from Fort de Chartres crossed the river to conduct the sale and draft an official record of the proceedings. When this agent, Joachim Gérard, arrived in Ste. Genevieve to fulfill his duties, he did, however, have a local base of operations; this was the residence of André Deguire, "captain of the militia."[1]

In 1752, at the time of the first census of Ste. Genevieve, André Deguire was clearly the wealthiest and the most important head-of-household in the new village, although there was no captain of the militia at that early time. Sometime between 1752 and 1755, André Deguire *dit* Larose was appointed captain of the militia at Ste. Genevieve. The body of militiamen in the new town must have been small indeed at that time, but the formal organization of such a body indicates that the townspeople viewed their community as a permanent and viable affair, which required some structure. Captain of the militia was the first official position to exist in Ste. Genevieve, even before that of parish priest. This office remained an important position throughout the colonial history of the town, for in addition to military duties the captains fre-

---

1. KM 55:3:17:1.

quently had civil and social responsibilities to fulfill.[2]

In the early 1760s, one of the most aristocratic and exotic characters ever to appear in the Mississippi Valley arrived in the Illinois Country and was eventually appointed commandant of Ste. Genevieve. Philippe François de Rastel, chevalier de Rocheblave, was born in the south of France and emigrated to Canada. He was a younger son of the marquis de Rocheblave and probably had entered the royal army in order to make his fortune; the pattern of primogeniture in French aristocratic inheritance practices left a younger son with few resources except his name. Rocheblave developed a knack for dealing with Indians and a skill in the guerilla style warfare of the American frontier, apparently not blanching at such Indian practices as scalping. He was a subordinate of the dashing partisan warrior Charles de Langlade when the latter destroyed Braddock's command near Fort Duquesne in 1755 and was one of the Frenchmen who escaped after the French and their Indian allies were defeated at Fort Niagara in 1759. After Montcalm's crushing defeat on the Plains of Abraham in 1759, the French-Indian War was all but over in the East, and there was little left to do for a young French officer with ambition and a talent for survival but head west.[3]

Rocheblave remains an enigmatic and elusive character. It is not known precisely when he arrived in the Illinois Country, although it was probably sometime during the first half of 1760; he witnessed a financial transaction at Kaskaskia in April of that year. In 1763 Rocheblave married Marie-Michel Dufresne, a local girl, at Kaskaskia. She was the daughter of an officer in the town's militia company. Provincial Marie-Michel must have been dazzled, marrying an aristocrat with a glamorous war record and fancy titles. She may have lived to regret the day, however, for her husband's difficult personality and adventuresome spirit disrupted their family life and created problems for Marie all the way from Ste. Genevieve to Quebec. The Rocheblaves were still living in Kaskaskia as late as January 1766.[4]

---

2. Deguire was probably appointed captain of the Ste. Genevieve militia by Major Macarty, commandant at Fort de Chartres, but no document has emerged to demonstrate this. More work needs to be done on the militia in French colonial North America (see Eccles, *France in America*, 69, n. 18).

3. Frégault, *Canada: The War of Conquest*, chap. ix; Kopperman, Braddock, 52, 252, 268, 269; Seineke, *The Clark Adventure*, passim; Mason, "Rocheblave," 360-81; Surveyor, "Rocheblave," 233-42.

4. KM 60:4:24:1; Belting, *Kaskaskia*, 91. A property transaction (Illinois State

Philippe-François Rastel de Rocheblave, first commandant of Ste. Genevieve. Artist unknown.

In July 1766, Rocheblave's daughter Marie-Louise was baptized in Ste. Genevieve, and her father was identified as "commandant of the post." Along with many other French-speaking families,

Archives, Kaskaskia Deed Book B:86; KM 60:9:13:1) that makes Rocheblave "commandant au village St. Joachim" in September 1760 was clearly miscopied. The original of this document (Kaskaskia Book B:100-01) has the correct date, Sep. 13, 1766. I am indebted to Raymond Hammes of Springfield, Illinois, for tracking down this information.

the Rocheblaves had evidently left the British side of the Mississippi in order to settle on the Spanish side of the river. Probably Rocheblave was appointed commandant of Ste. Genevieve by Louis St. Ange de Bellerive, the last French commandant of the Illinois Country. St. Ange evacuated Fort de Chartres late in 1765, leaving it to the newly-arrived British garrison, and crossed the Mississippi to St. Louis, which had been founded less than two years earlier. At St. Louis, St. Ange became de facto commandant of a region that was legally Spanish territory. A French chain-of-command thus persisted in Spanish Illinois during the mid-1760s despite the coming of Spanish sovereignty to the west bank of the Mississippi.[5]

When Spanish officials first arrived in the Illinois Country in the autumn of 1767 they stopped at Ste. Genevieve and picked up Rocheblave, who escorted them upriver to St. Louis. St. Louis, although probably smaller than Ste. Genevieve at that time, had been selected by the Spaniards as their seat of government in the Illinois Country because of its strategic location near the confluence of the Mississippi and Missouri rivers.[6]

In August 1768, the first Spanish governor of Louisiana, the hapless Don Antonio Ullua, reported that "at Missera or Ste. Genevieve, twenty leagues below Pencur [St. Louis], resides a special volunteer commandant. He is M. de Rocheblave, another retired French officer. Because this [i.e., Ste. Genevieve] is a well-populated place, it cannot get along without a commandant. . . . Until now the commandant has not received a salary, for until peace was concluded [1763] these places were very small, their inhabitants living on the side that is now English." Thus, in 1768 Ste. Genevieve was a growing Spanish colonial town, and Spanish authorities seemed to be well-pleased with the town commandant, M. de Rocheblave.[7]

The abortive revolt against Spanish sovereignty in Louisiana that flared up in and around New Orleans in 1768-69 did not catch on in the Illinois Country. The prudent policy of remaining loyal to Spain was in part due to the influence of men like St. Ange in St. Louis and Rocheblave in Ste. Genevieve. Rocheblave

5. SGPR, Baptisms A:18; Alvord and Carter (eds.), *The New Regime*, 111-114; Stirling to Gage, Dec. 15, 1765, in ibid., 124-27; Houck, *History of Missouri*, 212.

6. Francisco Ríu to Antonio Ulloa, Nov. 12, 1767, PC 109; Ulloa to Grimaldi, Aug. 4, 1768, AGI, Audiencia de Santo Domingo, legajo 2542.

7. Ulloa to Grimaldi, Aug. 4, 1768, ibid.

cherished no flag and was willing to serve any sovereign that suited his interests. In the late 1760s that happened to be the king of Spain. The decisive Alexandro O'Reilly arrived at New Orleans in the summer of 1769, and on behalf of Spain quashed the French revolt and executed its ringleaders. Thereupon, Rocheblave dashed off a congratulatory letter to O'Reilly and remarked that the two of them were in a sense compatriots since Rocheblave's mother had been a Dillon, and therefore Irish like O'Reilly himself.[8]

On 25 November 1769, Joseph Labuxière, a former French royal notary from the east bank of the Mississippi, wrote to O'Reilly from Ste. Geneviève and explained that "Monsieur de Rocheblave has taken charge of this post and all of its dependencies in the name of the king of Spain. Then I, functioning as judge, received in the name of his Catholic Majesty and in the presence of the commandant [i.e., Rocheblave] the oath of loyalty given by all of the inhabitants." Rocheblave by his own account, and it is credible enough, was a vigorous and conscientious commandant at Ste. Geneviève. When the citizens of the town complained that they were being abused by English soldiers on the east bank of the Mississippi, Rocheblave swiftly interceded on behalf of his people with the British command at Fort de Chartres.[9]

By the end of 1769, however, Rocheblave's position as commandant in Ste. Geneviève was already being undermined. Auguste Chouteau told Rocheblave there were rumors circulating in New Orleans that Rocheblave had tampered with official Spanish correspondence. Rocheblave articulately and vehemently denied these allegations, claiming that he was known as a man incapable of such baseness. He acknowledged that he had had some "difficulties" with Francisco Ríu, who in 1767 had led the first Spanish expedition to the Illinois Country; but, Rocheblave insisted, these had been honest disagreements between honest men, and he did think that Ríu was capable of trying to besmirch his reputation. It was, however, extremely difficult for a person in remote Ste. Geneviève to defend himself against calumnies being circulated in New Orleans, and Rocheblave lost the battle to influence Spanish authorities in the capital. In June 1770, Lieutenant Louis Dubreuil Villars, one of the many French officers to enter Spanish

8. Moore, *Revolt in Louisiana;* Trenfel, "Spanish Occupation of the Upper Mississippi Valley"; Rocheblave to O'Reilly, Oct. 9, 1769, PC 187.

9. Labuxière to O'Reilly, Nov. 25, 1769, PC 187; Rocheblave to O'Reilly, Nov. 26, 1769, ibid.

service in Louisiana, replaced Rocheblave as commandant in Ste. Genevieve. Several years later, Rocheblave, who had run into debt in Ste. Genevieve, moved back to the east side of the Mississippi, and in 1776 he became commandant of British Kaskaskia.[10]

An office almost parallel to that of town commandant was that of captain of the militia. Indeed, it is not always easy precisely to distinguish their functions, and occasionally during the Spanish regime one man filled both positions. Technically, the commandant held rank over the captain of the militia, but because of differing personalities and changing circumstances this was not always true in practice. Outsiders, even Spaniards, sometimes served as town commandants, while the captain of the militia was by definition always a local inhabitant.

Early in 1764, Neyon de Villiers, commandant at Fort de Chartres, reported to New Orleans: "I have permitted Sieur Vallé, captain of the militia at Ste. Genevieve, to descend to New Orleans in order to conduct some business. He is one of the richest and most industrious inhabitants of this region. Fortune seems to have recompensed him for being a good man [*honnest homme*]." Villiers' letter tells us that sometime between 1759 and 1764 François Vallé I had replaced André Deguire *père* as captain of the militia in Ste. Genevieve. As the town grew during the late 1750s and early 1760s it became necessary to have a leader who was literate, which Vallé was and Deguire was not. In his instructions to Lieutenant Governor Piernas of February 1770, Governor O'Reilly reaffirmed the office of militia captain in all the outposts of Upper Louisiana. For Ste. Genevieve, the autocratic Irishmen in the service of the Spanish monarchy appointed François Vallé captain, Henri Carpentier lieutenant, and François Duchoquette sub-lieutenant. These men represented the social economic power elite of the community; indeed, two of François Vallé's sons married daughters of Henri Carpentier. In 1770, Vallé *père* was not only militia captain, he was also "lieutenant particulier du juge à Ste. Geneviève." This title was more important than that of captain, for it meant that Vallé was the sole source of justice in town and decided all minor cases, both civil and criminal, as a one-man court. Serious cases were sent to St. Louis and sometimes to New Orleans. As "special lieutenant" in Ste. Genevieve Vallé received

10. Rocheblave to O'Reilly, Nov. 27, 1769, PC 187; Pedro Piernas to François Vallé, June 9, 1770, PC 212 A; Villars to O'Reilly, June 30, 1770, PC 187; Rocheblave to ?, June 6, 1776, PC 196; Mason, "Rocheblave," 366; Surveyor, "Rocheblave," 236.

François Vallé I, patriarch of Old Town Ste. Genevieve. Portrait by unknown artist in Guibourd-Vallé house, Ste. Genevieve, Missouri.

a salary of 100 pesos per year from the Spanish government.[11]

Papa Vallé got along famously with his Spanish overlords. When Don Francisco Ríu arrived in Ste. Genevieve in August 1767 on his way upriver to St. Louis, he was, in his own words, given "a very nice reception by Mr. Valet and the whole town was very pleased with the arrival of the arms of our Catholic Majestly." It may well be doubted if the citizens of Ste. Genevieve were in fact joyous over the arrival of the Spaniards, but Vallé had apparently prepared the town to give a warm welcome for the newcomers to the Illinois Country. During the next two years, while sedition was rife in lower Louisiana, Ste. Genevieve remained, under Vallé's tutelage, completely loyal to Spain. When Don Pedro Piernas arrived in the Illinois Country to become lieutenant governor at St. Louis, Vallé took good care of him and was thanked for his efforts by the Spanish authorities in New Orleans.[12]

The 1770s were tranquil years for the Old Town. Not until late in the decade did the American Revolution affect the Upper Mississippi Valley, and local government in Ste. Genevieve remained stable and adequately effective. Rocheblave, who had developed a reputation as a troublemaker, was replaced as commandant by Villars, who "took possession of the post of Ste. Genevieve" on June 15, 1770. Villars described the town at the time of his arrival as peaceful and "entirely law abiding." Papa Vallé controlled the civil government as *lieutenant particulier,* and Commandant Villars got along so well with Vallé that he married Vallé's daughter, Marie-Louise, in 1771. Relations between the powerful Vallé family and town commandants appointed from the outside would not always be so amicable.[13]

During the early 1770s, Don Pedro Piernas served as Spanish lieutenant governor in St. Louis. An interesting vignette of the harmonious relations that developed between Papa Vallé in Ste. Genevieve and his superior in St. Louis is provided in a letter that Piernas wrote to Vallé in 1771. Papa's wife, Marie Billeron Vallé had been in St. Louis conducting family business (as she often did), and Piernas wrote to Vallé:

---

11. Villiers to D'Abbadie, Feb. 3, 1764, *Favrot Papers,* 1:47; "General Instructions of O'Reilly . . . Feb. 17, 1770," *SRM,* 1:81; Contaduria of Louisiana, PC 538 B.

12. Ríu to Ulloa, Nov. 12, 1767, PC 109; Juan de Loyola to Vallé, May 12, 1769, referred to in Vallé to Loyola, Sep. 17, 1769, PC 187.

13. Villars to O'Reilly, June 15, 1770, PC 187; SGPR, Marriages, Book A :148.

> Madame Vallé's strong desire to rejoin you has deprived us
> of her agreeable company. We have tried everything in our
> power to make her remain awhile longer, but she was inflex-
> ible. We considered using force but out of fear that you might
> initiate a lawsuit we let her take her leave.[14]

A charming scene, which shows us how stability of government
in Spanish Illinois was buttressed by close personal relationships
within the power elite.

Don Francisco Cruzat replaced Piernas as lieutenant governor
in charge of Spanish Illinois in 1775, and Vallé's relations were
as cordial with him as they had been with his predecessor. Vallé
was of course too wealthy and too popular with the Spaniards not
to have some enemies in Ste. Genevieve. Don Bernardo de Gálvez
became governor of Spanish Louisiana in 1777, and shortly after
assuming power he received complaints from Ste. Genevieve that
Vallé was abusing his power as civil magistrate. Gálvez wrote to
Cruzat and explained that he had heard that Vallé was conducting
public auctions in such a way as to give unfair advantage to his
family. Spaniards were famous for their meticulous attention to
legality, and Gálvez was clearly upset about the alleged abuses
taking place in Ste. Genevieve. He ordered Cruzat closely to oversee Vallé's conduct. "In the event of other excesses of this kind,"
Gálvez wrote bluntly to Cruzat, "replace him."[15]

François Vallé was sorely threatened by the allegations circulating in New Orleans about his conduct as chief magistrate in Ste.
Genevieve. He well knew that if one of his enemies acquired cred-
ibility with the authorities in the capital the hierarchy of the
Spanish provincial government would work its way and he would
lose his position. Vallé wrote directly to Governor Gálvez justifying
his conduct as *lieutenant particulier* in Ste. Genevieve; his letter of
8 August 1778 is most interesting for what it reveals about government and the exercise of power in the town. Vallé's principal
accuser was one Joseph Tellier, who claimed among other things
that Vallé had auctioned off to one of his sons a family of black
slaves belonging to Tellier at less than the market value. Vallé
wrote to Gálvez that if he were not old and infirm he would travel
in person to New Orleans to defend himself against Tellier's accusations, which, according to Vallé, had been trumped up by a

14. Piernas to Vallé, Sep. 9, 1771, PC 194.
15. Gálvez to Cruzat, Aug. 12, 1777, PC 1.

"cabal of enemies." Vallé went on to point out that two lieutenant governors from St. Louis, Piernas and Cruzat, could testify to his honesty as magistrate in Ste. Genevieve, and that Vallé was dispatching to New Orleans the official documents that would demonstrate his integrity. He also offered either to return the slaves to Tellier or put them back on the auction-block for resale.[16]

Vallé finally played his trump card by suggesting to Gálvez that the cabal of his enemies was motivated by Vallé's refusal to become party to the anti-Spanish revolt that had erupted in Lower Louisiana. This was a deft stroke: Vallé thus informed Gálvez that the enemies of François Vallé were also the enemies of Spain and therefore of the Spanish governor of Louisiana, namely Gálvez. Whether Vallé's claim was true is not known, but the ploy seemed to work. Gálvez replied immediately and assured Vallé that he did not doubt his integrity, adding that if it became clear that the accusations against Vallé had been politically motivated Gálvez would severely punish the false accusers. The fate of Tellier and the other members of the anti-Vallé cabal is unknown, but it is clear that the Vallé grip upon power in Ste. Genevieve was not always unopposed by other factions.[17]

François Vallé *père* did not lose his position as *lieutenant particulier* in Ste. Genevieve in the furor over Tellier's accusations, and he may have been spared this loss by his close relationship to Pedro Piernas, former lieutenant governor in St. Louis, and to Francisco Cruzat, the current lieutenant governor. Piernas was in New Orleans when the Tellier case broke and probably he went to Gálvez in support of his old friend François Vallé. And Cruzat never abandoned Vallé. Even before Governor Gálvez exonerated Vallé, Cruzat did not hesitate to demonstrate his closeness to the *lieutenant particulier* of Ste. Genevieve. In May 1778, for example, Cruzat had heard that Vallé was short of liquor to cheer himself up while his position was in jeopardy. Cruzat thereupon wrote to Vallé that he had learned about "the scarcity of brandy in your town, and because I consider it absolutely essential to have some in your house, Madame Cruzat and I are sending you . . . a little barrel to show our affection for you and your family." Vallé's friends in St. Louis and New Orleans may have saved him during the Tellier

---

16. Vallé to Gálvez, Aug. 8, 1778, PC 1.
17. Draft of letter, Gálvez to Vallé, Aug. 28, 1778, PC 1.

affair of 1778.[18]

Don Fernando de Leyba replaced Cruzat as lieutenant governor at St. Louis in the summer of 1778. De Leyba, best known for his defense of St. Louis during the Anglo-Indian attack in May 1780, was an unpopular official in Spanish Louisiana, but Papa Vallé in Ste. Genevieve weathered the stormy two years of his lieutenant governorship without mishap. Indeed, as was seen in chapter three, Vallé's three sons — Charles, François, and Jean-Baptiste — served under De Leyba during the attack on St. Louis.

When De Leyba died suddenly at St. Louis in June 1780, Cruzat was reassigned to Upper Louisiana as his replacement. Cruzat required some time in New Orleans to prepare himself to return to St. Louis, but once he got on the river he made good time going upstream, making the trip in fifty-eight days. Cruzat was fortunate to make the trip up the Mississippi during relatively slack water (August and September), and François Vallé was lucky to have his old friends back in command at St. Louis. Vallé wrote to Piernas in New Orleans that everyone in Ste. Genevieve was glad to see Cruzat return, for by his auspicious conduct he had captured their "hearts and minds." As for Cruzat's attitude toward Vallé, he wrote expressing his regret that Papa's illnesses continued and his hope that they would not adversely affect Vallé's "zeal for the service." Cruzat had nothing to fear, for at that time, October 1780, Vallé wrote to Gálvez that "if anything could increase my zeal for the service of my prince [i.e., the king of Spain] and my attachment to his country, the marks of kindness for me that you expressed in your letter of last July 25 would be the surest means. . . ." Vallé had learned to express himself as well as any European aristocrat in the convoluted and sycophantic prose of Old Regime diplomacy, and it is clear that as he entered old age the *lieutenant particulier* of Ste. Genevieve was secure in his position from any threats either inside or outside of town.[19]

When François Vallé *père* died in 1783, François Vallé *fils* wrote to Governor Miró in New Orleans and asked the governor to maintain the office of *lieutenant particulier* in the Vallé family and suggested that his older brother Charles (Carlos) was the appropri-

---

18. On Piernas's friendship with Vallé, see, for example, Piernas to Vallé, Feb. 19, 1780, PC 147 A.

19. See Cruzat's instructions from Gálvez, July 25, 1780, *SRM*, 1: 171-72; Vallé to Pedro Piernas, Oct. 5, 1780, PC 193 B; Cruzat to Vallé, Oct. 31, 1780, PC 192; Vallé to Gálvez, Oct. 5, 1780, PC 193 B.

ate person to fill in the boots of the deceased Papa Vallé. This position was crucial to the Vallés for maintaining their control of government in Ste. Genevieve. Lieutenant Governor Cruzat in St. Louis, an old friend of the Vallés, supported François II's request, but Governor Miró in New Orleans refused to oblige the Vallés. Rather, the governor restructured the town government of Ste. Genevieve by suppressing the old French title of *lieutenant particulier* altogether. Henceforth, the town commandant would carry the title "Commandant Civil et Militaire," and both military and judicial authority rested in his hands.[20]

Silvio Francisco de Cartabona had replaced Louis Villars as town commandant at Ste. Genevieve in 1776, but it was only with the death of François Vallé I in 1783 that Cartabona became civil governor in town and began to place his signature on legal documents. Charles Vallé was appointed captain of the Ste. Genevieve militia in 1783, but his reduced powers and debauched personal life meant that his influence was a mere shadow of what his father's had been. For ten years the Vallé family was removed from the center of formal political power in Ste. Genevieve, although the wealth, ambition and social prominence of François II and Jean-Baptiste permitted them to exercise a good deal of power informally.[21]

Silvio de Cartabona, an Italian in the service of the Spanish monarchy, was the first genuine outsider to be thrust upon the citizens of Ste. Genevieve as town commandant. Cartabona's sojourn in Ste. Genevieve, first as military commandant (1776-83) and then as *Commandant Civil et Militaire* (1783-84), seems to have been relatively uneventful and unremarkable. He did lead the expedition to St. Louis when that post was attacked in 1780, but his activities in Ste. Genevieve are of little interest; he did not buy property in the town, marry a local girl, or establish any enduring personal or business contacts. Cartabona was merely a professional Spanish soldier who by happenstance was posted to Upper Louisiana and wound up as commandant at Ste. Genevieve. He apparently served adequately in that function but left no perma-

---

20. Vallé to Miró, Dec. 4, 1783, PC 9; Cruzat to Miró, Nov. 13, 1783, ibid.

21. Cartabona to Miró, Dec. 4, 1783, PC 9; Charles Vallé had in fact been serving as de facto captain of the Ste. Genevieve militia since December 1780 because of his father's illnesses (Cruzat to François Vallé I, Dec. 12, 1780, PC 193 B); the officers of the Ste. Genevieve militia in early 1784 were Captain Charles Vallé, Lieutenant François Vallé II, and Sub-lieutenant Jean-Baptiste Vallé (Miró to Cruzat, Mar. 26, 1784, PC 117 B).

nent mark on the town.[22]

Early in July 1784, Cartabona was replaced as civil and military commander of Ste. Genevieve by another outsider, Antonio de Oro. The similarity of the two men is unhappily attested to by both Rozier and Houck, each of whom presents them as one man "Don Silvio Francisco de Cartabona de Oro." Although misleading and aggravating, this error is understandable: both men were professional Spanish soldiers in Upper Louisiana; both served as commandants of Ste. Genevieve; both were outsiders to the community; and neither of them seems to have had a profound impact upon the history of the town. De Oro, as will be revealed in a later chapter, was, however, clearly the more important for our story because he served in Ste. Genevieve during the severe floods of the mid-1780s and because of his long dispute with the Vallé brothers, François and Jean-Baptiste.[23]

It is not surprising that there was tension between the Vallé family and the Spanish commandants of Ste. Genevieve; the remarkable thing is that it took so long for this tension to break to the surface. The Vallé men had wealth, social prominence, energy, ambition, and local connections. How were they to reconcile themselves to playing a subordinate role to the Spanish commandants imposed from the outside? From 1770 to 1783 this potential problem had been kept latent by the prudence and political skill of François Vallé I, and by the fact that the Spanish government had permitted him to retain the title and functions of *lieutenant particulier* of Ste. Genevieve. There is no evidence of friction between François Vallé I and the first two Spanish commandants, Louis Villars and Silvio de Cartabona.

During the mid-1780s, three events altered the structure and personnel of leadership in Ste. Genevieve: 1) François Vallé died in 1783 and the position of *lieutenant particulier* was suppressed. 2) Antonio de Oro succeeded Silvio de Cartabona as civil and military commandant in 1784. 3) Charles Valle, who had replaced his father as captain of the militia, left Ste. Genevieve for good in the late 1780s; his personal life was in a shambles and he moved

22. Cartabona himself said of Ste. Genevieve: "Nothing of great interest occurs in this town. Peace and tranquility have obtained since my arrival here (Cartabona to Gálvez, Feb. 4, 1778, PC 1)."

23. Rozier, *Early Settlement of the Mississippi Valley;* Houck, *History of Missouri,* 1:346-47. Breveted Captain Antonio de Oro left New Orleans by convoy in March 1784 and arrived at Ste. Genevieve in June (Miró to Cruzat, Mar. 10, 1774, PC 117 B; De Oro to Miró, July 26, 1784, PC 117 A).

to Opelousas in Lower Louisiana. These events left François II as scion of the Vallé family and placed a Spanish soldier, Antonio de Oro, in town who was accustomed to being obeyed. The tension between local power and Spanish authority, which had lain dormant for so long, was about to surface in Ste. Genevieve. This problem was not finally resolved until 1794, when François Vallé II became town commandant. With that occurrence local power and Spanish authority were finally wed, but before that union was consummated there was a decade of increasing political tension and strife within Ste. Genevieve.[24]

Difficulties between De Oro and François Vallé began in the spring of 1785. François, who was perhaps testing the recently arrived commandant, attempted to gain title to a small piece of land without going through the required formalities. De Oro was in fact not quite sure how to handle the situation and wrote to Cruzat in St. Louis for instructions. Cruzat, although he was an old friend and supporter of the Vallé family, was blunt and unequivocal in his reply: De Oro was never to permit that sort of "insubordination, most especially from a subject [i.e., François Vallé] who should be well-informed on the issue of subordination to one's superiors." Thus De Oro won the first round of the match. But the Spanish soldier was ill and isolated in Ste. Genevieve, and the Vallé brothers were young and aggressive.[25]

In October 1786, De Oro wrote to Lieutenant Governor Cruzat in St. Louis and expressed his dismay that many black slaves in Ste. Genevieve carried firearms. This practice was injurious to the community, De Oro claimed, for careless slaves belonging to a few important persons had killed domestic livestock in the Ste. Genevieve area. The carrying of firearms by slaves was indeed a violation of the law, and moreover, De Oro's Castilian sense of propriety was offended by the practice of permitting slaves to carry arms. Cruzat's initial reaction to De Oro's proposal, which seemed reasonable enough, was favorable. De Oro proceeded to post on the door of the parish church in Ste. Genevieve an ordinance prohibiting slaves to carry firearms; this door was the community bulletin board.[26]

---

24. On Charles Vallé's personal life, see above, chap. vi.

25. Cruzat to De Oro, Mar. 9, 1785, PC 117 B.

26. Cruzat to De Oro, Oct. 31,1786, PC 199; De Oro to Cruzat, Nov. 23, 1786, PC 12. Article XII of the Black Code ("Edit concernant les Nègres," 79) forbade slaves to carry "offensive weapons."

François and Jean-Baptiste Vallé, who were two of the largest slave holders in Ste. Genevieve, objected to De Oro's ordinance, claiming that when their slaves were working a league or two from the village they needed weapons with which to protect themselves from hostile Indians. Going over De Oro's head, the Vallé brothers sent a memorandum to Cruzat in which they articulated their objections to De Oro's ordinance. De Oro thereupon accused the Vallés of "disobedience and insubordination," and an inability "to recognize the superiority that His Majesty [the king of Spain] conveys upon a commandant." The long smoldering issue of Spanish commandant versus local power elite was thus first articulated in Ste. Genevieve.[27]

Cruzat had gotten himself in a bit of a pinch by agreeing to De Oro's ordinance before he knew what the Vallés thought about it. Cruzat responded to De Oro that he had, after serious reflection, found no trace of disobedience or insubordination in the Vallés' memorandum, but agreed to send the whole affair to New Orleans for final arbitration. De Oro himself wrote to Governor Miró and complained of the *habitants* of Ste. Genevieve, who, according to De Oro, wished to live "without restraints, in perfect freedom, oblivious to religion, and without recognizing the laws of justice." De Oro also sent Miró a lampoon that had appeared on the church door in Ste. Genevieve, which suggested that De Oro's wife wore the pants in their family. At this point, De Oro sensed that he was engaged in a dispute he would ultimately lose, and in late 1786 he asked Governor Miró to reassign him. Trying to govern Ste. Genevieve's independent power elite had proven too much for the old soldier.[28]

Once Governor Miró had assembled on his desk in New Orleans all the materials from Ste. Genevieve and St. Louis regarding the De Oro affair, it did not take the governor long to make a decision: De Oro and the influential citizens of Ste. Genevieve were utterly incompatible, and the town had to have a new commandant. In January 1787, Miró sent De Oro a dispatch ordering him to report to Lower Louisiana for reassignment. De Oro had bucked the Vallés and lost, and he would not be the last Spanish commandant

---

27. Vallé memorandum, Nov. 20, 1786, PC 12; De Oro to Cruzat, Nov. 23, 1786, ibid.

28. Cruzat to De Oro, Nov. 27, 1786, PC 199; Cruzat to Miró, Nov. 30, 1786, PC 12; De Oro to Miró, Dec. 5, 1786, PC 199; De Oro to Miró, Dec. 3, 1786, PC 199.

of Ste. Genevieve to wind up thus embarrassed.[29]

Before De Oro's replacement arrived in Ste. Genevieve, De Oro had become desperately ill. He died in Ste. Genevieve in August 1787, and he must have died with special bitterness knowing that the town he had come to despise would be his final resting place. Like Papa Vallé four years earlier, De Oro was buried in the Old Town cemetery, a long way from his native Spain. The inventory of De Oro's estate shows that, whatever his faults as commandant, he had lived modestly in Ste. Genevieve, with his wife and one black slave in a small house.[30]

Colonial Ste. Genevieve, located as it was on the far-flung frontier of European settlement on the North American continent, seems to have been a veritable catchbasin for exotic characters on the run from more civilized locales. One of the most interesting of these characters arrived in Ste. Genevieve in the summer of 1787. Henri Peyroux de la Coudrenière, a Frenchman with an aristocratic name, was a man of some intellectual and linguistic attainments. During the 1770s he had acquired a fortune in Louisiana and wrote a memoir on agriculture. His first established presence in Ste. Genevieve was on August 4, 1787, at which time he wrote to Governor Miró in New Orleans: "I have returned from St. Louis where I presented to Monsieur Cruzat the commission with which you have honored me. Monsieur de Oro is ill. He will recognize me as his successor tomorrow, August 5." Thus Governor Miró had appointed Peyroux commandant of Ste. Genevieve to replace De Oro, and Peyroux had journeyed to St. Louis to present his credentials to Lieutenant Governor Cruzat. Peyroux's appointment was a reward for his service to Spain in recruiting Acadian refugees to settle in Lower Louisiana.[31]

The correspondence by, to, and concerning Peyroux while he was commandant at Ste. Genevieve is voluminous. Unlike Cartabona and De Oro, who left but few documents, Peyroux spewed forth a surfeit of letters, dispatches, and memoranda upon which to reconstruct the history of his tenure as commandant; these documents also reveal something of Peyroux's personality and character.[32]

29. Miró to De Oro, Jan. 13, 1787, PC 200; Miró to De Oro, Apr. 20, 1787, ibid.

30. SGPR, Burials, Book 2:5; inventory of De Oro's estate printed in Billon (ed.), *Annals*, 1:246-47.

31. On Peyroux see Winzerling, *Acadian Odyssey*, chap. viii; Nasatir (ed.), *War Vessels*, passim, esp. 222-24; Peyroux to Miró, Aug. 4, 1787, PC 199.

32. Most of these letters are in AGI, PC.

Peyroux had a natural genius for alienating people. He fought with his subordinates, his superiors, his colleagues, and even his own family. He had not been commandant long in Ste. Genevieve before his personal quirks began to emerge. In January 1789, Governor Esteban Miró finally wrote to Peyroux and admonished him to adhere to the chain of command in the Spanish bureaucracy: "You must follow the orders of Monsieur Pérez [Lieutenant Governor in St. Louis]. You must address yourself to him as your immediate superior, and it is through him that I must be informed of everything. . . . Subordination requires this, and moreover, I do not have the time to do so much writing." Peyroux's ego must have been hurt by Miró's bluntness, but the governor was sick and tired of the flood of carping letters from Ste. Genevieve's importunate commandant.[33]

That Peyroux had succeeded in irritating Governor Miró became abundantly clear in a personal issue that arose between Peyroux and his brother Pierre-Charles. Pierre lived intermittenly in Ste. Genevieve and had left some personal property in town when he went downriver to New Orleans. Peyroux did not wish to attend to his brother's effects and informed him that if he did not return immediately to Ste. Genevieve to take care of his property Peyroux would place the articles in storage at his brother's expense. In New Orleans Pierre-Charles told Miró of this affair, and the governor forthwith wrote to Peyroux and forbade him to execute his plan, for, as the governor put it: "I cannot believe that you could be so inhumane to your brother; as commandant you must not do it, and as Monsieur Peyroux to do it would be cruel and shameful."[34]

It is a wonder that Peyroux lasted six years as commandant of Ste. Genevieve. He eventually destroyed himself by engaging in something that no man could do and survive in Ste. Genevieve — he entered into a long and bitter feud with the Vallé clan. It all began in December 1791 when Peyroux left town for a few days and François Vallé II, who was lieutenant of the Ste. Genevieve militia, served as post commandant *ad interim.* As soon as Peyroux departed town, Vallé discovered a man in prison about whom Peyroux had left no report or records. Vallé asked the corporal in charge of the man's confinement if the prisoner were a criminal and why he had been incarcerated. The corporal replied that the

---

33. Miró to Peyroux, Jan. 22, 1789, PC 202.
34. Miró to Peyroux, Jan. 20, 1789, PC 201.

man was no criminal but that he had been imprisoned by Peyroux for some small debt incurred in a commercial transaction. Upon hearing this, Vallé ordered the man released on his own recognizance pending Peyroux's return. When, just before Christmas 1791, Peyroux did return to Ste. Genevieve, he charged Vallé with the responsibility of paying the released man's debt. Vallé refused to pay, whereupon Peyroux flew into a rage and took the rash step of having Vallé arrested and jailed.[35]

This "outrageous action [*procede violent*]" was a *cause celèbre* in Upper Louisiana over the Christmas and New Year's holidays of 1791-92. François Vallé's brother, Jean-Baptiste, wrote to St. Louis on his brother's behalf. It was quickly apparent that the two most powerful persons in St. Louis, Lieutenant Governor Pérez and Auguste Chouteau, were on Vallé's side. A revealing letter was sent by Chouteau to François Vallé on January 2, 1792. Chouteau explained that both he and Pérez were terribly hurt by what had happened to François. But the key passage in Chouteau's letter, a passage that contained bad tidings for Peyroux, spoke of the great pleasure it would give Chouteau to avenge François, who could count for help upon all of Chouteau's friends. When Auguste Chouteau, a man who had friends and business associates the length and breadth of Spanish Louisiana, wrote in this vein to Vallé on January 2, Peyroux's position was seriously undermined. Peyroux had picked the wrong enemies. His acrimonious dispute with François Vallé was the beginning of the end for Peyroux as commandant in Ste. Genevieve.[36]

Peyroux left Ste. Genevieve again in February 1792. He proceeded downriver to New Orleans where he embarked on the brigantine *La Amable Maria* for Philadelphia. Peyroux's mission in the American capital was to make contact with "honorable German, Flemish, Dutch, or French families" and induce them to emigrate to Spanish Louisiana. The Spaniards were constantly striving to turn Louisiana into a viable colony by increasing its population through immigration. French Revolutionary wars in Europe doomed Peyroux's mission to failure. But while residing

---

35. François Vallé to Pérez, Dec. 21, 1791, PC 211; Vallé to Pérez, Dec. 23, 1791, ibid.

36. Copy of Jean-Baptiste Vallé's letter to Pérez, Dec. 29, 1791, PC 211; Pérez to François Vallé, Dec. 26, 1791 (two letters of this date), MHS, Vallé Collection, Box 1; Auguste Chouteau to Vallé, Dec. 26, 1791, ibid.; Chouteau to Vallé, Jan. 2, 1792, ibid.

in Philadelphia Ste. Genevieve's commandant had the opportunity to meet, among other dignitaries, Secretary of State Thomas Jefferson, who was already interested in the trans-Mississippian West.[37]

François Vallé had been released from jail and entirely vindicated by the time Peyroux departed Ste. Genevieve in February 1792, and Vallé once again became town commandant *ad interim.* How it must have galled Peyroux to turn his command over to Vallé. But given Vallé's position as the ranking officer in the town militia Peyroux had no choice but to turn Ste. Genevieve over to his heartiest enemy.[38]

Peyroux was absent from Ste. Genevieve for more than a year, not returning to town until the summer of 1793. In his absence Manuel Pérez was replaced as lieutenant governor in St. Louis by the French creole Zenon Trudeau. In Ste. Genevieve the Vallés began to cultivate Trudeau as soon as he arrived in Upper Louisiana in the autumn of 1792, and they were probably aided by their friend Auguste Chouteau. Even before Peyroux returned to Ste. Genevieve, Trudeau had become a friend of and advocate for Vallé. Trudeau wrote to the new governor in New Orleans, Hector de Carondelet, asking favors for Vallé and pointing out that Vallé was "a zealous servant of the king and the public welfare." While Peyroux traveled to Philadelphia, François Vallé was at home tending the store, and this assiduity, so characteristic of the Vallés, paid dividends.[39]

When Peyroux returned to Ste. Genevieve in July 1793 he was still officially civil and military commandant of the town. Trudeau, however, soon moved to whittle away his powers and to boost the position of François Vallé. The latter, who had been lieutenant of the militia, was promoted to captain, a position that for several years had been filled ex officio by the commandant. When Trudeau wrote to Vallé informing him of this promotion Trudeau remarked that he wished that he could do more, "but time will make you see that which I wish I could do for you and your family." Thus it is apparent that by August 1793 Trudeau had

37. Nasatir (ed.), *War Vessels,* 223, n. 77; Carondelet to Felix Trudeau, Apr. 17, 1792, PC 18; Carondelet to José Jaudenes and José de Viar, Apr. 17, 1792, PC 104 A; Jaudenes and Viar to Carondelet, June 5, 1792, PC 25 A; see also Peyroux's letters to Carondelet from Philadelphia, PC 206.

38. Vallé to Pérez, Feb. 23, 1792, PC 207 B.

39. Trudeau to Carondelet, Apr. 10, 1793, PC 26.

decided to replace Peyroux with François Vallé as commandant in Ste. Genevieve and that he was merely awaiting a convenient opportunity to do so.[40]

In September 1793 Trudeau traveled to Ste. Genevieve and spent a week in town attending to various affairs. This trip reinforced Trudeau's already negative estimation of Peyroux, and Trudeau commented unfavorably about Peyroux in his report to Carondelet. Peyroux was "presumptuous of his own knowledge and condemns everything that he himself has not thought of." Trudeau's visit finally alerted Peyroux to the fact that his position was tenuous, for during the visit Trudeau had ignored Peyroux and, in the latter's words, acted as if "he were absolute monarch here and I counted for nothing."[41]

Peyroux was at odds with Trudeau, with the entire Vallé family, and with the parish priest in Ste. Genevieve, Abbé de St. Pierre, whom Peyroux accused of being a "false priest." By November 1793 Peyroux felt threatened enough to launch a counterattack against his legion of enemies. He unburdened himself in a long letter to Governor Carondelet. According to Peyroux Ste. Genevieve was a stagnating town in the clutches of a corrupt power elite. And when he had tried to do something about it the wicked Vallé family had roped in the lieutenant governor and the local parish priest on their side in order to halt Peyroux's reform movement. The Vallés had even insulted Peyroux's wife and ignored his orders. François Vallé had finally become so insubordinate that Peyroux was obliged to confine him for twenty-four hours in the guardroom ("chambre du corporal").[42]

Coudrenière surely was an odd duck but he was also intelligent and energetic, and was perhaps the best educated person in Ste. Genevieve. There is some fragmentary evidence that Peyroux was in fact a defender of the poorer inhabitants against the interests of the power elite, which was led by the Vallés. The weight of the evidence suggests, however, that even though Peyroux may have been a reformer of sorts he was abrasive and abusive enough to undermine his position with most of the citizens of Ste. Genevieve and that his diatribe against the "corrupt" power elite was largely a fabrication of a difficult and slightly paranoid person.

---

40. Trudeau to Vallé, Aug. 24, 1793, MHS, Vallé Collection, Box 1.

41. Trudeau to Carondelet, Sep. 28, 1793, PC 208 A.

42. Peyroux to Trudeau, Aug. 14, 1793, PC 2363; Peyroux to Carondelet, Nov. 14, 1793, PC 207 B.

The final straw in the Peyroux affair came during the winter of 1793-94, when Peyroux's loyalty to the Spanish regime in Louisiana was called into doubt. While living in Philadelphia early in 1793 Peyroux had met Citizen Genêt, the ardent revolutionary who was French minister to the United States. Genêt was actively plotting to launch a joint Franco-American military invasion of Louisiana in order to seize the province from Spain, and there were rumors to the effect that Peyroux had been recruited for this anti-Spanish plot.[43]

With the threat of an invasion hanging over his head, Lieutenant Governor Trudeau wrote to François Vallé from St. Louis on January 6, 1794, and told Vallé to keep a watch on Peyroux, for he (Trudeau) had become suspicious of him. Then, a few days later, Trudeau concocted a clever stratagem by which to rid himself of Peyroux. He dispatched Peyroux with twelve militiamen from Ste. Genevieve to New Madrid for the ostensible purpose of bolstering the defenses of an exposed outpost during a critical juncture. Trudeau was even duplicitous enough to suggest to the ambitious Peyroux that he might expect to achieve "gloire" by serving at New Madrid, which had "a fort complete with artillery." On January 12, 1794, Peyroux set out for New Madrid with hopes of achieving that glory in defense of a Spanish outpost.[44]

But the day after Trudeau sent Peyroux his marching orders the lieutenant governor sent off a secret dispatch to the commandant at New Madrid, Thomas Portell, informing him that Peyroux's loyalty to Spain was in serious doubt. As soon as Peyroux's party of thirteen men from Ste. Genevieve arrived in New Madrid, Portell had Peyroux arrested and dispatched down the Mississippi under guard. The militiamen Portell sent back to Ste. Genevieve, for "since their arrival here three days ago they have been continuously drunk." Portell was not enthusiastic about the reinforcements he had received from Ste. Genevieve — one "traitor" and twelve militiamen on a binge.[45]

Trudeau had engineered Peyroux's expulsion from Ste. Genevieve without so much as consulting Governor Carondelet about it. But once he had set in motion his plot to get rid of

43. Liljegren, "Jacobinism," 42-43; Nasatir (ed.), *War Vessels,* 88, n. 5.

44. Trudeau to Vallé, Jan. 6, 1794, MHS, Vallé Collection, Box 1; Trudeau to Peyroux, Jan. 8, 1794, PC 207 A; Peyroux to Vallé, Jan. 12, 1794, MHS, ibid.

45. Trudeau to Portell, Jan. 9, 1794, PC 28; Portell to Gayoso de Lemos, Jan. 25, 1794, PC 42.

Peyroux he had to explain his actions to the governor. On January 15, 1794, Trudeau wrote that he was "suspicious of Peyroux's knowledge about the plan to invade this province [Louisiana]." And two weeks later Trudeau explained to Carondelet that "I find myself forced to dismiss Monsieur Peyroux from his command at Ste. Genevieve. His conduct had given me a right to think that he did not withdraw from America without having had knowledge of the project [Genêt's invasion plan] that threatens us."[46]

Four days after Trudeau wrote to Carondelet, Delassus de Luzières, leader of the settlement at New Bourbon, sent Carondelet a much more sweeping indictment of Peyroux. De Luzières drafted a nine-article bill of particulars against Peyroux, claiming that he was a security risk, that he was a divisive force in the community, that he refused to change his residence from the Old Town to the New Town of Ste. Genevieve, that he fought with the parish priest, and that he handled Indian relations poorly. According to De Luzières, Peyroux had done nothing right as commandant of Ste. Genevieve, and it seems likely that Trudeau and De Luzières had coordinated their attacks upon Peyroux. In any case, De Luzières' blast of February 1, 1794, surely persuaded Carondelet that Trudeau had been correct to relieve Peyroux as commandant. Yet Carondelet's terse acknowledgement of this action, which he penned to Trudeau on March 3, clearly suggests that the governor was not convinced that Peyroux was in fact a traitor.[47]

When Gayoso de Lemos, the Spanish lieutenant governor at Natchez, relayed Peyroux down to New Orleans in February 1794, he sensed that something odd was going on. Gayoso remarked to Carondelet that "besides public interest, the commandant in Illinois [i.e., Trudeau] must have something else against Peyroux." Gayoso was of course correct. Trudeau had tarred Peyroux with the brush of treason as a means of getting him out of Ste. Genevieve. Once Peyroux arrived in New Orleans, no formal charges were brought against him. Indeed, his reputation remained sufficiently intact for him later to be appointed commandant at New Madrid, from which post he was dismissed for insubordination in 1803. After a turbulent career of more than twenty

---

46. Trudeau to Carondelet, Jan. 15, 1794, PC 28; same to same, Jan. 28, 1794, PC 209.

47. De Luzières to Carondelet, Feb. 1, 1794, PC 210; Carondelet to Trudeau, Mar. 3, 1794, PC 21.

years in Spanish Louisiana, Peyroux left America to return to his native France, where he was swallowed up by the Napoleonic imperium. His older brother, Pierre-Charles, and his mother, Marguerite, with both of whom Peyroux had fought, died and were buried in Ste. Genevieve.[48]

Upon Peyroux's dismissal, Trudeau forthwith replaced him with his old friend and ally, François Vallé II. Vallé thus became civil and military commandant of the Ste. Genevieve District, which extended from Apple Creek (Rivière à la Pomme) north to the Meramec and from the Mississippi westward indefinitely. Vallé's service sheet, which Spanish authorities drafted in 1787, listed him as being endowed with only "poor capacity," but he had shown "great valor, application, and conduct" in serving the royal government. Moreover, as Trudeau explained in a letter of January 1794, François Vallé was "the only person who could be entrusted with the defense of Ste. Genevieve because the citizens trust him and because he has a special genius for handling the Indians, . . . qualities that Don Enrique Peyroux seemed to be lacking." After ten years of waiting and planning, the Vallés were back in the saddle as official rulers in Ste. Genevieve. Two commandants, Antonio de Oro and Peyroux de la Coudrenière, had crossed swords with the Vallé family and both lost. The Vallés had pursued their ambitions with tenacity, skill, and most importantly, with success.[49]

Whatever the machinations or motivations of Trudeau and Vallé in the Peyroux-Vallé conflict, François Vallé II's replacement of Peyroux as commandant of Ste. Genevieve in 1794 was surely a salutary change for the town. The decade that François *fils* governed Ste. Genevieve (1794-1804) was a tumultuous time for the town; a massive immigration of Anglo-Americans changed the demographic and ethnic basis of the community and the three-cornered rivalry — Spanish, French, and American — for control of Louisiana was played out. François Vallé II governed efficiently and effectively through this difficult decade. He got along well

---

48. Gayoso to Carondelet, Feb. 4, 1794, PC 42; Houck, *History of Missouri,* 2:125, 137. Regarding Peyroux's mother and brother, see above, chap. ix; Peyroux lived for several years at his Saline concession after he was dismissed as commandant. Peyroux's wife continued to live in Ste. Genevieve after her husband's departure for New Madrid.

49. Holmes (ed.), *Honor and Fidelity,* 225; Trudeau to Portell, Jan. 9, 1794, PC 28. On the boundaries of the Ste. Genevieve District, see Stoddard, *Sketches,* 214, and below, chap. xiv, n. 19.

with the citizens of the town, with his superiors in St. Louis and
New Orleans, and with his colleague, Pierre-Charles Delassus de
Luzières, who was commandant at neighboring New Bourbon
during the same period. Paul Alliot, who visited Ste. Genevieve
at the end of the colonial period, remarked that the town was
"governed by a commandant who always terminates amicably the
quarrels that arise among them [the citizens]." François II's salary
as commandant in Ste. Genevieve was 100 pesos (dollars) per year,
which was the same amount that his father had received as *lieutenant particulier*. Vallé asked for a captain's rank in the Spanish army,
but despite Governor Carondelet's support, the royal government
turned him down.[50]

In January 1804 the town of Ste. Genevieve awaited the official
cession of Louisiana to the United States. Commandant François
Vallé wrote to Lieutenant Governor Charles Delassus in St. Louis
on January 13 that he was waiting the arrival of newspapers and
noted that he suffered from "an inflammation of the chest." Vallé
had less than two months to live, although he was not yet fifty
years old. Perhaps the endemic malaria of the Mississippi Valley
had sapped his energies.[51]

Early in March, Delassus drafted an inventory of the men who
had served Spain well in Upper Louisiana and sent it to Captain
Amos Stoddard, the American who was about to become commandant of the entire vast and largely unknown region. Concerning
François Vallé, Delassus commented that "the fidelity of this family
under all the administrations; the must good service of this man
since his employment, the universal esteem of all the inhabitants
that he so justly deserves, cannot but cause regret that so useful
a man is about to depart life. . . ."[52]

François Vallé II died in Ste. Genevieve the very day that Delassus sent these remarks to Stoddard, March 6, 1804, just four days
before the town officially became American. François II was the
only commandant of colonial Ste. Genevieve to have been born
in the town (1758), live his entire life there, and die there. François
was buried, beneath his pew in the log church that had been
constructed in 1794, alongside his infant daughter Audile-Matilde,

50. Alliot, "Reflections," 133; Contaduria of Louisiana, PC 538 B; Vallé to
Carondelet, Nov. 5, 1795, PC 129; Carondelet to Luis de las Casas, Sep. 12,
1796, PC 1444; Conde de Santa Clara to Carondelet, Nov. 14, 1797, PC 153 B.

51. Vallé to Delassus, Jan. 13, 1804, PC 188 B.

52. Delassus to Stoddard, Mar. 6, 1804, printed in Billon (ed.), *Annals*, 1:365-71.

François Vallé II, who died just before Ste. Genevieve passed into American hands. Portrait by unknown artist in Guibourd-Vallé house, Ste. Genevieve, Missouri.

who had died a week earlier. Successive churches were built over his remains during the nineteenth century, and his grave is now marked with a bronze plaque embedded in the floor of the present edifice.[53]

The spring of 1804 was a lugubrious season for the citizens of Ste. Genevieve. Their commandant and the scion of the Vallé family, François II, was prematurely dead. Uncertainty at the local level was compounded by the coming of American sovereignty to all of Louisiana. No one in Ste. Genevieve was sure how the Anglo-American politicians on the eastern seaboard would treat the trans-Mississippian town with a French-speaking population. To their credit, however, the Americans started out on the right foot.[54]

Lieutenant Governor Delassus had been a friend of the Vallé family for ten years when he sent his report to Captain Stoddard in March 1804. In this report Delassus praised both the Vallé brothers, François II and Jean-Baptiste. Of Jean-Baptiste, Delassus wrote that he was "a very zealous officer. He has been employed in several different circumstances and always conducted himself well. Since the illness of his brother [François II], he has been temporarily in command at Ste. Genevieve." Jean-Baptiste was in fact a very able and cosmopolitan individual, who was equally at home on the streets of rustic Ste. Genevieve and in the drawing rooms of New Orleans. Captain Stoddard was wise to turn to Jean-Baptiste Vallé after François II died on March 6, 1804.[55]

On March 19, 1804, Jean-Baptiste wrote solemnly to Charles Delassus in St. Louis: "I felt that it was my duty to accept the position [civil commandant of Ste. Genevieve] that Monsieur Stoddard has offered me. . . . We are now all Americans. As such, I wish, as I would under any government, to devote my services to the country and to the well being of its citizens." Jean-Baptiste was not overjoyed with the thought of being an American, but his family had shown remarkable flexibility and adaptability in the face of changing circumstances, serving French, Spanish, and American regimes in turn without so much as batting an eye. Jean-Baptiste Vallé's commission as the first American commandant of Ste. Genevieve is in the Missouri Historical Society, dated

---

53. SGPR, Burials, Book 2:67.

54. On international politics in 1804, see above, chap. iii.

55. Billon (ed.), *Annals*, 1:368; Jean-Baptiste had been serving in fact as town commandant since the middle of February because of his brother's illness (Jean-Baptiste Vallé to Delassus, Feb. 14, 1804, PC 197).

Jean-Baptiste Vallé, first American commandant of Ste. Genevieve. Portrait by unknown artist in Guibourd-Vallé house, Ste. Genevieve, Missouri.

March 10, 1804, and signed by Captain Amos Stoddard. Events had moved swiftly in North America, for when Jean- Baptiste was born in 1760 the American Republic had not even been conceived.[56]

Colonial Louisiana never had clear and consistent codes of civil or criminal laws in statutory form. During the Spanish regime, justice was based upon a mishmash of ancient French customs and French royal statutes that the Spanish authorities continued to recognize; an assortment of decrees and edicts that emanated from Spanish officials in St. Louis and New Orleans; and finally local ordinances promulgated by the town commandants. When Captain Amos Stoddard arrived in Louisiana to take command of the territory for the United States, he remarked: "It would require the ability and industry of an able jurist to delineate even the leading traits of the laws, by which Louisiana was governed."[57]

The *coutume de Paris* was a fundamental law (really a congeries of various laws and precedents) that governed family property and inheritance practices in northern France. This customary law had been officially introduced to French Louisiana in 1712, and throughout Ste. Genevieve's colonial period the *coutume de Paris* regulated the use and disposal of property within families. Because the law did not exist as a single codified text, but merely as a compilation of customs, disputes among heirs sometimes arose. In such instances, the dispute was referred for judgment to the lieutenant governor in St. Louis.[58]

On August 18, 1769, the forceful General Alexandro O'Reilly arrived in New Orleans charged with the mission of imposing Spanish rule upon the colony of Louisiana. Three months later, O'Reilly formally abrogated all French laws for the colony and replaced them with "O'Reilly's Laws," which were based upon the Spanish Laws of the Indies. O'Reilly did reaffirm, however, the French law governing black slavery, the famous Black Code. Although some provisions of the Black Code were liberalized under the impact of Spanish law, the code continued to regulate black slavery in Louisiana throughout the colonial period.[59]

56. Vallé to Delassus, Mar. 19, 1804, PC 197. In November 1804, Jean-Baptiste Vallé was replaced as commandant of the Ste. Genevieve District by the American Major Seth Hunt, Carter (ed.), *Territorial Papers*, 13:54-55.

57. Stoddard, *Sketches*, 273.

58. On the *coutume de Paris*, see above, chap. vi.

59. Gayarré, History of Louisiana, 3:1-8, 37; Moore, *Revolt in Louisiana*, 216-18; Caughey, "Louisiana Under Spain"; more on the Black Code, above, chap. vii.

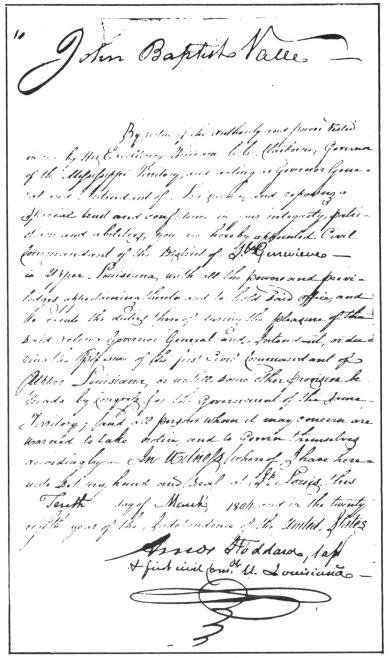

Captain Amos Stoddard's order of March 1804 naming Jean-Baptiste Vallé commandant of the Ste. Genevieve District. Courtesy Missouri Historical Society, St. Louis.

O'Reilly's "Laws" of November 1769, which at least in principle were applicable and enforceable from New Orleans to the Missouri River, contained some interesting provisions: jails were to be kept clean and healthy; a person on trial for a crime against whom only one witness testified could not be subjected to the penalty prescribed for that particular crime but would be punished more mildly at the discretion of the judge; anyone who reviled Christ or the Virgin Mary could have his or her tongue cut out; a couple found guilty of double adultery could be put to death by the *husband* of the wayward woman, although the wronged *wife* seemed to have no rights; a priest's concubine could be punished but not the fornicating priest, presumably because the latter would have fallen under the jurisdiction of canon law instead of the civil law; fornication between unmarried couples could lead to, if it were necessary to terminate the sin, banishment of the male and confinement of the female.[60]

To what extent "O'Reilly's Laws" were enforced, or even known of, in distant Ste. Genevieve is open to question. The legal historian Hans Baade has remarked that Spanish Louisiana was a "duel state" because Spanish laws promulgated in New Orleans reached the outposts of the colony only haltingly. Perhaps construction of Ste. Genevieve's jail, which seems to have occurred in 1771, was a consequence of Spanish legal requirements, for the town had had no jail whatsoever during the French regime. Violent criminals, if in fact any such specimens appeared in the tiny and homogeneous community during the 1750s and 1760s, were probably taken across the Mississippi to Kaskaskia or Fort de Chartres for incarceration.[61]

Laws that certainly were promulgated if not necessarily enforced in Ste. Genevieve were those drafted by the Spanish lieutenant governors in St. Louis. The posting of these laws on the door of the parish church in Ste. Genevieve conveyed their contents to the literate townspeople, and others were informed by word-of-mouth. Virtually complete sets of the ordinances that Lieutenant Governor Francisco Cruzat issued during both of his terms in office (1775-78 and 1780-87) are extant. Some of these were in-

60. Gayarré, 8-18; Caughey, 60-62; concerning Spanish colonial laws on sexual morality, see the fascinating article by Holmes, "Do It! Don't Do It!: Spanish Laws on Sex and Marriage," 19-42.

61. See SGA, Documents, no. 21; St. Ange de Bellerive to O'Reilly, Nov. 23, 1769, PC 187. Baade, "The Law of Slavery in Spanish Luisiana," 44.

Tombstone of Jean-Baptiste Vallé and his wife, Jeanne Barbeau Vallé, in historic cemetery at Ste. Genevieve, Missouri.

tended only for St. Louis, but most applied to Spanish Illinois in general, including Ste. Genevieve. Moreover, Cruzat twice traveled to Ste. Genevieve especially to post ordinances there. Because of repeated ordinances concerning them, four problem issues stand out in Cruzat's corpus of laws for Spanish Illinois: handling of the Indians; control of the behavior of black slaves; regulation of hunting and trapping; and maintenance of protective fencing around the enclosed arable agricultural lands. The last, fencing, was in fact overwhelmingly the single most important issue in Cruzat's ordinances and concerned the enclosed common fields of both St. Louis and Ste. Genevieve.[62]

Indeed, not only Cruzat but two of his successors in St. Louis, Manuel Pérez (1787-1792) and Zenon Trudeau (1792-1799), drafted ordinances concerning the fences (*clôtures*) around the Big Field Commons of Ste. Genevieve. The agricultural lands of the Big Field were the basis of the economy in colonial Ste. Genevieve; fences were essential to protect the arable fields from grazing animals; there were perennial problems in getting the local habitants to cooperate and coordinate for the purpose of building and maintaining fences and gates. The importance of the fences is made apparent by the fact that three successive lieutenant governors issued ordinances concerning the *clôtures* at Ste. Genevieve. Moreover, two of them, Cruzat and Trudeau, made special trips to Ste. Genevieve from St. Louis in order personally to try to deal with the fencing problem, Cruzat in September 1776 and Trudeau in September 1793.[63]

While most of the formal laws and ordinances that controlled the lives of people in colonial Ste. Genevieve emanated from New Orleans and St. Louis, the town commandants did possess limited powers of legislation. Reacting to a rash of illnesses in Ste. Genevieve during the summer of 1785, commandant Don Antonio

---

62. Cruzat's ordinances for the period 1775-1778 are in PC 2358; those for the period 1780-87 are in PC 2361; the second group has been printed in *SRM*, 1:240-52.

63. Cruzat issued an ordinance for fences in Ste. Genevieve on Sep. 7, 1776 (PC 2358) when he was in the town, and he issued another on the same subject from St. Louis Apr. 27, 1784 (SGA, Documents, no. 28); Pérez drafted an ordinance on Ste. Genevieve's fences in St. Louis Feb. 1, 1788, and Peyroux promulgated it in Ste. Genevieve five days later (SGA, Documents, no. 29); Trudeau visited Ste. Genevieve in September 1793 (Trudeau to Carondelet, Sep. 28, 1793, PC 208 A) and issued an ordinance on Ste. Genevieve's fences in November 1793 (SGA, Documents, no. 30).

de Oro issued a local ordinance ordering the citizens to dispose of all dead animals by throwing them into the Mississippi, for "dead animals could cause epidemic diseases in this post." Being aware of the contagious nature of many illnesses, De Oro also tacked a clause onto this ordinance that ordered "persons of all classes to inform [the commandant] when they leave town and when they return." Although this was perhaps an enlightened gesture, one may be sure that the townspeople ignored such a manifestation of arbitrary Spanish power. In any case, few laws were promulgated by the commandants of Ste. Genevieve. The powers of the commandants tended to be more executive and judicial than legislative, although neither the French nor the Spanish monarchies conceived of government in American tripartite terms.[64]

In neither French nor Spanish law was much distinction made between what was illegal, and/or immoral, and/or sinful. The Ste. Genevieve civil records contain a curious case from 1796, which reveals that local government did make some attempt to regulate private morality in accordance with the dictates of Spanish royal law. In the spring of 1794 there arrived at Ste. Genevieve an outsider named Louis Coyteaux. Coyteux was a literate person and received a land grant in the Bois Brûlé bottom area near Ste. Genevieve. There he built a small house, and took into his residence as a concubine an English woman named Josette Parker.[65]

In 1796 the parish priest of Ste. Genevieve, Abbé de St. Pierre, began to badger Coyteux about his sinful relationship with the woman. It is not known precisely what motivated the priest, whether it was the sexual immorality, the fact that Coyteux was living with a woman who was English and Protestant, or the fact that fornication was technically contrary to the civil laws of Spanish Louisiana. Probably St. Pierre had all of these things in mind. In any case, according to St. Pierre's own account, the priest asked Coyteux to stop after Sunday Mass to speak to him. Coyteux did not oblige the solicitous father. In his capacity as parish priest St. Pierre then sent Coyteux "an urgent note" asking him to pay a special visit in order to discuss the issue. Again Coyteux ignored the priest's entreaty. Finally St. Pierre went to Commandant François Vallé in order to bring the civil powers of the community in to support the church on this pressing matter of public morality.

---

64. SGA, Documents, no. 7.

65. Concerning Coyteux's arrival in Ste. Genevieve, see above, chap. iii.

St. Pierre delivered a formal written complaint to Vallé on August 8, 1796, but Vallé did not get around to acting on the matter until August 31. Probably the prudent commandant was reluctant to involve himself and the prestige of his office in such an issue, although the Spanish laws of Louisiana gave him every right to do so. But act Vallé finally did, by sending the reprobate Coyteux an order "to expell from [his] house an English woman within twenty-four hours because [their] cohabitation is contrary to the good morals and to the ordinances of His Majesty [i.e., the king of Spain]." Vallé explained that he was issuing the order because of the "repeated requests made by Monsieur de St. Pierre, curate of this parish."[66]

Coyteux buckled under the pressure brought to bear on him jointly by the religious and civil powers of Ste. Genevieve. He made an honest woman of Josette Parker, who became Josette Parker Coyteux on September 26, 1796. Spanish law and the official morality of the Catholic Church had triumphed.[67]

After General O'Reilly had overhauled the laws of Louisiana, he moved on to consider how local commandants would enforce the laws. In February 1770 O'Reilly drafted special instructions for the commandants of the various posts in the colony, including St. Louis and Ste. Genevieve. These instructions for the two principal settlements of Spanish Illinois contained thirty-one clauses, all of which, according to O'Reilly, were designed to ensure three fundamental things: "that the dominion and government of His Majesty [the king of Spain] be loved and respected; justice administered promptly, impartially, and according to the laws; and that commerce be protected and increased as much as possible." O'Reilly explicitly laid down the chain of governmental command reaching from New Orleans to Ste. Genevieve: governor general in New Orleans; lieutenant governor in St. Louis; and lieutenant in Ste. Genevieve. This last official, always called the civil and military commandant in the local records, was provided with the muscle of a corporal and seven regular soldiers.[68]

The instructions that Governor Esteban Miró issued for Peyroux de la Coudrenière in April 1787 provide some notion of the extent of the powers and jurisdiction of commandants in colonial Ste.

66. SGA, Miscellaneous, no. 50.

67. SGPR, Marriages, Book B:36.

68. General instructions of O'Reilly, Feb. 17, 1770, printed in *SRM*, 1:76-83.

Genevieve. First, he was reminded to obey all orders of the lieutenant governor in St. Louis. Peyroux could decide all civil cases
where the sum of money involved did not exceed fifty pesos (later
raised to 100 pesos), above which amount he was obliged to send
the case to St. Louis for judgment. He had a right to issue passports
to persons wishing to travel on the Mississippi, either across to
the American side or down to New Orleans, but only the lieutenant
governor could grant permits to conduct commerce. Peyroux was
authorized to allow new immigrants to settle in the Ste. Genevieve
District, provided they were Roman Catholics and the lieutenant
governor in St. Louis was kept informed. Peyroux's instructions
reveal that the Spanish government in Louisiana was determined
to make the chain-of-command function and that local commandants had to adhere to the hierarchy of the bureaucracy.[69]

The citizens of colonial Ste. Genevieve were a litigious people.
Although town commandants were encouraged by the authorities
in New Orleans to settle disputes out of court ("à l'aimable"), the
extant civil records contain nearly 300 civil suits of one kind or
another. There were no lawyers in colonial Ste. Genevieve, for
the French monarchy had kept them out of Lousiana on the
grounds that they bred contentiousness in society. Individuals,
however, sometimes drafted their own petitions, and illiterates
could have theirs drafted by the local notary or clerk. All judicial
proceedings were conducted in writing, and there was no opportunity to plead in person. Frequently civil cases had to be referred
to St. Louis because the sums involved were too large to be adjudi-
cated in Ste. Genevieve. But, for example, when Bernard Pratte
sued Joseph Peigne for a 100-piastre (100-dollar) debt in 1795,
Commandant François Vallé II handled the case locally.[70]

An interesting and revealing case arose at Cape Girardeau in
1801, which, although not bearing directly upon Ste. Genevieve,
provides a glimpse of how Spanish officials conceived of a town
commandant's civil powers. This case concerned custody of a
minor child, and Lieutenant Governor Charles Delassus wrote to
Louis Lorimier, commandant at Cape Girardeau:[71]

---

69. Miró's instructions to Peyroux, Apr. 20, 1787, printed in *SRM*, 1:238-39.

70. The royal instructions to Governc ' ¬nville of 1732 banned barristers
from French Louisiana (Baade, "Marri¬   ¬tracts," 10, n. 40); SGA, Litigations, no. 245.

71. Delassus to Lorimier, Apr. 15, 1801, ¬ C 218.

You will find enclosed a letter from Madame Richard to me in which she asks for custody of her son. Because the bad behavior of this woman could only have a prejudicial influence on the child you must strive to place him elsewhere. I will leave it up to you to act in this case in accordance with your position as *commandant and protector of the disadvantaged* [my italics], following the paternal intentions of Monsieur Richard for the well-being of his son.

Not enough is known of this case to ascertain if this was an instance of official discrimination against the female party, or if Madame Richard really was a bad woman. Nonetheless, the case does show clearly that town commandants in Spanish Illinois had power to intercede in family disputes for the sake of protecting minor children.

Governor Miró's instructions to Peyroux in 1787 contained a curious lacunae: there was no mention of the town commandant's powers in criminal cases. In 1788, Peyroux investigated a murder that had occurred at Anse à la Graisse (later New Madrid). During a drunken argument, one Pedro Armand *dit* Normand had killed a fellow reveler with a knife. Normand was escorted to Ste. Genevieve by a posse of three Delaware Indians and interrogated by Peyroux. Normand was evidently guilty, but the case had to be sent to New Orleans for disposition. When Peyroux took command at New Madrid in 1799, he was forbidden to handle any criminal case that might call for corporal punishment or banishment from the colony. Thus it is apparent that the jurisdiction of post commandants in Spanish Illinois was limited almost exclusively to investigation of crimes. No white person was ever executed, mutilated, whipped, or tortured in colonial Ste. Genevieve, for the commandant's powers were too circumscribed to inflict such punishments.[72]

The fact that commandants in Ste. Genevieve had virtually no authority to hear criminal cases did not significantly diminish their powers, for serious crimes were rarely committed in Spanish Illinois. The French-speaking citizens of Louisiana had a reputation for being law-abiding people. Captain Amos Stoddard remarked at the end of the colonial period that "in no country were aggravated crimes more rare than in Louisiana," and "the French attached more disgrace to punishments than any other people."

---

72. Miró's instructions to Peyroux, Apr. 20, 1787, printed in *SRM*, 1:238-39; LSM, Spanish Judicial Records, 1789012101; memorandum of Peyroux, Jan. 12, 1803, PC 220.

Crimes were of course committed, and there is fragmentary documentation on criminality and law enforcement in colonial Ste. Genevieve.[73]

There is no record of a complete criminal process — with investigation, charges, trial, verdict, and punishment — in colonial Ste. Genevieve. When lead miners, boatmen, or trappers got drunk and disorderly in town, which they certainly must have done, the community perhaps dealt with such reprobates without criminal proceedings. At the other end of the spectrum, in cases of murder or assault, the town commandant would conduct the investigation and then send the case to either St. Louis or New Orleans. In 1786, for example, a brawl took place in the quarters of the Spanish garrison in Ste. Genevieve. Pedro Larmona attacked Juan Garzia with an axe and severely wounded him. Town commandant Antonio de Oro investigated the case and sent it to Lieutenant Governor Cruzat in St. Louis, who in turn referred it to Governor Miró in New Orleans. The fact that a mere assault, even though the weapon involved made it aggravated assault, was forwarded all the way to New Orleans, surely indicates how seldom such crimes took place in Upper Louisiana.[74]

In the 1790s a criminal case occurred in Ste. Genevieve that tells much about criminal justice in Spanish Louisiana. A black slave named Philippe, who belonged to Louis Caron (brother-in-law to François Vallé II), had murdered in cold blood another black slave belonging to Jean-Baptiste Vallé. Lieutenant Governor Trudeau's investigation of the incident revealed that there was no question about Philippe's guilt. His owner, Caron, despite the fact that Philippe was his only slave and most valuable possession, testified against him. And Philippe himself admitted his guilt when Trudeau interrogated him. The murderer along with a complete record of the investigation were dispatched to New Orleans at the beginning of the year 1795, for not even the lieutenant governor in St. Louis had the power to conduct trials in capital cases.[75]

Louis Caron thus lost his valuable possession, which no doubt aggravated him enough. But to add insult to injury reports began to arrive in Ste. Genevieve from New Orleans that the slave Philippe, rather than having been promptly executed, was circulat-

---

73. Stoddard, *Sketches*, 282-83.

74. Cruzat to De Oro, Oct. 23, 1786, PC 117 A; Cruzat to Miró, Nov. 30, 1786, PC 12; Cruzat to De Oro, Dec. 2, 1786, PC 117 A.

75. De Luzières to Gayoso de Lemos, July 25, 1798, PC 215 A.

ing like a free man in the capital city. The last straw for the people of Ste. Genevieve came in the spring of 1798, when poor Louis Caron received a bill from the jailer in New Orleans asking Caron to pay living expenses for the ostensibly incarcerated Philippe. On Caron's behalf, Delassus de Luzières wrote a letter of great indignation, which François Vallé also endorsed, to the new governor, Gayoso de Lemos. De Luzières explained that such a miscarriage of justice would simply encourage slave owners to conceal crimes committed by their slaves, that the jailer in New Orleans must be an extortionist, and that Gayoso owed both Caron and De Luzières an explanation of the affair.[76]

Although the outcome of this case is not known, the facts of the matter warrant some comment. De Luzières' point that such instances of aborted justice would encourage slave owners to conceal crimes of their slaves can be elaborated upon by remarking that even without such a disspiriting precedent slave owners must routinely have covered up for their larcenous or felonious slaves; simple self-interest would have impelled them to do so. Secondly, it seems likely that Spanish authorities had adopted a policy of criminal justice that is already well known from the history of Anglo-American South: blacks could do physical violence to other blacks with relative impunity. This would explain the fact that Philippe, the black murderer from Ste. Genevieve, had been sent down to New Orleans for punishment at the beginning of 1796 and was still alive and well, and perhaps even free, more than two years later. It is of course conceivable that the wheels of justice simply turned that slowly in Spanish New Orleans, but the absence of jury trials usually expedited rather than impeded the execution of justice. Although Gayoso's response to De Luzières is unknown, we may be assured that the unfortunate Louis Caron never got his slave back.

If the criminal justice system in Spanish Illinois worked slowly with regard to black slaves who had killed other black slaves, it perhaps worked not at all with regard to whites who killed black slaves. The Ste. Genevieve civil records contain an inquest into the killing of a black slave at the Saline in 1783. The slave, Tacouä, had been working at the salt furnaces of his master, Jean Datchurut, and Datchurut's overseer, Jean-Baptiste Lacroix, struck Tacouä in the head with a pickax. Eighteen hours later, Tacouä died, and the town surgeon ruled that the blow to the head had

---

76. Ibid.

killed him. Although such a killing was in direct violation of Article XXXIX of the Black Code, there is no evidence that any action was taken against Lacroix. Perhaps Datchurut reprimanded his overseer, but it seems extremely unlikely that Lacroix was sent to St. Louis to face criminal charges. In 1787, four years after this incident, Lacroix was still a member of Datchurut's household. The other possibility for interracial murder, that of a black killing a white, apparently never occurred in colonial Ste. Genevieve.[77]

There is no comprehensive documentation on crimes in colonial Ste. Genevieve, but the extant documents reveal unmistakably that there was an increase in crime as the ethnic composition of the district began to change dramatically in the 1790s. With the flood of Anglo-American settlers crossing to the west side of the Mississippi, law enforcement became an increasing problem in the Ste. Genevieve District. The mobile Americans seemed to be more violent than the old French-speaking core of the community, and they certainly had a more casual attitude toward the law. In 1793, François Vallé had an American, John Peyne, locked in irons in the Ste. Genevieve jail because Peyne had stolen a mare from the locally-living Loup (Delaware) Indians. Peyne, a drifter from Kentucky, was released after the Indians got their horse back.[78]

The Ste. Genevieve jail held John Peyne, the horse thief, until his release, but the jail was not always so secure. In 1802 an American, Andrew Gibson, was arrested and incarcerated on charges that he had asked Louis Robitaille, a goldsmith in Ste. Genevieve, to make him a mold for counterfeiting Spanish piastres. Americans in the Illinois Country had been trying to counterfeit Spanish currency since at least as early as 1790. In any case, Gibson broke out of the Ste. Genevieve jail and slipped with impunity back to the east side of the Mississippi.[79]

But the Americans were more than mere horse thieves and counterfeiters. In 1801, an American named Stone murdered another American named O'Connor near Mine à Breton (Potosi). Despite François Vallé's attempts to apprehend him, Stone evaded Spanish justice, like Gibson a year later, by fleeing back to the American side of the Mississippi. Vallé asked for help from the

77. SGA, Slaves, no. 197.

78. François Vallé to Trudeau, May 16, 1793, PC 207 B.

79. Vallé to Delassus, May 24, 1802, PC 219; Vallé to Delassus, July 26, 1802, ibid.; Pedro Foucher to Miró, Oct. 20, 1790, PC 16; on counterfeiting in Spanish Louisiana see Holmes, *Gayoso*, 56-57.

American justice of peace, John Edgar, but Stone was never apprehended and brought to justice. At least the lawless Americans were killing each other instead of the established creole inhabitants of the Illinois Country.[80]

O'Connor's murder prompted Commandant Vallé to appoint Nicolas Caillot *dit* Lachance II as temporary *commissaire de police* at Mine à Breton in July 1801. Violence in the mining district continued, however, and in 1802 Joseph Decelle Duclos was made permanent police commissioner at Mine à Breton. Duclos's appointment was the direct result of a petition sent by residents of Mine à Breton to François Vallé asking for "an officer empowered and authorized to regulate domestic affairs." The petition, significantly written in English, prompted the first extension of Spanish colonial government into the hinterlands of Spanish Illinois.[81]

More important than the murder of one itinerant American by another was a rape that occurred in 1800. Widow Duff, an inhabitant of Bois Brûlé below New Bourbon, came to Delassus de Luzières to complain that her twelve-year-old daughter, Marie had been raped by one Thomas Allen. De Luzières might have turned the good widow away as a nuisance; after all, could not twelve-year-old girls be seducers? But no, De Luzières' aristocratic sense of honor was piqued, and he dashed off a flurry of orders: Marie was to be examined by two mid-wives in the presence of two witnesses; they confirmed the rape. Jeremiah Perell, police commissioner at the Saline, was ordered to lead a posse of three men, "well-mounted and well-armed," to seek out the violator, Allen, arrest him, and seize all of his belongings. Colonial Spanish law enforcement at the local level went into prompt and vigorous action. But once again it was all to no avail. Perell reported back to De Luzières that Allen had abandoned his lodgings at Bois Brûlé and fled. The rapist, like the murderer, probably disappeared on the American side of the Mississippi.[82]

Many of the difficulties of the law enforcement officers in the

---

80. There is an entire run of correspondence on the O'Connor case in François Vallé's letterbook (PC 217); see also Nasatir, "Pedro Vial," 103-05; Delassus gave Vallé permission to prosecute Stone should he be apprehended (Delassus to Vallé, May 29, 1801, MHS, Vallé Collection, Box 2).

81. Vallé to Nicolas Lachance, July 11, 1801, PC 217; Lachance's appointment, July, 23, SGA, Mines, no. 1; petition of July 3, 1802, PC 219; Vallé to Delassus, July 10, 1802, ibid.

82. SGA, Litigations, no. 114.

Ste. Geneviève District during the last decade of Spanish rule were rooted in a peculiar set of geo-political circumstances. On the western side of the Mississippi the colonial Spanish government ruled over a basically French-speaking community that was stable, traditional, and law-abiding. On the eastern side of the river was the wild, western frontier of the young American republic, the society of which was deracinated, mobile, and, if not downright criminal, at least scornful of all established authority. When these rambunctious Americans crossed to the west side of the Mississippi to pursue their fortunes, they carried their unruly habits with them; and when they committed violent crimes in Spanish Illinois they found ready sanctuary on the east side of the Mississippi. Given this set of circumstances, the West was conspicuously less wild than the East.

In pursuing the incomplete, though not insignificant, documentation that exists on the subject of crimes and law enforcement in colonial Ste. Geneviève, a salient fact emerges — there is no written record of a single instance in which an established member of the French-speaking community was accused of committing a crime of violence against the person of another member of that community. Shortly after the Louisiana Purchase, the French creoles of the Illinois Country were described to President Thomas Jefferson as "a civil quiet people," who could be "easily governed." The president must have been pleased to receive this characterization of his new American citizens.[83]

Instructions sent to Spanish Illinois from authorities in New Orleans define the judicial responsibilities of post commandants but do not dwell on the subject of political leadership except to note that the commandants should see to it that the Spanish monarchy was well-loved. For a government of divine-right monarchy, affection was sufficient popular participation in the political process. The Yankee Henry Brackenridge remembered the government of Ste. Geneviève as a despotism when he wrote his *Recollections of Persons and Places in the West*. Brackenridge remarked that "all politics, or discussions of the affairs of government, were entirely unknown: the commandant took care of all that sort of thing." And in another passage, where he managed to take a swipe at the Catholic religion as well as the government in Ste. Geneviève,

83. Rufus Easton to Jefferson, Jan. 17, 1805, Carter (ed.), *Territorial Papers*, 13:84.

Brackenridge observed that "this religion [Roman Catholicism] is admirably adapted to prevent them [the citizens of Ste. Genevieve] from becoming discontented under a despotism, as it is calculated to occupy so much of their time and attention, as to leave little for any but their private concerns." Brackenridge's Whiggish bias permeates these passages: kings are bad; Roman Catholics are worse; Spanish Roman Catholic kings are worst. Brackenridge was of course correct inasmuch as the Spanish colonial government of Ste. Genevieve did not foster or encourage political discussion or debate. Nevertheless, many major issues of public policy in colonial Ste. Genevieve were determined in a notably open and egalitarian manner.[84]

Regulation of the fences around the agricultural lands was the single most important issue of public policy in colonial Ste. Genevieve. Other major issues included construction and mainte-nance of roads, bridges, drainage ditches, levees, the parish church, and the rectory, At least as early as the 1770s, and probably before that time, all of these issues were handled in more or less democratic fashion — the town commandant would convene an assembly of the citizens, which would then proceed to select by a plurality vote "syndics" or "arbiters" to oversee the matter at hand. In the specific case of fencing the Big Field, it seems likely that the assembly of "habitants" included only those persons who owned arable land within the Big Field Commons, and in this sense the word "habitant" meant farmer. For issues of general concern, like the construction of a new parish church, the assembly included all "citoyens" and "habitants," which seems to have meant all local inhabitants who got word that an assembly was going to be held.[85]

On April 15, 1778, for example, an assembly of "habitants" met in the "chambre du gouvernement" of Ste. Genevieve in the pres-ence of Commandant Don Silvio de Cartabona in order to deal with the issue of fencing around the Big Field, The "chambre du gouvernement," the government room, was almost certainly the commandant's residence, which must have been bursting at the joints in holding this gathering of farmers. When all the citizens met, as opposed to this meeting of "habitants," the assemblies must have been held out-of-doors, and one can well imagine the

---

84. Instructions of O'Reilly, Feb. 17, 1770, *SRM* 1:76; Brackenridge, *Recollec-tions*, 25, 29.

85. See SGA, Documents, no. 26, no. 30.

commandant presiding from the vantage point of the gallery on the front of his house as the citizens milled about within the picket fence surrounding the property.[86]

In any case, on April 15, 1778, the "habitants" of Ste. Genevieve selected eight syndics. The eight selected were, in the order that they signed the regulations: Charles Vallé, Louis Delorier, Jean Datchurut, François Vallé, Louis Lasource, André Deguire (mark), Nicholas Roussin (mark), and Jean-Baptiste Couturier (mark). These eight syndics did not directly oversee the maintenance of the fences but were rather charged with enforcing the eighteen different specific clauses of the regulations. The first, and most important, of these clauses called for an assembly of all "habitants" in the "chambre du gouvernement" every year on January 1. And at this assembly one syndic and six arbiters would be elected to inspect the fences and oversee their maintenance. Thus in democratic fashion two groups of citizens were selected, one to enforce the regulations pertaining to the fences and the other to oversee the actual work at the site.[87]

Almost precisely the same procedure was employed to deal with the issue of maintaining the streets, bridges, and canals in and around Ste. Genevieve. On April 15, 1784, for example, an assembly of citizens elected eight syndics (the same as listed above) to oversee the regulations regarding public works. In this case the regulations stipulated that on January 1 of every year "two syndics or general inspectors" would be elected directly to oversee the maintenance of streets, bridges, and canals in town.[88]

These rather complicated processes hardly smack of the despotic government of which Brackenridge complained. Rather, important issues of public policy in colonial Ste. Genevieve were resolved much as they were in New England town hall meetings, in a mode that has been called "consensual communalism." Amazingly enough, even French Roman Catholics could gather together, deliberate, and exercise their franchise responsibly, behaving in just as civilized a fashion as Anglo-Saxon Protestants.[89]

---

86. Ibid., no. 26.

87. Ibid.

88. Ibid., no. 28.

89. Zuckerman, *Peaceable Kingdoms*, 189.

Chapter XII

Priests and Parishioners: The Catholic Church in Ste. Genevieve

N O TRAVELER WHO TURNS EAST off of U.S. Highway 61 and descends into contemporary Ste. Genevieve via the Old Plank Road can fail to be impressed by the looming presence of the Roman Catholic Church. The two most imposing edifices in town are the Knights of Columbus building and the parish church, both late Victorian-era structures. Indeed, there is a distinctly Old Worldly and Old Regime quality about the nucleus of contemporary Ste. Genevieve, with the towering neo-Gothic church standing triumphant above the humble Ste. Genevieve County courthouse.

Ste. Genevieve is today heavily Roman Catholic, and colonial Ste. Genevieve was even more so. Until the end of the colonial period, when Spanish officials allowed a scattering of Anglo-American Protestants to enter Upper Louisiana, Ste. Genevieve was inhabited almost exclusively by Roman Catholics. Moreover, the townspeople were not merely nominal Catholics; they took their religion seriously. As Francis J. Yealy noted in his study of Ste. Genevieve, "we shall not understand the character of these French pioneers, unless we appreciate the profound effect which religion had on their lives."[1]

Colonial Louisiana practiced none of the separation of church and state upon which Americans pride themselves. Civil and religious authorities complemented and reinforced one another in

---

1. Protestants had never been accepted in Spain or its colonies. Louis XIV outlawed Protestantism (Edict of Fontainebleau, 1685) in all French dominions. Article I of the Black Code ("Edit concernant les Nègres . . . à la Louisiane," 76) outlawed Jews in Louisiana. Yealy, *Ste. Genevieve,* 86.

Louisiana as they did in the Bourbon homelands of France and Spain. This mutuality of state and church was evident when Ste. Genevieve was an embryo community, for the French land grants of 1752 were made contingent upon the grantees furnishing materials to construct a chapel. Ideally, civil and religious affairs were managed as coordinate components of an harmonious whole in colonial Ste. Genevieve, although the ideal was not always realized.[2]

By the mid-1750s, Ste. Genevieve had its own vertical-log church. This first religious structure in the pioneer community was a mission chapel rather than a parish church, for Ste. Genevieve was at that time merely a satellite of the parish of the Immaculate Conception in Kaskaskia. In 1759 Ste. Genevieve acquired its own parish register, and several years later it received a resident priest. Philibert Watrin, the Jesuit father from Kaskaskia who made the first entries in the Ste. Genevieve parish records, provided the best description of religious life in early Ste. Genevieve. Watrin wrote this in 1764, one year after the suppression of the Jesuit Order and his departure from the Illinois Country:[3]

> The curé of Cascakias found himself obliged to go there [i.e., Ste. Genevieve] to administer the sacraments, at least to the sick; and, when the new inhabitants saw their houses multiplying, they asked to have a church built there. This being granted them, the journeys of the missionary [i.e., Watrin himself] became still more frequent, because he thought that he ought then to yield himself still more to the willingness of his new parishioners, and to their needs. However, in order to go to this new church he must cross the Mississippi, which, in this place, is three-eighths of a league wide; he sometimes had to trust himself to a slave, who alone guided the canoe; it was necessary, in fine, to expose himself to the danger of perishing, if in the middle of the river they had been overtaken by a violent storm. None of these inconveniences ever prevented the curé of Cascakias from going to Sainte Genevieve when charity called him thither, and he was always charged with this care until means were found to place at Sainte Genevieve a special curé, which occurred only a few years ago, when the inhabitants of the place built a house for the pastor.

2. O'Neill, *Church and State in French Colonial Louisiana;* land grants in MHS, Guibourd Collection.

3. "Banishment of the Jesuits," July 9, 1763, printed in *JR*, 70:233-35. Thwaites identified Watrin as the author of this document, ibid., 13.

Watrin's account of religious life in Ste. Genevieve was patently a justification of himself and the Jesuit Order. Nonetheless, the account seems accurate enough, and it reveals that the lives of the Jesuit fathers from Kaskaskia who served the new settlement of Ste. Genevieve were little different from those of the first heroic missionaries to serve in the upper Mississippi Valley — Marquette, Hennepin, Membré, and Ribourde.

Watrin indicated that when he kept the church records for Ste. Genevieve (1759-1761) he was still merely a missionary, who periodically crossed the river from Kaskaskia to minister to the spiritual needs of the new settlement on the west bank of the Mississippi. Ste. Genevieve's first resident pastor, for whom the townspeople built a rectory, was probably Jean-Baptiste de La Morinie, who like Watrin was a Jesuit from the Society's establishment at Kaskaskia. When in 1764 Watrin wrote that a "special curé" was placed at Ste. Genevieve "a few years ago" he was likely referring to La Morinie, who maintained the parish register in Ste. Genevieve from 1761-63 and must be considered the town's first parish priest.[4]

La Morinie was born in France, and his name suggests that he came from a family of the lesser nobility. He joined the Society of Jesus before leaving the Old World for New France, which he probably did in 1736. During the 1740s and 1750s, La Morinie served as missionary priest in Upper Canada (Michigan) and, like Ste. Genevieve's first military commandant, Rocheblave, was driven west by the upheavals of the French and Indian War (1755-1763). It is not known when La Morinie arrived in the Illinois Country, but by the autumn of 1761 he was keeping the parish register in Ste. Genevieve, his first entry being November 10 of that year.[5]

Watrin wrote that La Morinie "had taken charge of the church of Ste. Genevieve through the motive of a zeal that refuses itself to nothing." This may be true, but more likely La Morinie, as a newcomer to the Jesuit house at Kaskaskia, was assigned the duty that none of his colleagues wanted — to serve as resident pastor at the tiny and isolated parish of Ste. Genevieve. And Watrin, whose onerous duties La Morinie assumed, graciously complimented his unfortunate confrere.[6]

---

4. Ibid.; Thwaites (ed.), *Wisconsin State Historical Collections,* 18:474-75; Palm, *Jesuit Missions,* 79, 88.

5. Rothensteiner, *Archdiocese of St. Louis,* 83,; Yealy, 30.

6. Watrin, "Banishment of the Jesuits," 277.

Little is known of La Morinie's life and service during his two years of residence in Ste. Genevieve. He baptized, married, and buried the pioneers who made up his flock; he kept the parish register; he lived in a rectory built for him by his parishioners. Events were transpiring in eastern North America and Europe during 1761-63 that would have a profound effect upon Ste. Genevieve's future, but La Morinie's uneventful tenure as town priest reflects an apparently quiet period in the community's history.

In 1763 the Society of Jesus was suppressed in France and in all French colonies, including Louisiana. Civil authorities from Fort de Chartres seized the Jesuit properties at Kaskaskia and auctioned them off in November 1763 (Jean-Baptiste Bauvais was the chief purchaser), and within a matter of days the six Jesuit fathers who had been based at Kaskaskia, including Father La Morinie, were in route downriver to New Orleans. Thus came to a sudden end nearly a century of Jesuit missionary activity in the Illinois Country. Father Philibert Watrin, who had made the first entries in the Ste. Genevieve church records, was one of the dispossessed Jesuits. In his touching apology for his order's accomplishments in America, he chronicled with bitterness that "it was ordained . . . that the chapel ornaments and sacred vessels of the Jesuits living in the country of the Illinois should be delivered up to the Royal procurator for that country, and that the chapels should be demolished; and that, finally, the afore-said Jesuits, so-called, should return to France. . . ." The French royal government intended the dissolution of the Jesuit Order to be total and final.[7]

When Louis XV's government at distant Versailles decided to suppress the Society of Jesus, it surely did not consider the impact that this decision would have upon the Illinois Country. Indeed, it is probably a safe bet that King Louis and his principal advisor at the time, duc Etienne de Choiseul, had never heard of a settlement called Ste. Genevieve of the Illinois Country. Five of the six Jesuit fathers who descended the Mississippi in November 1763 had made entries in the Ste. Genevieve parish register. The first church in Ste. Genevieve may have amounted to little more than a mission chapel of the Jesuit Order in Kaskaskia, but when this order was suppressed it had a grave impact upon the religious

7. Ibid. 219; Palm, 86-97; Rothensteiner, 86-95; Alvord and Carter (eds.), *The Critical Period*, 62-133.

life of the town — La Morinie's departure for New Orleans left
Ste. Genevieve sorely in need of a parish priest. The citizens of
Kaskaskia pleaded with the commandant at Fort de Chartres to
allow them to retain their pastor, Father Aubert, who was one of
the Jesuits, and doubtless the townspeople of Ste. Genevieve
wished to retain La Morinie. But the commandant had no powers
to countermand the orders of the monarch, and the parish priests
in the Illinois Country were swept away along with the Jesuit
mission.[8]

Although finished as Jesuits, the six priests who descended the
Mississippi in the autumn of 1763 had not completed their lives
as spiritual servants of mankind. Five of them returned to France
and wound up in such far-flung dioceses as Nancy and Grenoble.
One of them returned upriver to the Illinois Country. Father
Sebastian-Louis Meurin was given permission by the Superior
Council of Louisiana to return to the Illinois Country on two
conditions: that he accept the Superior of the Capuchin Order in
New Orleans as his religious master and that he reside in Ste.
Genevieve, which was located in territory that had just passed *de
jure* to Spanish sovereignty. The French and Indian War had
ended the same year (1763) in which the Society of Jesus was
suppressed, and with this coincidence the religious and political
history of the Illinois Country became tightly intertwined.[9]

In the person of Father Meurin, we have the first parish priest
of Ste. Genevieve whom we can know as a historic personage of
flesh and blood and personality. Like La Morinie, Meurin was
French rather than French Canadian. He had arrived in the Illinois
Country sometime during the 1740s, and from 1749 to 1753 spent
most of his time at the Vincennes post. In 1753 he moved to the
Jesuit house at Kaskaskia where for ten years he did missionary
work with the neighboring Kaskaskia Indians. Indeed, it was probably a desire to continue service among the Indians that impelled
Meurin to ask permission to return to the Illinois Country late in
the year 1763. Political changes wrought by the French and Indian
War turned Father Meurin from Indian missionary to parish priest
of Ste. Genevieve, for the orders he received in New Orleans

8. On the decision of Louis XV to suppress the Society of Jesus in all French
territory see Henri Carré in Lavisse (ed.), *Histoire de France*, vol. 8, pt. 2:319-32;
the five were Philibert Watrin, Jean-Baptiste de La Morinie, Jean-Baptiste Aubert, Jean-Baptiste de Salleneuve, and Sebastien Meurin; Palm, 88; Yealy, 37;
Rothensteiner, 93-94.

9. Palm, 90-92; Rothensteiner, 115-23; Yealy, 39-40.

forbade him to resettle on the east side of the Mississippi, which had become British territory.[10]

Meurin left New Orleans for Upper Louisiana in February 1764. By eighteenth-century standards Meurin was already an old man (fifty-seven) at this stage of his career. To abandon the relative comfort and security of New Orleans for the harsh frontier of the upper Mississippi Valley was, as his former colleague Watrin put it, "a brave resolution." Meurin stopped at the Arkansas Post on his way up-river to baptize thirteen neophytes in March 1764. His stay there must have been brief, however, for he recorded his baptism of a child (a black slave belonging to Jean-Baptiste Bauvais) in Ste. Genevieve on May 13. Meurin had thus accomplished the trip up the Mississippi from New Orleans to Ste. Genevieve via the Arkansas Post in less than three months, which was a punishing pace for the 1760s. The former Jesuit who became pastor in Ste. Genevieve in the spring of 1764 was a tough old nut in both body and spirit.[11]

Shortly before the first British troops arrived at Fort de Chartres from Fort Pitt on October 9, 1765, the Recollect Father Luc Collet died at Nouvelle Chartres. This left the entire Illinois Country — both the British and the Spanish divisions — with but one priest, Father Meurin, to minister to the overwhelmingly Roman Catholic population. The British Captain Thomas Stirling described the situation in December 1765:[12]

> The inhabitants [of Illinois] complain very much for want of Priests. There is but one man remains, the rest either having died or gone away. He stays on the other side; he was formerly a Jesuit and would have been sent away likewise if the Kaskaskias Indians, to whom he was a Priest, had not insisted on his staying, which the French allowed him to do, upon his renouncing Jesuitism. . . .

The coincident suppression of the Jesuits and the political transformations in the Illinois Country had clearly wreaked devastation upon the religious life of the region. Poor old Meurin needed help, and he began to plead for it. His letter of March 23, 1767

---

10. Alvord and Carter (eds.), *The Critical Period*, 103, n. 2; Palm, 90.

11. Watrin, "Banishment," 291; Rothensteiner, 116.

12. Stirling to General Thomas Gage, Dec. 15, 1765, printed in Alvord and Carter (eds.). *The New Regime*, 124-25.

to Bishop Jean-Olivier Briand of Quebec provides a good overview of the religious situation in the Illinois Country at the time:[13]

> St. Joachim or Ste. Genevieve is the place of my residence as it was ordained by the conditions of my return to the Illinois country. It is from there that I come every springtime and go through the other villages for Easter. I return thither again in the autumn and every time that I am called for the sick. This is all that my infirmities and my means can permit me.

Meurin's letters to the bishop of Quebec became increasingly pitiful. In a missive of May 9, 1767 he lamented the hardships of his missionary work and remarked that he could no longer singlehandedly serve the religious needs of the Illinois Country, which was too difficult an area for even "the most robust man." Meurin wrote this letter from Cahokia, where he had been for several days and was preparing to depart for Ste. Genevieve in order to comfort a "dangerously ill person." Four priests were required adequately to minister to the villages of the Illinois Country according to Meurin, but an additional one, for the east side of the Mississippi, was absolutely essential so that Meurin would not have to cross "a very rapid and dangerous river."[14]

Bishop Briand of Quebec, unable to send Meurin meaningful assistance, sent him instead a grandiose, meaningless, and dangerous title — Grand Vicar of all former French Louisiana. Briand as bishop of British Quebec had no authority to grant Meurin this title, which immediately cast Meurin in a bad light with Spanish officials in New Orleans. From their viewpoint Meurin's mere correspondence with Briand was suspect, and Meurin's title of Grand Vicar, which technically gave him powers even in New Orleans, was an outrage.[15]

Meurin himself acknowledged that he had erred in exercising religious authority under the jurisdiction of the bishop of Quebec, for this was a technical violation of the written declaration he had presented to the Superior Council in New Orleans before he returned to the Illinois Country in the spring of 1764. Meurin had promised that he would serve in Ste. Genevieve exclusively as vicar

---

13. Meurin to Briand, Mar. 23, 1767, ibid., 523.

14. Meurin to Briand, May 9, 1767, ibid., 568-69.

15. Briand to Meurin, Apr. 28, 1767, Alvord and Carter (eds.) *The New Regime,* 563-64; Palm, 92-93; Rothensteiner, 117-20.

of the Capuchins in New Orleans, "subject to their visits, their reprimands, and corrections. . . ." As Yealy has pointed out, however, the authorities in New Orleans never fulfilled their end of the bargain by confirming Meurin in his position and providing him with a stipend. Meurin must have found the complexities of this jurisdictional issue monumentally irrelevant to his exhausting work as sole priest in the entire Illinois Country.[16]

Spanish officials in New Orleans did not find it irrelevant, however, and they initiated action against Ste. Genevieve's pastor. St. Ange de Bellerive, the last French commandant at Fort de Chartres and interim Spanish commandant at St. Louis in 1765, notified Governor Antonio de Ulloa in New Orleans that he had dutifully "served the order that you sent me, . . . and Meurin the priest submitted immediately and crossed to the English side [of the Mississippi]." Meurin's own account, which he presented in a letter to Bishop Briand, stated that the Spanish government in Louisiana had initiated proceedings against him and he fled Ste. Genevieve for the east bank of the river in order to avoid prosecution. The precise circumstances of Meurin's departure from Ste. Genevieve will never be known, but there is no doubt that he left Spanish for British Illinois before the autumn of 1768. In October, General Thomas Gage, commander of all British forces in North America, wrote that "the Priest who retired to the West Side of the River when the King's Troops took possession of Fort-Chartres, has had some quarrel with the Spaniards, and is returned again, and become a Subject to His Majesty."[17]

Historians have criticized Philippe de Rocheblave, commandant at Ste. Genevieve, for having been harsh with Meurin. There is in fact no firm evidence that this was the case. Indeed, as late as July 1768 Rocheblave wrote to New Orleans on Meurin's behalf, requesting a pension for Meurin, who was "old, infirm, and needy." Meurin was not driven out of Ste. Genevieve by Rocheblave but by distant authorities who were ignorant of the needs of the Illinois Country.[18]

---

16. Rothensteiner, 121; Yealy, 44.

17. St. Ange to Ulloa, June 23, 1768, PC 187; Meurin to Briand, June 11, 1768, printed in Alvord and Carter (eds.), *Trade and Politics*, 300-10; Gage to Hillsborough, Oct. 9, 1768, ibid., 414-16.

18. On the Rocheblave issue see: Alvord, *Illinois Country*, 318-19; Lahey, "Catholic Church," 19 23; Mason, "Rocheblave," 364; Shea, *Archbishop Carroll*, 120; Schlarman, *Quebec to New Orleans*, 442-43; Surveyor, "Rocheblave," 235-36; Yealy, 44; Rocheblave to Ulloa?, July 13, 1768, PC 187.

Although Meurin sometimes returned clandestinely to Ste. Genevieve to serve his former parishioners, his expulsion from Spanish territory left the town — indeed, left all of Spanish Illinois — without a resident priest. But in the autumn of 1768 a new priest arrived in the Illinois Country. Pierre Gibault was dispatched from Quebec by Bishop Briand in response to Meurin's persistent pleas for assistance. With Gibault's arrival in the Illinois Country religious life in Ste. Genevieve became regular in its irregularity. That is, both old Meurin and young Gibault resided in British Illinois, the former principally at Cahokia and the latter at Kaskaskia, and they both regularly, although unofficially, crossed the Mississippi to serve the inhabitants of St. Louis and Ste. Genevieve.[19]

Meurin, old and infirm, reported to Bishop Briand in June 1769 that "I can only be counted among the dead." Moreover, because Meurin was *persona non grata* on the Spanish side of the river and lived mostly at Cahokia, Ste. Genevieve became largely Gibault's responsibility. In February 1769, Gibault wrote to Briand that he had "always officiated at Ste. Genevieve, which is two leagues distant from my parish on the other bank of the Mississippi [i.e. Kaskaskia]." Thus for five years, 1768-1773, the citizens of Ste. Genevieve had no pastor of their own; they instead had to rely upon Gibault to, in his words, "visit the sick and perform marriages and baptisms." When Gibault could not get to town, provisional baptisms were done by the parish chanter, who in the early 1770s was François Lalumandière.[20]

Gibault and Meurin, both of whom made entries in the Ste. Genevieve parish register between 1768 and 1772, did not always get along as co-shepherds of the flock in the Illinois Country. The old man felt that Gibault confined himself too much to Kaskaskia and neglected the people in outlying areas like Ste. Genevieve, who "are as much his parishioners as those of Kaskaskia." Gibault on the other hand reported to Briand that Meurin was senile and, because he was a former Jesuit, was despised by many villagers. Despite their periodic squabbles, however, all the evidence indicates that Meurin and Gibault were brave, honorable, and devoted servants of the Catholic Church and the flock that they tended.

---

19. Palm, 92 93; Rothensteiner, 124-31.

20. Meurin to Briand, June 14, 1769, in Alvord and Carter (eds.), *Trade and Politics*, 549; Gibault to Briand, Feb. 15, 1769, ibid., 502; SGPR, Baptisms, Book A. See also Donnelly, "Pierre Gibault."

They were the last in a series of great Catholic missionaries in the Illinois Country running back to Marquette, who partook of the spiritual drive of the French Catholic Reformation. The citizens of early Ste. Genevieve were fortunate to have had such men as occasional pastors. The colonial town was not always to be so lucky in the draw of spiritual attendants.[21]

Meurin finally died at Prairie du Rocher in 1777, and Gibault buried him in the church there. His bones were later removed to the cemetery of the Jesuit novitiate in Florissant, Missouri. Gibault lived on for decades and continued to influence men and affairs in Upper Louisiana until his death at New Madrid in 1802.[22]

For five full years, from the autumn of 1768 to the autumn of 1773, Gibault regularly crossed the Mississippi from his parish of Kaskaskia to serve the spiritual needs of the people of Ste. Genevieve and maintain their church records. Ste. Genevieve had no resident pastor, but Gibault filled in as best he could. The townspeople showed their appreciation of Gibault's efforts by granting the priest a goodwill offering in lieu of the tithes due to an official pastor. Probably no one was more deserving of such small pecuniary reward. Accurately, with but a touch of self-pity, Gibault described his miserable existence at that time. Over-worked, fever-ridden, and threatened by hostile Indians, Gibault made his rounds armed with musket and two pistols, "never sleeping four nights in a year in my own bed. . . ." No wonder that Gibault began to comfort himself with regular doses of tafia and *eau-de-vie*.[23]

Spain had acquired *de jure* sovereignty over Louisiana in 1762 but did not secure substantial *de facto* political power in the colony until General Alexandro O'Reilly crushed an anti-Spanish revolt in 1769. The ecclesiastical position of the newly acquired Spanish colony was not resolved until 1772, when Louisiana was formally placed under the jurisdiction of the diocese of Santiago de Cuba. These circumstances help to explain why Ste. Genevieve was left for so long without an official pastor sent from Spanish New Orleans, instead had to rely upon bootleg spiritual attention from across the Mississippi. This irregular situation ended in October

---

21. Meurin to Briand, June 14, 1769, in Alvord and Carter (eds.), *Trade and Politics*, 553; Gibault to Briand, Feb. 15, 1769, ibid., 502-03.

22. Palm, 93; Rothensteiner, 131.

23. Gibault to Briand, Oct. 1769, in Alvord and Carter (eds.), *Trade and Politics*, 608-25.

1773 with the arrival in Ste. Genevieve of Father Hilaire de
Géneveaux.[24]

There is more documentation on Hilaire as parish priest in Ste.
Genevieve (1773-1777) than for any of the other men who served
in that capacity during the town's colonial history. Yet when the
Reverend John E. Rothensteiner published his *History of the Archdiocese of St. Louis* in 1928, he chose not to deal with the history
of Father Hilaire's tenure as priest in Ste. Genevieve; probably
Rothensteiner found the material on Hilaire ill-suited for his inspi-
rational brand of history. Reverend Francis Yealy, who possessed
more intellectual honesty than Rothensteiner, broached the
Hilaire affair when he published his study of Ste. Genevieve in
1935. With grace and tact Yealy summarized the case in these
words: "The story of his [Hilaire's] misadventures is not set down
here to invite sneers at this unhappy priest who has long ago
rendered his account to God." Less gracefully and more clinically,
it can be said that Hilaire was a severely neurotic person who was
bound to create a turmoil wherever he served.[25]

Hilaire was a Capuchin friar who had been active in Louisiana
since the early 1750s. During the late 1760s and early 1770s,
Hilaire competed bitterly with Father Dagobert for the position
of superior of the Capuchin Order in New Orleans, and in 1773
Governor Luis de Unzaga decided in favor of Dagobert. Unzaga
thereupon attempted an administrative finesse that would kill two
birds with one stone: he posted Hilaire to Ste. Genevieve, thereby
providing the town with resident pastor and simultaneously removing the difficult priest from New Orleans. The citizens of Ste.
Genevieve were soon to pay for Unzaga's cleverness.[26]

Hilaire left New Orleans at the end of July or the beginning of
August 1773. Perhaps he was pleased to be leaving the muggy
lower Mississippi at that time of year in order to arrive in the
Illinois Country for a fine autumn season. In any case, he arrived
in Ste. Genevieve on October 27, when the leaves on the hardwoods
still had good color, and took up residence in the François Vallé
household while waiting his own quarters; apparently the old rectory, which had been built in the early 1760s, was no longer
habitable. Although François offered Hilaire the famous Vallé

24. Gayarré, *History of Louisiana*, 3:55-58; Moore, *Revolt in Louisiana*, 222-23.
25. Yealy, 53.
26. Gayarré, 3:50-90; Lahey, 31-40; Pedro Piernas to ?, Aug. 2, 1773, PC 111.

hospitality, relations between the two men were soon to sour.[27]

Troubles between Hilaire and his parishioners began almost immediately. In the summer of 1774 the townspeople of Ste. Genevieve began to complain about their new pastor to Lieutenant Governor Piernas in St. Louis: Hilaire was demanding a literal tithe of one-tenth of his parishioners' incomes instead of the one-twenty-sixth that had been customary in all French colonies in North America. Hilaire was not instructing the youth in the faith and delivering sermons. Hilaire had forbidden his flock to see the priest from across the Mississippi (i.e., the popular Gibault). In June 1774 more than thirty citizens of Ste. Genevieve petitioned Piernas to straighten Hilaire out. The petitioners even suggested that the priest might wish to leave the parish; and, two months later, fifteen of the bolder citizens demanded outright that Hilaire be removed from Ste. Genevieve because he was an incorrigible troublemaker.[28]

The stickiness of the Hilaire affair was soon apparent, for Piernas referred the case to Governor Unzaga rather than try to cope with it in St. Louis. Learning of his parishioners' gathering hostilities, Hilaire himself wrote to the governor and complained about his lack of servants and his financial distress. Hilaire's personal plight was certainly real, and he continued to live with François Vallé, apparently for lack of wherewithal to maintain his own lodgings.[29]

Governor Unzaga answered both Piernas and Hilaire from New Orleans in February 1775: Hilaire could not alter the customary tithe of one-twenty-sixth on his parishioners but he would receive an annual stipend of fifty pesos to cover the cost of maintaining a domestic servant. Unzaga also informed Hilaire that it was vital to have someone administer the sacraments should he not be available to do so. This gave Gibault tacit permission to cross the Mississippi from time to time to see his old friends in Ste. Genevieve. Unzaga was trying hard to salve things over in troubled Ste. Genevieve, and he was obviously not prepared to take the drastic measure of removing Hilaire from office. After all, where could the cranky Capuchin be sent in Spanish North America that

---

27. Hilaire to Unzaga, Dec. 19, 1773, PC 192.

28. Piernas to Unzaga, July 9, 1774, PC 2357; petition June 6, 1774, in *SRM*, 1:121-23; petition Aug. 6, 1774, PC 196.

29. Hilaire to Unzaga, Nov. 19, 1774, PC 81.

was more remote than Ste. Genevieve?[30]

The petitioners from St. Genevieve were, however, ultimately correct in their judgment. They knew their man and they recognized that he was not the sort of character to let the dust settle. Turned down for advancement in New Orleans, cast away to the distant Illinois Country, unable to impose his will even in provincial Ste. Genevieve, if Father Hilaire could do nothing else he could at least raise a little hell. His fatal mistake, however, the same mistake that De Oro and Peyroux later made, was to choose a member of the Vallé family with whom to pick a fight. One could not do this and survive in colonial Ste. Genevieve.

The roots of Hilaire's animosity toward François Vallé I cannot be ascertained. Vallé had taken the priest in, housed and fed him, and refused out of a sense of hospitality to his houseguest to sign the petitions demanding Hilaire's removal. Perhaps it was a case of a neurotic biting the hand that had fed him, for Hilaire had lived *chez* Vallé for at least a year. In any case, Hilaire's peculiar personality blossomed out bizarrely in the affair of the missing church pew.

Both Louis Villars, town commandant, and François Vallé I, civil judge and commander of the local militia, had special pews installed at the front of the parish church in Ste. Genevieve. In June 1775 Vallé's pew came up missing. Villars, Vallé's son-in-law, reported to the new lieutenant governor in St. Louis, Cruzat, that Father Hilaire had spirited it away while Vallé was ill and indisposed. Cruzat must have wondered what on earth was going on down in Ste. Genevieve, but on July 3, 1775 he sent orders to both Villars and Hilaire that Vallé's pew would forthwith be returned to its customary place in the church. Cruzat already sensed that in the person of Father Hilaire he had a strange case on his hands and he begged the priest to "restrain yourself to avoid such scandals."[31]

Hilaire turned a deaf ear to Cruzat's plea however. Commandant Villars had soldiers from the Spanish garrison in Ste. Genevieve conduct a house to house (including the rectory) search for Vallé's pew, and the pew was found behind the rectory smashed to bits. Everyone knew that Hilaire was responsible for this outrage, but

30. Unzaga to Piernas, Feb. 20, 1775, PC 2357; Unzaga to Hilaire, Feb. 20, 1775, PC 81.

31. Villars to Cruzat, June 23, 1775, PC 81; Villars to Cruzat, June 24, 1775, ibid.; Cruzat to Villars, July 3, 1775, ibid.; Cruzat to Hilaire, July 3, 1775, ibid.

because there was no proof the cost of building Vallé a new pew was borne by general parish funds. Indeed, it is conceivable that disgruntled parishioners framed Hilaire in this case, although his future conduct would suggest that he was the guilty party. While Vallé's new pew was being built, Villars magnanimously turned his personal pew over to his aging father-in-law.[32]

The tormented Father Hilaire continued his shenanigans, which would be more humorous were they not so clearly the products of a troubled mind. A local woman, Madame Truteau, had developed the pious custom of baking a special loaf of bread to bring to church on Christmas Eve. After being blessed by the priest, the *pain bénit* was broken and distributed to the parishioners, who derived special satisfaction from this communal rite. On Christmas Eve 1775, Father Hilaire refused to bless Madame Truteau's bread and then, adding insult to injury, justified his refusal at Christmas Mass the next day by explaining that the bread had come from profane and sacrilegious hands. Hilaire's parishioners were outraged by this and complained to St. Louis. Lieutenant Governor Cruzat relayed the story on to Governor Unzaga in New Orleans with the comment that he wished "to God that Father Hilaire would stop his bad behavior." Poor Unzaga! He had posted Hilaire to remote Ste. Genevieve in order to rid himself of the troublesome friar, but Hilaire had a special knack for making his presence known — all the way down the Mississippi River.[33]

In the spring of 1776 Ste. Genevieve got a new military commander, Don Silvio Francisco de Cartabona. Cartabona soon reported to Unzaga that Father Hilaire was concocting new quarrels, disputes, and insults every day; he was disturbing the tranquility of the town; he refused to give extreme unction to one of Vallé's dying slaves — he had made public utterances that a negro would not dare to make. In short, wrote Cartabona, "this town would be much better off without a priest." This difficult, virtually impossible, situation simmered on for one more year, when Hilaire's actions and a new governor general in New Orleans finally brought things to a head in Ste. Genevieve.[34]

The church wardens (*marguilliers*) were important elected officials. Three usually served in Ste. Genevieve, and collectively they constituted the *fabrique,* or parish administration. This was a system

---

32. Villars to Cruzat, July 13, 1775, PC 81.

33. Cruzat to Unzaga, May 25, 1776, ibid.

34. Cartabona to Unzaga, June 12, 1776, ibid.

of lay trusteeship, and the wardens were charged with directing the *temporal* side of the Ste. Genevieve parish. They received tithes, collected rent for places in the pews, appointed the chanter and sacristan, kept the church and rectory in repair, oversaw the church real estate, including several parcels of land in the Big Field, and paid the priest's salary. In the spring of 1777, Father Hilaire refused to cooperate in the selection of new church wardens, (Jean Datchurut, Louis Bolduc *père*, and Jean-Baptiste Pratte) but the townspeople selected them anyway. Furthermore, Hilaire accused François Vallé's niece of stealing alms from the church and would not, for lack of time he claimed, hear confessions, offer vesper services, or teach the catechism to the children. In April 1777 the citizens gathered in Cartabona's residence and drafted a formal complaint to Lieutenant Governor Cruzat, spelling out Hilaire's eccentricities and delinquencies and requesting his removal. Virtually every adult male in town signed (or affixed his mark) to this document.[35]

Hilaire knew that he was under attack (perhaps in fact enjoyed it) and took the offensive by launching a literally incredible assault upon François Vallé. Hilaire wrote to the new governor general of Louisiana, Don Bernardo de Gálvez, and accused Vallé (and his wife) of being "proven heretics of the Presbyterian sect," and of "usurping almost all the rights and privileges of the bishops and priests of the Holy Roman Church." Vallé defended himself, stating flatly that both he and his wife were "Apostolic and Roman Catholics," the church wardens Datchurut and Pratte requested Hilaire's removal. By mid-August 1777 Governor Gálvez had on his desk in New Orleans an entire dossier of information regarding the ecclesiastical situation in distant Ste. Genevieve.[36]

Precisely what ran through Gálvez's mind as he perused the file on the Hilaire affair is not known, but the governor had little need to read anything other than Hilaire's own preposterous letter

---

35. The parishioners of Ste. Genevieve attempted to elect new church wardens in March 1777 but were thwarted by Father Hilaire; see pertinent documents in PC 81. Régis Lasource was the retiring warden who was charged with arranging the election of new wardens. Citizens of Ste. Genevieve to Cruzat, Apr. 30, 1777, PC 1; see also Lahey, 35-36. Lay trusteeship no longer exists in the American Catholic Church, but the Archdiocese of St. Louis still owns agricultural land in the Big Field (personal communication, Father Gregory Schmidt).

36. Hilaire to Gálvez, June 14, 1777, PC 1; Vallé to Galvez, June 23, 1777, ibid.; Cruzat to Gálvez, July 2 and 7, 1777, ibid.; Datchurut and Pratte to Gálvez, July 11, 1777, PC 190; Cartabona to Gálvez, July 12, 1777, PC 1.

in order to make his decision. Hilaire's words, "hérétiques de la secte des presbytériens" fairly leap off the page, and they must have galvanized the attention of a Spanish Catholic like Gálvez. Hilaire's "proof" that Vallé and his wife were vile Presbyterians was that during a period of severe illness Vallé had had a "priest of that sect from the English side [of the Mississippi] administer him the holy sacrament." This "Presbyterian priest" was of course none other than Vallé's old friend, Father Gibault of Kaskaskia, whom Vallé indeed had summoned to Ste. Genevieve to minister to him in his illness. With such an accusation against a man like Papa François Vallé, Gálvez knew that Hilaire was finished in Ste. Genevieve. The governor drafted a terse order to Cruzat on August 11, 1777: send Hilaire down to New Orleans forthwith, allowing him only enough time to pack his bags before embarking. Gálvez it seems knew his man well enough to make this last prudent recommendation. But Hilaire was too quick for the governor.[37]

Mail went swiftly down the Mississippi during the eighteenth century, almost always moving from the Illinois Country to New Orleans in less than a month. Movement upriver was of course a different matter, and letters often took four months to reach St. Louis and Ste. Genevieve from New Orleans. Gálvez sent his dismissal orders for Hilaire on August 11, Cruzat received them in early December 1777, and by the end of the year Hilaire was on his way down river. But between the time that Galvez posted Hilaire's dismissal orders and the time that the orders arrived in the Illinois Country the priest was engaged in yet another startling escapade.[38]

On October 16, 17, and 18 Commandant Cartabona of Ste. Genevieve interrogated more than twenty *habitants* and black slaves concerning an issue of vandalism perpetrated against the parish rectory and church. These structures belonged to the community of parishioners in Ste. Genevieve and damage to them was thus a matter of public concern. The testimony of Cartabona's witnesses revealed that Hilaire had directed his own negress slave, and other black slaves whom he had engaged in return for some tafia, to wreak devastation upon the parish property: they razed the rectory stable, tore down the picket fence surrounding the rectory, ripped window frames out of both church and rectory, and knocked down an interior wall in the rectory. The lumber accumulated from

---

37. Gálvez to Cruzat, Aug. 11, 1777, ibid.
38. Cruzat to Gálvez, Dec. 16, 1777, PC 2358

these various demolition projects was chopped into firewood and stacked in Hilaire's shed, for, according to Hilaire's domestic slave, the rectory was short on firewood.[39]

In a dramatic and destructive fashion, Hilaire was making two points: the church and rectory in Ste. Genevieve were not suitable structures for a person of *his* status; the parishioners in town were not taking adequate care of *his* needs, firewood in this instance. The church wardens were not sympathetic to Hilaire's manner of stating his case and they asked Cruzat that "the person" guilty of the vandalism be obliged to "pay in cash or have his effects confiscated."[40]

In December 1777, Commandant Cartabona, two witnesses, Michel Laroche and Louis Chamard, and three appraisers — Pierre Aubuchon, Louis Lacroix, and Michel Placet — inspected the devastated parish property. Their estimate of total damages was 550 livres, the price of a small lot with a modest house in Ste. Genevieve at that time. It seems likely that Hilaire fled town before any pressure could be brought to bear upon him to pay for the vandalism. Indeed, as a cleric Hilaire was technically immune from civil prosecution in any case. The townspeople of Ste. Genevieve were simply left holding the bag for Father Hilaire's debts, both material and spiritual.[41]

In April 1778 Governor Gálvez posted Father Hilaire as curate to the Natchez Post. Ste. Genevieve's gain was Natchez's loss. It does seem fantastic that disturbed incompetents like Hilaire could find refuge and hold position in the Catholic Church of colonial Louisiana; but then the Mississippi frontier was on the far fringes of European civilization, and educated persons of any kind were difficult to find. Literate misfits, a priest like Hilaire or a commandant like Peyroux, could survive in remote Ste. Genevieve — at least for awhile.[42]

Ste. Genevieve was again without a parish priest. But the situation was worse than that, for Hilaire had left debris and chaos in his wake. He had not only vandalized the church and the rectory

---

39. The vandalism started in September 1777; see memorial of Pratte and Datchurut to Cruzat, Sep. 5, 1777, PC 1; depositions taken by Cartabona, Oct. 16, 17, 18, 1777, ibid.

40. Pratte and Datchurut to Cruzat, Oct. 20, 1777, ibid.

41. Statement of damages, Dec. 21, 1777, ibid.

42. Hilaire was posted to Natchez in April 1778 (Gálvez to Grandpré, Apr. 3, 1778, PC 1).

but had also neglected to maintain complete and accurate parish records. Father Bernard de Limpach, who had become parish priest at St. Louis in 1776, traveled to Ste. Genevieve in September 1778 to straighten out the church register and fill in the missing entries.[43]

Father Bernard remained in Ste. Genevieve for several weeks to deal with various religious issues, one of which was the planning of a new parish church. Ste. Genevieve probably had its first vertical-log church by the mid-1750s. This structure may have lasted until 1773, when, according to François Vallé's letter of self-defense written on June 23, 1777, a new church was built for Father Hilaire. Already by 1778 that church needed to be replaced, for during Hilaire's rampage in the autumn of 1777, several of the windows had been ripped out; and, more seriously, the Mississippi had taken a capricious turn toward the town in the mid-1700s and the church built in 1773 was threatened by floodwaters. On September 27, 1778, the inhabitants of Ste. Genevieve met in the abandoned rectory, with Cartabona, Vallé, and Father Bernard all present. This assembly decided to build a new church on higher ground. The problems of the devastated rectory, which had been built for Father Hilaire in 1774 did not come up at this meeting, for with no resident priest a new rectory was not an urgent issue.[44]

We know little about the church that was presumably erected in the autumn of 1778. Certainly it was of vertical-log construction, like those that preceded it and succeeded it, and had a wooden-shingled roof. Within the sanctuary Commandant Cartabona and *lieutenant particulier* François Vallé had special pews (*bancs*) draped with blue tapestries, and the town's other leading citizens (the church wardens and the militia officers, for example) also had their own individualized pews up front toward the altar but behind those of the two governors. In back there was standing room for the baptized black slaves who wished to attend Mass. This edifice was the next to the last church built in the Old Town, and it remained in use for ten years.[45]

---

43. Yealy, 56; SGPR, Baptisms, Book A:80. For the purposes of this study, many errors in the original SGPR have been corrected using the annotated Ida Schaaf transcripts (MHS) and other sources such as estate papers (SGA).

44. Vallé to Gálvez, June 23, 1777, PC 1; see also Piernas to Unzaga (July 13, 1773, PC 81) concerning proposal for new church in Ste. Genevieve; SGA, Documents, no. 32.

45. Father Bernard wrote to Governor Unzaga (Oct. 10, 1776, PC 196) from St. Louis and mentioned the special pews in the church at Ste. Genevieve.

Father Pierre Gibault, who served Ste. Genevieve frequently during the 1770s and 1780s but was never canonical priest of the parish.

Lacking their own parish priest, the townspeople of Ste. Genevieve had to rely upon the reliable Father Pierre Gibault, whom François Vallé described as "curate of Kaskaskia and our usual [spiritual] director when there is no curate in this post." Gibault was of course an appointee of Quebec and technically had no official status or business in Spanish Illinois. He persisted in crossing the Mississippi on spiritual errands, however. In 1774, for example, François Vallé was gravely ill, and Gibault traveled to Ste. Genevieve to comfort and confess his old friend.[46]

Gibault was finally drawn directly into affairs on the Spanish side of the river when in 1777 Hilaire accused him of being a Presbyterian preacher. In a letter addressed to "Monsieur" (probably Governor Bernardo de Gálvez), dated July 12, 1777 from Kaskaskia, Gibault defended himself against Hilaire's calumnies. The charge that he was a heretic was absurd, Gibault explained, and Hilaire's accusation was unconscionable because at one time the two priests had confessed one another. Yes, he had given the sacraments on the Spanish side, but only because Hilaire's dereliction of duty compelled him to do so. Indeed, both the civil and religious authorities in St. Louis had agreed to let him serve unofficially in Spanish territory, and his best character reference was none other than former lieutenant governor of Spanish Illinois, Don Pedro Piernas.[47]

It is clear that Gibault did not like living on the east side of the Mississippi in British territory. His aid to General George Rogers Clark in securing Kaskaskia and Vincennes for the American cause in 1778-79 is well known. But once the east side of the river had become American Gibault did not like it any better. American Illinois had an increasingly deracinated and lawless population, and Gibault wanted to move to Ste. Genevieve on the Spanish side of the Mississippi, where as a European Roman Catholic he would feel more at home. Gibault finally wrote to Governor Miró in New Orleans and proclaimed his desire to take possession of the parish of Ste. Genevieve, for American Illinois was "without commandant, soldiers, or laws," and was "in the greatest spiritual and temporal disorder."[48]

---

46. Vallé made these remarks in his letter of self-defense (Vallé to Gálvez, June 23, 1777, PC 1) after Hilaire had attacked him and Gibault.

47. Gibault to Gálvez, July 12, 1777, PC 190.

48. Donnelly, "Pierre Gibault," 81-92; Rothensteiner, 132-39; Gibault to Miró, July 29, 1782, *SMV*, 3:47-48.

In February 1783 Miró informed Cruzat in St. Louis that as far as he was concerned Gibault was welcome to remain in Ste. Genevieve but that he was speaking only for himself as governor and not for the Roman Catholic Church. There is no evidence that this conundrum over ecclesiastical jurisdiction was ever resolved, and Gibault's position in Ste. Genevieve remained officially irregular.[49]

Although Gibault was not canonical priest of the community, he had taken up residence at Ste. Genevieve by the early 1780s. In the autumn of 1782, Gibault was smitten by a serious illness and drafted a last will and testament in Ste. Genevieve. He wished to be buried in the parish church, "the customary sepulcher for priests," and he bequeathed his two black slaves to his sister and her husband. Priests in the Illinois Country customarily used black slaves as domestic servants, but Gibault's testament reveals an interesting glimpse of his humanity: the two slaves could, should Gibault die, sell themselves if they wished to another master and only the proceeds of the sale would go to the priest's sister and her husband. Gibault perhaps suspected his brother-in-law of cruelty and wished to afford his house slaves the opportunity of having a better master.[50]

Gibault was not a good manager of money, and his pitiful income from tithes, alms, and stipends, often left him in difficult financial straits. In 1783, a creditor from Montreal dunned him for a thirty-three-livre debt going back to 1768. And a year later, Antonio de Oro, the new commandant in Ste. Genevieve, had Gibault's slaves sequestered in the town jail until the priest paid his debts to two ferryboatmen; Gibault was compelled to sell the slaves to pay this debt. By all accounts Gibault was a popular priest in Ste. Genevieve, but on issues of money the townspeople were cold-blooded businessmen. It is possible that Gibault's drinking habits were already making their mark on his life, although his portrait also suggests a personality too-abstracted from mundane affairs to be adept at handling finances.[51]

---

49. Miró to Cruzat, Feb. 10, 1783, PC 9; Cruzat seems not to have received this letter and informed Gibault of it until the autumn of 1783; see Cruzat to Miró, Nov. 13, 1783, ibid.

50. MHS, New Madrid Archives, 1431-19. Gibault's disposition of his slaves was in accord with Spanish rather than French practice (Baade, "The Law of Slavery," 75).

51. Alexis Réaume to Gibault, Aug. 27, 1783, ibid.; SGA, Litigations, no. 161,

Restored chapel at Cahokia, Illinois. Built in the late eighteenth century, this chapel probably looks much like the first parish churches in colonial Ste. Genevieve.

Gibault left Ste. Genevieve late in the year 1784 to establish himself as pastor in Vincennes, an outpost he knew from his circuit-riding days. Perhaps he simply became weary of his irregular status in Ste. Genevieve; or perhaps his financial difficulties in town had generated friction between himself and his parishioners. Gibault spent almost seven unhappy years in the new American republic. Unhappy because he was caught up in the jurisdictional dispute between Bishop Hubert of Quebec and Bishop Carroll of Baltimore, and unhappy because, in his words, "one must all the time endure terrible affronts for the faith"; apparently Protestant settlers on the American frontier were abusing Roman Catholics.[52]

Sep. 7, 1784; Cruzat to De Oro, Sep. 18, 1784, PC 117A; SGA, Slaves, no. 73, 18 Sep. 1784; ibid., Sep. 27, 1784.

52. Gibault to La Tulippe, June 25, 1791, PC 17; according to Houck (*SRM*, 2:372) La Tulippe was a stonemason who had moved from Vincennes to Spanish Illinois.

In 1792 Gibault left the east side of the Mississippi once again. He abandoned the parish at Vincennes and moved to the new settlement of New Madrid, founded by the American George Morgan on Spanish territory in 1789. Gibault finally acquired the position of canonical pastor at New Madrid in 1793, a position he had never achieved in all his years of service in Ste. Genevieve, and he remained there until his death in 1802. American sovereignty was about to descend upon Louisiana, and Gibault, if he had known, would have died content in the knowledge that he had narrowly missed becoming an American once again.[53]

Gibault's last years in Upper Louisiana, like many of his first years, were miserable. He had never been able to endure the hardships of missionary life on the Mississippi frontier without some comfort from the bottle, and by the late 1790s his consumption had risen to a quart of spirits per day. Some of this alcohol was used to buffer the pain inflicted upon him by his new superior, Father James Maxwell, the bullying curate of Ste. Genevieve and vicar general of Upper Louisiana. Gibault had spent half his life in the Illinois Country, a life of drudgery, hardship, and self-effacement. His only ambition seems to have been to serve man's spiritual needs. Gibault's reputation should rest upon his work as a comforter of souls rather than upon his brief service to the American cause during the Revolutionary War.[54]

After Gibault left Ste. Genevieve in 1784 he was temporarily replaced by another one of the curiously cosmopolitan, itinerant adventurers whose lives punctuate the history of the colonial town. Paul von Heiligenstein (de St. Pierre in French) was a German Carmelite who had served as a chaplain in the French expeditionary force during the American Revolution. A German in the service of the King of France, he witnessed George Washington's victory at Yorktown and later became priest in Ste. Genevieve. By such characters is the colonial history of the Illinois Country enlivened. During his first tour of duty in Ste. Genevieve (summer of 1785 to summer of 1786), Father St. Pierre, as he was called in Louisiana, was merely interim pastor. He had been sent to the Illinois Country by the famous American Bishop John Carroll of Baltimore and was residing in Ste. Genevieve ("a Spanish parish," he called it) only until a residence was put in shape for him at

---

53. Donnelly, "Gibault," 90 91; Houck, History of Missouri, 2:310-11; Gibault swore allegiance to Spain at New Madrid in December 1793 (*SRM*, 1:336).

54. Gibault's liquor bills, MHS, New Madrid Archives, 1431-57.

Cahokia on the American side of the Mississippi. Although he wished to remain in Ste. Genevieve and would return there in a few years time, in the summer of 1786 St. Pierre was replaced by a Spanish appointee dispatched from New Orleans.[55]

Father Louis Guignes was a Capuchin friar, as Father Hilaire had been. In April 1786 Governor Miró wrote to Lieutenant Governor Cruzat that he was sending "a monk and not a meddler" (an invidious allusion to Hilaire?) to take charge of the parish of Ste. Genevieve. Father Guignes traveled up the Mississippi by riverboat as far as the Arkansas Post and then proceeded northward on foot, arriving at Ste. Genevieve in August 1786.[56]

Father Guignes was a quirky personality, and he soon informed Governor Miró that the townspeople of Ste. Genevieve were not living up to his expectations. The reverend father was likewise not meeting the expectations of the citizens, who began to make Guignes the butt of their ridicule. Governor Miró wrote to Cruzat in St. Louis and criticized the people of Ste. Genevieve for not using the established chain of command for their complaints — town commandant and lieutenant governor — instead of "employing ridicule," which was an "ugly and detestable means of complaining." It would be fascinating to know precisely what techniques the townspeople used to ridicule Guignes, but it can safely be assumed they employed that talent for mimicry in which the premodern world was so rich.[57]

Lieutenant Governor Cruzat knew the situation in Ste. Genevieve better than Governor Miró, and it is apparent from Cruzat's letters to town commandant De Oro that the lieutenant governor had sided with the townspeople against their priest. By the end of the year 1788 Louis Guignes was on his way back to New Orleans without having left much of a mark on Ste. Genevieve. The townspeople meanwhile had shown themselves willing and able to exercise power locally, even though Ste. Genevieve was a dependency of the autocratic Spanish monarchy and, ecclesiastically, was subject to the diocese of Cuba.[58]

---

55. For an introduction to St. Pierre, see Nasatir, *War Vessels*, 317, n. 61; Yealy, 57, 63-64; Rothensteiner, 156-76; St. Pierre to Tardiveau, Sep. 27, 1787, in Alvord (ed.), *Kaskaskia Papers*, 571.

56. Miró to Cruzat, Apr. 26, 1786, PC 117 B; De Oro to Miró, Aug. 9, 1786, PC 199; Cruzat to Miró, Aug. 23, 1786, *SMV*, pt. 2:186-87.

57. Miró to Cruzat, Jan. 25, 1787, PC 118.

58. Cruzat to De Oro, Apr. 25 and May 18, 1787, PC 118.

There is much evidence that most law-abiding persons with Continental European backgrounds found American Illinois of the late eighteenth century an inhospitable place. The late 1780s and early 1790s saw a large migration of French Canadian families from Kaskaskia to the New Town of Ste. Genevieve, for the American side of the Mississippi was in chaos. Pierre Gibault left Vincennes to seek a haven in New Madrid, and Abbé de St. Pierre wished to leave Cahokia to return to his one-time parish in Spanish Ste. Genevieve.

The confusion over ecclesiastical jurisdiction in the western (trans-Mississippian) Illinois Country had been cleared up in the early 1770s, when Rome decreed that all of Louisiana was within the jurisdiction of the Spanish church. During the 1780s, the head of the Spanish church in Louisiana was Bishop Cyrillo de Barcelona, who resided in New Orleans and exercised episcopal functions under the authority of the diocese of Cuba. From his parish at Cahokia St. Pierre wrote to New Orleans in the spring of 1789 and asked to be appointed canonical pastor either at Ste. Genevieve, which he noted had had no pastor since Guignes' departure, or at the new settlement of New Madrid. St. Pierre had done well under difficult circumstances as priest in Cahokia. He was popular with his parishioners, and under his guidance they began to erect a new parish church, which has now been handsomely rebuilt. But St. Pierre wanted to leave the United States and he was willing to take virtually *any* post in Spanish territory.[59]

St. Pierre did not like living on the American frontier. Furthermore, he was having troubles with Father Huet de La Valinière, whom Bishop Carroll of Baltimore had appointed curate in Kaskaskia and vicar general of American Illinois in 1786. While St. Pierre was a German Carmelite, La Valinière was a French Sulpician and as vicar general he was St. Pierre's superior. La Valinière had a reputation for being an odd duck. The new Spanish lieutenant governor in St. Louis, Don Manuel Pérez, claimed that La Valinière had fallen from his horse, "striking his head, and the fall caused a change in his mind which increases or diminishes according to the season, but never ceases." Perhaps St. Pierre first met him during a bad season, for the two men were soon bitter enemies.[60]

59. St. Pierre to Antonio de Sedella, May 1, 1789, UNDA, New Orleans Diocesan Collection, IV-4-e; Rothensteiner (170) printed this letter but got the date and the addressee wrong.

60. Rothensteiner 161-64; Pérez to Miró, Nov. 18, 1788, *SMV*, pt. 2:261.

Bishop Cyrillo finally granted St. Pierre's request and assigned him to the parish of Ste. Genevieve in the autumn of 1789. But before St. Pierre left the American side of the Mississippi his enemy La Valinière began allegations that would haunt St. Pierre for the remainder of his career in the Illinois Country: La Valinière suggested in letters sent to religious authorities in both Baltimore and New Orleans that St. Pierre was not a properly accredited priest, that he was a "false or at least a bad priest." The evil seeds planted by La Valinière eventually took root.[61]

When Father Guignes arrived at Ste. Genevieve in August 1786, the townspeople had created a rectory for him by purchasing a lot and a house from Nicholas Roussin and refitting the house for the priest's use. This house was almost certainly in the Old Town. Several years of severe flooding had already afflicted the town, but the parish church was still located there, and, in 1786, so was the majority of the population. Indeed, in the late 1780s a new parish church was built in the Old Town. St. Pierre probably moved into Guignes' vacated rectory when he returned to Ste. Genevieve in 1789, even though the Old Town was then rapidly decaying. In 1792 St. Pierre bought a residence in the New Town, established a chapel there (the parish church was not built until late in 1794), and became an advocate for the new community of Petites Côtes.[62]

Indeed, it was St. Pierre's advocacy of the New Town of Ste. Genevieve that first created problems for him in Ste. Genevieve. Two years before St. Pierre's return to Ste. Genevieve in 1789, the willful Peyroux de la Coudrenière had become town commandant, and Peyroux wanted the Saline to replace the dying Old Town as the seat of government in the Ste. Genevieve District. In 1788 Peyroux and St. Pierre had been allies in league against the peculiar Father La Valinière of Kaskaskia. But in the summer of 1793 Peyroux returned to Ste. Genevieve from an extended trip to the United States to discover that during his absence St. Pierre had moved his residence and, in cooperation with François Vallé II, transferred the parish organization to the New Town. Peyroux

61. Lahey, 60; St. Pierre began to record baptisms in Ste. Genevieve during September 1789, SGPR, Baptisms, Book B; La Valinière to Miró, Feb. 23, 1788, *SMV*, pt. 2:242-44.

62. SGA, Documents, no. 35; Trudeau remarked that a new church had been built at Ste. Genevieve six years earlier (Trudeau to Carondelet, Sep. 1, 1794, PC 197); SGA, Deeds, no. 321, Dec. 20, 1792; see also below, chap. xiii.

was thenceforth St. Pierre's bitter and unrelenting enemy.[63]

In August 1793, Lieutenant Governor Trudeau, who was a supporter of Vallé, wrote to Peyroux and urged the commandant to live amicably with Father St. Pierre, whom Trudeau insisted was a worthy pastor. Peyroux replied to Trudeau's letter with a blast against St. Pierre, calling him "an adventurer, a false priest, [and] a vagabond." Disingenuously, Peyroux fulminated against St. Pierre. Peyroux's anger with the priest had in fact been aroused by St. Pierre's friendship with the Vallés and his decision to move the parish to the New Town. Peyroux insisted that a majority of the citizens wished to maintain the parish in the Old Town and had resisted St. Pierre's move to Petites Côtes. This was patently untrue.[64]

Peyroux learned during Trudeau's visit to Ste. Genevieve in September 1793 that the lieutenant governor was supporting the Vallé-St. Pierre faction against him, and he reacted by going over Trudeau's head directly to authorities in both Baltimore and New Orleans. Peyroux was, as we have seen, about to lose his own position as town commandant, but during his last few months in office he spread poison about St. Pierre as fast and as far as he could. Because Peyroux was intelligent, educated, well-traveled, and well-known his poison had just sufficient potency to help destroy St. Pierre as pastor in Ste. Genevieve, although the destruction proceeded with slow agony.[65]

The first indication that St. Pierre was likely to lose his curacy in Ste. Genevieve came in the spring of 1795, when St. Pierre received an ominous letter from the grand vicar of all Louisiana, Patrick Walsh. Walsh urged St. Pierre to abandon the parish of Ste. Genevieve and descend to New Orleans where he would be assigned a new curacy. This news, as Delassus de Luzières explained in a letter to his friend Governor Carondelet, perturbed the townspeople of Ste. Genevieve, who were exceedingly fond of their pastor. De Luzières was correct, for one week later more than fifty citizens of Ste. Genevieve signed a petition that implored Carondelet to intercede with the religious authorities in New Orleans so that "the Reverend Father St. Pierre, our worthy pastor,"

---

63. Pérez to Miró, Nov. 18, 1788, *SMV*, pt. 2:361-63; on Peyroux, see above, chap. xi.

64. Trudeau to Peyroux, Aug. 7, 1793, PC 207 A; Peyroux to Trudeau, Aug. 14, 1793, PC 2363.

65. Peyroux to Carondelet, Sep. 10, 1793, PC 208 B.

might remain as curate in Ste. Genevieve. François Vallé II, who had replaced Peyroux as military and civil commandant of the Ste. Genevieve District, witnessed the signatures and swore that the petition represented the "general opinion of the citizens of this parish."[66]

Despite the force of this petition, Carondelet ordered St. Pierre to descend to New Orleans for investigation. The governor's orders arrived in Ste. Genevieve in the autumn of 1795, and the townspeople again moved to defend their pastor — they asked Lieutenant Governor Trudeau to act on their behalf. Trudeau responded by sending Carondelet a detailed certification of St. Pierre's religious and civic qualifications, pointing out that the priest had always helped to maintain a harmonious community. Ten days later Trudeau wrote the governor on his own account and praised St. Pierre's virtues: he was loved and respected by his parishioners; he spoke German, English, French, and also a little Spanish; he knew the principles of good agriculture and gave advice on its practice; he concerned himself with the development of the district; his removal from office would be a great loss for Ste. Genevieve. Trudeau was telling the governor general that St. Pierre was a boon to the whole Spanish plan for populating and developing Upper Louisiana.[67]

On December 3, 1795 town commandant François Vallé II wrote two letters to Carondelet. Although Vallé must have been charged with emotion when he wrote it, the first letter was a dry and matter-of-fact official dispatch: he had personally served St. Pierre with Carondelet's orders, and the priest was on his way downriver in Chouteau's barge. "God grant you [Carondelet] a long life." The second letter on the other hand was a rare one, for against all of his political instincts and his usual habits of mind Vallé allowed his personal feelings to spill out onto the page: "As commandant and long-time citizen of this post I must tell you about the upright life and actions of this pastor, of his selflessness and his eagerness to help the poor and the sick, and his extreme

---

66. De Luzières to Carondelet, Mar. 15, 1795, PC 211; petition of citizens of Ste. Genevieve, Mar. 22, 1795, PC 210. Patrick Walsh served as grand vicar under Luis Peñalver y Cárdenas, who was appointed bishop of Louisiana and the Floridas in 1793. Louisiana and the Floridas had been established as a diocese independent of Cuba in 1791.

67. Carondelet to François Vallé, July 14, 1795, MHS, Vallé Collection, Box 2; Trudeau to Carondelet, Nov. 20, 1795, PC 139; Trudeau to Carondelet, Nov. 30, 1795, PC 211. St. Pierre of course knew Latin as well.

vigilance and care to fulfill his pastoral duties. . . . I add, Monseigneur, my personal pleas to those of our citizens for the speedy return to our parish of this good and worthy pastor."[68]

With such recommendations one might have thought that St. Pierre would indeed have been posted quickly back to Ste. Genevieve. As he plunged southward down the Mississippi in Chouteau's barge St. Pierre probably thought the same thing, for he knew that he was innocent of whatever charges were being leveled against him.

But when St. Pierre arrived in New Orleans at the end of the year 1795 he discovered that his replacement, Father James Maxwell, had already been dispatched for Ste. Genevieve; the two priests must have crossed paths somewhere on the lower Mississippi. St. Pierre also discovered, as he explained in a letter to his friend François Vallé, that "atrocious calumnies" were being spread in New Orleans to the effect that the bishop of Baltimore (John Carroll) had forbidden St. Pierre to function as a priest and had had him expelled from American Illinois. Because these slanders were in fact without foundation — indeed, Bishop Carroll had defended St. Pierre during his row with La Valinière — St. Pierre felt compelled to go to Baltimore in order to obtain affirmation of his sound credentials. St. Pierre, in addition to his other virtues, was obviously a patient and determined fellow. Determined to return home to Ste. Genevieve, for he had promised his parishioners that he would accept no other parish in exchange for theirs.[69]

St. Pierre did in fact travel to Baltimore from New Orleans in the winter of 1796 and did succeed in having his name cleared — at least for the time being. After a six-month absence, he returned to Ste. Genevieve "triumphant" (Trudeau's adjective) in May 1796. That St. Pierre still possessed religious authority and moral force in the community is evident in an incident concerning public morality that transpired in August 1796, when St. Pierre compelled Louis Coyteux to marry the woman with whom he was living.[70]

68. Vallé to Carondelet, Dec. 3, 1795, PC 211; Vallé to Carondelet, Dec. 3, 1795, PC 214.

69. St. Pierre to François Vallé, Jan. 20, 1796, SGA, Misc. 2, no. 51; Bishop Carroll to La Valinière, Jan. 11, 1789, UNDA, Records of the Diocese of Louisiana and the Floridas, 1756-1803, V-1-c, 9-12.

70. De Luzières to François Vallé, May 22, 1796, MHS, François Vallé Collection, Box 2; Trudeau to Carondelet, July 3, 1796, PC 212 B; on Coyteux case, see above, chap. xi

St. Pierre's triumph was short-lived, however. When he returned to Ste. Genevieve late in May 1796, he discovered that Father James Maxwell had arrived before him from New Orleans with the fancy title of vicar general of Upper Louisiana. Indeed, Maxwell had already begun to make entries in the Ste. Genevieve parish register. Moreover, unbeknown to St. Pierre, Bishop Carroll of Baltimore had written a rather duplicitous letter to Bishop Peñalver of New Orleans, suggesting that St. Pierre might in fact be a delinquent priest. In any case, the townspeople of Ste. Genevieve had often struggled along with no priest of their own, and now suddenly in 1796 they had a surfeit of the reverend fathers, one anomaly replacing the other. Sometime in late May or early June 1796 Maxwell discreetly retired to St. Louis to bide his time, apparently confident that he would soon supplant St. Pierre as curate in Ste. Genevieve.[71]

In February 1797 St. Pierre made his last entries in the Ste. Genevieve parish records and by early April he was on his way back downriver to New Orleans — never to return. The charges against him had been renewed, and this time the authorities in New Orleans were determined to make them stick. St. Pierre must have sensed this, for he sold his house, slaves, and real estate to Vital Bauvais in February.[72]

Yet St. Pierre's reputation remained untarnished in the Illinois Country. Indeed, there was a veritable competition among the communities of Ste. Genevieve, New Bourbon, and Kaskaskia for the privilege of retaining St. Pierre as pastor. When St. Pierre descended the Mississippi in April 1797, he went armed with a petition that the church wardens in Ste. Genevieve (Vital Bauvais and Jean-Baptiste Bauvais at that time) had written on behalf of all the parishioners. This petition heaped praise upon St. Pierre and implored him to return to Ste. Genevieve. And as soon as the Catholic citizens of Kaskaskia heard that St. Pierre might be forced to leave his curacy in Ste. Genevieve, they unanimously petitioned him (May 6, 1797) to become pastor of their community and even offered to defend St. Pierre should any allegations be brought

---

71. Maxwell's first entry in the Ste. Genevieve parish records was a baptism on May 15, 1796; see SGPR, Baptisms, Book B:67; Bishop Carroll to Bishop Peñalver, Apr. 7, 1796, in Hanley (ed.), *Carroll Papers*, 2:169-70. Carroll's motives in writing this letter seem to have been largely political; that is, he wished to establish a good relationship with Bishop Peñalver of New Orleans, who was investigating St. Pierre. See also Rothensteiner, 198-99, on Maxwell.

72. SGPR, Baptisms, Book B:74; SGA, Deeds, no. 349.

against him. During more than a decade's residence in the Illinois Country, St. Pierre had celebrated Mass many times in Kaskaskia, and he was well-remembered there. Petitions from people who knew St. Pierre best, parishioners and former parishioners, could not save him, however, once the bureaucracy of the Catholic Church took hold. St. Pierre departed Ste. Genevieve in April 1797 and he never returned to the Illinois Country, a country he had learned to love.[73]

Upon his arrival in New Orleans, St. Pierre became a houseguest in the residence of the Vallé family attorney, Berte Grima. This commodious home must have provided the weary cleric with some comfort while he underwent tedious interrogation and investigation by Bishop Peñalver. The manuscript record of this ecclesiastical process runs to 199 pages and includes depositions from townspeople in Ste. Genevieve that Father James Maxwell recorded.[74]

As the investigation of St. Pierre dragged on through the sweltering New Orleans summer and into the autumn of 1797, it became increasingly apparent that the priest from Ste. Genevieve was innocent of any of the serious allegations that had been made: he had not forged documents; he was not a false priest; he had not broken his priestly vows by engaging in sexual intercourse. Apparently St. Pierre finally tired of the whole ordeal and began to snap back at his interrogators. On October 24, 1797 Bishop Peñalver removed St. Pierre's sacerdotal powers; henceforth St. Pierre could not celebrate the Mass in Spanish Louisiana. The next day, in a dramatic and defiant gesture, St. Pierre fled Louisiana to seek refuge at Natchez, in American territory.[75]

Proof positive that St. Pierre was in fact a worthy priest and a good man came in 1800 when he was allowed to return to Spanish Louisiana and was given the parish of St. Francis at Pointe Coupée. Although lost forever to the people of Ste. Genevieve, St. Pierre distinguished himself as a priest in Louisiana until his death in

---

73. Both of these petitions are in the archives of the Archdiocese of Baltimore in Baltimore, Maryland; a copy of that from the citizens of Kaskaskia is also found in PC 214; on St. Pierre's popularity, see also De Luzières to Carondelet, Apr. 22, 1797, PC 213.

74. Berte Grima to François Vallé, June 6, 1797, MHS, François Vallé Collection, Box 2; UNDA, Diocese of Louisiana, V-1-c; depositions in ibid., 113-23.

75. Peñalver's decree in ibid., 193-94. Because St. Pierre fled New Orleans without a passport the civil authorities were also pursuing him; see Gayoso to Peñalver, Oct. 27, 1797, ibid., 197-98; Gayoso to Trudeau, Oct. 26, 1797, PC 131 A.

1826. In his last parish, St. Gabriel of Iberville, he was affectionately called "le brave et bon de St. Pierre."[76]

There is something slightly odd about St. Pierre's persecution and removal from the parish of Ste. Genevieve. He was the most popular priest in the entire colonial history of the town, a town that was hard on its priests; he had broad public support and the support of the powerful men in Upper Louisiana — Zenon Trudeau in St. Louis, François Vallé II in Ste. Genevieve, and Delassus de Luzières in New Bourbon. St. Pierre was the priest of Henry Brackenridge's fond boyhood memories of Ste. Genevieve, the priest who had baptized the American boy Roman Catholic to please Brackenridge's pious guardian, Madame Vital Bauvais. Although St. Pierre had gotten caught up in the jurisdictional confusion created by the political complexity of colonial North America, it was obvious that he was not a "false priest" as his detractors alleged.

Why then did St. Pierre fall? He could be, as several of his letters reveal, a brusque and sarcastic man. He did manage to make some articulate and persistent enemies, although it is apparent that none of these — Peyroux and La Valinière, for example — were as worthy a person as he. He had fought acrimoniously with the three peculiar French nuns whom De Luzières had brought to Ste. Genevieve, and when the nuns returned to New Orleans they campaigned against him. It is also possible that the two Irishmen, Patrick Walsh and Thomas Hassett, who were Bishop Peñalver's chief administrators in New Orleans, wanted one of their own as vicar in Spanish Illinois and therefore engineered St. Pierre's removal from Ste. Genevieve to make room for James Maxwell; Maxwell, after all, was dispatched with unseemly haste upriver to Illinois even before St. Pierre had a chance to plead his case. These Irish ecclesiastics serving the Spanish church were known manipulators, and St. Pierre may well have been a victim of their political machinations.[77]

St. Pierre's last doleful appearance in the Ste. Genevieve local records came with the auction sale of his remaining personal effects in March 1798. James Maxwell was one of the principal

---

76. Proceedings for appointment of St. Pierre as pastor of Punta Cortado, UNDA, Diocese of Louisiana, V-2-i; Rothensteiner, 177.

77. For a sharp-tongued letter of St. Pierre, see St. Pierre to Bishop Carroll, Apr. 1, 1797, archives of the Archdiocese of Baltimore; St. Pierre himself thought that the French nuns had done him the most harm (St. Pierre to Carroll, 1798?, ibid.); see also Lahey, 84; Melville, *John Carroll*, 238.

purchasers. St. Pierre had been a worthy and popular pastor in Ste. Genevieve and was probably involved in establishing the first elementary school in town, the school that young Brackenridge attended while he resided *chez* Bauvais. His most enduring contribution to the community, however, was his transfer of the parish from the Old Town to the New Town in 1793. As François Vallé II moved the civil government to Nouvelle Ste. Genevieve, so St. Pierre moved the ecclesiastical regime. The church he had built there in 1794 lasted, with some alterations, until 1837.[78]

Before St. Pierre made his final departure from Ste. Genevieve in April 1797, James Maxwell had returned to town in March and taken charge of the parish register. For at least a month during the spring of 1797, both St. Pierre and Maxwell were living in Ste. Genevieve. Despite his many saintly qualities, St. Pierre surely harbored some bitterness for Maxwell, the interloper with the grand title of vicar general; tension between the two priests in town must have been palpable. Maxwell's pastorate in Ste. Genevieve, 1797-1814, fell largely in the territorial period of Ste. Genevieve's history. Nonetheless, Maxwell was the last colonial pastor of the town, and the man and his activities warrant some comment in this study.[79]

Since the governship of Alexandro O'Reilly during the late 1760s, Louisiana had received substantial numbers of Irish priests trained in the renowned Irish College of the University of Salamanca in Spain. Maxwell was one of these cosmopolitan Catholic priests, as were his friends at diocesan headquarters in New Orleans, Walsh and Hassett. Maxwell's appointment as pastor in Ste. Genevieve and as vicar general of Upper Louisiana was political in two respects: Governor Carondelet wanted an Irishman like Maxwell in those offices in order to help attract Irish-American Catholics to Spanish Illinois; Maxwell's friends were the chief administrative officers of the diocese of Louisiana and had the power to make his appointment. In any case, it is clear that Maxwell did not become pastor in Ste. Genevieve on the basis of any outstanding spiritual qualities. He was and remained basically a politico.[80]

Indeed, as soon as Maxwell became ensconced in Ste. Genevieve

---

78. SGA, Miscellaneous 2, no. 55.

79. SGPR, Baptisms, Book B:74.

80. The British Government did not permit Catholic seminaries in Ireland, and thus many Irishmen trained for the priesthood in Spain; see Rothensteiner, 198.

as curate and vicar general he demonstrated a keen sense of hierarchy, territoriality, and power. Poor old alcoholic Pierre Gibault, the last of the frontier missionary priests in Upper Louisiana, was pastor in New Madrid at the time of Maxwell's arrival in Spanish Illinois; and Maxwell as vicar general was Gibault's superior. Maxwell soon came down hard on Gibault for being too lenient in performing marriages without proper publication of bans, principally for non-Catholics. It was not precisely marriages without bans to which Maxwell objected but rather that Gibault was not collecting the twenty-four-piastre (dollar) fee, twelve for the first two and twelve for the third, required to permit dispensing with the marriage bans. Of course the handsome fee for dispensation was to be remitted directly to none other than the vicar general of Upper Louisiana himself.

In a brutal letter of October 1797, Maxwell reprimanded Gibault, who had himself once been vicar general of the Illinois Country under the jurisdiction of Quebec. Maxwell expressed his hope that "you do not give me cause to be discontent with you, for . . . having been so long grand vicar in this region you should know the laws that apply here." Maxwell, the Irish mercenary churchman, loved to rub salt into old Gibault's wounds by reminding him how far he had fallen in status. And in 1801, only one year before Gibault's death, Maxwell jumped on the indulgent pastor of New Madrid once again for granting dispensation of marriage bans too freely. Maxwell informed Gibault that he had been kind to him in the past (!) but that he had about had his fill and was considering sending an unfavoral evaluation of Gibault to the bishop in New Orleans. The reader of Maxwell's letters to Gibault is struck both by their brutality and their cupidity. Incredibly, this is the man whom Rothensteiner characterized as "lovable" in his *History of the Archdiocese of St. Louis.*[81]

How well James Maxwell functioned as pastor in Ste. Genevieve and what his parishioners thought of him is not clear. His letters show him to have been intelligent and articulate, and Andrew Ellicott, who met Maxwell in New Madrid, described him as "a well-informed, liberal gentleman." Houck called Maxwell "a very active and enterprising man," which he certainly was. It is noteworthy that no one who met Maxwell had anything complimentary to say about his *priestly* qualities. When Henry Brackenridge revis-

---

81. Maxwell to Gibault, Oct. 6, 1797, MHS, New Madrid Archives, 1431-52; Maxwell to Gibault, Oct. 28, 1801, ibid., 1431-67; Rothensteiner, 199.

ited Ste. Genevieve in 1811 after a fifteen-year absence he expressed regret that Father St. Pierre, of whom he had been so fond,
was gone and had been replaced by "an Irish priest who took
more pleasure in his dog and gun than in the celebration of mass
for his flock." This description of Maxwell evokes visions of
Chaucer's worldly monk "that loved venerie." In 1810 charges
surfaced that Maxwell was spending much of his time gambling
and attending dances. Maxwell sent a spirited defense of himself
to Bishop Carroll of Baltimore, who was then his superior, and
Carroll dropped the issue. Another priest who visited Ste.
Genevieve at that time, however, observed that "it would be better
if he [Maxwell] were not there at all, for he spends his time at
hunting and horse racing and his nights playing cards." Maxwell
was obviously not leading a monkish existence, but there is no
evidence that his life-style in Ste. Genevieve was genuinely debauched or immoral.[82]

As parish priest in Ste. Genevieve and vicar general of Upper
Louisiana, Maxwell received a salary of forty pesos (dollars) per
month. This was not an insignificant sum, considering that François Vallé II's salary as town commandant was only 100 pesos per
annum, and that St. Pierre's salary as curate had been twenty
pesos per month. At some point, probably about 1800, Maxwell
moved from Ste. Genevieve to New Bourbon, which was within
the parish of Ste. Genevieve. He may have done this the better
to exploit an 800-arpent (680 acres) tract of land that he had
purchased near New Bourbon in 1799. When Paul Alliot visited
Ste. Genevieve toward the end of the colonial period, Maxwell
was conspicuous for his absence, and Alliot observed that the town
made do without a priest.[83]

If not scandalous, Maxwell's life in the Ste. Genevieve District
was apparently more secular than spiritual. It is curious to find
Rothensteiner remarking that "Father Maxwell was above all
things a true priest," and then spend an entire page discussing
the priest's very extensive land holdings, a reminder of which is
Maxwell's Hill on the northern edge of present-day Ste. Genevieve.

82. Ellicott quoted in Houck, *History of Missouri,* 2:305, no. 46; Houck, ibid.;
Brackenridge quoted in Yealy, 97; Bishop Carroll to Maxwell, May 30, 1810, in
Hanley (ed.), *Carroll Papers,* 3:177; Maxwell to Carroll, Nov. 17, 1810, Archives
of the Archdiocese of Baltimore; Father Urban Guillet to Bishop Plessis of
Quebec, May 4, 1810, printed in McDermott, *Old Cahokia,* 302.

83. Nasatir, "Government Employees and Salaries," 64, 154; SGA, Deeds no.
435; Alliot, 133.

In addition to real estate, Maxwell had a lively interest in politics and enjoyed wielding power and influence. In 1805, Ste. Genevieve was described to President Thomas Jefferson as the "only village over which a Priest can have any influence." Maxwell was able enough politically to preside over the first session of the legislative council of the Missouri Territory in January 1814. Shortly thereafter, he died of injuries sustained in a riding accident, a not unusual cause of death at that time. Probably the citizens of Ste. Genevieve missed their energetic priest, but there is no evidence that they mourned him. James Maxwell is buried beneath the nave of the parish church.[84]

Maxwell's pastorate is most instructive for delineating the great change that occurred in the priesthood of the Illinois Country during the second half of the eighteenth century. Early colonial Ste. Genevieve was served by Jesuit missionaries whose lives were devoted, arduous, and bordered on the heroic, as they faced long distances, bitter weather, and hostile Indians to carry out their spiritual mission. By 1800 Ste. Genevieve had a parish priest who viewed his pastorate as a political sinecure from which to extend his power and influence in the temporal world.

To depict the pastorates of the various priests who served in colonial Ste. Genevieve is one thing; to characterize the spiritual lives of the townspeople is quite another. Outsiders, both Catholics and Protestants, tended to deprecate the religious lives of Ste. Genevieve's citizens. Don Pedro Piernas, the Spanish lieutenant governor at St. Louis (1768-74), wrote in 1769 that the townspeople of Ste. Genevieve "totally neglected" their religion. But Piernas knew the townspeople only superficially, and, moreover, was a Spanish Catholic zealot with a strong streak of self-righteousness in him.[85]

General Georges-Victor Collot, who visited Ste. Genevieve briefly in 1796, labeled the French creoles of the Illinois Country "superstitious." This epithet coming from a French Revolutionary general probably meant "devoutly religious." To Collot, as to most eighteenth century intellectuals, devout Roman Catholics were by definition superstitious. Collot's view of religion in colonial Ste.

---

84. Rothensteiner, 200, 203; Yealy, 96-97; Rufus Easton to Jefferson, Jan. 17, 1805, Carter (ed.), *Territorial Papers,* 13:84.

85. Piernas to O'Reilly, Oct. 31, 1769, in *SRM,* 1:70-71.

Genevieve is no more valid than his careless map of the middle Mississippi Valley.[86]

Christian Schultz, the traveler from New York State who visited Ste. Genevieve in 1808, sneered repeatedly at the religion of the townspeople. Schultz's rationalized Protestant bias oozed from his pen when he ridiculed the religious effigies in the parish church and alleged that the townspeople lived in a state of "the most abject ignorance of every thing either human or divine."[87]

The persistent Anglo-Protestant prejudice against Mississippi Valley French society and culture pervaded the writings of Henry Schoolcraft. Schoolcraft visited the Missouri Territory in 1818 and remarked that "the French constitute a considerable proportion of the whole population, and it is but repeating a common observation to say, that in morality and intelligence they are far inferior to the American population. The French are uniformly members of the Roman Catholic Church." Perhaps such bigotry was an essential part of the confidence required for Americans to conquer the continent.[88]

Piernas, Collot, Schultz, and Schoolcraft were all outsiders, who viewed religion in Ste. Genevieve through the prism of their respective biases. Henry Brackenridge was also an outsider, but he lived in Ste. Genevieve long enough to view the community from the inside and with some sympathy. In good humor, Brackenridge recalled that Madame Bauvais had "felt some repugnance at putting a little heretic into the same bed with her own children." In a more serious vein, Brackenridge termed the townspeople "exemplary Catholics," and in another passage noted they were "very far from being bigoted or superstitious." Father Maxwell, who had traveled wide and far, wrote to Bishop Peñalver in New Orleans and said that Ste. Genevieve had more religion and better morals than any other community in Louisiana. Brackenridge and Maxwell are surely more reliable witnesses about spiritual life in Ste. Genevieve than are Piernas, Collot, Schultz, and Schoolcraft.[89]

The evidence strongly suggests that the people of colonial Ste. Genevieve were good Catholics. They wanted a priest to administer the sacraments, which they deemed necessary for salvation; they

---

86. Collot, *A Journey in North America,* 1:232.

87. Schultz, *Travels,* 61-63.

88. Schoolcraft, *Lead Mines,* 39.

89. Brackenridge, *Recollections,* 26-27; Brackenridge, *Views of Louisiana,* 135; Maxwell to Peñalver, Apr. 22, 1797, UNDA, Diocese of Louisiana, V-1-c, 199-200.

wanted their children raised as Roman Catholics and taught the catechism; they believed in the intercession of the saints on their behalf, especially those saints to whom they felt closest: Ste. Genevieve, St. Joachim, Ste. Anne, and the Virgin Mary; they wanted a parish church, which remained the central edifice in town throughout the entire colonial period. The townspeople of Ste. Genevieve were neither sanctimonious nor self-righteous and they could not abide those attributes in others. In their rough, although apparently justifiable, treatment of several of their priests, the townspeople showed that they had no great reverence for clerics. But, as medieval people demonstrated in their simultaneous building of cathedrals and telling of ribald tales about priests, anti-clericalism is often a touchstone for the most profoundly religious mentalities. The Roman Catholicism in colonial Ste. Genevieve was earthy and robust, and, like that described in François Mauriac's novels set in the French countryside, was rooted in the rhythms of life in an agricultural community. Lieutenant Governor Piernas, a Spaniard who was ignorant of French Canadian culture, simply mistook rusticity and informality in religious practice for neglect of religion.

Chapter XIII
The New Towns:
Nouvelle Ste. Geneviève
and Nouvelle Bourbon

L IFE IN STE GENEVIEVE is no longer continuously influenced by the presence of the Mississippi River. Levees have largely tamed the destructive forces of the river, and commodities and people now move into and out of Ste. Genevieve via road and rails instead of by riverboat. The routine of daily life in modern Ste. Genevieve would not be materially altered if the town were located ten miles inland.

Things were different for colonial Ste. Genevieve, which, more than anything else, was a river town. The Mississippi played a dominant role in shaping Ste. Genevieve's destiny during the eighteenth century. That the town's citizens were largely of French Canadian extraction and spoke French, and that the government was first French and then Spanish, were facts of small consequence compared to the omnipresence of the mighty river, which was both a giver and a taker of life. Like the Nile in Egypt, the Mississippi had deposited rich alluvial soils to support a bountiful agriculture and periodically revivified these soils with spring floods; and, like many great rivers in the preindustrial world, the Mississippi served as an umbilical cord for the towns and cities strung along its course. The great bulk of all goods and people moving into and out of Ste. Genevieve traveled upon the surface of the river.

On the other hand, the Janus-faced Mississippi was the great destructive force in the lives of the townspeople, for the same flood waters that brought fertility to the soil swept away crops, houses, and cattle. Furthermore, the stagnant pools left on the alluvial plain after the flood waters had receded were breeding places for the clouds of mid-summer mosquitos that carried yellow fever and malaria, two of the peskiest diseases in colonial Ste. Genevieve. For the citizens of the town the presence of the river was eternal, essential, and often devastating. Gregory M. Franzwa was astute to begin his brief history of the town with a chapter on the river. The river was responsible for the birth, growth, and death of the Old Town of Ste. Genevieve, and it was responsible for the founding of the New Town.[1]

When the Englishman John Bradbury visited the Mississippi Valley early in the nineteenth century he noticed something unusual about the topography of the valley. In his *Travels in the Interior of America* he remarked that St. Louis "has a decided advantage over any of the other towns, on account of its being situated on a rock, but little elevated above the high floods of the river, and immediately on its border. Such situations are very rare, as the Mississippi is almost universally bounded either by high perpendicular rocks or loose alluvial soil, the latter of which is in continued danger of being washed away by the annual floods. . . ." That then was the problem that the citizens of eighteenth-century Ste. Genevieve faced — how could they locate themselves close enough to the river to utilize it and at the same time protect themselves from its rampaging flood waters. This was a preoccupying issue for the colonial community and the one that prompted the founding of the New Town.[2]

Henry M. Brackenridge visited the upper Mississippi Valley on two occasions, the first time as a schoolboy in Ste. Genevieve during the 1790s and the second time in 1811 as veteran traveler. After the second sojourn, Brackenridge was moved to write *Views of Louisiana,* which was published in 1814. In this book Brackenridge provided the first published history of the two colonial Ste. Genevieves, Old Town and New Town. Brackenridge was a keen observer and possessed a lively awareness of the impact of geography upon human society. In presenting his brief history of Ste. Genevieve he made the following observations:[3]

> It is situated about one mile from the Mississippi, between the two branches of a stream called *Gabourie,* on a flat of about one hundred acres, and something higher than the river bot-

1. Franzwa, *Story of Old Ste. Genevieve.* On malaria and yellow fever, see above, chap. viii.

2. Bradbury, *Travels,* 266.

3. Brackenridge, *Views of Louisiana,* 124-25.

tom. There is a second bank about twenty feet higher than
this, upon which the town begins at present to extend; this is
merely a slip, however, and bounded by a third bank, eighty
feet above the level of the river: there are also scattered houses
for some distance up each branch of the Gabourie. . . . Ste.
Genevieve was formerly built immediately on the Mississippi,
but the washing away of the bank, and the great flood of 1782
(*l' anné des eaux*) [*sic*] caused the inhabitants to choose a higher
situation. The ruins of the old town may be still seen, and
there are several orchards of fine fruit yet remaining.

Brackenridge's account contains the first published version of
the phrase, "l'anné des eaux," year of the waters, although Brackenridge gave the wrong date for the big flood. The well-known
minutes of Theodore Hunt, who was recorder of land titles in the
Ste. Genevieve region in 1825, contain a slightly different version
of the phrase, "l'anné des Grandes Eaux," year of the big waters.
On that occasion, according to Hunt's prize witness, Julien Labrière, the flood waters were so high in the Old Town, some twelve
to fifteen feet deep, that riverboats moored up at chimneys atop
the houses in town.[4]

The signs on many historic houses in Ste. Genevieve, which
proclaim 1784 or 1785 as the date when the houses were built,
erroneously suggest that the New Town arose rapidly in a mere
year or two as a result of *the* big flood. This is too simple a story
of the demise of the Old Town and birth of the New Town, for
births and deaths of human communities rarely occur with such
suddenness. Human beings are too much creatures of habit for
this to happen; a single bad year would not have persuaded many
persons to abandon their homesteads and flee to higher ground
in order to create a new community. Rather, it was the frustration
of being flooded out time and again that finally drove the settlers
out of the Old Town and impelled them to develop the New Town
at Petites Côtes.

It is difficult to say exactly when the Mississippi had cut its way
inland to the point of being a clear and present danger to the Old
Town settlement, for the river works its way against the soil capriciously rather than uniformly and continuously. The earliest
document to deal with this question seems to be a request for a
land grant dating from 1771. Claude Caron, "habitant de Ste.

---

4. Ibid., 127; Hunt's "Minutes," 1825, typescript in MHS. The original of this
valuable document is in the Missouri State Archives in Jefferson City, Missouri.

Geneviève," asked the town authorities, Louis Villars and François Vallé, for a new residential lot in town because his property "close to the Petite Rivière" was being washed away and Caron would soon have to abandon it. Villars and Vallé granted Caron's request and ceded him a new *terrain* further away from the encroaching river but still within the limits of the Old Town. At least four persons were granted town lots upon request during the last week of April 1771, but only Caron specifically adduced erosion by the Mississippi as the basis for his request. Perhaps that reason was so obvious that the other supplicants did not bother to mention it, or perhaps the river was at that time only cutting into the Old Town at isolated points, without presenting a general threat to the settlement.[5]

By 1778 the situation had changed dramatically. In January of that year thirty-five citizens of Ste. Genevieve signed (the illiterate half with their marks) a petition asking permission to relocate "les Clôtures de la Commune," the community fences. This petition began with a terse pronouncement: "The inroads that the Mississippi has recently made against their settlements oblige [the petitioners] to abandon them entirely in order to settle further away." If this statement were to be taken literally and out of context, one might conclude that the petitioners were indeed planning to create a veritable new town in 1778.[6]

This, however, was not the case, for the petition went on to ask only that the fences along the east side of the arable fields be pushed back from the Mississippi in order to make room for new residential development. François Vallé, to whom as *lieutenant particulier* the petition was addressed, clarified the issue with an explanatory note when he forwarded the petition to Lieutenant Governor Cruzat in St. Louis. Vallé explained that there was a need to relocate "part of the town fences in order to facilitate the settlement of persons whose concessions are daily being consumed by the Mississippi, and to provide free passage to the *habitants* and their cattle." The issue was thus to move the fence facing the river back toward the hill-line, creating additional residential property, road space, and communal grazing land at the expense of the arable fields. As the Mississippi cut seriously into the Old Town settlement during the 1770s (the petition speaks of the inroads made *recently* by the river), the first reaction of the townspeople

---

5. SGA, Concessions, no. 19, no. 55, no. 59, no. 97.

6. SGA, Documents, no. 26.

was not to relocate *en masse* and establish a new town but rather
to accommodate themselves piecemeal by converting some of their
abundant plowland into lots for house sites.[7]

By the end of the 1770s the Old Town of Ste. Genevieve was
a mature community, with little or no residential real estate left
for new settlers. The surge of immigrants who had arrived from
the east side of the Mississippi during the 1760s, the encroach-
ments of the river during the 1770s, plus the fact that most of
the bottomland was enclosed for agriculture meant that land for
new homesteaders was virtually non-existent. Thus, when seven
Anglo-Americans petitioned the authorities at Ste. Genevieve for
concessions upon which to settle in 1779, they asked for land on
the Bois Brûlé bottom several miles downriver from the Old Town
itself. It is conceivable that the Anglo-Americans simply did not
wish to mingle with the French-speaking citizens of the Old Town
and therefore chose to settle some miles away. But given the
danger presented at that time by hostile Indians, it seems likely
that the newcomers to the west bank of the Mississippi would have
settled in town if land had been available there. Thomas Tyler
was the only one of these seven petitioners able to sign his name
and he was clearly the leader of the group. Lieutenant Governor
De Leyba granted land to the seven men, but Tyler soon moved
on to settle near the Meramec River.[8]

In 1784, the citizens of the Old Town decided to take the offensive against the Mississippi. Eight syndics elected by the general
assembly of citizens on April 15, 1784 drafted nine articles of
regulations for public works in Ste. Genevieve, and two of the
articles dealt specifically with levees to contain the Mississippi and
protect the town; they were to be erected as soon as possible and
were to be built and maintained at public expense. These were
brave and resolute words as they appear on paper, but the Mississippi was not to be so easily tamed, and the efforts to throw up
effective levees with human muscles and teams of oxen must have
been pitiful indeed. The proposal to build levees in 1784 was a
desperate attempt to preserve the Old Town as a viable community, for the inhabitants would soon abandon the town in droves,
most of them to resettle in the new community called Petites Côtes,
Little Hills. This new settlement — which was located up the Mis-

_____

7. Ibid.; see also Cruzat to Vallé, Feb. 6, 1778, PC 131, in which the lieutenant
governor granted the request.

8. SGA, Concessions, no. 100.

sissippi, across the Big Field from the Old Town, by the forks of Gabouri Creek — was destined to become the New Town of Ste. Genevieve.[9]

Although a succession of floods prompted the townspeople of Ste. Genevieve to begin a new community on higher land, there was one particularly devastating flood, which more than any other provoked an exodus from the Old Town. "The year of the big waters" was 1785, when the flooding Mississippi swept over its banks, across the Big Field, and through the Old Town. The flood waters began to rise in late April and by May 1 they were wreaking havoc. This disastrous springtime flood was especially unfortunate, for the Big Field had already been sown in maize and wheat; virtually the entire crop was lost. On June 6, 1785, Lieutenant Governor Cruzat reported to New Orleans that "the waters have risen so greatly . . . that they have entirely submerged the village of Santa Genoveva. All its inhabitants having been obliged to retire with great haste to the mountains which are one league away from the said village. . . . Although the waters have now fallen, those inhabitants remain along the said coast without yet knowing where they can settle." In point of fact, most of the inhabitants, including the town commandant, Antonio de Oro, returned to live in the Old Town. Nevertheless, the year 1785 was a turning point in the history of colonial Ste. Genevieve, and in the following two years De Oro granted numerous concessions of land near the forks of Gabouri Creek, where the nucleus of New Ste. Genevieve was forming.[10]

Julien Labrière, land recorder Hunt's witness in 1825, stated that "about fifty years ago [1775], the Bank having caved in very much, compelled the Inhabitants to think of removing from the Old Village, and A D One thousand seven hundred and Eighty four three men named Loisel, Maurice Chatillon and Jacque Boyer removed from the old village and established the present village of S'Genevieve. . . ." Labrière's testimony is in rough accord with the source documents: the Old Town was a fully mature settlement by the mid-1770s, but in the mid-1780s erosion by the Mississippi had stimulated the birth of a new settlement, Petites Côtes, later New Ste. Genevieve; and the first persons settled in the new community during 1783-84.[11]

9. SGA, Documents, no. 5.

10. Cruzat to Miró, June 6, 1785, PC 11. There is a mass of correspondence in the PC concerning the great flood of 1785, much of it in legajos 11 and 117.

11. Hunt's "Minutes."

Labrière's recollection was even correct concerning the names of the first settlers. In 1787 one Joseph Loisel requested a concession of agricultural lands "on the hills," and described himself as one who had been "settled for several years at the foot of the hills." Houck stated that the first settlers in the New Town were Jacques Boyer and "one Loisette [obviously Loisel]." If Boyer and Loisel were two of the earliest settlers in the New Town, a strong case can be made for including Chatillon along with them; Jacques Boyer was married to the daughter of Jean-Baptiste Maurice *dit* Chatillon, and this Chatillon sold his house in the Old Town in October 1783. It seems in fact likely that Chatillon was the oldest and earliest of Labrière's first three settlers in the New Town and that he moved to the Petites Côtes along with his daughter and son-in-law Jacques Boyer late the year 1783; their friend Loisel either accompanied them or followed shortly afterward, perhaps not until after the flood of 1784.[12]

We thus see the nucleus of the New Town emerging in much the same manner as had that of the Old Town — a small group of friends and relatives looking for a better place to live and till the land. The catalyst and leading member of this small group in the New Town was probably Jean-Baptiste Maurice *dit* Chatillon, as André Deguire *dit* Larose *père* had been in the Old Town.

It is difficult to trace the history of settlement patterns and land ownership in either of the early Ste. Genevieves. First, many of the original records, land grants and deeds, are missing. And second it is apparent that many of the residents in both the Old Town and the New Town were homesteaders of a sort. That is, their rights to the property upon which they resided were prescriptive and customary rather than written and formal. We have, for example, no official concessions of residential property in the New Town for any one of our three pioneer settlers: Maurice *dit* Chatillon, Jacques Boyer, or Joseph Loisel. Loisel's request for land in 1787 was for "terre," agricultural land, and not for a "terrain" or lot. It was more important to make formal application for agricultural land than for residential land, as is made clear in a property deed of 1792.[13]

---

12. SGA, Concessions, no. 62; Houck, *History of Missouri,* 1:352; SGA, Marriage Contracts, no. 21; SGA, Deeds, no. 427.

13. The procedures for granting of land in and around Ste. Genevieve changed from the French to the Spanish regime and also varied with different officials in St. Louis and Ste. Genevieve. The first land grants at Ste. Genevieve were conveyed during the late 1740s and early 1750s by the then French commandants

In November of that year, Jean-Baptiste Sainte Marie sold a lot and a house in the New Town. The deed of transfer substantiated his ownership of the property by noting that Sainte Marie had purchased it from Jacques Boyer, who had "no concession except the house that he built, . . . which, pursuant to government practice [*usage*] conveys ownership." The building of a residence was a man's claim to his residential property, whereas agricultural land, with no house on it, required a formal concession of ownership. The Spanish government in Louisiana had no statutory homestead law, but Spanish authorities were eager to promote immigration to the colony and had therefore permitted, as this deed of 1792 indicates, a customary homestead usage or practice to develop. It was by this practice that many of the first settlers in the New Town acquired their residential lots.[14]

In any case, by 1787 a firm nucleus for the New Town had been established. In January of that year, six illiterates (Labaux, St. Aubain, Delinel, Bequet, Gravel, and Morisseau), who were described as "habitants residents," resident farmers, of the Petites Côtes district of "this post," i.e. Ste. Genevieve, applied to Commandant Antonio de Oro for a land grant. They asked for 11½ arpents of agricultural land on the south bank of Gabouri Creek facing the Mississippi. The petitioners had been sowing the land for several years, because of "the disaster occasioned by the flooding of the Mississippi." This was a request for plowland on the

---

at Fort de Chartres (KM 55-2-3-1; MHS, Guibourd Collection). During the early phases of the Spanish regime in the Illinois Country, before Spanish authorities arrived in St. Louis, St. Ange de Bellerive, acting commandant in Upper Louisiana, granted land at Ste. Genevieve on his own accord (SGA, Concessions, no. 57). During the 1770s, the military commandants at Ste. Genevieve (Louis Villars and Silvio de Cartabona), in conjunction with *lieutenant particulier* François Vallé I granted land under the authority of Lieutenant Governor Francisco Cruzat (ibid., no. 2). During the late 1780s, town commandant Peyroux de la Coudrenière seems to have had authority to grant land at Ste. Genevieve on his own accord (ibid., no. 92). When in the early 1790s François Vallé II became town commandant, he granted land with the approval of Lieutenant Manuel Pérez (ibid., no. 93), but later Lieutenant Governor Zenon Trudeau gave Vallé the authority to grant land on his own accord (ibid., no. 14). Finally, when Moses Austin asked for an entire square league of land in the lead mining region in 1797, he went directly to Governor General Carondelet with his request (see above, chap. vi). For general accounts of Spanish land grants in Upper Louisiana, see Pelzer, "Spanish Land Grants," 3-37; Violette, "Spanish Land Claims," 167-200.

14. SGA, Deeds, no. 335.

flood plain, but it is apparent that the petitioners had built their residences further up on the hills. In other words, they were some of the first residents of the present town of Ste. Genevieve, which in 1787 was called simply Little Hills.[15]

Seven *habitants* formally objected to their fellow citizens' request for the 11½ arpents of arable land. Their objection claimed that the land was a valuable part of the communal grazing area and should not be granted to individuals. De Oro referred the matter to Lieutenant Governor Cruzat, who decided in favor of the petitioners because they had been tilling the land since 1784 and because it was sound policy to encourage the extension of agriculture.[16]

In April 1787 there was a flurry of land-granting activity as petitioner after petitioner, including Joseph Loisel, requested new agricultural land outside the confines of the Old Town settlement. Much of the requested land was near Gabouri Creek. De Oro and Cruzat granted all of these requests, with the provision that the strips of land, one and one-half to four arpents (one arpent equals about 192 feet) wide, would extend only forty arpents deep. There are no extant records from the mid-1780s for concessions of residential property, *terrains*, either because these documents have disappeared over the years, or because the informal homesteading practice rendered such documents superfluous.[17]

Antonio de Oro was commandant in Ste. Genevieve from the summer of 1784 until the summer of 1787, when he died in the Old Town. He was unlucky enough to govern the community during some of the worst flood years in the town's history, when the Old Town settlement was succumbing to the ravages of the Mississippi. De Oro also presided over the first moves to the New Town by forwarding legitimate requests for land on to Lieutenant Governor Cruzat in St. Louis.

In August 1787 Henri Peyroux de la Coudrenière replaced the dying De Oro as town commandant, and although Peyroux turned out to be a difficult and unsuccessful leader, he had one habit that endears him to historians: he loved to write letters, especially to the governor in New Orleans. Many of these letters have sur-

15. SGA, Concessions, no. 8; Cruzat to De Oro, Feb. 9, 1787, PC 118.

16. Ibid.

17. Ibid., no. 62, no. 77, no. 58a, no. 101, no. 9, no. 2; Cruzat to De Oro, Apr. 14, 1787, PC 118; Cruzat to De Oro, Apr. 25, 1787, ibid.; Cruzat to De Oro, May 18, 1787, ibid.

vived and they are invaluable sources on the history of Ste. Genevieve during the critical transition period 1787-1792; this was the five-year period when the basic move from Old Town to New Town was accomplished.[18]

In March 1788 Peyroux wrote to Governor Miró and painted a bleak picture of the Old Town. The location was abominable, "an infectious marsh, which is undermined daily by the Mississippi. The soldiers' quarters are located on eroding land about one hundred feet from the bank, which places them in the greatest danger. My house is scarcely safer." Peyroux, whose mind was always rich with expedients, advocated moving the settlement to one of two nearby sites:

> One of them is that of the Saline, located one hundred arpents [about 1920 feet] lower than Ste. Genevieve; the other one is that of the Petites Côtes on the road to St. Louis, one league from Ste. Genevieve. The [latter] village is twenty arpents [about 3840 feet] distant from the Mississippi, and situated along a muddy stream [Gabouri Creek]. The other one is placed at the mouth of a river abounding in fish and on a high and solid terrain. This position of the village of Saline along the Mississippi seems to have the advantages necessary to a central point for this district.

For an entire page Peyroux extolled the virtues of the Saline as the best alternative site for the crumbling Old Town.[19]

Peyroux was of course correct to point out that the Old Town's days were numbered, but his advocacy of the Saline was based largely upon self-interst: Peyroux owned an enormous tract of land, a square league, at the mouth of the Saline Creek. Should the Saline become the new administrative center for the Ste. Genevieve District, with Apple Creek as its southern boundary and the Meramec River its northern boundary, Peyroux would instantaneously become the wealthiest man in the district. Peyroux was trying to turn the Old Town's misfortune into a windfall for himself.[20]

The spring flood of 1788 provided Peyroux with an occasion to make his pitch for the Saline more dramatic. He wrote to Miró on April 29:[21]

18. On Peyroux's tenure as town commandant, see above chap. xi.

19. Peyroux to Miró, Mar. 8, 1788, PC 201.

20. Concerning Peyroux's Saline concession, see documents in PC 215 A, including a copy of Peyroux's original concession from Lieutenant Governor Pérez in 1787.

21. Peyroux to Miró, Apr. 29, 1788, PC 201.

I have the honor of writing to you at a critical moment for the village of Ste. Genevieve. The Mississippi is covering the grain and threatens us with an inundation like the one of three years ago. The inhabitants have already sent their cattle to the hills and they fear that they will soon have to abandon their houses. . . .

All of these misfortunes surely support the reasons that I have adduced for Your Lordship in favor of making the village of the Saline the center [*chef lieu*] of this settlement.

The flood of 1788 was not as severe as that of 1785. But Ste. Genevieve's problems were compounded in April when the mill-race of a water mill on South Gabouri Creek washed out and a torrent gushed out onto the Big Field, which had already been sown. When Governor Miró heard about this, he officially granted the "unfortunate citizens" of Ste. Genevieve permission to move their residences from the flood plain up onto the neighboring hills. Meanwhile, Peyroux seized the opportunity presented by the calamity to continue his arguments for development of the Saline.[22]

Peyroux was a clever and ambitious fellow who was moving swiftly and adroitly to create a fiefdom for himself at the Saline, where he would be both commandant and the richest citizen. Spanish administrative correspondence for Louisiana during 1788 shows that Peyroux very nearly succeeded in fulfilling his ambitions. Governor Miró liked and approved Peyroux's plan to move the governmental center of the Ste. Genevieve District to the Saline and he forwarded the plan to Lieutenant Governor Manuel Pérez. Pérez, who had replaced Cruzat at St. Louis in the autumn of 1787, was positively enthusiastic about the idea. The Saline was a better location than the Old Town, which was being carried away by the Mississippi. Moreover, the move would cost the Spanish government nothing because Peyroux had offered to build a new barracks for the small garrison and rent it at the same price being paid in Ste. Genevieve. Old and decrepit Pérez, who had served the Spanish monarchy for nearly forty years, was putty in Peyroux's hands, and at the end of 1788 the latter's plans for the Saline were about to come to fruition. Yet they did not. The settlement at the Saline remained a sleepy and sparsely populated place while a New Town of Ste. Genevieve arose on the hills to take the place of the Old Town as the center of the Ste. Genevieve

22. Ibid.; Miró to Pérez, Sep. 5, 1788, PC 5.

District in Spanish Illinois.[23]

Precisely why Peyroux's plans for the Saline aborted is not clear. There is no evidence that Peyroux or the Spanish officials in St. Louis and New Orleans changed their minds and decided against the Saline. Peyroux's plans were, however, almost certainly opposed by the traditional power elite in Ste. Genevieve. This group was led by the Vallés, who had fought bitterly with Peyroux for years over various issues. As we have seen, François Vallé II was soon to replace Peyroux as town commandant. Just how this group thwarted Peyroux we do not know, perhaps simply by discouraging people from settling at the Saline and urging them to settle elsewhere. François Vallé set an example by moving to the Petites Côtes himself. After all, Peyroux could not establish his administrative center in a vacuum; he had to generate a wave of settlement at the Saline, and this he was never able to do.[24]

The severe flooding of the mid-1780s had stimulated a veritable exodus from the Old Town. The refugees from this flight together with a new wave of immigration from the east side of the Mississippi created a complex of communities by 1790. The Old Town was no longer the undisputed nucleus of the Ste. Genevieve District, but it was not perfectly clear what would replace it: the Saline, the new community of Petites Côtes, or a third choice, which was first described by Peyroux in September 1790. He wrote to Miró that "little by little the inhabitants are building fine settlements on the hills, and I hope that in a few years the diseased marsh of Ste. Genevieve will be uninhabited. A new village has just been founded at a very high spot between the Saline and the village of Gabouri River [i.e. Petites Côtes]. The new village has been named Calvary." Thus was first mentioned the village that would become New Bourbon. After passing reference to Petites Côtes, against which Peyroux had a distinct bias, he went on to speak glowingly of Calvary: "The water is good there, and there is one of the most beautiful views in the world. . . . The habitants . . . have just harvested the finest wheat that is possible to see." Interestingly, this letter of Peyroux's contains no mention of the Saline; perhaps Peyroux had already seen the handwriting on the wall and decided that his big plans of 1788 were doomed to fail after all.[25]

---

23. Miró to Peyroux, Apr. 30, 1788, PC 201; Pérez to Miró, Nov. 15, 1788, *SMV*, 2:260.

24. It is not known precisely when François Vallé II moved from the Old Town to Petites Côtes. Probably it was about 1790.

25. Peyroux to Miró, Sep. 2, 1790, PC 203.

Abbé de St. Pierre, curate of Ste. Genevieve during the early 1790s, provided a detailed picture of the complex of settlements within his parish in 1792. In a letter to the newly-appointed Governor Carondelet in October of that year, St. Pierre claimed that his parish was composed of three villages:[26]

> The first is old Ste. Genevieve, sad remains of the [flood] waters, which consists of a propped up church, an old rectory, miserable quarter for seven and one-half [sic] soldiers. They are without a tambour or a drum, without canon, and without powder, which are necessary in case of an attack in order to call together the eight or ten families that live rather far apart. Half of these are fed up and will move to the new settlement next spring, and the rest are only waiting for the departure of the curate, the government, and the troops. The large numbers of thieves and vagabonds who roam on the other bank [of the Mississippi] have obliged me to remove the sacred vessels from the church, which is located seven arpents [about 1,344 feet] from the barracks and four [about 768 feet] from the closest neighbor. As for myself, I risk being robbed and murdered, which is why I am begging the Reverend Vicar General to move the curate to New Ste. Genevieve. The second [village] is Mont Généreux [later New Bourbon], which village of twenty hearths is very well situated for agriculture and is located only half a league from New Ste. Genevieve; a chain of habitations will join the two of them. The third [village] is therefore New Ste. Genevieve. It is located twelve arpents [about 4,306 feet] from the Mississippi along a small river [Gabouri Creek] that is navigable for a good half of the year; it has an eminence that would be very suitable for a fort and a small garrison capable of defending the entire village against enemy threats. A chapel has been built there to serve until our august king . . . has a church constructed.

This is the only good description we have of the Ste. Genevieve area during the transitional period of the early 1790s, when the Old Town was rapidly disintegrating and the new settlements up on the hills, New Bourbon to-be, and the New Town of Ste. Genevieve were taking shape. St. Pierre was clearly an advocate for the New Town, as Peyroux had been for the Saline, but the future was on St. Pierre's side: within a year from the time he wrote this letter in October 1792, the New Town had become the

26. St. Pierre to Carondelet, Oct. 1, 1792.

seat of government for the Ste. Genevieve District. St. Pierre's letter is also one of the first, perhaps the first, documents to use the appellation "Nouvelle Ste. Geneviève," instead of one of the earlier names: Petites Côtes, Petites Côtes de Ste. Geneviève, village de la rivière Gabourie, or village des Petites Côtes de la fourche [i.e., the forks of Gabouri Creek].[27]

During the second half of 1789, the first burials were performed in the new cemetery at Petites Côtes. This is now the old historic cemetery in Ste. Genevieve. A sure sign that the Old Town was moribund came in February 1793 when François Leclerc's body was exhumed from its grave in the Old Town and reburied in the cemetery of Petites Côtes. Leclerc, who had been the husband of François Vallé's niece, Marie-Louise Vallé, had died in June 1789, but at that time it was not clear that Petites Côtes would be the principal community of the future. Such exhumations and reburials were rare events, and the remains of most of those persons who were buried in the Old Town are either still beneath the soil of the Big Field or have been washed away by the Mississippi.[28]

New Ste. Genevieve and New Bourbon grew apace during the 1790s as the thriving twin towns of the Ste. Genevieve District. They were close together, less than two miles apart according to Abbé St. Pierre, a road (now St. Mary's Road) lined by houses connected them, and they had much in common. Yet they were distinct communities, with their own respective commandants, populations, and identities. One was to die and the other to live, but these different destinies were apparent to no one during the 1790s.

By the early 1790s, two of the pioneer settlers in the New Town — Loisel and Chatillon — had sold and moved on to the new community of Carondelet near St. Louis. But if some persons were leaving New Ste. Genevieve yet more were moving in. Families continued to move up from the Old Town until its final abandonment in 1794. Moreover, new residents were arriving from outside of the community. In the late 1780s and early 1790s there was a second wave of immigration by French creoles from the east side of the Mississippi. The first wave, which took place during the 1760s when the east bank of the river became British, had helped to create the mature Old Town of the early 1780s.

27. Lieutenant Governor Trudeau ordered the town government moved to Petites Côtes in September 1793 (Trudeau to Carondelet, Sep. 16, 1793, PC 27 B).

28. SGPR, Burials, Book 2:11; ibid., p. 20.

The second wave was instrumental in populating the New Town of the 1790s. This immigration occurred in response to the reigning anarchy in American Illinois, which was most crippling between 1786 and 1790.[29]

On the American side of the Mississippi there were marauding Indians and lawless Americans, and there was no effective government to deal with violence and civil disorders. The sometime priest at Ste. Genevieve, Pierre Gibault, wrote from American Kaskaskia that "in Canada all is civilized, here all is barbarous. You are in the midst of justice, here injustice dominates. . . . Wantonness and drunkenness pass here as elegance and amusements quite in style. Breaking of limbs, murder by means of a dagger, sabre, or sword are common, and pistols and guns are but toys in these regions." Indeed, some of the creators of chaos on the American side of the Mississippi moved to Spanish Illinois. The notorious John Dodge, for example, settled near Ste. Genevieve in the late 1780s.[30]

But American sovereignty east of the Mississippi cut in different and contradictory ways in the minds of the creole citizens in American Illinois, for there was fear of too *much* American government as well as fear of too little. Although the American government had shown no capacity to impose law and order in Illinois, there were widespread rumors that it intended to free the black slaves. Thus the French creoles living in American Illinois who did not fear for their lives did fear the loss of their property. Spanish officials on the west side of the river were, of course, pleased to exploit for their own purposes the dismal situation on the east side.[31]

In their quest to populate Upper Louisiana and thereby create a viable and vigorous colony, Spanish officials had persistently looked to the creoles living east of the Mississippi as desirable settlers for Spanish Illinois. In 1778, Governor Bernardo de Gálvez wrote to Spain from New Orleans and said that he had "directed the lieutenant governor of Illinois [Cruzat at that time] to endeavor

29. Houck, *History of Missouri*, 1:386; *SRM*, 2:370, n. 39. On the growth of the Old Town, see above, chap. ii.

30. Gibault to Bishop Briand, June 6, 1786, Alvord (ed.) *Kaskaskia Records*, 542-44. In the autumn of 1788, Lieutenant Governor Pérez (Pérez to Miró, Oct. 12, 1788, PC 14) stated that John Dodge had settled at Ste. Genevieve two and one-half years earlier. Concerning Dodge's activities at that time see Alvord, *The Illinois Country*, 366-68. It has been reckoned (Alvord [ed.], *Cahokia Records*, cxliv) that Kaskaskia lost seventy-seven percent of its French citizens between 1783 and 1790.

31. Alvord (ed.), *Cahokia Records*, cxli.

to increase the population of the settlements committed to his charge, especially with French Canadian families living among the English." When eastern Illinois became American, beginning with George Rogers Clark's capture of Kaskaskia in 1778, the Spanish authorities increased their efforts to draw the creole population from the east side of the Mississippi to the west side. Writing from Kaskaskia in October 1789, John Rice Jones, who moved to Ste. Genevieve early in the American period, said that "every effort is made use of by the Spanish Government to depopulate this side. . . ."[32]

In March 1788 Commandant Henri Peyroux of Ste. Genevieve informed Governor Miró (Gálvez's successor) that "several Catholic families have already left American territory in order to live under the Spanish flag, and a large number of other families are prepared to do so." Two years later, Lieutenant Governor Pérez drafted a special census that enumerated all the immigrants from the east side of the Mississippi who had come to St. Louis and Ste. Genevieve during the period December 1, 1787 to December 31, 1789. The list for Ste. Genevieve included thirteen heads of family, most of whom brought with them their wives, children, and slaves. These families totaled 135 human beings of all categories, which represented a whopping twenty percent increase in the population for the Ste. Genevieve area during the years 1788-89, the very time that the New Town was superseding the Old Town as the metropole of the district.[33]

However, it was not only sheer numbers that made this massive immigration of the late 1780s so important to the future of the New Town, for among the immigrants were men of character and substance. These men — Jean-Baptiste St. Gemme Bauvais, his brother Vital St. Gemme Bauvais, Nicolas Janis (whose daughter Félicité was the wife of Vital Bauvais), and Nicolas Caillot *dit* Lachance — represented an important infusion of new blood into the traditional power elite of Ste. Genevieve. The Bauvais brothers were sons of the late Jean-Baptiste St. Gemme Bauvais *père,* who had immigrated from Canada to Kaskaskia in 1725 and risen to become the wealthiest man in the Illinois Country. Jean-Baptiste

---

32. Bernardo de Gálvez to Joseph de Gálvez, Jan. 27, 1778, SRM, 1:152-53. John Rice Jones to John Hamtramck, Oct. 29, 1789, Alvord (ed.) *Kaskaskia Records,* 515-16.

33. Peyroux to Miró, Mar. 8, 1788, PC 201; Pérez to Miró, Mar. 1, 1790, PC 16; census printed in *SMV,* 2:290.

père had owned land and even maintained a residence in the Old Town, but he had raised his family principally in Kaskaskia. His sons married and began their families there before moving to Ste. Genevieve in 1787. When Jean-Baptiste *fils* crossed the Mississippi with his family to settle in the New Town he brought with him thirty slaves as a measure of his wealth. His daughter, Marie-Louise married Louis Bolduc *fils* in 1797. Vital Bauvais, the younger brother of Jean-Baptiste *fils*, also moved to the New Town, after having established himself temporarily at the Saline. He owned twenty-two black slaves. Vital's son, Vital *fils*, married Thérèse Pratte, daughter of the wealthy Jean-Baptiste Pratte, at Ste. Genevieve in 1798. Nicholas Janis, who was part of the Bauvais clan through his daughter's marriage to Vital Bauvais, was an old man when he moved to the New Town in 1788, but he had owned real estate on the west side of the Mississippi for decades. He was well-to-do, commanding nineteen black slaves. Nicolas Caillot *dit* Lachance was also an old and distinguished citizen of Kaskaskia; serving as both captain of the militia and civil magistrate when he decided to move to the Ste. Genevieve District during the winter of 1787-88. Lachance brought with him fourteen slaves and numerous sons, one of whom was named commissioner of police at Mine-à-Breton (Potosi) in 1801. Finally, there was Jean-Baptiste Laffont, Kaskaskia's surgeon, whom Pérez neglected to include on his list of immigrants. Laffont had assisted George Rogers Clark with his conquest of British Illinois, but then, as so many other creoles, became fed up with the Americans. After moving from Kaskaskia to Vincennes, Laffont finally settled at Ste. Genevieve with his family and a black slave in the spring of 1788.[34]

These five heads of family, all of whom moved to Ste. Genevieve and its environs during the time that the New Town was fast developing, were all wealthy and had all been prominent citizens of Kaskaskia. They preferred to live out their lives under Spanish Catholic rule rather than in the turbulent young American republic. Their departure from the east bank of the Mississippi was a big loss for Kaskaskia but a boon for the New Town of Ste. Genevieve, which thus acquired both wealth and leadership during a critical juncture in its development. And once again we see the reoccurring pattern of French Canadian families moving to new locations as tightly knit groups of friends and relatives.

---

34. Ibid.; on Laffont, see Alvord (ed.), *Kaskaskia Records*, xxx; Alvord, *The Illinois Country*, 328; Miró to Peyroux, Sep. 6, 1788, PC 201.

When in March 1788 Commandant Peyroux informed Governor Miró about the substantial immigration from the east side of the Mississippi, Miró was delighted. He replied to Peyroux that "the new French families from the American side moving to our side pleases me. I have given Monsieur Pérez [lieutenant governor in St. Louis] orders to admit American families as well." Miró's order to Pérez reveals the sharp anxiety of Spanish authorities that they could not hold the colony of Louisiana if they did not succeed in attracting new immigrants, for the admission of Americans to Spanish Illinois raised serious problems for the Spaniards. The issue of American immigration to Spanish Illinois was entangled with complex military, diplomatic, and religious matters dealt with elsewhere in this book. It is sufficient to remark here that Spanish officials attempted a compromise by encouraging Americans to move to the west side of the Mississippi but also encouraging them to become good Roman Catholics.[35]

In the early 1790s, at the same time that some Americans began to arrive in the Ste. Genevieve District, a smaller and more exotic group also came to settle on the hills above the Big Field and along the banks of Gabouri Creek. This group consisted of *émigrés* who came to the Illinois Country in flight from the French Revolution. These persons were not numerous but they were influential, and they helped to create the towns of New Ste. Genevieve and New Bourbon as they existed at the end of the colonial period. The creoles and French Canadians of the Illinois Country had a traditional caste of mind and a reputation for being sound royalists. The criticisms of absolute, divine-right monarchy that circulated in the Paris of the Enlightenment did not find sympathetic ears in a community like Ste. Genevieve, where virtually no one read books. Why should not French *émigrés* find an expatriot refuge in French-speaking Spanish Illinois?

The most prominent of the French royalist *émigrés* to settle in the Ste. Genevieve District during the 1790s was Chevalier Pierre Charles de Hault Delassus de Luzieres. He arrived in the Illinois Country in the spring of 1793 and became the leader of the fledgling settlement on the hills above the Old Town. This he christened New Bourbon in honor of the dynasty that had just been bloodily removed from the throne of France but which continued to rule

---

35. Peyroux to Miró, Mar. 8, 1788, PC 201; Miró to Peyroux, Apr. 30, 1788, ibid. On the issue of religion and American immigration to Spanish Illinois, see below, chap. xiv.

Spain. De Luzières' son, Charles Delassus, was appointed commandant at New Madrid in 1796 and in 1799 became lieutenant governor in St. Louis, replacing Zenon Trudeau. The most conspicuous French émigré to settle in Ste. Genevieve proper was the
young Breton gentleman, Augustin-Charles Frémon de Laurière,
who possessed the impeccable royalist credentials of having fought
in the anti-Revolutionary army of the Vendée. As we have seen,
Frémon was for a time headmaster of an elementary school in
Ste. Genevieve and also served for several years as town *greffier*,
clerk. He later moved on to St. Louis, but during his more than
ten years in Ste. Genevieve Frémon was perhaps the most learned
person in town.[36]

It is a curious fact that those far-off political upheavals, the
American and French Revolutions, had much to do with the development of the Ste. Genevieve District during the 1790s. The
first created conditions on the east side of the Mississippi that
impelled the creole settlers there to seek sanctuary across the river,
and the second forced Frenchmen who had never dreamt of emi-
grating to America to flee the blade of the guillotine and wind up
in royalist Spanish Illinois. Although French-speaking and under
the Spanish flag, the Ste. Genevieve District of the 1790s had
something quintessentially American about it — it was a home for
political refugees looking to escape violence and oppression.

Population figures from the eighteenth century must be taken
with a grain of salt, but the Spanish censuses for Ste. Genevieve
and New Bourbon from 1772 to 1799 are revealing even if they
are not entirely accurate. The following figures are inclusive, com-
prehending whites, blacks, and mulattoes, free and slave, adults
and children:[37]

```
1772 . . . . .  691 for the Old Town
1779 . . . . .  698 for the Old Town
1787 . . . . .  670 for the Old Town and Petites Côtes
1791 . . . . .  923 for the Old Town and Petites Côtes
1795 . . . . .  849 for New Ste. Genevieve
                153 for New Bourbon
```

---

36. For an introduction to the De Luzières family, see McDermott, "Diary of
Charles de Hault de Lassus," 359-69; on Frémon de Laurière, see above, chap. ix.

37. Census of 1772, *SRM*, 1:53; census of 1779, PC 193 A; census of 1787,
MHS, archives; census of 1791, *SRM*, 2:365-68; census of 1795, *SRM*, 1:323-36;
census of 1796, *SRM*, 2:140-41; census of 1800, *SRM*, 1:facing 414.

1796 . . . . . 773 for New Ste. Genevieve
383 for the New Bourbon District
(including the Saline)
1800 . . . . 1,163 for New Ste. Genevieve
630 for the New Bourbon District

A number of important facts are apparent from these figures, approximate though they are: the Old Town was more or less stagnant during the 1770s and throughout most of the 1780s. In the late 1780s, with increasing chaos on the American side of the Mississippi and the foundation of the settlement of Petites Côtes, population began to rise. Indeed, the period 1787-91 was a time of veritable demographic boom, based largely upon massive migration from the east side of the Mississippi. In the mid-1790s, after the founding of New Bourbon in 1793, the population of the Ste. Genevieve District as a whole continued to grow, although De Luzières' settlement of New Bourbon siphoned off some numbers from New Ste. Genevieve. Then, following Governor Carondelet's decision to liberalize immigration policy for Spanish Louisiana in 1796, there was a surge of Anglo-Americans into both the Ste. Genevieve and New Bourbon Districts. Although New Ste. Genevieve and New Bourbon were closely associated communities, they were distinct entities with their own respective governments, and they shall be examined in turn.

It was first called New Ste. Genevieve in 1792, and by 1793 that had become the standard appellation, replacing such earlier names as Petites Côtes. The New Town grew with its nucleus between the north and south branches of Gabouri Creek, where the center of town still lies. Many of the first residences were strung out along South Gabouri Creek and the road running from the Old Town north to St. Louis. This road, now St. Mary's Road and Main Street, was called La Grande Rue during the late eighteenth and early nineteenth centuries and was clearly the most important street in the New Town. Indeed, it was the only street to be dignified with a particular name, the others being referred to as, "a cross street," of "the street that goes to the church," or "the street that separates so-and-so's lot from so-and-so's lot." Roads radiated from the center of the New Town down to the Mississippi, south to the Saline via New Bourbon, to the Old Town where there was still an important river port, north to St. Louis via Little Rock Landing, and west to Mine-à-Breton. All roads were unimproved and often impassable, and the Mississippi River remained over-whelmingly the town's most important means of communication with the outside world. The river was the fastest and easiest avenue of direct contact with St. Louis, New Orleans, and the United States. Ste. Genevieve was linked to the east bank of the Mississippi by ferries that docked at Little Rock Landing, just north of town, and at the Old Town landing, just south of the New Town.[38]

The appellation "New Town" suggests rationality and planning. This was not true in the case of Nouvelle Ste. Geneviève. Paradox-ically, in its early phases the New Town of Ste. Genevieve grew in a more helter-skelter and ad hoc fashion than had the Old Town. François Saucier, the royal French engineer who had worked on the stone Fort de Chartres, laid out the Old Town according to a rational plan in the early 1750s. And surveyors from Nouvelle Chartres and Kaskaskia, such as Jean-Baptiste Bar-rois, measured off town lots and agricultural fields in toises and arpents. Although the New Town eventually (probably by 1795) had a public square to serve as a municipal focal point, its early development was organic and unplanned. There was no *arpenteur* (surveyor) at all in town until Antoine Soulard arrived in February 1794 to help plan the fort that was built on the hill overlooking South Gabouri Creek, and the New Town grew without the aid of trained engineers. Although measurements of some sort were obviously made, the amateurish quality of the work is still apparent in the street grid of the nucleus of Ste. Genevieve: none of the streets is quite straight; none of the corners quite a right angle; and none of the city blocks precisely the same size as any other. These characteristics convey a bit of Old Worldly charm to the present city.[39]

The official transfer of civil, military, and religious authority from the Old Town to the New was a complex affair that revolved around a threat of foreign invasion and the difficult personality of Henri Peyroux, who was officially town commandant in 1793.

---

38. The parish priest, Abbé St. Pierre, may have been the first person to use (St. Pierre to Carondelet?, Oct. 1, 1792, PC 206) the name "Nouvelle Ste. Geneviève." From Little Rock Landing, the main route north crossed the Missis-sippi, proceeded up to Cahokia, and then recrossed the river to St. Louis.

39. On the early planning of the Old Town, see above, chap. ii. Soulard himself claimed that he arrived in Ste. Genevieve to help with the fort (Soulard to Gayoso, Dec. 15, 1797, PC 213), but there is no evidence that he did other surveying while in town. In its unplanned quality, the New Town of Ste. Genevieve differed from other Spanish colonial towns (see Crouch, *Spanish City Planning*).

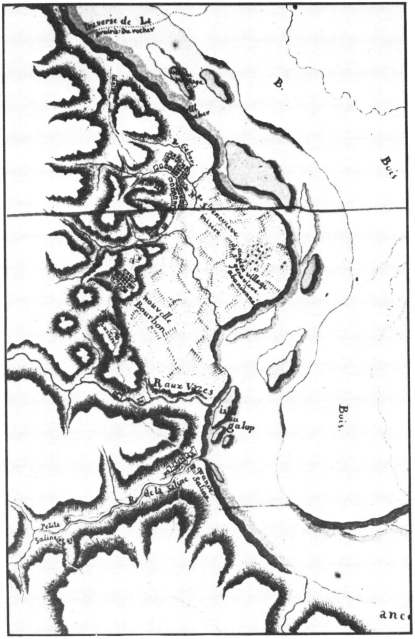

Detail of the Nicolas de Finiels map (1797), showing the Ste. Genevieve region. The Old Town, "ancient village," is shown as abandoned. Looking closely at the New Town, "Nouvelle Ste. Geneviève," one can discern the town square, the row of houses leading toward "Nouvelle Bourbon," and the fort on the hill above the town.

On April 14, 1793, Governor Carondelet posted orders in New Orleans for Lieutenant Governor Trudeau in St. Louis. Trudeau was told to relocate Ste. Genevieve, moving the commandant's residence (sometimes called "la chambre du gouvernement"), the parish church, and the rectory from the Old Town to the New. There is no doubt that by 1793 the New Town was the major locus of population in the Ste. Genevieve District; the Old Town, the Saline, and New Bourbon were secondary centers.[40]

Indeed, much of what Governor Carondelet ordered on April 14 had already occurred *de facto*. Abbé St. Pierre, the parish priest, had purchased a residence in the New Town in December 1792 and thus the rectory was no longer in the Old Town. In March 1793, St. Pierre, with Trudeau's permission, had removed the holy vessels and ornaments from the church in the Old Town to the chapel in the New Town, which seems to have been built in the late 1780s. At about the same time, late winter or early spring 1793, Trudeau also moved the garrison up to the New Town to protect the bulk of the region's citizens from possible attack either by Osages or "bandits from the Cumberland [i.e., Tennessee]." Because François Vallé already lived in the New Town and was acting commandant, Carondelet's order to move the commandant's residence was in a sense superfluous. Yet the governor's orders of April 14 were significant for two issues, the building of a new parish church and the disposition of the eccentric Peyroux, who returned to Ste. Genevieve as commandant in July 1793.[41]

Peyroux still lived in the Old Town and he was adamantly opposed to recognizing the New Town by moving the government and the church there. He wrote to Governor Carondelet in July 1793 and accused St. Pierre of engineering the move to the New Town simply because the priest had purchased a residence there. Peyroux, as it turned out, badly misjudged his opposition, for virtually everyone of substance was against him — St. Pierre to be sure, but also the Vallés, Lieutenant Governor Trudeau, and Governor Carondelet. The issue of where the commandant of Ste. Genevieve would live — Old Town or New Town — was resolved definitively when François Vallé II replaced Peyroux as commandant early in 1794. Henceforth New Ste. Genevieve was *the* Ste.

---

40. Lieutenant Governor Trudeau received the governor's orders in September and put them into effect (Trudeau to Carondelet, Sep. 16, 1793, PC 27 B).

41. SGA, Deeds, no. 312; St. Pierre to Carondelet, May 29, 1793, PC 208 A; Trudeau to Carondelet, Aug. 18, 1793, PC 2363.

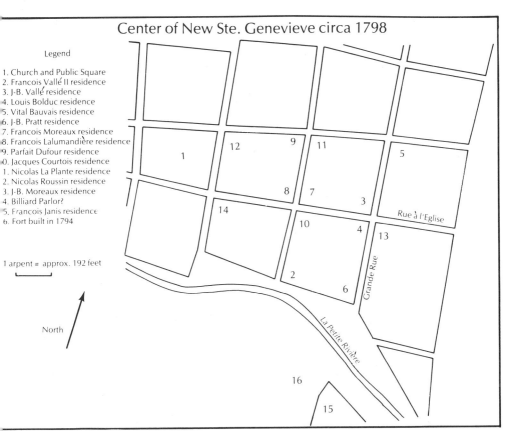

Center of New Ste. Genevieve circa 1798

Legend

1. Church and Public Square
2. Francois Vallé II residence
3. J-B. Vallé residence
4. Louis Bolduc residence
5. Vital Bauvais residence
6. J-B. Pratt residence
7. Francois Moreaux residence
8. Francois Lalumandière residence
9. Parfait Dufour residence
10. Jacques Courtois residence
11. Nicolas La Plante residence
12. Nicolas Roussin residence
13. J-B. Moreaux residence
14. Billiard Parlor?
15. Francois Janis residence
16. Fort built in 1794

1 arpent = approx. 192 feet

North

Genevieve.[42]

The orders that Carondelet dispatched to Trudeau from New Orleans in April seem to have arrived in St. Louis either in late August or early September, for on September 7, 1793 Trudeau betook himself to Ste. Genevieve to deal in person with the issue of where and how a new parish church would be built. Significantly, Trudeau traveled directly from St. Louis to New Ste. Genevieve and called an assembly of all the citizens in the presence of "the Reverend Father St. Pierre, curate of the parish," and François and Jean-Baptiste Vallé, "officiers in the militia." Trudeau pointedly shunned and eschewed Peyroux and the Old Town, although he spent an entire week in New Ste. Genevieve. This visit by the lieutenant governor was both practical and symbolic and placed the weight of the Spanish government squarely behind the New Town and its new commandant-to-be, François Vallé II. Although Peyroux technically clung to his position as commandant for another six months, he was effectively emasculated by Trudeau's visit to Ste. Genevieve during the second week

42. Peyroux to Carondelet, July 12, 1793, PC 208 B. On the Peyroux-Vallé struggle for leadership in Ste. Genevieve, see above, chap. xi.

in September 1793.[43]

Building a new church turned out to be a more difficult task than ousting Peyroux from office and moving the government to the New Town. At the assembly of citizens convened by Trudeau in September 1793, Nicolas Caillot *dit* Lachance, Jean-Baptiste Pratte, and Louis Bolduc *père* were chosen by a plurality of voices as syndics to oversee the building of a new church. Their principal function as syndics in this case was to make an equitable assignment of the labor and materials that each citizen would contribute to the effort. The syndics failed in their first effort. There was sharp disagreement within the community both about the location of the new church and about fair apportionment of the labor and materials for its construction. By the summer of 1794 no church had been built and at least one lawsuit flared up when Augustin Bertau insisted that he had been assigned too large a share of labor and materials for the building. From the bitterness of the dispute, it is apparent that the litigious urge of many of Ste. Genevieve's citizens was not tempered by the holy nature of the undertaking at hand. Trudeau had to make a second trip to Ste. Genevieve, in August 1794, before all of the disputes were resolved and construction of the church could begin.[44]

Seventeen ninety-four was a big year for construction in the New Town. The new church was erected in the autumn of the year, and the fort had been built during the preceding spring. Apparently it was easier to get the citizens to agree on contributing labor and materials for the protection of their skins than for the salvation of their souls. The fort was built on the hill just south of South Gabouri Creek as can be seen on the Finiels map. It may have housed the small Spanish garrison in town, but it never saw military action, and by 1804 it was in a shambles, a decaying vestige of Spanish power in the upper Mississippi Valley.

For the purpose of writing sound history — as well as out of concern for historic preservation, restoration, and educated tourism — there must be some attempt to assign accurate dates of construction to the existing colonial houses in Ste. Genevieve. This sort of dating requires the most detailed and painstaking research in source documents as well as expert analysis of surviving structures. Some of this has been done, and more is being con-

43. SGA, Documents, no. 33.

44. Ibid., Documents, no. 33, no. 34; ibid., Litigations, no. 25; Trudeau to Carondelet, Sep. 1, 1794, PC 197.

View of Ste. Genevieve about 1840. Some of the large lots, houses, and picket fences of the colonial period are still discernible in this view. Notice the smoke stacks of the steamboat docked at Little Rock Landing. Photo courtesy of the Missouri Historical Society of St. Louis.

ducted at this time. For the present, one must be content with several general observations and criticisms without pretending to offer precise dates for the historic buildings.[45]

The dates that have been assigned to many of the historic houses are too early by from five to as much as twenty years. Most of the famous remaining houses — Vallé, Bolduc, Bauvais, Guibourd — belonged to leading families of colonial Ste. Genevieve. But the records make it clear that the leading families of town did *not* lead the migration from the Old Town to the New Town in the wake of the bad floods of 1784 and 1785. The first persons to move to the forks of the Gabouri or to Petites Côtes were from lesser families: Boyer, Chatillon, Loisel, Ratte, Gravel, Lacombe, Roussin, Delinel. None of their residences seem to have survived.

François Vallé II received a two-arpent grant of land in the village of Ste. Genevieve from Antonio de Oro, but the precise date of the grant is not known. De Oro was replaced by Peyroux as town commandant in August 1787, and therefore it is possible that this grant to Vallé was in the New Town. It is even conceivable

---

45. A team of investigators from the University of Missouri- Columbia, led by Professor Osmund Overby, is trying to date the historic houses in Ste. Genevieve.

that François Vallé had built a residence in the New Town and moved there by 1787. But if he had, it is curious that when Jean Datchurut's house was auctioned off in the Old Town in March, 1790 Vallé bid on it. It seems more likely that Vallé moved to the New Town in 1790 or 1791, at which time he probably built the house on the north side of Gabouri Creek that still stands, although much altered.[46]

Jean-Baptiste Vallé, François's younger brother, bought his sister's share in their father's (François Vallé I) house in the Old Town in October 1785, which suggests that Jean-Baptiste was probably living in the "paternal house" at that time. Jean-Baptiste also bid, much higher than his brother, on Datchurut's house in the Old Town in 1790. Once again, a good guess would be that Jean-Baptiste left the Old Town and built the nucleus of the present Jean-Baptiste Vallé House in the New Town during the early 1790s.[47]

When residents of Ste. Genevieve were moving to the New Town, they sometimes salvaged components from structures in the Old Town and reused them. Vertical-log buildings, which contained large but relatively few components fixed together with pegs, lent themselves to such salvaging projects. Occasionally, entire structures were disassembled, moved, and reassembled. In 1774, for example, a house was dismantled near Fort de Chartres, transported in pieces down the Mississippi, and re-erected at Ste. Genevieve. And in 1789 Lieutenant Governor Pérez reported that the residents of Ste. Genevieve had decided to "move their houses to the foot of the hills."[48]

The house of Louis Bolduc *père* because of its splendid restoration generates much speculation. Extant records, unfortunately, do not present many leads as to when it was originally built. It has been repeatedly suggested that the Bolduc House was first erected in the Old Town and then disassembled and moved to the New. This is surely incorrect. The house that Louis Bolduc had built at the Old Town in 1770 (the building contract survives) had different dimensions than the house that now stands in Ste. Genevieve. Perhaps Bolduc utilized some components from his Old-Town house when he built in the New Town. However, that

---

46. *American State Papers, Public Lands*, 3:323; SGA, Estates, no. 78.

47. Ibid.; SGA, Deeds, no. 122.

48. Pedro Piernas to François Vallé, Apr. 22, 1774, PC 189 A; Pérez to Miró, May 1, 1789, PC 15 A.

house was about twenty years old when Bolduc moved and had been subjected to repeated flooding. It is questionable how much of Bolduc's 1770 residence was worth salvaging. It seems likely that the restored Bolduc House was first built about 1790 and was made very largely of newly cut components.[49]

Vital St. Gemme Bauvais apparently gathered up his family and slaves and left Kaskaskia toward the end of 1787, which was a time of vicious anarchy on the American side of the Mississippi. According to Peyroux de la Coudrenière, who was then commandant in Ste. Genevieve, Vital Bauvais first settled at the Saline. He did not remain there long, however, and soon moved on to New Ste. Genevieve. Not long thereafter, he built the house that still stands, though much altered, on Main Street. The Vital Bauvais House is one of only three remaining houses built in the *poteaux-en-terre* manner and is clearly one of the oldest structures in Ste. Genevieve.[50]

In 1793, town commandant Peyroux, remarked that "the two villages, New Bourbon and New Ste. Genevieve, are joined by a row of houses. . . ." That row of residences, clearly shown on Finiels' map of 1797-98, was located along the road that ran south from Gabouri Creek toward New Bourbon just below the bluff line. The route is today delineated by St. Mary's Road and U.S. Highway 61. There is still an impressive scattering of historic structures along the west side of St. Mary's Road, and several of these were perhaps there when Peyroux observed the row of houses in 1793. Beginning near Gabouri Creek and proceeding south on St. Mary's Road, these historic structures are, in order: the Janis-Zeigler House (Green Tree Tavern); the Amoureaux House; the Bequette-Ribault House; and the Pierre Dorlac House. All four of these houses have walls of vertical logs in the French creole style, and all of them date from the colonial era or shortly thereafter.[51]

The handsome Guibourd House is a transitional monument for the history of architecture in old Ste. Genevieve. This house was

---

49. SGA, Contracts, no. 5.

50. On Mar. 8, 1788, town commandant Peyroux de la Coudrenière reported (Peyroux to Miró, PC 201) that Vital Bauvais had left Kaskaskia to settle at the Saline. When Vital moved on to the New Town has not been established.

51. Peyroux to Miró, Sep. 10, 1793, PC 208 B. Dendro dating by Richard P. Guyette and Osmund Overby (personal communication, Osmund Overby) suggests that the Bequette-Ribault House was built ca. 1808.

the first major residence built in Ste. Genevieve under American sovereignty. Jacques Guibourd arrived in the upper Mississippi Valley in 1799 as a refugee from the slave rebellion on St. Domingue. Because of his wealth, breeding, and education he was quickly welcomed into the power elite in Ste. Genevieve. In June 1799 Commandant François Vallé II accorded him a large grant of land near the parish church. This grant probably constituted the entire city block upon which the Guibourd House now stands. But Guibourd did not immediately erect a house on the property. Guibourd and his family needed a place to live, and they bought a house from Jean-Baptiste Vallé in February 1800. It was probably while living in this house that Jacques Guibourd proceeded with the construction of a new residence on his near the parish church. This edifice, the well-known Guibourd House, seems to have been completed only in the autumn of 1806, at which time the Guibourds sold the house they had purchased from Vallé in 1800. There is no shred of evidence that the Guibourd House was moved to its present site from an earlier location. The original roof of the house was hipped in pure creole fashion, and the style was later altered with the addition of gabled ends.[52]

The historic houses of Ste. Genevieve are an architectural heritage of the first importance. Nothing is served by trumping up artificially early dates in order to promote the houses. These finely wrought structures do not need that kind of puffery.

In 1797, François Vallé II remarked that because "the *habitants* of my two posts [i.e., Ste. Genevieve and New Bourbon] have the same interests and occupations, everything that is advantageous for one is likewise for the other." Regarding New Bourbon, Ste. Genevieve's sister village of the 1790s, there is both more data and less data. Except for the undoubted archaeological riches that shall one day be exploited, there are no physical remains of the once flourishing village. On the other hand, we have the marvelously detailed and comprehensive census that De Luzières compiled for New Bourbon in 1797, of which there is no equivalent for Ste. Genevieve.[53]

New Bourbon was located on the "grandes côtes" directly above

---

52. SGA, Concessions, no. 35, no. 70; Ste. Genevieve Deed Book A:122-24; Peterson, "Early Ste. Genevieve," 231-32.

53. Vallé to Gayoso, Dec. 2, 1797, PC 214; New Bourbon census of 1797, PC 2365.

The Amoureaux House on St. Mary's Road. This poteaux-en-terre *house is one of the oldest structures in Ste. Genevieve and originally had a hipped roof. Its present gabled roof reflects one of the stylistic changes that occurred in domestic architecture in Ste. Genevieve during the nineteenth century.*

the Big Field, in contrast to Ste. Genevieve, which was located on the "petites côtes" along Gabouri Creek. New Bourbon-to-be was established as an embryo community in the mid-1780s for the same reasons as New Ste. Genevieve: repeated flooding of the Old Town, a favorable birth rate within the creole population, and heavy immigration across the Mississippi from the American side. The village on the "grandes côtes" was first called Calvary in memory of Christ's death; then "Mont Généreaux," Generous Mountain, in recognition of the fertile fields that surrounded the settlement; and finally, as will be seen, Nouvelle Bourbon.[54]

The settlement on the high hills would have amounted to little worthy of mention had it not been for the French Revolution and the flight to America of Pierre-Charles de Lassus de Luzières. His first home in America was in the United States, at Pittsburgh, which because of its site at the commencement of the Ohio River was a jumping off point for Upper Louisiana. While at Pittsburgh, De Luzières developed a plan to bring one hundred French families from Gallipolis (City of the French) on the Ohio, who

54. Peyroux to Miró, Sep. 2, 1790, PC 203.

had been duped in a land development scheme, to the Illinois Country for resettlement.[55]

De Luzières first visited Ste. Genevieve in 1792. He reconnoitered the area and probably boarded with François Vallé, who was serving as interim commandant while Peyroux was absent on a trip to Philadelphia. Little is known about this first visit, but by the spring of 1793 De Luzières was in New Orleans laying out grandiose plans to Governor Carondelet. De Luzières and his colleagues decided to name the new community New Bourbon in honor of the Bourbon king of France who had recently lost his head on the guillotine: "We desire that the principal town of the new colony may be dedicated to the memory of the unfortunate Louis XVI, under the name of Nouvelle Bourbon." Incidentally, a Bourbon king, Charles IV, still ruled in Spain.[56]

De Luzières correspondence while he was in New Orleans in the spring of 1793 reveals the grand plans he had for the fledgling settlement that was perched on the hills above the Big Field. De Luzières would take his family to the Illinois Country; he would bring large numbers of immigrants, both from Gallipolis and directly from Revolution-wracked France; he would exploit the rich agricultural lands of the Illinois Country with the help of "the productive method of agriculture used in . . . the province of Hainaut [Flanders]"; he would develop the lead mines and build water mills; he would bring in a doctor and a new midwife from Gallipolis. In brief, De Luzières, a French aristocrat, was planning to descend upon the sleepy, illiterate, backward Ste. Genevieve District, and shake it to its very teeth with an ambitious program of modernization.[57]

It is a curious spectacle to see this counter-revolutionary aristocrat laying out a program of enlightenment and self-improvement that would have had the hardy approval of all of the Revolutionary leaders in France. De Luzières would soon discover, to his deep

---

55. McDermott, "Diary of Charles de Hault de Lassus," 360-61.

56. De Luzières et al. to Carondelet, Apr. 17, 1793, *SRM*, 1:392.

57. Some of the correspondence concerning the plans for settling New Bourbon is available in *SRM*, 1:359-95; see also De Luzières to Carondelet, May 1, 1793, PC 214. The land upon which the town of New Bourbon was erected had belonged to François Vallé and then to John and Israel Dodge (De Luzières to Carondelet, Apr. 30, 1793, PC 214; SGA, Documents, no. 23). A University of Missouri research team believes that it has discovered De Luzières' residence just under the bluffs south of Ste. Genevieve (personal communication, Osmund Overby).

The Janis-Zeigler House (Green Tree Tavern) as it looks today. This house was built be Nicolas Janis ca. 1790.

chagrin, that the basic structures of human existence — which are determined by traditions, geography, and climate — do not readily lend themselves to molding by visionaries on either side of the Atlantic. Revolutionaries in France would learn the same thing at about the same time.

De Luzières left New Orleans in May 1793 and arrived in the Ste. Genevieve District in August of that year. When Lieutenant Governor Trudeau made his momentous visit to Ste. Genevieve in early September 1793, he met De Luzières and was favorably impressed by him as "a virtuous man." Trudeau also pitied him, for De Luzières was laid low with either yellow fever or malaria, those debilitating diseases of the early Mississippi Valley. Rumors were already circulating that De Luzières had expired, and Trudeau was afraid that his family might arrive only to find him dead.[58]

De Luzières overcame his first bout with river-valley fevers, however, and his extended family — including his wife, two sons, a pregnant daughter, a son-in-law, and servants — arrived at New Bourbon in February 1794 via the Ohio and Mississippi rivers.

58. Trudeau to Carondelet, Sep. 28, 1793, PC 208 A.

Sometime later, Moses Austin described his visit to the De Luzières household at New Bourbon:[59]

> One Mile from St Genevieve Down the River is a Small Village Called New Bourbon of about 20 Houses. At this place, I was Introduced to The Chevaleer Pierre Charles De Hault De Lassus, a French Nobleman Formerly of the Council of the late King of France. . . . Madame De Lassus did not appear to support the Change of Situation so well as the Chevalier. I was examining a larg Piece of painting, which was in Madame De Lassus Bed Chamber, representing a grand Festival given by the citizens of Paras, . . . on the birth of the Dauphin and a Parade of all the Nobles on the same Occation. She came to me and putting her finger on the Picture pointing out a Coach There said, . . . my situation is now strangly Chang'd.

There is something chilling about Madame de Luzières' understatement that her situation in New Bourbon was "strangely Chang'd" from that which it had been in Paris. It almost seems that the flight from revolution — which had taken Madame de Luzières from Paris to Pittsburgh to New Bourbon — had induced a culture shock making madame slightly daft. As Moses Austin's curiosity in her painting demonstrates, the canvas that Madame de Luzières had lugged across the Atlantic Ocean and halfway across North America was a strange apparition on the trans-Mississippian frontier. Perhaps madame kept body and soul together by fixing her attention upon that precious relic of a lifestyle shattered.

Pierre-Charles de Luzières was destined to live out his mortal days in his new settlement, dying at New Bourbon as a reluctant American in 1806. De Luzières' remains rest in the historic Ste. Genevieve cemetery. His oldest son, Charles de Hault Delassus, served effectively as the last Spanish lieutenant governor (1799-1804) in St. Louis, and his son-in-law, Pierre Derbigny, moved to New Orleans and later served briefly as governor of the State of Louisiana.

Throughout the 1790s, De Luzières sent out a stream of lengthy missives from his residence in New Bourbon. A man with his background was obviously isolated and lonely on the upper Mississippi Valley frontier, and he consoled himself with epistolary

---

59. François Vallé to Trudeau, Feb. 14, 1794, PC 209; Garrison (ed.), "A Memorandum of Moses Austin's Journey," 541-42.

The Jean-Baptiste Vallé House as it looks today, after having been altered several times during the nineteenth century. Vallé, who was appointed American commandant of Ste. Genevieve in 1804, built this house in the New Town at the corner of La Grande Rue and Rue à l'Eglise.

exercises. De Luzières' letters from New Bourbon consist of a virtually unbroken jeremiad. He complained of "violent and stubborn fevers," crops destroyed by floods, backward technology, lack of medical facilities, pesky Indians, and an unsympathetic Spanish bureaucracy. De Luzières was by nature neither a hypochondriac nor a complainer. His problems on the frontier were real and persistent, and, on balance, he must be admired for his tenacity in coping with them.[60]

There were occasional bright spots for De Luzières in Spanish Illinois. His oldest son, Charles de Hault Delassus, rose swiftly in the Spanish colonial service. The Mississippi obligingly stayed within its banks during the spring of 1795, and in June of that year De Luzières predicted a harvest of wheat and maize the likes of which the Illinois Country had not seen in thirty years. And in the spring of 1798 the New Bourbon area produced 8,000 livres worth of "very fine" maple syrup. In 1797, Governor Carondelet, in a parting gesture to his old acquaintance and countryman

60. De Luzières to Carondelet, Sep. 1, 1794, PC 210; De Luzières to Carondelet, June 12, 1797, PC 214; De Luzières to Carondelet, Sep. 21, 1797, ibid.; De Luzières to Gayoso, Jan. 7, 1798, PC 215 A; De Luzières, "Observations . . ." attached to the New Bourbon census of 1797, PC 2365.

(Carondelet was also from Flanders) as he left the governorship of Spanish Louisiana, created a separate jurisdiction for New Bourbon and made De Luzières civil and military commander. Henceforth, his name would be: Don Pierre-Charles de Hault, Seigneur de Lassus, de St. Vrain, and de Luzières, Chevalier de Grand Croix de l'Ordre Royal de St. Michel, Captain and Civil and Military Commandant of New Bourbon. Quixotically, as European aristocrats lost their power and wealth their names became more grandiose. This was a strange handle with which to be saddled for a frontiersman in the American West.[61]

The administrative district of New Bourbon, as created by Governor Carondelet in 1797 and given to De Luzières to command, was a large swath of territory located between the Ste. Genevieve District to the north and the Cape Girardeau District to the south. De Luzières claimed that three-fourths of the population in his district lived not in New Bourbon as such but rather on the Saline and Aux Vases rivers and on the Bois Brûlé bottom lands along the Mississippi. These settlements were in fact at least as far removed from the village of New Bourbon as was New Ste. Genevieve. The only real explanation for Carondelet's creation of a New Bourbon District separate from the Ste. Genevieve District was, as Trudeau put it in a report of 1798, "in order to give its command to Monsieur de Luzières." In any case, this study is concerned with the village and not the district of New Bourbon.[62]

New Bourbon was located "a small league" (about three miles) south of New Ste. Genevieve and at a slighter higher elevation on the "grandes côtes" above the Big Field. In 1793, Peyroux de la Coudreniere deprecatingly remarked that "this hamlet is located very high up and the view from there is charming. But a fine view is not enough to create a great settlement." Peyroux's prediction was ultimately borne out. From the village of New Bourbon roads ran north to Ste. Genevieve, south to the Saline, and east over the Big Field and past the remains of the Old Town to the Mississippi, some two miles distant.[63]

---

61. De Luzières to Carondelet, June 9, 1795, PC 211; De Luzières to Gayoso, Mar. 6, 1798, PC 2371; Carondelet to François Vallé, May 31, 1797, PC 214; De Luzières to Carondelet, Sep. 21, 1797, ibid. For De Luzières' full titles, see "Contributions patriotiques," 1799, PC 216 B.

62. De Luzières to Carondelet, Sep. 21, 1797, PC 214; New Bourbon census of 1797, PC 2365; Trudeau's report of 1798, *SRM*, 2:248. The New Bourbon District was abolished by the Americans, Carter (ed.), *Territorial Papers*, 13:51-52.

63. Peyroux to Carondelet, Nov. 14, 1793, PC 207 B.

The Guibourd House as it looks today, after having been much altered. When it was built ca. 1806 it had the distinctive hipped roof popular in colonial Louisiana.

Early nineteenth-century plat maps show the village limits of New Bourbon and reveal Father James Maxwell's large adjacent land holdings. Because there are no visible physical remains of the village and no good contemporary descriptions of it, it is impossible at this time to describe the village with any accuracy. A chapel was planned for New Bourbon in 1794, but the plan probably never came to fruition. When in 1797 Governor Carondelet turned New Bourbon into the seat of government for the New Bourbon District, De Luzières commented that he would have to establish a place for public assemblies that would have a bulletin board to post ordinances and other public announcements. Thus New Bourbon probably had some sort of a town square or village commons. In 1795, Pierre-Charles Peyroux, Henri's brother, drafted a will and in which he left a building site at New Bourbon for a hospital, and also donated all of his medicines and medical books to the envisioned establishment. The hospital was of course never built, and no one knows what became of Pierre Peyroux's medical library.[64]

Far and away the most valuable document available for studying colonial New Bourbon is the census that De Luzières compiled in November 1797. This census comprehended the entire district, including Bois Brûlé and the Saline, but the following data are for the village of New Bourbon only:[65]

Heads of Household in New Bourbon

Name	Nationality	Religion	Occupation
Pierre-Charles De Luzières	French	Catholic	Commandant
André Deguire [III]	Creole	Catholic	Agriculturalist
Israel Dodge	American	Catholic	Agriculturalist
Widow John Dodge	American	Protestant	Agriculturalist
Job Westover	American	Protestant	Agriculturalist
Joseph Fenwick	American	Catholic	Agriculturalist
George Hamilton	American	Catholic	Agriculturalist
Nicolas Caillot *dit* Lachance	French	Catholic	Carpenter
Baptiste Lachance	Creole	Catholic	Agriculturalist
François Lachance	Creole	Catholic	Agriculturalist
Antoine Lachance	Creole	Catholic	Agriculturalist
Gabriel Lachance	Creole	Catholic	Agriculturalist
Joseph Lachance	Creole	Catholic	Agriculturalist
Gabriel Nicole	Creole	Catholic	Agriculturalist
Widow Thibault	Creole	Catholic	Agriculturalist
Thomas Madden	Irish	Anglican [not quite Protestant]	Surveyor and Agriculturalist
Paul Deguire	Creole	Catholic	Agriculturalist
Louis Tonnellier	French	Catholic	Agriculturalist
Pierre Chevalier	Creole	Catholic	Agriculturalist
Alexis Griffard	Canadian	Catholic	Saltmaker
Joseph Tissereau	Canadian	Catholic	Agriculturalist
Etienne Gouvereau	Creole	Catholic	Agriculturalist
François Simoneau	Canadian	Catholic	Agriculturalist
Widow Bernier	Canadian	Catholic	Agriculturalist
François Bernier	Canadian	Catholic	Agriculturalist

64. Trudeau to Carondelet, Apr. 24, 1794, PC 28; De Luzières to Carondelet, June 12, 1797, PC 212; De Luzières to Carondelet, Sep. 21, 1797, PC 214; SGA, Wills, no. 38.

65. New Bourbon census of 1797, PC 2365.

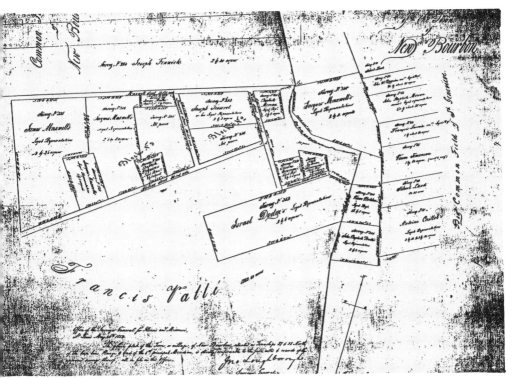

Plat map of New Bourbon in the early nineteenth century. Notice large tracts of land owned by "Françis Vallé" and "James Maxwell's legal representatives." Father Maxwell was the parish priest of Ste. Genevieve, 1797-1814. Photo courtesy of the Missouri Historical Society of St. Louis.

Widow Belmar	Creole	Catholic	Agriculturalist
Louis Lacombe	Creole	Catholic	Agriculturalist
Jerome Métis	Creole	Catholic	Agriculturalist
Charles Aimé	Creole	Catholic	Agriculturalist
John Bives	American	Catholic	Agriculturalist
François Portugais	Portuguese	Catholic	Agriculturalist
Louis Julien	Canadian	Catholic	Agriculturalist
François Lacroix	Canadian	Catholic	Agriculturalist
Joseph Perdot	Creole	Catholic	Agriculturalist
Joseph Montmirel	Canadian	Catholic	Agriculturalist
Jacob Weiser	German	Protestant	Miller
David Montgomery	American	Protestant	Blacksmith

The total population of the village of New Bourbon was 270 persons, adults and children, whites and blacks, free and slave. There were eighty-three black slaves, including men, women, and children. Joseph Fenwick of Kentucky, the father of Doctor Walter Fenwick, was the largest slaveholder, owning sixteen blacks. The thirty-eight heads of family came from diverse regions, but the majority were from the Illinois Country. Grouped by place of origin, they numbered as follows: sixteen French creoles, nine French Canadians, seven Americans, three French, one Irish, one German, and one Portuguese. New Bourbon obviously had a higher percentage of Americans than did Ste. Genevieve. The single Portuguese was a former soldier from the Spanish garrison. Many heads-of-household at New Bourbon in 1797 are familiar as former residents of Ste. Genevieve: André Deguire III, Louis Tonnellier, Alexis Griffard, Etienne Gouvereau, François Simoneau, François Bernier, Louis Lacombe, Charles Aimé, and François Lacroix all moved to New Bourbon from neighboring Ste. Genevieve.

A variety of occupations were represented, but the overwhelmingly majority of New Bourbon's citizens were "cultivateurs." De Luzières used that word rather than the ambiguous *habitants* (meaning either citizen or farmer) to designate planters and farmers. It is apparent that New Bourbon, to an even greater extent than Ste. Genevieve, was an agricultural community.[66]

The detailed census of 1797 brings the New Bourbon of that year close to one's senses: the community of farmers, millers, carpenters, blacksmiths, and slaves comes vividly alive. But by 1806 its leader, Pierre-Charles de Luziéres, had died and been buried in a plot that was a long way from his native Flanders. And within fifty years the entire community had disappeared, the people having either emigrated or died and the buildings crumbled. It would be a worthy project in historical archaeology to locate and excavate the old New Bourbon town site, for beneath the soil on the hill with the fine view of the Mississippi Valley lies a time capsule of life on the river frontier in colonial times.[67]

The New Town of Ste. Genevieve can be distinguished from the Old Town in a number of important ways: first, it did not cling precariously to the bank of the Mississippi, for it was located a mile inland and upon ground about twenty-five feet higher. This location was certainly healthier than the swampy site of the

---

66. Vallé to Gayoso, Dec. 2, 1797, PC 214.

67. De Luzières died in December 1806 (SGPR, Burials, Book 2:79) and his wife died in July of that year (ibid., 78). They were both buried in the New Town cemetery.

Old Town. By the end of the colonial era the New Town had a larger population than the Old Town had ever had. And this larger population was more diverse — in ethnic background, in religion, in vocations — and was better educated. The New Town had an armed fort, which though never used in defense, gave the residents of the community some measure of psychological security that the residents of the Old Town had never had. Because of increased river traffic and a network of roads, primitive though they were, the New Town was more open to the outside world and its influences — economic, cultural, and political — than the Old Town had been.

Architecturally there was little to distinguish the two colonial Ste. Genevieves: the houses in both were for the most part relatively small, built of vertical posts, roofed with wooden shingles, and situated on large, fence-enclosed lots. The New Town had a town square, the Place de l'Eglise, that the Old Town had not had, but in both towns the parish church was the focal point of community life.

During the late 1780s, there were acrimonious disputes about where Nouvelle Ste. Geneviève would be located. But about one thing there was no disagreement — there *would be* a new Ste. Genevieve. The move from the Old Town to the New Town was significant because it signaled the resolve of the townspeople to maintain a community and a parish in that particular region of the Mississippi Valley. The river had repeatedly demonstrated its capacity to wreak havoc with any settlement located upon the flood plain. But by the 1780s, Ste. Genevieve had enough tradition, strength of purpose, and identity not to be eradicated by destructive flood waters. In their determination to maintain their community, the townspeople successfully rebuilt Ste. Genevieve on higher ground. The citizens of neighboring Kaskaskia lacked that determination, and their town was destined to be swallowed up by the rapacious river.

Chapter XIV
Conclusion: Changing Times

IT IS COMMON HISTORICAL KNOWLEDGE that modern Western civilization is a product of a long period of gestation going back to the ancient and medieval worlds, and that certain catalytic developments during the Early Modern Period (1500-1815) brought about its birth. These stimulating developments are customarily labeled Renaissance, Reformation, Scientific Revolution, Enlightenment, Agricultural Revolution, Industrial Revolution, and French Revolution. By 1815 all of the basic structures of modernity — intellectual, religious, scientific, economic, social, and political — were in place, and Western history since 1815 has simply been the elaboration of these structures. The colonial town of Ste. Genevieve was overwhelmingly a premodern society, but in the decade preceding the Louisiana Purchase. This community was being wrenched toward modernity. This proposition can be examined briefly from several different perspectives.

Demography

All of the classic aspects of a premodern society characterized birth and death in colonial Ste. Genevieve. There was little or no contraception; repeated pregnancies for fecund couples; high rates of infant and child mortality; and short life spans, especially in women. In all of these respects, life in colonial Ste. Genevieve was not substantially different from life in medieval France, or from that in many third-world countries today.

Economy

The economy of colonial Ste. Genevieve was largely agricultural and depended heavily upon slave labor. Moreover, the system of exploiting the soil practiced by the creole habitants was primitive and inefficient. This was partly because the rich soil of the Big Field permitted inefficiency and partly because the *habitants* were ignorant of innovations in agriculture that were being introduced in some places in Europe during the eighteenth century. The *habitants* had no knowledge of sophisticated crop rotation, no knowledge of nitrogen-fixing crops like clover, and employed only heavy medieval-style plows. And once the cereal grains — overwhelmingly maize and wheat — were harvested, the grain was milled largely with horse mills, the technology of which went back to the Babylonians. Some small water mills were in use, but apparently no windmills.

Ste. Genevieve's commercial contacts with the outside world, maintained largely through New Orleans, were dominated by the mercantile policies of France and Spain. Thus Ste. Genevieve assumed a classical colonial position, exporting raw materials and importing finished products. Looms and weavers, for example, did not exist in town because it was a colonial community's obligation to purchase manufactured cloth from the mother country.

Religion

During most of the colonial history of Ste. Genevieve the religious ideas and practices of the townspeople were entirely traditional. They were conventional Roman Catholics, who would not have been able to describe a Protestant, although they had perhaps heard of such creatures. Ste. Genevieve's first priests were all Jesuits. But the townspeople probably knew nothing of the Catholic Reformation, from which the Jesuit order had sprung, and surely knew nothing about the heated Jesuit-Jansenist debate that was rending the French Catholic Church at that time. Deism, the religion of eighteenth-century intellectuals, was altogether foreign to colonial Ste. Genevieve, and atheism was not in the townspeople's vocabularies. Although their marriages were performed in accordance with the decrees of the Council of Trent, the citizens of Ste. Genevieve had certainly not heard of the assembly that created the modern Roman Catholic Church. Until a scattering of American Protestants arrived in the 1790s, religion in colonial Ste. Genevieve was for all intents and purposes medieval in conscience and practice.

Mentalities

The townspeople of colonial Ste. Genevieve were oblivious of the intellectual and cultural movements that brought about the modern world: they had not heard of the Renaissance; the Copernican-Newtonian revolution in science; or the Enlightenment, which was in full bloom in Paris at the time that Ste. Genevieve was founded. The overwhelming majority of townspeople thought that the sun revolved around the earth and that the Mississippi River flowed to the Gulf of Mexico because the waters of the river had an irresistible desire to join with those of the ocean.

In more mundane ways the mental structures of the Ste. Genevieve townspeople were also premodern. Their sense of orientation in time and space was different than ours. As Robert Mandrou has pointed out, time and space are "constructions of the human mind, efforts of man." The townspeople construed time and space differently than twentieth-century man. Issues about which we demand great precision and specificity were of little consequence to them. People today know their exact ages and the ages of those close to us — family, friends, and relatives. But in 1783 when Pélagie Vallé petitioned for custody of her daughter, the best she could do was identify her as "about ten years old" (she was in fact nine years old). Nowadays, should a mother make such a plea in a divorce court, the judge would immediately declare her an unfit parent. The numerous inaccuracies in the detailed Ste. Genevieve census of 1787 make it clear that neither census-taker nor citizens cared a fig about precise records.[1]

Various and sundry visitors passed through Ste. Genevieve and remarked in their writings about the founding of the town. These writings reveal that by the end of the colonial era the townspeople did not have the faintest idea when their community had been established. Lieutenant Governor Trudeau reported that Ste. Genevieve had been founded sometime in the 1730s, while Captain Amos Stoddard wrote that the town had been founded "soon after the peace of 1763." Unaware that future scholars would lavish much time on their community, the townspeople were blithely forgetful about epochal events in their past.[2]

Even the exact year of *the* great flood, *l'année des grandes eaus,*

---

1. Mandrou, *Introduction à la France moderne,* 92; concerning the Vallé custody case, see above, chap. vi.

2. Trudeau's report of 1798, *SRM,* 2:248; Stoddard, *Sketches,* 215.

was apparently soon forgotten by Ste. Genevieve's citizens. Both Perrin du Lac and Brackenridge, for example, placed the great flood in 1782 instead of 1785. A general lack of concern with precise data plus an overwhelmingly oral tradition meant that even landmark dates were fuzzy in the townspeople's memories. The French general, Georges-Victor Collot, remarked about the creole inhabitants of the Illinois Country that "they have even forgotten the regular division of the months, and of time itself, according to the calculations of civilization. If you ask them when a particular event happened, they will answer, that it was when the waters were high, when the strawberries were ripe, or in the corn and potato season."[3]

If the citizens of colonial Ste. Genevieve had only a blurred sense of their place in time, their sense of their place in space was also impressionistic, relative and imprecise. The streets in neither the Old Town nor the New Town were named (except for the Grande Rue), and the houses not numbered. Pieces of real estate were not located absolutely in a geographical framework with fixed reference points. Overwhelmingly, lots were identified relative to so-and-so's land, and as real estate changed hands and persons died the situation became complex and confused. The citizens viewed their community organically and in detail rather than in absolute abstract terms.

Government

Although a few persons in Ste. Genevieve must have occasionally wondered about the republican political system in the United States, which they had in fact helped to create by aiding the American revolutionaries, government in the colonial town was old-fashioned and traditional. Ste. Genevieve was an appendage of an absolute, divine right monarchy that had no interest in civil liberties or inalienable rights and that ruled through a heirarchical chain of command that brooked no interference. This was true despite the fact that some issues of urgent local importance — the fencing around the Big Field for example — were often handled more or less democratically in assemblies of the *habitants*. Such assemblies were of course convened at the pleasure of the royal bureaucracy and were not matters of rights inherent in the people.[4]

---

3. Perrin du Lac, *Voyage*, 167; Brackenridge, *Views of Louisiana*, 126; Collot, *Journey in North America*, 1:232-33.

4. Concerning community assemblies, see above, chap. xi.

Society

Of all aspects of life in colonial Ste. Genevieve, the social structure was the most modern. Although society was to some extent hierarchically ordered, and there were large numbers of slaves, the structure of society was not rigid: there were no hereditary castes as in Asia, nor even any estates (clergy, nobility, and commoners) as in metropolitan France. The Vallé men were called by the Spanish aristocratic title, *don*, and were in a sense the local *seigneurs*. But in more American than European fashion, it was their wealth and ability that made them powerful and not their bloodline. If somehow the Vallé family fortune had been destroyed, and the family members been unable to recoup it, the Vallé family would have shriveled into insignificance almost immediately. When, for example, Charles Vallé destroyed with debauchery his fortune and his capacities, he became a broken man and was obliged to leave the community in disgrace. His family name could not save him.

And for some persons, even for slaves, there was social mobility. Pierre Viriat was a rough and ready lead miner who through skill and industry had made some money. He freed his female black slave, Roddé Christi, and married her in 1801, and virtually the entire power elite of Ste. Genevieve turned out for the ceremony. This, to be sure, was an unusual case: the traditional economy of Ste. Genevieve did not lend itself to rapid economic advancement, and few freed slaves married their ex-masters. Nonetheless, the Viriat case is instructive because it demonstrates the possibilities for advancement in the society of the colonial town. In this regard the trans-Mississippian frontier of Spanish Illinois was perhaps more American than America in the late eighteenth century, for the residents of Ste. Genevieve were largely free of caste, class, or racial stereotypes.[5]

Anglo-American immigration to Louisiana, which began in earnest following the American Revolution, wrought profound changes in the Illinois Country. The imminent historian of early Illinois, Clarence Walworth Alvord, remarked that "the occupation of the great Mississippi valley by men of English speech was the most important event in the history of the United States and

---

5. The Viriat-Christi marriage is dealt with above, chap. vii.

one of the most momentous in the history of humanity." Spanish attitudes about this momentous event were complex and vacillating during the 1780s and '90s. Much of the vacillation centered upon religious issues, for Anglo-American settlers were likely to be Protestants, and Spaniards tried more diligently than any other people in the eighteenth century to do their duty to the God of their Catholic Church and to their king, whose title was "His Most Catholic Majesty."[6]

Governor O'Reilly 1769-70 had attempted to expel Protestants from Louisiana, although at that time there were but few Protestants in the colony. Under Miró (1784-91), religious policy in Louisiana, which bore directly on the issue of American immigration, was liberalized. Protestant churches, Protestant worship services, and Protestant preachers remained outlaws, but persons were not *compelled* to become Roman Catholics. In November 1789, fourteen Americans swore allegiance to "His Catholic Majesty," the king of Spain, but the text of the oath contained nothing about religion as such. A kind of *de facto* liberty of conscience thus prevailed in Miró's Louisiana. And during the last years of Miró's administration a significant number of Americans settled in the Genevieve region, if not in the New Town itself.[7]

But the issue of American immigration to Louisiana caught Spanish colonial officials on the horns of a dilemma: populate the colony or lose it to enemy attack and internal atrophy; populate the colony with Americans and run the risk of losing it to cultural submersion or political and religious subversion. From the Spanish point of view it was therefore best to try to find immigrants of European stock to settle in Louisiana. This idea prompted the commandant of Ste. Genevieve, Peyroux de la Coudrenière, to go to Philadelphia in 1792. Peyroux hoped that from Philadelphia he could make contact with Frenchmen, especially Acadians who had resettled in France, whom he would persuade to emigrate to Spanish Louisiana.[8]

Peyroux did manage to send some Frenchmen to Lower Louisiana, but Governor Carondelet was not pleased with the sort

---

6. Alvord, *The Illinois Country*, 414.

7. Concerning Governor Miro's policies, see Burson, *The Stewardship of Don Esteban Miro;* oath printed in *SRM*, 1:319-20.

8. On Peyroux's trip to Philadelphia, see above, chap. xi. Peyroux had been active in the 1770s and 1780s recruiting Acadians to settle in Louisiana (Winzerling, *Acadian Odyssey*, chap. viii).

of immigrants that Peyroux had recruited. In September 1792 Carondelet wrote to Peyroux, who was still in Philadelphia: "Of all the settlers you have sent me, very few are appropriate for bolstering the population of this colony, which has need for farmers and useful workers but not for actors, wigmakers, musicians etc., who are for the most part persons of bad morals." Whatever the quality of Peyroux's French settlers, political events in Europe soon aborted Peyroux's mission to Philadelphia. Peyroux himself acknowledged that once the French Revolutionary government had executed Louis XVI (January 1793) and provoked a war with Bourbon Spain, large-scale emigration from France to Spanish Louisiana was impossible. Only a handful of French royalist *émigrés*, like Delassus de Luzières, came to Louisiana during the mid-1790s.[9]

In August 1793, Jacques Clamorgan, the well-known entrepreneur from St. Louis who often did business in Ste. Genevieve, wrote Governor Carondelet an interesting memorandum on the subject of Louisiana and its population. Clamorgan's basic point was that the colony desperately needed people, especially agriculturalists, in proportion to its vast area, but that immigrants should be of continental European stock. Above all, Clamorgan wanted to attract German farmers to Louisiana, for the Germans who had settled during the 1720s at the famous Côtes des Allemands in Lower Louisiana had proven exemplary colonists. Clamorgan did not want Louisiana populated with Americans because he correctly foresaw that demographic and economic changes precipitate political changes; a Louisiana inhabited by Americans would soon be absorbed by the United States. This prospect Clamorgan found odious. Clamorgan's proposal was, however, premature, for the massive German immigration to North America did not begin until the 1830s. On the other hand, hordes of Americans were already in the Mississippi Valley by the mid-1790s.[10]

By 1793 there were perhaps a dozen Americans living in Ste. Genevieve and its environs who had taken oaths of loyalty to the king of Spain. The most important of these were the Dodge brothers, John and Israel, who were welcomed in Spanish Illinois even though they were known as troublemakers in American Il-

---

9. Carondelet to Peyroux, Sep. 24, 1792, PC 205; Peyroux to Carondelet, Nov. 14, 1793, PC 207 B.

10. Clamorgan to Carondelet, Oct. 4, 1793, *SMV*, 3:208-211; see Carondelet's favorable reply to Clamorgan, July 22, 1794, *ASP, Public Lands*, 8:234.

linois. The Dodge brothers soon settled at New Bourbon, which had a higher percentage of Americans than Ste. Genevieve proper.[11]

Carondelet, who became governor general of Spanish Louisiana in 1792, had profound reservations about permitting Anglo-Americans to settle in the colony. When the governor received news that a group of Americans had settled without official permission on the Meramec (Big) River some twelve leagues from Ste. Genevieve, he ordered Lieutenant Governor Trudeau to root them out before they seized any land. It is not known what happened on this occasion, but Carondelet told Trudeau that, if necessary, he should call in some Indians to harass the American settlers.[12]

As late as November 1794, when Carondelet drafted his well-known military report on Louisiana, the governor expressed serious anxiety about the coming Americans, "a new and vigorous people, hostile to all subjection, advancing and multiplying . . . with a prodigious rapidity." But Pinckney's Treaty (October 27, 1795) gave Americans unfettered access to the Mississippi; and in 1796 Carondelet, who, according to Thomas Jefferson, "had once seen the folly of settling the Goths at the gates of Rome," began positively to encourage Americans to settle in Spanish Louisiana by promising them large grants of land. Of course Carondelet did not want ne'er-do-wells settling in his colony, and he threatened Commandant François Vallé with a 500-piastre fine should he permit anyone who was not "a good worker and honest person" to settle in the Ste. Genevieve District. Vallé replied that he was doing his best to keep all the "vagabonds" out and that he was accepting "Catholics and well-to-do persons, especially those owning negros." Vallé felt obliged to observe, however, "the increase of population and the mixture of nations make it more difficult to maintain good order." Commandant Vallé, who knew at first hand the aggressive and lawless Americans pushing into Spanish Illinois, must have raised his eyes to heaven over Carondelet's naïveté. The Americans, including Goths and Protestants, were arriving in numbers.[13]

The Vallés did not like the arrival of masses of Americans in

---

11. The New Bourbon census of 1797 (PC2365) provides a place of origin for each resident listed. Concerning John Dodge's exploits at Kaskaskia, see Alvord, *The Illinois Country*, 362-72.

12. Carondelet to Trudeau, June 8, 1792, PC 18.

13. Carondelet's "Military Report," Nov. 24, 1794, Robertson (ed.), *Louisiana*

Spanish Illinois any more than anyone else, for the newcomers threatened to destroy a culture and way of life within which the Vallé family had prospered. But the Vallés had not risen to prominence by burying their heads in sand and ignoring facts of life. And plain facts of life for the Ste. Genevieve District in the 1790s were that an energetic American republic existed just across the Mississippi and that many Americans were immigrating to the west side of the river. Perhaps no one could have predicted with certainty as early as 1796 that Spanish Illinois was on the verge of becoming American territory, but François Vallé II had a strong suspicion that this would soon occur. He prepared his family for this eventuality by sending his son and namesake, seventeen-year-old François Vallé III, to New York to study the language of the Americans.

In September 1796, Delassus de Luzières remarked that "Monsieur Clamorgan is charged with conducting to the United States of America the only [surviving] son of Monsieur François Vallé, our brave commandant of Ste. Genevieve; he will place him in one of the best colleges to learn there the English language." Vallé may not have liked Americans very much, but in 1796 he was already betting on them to win the North American sweepstakes, which had as its prize the vast territory of Louisiana. In June 1797 Commandant Vallé heard that his son had arrived safely in New York City. There François III began to prepare himself to lead his family into the American era of Ste. Genevieve's history.[14]

François Vallé II claimed that the population of the Ste. Genevieve District nearly doubled during the first half of 1797, and in June of that year he requested an English interpreter in order to deal more effectively with the newly arrived Americans. Moses Austin, who was one of the immigrants that arrived from the United States in 1797, later wrote that "the commencement of the American emigration may be dated back from the Fall of '96 and the Spring of '97." The comments of Vallé and Austin may not be precisely accurate, but it is a matter of historical fact that masses of Americans settled in Spanish Illinois during 1796-97.[15]

Under the Rule of Spain, France, and the United States, 1:297; Whitaker, *The Spanish-American Frontier,* 103; Carondelet to Vallé, June 1, 1796, PC 214; Vallé to Carondelet, Nov. 10, 1796, PC 212 A.

14. De Luzières to Carondelet, Sep. 29, 1796, PC 48; Vallé to Carondelet, June 23, 1797, PC 214.

15. Vallé to Carondelet, June 7, 1797, PC 214; Barker (ed.), *Austin Papers,* vol. 2, pt. 1:115.

In August 1797, Gayoso de Lemos succeeded Carondelet as governor general of Spanish Louisiana, and Gayoso moved quickly to restrict American immigration to Spanish Louisiana. In September 1797, Gayoso dispatched to the commandants of all settlements in Louisiana "Instructions . . . Relative to the Admission of New Colonists." Probably more for political than religious reasons as such, Gayoso wanted Spanish Illinois to become uniformly Roman Catholic. Article 7 of his instructions forbade the admittance of non-Catholics to Illinois, and Article 6 decreed that children of non-Catholics already settled in Illinois absolutely had to be raised as Roman Catholics. Protestant settlers found Article 6 especially autocratic and odious.[21]

Serious and loyal men in Spanish Illinois, including Lieutenant Governor Trudeau, objected to these articles on the grounds that they were difficult to enforce and, if they could be enforced, would have a baleful impact upon the colony. Gayoso stuck to his policy of discriminating against Protestant settlers, however, and his orders slowed down American immigration into the Ste. Genevieve region for several years. In 1798 Trudeau even claimed that some wealthy Protestant settlers in Spanish Illinois had for religious reasons moved back to the east side of the Mississippi. When John Matthews of North Carolina settled at New Bourbon in 1800, he not only swore loyalty to the king of Spain, he also proclaimed that he and his entire family were Roman Catholics. For Gayoso, Roman Catholicism implied political loyalty.[17]

Despite the influx of Anglo-Americans into Spanish Illinois during the 1790s, Ste. Genevieve proper remained largely ethnic French at that time. The Americans tended to settle in the New Bourbon District, at the Saline, in the valleys of the Big and Meramec rivers, at Plattin Creek, and at Mine à Breton. A comparison of the 1796 civil census of the *town* of Ste. Genevieve with the census that Abbé St. Pierre took of the entire *parish* the same year reveals that already the outlying areas had almost as many white and black residents as did the town itself: the town contained 772 persons and the parish 1,214, excluding Indians whom St. Pierre also tabulated.[18]

---

16. Gayoso's regulations arrived in Ste. Genevieve in the spring of 1798, SGA, Documents, no. 13.

17. Trudeau to Gayoso, Aug. 23, 1798, BL; James Mackay to Gayoso, Nov. 28, 1798, PC 2365; Trudeau's report of 1798, *SRM*, 2:256; SGA, Documents, no. 82.

18. Census of 1796, *SRM*, 2:141-42; St. Pierre to Bishop Peñalver, Sep. 30,

When Captain Amos Stoddard arrived to take command of Upper Louisiana for the United States Government in 1804, he estimated the population of the Ste. Genevieve District (within which Stoddard included the New Bourbon District) to be 2,350 white persons. This was not a casual estimate, for Stoddard used the Spanish census of 1800 and then added the estimated increase between 1800 and 1804. The census of 1800 showed 1,326 whites in the Ste. Genevieve and New Bourbon districts, which means that Stoddard reckoned that approximately 1,000 additional white persons arrived, or were produced by a favorable birth/death ratio, in the area between 1800 and 1804. If François Vallé was more or less correct when in 1797 he remarked that the population of the Ste. Genevieve District had nearly doubled during the first six months of 1797; if we assume that most of the immigrants, both in 1797 and between 1800 and 1804, were Americans, which was probably true; and if we take the census figures from 1800 as roughly accurate for 1797, we can suggest that at the time of the Louisiana Purchase about seventy-one percent of the white persons in the Ste. Genevieve District were Americans. This percentage is likely a bit low, for between 1797 and 1800 some Americans settled in the area despite Gayoso's religious restrictions. In any case, by 1804 a clear majority of the population in the Ste. Genevieve District (not in the town itself) was American.[19]

Many, of the profound changes that Ste. Genevieve experienced during the last decade of the colonial era were related to the demographic transformation taking place at that time in Upper Louisiana. The arrival in the Ste. Genevieve and New Bourbon Districts of large numbers of Americans spread human habitation to many areas beyond the two principal villages, and indeed created a third village — Mine à Breton.

Lieutenant Governor Trudeau remarked in 1798, that the influx of Americans to Spanish Illinois had important qualitative as well as quantitative consequences, for the Americans brought with them improved agriculture and technology. They sowed their

1796, UNDA, New Orleans Diocesan Collection, IV-5-1.

19. Stoddard, *Sketches*, 217; census of 1800, *SRM*, 1:facing 414. Stoddard's figures as presented here were based upon a Ste. Genevieve District with the Meramec River as a northern boundary. In another place, Stoddard used Plattin Creek as a northern boundary, thus reducing the population of the district; see Carter (ed.), *Territorial Papers*, 13:18.

crops on the uplands instead of merely on the Mississippi flood plain, and they built better mills; the Dodge mill on Dodge Creek was one of these. As we have seen, Moses Austin, originally a Connecticut Yankee, also revolutionized the lead mining industry at the end of the colonial period.[20]

Most of the American immigrants to Spanish Illinois were Protestants, which created greater religious diversity in the region and served to educate the creole inhabitants: all Christians were not necessarily Roman Catholics. The Protestants did not have their own church in town until well into the nineteenth century and had to be married by the local Catholic priests. By 1799, Father Jacques Maxwell was marrying in the Ste. Genevieve District more Protestant or mixed couples than Roman Catholic couples.[21]

The Anglo-Americans were also generally more literate than the native *habitants* of Spanish Illinois. This fact not only raised the percentage of literate persons in the Ste. Genevieve District but also put pressure upon the older residents to educate their children. It is possible that the school over which Fremon de Lauriere presided in 1797-98 was an attempt to produce youngsters educated enough to compete with the newcoming Americans. The Dodge brothers, for example, were literate, aggressive entrepreneurs, and certainly would have been both a model and a threat to the established creole families.

The increased American influences — because of American immigrants and traders, and because someone like François Vallé III went off to school in the United States — must also have wrought more subtle but nonetheless important changes in Ste. Genevieve. By 1804 some persons in town perhaps had become interested in trying the American republican system of government, although they could not express such interests while they remained subjects of the king of Spain. And by 1802 smallpox vaccination was available (though not used) in Ste. Genevieve, which indicated that modern science had finally arrived in the upper Mississippi Valley. Perhaps someone like Dr. Walter Fenwick even brought news about the heliocentric universe. There was no newspaper or printing press in either St. Louis or Ste. Genevieve until well after the Louisiana Purchase, although Amer-

---

20. Trudeau's report of 1798, *SRM*, 2:248; concerning Moses Austin, see above, chap. v.

21. SGPR, Marriages, Book D.

ican newspapers sometimes made their way into Spanish Illinois from across the Mississippi.[22]

In short, the period 1974-1804 witnessed the beginning of the destruction of the tightly knit French Canadian and creole community that had remained more or less intact until the early 1790s. The French colonial flavor of Ste. Genevieve did not disappear overnight — either with the coming of American settlers to the area in the late 1790s, or with the arrival of American sovereignty in 1804. As late as 1810 Christian Schultz still viewed Ste. Genevieve as an insular community: "There is a small circle of Frenchmen, who, from a familiar intercourse with the Americans, have conquered both their local and religious prejudices, and may be considered as agreeable society." There is no need to dwell upon Schultz's own marked prejudices, of which he was naturally entirely unconscious. In any case, only in the second quarter of the nineteenth century did the French-speaking population and the French language lose their positions of preponderance, and French creole architecture become subordinate to Anglo-American and German styles. These changes — given the large forces that were transforming early nineteenth-century America — were inevitable, and may even be viewed as progressive. But the remains of French Canadian and creole Ste. Genevieve, architectural and documentary, continue to be the town's most important cultural heritage, a heritage that for its antiquity and power to provide aesthetic delight is unrivaled in the Midwest.[23]

It has been almost a century since Frederick Jackson Turner first broached his frontier thesis of American history. This thesis stimulated an enormous amount of interest in the impact of environment upon the development of human societies. Ray Allen Billington has summarized the Turner thesis in this way: "The European heritage . . . accounted for the similarities between European and American society; to explain the . . . differences historians must look to the distinctive environment of the United States." This general advice can be applied to the study of colonial Ste. Genevieve, although many of Turner's specific notions about

22. On smallpox vaccination and Dr. Fenwick, see above, chap. viii.

23. Schultz, *Travels*, 67. Rohrbough (*Trans-Appalachian Frontier*, 143-44) has recently commented upon the cultural differences between the French creoles and the Anglo-Americans in the Mississippi Valley.

the frontier are not relevant to the French Illinois Country.[24]

The townspeople and their forebears and brought with them from Canada and France certain physical characteristics, religious practices, political ideas, social customs, and habits of mind, but these were shaped and molded by the particular environment that they encountered in the Mississippi Valley. Eighteenth-century persons were themselves aware how the surroundings had shaped the people of the Illinois Country. The would-be spy, Bonnevie de Pogniat, wrote in 1795 that the men of Upper Louisiana "love to hunt in the forest among the Indians. The hard labor of rowing up the [Mississippi] river make them incomparably stronger and less susceptible to fatigue than Europeans. And because the height of glory in that region is to excel at hunting and rowing they are inclined to scorn Europeans, whom they surpass in those activities."[25]

While Bonnevie praised the inhabitants of the Illinois Country, another Frenchman, Perrin du Lac, thought that the geography of that region had induced a certain slothfulness in the people: "The citizens of Ste. Genevieve . . . seem to be born without ambition or desires. They possess a portion of the earth whose fertility transcends the imagination; in a few days they sow and harvest their subsistence for the entire year." Thus Du Lac felt that the bountiful earth of Ste. Genevieve's Big Field had made the townspeople lazy.[26]

Henry Brackenridge also noticed that there was a distinct difference in temperament between French creoles and metropolitan Frenchmen. Like Du Lac, Brackenridge thought that this difference was due to geography and agriculture; "the necessaries of life were easily procured . . ." in Ste. Genevieve. Unlike Du Lac, however, Brackenridge found the creoles of Ste. Genevieve attractive people: "In the character of these people, it must be remembered, that they are essentially Frenchmen; but, without that restlessness, impatience and fire, which distinguishes the European. . . . From the gentle and easy life which they led, their manners, and even language, have assumed a certain degree of softness and mildness: the word *paisible,* expresses this characteristic." Thus

---

24. Billington, *Westward Expansion,* 1.

25. Bonnevie de Pogniat, "Mémoire sur la Louisiane et les Illinois," AN, section Outre-Mer, DFC Louisiane 26:29.

26. Perrin du Lac, *Voyage,* 172.

beauty was in the eye of the beholder, and what Du Lac took for indolence Brackenridge called gentleness.[27]

It can be seen that the physical environment of the Illinois Country helped to create a distinctive inhabitant, as it helped to produce a distinctive architecture: not quite French, not quite Canadian, not quite Lower-Louisiana creole, but uniquely Illinoisan in shape and character. These citizens of colonial Ste. Genevieve were tough in body and mind, slave holders but not racists, Roman Catholics but not bigots, exploiters of the land but not imperialists. They had come to terms with their environment and by dint of effort had established the first permanent white community west of the Mississippi in Upper Louisiana.

---

27. Brackenridge, *Views of Louisiana*, 134.

Appendixes

Appendix A

Charles La Vallée = Geneviève Marcou (married in Canada, 1707)
  (1679-1753)   (1682-1756)
               (A) Charles Vallé
               (B) François Vallé I

(A)
Charles Vallé = Geneviève Crête (married in Canada, 1732)
   (1709-?)   (1714-1759)
            Marie-Louise Vallé = François Leclerc (married in Ste.
            (1739-1826)   Genevieve, 1776)
            Charles Vallé = (1) Elizabeth Couturier (married in Ste.
            (1748-1814)   Genevieve, 1780)
                     = (2) Marianne Corset (married in Ste.
                              Genevieve, 1791)

(B)
François Vallé I = Marianne Billeron (married in Kaskaskia, 1748)
  (1716-1783)   (1729-1781)
           Marie-Louise Vallé = Louis Villars (married in Ste.
                           Genevieve, 1771)
           Charles Vallé = Pélagie Carpentier (married in Ste.
            (1751?-1796)   Genevieve, 1769, separated 1783)
           Joseph Vallé
           (1756? — killed by Indians at Mine La Motte, 1774)
           (C) François Vallé II
           (D) Jean-Baptiste Vallé
           Marguerite (illegitimate) = Louis Caron (married in
           (?-1804)   Ste. Genevieve, 1778)

(C)
François Vallé II = Marie Carpentier (married in Ste. Genevieve, 1777)
  (1758-1804)
            ┌─ Marie Vallé = Joseph Pratte (married in Ste.
            │   (1778-1841)   Genevieve, 1796)
            ├─ François Vallé III = Mary Kerlegan (married in Ste.
            │   (1779-?)   Genevieve, 1828)
            └─ Julie Vallé = Walter Fenwick (married in Ste.
                 (1786-1815)   Genevieve, 1801)

(D)
Jean-Baptiste Vallé = Jeanne Barbeau (married in Prairie du Rocher, 1783)
  (1760-1849)
            ┌─ Jean-Baptiste Vallé II
            │   (1783-1837)
            ├─ François-Baptiste Vallé
            │   (1785-1851)
            └─ Louis Vallé (appointed to West Point, 1805)
                 (1789-1833)

Appendix B

Governors General of Louisiana, 1743-1803

Vaudreuil-Cavagnial, Pierre de Rigaud, marquis de	1743-1753
Kerlérec, Louis-Billouart, chevalier de	1753-1763
Abbadie, Jean-Jacques d'	1763-1765
Aubry, Charles-Philippe de	1765-1766
Ulloa, Antonio de	1766-1768
O'Reilly, Alexandro	1769-1770
Unzaga, Luis de	1770-1776
Gálvez, Bernardo de	1776-1783
Miró, Esteban	1783-1791
Carondelet, Francisco Luis Hector	1792-1797
Gayoso de Lemos, Manuel	1797-1799
Casa Calvo, Sebastián Calvo de	1799-1801
Salcedo, Juan Manuel de	1801-1803

Appendix C

Commandants and Lieutenant Governors of Upper Louisiana, 1742-1803

Bertet, Chevalier de	1742-1749
St. Claire, Jean-Baptiste Benoist (interim)	1749-1751
Macarty, Jean-Jacques	1751-1760
Villiers, Pierre-Joseph Neyon de	1760-1764
St. Ange de Bellerive, Louis (Fort de Chartres)	1764-1765
St. Ange de Bellerive, Louis (St. Louis)	1765-1770
Piernas, Pedro Joseph	1770-1775
Cruzat, Francisco (first term)	1775-1778
Leyba, Fernando de	1778-1780
Cruzat, Francisco (second term)	1780-1787
Pérez, Manuel	1787-1792
Trudeau, Zenon	1792-1799
Delassus, Charles (Carlos) Dehault	1799-1803

Appendix D

Commandants of Ste. Genevieve, 1760-1804

Rocheblave, Philippe Rastel de	1760-1770
Villars, Louis Dubreuil de	1770-1776
Cartabona, Silvio de	1776-1784
Oro, Antonio de	1784-1787
Peyroux de la Coudrenière, Henri	1787-1794
Vallé, François II	1794-1804

Appendix E

Captains of the Militia at Ste. Genevieve, 1752-1804

Deguire, André *père* . . . . 1752-1760?
Vallé, François I (also *lieutenant partculier*) 1760-1783
Vallé, Charles 1783-1787
Peyroux de la Coundrenière, Henri 1787-1793
Vallé, François II 1793-1804

Appendix F

Catholic Priests at Ste. Genevieve, 1759-1814

Watrin, Philibert (Jesuit from Kaskaskia) 1759-1761
La Morinie, Jean-Baptiste de (Jesuit from Kaskaskia) 1761-1763
Meurin, Sebastian-Louis 1764-1768
Gibault, Pierre 1768-1773
Geneveaux, Hilaire de 1773-1777
Limpach, Bernard de (visiting from St. Louis) 1778
Gibault, Pierre 1778-1784
St. Pierre, Paul de 1785-1786
Guignes, Louis 1786-1788
St. Pierre, Paul de 1785-1786
Maxwell, Jacques (James) 1796-1814

Appendix G

Weights and Measures

French livre equivalent to 1.08 English pounds
French quintal equivalent to 100 livres or 108 English pounds
French pied equivalent to 12.76 English inches or 1.063 English feet
French pouce equivalent to 1.063 English inches
French toise equivalent to 6 French pied or 6.38 English feet
French linear arpent equivalent to 191.86 English feet
French square arpent equivalent to .845 acre

Appendix H

Currencies and Prices

French livre equivalent to .20 American dollar, Spanish peso, Spanish piastre
French sou (or sol) equivalent to .05 livre, .01 Spanish peso or piastre, .01 American dollar
Spanish piastre equivalent to Spanish peso, American dollar, 5 French livres
Spanish real (or escalin) equivalent to .125 Spanish peso or piastre or American dollar

Values of principal commodities at Ste. Genevieve, 1765-1795:

Plowland in the Big Field . . . . 40-1000 livres per facing arpent
Flour . . . . 15-40 livres per quintal
Wheat . . . . 4-10 livres per minot
Maize . . . . 1-2 livres per minot
Pork bellies . . . . 3-4 livres per livre
Lead . . . . 5-15 sols per livre
Tobacco . . . . 40 livres per quintal
Salt . . . . 40 livres per quintal
Deer hides . . . . 20-40 sols per livre

Bibliography

Bibliographies, Finding Aids, and Reference Books

Alvord, Clarence W. "Eighteenth-Century French Records in the Archives of Illinois," *American Historical Association Annual Report* 1 (1905), 353-66.

Astoquia, Madeline, et al. *Guide des sources de l'histoire des Etats Unis dans les Archives françaises* (Paris, 1976).

Barron, Bill. *The Vaudreuil Papers: A Calendar and Index of the Personal and Private Records of Pierre de Rigaud Vaudreuil, Royal Governor of the French Province of Louisiana, 1743-1753* (New Orleans, 1975).

Beers, Henry P. *The French and British in the Old Northwest: A Bibliographical Guide to Archive and Manuscript Sources* (Detroit, 1964).

_____ . *The French in North America: A Bibliographical Guide to French Archives, Reproductions, and Research Missions* (Baton Rouge, 1957).

Belisle, Louis-Alexandre. *Dictionnaire général de la langue française au Canada* (Quebec, 1954).

Conrad, Glenn R. and Brasseaux, Carl A. (eds.). *A Selected Bibliography of Scholarly Literature on Colonial Louisiana and New France* (Lafayette, Louisiana, 1982).

DeVille, Winston. "Manuscript Sources in Louisiana for the History of the French in the Mississippi Valley," in John Francis McDermott (ed.), *The French in the Mississippi Valley* (Urbana, Illinois, 1965), 209-16.

Early Missouri Archives, compiled by Missouri Historical Records Survey, Works Progress Administation (St. Louis, 1941).

Genêt, Nicole, et al. *Les objets familiers de nos ancêtres* (Ottawa, 1974).

Hebert, A. Otis. "Resources in Louisiana Depositories for the Study of Spanish Activities in Louisiana," in John Francis McDermott (ed.), *The Spanish in the Mississippi Valley, 1762-1804* (Urbana, Illinois, 1974), 26-37.

Hill, Roscoe R. *Descriptive Catalogue of the Documents Relating to the History of the United States in the Papeles Procedentes de Cuba Deposited in the Archivo General de Indias at Seville* (Washington, D.C., 1916).

Holmes, Jack D.L. *A Guide to Spanish Louisiana, 1762-1806* (New Orleans, 1970).

Leland, W.G. *Guide to the Materials for American History in the Libraries and Archives of Paris,* vol. 1 (Washington, D.C., 1943).

Lessard, Michel and Marquis, Huguette. *Encyclopédie des antiquités du Québec: Trois siècles de production artisanale* (Ottawa, 1971).

Marion, Marcel. *Dictionnaire des institutions de la France au XVIIe et XVIIIe siècles* (Paris, 1923).

McDermott, John Francis. *Glossary of Mississippi Valley French 1673-1850* (St. Louis, 1941).

Menier, Marie-Antoinette, et al. *Inventaire des Archives Coloniales: Correspondance à l'arrivée en provenance de la Louisiane,* vol. 1 (Paris, 1976).

Nasatir, Abraham P. and Liljegren, Ernest R. "Materials Relating to the History of the Mississippi Valley," *Louisiana Historical Quarterly* 21 (1938), 3-73.

O'Neill, Charles E., et al. *Catalogo de documentos del Archivo General de Indias, seccion V, Gobierno, Audencia de Santo Domingo sobre la epoca española de Luisiana* (New Orleans, 1969).

Pease, Marguerite Jenison. *Guide to Manuscript Materials Relating to Western History* in Foreign Depositories Reproduced for the Illinois Historical Survey (Urbana, Illinois, 1956)

Read, William A. *Louisiana-French* (Baton Rouge, 1963).

Robertson, James A. *List of Documents in Spanish Archives Relating to the History of the United States* (Washington, D.C., 1910).

Ste. Genevieve Flood Control Study, 3 vols. (U.S. Army Corps of Engineers, St. Louis, 1983).

Surrey, Nancy Miller. *Calendar of Manuscripts in Paris Archives and Libraries Relating to the History of the Mississippi Valley to 1803,* 2 vols. (Washington, D.C., 1926, 1929).

Tanguay, L'Abbé Cyprien, *Dictionnaire généalogique des familles Canadiennes depuis la fondation de la colonie jusqu'à nos jours,* 7 vols. (Montreal, 1871-1890).

Trudel, Marcel. *An Atlas of New France* (Quebec, 1968).

Archival Materials

Archives of Canada
Archives de l'Archidiocèse de Québec, Quebec
Correspondence of Jean-Olivier Briand

Archives nationales de Québec à Montréal
Notarial records

Archives of France
Archives du Ministère des Affaires Etrangères, Paris
Mémoires et Documents, Amérique

Archives du Ministère de Guerre, Vincennes
Series A^1 2592
Cartes et plans

Archives Nationales, Paris
Archives des Colonies, series C^{13}A, D^{2}C, F^{2}A, F^3, G^1 (microfilm in Library of Congress)
Archives nationales, section Outre-Mer, DFC Louisiane 26
Archives du Service Hydrographique de la Marine, series JJ

Bibliothèque Nationale, Paris
Salle des manuscrits, nouvelles acquisitions françaises 9310

The French manuscript collections contain little information pertaining directly to Ste. Genevieve, but they do contain masses of collateral materials relating to the Mississippi Valley in general.

Archives of Spain
Archivo General de Indias, Seville
Audencia de Sto. Domingo, legajos as cited in footnotes
Papeles Procedentes de Cuba, legajos as cited in footnotes

With a few exceptions, the materials from Spanish archives used in this study came from Professor Abraham P. Nasatir's monumental collection of transcripts from the Archivo General de Indias.

Archives of the United States
Archives of the Archdiocese of Baltimore
Letters of Father James Maxwell

Archives of the University of Notre Dame, South Bend, Indiana
Records of the Diocese of Louisiana and the Floridas, 1576-1903 Abbé de St. Pierre Papers

Bancroft Library, Berkeley, California
Louisiana Collection, 1765-1804. Lawrence Kinnaird has translated and published this collection for the years 1765 through 1794 (see bibliography below). These documents were originally part of the Papeles de Cuba collection, but were removed from Cuba before that collection was sent to Seville.

Huntington Library, San Marino, California
Loudun Papers: 426, 568

Illinois Historical Survey, Urbana, Illinois
Contains masses of transcripts, photostats, and microfilms pertaining to the eighteenth-century Illinois Country, including Ste. Genevieve.

Illinois State Archives, Springfield, Illinois
Draper Collection (microfilm)
Kaskaskia Deed Books A and B

Louisiana State Museum, New Orleans
Records of the French Superior Council for Louisiana to 1769
Spanish Judicial Records for Louisiana, 1770 to 1803

Missouri Historical Society, St. Louis
Census of Ste. Genevieve, 1787. This is a manuscript copy made by Walter B. Douglas from a copy made of the original at the Archivo Nacional de Cuba in 1905.
Chouteau Collection
Delassus Collection
François Vallé Collection
Guibourd Collection
Theodore Hunt's "Minutes," typescript
Kaskaskia Parish Records, transcripts
New Madrid Archives
St. Charles Archives
St. Charles Parish Records
Ste. Genevieve Archives (microfilm). The originals of these valuable civil records, which are now in the Ste. Genevieve County courthouse, were housed in the archives of the Missouri Historical Society in St. Louis until 1968. An excellent finding aid (containing a few minor errors) was prepared and the records were microfilmed. These records have now been reorganized and re-microfilmed by the Western Historical Manuscripts Collection librarians in Columbia, Missouri. All of the citations to the Ste. Genevieve Archives in this study refer to the original organization as accomplished by the Missouri Historical Society.
Ste. Genevieve Parish Records, transcript by Ida Schaaf.

Randolph County Courthouse, Chester, Illinois
Kaskaskia Manuscripts, 1721-1765 (available on microfilm)

St. Charles Historical Society, St. Charles, Missouri
St. Charles Deed Book A

Ste. Genevieve County Courthouse, Ste. Genevieve, Missouri
Contains the original Ste. Genevieve colonial civil records.
Original Deed Books A and B.

Ste. Genevieve Parish Rectory, Ste. Genevieve, Missouri
Contains the original parish records. These are now available, except for the first book of burials (1766-84), on microfilm through the Western Historical Manuscripts Collection, Columbia, Missouri.

Printed Source Materials

Alliot, Paul. "Historical and Political Reflections on Louisiana," in James A. Robertson (ed.), *Louisiana Under the Rule of Spain, France, and the United States, 1785-1807*, 2 vols. (Cleveland, 1911).

Alvord, Clarence W. (ed.). *Cahokia Records 1778-1790*. Vol. 2: *Collections of the Illinois State Historical Society* (Springfield, 1907).

Alvord, Clarence W., and Carter, Clarence E. (eds.). *Kaskaskia Records, 1778-1790*. Vol. 5: *Collections of the Illinois State Historical Society* (Springfield, 1909).

————(ed.). *The Critical Period, 1763-1765*. Vol. 10: *Collections of the Illinois State Historical Society* (Springfield, 1915).

————ed.). *The New Regime 1765-1767*. Vol. 11: *Collections of the Illinois State Historical Library* (Springfield, 1916).

————(ed.). *Trade and Politics 1767-1769*. Vol. 16: *Collections of the Illinois State Historical Library* (Springfield, 1921).

American State Papers, Public Lands, vols. 1-8 (Washington, D.C., 1832-1861).

Arthur, Stanley C. (ed.). *Index to the Dispatches of the Spanish Governors of Louisiana, 1766-1792* (New Orleans, 1957).

Austin, Moses. *A Summary Description of the Lead Mines in Upper Louisiana.* (Washington, D.C., 1804).

Auxerre, Louis Léger d'. *La nouvelle maison rustique*, 2 vol. (Paris, 1763).

Barker, Eugene C. (ed.). "The Austin Papers," *Annual Report of the American Historical Association for the Year 1919*, vol. 2, pt. 1 (Washington, D.C., 1924).

Billon, Frederick L. (ed.). *Annals of St. Louis in Its Early Day Under the French and Spanish Dominations, 1776-1804* (St. Louis, 1886).

Bossu, Jean Bernard. *Travels in the Interior of North America, 1751-1762*, trans. and ed. Seymour Feiler (Norman, Oklahoma, 1962).

Brackenridge, Henry. *Recollections of Persons and Places in the West* (Philadelphia, 1834).

————. *Views of Lousiana: Together with a Journal of a Voyage up the Missouri River in 1811* (Pittsburgh, 1814).

Bradbury, John. *Travels in the Interior of America* (1817; reprint Ann Arbor, 1966).

————. *Travels in the Western Country, 1818-1819* (Philadelphia, 1820).

Brown, Margaret K. and Dean, Lawrie C. (eds.). *The Village of Chartres in Colonial Illinois, 1720-1765* (New Orleans, 1977).

Carondelet, Baron Hector de. "Military Report on Louisiana and West Florida, November 24, 1794," in James A. Robertson (ed.), *Louisiana Under the Rule of Spain, France, and the United States, 1785-1807*, 2 vols. (Cleveland, 1911), 1:291-345.

Carter, Clarence E. (ed.). *The Territorial Papers of the United States:* Vol. 7, *Indiana, 1800-1810;* vol. 13, *Louisiana-Missouri, 1803-1806* (Washington, D.C., 1939, 1948).

Catterall, Helen T. and Hayden, James J. (eds.). *Judicial Cases Concerning American Slavery and the Negro.* 5 vols. (1926; reprint New York, 1968).

Charlevoix, Pierre-François Xavier de. *Histoire et description générale de la Nouvelle France avec le Journal Historique d'un Voyage fait par ordre du Roi dans l'Amérique Septentrionale*, 6 vols. (Paris, 1744).

Clément, Pierre (ed.). *Lettres, instructions et mémoires de Colbert*, 7 vols. (Paris, 1861-1882).

Collot, Georges-Victor. *A Journey in North America,* 2 vols. and atlas (Paris, 1826; reprint Florence, Italy, 1924).

Dart, Henry P. (ed.). "Marriage Contracts of French Colonial Louisiana," *The Louisiana Historical Quarterly* 17 (1934), 229- 241.

Dart, Henry P., and Prince, Edith Dart (ed. and trans.). "Inventory of the Estate of Sieur Jean-Baptiste Prévost, Deceased Agent of the Company of the Indies, July 13, 1769," *Louisiana Historical Quarterly* 9 (1926), 411-98.

Davenport, Frances G., and Paullin, Charles O. (eds.). *European Treaties Bearing on the History of the United States and its Dependencies,* 21 vols. (Gloucester, Massachusetts, 1967).

Dumont de Montigny, Jean-François Benjamin. *Mémoires historiques sur la Louisiane.* 2 vols. (Paris, 1753).

"Edit concernant les Nègres à la Louisiane," *Publications of the Louisiana Historical Society* 4 (1908), 75-90.

Favrot Papers, 1695-1803. Prepared by Historical Records Survey, Division of Professional and Service Projects, Works Projects Administration, 7 vols. (New Orleans, 1940-42).

Flagg, Edmund. "The Far West, 1836-1837," in Reuben G. Thwaites (ed.) *Early Western Travels, 1748-1846,* 32 vols. (Cleveland, 1906), 27: 19-121.

Flint, Timothy. *Recollections of the Last Ten Years, passed in occasional residences and journeyings in the valley of the Mississippi* (Boston, 1826).

Forbes, S. A. "The Gui Année in Illinois," typescript in the Illinois Historical Survey (Urbana, Illinois, 1896).

Garrison, George P. (ed.). "A Memorandum of Moses Austin's Journey, 1796-1797," *American Historical Review* 5 (1900), 518-42.

Hanley, Thomas O'Brien (ed.). *The John Carroll Papers,* 3 vols. (Notre Dame, Indiana, 1976).Houck, Louis (ed.). *The Spanish Regime in Missouri; a Collection of Papers and Documents relating to Upper Louisiana, Principally within the Present Limits of Missouri, During the Dominion of Spain, from the Archives of the Indies at Seville,* 2 vols. (Chicago, 1909).

Kalm, Peter. *The America of 1750: Peter Kalm's Travels in North America,* ed. Adolph B. Benson, 2 vols. (New York, 1937).

Holmes, Jack D.L. (ed.). *Documentos Ineditos para la Historia de la Louisiana 1792-1810* (Madrid, 1936).

———. *Honor and Fidelity, The Louisiana Infantry Regiment and the Louisiana Militia Companies, 1766-1821* (Birmingham, Alabama, 1965).

Hutchins, Thomas. *A Historical and Topographical Description of Louisiana and Western Florida,* ed. Joseph G. Tregle, Jr., (1784; facsimile Gainesville, Florida, 1968).

———. *A Topographical Description of Virginia, Pennsylvania, Maryland, and North Carolina,* ed. Frederick C. Hicks, (1778; reprint Cleveland, 1904).

Imlay, Gilbert. *A Topographical Description of the Western Territory of North America* (London, 1797).

James, James A. (ed.). *The George Rogers Clark Papers.* Vols. 8 and 19: *Collections of the Illinois State Historical Library,* 2 vols. (Springfield, 1912, 1926).

Jefferys, Thomas. *The American Atlas* (London, 1775).

Kellogg, Louise Phelps (ed.). *Early Narratives of the Northwest, 1634-1699* (New York, 1917).

Kinnaird, Lawrence (ed.). "Clark-Leyba Papers," *American Historical Review* 41 (1935), 92-112.

_____ . *Spain in the Mississippi Valley, 1765-1794.* Vols. 2, 3, and 4, pts. 1, 2, and 3: *American Historical Association Report for 1945* (Washington, D.C., 1946-49).

La Harpe, Bernard de. *Journal historique de l'éstablissement des français à La Louisiane* (New Orleans, 1831).

Le Page de Pratz, Antoine Simon. *The History of Louisiana,* ed. Joseph C. Tregle, Jr., (1774; facsimile Baton Rouge, 1975).

Maduell, Charles R., Jr. (comp. and trans.). *The Census Tables for the French Colony of Louisiana from 1699 through 1732* (Baltimore, 1972).

Margry, Pierre (comp. and ed.). *Découvertes et établissements des français dans le sud de l'Amérique Septentrionale* (1614-1754), 6 vols. (Paris, 1876-1886).

Marshall, Thomas (ed.). *The Life and Papers of Frederick Bates,* 2 vols. (St. Louis, 1926).

Mason, Edward G. (ed.). "Rocheblave Papers," in Edward G. Mason (ed.), *Early Chicago and Illinois* (Chicago, 1890), 382-418.

Mereness, Newton D. (ed.). *Travels in the American Colonies* (New York, 1916).

Nasatir, Abraham P. (ed.). *Before Lewis and Clark,* 2 vols. (St. Louis, 1952).

_____ (ed.). *Spanish War Vessels on the Mississippi, 1792-1796* (New Haven, 1968).

Pargellis, Stanley (ed.). *Military Affairs in North America, 1748-1765: Selected Documents from the Cumberland Papers in Windsor Castle* (New York, 1936).

Pease, T. C. (ed.). *Illinois on the Eve of the Seven Years' War, 1747-1755.* Vol. 29: *Collections of the Illinois State Historical Society* (Springfield, 1940).

Pénicaut, André. *Fleur de Lys and Calument: Being the Pénicaut Narrative of French Adventures in Louisiana,* ed. and trans. Richebourg Gaillard McWilliams, (Baton Rouge, 1953).

Perrin du Lac. *Voyage dans les deux Louisianes* (Lyons, 1805).

Pitot, James. *Observations on the Colony of Louisiana from 1796-1802* (Baton Rouge, 1979).

Pittman, Philip. *The Present State of the European Settlements on the Mississippi,* ed. Robert Rea (1770; facsimile Gainesville, Florida, 1973).

"Publications of the Louisiana Historical Society," 4 (1908), 75-90.

Robertson, James Alexander (ed.). *Louisiana Under the Rule of Spain, France, and the United States, 1785-1807,* 2 vols. (Cleveland, 1911).

Rowland, Dunbar, and Sanders, Albert G. (trans. and eds.). *Mississippi Provincial Archives,* 3 vols. (Jackson, Mississippi, 1927-32).

Rowland, Dunbar; Sanders, Albert G.; and Galloway, Patricia K. (trans. and eds.) *Mississippi Provincial Archives,* vols. 4 and 5 (Baton Rouge, 1984).

Schaaf, Ida (trans. and ed.). *Sainte Genevieve Marriages, Baptisms, and Burials from the Church Registers, 1759-1839* (St. Louis, 1911).

Schoolcraft, Henry R. *A View of the Lead Mines of Missouri* (New York, 1972).

Schultz, Christian. *Travels on and Inland Voyage . . . performed in the years 1807 and 1808,* 2 vols. in 1 (New York, 1810).

Shea, John Gilmary (ed.) *Discovery and Exploration of the Mississippi Valley: with the Original Narratives of Marquette, Allouez Membré, Hennepin, and Anastase Douay.* (New York, 1852).

_____ . *Early Voyages up and down the Mississippi by Davelier, St. Cosme, Le Sueur, Gravier, and Guignes.* (Albany, 1861)

Stoddard, Amos. *Sketches, Historical and Descriptive of Louisiana* (Philadelphia, 1812).

Stiles, Henry Reed (ed.). *Joutel's Journal of La Salle's Last Voyage, 1684-87* (New York, 1906).

Thwaites, Reuben G. (ed.). *Early Western Travels, 1748-1846,* 32 vols. (Cleveland, 1904-07).

———— (ed.). *The French Regime in Wisconsin-I. 1634-1727.* Vol. 16: *Collections of the State Historical Society of Wisconsin* (Madison, 1902).

———— (ed.). *The French Regime in Wisconsin-II, 1727-1748.* Vol. 17: *Collections of the State Historical Society of Wisconsin* (Madison, 1906).

———— (ed.). *The French Regime in Wisconsin-III.* Vol. 18: *Collections of the State Historical Society of Wisconsin* (Madison, 1908).

———— (ed.). *The Jesuit Relations and Allied Documents,* 73 vols. (Cleveland, 1896-1901).

Tucker, Sara J. and Temple, Wayne C. (comps. and eds.). *Indian Villages of the Illinois Country, Atlas.* Vol. 2: *Scientific Papers, Illinois State Museum* (Springfield, 1942, 1975).

United Nations. *Demographic Yearbook,* 1970 (New York, 1971).

Württemberg, Duke Paul Wilhelm of. *Travels in North America, 1822-1824,* trans. W. Robert Nitske, ed. Savoie Lottinville, (Norman, Oklahoma, 1973).

Secondary Materials

Ackerknecht, Erwin H. *History and Geography of the Most Important Diseases* (New York, 1965).

————. *Malaria in the Upper Mississippi Valley, 1760-1900* (Baltimore, 1945).

Adair, E. R. "The French-Canadian Seigneury," *The Canadian Historical Review* 35 (1954), 187-207.

Adair, James. *The History of the American Indians, Particularly those Nations Adjoining to the Mississippi, East and West Florida, Georgia, South and North Carolina, and Virginia* (London, 1775).

Aiton, Arthur S. "The Diplomacy of the Louisiana Cession," *American Historical Review* 36 (1931), 701-20.

Alden, John R. *John Stuart and the Southern Colonial Frontier: A Study of Indian Relations, War, Trade, and Land Policies in the Southern Wilderness, 1754-1775* (Ann Arbor, 1944).

Allain, Mathé. "L'Immigration française en Louisiane 1718-1721," *Revue Histoire de l'Amérique* 28 (1975), 555-64.

————. "Slave Policies in French Louisiana," *Louisiana History* 21 (1980), 127-37.

Alvord, Clarence W. *The Illinois Country, 1673-1818,* (Springfield, 1920).

Ariès, Philippe. *Centuries of Childhood,* trans. Robert Baldick, (New York, 1962).

Arthur, Stanley and Kerwin, George. *Old Families of Louisiana* (New Orleans, 1931).

Axtell, James. "The Ethnohistory of Early America: A Review Essay," *William and Mary Quarterly* 35 (1978), 110-44.

————. "The White Indians of Colonial America," *William and Mary Quarterly,* third series, 32 (1975), 55-88.

Baade, Hans. "Marriage Contracts in French and Spanish Louisiana: A Study in 'Notarial' Jurisprudence," *Tulane Law Review* 53 (1978), 1-92.

————. "The Law of Slavery in Spanish Louisiana, 1769-1803," in Edward F. Hass (ed.), *Louisiana's Legal Heritage* (New Orleans, 1983), 43-86.

Baker, Vaughan et al. "Le Mari Est Seigneur: Marital Laws Governing Women in French Louisiana," in Edward F. Haas (ed.), *Louisiana's Legal Heritage* (New Orleans, 1983), 7-18.

Baldick, Robert. *Centuries of Childhood: A Social History of Family Life* (New York, 1962).

Bannon, John F. "Black-Robe Frontiersman: Gabriel Marest, S.J.," *Bulletin of the Missouri Historical Society* 10 (1954), 351-66.

Barbeau, Albert, *La vie rurale dans l'ancienne France* (Paris, 1885).

Barbeau, Marius. "Voyageur Songs of the Missouri," *Bulletin of the Missouri Historical Society* 10 (1954), 336-47.

Belting, Natalia M. *Kaskaskia Under the French Regime* (Urbana, Illinois, 1948).

Bemis, Samuel Flagg. *Jay's Treaty: A Study in Commerce and Diplomacy* (New York, 1923).

————. *Pinckney's Treaty: America's Advantage from Europe's Distress, 1783-1800* (Westport, Connecticut, 1960).

Bender, Prosper. "Holidays of the French Canadians," *Magazine of American History* 20 (1888), 461-68.

————. "The Historic Games of Old Canada," *Magazine of American History* 26 (1891), 367-74.

Bett, W. R. *The History and Conquest of Common Diseases* (Norman, Oklahoma, 1954).

Billington, Ray A. *Westward Expansion: A History of the American Frontier* (New York, 1950).

Bjork, David K. "The Establishment of Spanish Rule in the Province of Louisiana, 1762-1770," Ph. D. Thesis, University of California, Berkeley, 1923.

Bloch, Marc. *French Rural History, an Essay on its Basic Characteristics*, trans. Janet Sondheimer (Berkeley, 1966).

Boily, Lise and Blanchette, Jean-François, *Les fours à pain au Québec* (Ottawa, Canada, 1976).

Bolton, Herbert E. *Rim of Christendom* (New York, 1936).

Bourdieu, Pierre. "Marriage Strategies as Strategies of Social Reproduction," in Robert Forster and Orest Ranum (eds.), *Family and Society* (Baltimore, 1976), 117-44.

Brasseaux, Carl A. "The Administration of Slave Regulations in FrenchLouisiana, 1774-1776," *Louisiana History* 21 (1980), 139-58.

Braudel, Fernand. *Capitalism and Material Life, 1400-1800*, trans. Miriam Kochan (New York, 1967).

_____. *The Structures of Everyday Life, The Limits of the Possible*, trans. Sian Reynolds (New York, 1979).

Breese, Sidney. *The Early History of Illinois from Its Discovery by the French in 1673, until Its Cession to the Great Britain in 1763, Including the Narrative of Marquette's Discovery of the Mississippi* (Chicago, 1884).

Bridges, Roger D. (ed.). "John Mason Peck on Illinois Slavery," *Journal of the Illinois State Historical Society* 75 (1982), 179- 217.

Burson, Caroline M. *The Stewardship of Don Esteban Miró, 1782-92* (New Orleans, 1940).

Calderon Quijano, Jose Antonio. *Fortificationes en Nueva España* (Seville, 1953).

Caldwell, Norman W. "The Chickasaw Threat to French Control of the Mississippi in the 1740's," *Chronicles of Oklahoma* 16 (1938), 465-92.

_____. *The French in the Mississippi Valley, 1740-1750.* (Urbana, 1941).

Carless, William. *The Arts and Crafts of Canada* (Montreal, 1925).

Carter, Clarence E. *Great Britain and the Illinois Country, 1763-1774* (Washington, D.C., 1910).

Caruso, John Anthony. *The Mississippi Valley Frontier: The Age of French Exploitation and Settlement* (New York, 1966).

Caughey, John W. Bernardo de Gálvez in Lousiana, 1776-1783 (Berkeley, 1934).

_____. "Louisiana Under Spain, 1762-1783," Ph. D. Thesis, University of California, Berkeley, 1928.

Chapman, Carl H. "The Indomitable Osage in the Spanish Illinois (Upper Louisiana), 1763-1804," in John Francis McDermott (ed.), *The Spanish in the Mississippi Valley, 1762-1804* (1974), 287-313.

Charbonneau, Hubert. *Vie et mort de nos ancêtres* (Montreal, 1975).

Chittenden, Hiram M. *The American Fur Trade of the Far West* (New York, 1902).

Clark, John G. *New Orleans, 1718-1812: An Economic History* (Baton Rouge, 1969).

_____. "The Role of the City Government in the Economic Development of New Orleans: Cabildo and City Council, 1783-1812" in John Francis McDermott (ed.), *The Spanish in the Mississippi Valley, 1762-1804* (1974), 133-48.

Coker, William S.; Holmes, Jack D. L.; Proctor, Samuel; and Wright, J. Leitch Jr. "Research in the Spanish Borderlands," *Latin American Research Review* (1972), 3-94.

Coughlin, Frances A. "Spanish Galleys on the Mississippi, 1792-1797," M.A. Thesis, Claremont Graduate School, 1945.

Crane, Verner W. *The Southern Frontier, 1670-1732* (Durham, North Carolina, 1928).

Crouch, Dora P.; Garr, Daniel J.; and Mundigo, Axel I. *Spanish City Planning in North America* (Cambridge, Massachusetts, 1982).

Curtin, Philip. *The Atlantic Slave Trade* (Madison, Wisconsin, 1969).

Dalton, Mary L. "Notes on the Geneology of the Vallé Family," *Missouri Historical Society Collections* 2 (1906), 54-82.

Darling, Arthur B. *Our Rising Empire, 1763-1803* (New Haven, 1940).

Dart, Henry P. "The First Cargo of African Slaves for Lousiana, 1718," *Louisiana Historical Quarterly* 14 (1931), 163-77.

Davis, David B. *The Problem of Slavery in Western Culture* (Ithaca, New York, 1966).

Davis, Natalie Z. *The Return of Martin Guerre* (Cambridge, Massachusetts, 1983).

DeConde, Alexander. *This Affair of Lousiana* (New York, 1976).

Deffontaines, Pierre. "The Rang-Pattern of Rural Settlement in French Canada," in Marcel Rioux and Yves Martin, (eds.), *French- Canadian Society* (Toronto, 1964), 3-18.

Degler, Carl N. *Neither Black nor White: Slavery and Race Relations in Brazil and the United States* (New York, 1971).

Denman, David D. "French Peasant Society in Flux and Stress: The Reintegration of Traditional Village Communal Activity in Ste. Genevieve, 1703-1830," M.A. Thesis, University of Missouri, Columbia, 1980.

————. "History of 'La Saline': Salt Manufacturing Site, 1675-1825," *Missouri Historical Review* 73 (1979), 307-20.

Diamond, Sigmund. "An Experiment in 'Feudalism': French Canada in the Seventeenth Century," *The William and Mary Quarterly* 18 (1961), 3-34.

Din, Gilbert C. "Early Spanish Colonization Efforts in Louisiane," *Louisiana History* 11 (1972), 31-49.

————and Nasatir, Abraham P. *The Imperial Osages, Spanish-Indian Diplomacy in the Mississippi Valley* (Norman, Oklahoma, 1983).

————. "Loyalist Resistance After Pensacola," in William S. Coker and Robert R. Rea (eds.), *Anglo-Spanish Confrontation on the Gulf Coast During the American Revolution* (Pensacola, 1982), 159-70.

————. "Spain's Immigration Policy and Efforts in Louisiana During the American Revolution," *Louisiana Studies* 14 (1975), 241-57.

————. "Spanish Immigration to a French Land," *Revue de Louisiane / Louisiana Review* 5 (1976), 63-80.

Donnelly, Joseph P. "Pierre Gibault and the Critical Period of the Illinois Country, 1768-78," in John Francis McDermott (ed.), *The French in the Mississippi Valley* (Urbana, 1965), 81-92.

Dorn, Walter. *Competition for Empire, 1740-1763* (New York, 1940).

Dorrance, Ward. *The Survival of French in the Old Sainte Genevieve District*. Vol. 10: *University of Missouri Studies* (Columbia, 1935).

Douglas, R. S. *History of Southeast Missouri*, 2 vols. (Chicago, 1912).

Drake, Daniel. *Systematic Treatise on the Principal Diseases of the Interior Valley of North America* (Cincinnati, 1850).

Drury, John. *Historic Midwest Houses* (Minneapolis, 1947).

Duby, Georges. *Rural Economy and Country Life in the Medieval West*, trans. Cynthia Postan (Columbia, South Carolina, 1968).

_____. *The Three Orders*, trans. Arthur Goldhammer (Chicago, 1980).

Duffy, John. *Epidemics in Colonial America* (Baton Rouge, 1953).

Earle, Alice M. *Home Life in Colonial Days* (Stockbridge, Massachusetts, 1974).

Eccles, William J. *The Canadian Frontier, 1534-1760* (Albuquerque, 1974).

_____. *France in America* (New York, 1972).

Echeverria, Durand. "General Collot's Plan for a Reconnaissance of the Ohio and Mississippi Valleys, 1796," *William and Mary Quarterly*, third series, 9 (1952), 512-20.

Ekberg, Carl J. "Antoine Valentin de Gruy, Early Missouri Explorer," *Missouri Historical Review* 76 (1982), 136-50.

_____. "Ste. Genevieve-St. Joachim, A Case of Mistaken Identity," *Historic Illinois* 3 (1981), 12-14

Ekberg, Carl J.; Smith, Charles R.; Walter, William D.; Lange, Frederick W. "A Cultural, Geographical, and Historical Study of the Pine Ford Lake Project Area," Illinois State University Archaeological Surveys, research report no. 2 (Normal, Illinois, 1981).

Elkins, Stanley M. *Slavery: A Problem in American Institutional and Intellectual Life* (New York, 1959).

Espinosa, J. Manuel. "Spanish Louisiana and the West: The Economic Significance of the Ste. Genevieve District," *Missouri Historical Review* 32 (1938), 287-97.

Everett, Donald E. "Free Persons of Color in Colonial Louisiana," *Louisiana History* 7 (1966), 21-50.

Farlarleau, Jean-Charles. "The Seventeenth-Century Parish in French Canada," in Marcel Rioux and Yves Martin (eds.), *French-Canadian Society* (Toronto, 1964), 19-31.

Febrvre, Lucien. *Life in Renaissance France*, trans. Marian Roghstein, (Cambridge, Massachusetts, 1977).

Fenton, W. et al. *American Indian and White Relations to 1830: Needs and Opportunities for Study* (Chapel Hill, 1957).

Fieher, Thomas M. "The African Presence in Colonial Louisiana: An Essay on the Continuity of Caribbean Culture," in Robert MacDonald et al. (eds.), *Louisiana's Black Heritage* (New Orleans, 1979), 3-31.

Fite, Emerson D., and Freeman, Archibald. *A Book of Old Maps Delineating American History* (New York, 1969).

Flandrin, Jean-Louis. *Familles: Parenté, maison, sexualité, dans l'ancienne société* (Paris, 1976).

Foley, William E. *The First Chouteaus: River Barons of Early St. Louis* (Urbana, Illinois, 1983).

_____. *A History of Missouri, 1673-1820* (Columbia, 1971).

_____. "Slave Freedom Suits Before Dred Scott: The Case of Marie Jean Scypion's Descendents," *Missouri Historical Review* 79 (1984), 1-23.

Folmer, Henry. *Franco-Spanish Rivalry in North America, 1524-1763* (Glendale, 1953).

Fortier, Alcée. *A History of Louisiana*, 4 vols. (New York, 1904).

Franzwa, Gregory M. *The Story of Old Ste. Genevieve* (St. Louis, 1967).

Frégault, Guy. *Iberville le conquérant* (Montreal, 1944).

_____. *Le Grand Marquis: Pierre de Rigaud de Vaudreuil et la Louisiane* (Montreal, 1952).

Gagné, Madame Charles. *Recettes typiques de la Côte-du-Sud* (Ottawa, 1970).

Gardner, James A. *Lead King: Moses Austin* (St. Louis, 1980).

Garraghan, Gilbert J. "Earliest Settlements of the Illinois Country," *Catholic Historical Review* 15 (1930), 351-62.

Gay, Peter. *Voltaire's Politics* (New York, 1959).

Gayarré, Charles, *History of Louisiana* (New Orleans, 1885).

Geggus, David P. *Slavery, War, and Revolution: The British Occupation of Saint Domingue, 1793-1798* (Oxford, 1982).

Genovese, Eugene D. *Roll, Jordan, Roll: The World the Slaves Made* (New York, 1976).

Gibson, Arrell M. *The Chickasaws* (Norman, 1971).

Giraud, Marcel. "France and Louisiana in the Early Eighteenth Century," *Mississippi Valley Historical Review* 36 (1950), 657-74.

————. *Histoire de la Louisiane Française*, 4 vols. (Paris, 1953-1974).

Glass, D. V., and Eversley, D. E. C. (eds.). *Population in History: Essays in Historical Demography* (Chicago, 1965).

Goubert, Jean-Pierre. *Malades et médecins en Bretagne, 1770-1790* (Paris, 1974).

Goubert, Pierre. "Historical Demography and the Reinterpretation of Early Modern French History," *Journal of Interdisciplinary History 1* (1970), 37-48.

————. *L,Ancien Régime.* Tome 1: *La Société* (Paris 1969).

Gravier, Henri. *La Colonization de la Louisiane à l'époque de Law; Octobre 1717-Janvier 1721* (Paris, 1904).

Green, M. Susan. "The Material Culture of a Pre-enclosure Village in Upper Louisiana: Open Fields, Houses, and Cabinetry in Colonial Ste. Geneviève, 1750-1804," M.A. Thesis, University of Missouri, Columbia, 1983.

Haas, Edward F. (ed.). *Louisiana's Legal Heritage* (New Orleans, 1983).

Hagan, William T. *The Indian in American History,* (New York, 1963).

————. *The Sac and Fox Indians.* (Norman, 1958).

Hand, John P. "Negro Slavery in Illinois," *Transactions of the Illinois State Historical Society for the Year 1910* (Springfield, 1913), 42-48.

Hanley, Lucy E. "Lead Mining in the Mississippi Valley During the Colonial Period," M.A. Thesis, St. Louis University, 1942.

Hardy, James D. Jr. "The Transportation of Convicts to Colonial Louisiana," *Louisiana History* 7 (1966), 207-22.

Harris, Richard C. *The Seigneurial System in Early Canada, A Geographical Study* (Madison, Wisconsin, 1966).

Heinrick, Pierre. *La Louisiane sous la Compagnie des Indes, 1717-1731* (1908).

Henripin, Jacques. *La population Canadienne au début du XVIII siècle* (Paris, 1954).

Henripin, Jacques, and Péron, Yves. "The Demographic Transformation of the Province of Quebec," in D. V. Glass and Roger Revelle (eds.), *Population and Social Change* (London, 1972), 213-32.

Higginbotham, Jay. *Old Mobile: Fort Louis de la Louisiane, 1702-1711* (Mobile, 1977).

"Historic American Buildings Surveys," Bolduc House, Mo-1105; Bequette-Ribault House, Mo-1114 (Washington, D.C., 1948).

Hodge, F. W. *Handbook of American Indians North of Mexico* (Washington, D.C., 1910).

Hoffman, Richard C. "Medieval Origins of the Common Fields," in William N. Parker and Eric L. Jones (eds.), *European Peasants and Their Markets: Essays in Agrarian Economic History* (Princeton, 1975), 23-71.

Holmes, Jack D. L. "The Abortive Slave Revolt in Pointe Coupée, Louisiana, 1975," *Louisiana History* 11 (1970), 341-62.

_____. "Do It! Don't Do It!: Spanish Laws on Sex and Marriage," in Edward F. Haas (ed.), *Louisiana's Legal Heritage* (New Orleans, 1983), 19-42.

_____. *Gayoso: the Life of a Spanish Governor in the Mississippi Valley, 1789-1799* (Baton Rouge, 1965).

_____. "Maps, Plans, and Charts of Louisiana in Paris Archives: A Checklist," *Louisiana Studies* 4 (1965), 200-21.

_____. "Medical Practice in the Lower Mississippi Valley During the Spanish Period, 1769-1803," *Alabama Journal of Medical Sciences* 1 (1964), 332-38.

_____. "Spanish Regulation of Taverns and the Liquor Trade in the Mississippi Valley," in John Francis McDermott (ed.), *The Spanish in the Mississippi Valley, 1762-1804* (Urbana, Illinois, 1974), 149-82.

Horsman, Reginald. *Expansion and American Indian Policy, 1783-1812* East Lansing, 1967).
ing, 1967).

Houck, Louis. *A History of Missouri from the Earliest Explorations and Settlements until the Admission of the State into the Union*, 3 vols. (Chicago, 1908).

_____. *Memorial Sketches of Pioneers and Early Residents of Southeast Missouri* (Cape Girardeau, 1915).

Hunt, George T. *The Wars of the Iroquois: A Study in Intertribal Relations* (Madison, 1940).

Jacobs, Wilbur R. *Dispossessing the American Indian: Indians and Whites on the Colonial Frontier* (New York, 1972).

Jaenen, Cornelius J. *Friend and Foe: Aspects of French-American Cultural Contact in the 16th and 17th Centuries* (New York, 1976).

James, James A. *The Life of George Rogers Clark* (Chicago, 1928).

_____. *Oliver Pollock: The Life and Times of an Unknown Patriot* (New York, 1937).

Jennings, Francis. *The Ambiguous Iroquois Empire* (New York, 1984).

_____. *The Invasion of America: Indians, Colonialism, and the Cant of Conquest* (New York, 1975).

Jordan, Winthrop D. *White Over Black: American Attitudes Toward the Negro, 1550-1812* (Chapel Hill, 1968).

Kaplan, Lawrence S. *Colonies into Nation: American Diplomacy, 1763-1801* (London, 1972).

Kedro, Milan. "The Three Notch Road Frontier: A Century of Social and Economic Change in the Ste. Genevieve District," *Missouri Historical Society* 29 (1973), 189-204.

Kenny, Laurence. "Missouri's Earliest Settlement and Its Name," *St. Louis Catholic Historical Review* 1 (1919), 151-56.

King, Grace E. *Creole Families of New Orleans* (New York, 1921).

_____. *New Orleans, The Place and the People* (New York, 1928).

Kinietz, W. V. *The Indians of the Western Great Lakes, 1615-1760* (Ann Arbor, 1940).

Kinnaird, Lawrence. "American Penetration into Spanish Louisiana," in George P. Hammond (ed.), *New Spain and the Anglo-American West* (Lancaster, Pennsylvania, 1932), 211-37.

_____. "American Penetration into Spanish Territory (1776- 1802)." Ph.D. Thesis, University of California, Berkeley, 1929.

_____. "The Spanish Expedition against Fort St. Joseph in 1781: A New Interpretation," *Mississippi Valley Historical Review* 19 (1932), 173-81.

Kniffen, Fred. "The Outdoor Oven in Louisiana," *Louisiana History* 1 (1960), 25-35.

Kopperman, Paul E. *Braddock at the Monongahela* (Pittsburgh, 1977).

Kroeber, A. L. *Cultural and Natural Areas of Native North America* (Berkeley, 1963).

Kyte, George W. "A Spy on the Western Waters: The Military Intelligence Mission of General Collot in 1796," *Mississippi Valley Historical Review* 34 (1947), 427-42.

Lahey, Mary C. "The Catholic Church on the Frontier of Spanish Illinois, 1763-1804," M.A. Thesis, San Diego State College, 1966.

Langer, William L. "Infanticide: A Historical Survey," *History of Childhood Quarterly* 1 (1974), 353-65.

Lauber, Almon W. *Indian Slavery in Colonial Times Within the Present Limits of the United States* (New York, 1913).

Lavisse, Ernest (ed.). *Histoire de France des origines jusqu'à la Révolution,* vol. 8, pt. 2 (Paris, 1926).

Lemieux, Donald J. "The Mississippi Valley, New France, and French Colonial Policy," *Southern Studies* 17 (1978), 30-56.

Le Page du Pratz, Antoine Simon. *The History of Louisiana,* ed. Joseph G. Tregle Jr. (1774, facsimile Baton Rouge, 1975).

Liljegren, Ernest R. "Frontier Education in Spanish Louisiana," *Missouri Historical Review* 35 (1941), 345-72.

———. "Jacobinson in Spanish Louisiana, 1792-1797," *Louisiana Historical Quarterly* 21 (1939), 47-97.

———. "Lieutenant-Colonel Don Calos Howard and the International Rivalry for the Mississippi Valley: 1796-1798," M.A. Thesis, University of Southern California, 1939.

Lockridge, Kenneth. *Literacy in Colonial New England* (New York, 1974).

Loomis, Noel M., and Nasatir, Abraham P. *Pedor Vial and the Roads to Santa Fe* (Norman, Oklahoma, 1967).

Lyon, E. Wilson. *Louisiana in French Diplomacy, 1759-1804* (Norman, Oklahoma, 1934).

Magnaghi, Russell M. "The Role of Colonial Indian Slavery in St. Louis," *Bulletin of the Missouri Historical Society* 31 (1975), 264-72.

Mandrou, Robert. *Introduction à la France moderne: Essai de psychologie historique* (Paris, 1961).

Marshall, Thomas. *The Life and Papers of Frederick Bates,* 2 vols. (St. Louis, 1926).

Martin, François-Xavier. *The History of Louisiana from the Earliest Period* (New Orleans, 1827-29).

Martin, Gaston. *Histoire de l'esclavage dans les colonies françaises* (Paris, 1948).

Mason, Edward G. "British Illinois — Philippe de Rocheblave," in Edward G. Mason (ed.), *Early Chicago and Illinois* (Chicago, 1890), 360-81.

Mathews, John J. *The Osages* (Norman, Oklahoma, 1961).

Mathieu, Jacques. "Familles et colonisation au XVIIe siècle," paper presented at French Colonial Historical Society (Evanston, Illinois, 1982).

McCann, Elizabeth. "Pénicaut and his Chronicle of Early Louisiana," *Mid-America* 23 (1941), 288-304.

McDermott, John F. "Culture and the Missouri Frontier," *Missouri Historical Review* 50 (1956), 355-70.

———. "Diary of Charles Dehault Delassus from New Orleans to St. Louis, 1836," *Louisiana Historical Quarterly* 30 (1947), 359-438.

——— (ed.). *Frenchmen and French Ways in the Mississippi Valley* (Urbana, Illinois, 1969).

_____ (ed.). *The French in the Mississippi Valley* (Urbana, Illinois, 1965).

_____ . "The Myth of 'The Imbecile Governor' Captain Fernando de Leyba and the Defense of St. Louis in 1780," in John Francis McDermott (ed.), *The Spanish in the Mississippi Valley 1762-1804* (Urbana, Illinois, 1974), 314-405.

_____ . "Myths and Realities Concerning the Founding of St. Louis," in John Francis McDermott (ed.), *The French in the Mississippi Valley* (Urbana, 1965), 1-16.

_____ . *Old Cahokia: A Narrative and Documents Illustrating the First Century of its History* (St. Louis, 1952).

_____ . *Private Libraries in Creole St. Louis* (Baltimore, 1938).

_____ (ed.). *The Spanish in the Mississippi Valley, 1762-1804* (Urbana, Illinois, 1974).

MacDonald, Robert R. et al. (eds.). *Louisiana's Black Heritage* (New Orleans, 1979).

McGowan, James T. "Creation of a Slave Society: Louisiana Plantations in the Eighteenth Century," Ph.D. Dissertation, University of Rochester, 1976.

_____ . "Planters Without Slaves: Origins of a New World Labor System," *Southern Studies* 16 (1977), 5-26.

McKinley, E. B. *Geography of Diseases* (Washington, D.C., 1935).

McNeill, William H. *Plagues and People* (New York, 1976).

Melville, Annabelle M. John Carroll of Baltimore (New York, 1955).

Meuvret, J. "Demographic Crisis in France from the Sixteenth to the Eighteenth Century," in D. V. Glass and D. E. C. Eversley (eds.), *Population in History: Essays in Demographic History* (Chicago, 1965), 507-22.

Miller, John C. *The Federalist Era, 1789-1801* (New York, 1960).

Moogk, Peter N. *Building a House in New France* (Toronto, 1975).

_____ . "Rank in New France: Reconstructing a Society from National Documents," *Histoire Sociale-Social History* 8 (1975).

_____ . "'Thieving Buggers' and 'Stupid Sluts': Insults and Popular Culture in New France," *The William and Mary Quarterly*, third series, 36 (1979).

Moore, John P. *Revolt in Louisiana: The Spanish Occupation, 1766-1770* (Baton Rouge, 1976).

Mueller, Raymond. "The Blount Conspiracy," M.A. Thesis, San Diego State College, 1939.

Musick, James B. *St. Louis as a Fortified Town* (St. Louis, 1941).

Nasatir, Abraham P. "The Anglo-Spanish Frontier in the Illinois Country During the American Revolution, 1779-1783," *Journal of the Illinois State Historical Society* (1928), 291-358.

_____ . *Borderland in Retreat: From Spanish to the Far Southwest* (Albuquerque, 1976).

_____ . "Government Employees and Salaries in Spanish Louisiana," *Louisiana Historical Quarterly* 29 (1946), 3-158.

_____ ."Jacques Clamorgan: Colonial Promoter of the Northern Border of New Spain," *New Mexico Historical Review* 17 (1942), 101-12.

_____ . "More on Pedro Vial in Upper Louisiana," in John Francis McDermott (ed.), *The Mississippi Valley, 1762-1804* (Urbana, Illinois, 1974), 100-19.

_____ . "St. Louis During the British Attack of 1780." in George P. Hammond (ed.), *New Spain and the Anglo-American West* (Lancaster, Pennsylvania, 1932), 239-61.

_____ . "Trade and Diplomacy in Spanish Illinois, 1763-1792," Ph.D. Dissertation, University of California, Berkeley, 1926.

Nash, Gary B. *Red, White, and Black: The Peoples of Early America* (Englewood Cliffs, New Jersey, 1974).

Oberholzer, Emil. "The Legal Aspects of Slavery in Missouri," *Bulletin of the Missouri Historical Society* 6 (1950), 139-61, 333-51, 540-45.

Ogg, Frederick Austin. *The Opening of the Mississippi: A Struggle for Supremacy in the American Interior* (New York, 1904).

Olivier-Martin, François Jean Marie. *Histoire de la Coutume de la Prevoté et Vicomté de Paris*, 3 vols. (Paris, 1922-30).

O'Neill, Charles E. *Church and State in French Colonial Louisiana: Policy and Politics to 1732* (New Haven, Connecticut, 1966).

Palm, Mary B. *Jesuit Missions of the Illinois Country, 1673-1763* (Cleveland, 1933).

Patterson, Orlando. *Slavery and Social Death* (Cambridge, Massachusetts, 1982).

Pelzer, Louis. "The Spanish Land Grants of Upper Louisiana," *The Iowa Journal of History and Politics* 11 (1913), 3-37.

Peterson, Charles E. "Early Ste. Genevieve and its Architecture, *Missouri Historical Review* 35 (1941), 207-32.

————. *A Guide to Ste. Genevieve, with Notes on its Architecture* (St. Louis, 1940).

————. "The Houses of French St. Louis," in John Francis McDermott (ed.), *The French in the Mississippi Valley* (Urbana, Illinois, 1965), 17-40.

Philback, Francis S. *The Rise of the West, 1754-1830* (New York, 1965).

Phillips, Paul C. *The Fur Trade*, 2 vols. (Norman, Oklahoma, 1961).

Porterfield, Neil H. "Ste. Genevieve, Missouri," in John Francis McDermott (ed.), *Frenchmen and French Ways in the Mississippi Valley* (1969), 141-79.

Price, Anna. "The Three Lives of Fort de Chartres: French Outpost on the Mississippi," *Historic Illinois* 3 (1980), 1-4.

Price, Richard (ed.). *Maroon Societies: Rebel Slave Communities in the Americas* (Garden City, 1973).

Raboteau, Albert J. *Slave Religion: The "Invisible Institution" in the Antebellum South* (New York, 1978).

Rétif de la Bretonne. *La vie de mon père* (Paris, 1970).

Reynolds, John. *Pioneer History of Illinois* (Belleville, 1852).

Ribotti, Frances D. and Peter J. *French Cooking in the New World* (Garden City, New York, 1967).

Robinson, Percy J. (ed.). *Toronto During the French Regime: A History of the Toronto Region from Brûle to Simcoe, 1615-1793* (Chicago, 1933).

Rohrbough, Malcolm J. *The Trans-Appalachian Frontier* (New York, 1978).

Rothensteiner, John E. *History of the Archdiocese of St. Louis*, 2 vols. (St. Louis, 1928).

————. "Earliest History of Mine la Motte," *Missouri Historical Review* 20 (1925), 199-213.

Rozier, Firman A. *History of the Early Settlement of the Mississippi Valley* (St. Louis, 1890).

Rutman, Darrett B. and Anita H. "Of Agues and Fevers: Malaria in the Early Chesapeake," *William and Mary Quarterly*, third series, 33 (1976), 31-60.

Schaaf, Ida M. "The First Roads West of the Mississippi," *Missouri Historical Review* 29 (1935), 92-99.

————. "The Founding of Ste. Genevieve, Missouri," *Missouri Historical Review* 27 (1933), 145-50.

Schlarman, Joseph H. *From Old Quebec to New Orleans* (Belleville, Illinois, 1929).

Seineke, Katherine W. *The George Rogers Clark Adventure in the Illinois* (New Orleans, 1981).

Seguin, Robert-Lionel. *La civilisation traditionelle de "l'habitant" aux 17e et 18e siècles* (Montreal, 1967).

Shea, John G. *Catholic Church in Colonial Days* (New York, 1886).

———. *Discovery and Exploration of the Mississippi Valley* (New York, 1852).

———. *Life and Times of Archbishop Carroll* (New York, 1888).

Shepherd, W. R. "The Cession of Louisiana to Spain," *Political Science Quarterly* 19 (1904), 439-58.

Shorter, Edward. *The Making of the Modern Family* (New York, 1975).

Slicher van Bath, B. H. *The Agrarian History of Western Europe, A.D. 500-1850,* trans. Olive Ordish (London, 1963).

Smith, Henry N. *Virgin Land: The American West as Symbol and Myth* (Cambridge, 1950).

Sosin, Jack M. *The Revolutionary Frontier, 1763-1783* (New York, 1967).

Stacey, C. P. *Quebec 1759: The Siege and the Battle* (Toronto, 1959).

Stoddard, T. L. *The French Revolution in San Domingo* (Boston, 1914).

Sturtevant, William C. (gen. ed.). *Handbook of North American Indians,* 28 vols. projected (Washington, D.C., 1978-). Vol 15: *The Northeast,* ed. Bruce G. Trigger.

Surrey, Nancy M. *The Commerce of Louisiana During the French Regime, 1699-1763* (New York, 1916).

Surveyer, Justice E. Fabre. "Philippe-François de Rastel de Rocheblave," in Percy J. Robinson (ed.), *Toronto During the French Regime* (Toronto, 1933), 233-42.

Swartzlow, Ruby J. "The Early History of Lead Mining in Missouri," *Missouri Historical Review* 28 (1934), 184-94, 287-95; 29 (1935), 27-34, 109-14, 195-205.

Tannenbaum, Frank. *Slave and Citizen: The Negro in the Americas* (New York,1946).

Temple, Wayne C. *Indian Villages of the Illinois Country* (Springfield, Illinois, 1977).

Thurman, Melburn D. *Building a House in 18th-Century Ste. Genevieve* (Ste. Genevieve, 1984).

———. "Cartography of the Illinois Country: An Analysis of Middle Mississippi Maps Drawn During the British Regime," *Journal of the Illinois State Historical Society* 75 (1982), 277-88.

Traquair, Ramsay. *Old Architecture of French Canada* (Montreal, 1932).

Trenfel, Jacqueline T. "Spanish Occupation of the Upper Mississippi Valley, 1765-1770," M.A. Thesis, University of California, Berkeley, 1941.

Trexler, Harrison Anthony. *Slavery in Missouri, 1804-1865* (Baltimore, 1914).

Trudel, Marcel. *The Beginnings of New France 1534-1663* (Toronto, 1973).

———. *L'esclavage au Canada français: Histoire et conditions de l'esclavage* (Quebec, 1960).

Turner, Frederick J. "English Policy Toward America in 1790-91," *American Historical Review* 7 (1902), 704-35.

———. *The Frontier in American History* (New York, 1920).

———. "The Origins of Gênet's Projected Attack on Louisiana and the Floridas," *American Historical Review* 3 (1898), 650-71.

———. "Policy of France toward the Mississippi Valley in the Period of Washington and Adams," *American Historical Review* 10 (1905), 249-79.

Usner, Daniel H. Jr. "From African Captivity to American Slavery: The Introduction of Black Laborers to Colonial Louisiana," *Louisiana History* 20 (1979), 25-48.

——— "Frontier Exchange in the Lower Mississippi Valley: Race Relations and Economic Life in Colonial Louisiana, 1699-1783," Ph.D. Thesis, Duke University, 1981.

Van Ravensway, Charles. "The Creole Arts and Crafts of Upper Louisiana," *Bulletin of the Missouri Historical Society* 12 (1956), 213-48.

Viles, Jonas. "Population and Settlement Before 1804," *Missouri Historical Review* 5 (1911), 189-213.

Villiers du Terrage, Marc de. *Les dernières années de la Louisiane française* (Paris, 1904).

_____. "La Salle Takes Possession of Louisiana," *Louisiana Historical Quarterly* 14 (1931), 301-15.

Vinovskis, Maria A. "Mortality Rates and Trends in Massachusetts Before 1760," *Journal of Economic History* 33 (1972), 184-213.

Violette, Eugene M. "Early Settlements in Missouri," *Missouri Historical Review* 1 (1906), 38-52.

_____. *History of Missouri* (1918).

_____. "Spanish Land Claims in Missouri," *Washington University Studies* 8 (1921), 167-200.

Vogel, Claude L. *The Capuchins in French Louisiana* (1722-1766) (New York, 1928).

Waddington, Richard. *La Guerre de Sept Ans,* 5 vols. (Paris, 1899-1914).

Walsh, Lorens S. and Menard, Russell R. "Death in the Chesapeake: Two Life Tables for Men In Early Colonial Maryland," *Maryland Historical Magazine* 69 (1974), 211-27.

Webre, Stephen. "The Problem of Indian Slavery in Spanish Louisiana, 1769-1803," *Louisiana History* 25 (1984), 117-35.

Wells, Robert V. *The Population of the British Colonies in America Before 1776* (Princeton, 1975).

Wheaton, Robert and Hareven, Tamara K. *Family and Sexuality in French History* (Philadelphia, 1980), 3-253.

Wilder, Laura I. *Little House in the Big Woods* (New York, 1953).

Whitaker, Arthur P. *The Mississippi Question, 1795-1803: A Study in Trade, Politics, and Diplomacy* (New York, 1934).

_____. *The Spanish American Frontier, 1783-1795* (Boston, 1927).

Wilson, Samuel Jr. "Colonial Fortifications and Military Architecture in the Mississippi Valley," in John F. McDermott (ed.), *The French in the Mississippi Valley* (Urbana, Illinois, 1965), 103- 22.

_____. "Ignace François Broutin," in John F. McDermott (ed.), *Frenchmen and French Ways in the Mississippi Valley* (Urbana, Illinois, 1969), 231-94.

Winzerling, Oscar W. *Acadian Odyssey* (Baton Rouge, 1955).

Woodward, C. Vann (ed.). *Mary Chesnut's Civil War* (New Haven, Connecticut, 1981).

Wright, J. Leitch Jr. *Britain and the American Frontier, 1783-1815* (Athens, Georgia, 1975).

Wrigley, E. A. *Population and History* (New York, 1969).

Yealy, Francis J., S. J. *Sainte Genvieve, The Story of Missouri's Oldest Settlement* (Ste. Genevieve, 1935).

Zeller, Gaston. *Les temps moderne: de Louis XIV à 1789.* Vol. 3: *Histoire des relations internationales,* Pierre Renouvin (ed.) (Paris, 1955).

Zinsser, Hans. *Rats, Lice and History* (Boston, 1935).

Zuckerman, Michael. *Peaceable Kingdoms: New England Towns in the Eighteenth Century* (New York, 1970).

Index

INDEX

The following abbreviations are used: Ill.--Illinois, Kas. -- Kaskaskia, La.--Louisiana, N.O.--New Orleans, S.G.--Ste. Genevieve, S.L.--St. Louis, U.S.--United States. Italic numbers refer to maps, figures, or illustrations.

I wish to thank Julie Barr, Gloria Ekberg, Mark Feaster, Edit Semsei, and Dianne True, all of whom helped to compose this index.

Also from The Patrice Press

The Story of Old
Ste. Genevieve

by Gregory M. Franzwa

177 pp. 76 photos, 3 maps
$4.95 plus $2 shipping
Mo. residents add 26¢ sales tax